17,00

The Developmental Psychopathology of Anxiety

The Developmental Psychopathology of Anxiety

MICHAEL W. VASEY
MARK R. DADDS

Editors

OXFORD

UNIVERSITY PRESS

2001

OXFORD

UNIVERSITY PRESS

Oxford   New York
Athens   Auckland   Bangkok   Bogotá   Buenos Aires   Calcutta
Cape Town   Chennai   Dar es Salaam   Delhi   Florence   Hong Kong   Istanbul
Karachi   Kuala Lumpur   Madrid   Melbourne   Mexico City   Mumbai
Nairobi   Paris   São Paulo   Shanghai   Singapore   Taipei   Tokyo   Toronto   Warsaw

and associated companies in
Berlin   Ibadan

Library of Congress Cataloging-in-Publication Data
Vasey, Michael W.
The developmental psychopathology of anxiety / edited by Michael W. Vasey and
Mark R. Dadds.
p. cm.
Includes bibliographical references and index.
ISBN 0-19-512363-8
1. Anxiety in children. 2. Anxiety—Etiology. I. Dadds, Mark R. II. Title.

RJ506.A58 V37 2000
618.92'85223–dc21   00-020480

3 5 7 9 8 6 4 2

Printed in the United States of America
on acid-free paper

To Paula, Katie, Libby, and my parents:
For their patience, support, and the many things
I have learned in their company.
M.W.V.

To my very special family (Paula, Ana, and Tom),
my students, and the many children and families
I have worked with clinically:
All have taught me so much.
M.R.D.

PREFACE

Before the 1980s, childhood anxiety problems received surprisingly little attention from researchers and clinicians relative to the large amounts of attention devoted to externalizing problems of childhood, such as aggression and hyperactivity. To a large extent, this relative neglect reflected the view that childhood anxiety problems, along with other internalizing problems, were typically transient developmental phenomena that had little importance for children's long term adjustment. However, subsequent to DSM-III's introduction of several childhood anxiety disorder categories into the psychiatric nomenclature, interest in clinical forms of childhood anxiety has increased substantially.

Surprisingly, although this growth in interest has coincided with the advent of the developmental psychopathology perspective, comprehensive and integrative discussions of the developmental psychopathology of anxiety remain rare. Understanding of the pathways by which childhood anxiety disorders develop requires consideration of a wide array of developmental influences and, more important, their potential for complex, reciprocal inter-actions over time (i.e., transactions). Work that considers such issues has begun to appear but, reflecting the broad range of factors that seem likely to contribute to such disorders, it remains widely scattered across disparate literatures within similarly diverse fields, including developmental psycho-logy, clinical psychology, and psychiatry. Further, although a number of excellent books on childhood anxiety and its disorders have appeared in the past few years, they have generally devoted more space to descriptive, assessment, and treatment issues than to considering issues related to the developmental psychopathology of anxiety. To foster understanding of such issues, we felt that a book was needed that reviews and integrates current research and theory on the major factors that may predispose to, protect against, precipitate, maintain, or ameliorate anxiety disorders in childhood and the developmental variations that may exist in those factors and in their operation as well as in the manifestations and prevalence of anxiety disorders in childhood, and across the lifespan.

In keeping with the overall aims of the volume, contributors were encour-aged to consider the tenets of the developmental psychopathology perspec-tive (see chapter 1) when preparing their chapters. Because the study of many of the issues and factors considered in this volume remains in its infancy, we urged contributors to go beyond the extant data and speculate regarding the implications of a developmental perspective for a given factor or its potential for transactional relations to other factors. The result is a series of very creative contributions that we are confident will stimulate further theoretical and empirical efforts regarding these important issues and which will be of interest to researchers and clinicians alike.

The book is divided into three parts. Part I contains two chapters which lay the foundations for the remainder of the book. In chapter 1, we review the major tenets of the developmental psychopathology perspective and, based upon them, we offer a conceptual framework for conceptualizing the development of childhood anxiety disorders. In chapter 2, Weiss and Last review the research on age, sex, and developmental variations in the major childhood anxiety disorders. As they note, research on anxiety disorders across the lifespan requires clear understanding of the different forms taken by such disorders at different points in the lifespan. Further, any adequate theory of the developmental psychopathology of anxiety must explain the patterns of change seen in the prevalence rates and manifestations of anxiety disorders across the lifespan. Such changes are central phenomena to be explained, and they also offer important clues regarding the factors that may contribute to the development of anxiety disorders and how they may differ across age groups.

Part II is devoted to the major factors that may play predisposing, protective, maintaining, and ameliorating roles in the development of childhood anxiety disorders and the processes by which they may play such roles. To begin the part, Eley provides in chapter 3 a comprehensive review of the rapidly growing behavioral genetics research literature concerning childhood anxiety. She concludes that there is a significant genetic risk for anxiety in childhood, and this risk appears to be common to depressive symptoms as well. Intriguingly, she also reports that there is strong evidence for shared environmental influences in childhood anxiety, a finding that stands in stark contrast to the consistent failure to find such influences in studies of adults.

Lonigan and Phillips (chapter 4) provide a comprehensive review of temperamental influences related to childhood anxiety. In this context, they articulate an innovative theory of temperamental vulnerability in which risk for anxiety is related not to a single dimension of temperament but, instead, to the interaction of two dimensions which operate in complex transaction with a host of other influences.

In chapter 5, Reiss, Silverman, and Weems review the theory and evidence underlying the construct of anxiety sensitivity and discuss its role as a risk factor for childhood and adult anxiety disorders. Worthy of particular note is their discussion of exciting preliminary evidence that increasing levels of anxiety sensitivity in childhood are associated with heightened risk for the development of panic disorders.

In chapter 6, Chorpita reviews evidence for an association between early control experiences and risk for anxiety disorders across the lifespan. According to the theory offered by Chorpita, the risk and protective influences attributable to such experiences are mediated by a variety of transactionally related factors, which include psychological, social, and biological variables.

In chapter 7, Gunnar offers a critical analysis of evidence for a theory which argues that biological factors play an important role in the onset and maintenance of anxiety disorders. Specifically, she considers the hypothesis that increased release of glucocorticoids and neuropeptides during fear increases the excitability of fear circuits and plays a role in the organization of pathological anxiety in humans and animals.

In chapter 8, Thompson considers risk for childhood anxiety disorders from the perspectives of emotion regulation and attachment theory. In doing so, he offers valuable insights regarding the development of anxiety regulation strategies and capacities in both normal and excessively anxious children.

Menzies and Harris review in chapter 9 the evidence for nonassociative influences in the etiology of childhood phobias. They conclude that, although associative conditioning influences play a role in the etiology of many phobias, such influences are clearly lacking in many other cases. Nonassociative theory suggests that those other cases often represent failures to master pre-existing fears owning to temperamental and parental influences.

In chapter 10, Dadds, Davey, and Field provide an overview of modern respondent conditioning theory and then offer an innovative discussion of such associative conditioning processes from a developmental perspective. Because cognition figures strongly in current conceptualizations of respondent conditioning, there are numerous ways in which cognitive development may be relevant to understanding the operation of such processes in childhood and their relevance for understanding the etiology, maintenance, and amelioration of childhood anxiety disorders.

Paralleling the discussion by Dadds and colleagues, Ollendick, Vasey, and King discuss in chapter 11 the potential roles played by operant conditioning influences in the etiology, maintenance, and amelioration of childhood anxiety disorders. They argue that the influence of many environmental factors on childhood anxiety can be understood in operant conditioning terms.

In chapter 12, Vasey and MacLeod review evidence for information-processing biases related to childhood anxiety. They conclude that it is now beyond doubt that anxious children show an attentional bias in favor of threat-relevant stimuli, and more sparse evidence suggests that such children additionally show a variety of other cognitive biases. However, important questions remain to be answered regarding the development of such biases. In the context of biased attentional processes, Vasey and MacLeod consider several developmental models which must be examined in future research.

In chapter 13, Dadds and Roth consider family processes in the development of childhood anxiety problems. They review evidence for a variety of family-based influences, and conclude by offering an integrative model that draws attention to the interconnected influence of child temperament, parent–child attachment, and family-based social learning processes when anxiety-prone children are exposed to challenging situations.

In chapter 14, Barrett considers the current state of knowledge regarding the treatment of childhood anxiety disorders. Current conceptualizations of maintaining and ameliorating factors have led to the development of highly efficacious interventions for childhood anxiety disorders. However, a variety of issues remain to be explored, more notably, the implications of development for the design of optimal intervention programs.

In chapter 15, Spence discusses efforts to prevent the development of childhood anxiety disorders. She concludes that, based on our knowledge of risk and protective factors, we are now able to identify children at risk for anxiety problems and to create effective preventive programs.

The chapters in the third part of the book are meant to showcase ongoing efforts in the field to build and test integrative models of childhood anxiety problems. These chapters illustrate how researchers are beginning to pull together many of the individual factors or processes discussed in the second part of the book to build theories that recognize the diverse influences and their complex transactions that lead to childhood anxiety disorders. The contributors to this part were selected because of their expertise and innovative work on specific clinical forms of childhood anxiety. In chapter 16, Muris and Merckelbach present their multifactorial model of the etiology of childhood specific phobias. Vernberg and Varela, in chapter 17, present a developmental perspective on posttraumatic stress disorder. In chapter 18, Rubin and Burgess provide a discussion of social withdrawal and its relations to childhood anxiety disorders. Related to this, in chapter 19, Morris presents a developmental model of social phobia. In chapter 20, Silove and Manicavasagar discuss their theory regarding early separation anxiety and its relationship to adult anxiety disorders. Finally, in chapter 21, Rapee presents his comprehensive and integrative theory of the development of generalized anxiety disorder in childhood.

In conclusion, although the chapters in this volume make it clear that we have learned much regarding the developmental psychopathology of anxiety, there is much that remains to be learned. It is our hope that this volume will help stimulate and guide future work in this area.

Michael W. Vasey
Mark R. Dadds

ACKNOWLEDGMENTS

We are indebted to the many people who have made this volume possible, especially the book's contributors for finding time in their already over-loaded schedules to participate in this project. From the start, we had no doubt that this group of outstanding scholars would produce interesting and valuable contributions. However, the creative, integrative, and stimulating chapters they have produced exceeded our highest expectations.

We are also particularly indebted to Joan Bossert and her staff at Oxford University Press, who have helped to shepherd this volume through its long and sometimes difficult developmental course.

Finally, thanks are extended to Rebecca Hazen for her tireless and amazingly rapid proofreading efforts and to the copyeditor at Keyword.

CONTENTS

CONTRIBUTORS

Paula Barrett
School of Applied Psychology
Griffith University, Gold Coast
Campus, Australia

Kim B. Burgess
Department of Psychology
University of Maryland at
College Park

Bruce F. Chorpita
Department of Psychology
University of Hawaii at Manoa

Mark R. Dadds
School of Applied Psychology
Griffith University, Nathan Campus,
Australia

Graham C. L. Davey
Cognitive and Computing Sciences
University of Sussex, Brighton, UK

Thalia C. Eley
Institute of Psychiatry
University of London, UK

Andy P. Field
Cognitive and Computing Sciences
University of Sussex, Brighton, UK

Megan R. Gunnar
Institute of Child Development
University of Minnesota

Lynne M. Harris
Department of Behavioural Sciences
University of Sydney, Australia

Neville J. King
Faculty of Education, School of
Graduate Studies
Monash University, Australia

Cynthia G. Last
Department of Psychology
Nova Southeastern University

Christopher J. Lonigan
Department of Psychology
Florida State University

Colin MacLeod
Department of Psychology
University of Western Australia

Vijaya Manicavasagar
Psychiatry Research & Teaching Unit,
Liverpool Hospital, Australia

Ross G. Menzies
Department of Behavioural Sciences
University of Sydney, Australia

Harald Merckelbach
Department of Psychology
Maastricht University
The Netherlands

Tracy L. Morris
Department of Psychology
West Virginia University

Peter Muris
Department of Psychology
Maastricht University
The Netherlands

Thomas H. Ollendick
Department of Psychology
Virginia Polytechnic Institute and
State University

Beth M. Phillips
Department of Psychology
Florida State University

Ronald M. Rapee
School of Behavioural Sciences
Macquarie University, Australia

Steven Reiss
Department of Psychology
Ohio State University

Janet H. Roth
School of Applied Psychology
Griffith University, Nathan Campus,
Australia

Kenneth H. Rubin
Department of Psychology
University of Maryland at
College Park

Derrick Silove
School of Psychiatry
University of New South Wales,
Australia

Wendy K. Silverman
Department of Psychology
Florida International University

Susan H. Spence
School of Psychology
University of Queensland, Australia

Ross A. Thompson
Department of Psychology
University of Nebraska

R. Enrique Varela
Department of Psychology
University of Kansas

Michael W. Vasey
Department of Psychology
Ohio State University

Eric M. Vernberg
Department of Psychology
University of Kansas

Carl F. Weems
Department of Psychology
Florida International University

Danielle D. Weiss
Department of Psychology
Nova Southeastern University

I

PRELIMINARY ISSUES

1

An Introduction to the Developmental Psychopathology of Anxiety

MICHAEL W. VASEY and MARK R. DADDS

Although anxiety disorders in childhood and adolescence received little attention from researchers until the mid-1980s, subsequent research has shown that such disorders warrant considerable concern. First, anxiety disorders are among the most prevalent forms of psychopathology affecting children and adolescents (Anderson, Williams, McGee, & Silva, 1987; Kashani & Orvaschel, 1990; Kashani, Orvaschel, Rosenberg, & Reed, 1989). Second, although many forms of anxiety are normal and transient developmental phenomena and childhood anxiety disorders typically remit within three to four years (Last, Perrin, Hersen, & Kazdin, 1996), a significant proportion of such disorders either have a chronic course or change form (Keller, Lavori, Wunder, Beardslee, & Schwartz, 1992; Last et al. 1996; Ollendick & King, 1994; Orvaschel, Lewinsohn, & Seeley, 1995). Further, many adult anxiety disorders have their onset in childhood or adolescence (Burke, Burke, Regier, & Rae, 1990; Kendler, Neale, Kessler, Heath, & Eaves, 1992; Öst, 1987). Third, anxiety symptoms and disorders in childhood appear to carry or signal significant risk for other disorders, particularly other anxiety disorders, dysthymia, and depression (Cole, Peeke, Martin, Truglio, & Serocynski, 1998; Last et al., 1996; Orvaschel et al., 1995). Finally, anxiety disorders have substantial potential to interfere significantly with children's adaptive functioning in a wide range of domains (Dweck & Wortman, 1982; Last, Hanson, & Franco, 1997; McGee & Stanton, 1990; Strauss, Frame, & Forehand, 1987).

Despite substantial gains in our knowledge of childhood anxiety disorders since the 1980s, much remains unknown. Whereas the majority of empirical and theoretical work to date has tended to focus on single factors operating in isolation, often with little regard to the potential impact of development, understanding the pathways by which childhood anxiety disorders develop, persist, and remit is likely to require consideration of a wide range of influences and, more importantly, their potential for complex dynamic, transformational interactions (i.e., transactions) across development. One approach which emphasizes consideration of such complex transactional pathways is the developmental psychopathology perspective. Over the past two decades, this perspective has emerged as a major organizational framework for the study of psychological disorders in childhood (Cicchetti

& Cohen, 1995). Unfortunately, this perspective has had surprisingly little impact on the study of childhood anxiety disorders which have, until recently, been approached primarily through downward extensions of adult theories and with little consideration of the complexities of development. Although developmental and transactional issues have recently begun to be emphasized by childhood anxiety researchers (e.g., Chorpita & Barlow, 1998; Manassis & Bradley, 1994; Stemberger, Turner, Beidel, & Calhoun, 1995; Vasey, 1993), there remains a need for a comprehensive discussion of childhood anxiety disorders from a developmental psychopathology perspective.

A well-defined set of tenets provide the foundations for the developmental psychopathology perspective (Cicchetti & Cohen, 1995; Kazdin & Kagan, 1994; Masten & Braswell, 1991). Although many of these are not unique to this perspective, as organized within it they provide a unique, broad, integrative framework within which the contributions of separate theories and disciplines regarding the nature, etiology, and course of anxiety disorders across the lifespan may be conceptualized. These axioms, if correct, help to explain the failure of simplistic main-effect models to account for variations in the manifestations of psychopathology within and between individuals and populations. Further, they imply that complexity and dynamic interactions between variables are the rule. However, it should be noted that the history of medicine reveals previous occasions when multifactorial models were invoked and later found to be unnecessary. For example, in the case of pellagra, complex variations in clinical presentation led theorists to argue that it was a complex, heterogeneous disorder with diverse causes. However, ultimately, the cause was found to be unitary (i.e., a deficit in vitamin B). Although it is unlikely that anxiety disorders have a unitary etiology, such historical examples alert us to the possibility that apparent complexity can reflect ignorance as well as a truly complex phenomenon under investigation. Of contemporary relevance is the fact that current systems of classifying and differentiating outcomes (i.e., psychiatric disorders) are crude at best, and this inherently leads to ambiguity and complexity in identifying etiologies. Nevertheless, it appears likely that childhood anxiety disorders are complex, multidetermined phenomena, even if they may not be as complex as they sometimes appear given our limited understanding.

Our principal goal in this chapter is to review the tenets of the developmental psychopathology perspective and to consider their implications for understanding the development, maintenance, and amelioration of childhood anxiety disorders. Subsequently, based on these tenets, the chapter will describe a broad framework for conceptualizing the various pathways associated with the development of childhood anxiety disorders.

The Developmental Psychopathology Perspective

Following the lead of Cicchetti and Cohen (1995) and Masten and Braswell (1991), the major concepts and tenets of the developmental psychopathology perspective can be subsumed under several major headings. Each of these is discussed below and its implications for understanding the development of childhood anxiety disorders are considered.

Diverse Developmental Pathways: Risk and Protective Factors in Dynamic Transaction

One of the major tenets of the developmental psychopathology perspective is the assumption of multideterminism, under which most forms of psychopathology are seen as resulting from multiple causal influences. Universal or main-effect models are viewed as generally untenable and, thus, single or sufficient causes are assumed to be unlikely. Instead, many factors are likely to contribute to the onset, maintenance, or amelioration of psychopathology, with most being insufficient and few, if any, being necessary to produce or prevent any given outcome. Thus, such influences are conceptualized as risk and protective factors, with each probabilistically related to various outcomes. Further, it is assumed that the effects of these factors are typically not merely additive, but rather that each is likely to influence others and, in turn, is likely to be influenced by them as well. Thus, the interactions between risk and protective factors are assumed to be dynamic and transformational (i.e., transactional) rather than static and non-transformational, with each factor potentially changing and changed by other factors over time in ways that increase or decrease cumulative risk.

Within the complex transactions among these diverse factors, it is unlikely that any given factor will invariably produce the same effect regardless of the configuration of other factors also in operation. This is the principle of *multifinality*. This principle states that any given factor will function differently and lead to multiple outcomes depending on the organization of the system in which it operates (Cicchetti & Cohen, 1995). Depending on the constellation of environmental stressors and supports coupled with the child's temperament and competencies (e.g., coping capacities), a given factor may produce a wide range of effects.

Consistent with this view, main-effect models concerning the origins of anxiety disorders have proven inadequate. For example, serious problems exist for a main-effect model of direct traumatic classical conditioning in the etiology of phobias. The failure of the direct classical conditioning model and other main-effect models to account for even circumscribed anxiety disorders like specific phobias is consistent with the developmental psychopathology principle of multifinality. Traumatic conditioning experiences may produce no phobia in one child, a highly specific or transient phobia in another, and a much more generalized or chronic phobia in a third depending on other factors operating in each case (Merckelbach, de Jong, Muris, & van den Hout, 1996). Further, children may develop phobias in the absence of direct traumatic conditioning experiences (Menzies & Clark, 1995). Similarly, recent findings regarding the etiology of posttraumatic stress disorder make it clear that the role of conditioning influences can be understood only in the context of additional influences such as the child's temperament, coping capacities, and environmental supports (La Greca, Silverman, & Wasserstein, 1998; La Greca, Silverman, Vernberg, & Prinstein, 1996; Lonigan, Shannon, Taylor, Finch, & Sallee, 1994; Vernberg, La Greca, Silverman, & Prinstein, 1996).

Just as a single factor may be associated with multiple outcomes, any given outcome may be reached by multiple pathways. Thus, neither a single cause nor a single set of causes (i.e., a single pathway) should be expected for most forms of psychopathology. Instead, multiple pathways to a given disorder should be expected. This is the principle of *equifinality*, which states that a diversity of paths may lead to the same outcome. Thus, rather than expecting a single or even primary path, we should expect a variety of pathways to a disorder.

From this perspective, anxiety disorders can be seen as emerging from multiple deviant developmental pathways or trajectories that reflect complex transactions over time between diverse characteristics of children and their environments. Indeed, it is becoming increasingly clear that there are multiple pathways associated with many anxiety disorders. For example, even within a given type of specific phobia, etiological heterogeneity is likely to be the rule, with some related to direct or indirect respondent conditioning whereas others may instead be linked to operant conditioning or nonassociative influences (see Dadds, Davey, & Field, this volume; Menzies & Harris, this volume; Muris & Merckelbach, this volume; Ollendick, Vasey, & King, this volume).

Although the possibility should be considered that there may be multiple pathways to a given disorder, in some cases such heterogeneous paths may signal that there are two or more variants of a disorder. For example, Stemberger et al. (1995) reported evidence for two distinct pathways in the etiology of general versus specific social phobia. In their study of the offspring of social phobia patients, they found that children with a generalized form of social phobia were more neurotic and introverted and more likely to have a history of shyness than those with specific social phobia. In contrast, the latter group was no different from normal controls in their history of shyness or their levels of neuroticism or introversion. Instead, they were more likely than normal controls to report specific traumatic events preceding their social phobias. Thus, it appears likely that there are at least two paths to the acquisition of social phobia, one in which generalized social phobia slowly evolves out of temperamental shyness and another in which specific social phobias are acquired through respondent conditioning mechanisms. However, there are likely to be other pathways to the development of either of these types of social phobia or any other anxiety disorder in childhood. Failing to consider the possibility of multiple paths to a given disorder may obscure important differences that have important implications for that disorder's prevention and treatment (Stemberger et al., 1995).

Risk and protective influences may be either transient or enduring in nature (Cicchetti & Cohen, 1995). Vulnerabilities are enduring characteristics or life circumstances that promote maladaptation. Enduring protective influences may either compensate for the effects of known risk factors in an additive manner, or they may operate interactively, moderating the effects of those risks. Because they are enduring features, such vulnerabilities and protective influences may play important roles at all points on a child's developmental pathway. In contrast, other risk and protective influences may be more transient in nature, thus playing a role at only one point in the development of a disorder. However, despite their transience, such events (e.g., a traumatic experience) may have important positive or negative impact on a child's developmental trajectory. Whether enduring or transitory, a given risk or protective factor may function differently depending on the point in development at which it occurs. However, more than for enduring factors, the effects of transitory factors will depend on when in the child's development they occur.

Outcomes are dependent on the dynamic balance between risk and protective factors. Psychopathology is more likely in a child for whom vulnerabilities heavily outweigh protective influences. For example, the child with limited coping capacity who is already organized in an anxious manner is more likely to develop posttraumatic stress disorder (PTSD) subsequent to trauma (La Greca et al., 1998; Lonigan et al., 1994).

Understanding of the many factors that may be involved in the diverse pathways to childhood anxiety disorders is fostered by distinguishing between the various roles that such factors may play. Roles played by risk factors include predisposing to, precipitating, maintaining, or intensifying maladaptation and psychopathology. In contrast, protective influences serve to protect against the development of childhood anxiety disorders or to foster a return to a normal developmental pathway subsequent to their onset. Many, if not most, factors are likely to play more than one of these roles. For example, a given factor may play different roles at different points in the development of the disorder that is considered. What serves to predispose to the onset of an anxiety disorder may later contribute to its maintenance or intensification. For example, temperamental factors may predispose to the onset of anxiety disorders but, subsequent to their onset, such factors may also contribute to their maintenance (Rothbart, Posner, & Hershey, 1995). However, it is noteworthy that the specific aspects that predispose to anxiety may be different from those that contribute to its maintenance. For example, although genetic factors may predispose to clinical forms of anxiety and their maintenance, these roles may be played by different genetic factors. Similarly, temperamental factors may contribute to the etiology of an anxiety disorder through heightened conditionability but contribute to its maintenance through resistance to habituation of anxiety responses.

To the extent that current anxiety disorder categories possess construct validity, each is presumably associated with at least one unique developmental pathway. However, many of the influences that comprise any given path may be shared with pathways to other anxiety disorders and to other forms of psychopathology, most notably depressive disorders (Brady & Kendall, 1992; Cole et al., 1998; Last et al., 1996; Orvaschel et al., 1995). Thus, many of the influences on the etiology and maintenance of specific childhood anxiety disorders may pertain to general risk for anxiety or psychopathology in general rather than to specific anxiety disorders. The same may be expected of protective and ameliorative factors. The specificity of pathways may rest either on the influence of one or more disorder specific factors or on unique organization and timing of the general influences involved. Kazdin and Kagan (1994) refer to these unique configurations of influences as "packages." Unfortunately, at present, the configurations or packages of factors that comprise pathways to specific childhood anxiety disorders are largely unknown.

The task of identifying such pathways is complicated by the fact that the specific categories of anxiety disorders in childhood remain the subject of some controversy. The high levels of comorbidity routinely observed among childhood anxiety disorders (Anderson, 1994) suggests to some researchers that current anxiety disorder categories lack discriminant validity among children and reflect artificial boundaries (Perrin & Last, 1995). Alternatively, these categories may be valid but co-occur frequently because they stem from common etiological factors, such as a common genetic vulnerability (Spence, 1997). In either case, consideration of the broad array of factors that may combine to form specific pathways is important for validating or improving the construct validity of anxiety disorder categories when applied to children (Garber & Strassberg, 1991).

Emphasis on Successful and Unsuccessful Adaptation

A second major tenet of the developmental psychopathology perspective is that the study of adaptation in all its forms, successful and unsuccessful, is important to understanding psychopathology (Cicchetti & Cohen, 1995). Meaningful interpretation of deviant developmental pathways is dependent on adequate understanding of normal patterns of development and the normal developmental contexts within which they occur. Thus, it is important to understand the normal development of children's skills for coping with anxiety and potentially anxiety-provoking situations and the environmental contexts in which children normally develop such skills. However, as Cicchetti and Cohen noted, understanding of normal developmental pathways and contexts is often difficult to achieve except through comparisons to deviant pathways. Thus, research on pathways to normal and abnormal anxiety in childhood must proceed simultaneously, with each enhancing the study of the other. By reference to normative patterns of development, we may be able to identify pathways prior to the onset of diagnosable disorder that represent adaptational failures that predict later onset of disorder (Cicchetti & Cohen, 1995).

It is mainly by studying pathways to successful adaptation that occurs despite exposure to enduring or transient risk factors that we can identify important protective influences. Thus, we should be equally interested in children who are at risk for anxiety disorders but do not develop them as we are in those who actually develop such disorders. This highlights numerous important questions. For example, why don't all children who are high in trait anxiety (i.e., highly anxiety-prone) develop posttraumatic stress disorder when they are exposed to traumatic events (La Greca et al., 1998)? Knowing how some children who are exposed to risk factors avoid developing anxiety disorders is essential for developing effective prevention programs. Similarly, although many childhood anxiety disorders remit over time, many do not and, of those that do remit, a substantial proportion either relapse or go on to develop other anxiety (or depressive) disorders (Last et al., 1996). Studying children whose anxiety disorders remit and do not relapse or lead to other disorders in comparison with those whose anxiety disorders remit but then return versus those who never remit would be an excellent strategy for understanding ameliorating factors and, more importantly, possible critical points on developmental paths when they may be most likely to return a child to a normal developmental trajectory.

Psychopathology Occurs in a Developing Organism

A third set of developmental psychopathology principles and concepts reflect the fact that psychopathology occurs in a developing organism. As Masten and Braswell (1991, p. 37) noted: "Particularly in childhood and adolescence, when developmental changes are pronounced, it is essential to consider the role of development in the origins, symptoms, and course of psychopathology, and, concomitantly, in classification, assessment, and treatment of childhood disorders." The implications of this touch on all aspects of the study of childhood psychopathology.

To begin with, substantial variability should be expected in the signs and symptoms that define a disorder (Garber & Strassberg, 1991). The potential for the clinical manifestations of anxiety disorders to vary with development raises questions about the DSM-IV (American Psychiatric Association, 1994) approach of applying adult-based diagnostic criteria to children. Assuming molecular continuity in symptoms of anxiety disorders across the age span carries serious risk that researchers may focus their attention too narrowly on those children who meet adult criteria "while missing a potentially larger group of children who display developmental variants of the symptomatology" (Garber & Strassberg, p. 229). The core symptoms of the disorders may be similar at a molar level of analysis, but not at the molecular level of specific behaviors. For example, avoidance responses may be similar at a molar level of analysis (i.e., they serve the same function), despite taking different specific forms (e.g., overt and crude responses such as hiding in a young child versus subtle and refined responses such as self-distraction in an older child). Alternatively, the core symptoms of the disorder may be different across development even at a molar level of analysis.

For example, this would seem to be the basis for the decision to subsume the category of avoidant disorder of childhood, first introduced in DSM-III (American Psychiatric Association, 1980), under the category of social phobia in DSM-IV. This change apparently reflects the assumption that these two categories are merely different developmental manifestations of the same basic phenomenon, with the expression of the central problem evolving from avoidance of unfamiliar people in childhood to fear of negative social evaluation in early adolescence (Francis, Last, & Strauss, 1992). Indeed, several recent studies suggest that shyness and behavioral inhibition in childhood may predict later social phobia (Hayward, Killen, Kraemer, & Taylor, 1998; Kagan, 1997; Stemberger et al., 1995).

Second, the fact that anxiety disorders occur within a developing organism highlights the importance of studying age differences in the prevalence and age of onset of various anxiety disorders. Why do anxiety disorders have their typical age of onset when they do? For example, why do phobias typically have their onset between the ages of 6 and 8 years? Why is the onset of social phobia typically later? Answers to these questions may involve identification of different risk factors for each that begin to operate at the age in question. Alternatively, it may be that a specific stress or mechanism may lead to very different behavioral difficulties depending on the point in development at which it occurs (Cicchetti & Cohen, 1995). Or it may be that such questions lead to discovery that the premise is wrong—perhaps social phobia can be found in younger children, but it doesn't look the same owing to the inability of younger children to show the cardinal feature of social phobia, fear of negative evaluation. As noted in the previous section, the decision to subsume the category of avoidant disorder of childhood under the category of social phobia reflects growing belief that behavioral inhibition to unfamiliar people in early childhood predicts fear of negative evaluation in adolescence.

Considering such age differences, particularly in interaction with sex differences, draws attention to important patterns for which etiological theories must account. Age and gender differences in the onset and prevalence of childhood anxiety disorders may provide important clues regarding the role of developing biological, social, cognitive, and emotional factors in the etiology of these disorders. Such differences may signal important age-related changes or gender-related differences in the prevalence or operation of risk factors (Daleiden, Vasey, & Brown, 1999). In other words, the degree to which certain factors operate or the manner in which they operate may depend on the age of the child.

The fact that the prevalence rates of some childhood anxiety disorders decrease with age whereas others increase highlights the need to test hypotheses about the transformation of one disorder into another, much as oppositional defiant disorder evolves into conduct disorder in some children (Vasey & Ollendick, 2000). For example, evidence suggests that separation anxiety disorder (SAD) is a significant predictor of later panic disorder and potentially a broad range of other anxiety disorders in adulthood

(Silove, Manicavasagar, Curtis, & Blaszczynski, 1996). Consistent with this possibility, previously anxious children are at risk to develop new anxiety disorders, although the majority of childhood anxiety disorders remit within three to four years (Last et al., 1996).

The finding that specific phobias are more prevalent among girls than boys provides an example of the heuristic value of studying gender differences. One possible explanation for this difference is that sex hormones may be important in the etiology of phobias (Merckelbach et al., 1996). If so, variations in such gender differences should exist, with the gender difference being greater following puberty. Alternatively, boys and girls may differ in the level of exposure to many anxiety-provoking or potentially phobic stimuli with boys greater exposure making them more resistant to fear conditioning through latent inhibition (see Dadds et al., this volume) or providing more opportunities for habituation or learned mastery of normal fears (see Menzies & Harris, this volume and Ollendick et al., this volume).

Third, an important aspect of the organization of the system that is likely to influence the impact of a given factor or the role that factor plays is the child's developmental level. Just as the nature and meaning of symptoms may vary across development, similar outcomes at different points in children's development may reflect the influence of different risk and protective factors (Cicchetti & Cohen, 1995). Conversely, very different outcomes (e.g., different disorders or disorder versus succesful adaptation) may result from the same risk and protective influences operating at different points in development. Thus, the potential for there to be diverse pathways to a given disorder may, in part, reflect developmental differences. However, it is also important to be alert to the possibility that, although factors operating at different points may be different at a molecular level, they may be similar at a molar level of analysis (Cicchetti & Cohen, 1995). For example, when considered at the molecular level, there appear to be differences in the types of experiences that lead to the onset of phobias in younger and older children. Öst (1987) found that modeling and information transmission modes of acquisition were associated with early age of onset, in contrast to direct conditioning which was associated with later age of onset. However, despite their differences, these different types of experiences remain understandable at a molar level as examples of respondent conditioning.

Fourth, the course and prognosis of a disorder may vary depending on the point in development at which onset occurs and the level of competence achieved prior to onset. Thus, just as there are important differences in the pathways associated with early- and late-onset forms of conduct disorder (Moffitt, 1993), an anxiety disorder having an early onset may be associated with different pathways and have different outcomes from forms having later onset. Similarly, it appears that childhood-onset depression may carry greater risk for later depression than depressions with later onset (Kovacs, Feinberg, Crouse-Novak, Paulauskas, & Finkelstein, 1984; Lewinsohn, Clarke, Seeley, & Rohde, 1994). This reflects another tenet of developmental psychopathology, that prior adaptation constrains subsequent adaptation (Cicchetti & Cohen, 1995).

The above point is illustrated by the risk of relapse associated with child-hood anxiety disorders, as well as the risk they carry for additional anxiety disorders and depression (Last et al., 1996). To the extent that a child on a deviant developmental pathway is unable to enter developmental contexts in which important skills are learned or honed, adaptation to future develop-mental challenges is jeopardized. Therefore, the longer a child is on a deviant developmental pathway, the less likely and more difficult it should be for the child to return to a normal trajectory. Thus, to the extent that anxiety disorders are associated with reduced access to critical developmental experi-ences, they are likely to persist or lead to other forms of psychopathology, owing to the child's failure to acquire important skills or to acquisition of forms of adaptation that reduce the likelihood that the child can experience important skill-promoting developmental contexts in the future. For example, because anxious children rely heavily on avoidance as a coping response, they may not gain important experiences, leading to serious skill deficits that make it difficult for them to be successful later in their develop-ment. Such a pathway is similar to the notion of "limited shopping" in Patterson's theory of antisocial behavior (Patterson, Reid, & Dishion, 1992). Like antisocial children, anxious children may suffer the cumulative effects of limited contact with important developmental contexts, owing to such influences as their own avoidant behavior (see below), their parents' tendency to limit their experiences or opportunities (see Dadds & Roth, this volume, and Menzies & Harris, this volume), or perhaps their tendency to process information about the world in biased and distorted fashion (see Vasey & MacLeod, this volume).

Summary

The tenets of the developmental psychopathology perspective have consider-able relevance for understanding the development, maintenance, and amelioration of childhood anxiety disorders. However, although considera-tion of these issues leads to many important questions, many remain as yet unaddressed by research. In an effort to foster research on such issues, the remaining section of this chapter describes a heuristic framework for con-ceptualizing the various pathways associated with the development of child-hood anxiety disorders.

An Integrative Framework for Conceptualizing the Diverse Developmental Pathways to Childhood Anxiety Disorders

The goal of this section of the chapter is to provide a heuristic framework for conceptualizing the development of anxiety disorders that reflects the

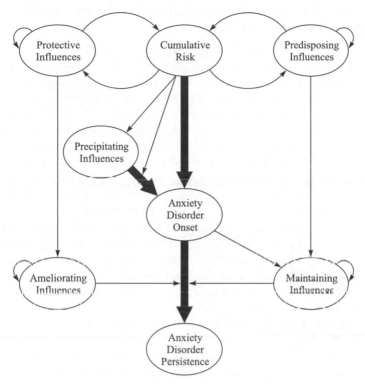

Figure 1.1. Major categories of influence, their transactional relations, and their role in the development, maintenance, and amelioration of anxiety disorders across time.

principles discussed in the previous section. This section begins with description of a model of the major categories of influence and their transactional relations to the development, maintenance, and amelioration of anxiety disorders across time. Owing to space limitations and the fact that detailed discussions of the major specific influences within these categories can be found elsewhere in this volume, they are discussed here only briefly. Instead, the focus is on the potential for transactional relations among these influences.

The proposed framework is depicted in fig. 1.1. This diagram highlights some of the potential relations among these elements and helps to clarify the diverse pathways by which children may develop and maintain anxiety disorders, resist their onset, or return to more adaptive developmental trajectories. It should be noted that several important aspects are not represented in fig. 1.1. First, such a diagram cannot easily depict the potential for variations in the specific forms taken by various risk and protective factors and in the pathways followed depending on a child's level of development. Second, the figure does not depict the potential for variation in the signs and symptoms associated with anxiety disorders at different points in the developmental sequence.

Cumulative Risk for Anxiety: Predisposing and Protective Factors in Dynamic Transaction

A wide range of factors may predispose to or protect against the development of anxiety disorders. The major candidates include, but likely are not limited to, those listed in table 1.1. For a more thorough discussion of each, the reader is referred to the relevant chapters in the present volume.

As depicted in fig. 1.1, cumulative risk reflects the balance between predisposing and protective influences. The dynamic, transactional nature of this balance is illustrated by virtue of the arrows from cumulative risk to protective and predisposing factors. The likelihood of occurrence or the impact of either type of factor may be increased or decreased depending on what other factors are operating and the balance between them at any given point in development. Dynamic, transactional relations are also expected among the specific factors operating within the broad categories of predisposing and protective factors. These relations are illustrated by the self-recursive arrows associated with the ovals representing predisposing and protective influences. Thus, cumulative risk is a dynamic function of the transactions between predisposing and protective influences, which themselves are shifting dynamically over time.

Although none of the predisposing factors listed in table 1.1 appears to be necessary for the development of an anxiety disorder, it seems likely that most anxious children travel a pathway that begins with one or more of these factors. Furthermore, as indicated by the self-recursive arrow associated with predisposing factors in fig. 1.1, because many predisposing factors seem likely to increase the probability that others will also occur, pathways involving several are likely to be the most common. Examples of this sort of synergistic relation are easily generated. First, children who are behaviorally inhibited or high in negative affectivity (see Lonigan & Phillips, this volume) may increase their exposure to environmental risks. For example, by virtue of their tendency to avoid such contexts and to punish, with anxious outbursts, those who attempt to encourage exposure, such children may limit their opportunities to habituate and master such contexts. Calkins (1994) argued that continuity in extreme inhibited temperament may be due partly to the fact that more extremely inhibited infants and toddlers will foster more accommodating responses from caregivers. This may reflect the parents' wish to protect their child from intense fear but may also be a response to the punishing qualities of such reactions and the negative reinforcement likely to follow their termination.

Second, anxiogenic cognitive biases and distortions are likely to be magnified by exposure to environmental risks such as punishment and failure, but in turn they may increase a child's exposure to such risks. For example, children who have low self-efficacy or low perceived control may give up sooner than most children when faced with challenges, and thus experience low control even in situations where there is potential for complete control (Skinner, 1995).

Table 1.1. Factors that may Predispose to or Protect Against Anxiety Disorders

Factor	Potential influences
Genetic factors	Child-based twin studies support a moderate genetic risk for symptoms of anxiety which may also be common to depression (see Eley, this volume).
Neurobiological factors	As reviewed by Gunnar (this volume), extant data, although sparse, suggest that increased stress hormones during fear enhance the excitability of fear circuits and contribute to increased susceptibility to pathological anxiety. The effects of such changes may include activation of genes associated with vulnerability to anxiety.
Temperament	Risk for anxiety (and depression) appears to be associated with high levels on the temperamental dimension of negative affectivity and extremes of behaviorally inhibited temperament (see Lonigan & Phillips, this volume). In contrast, uninhibited temperament may protect against anxiety disorder.
Emotion regulation skills	Deficient emotion regulation skills and maladaptive emotion regulation efforts may place children at risk for anxiety disorder, whereas adequate skills and parental supports may protect against their onset (see Thompson, this volume).
Cognitive biases and distortions	Childhood anxiety is associated with a variety of cognitive biases and distortions (see Vasey & MacLeod, this volume). These appear to exist prior to the onset of anxiety disorders and have significant potential to contribute to their development.
Early control experiences	Mastery experiences—opportunities to control significant aspects of the environment (e.g., access to food)—reduce risk for anxiety. In contrast, limitations on such control experiences may increase risk (see Chorpita, this volume).
Parental responses	Parents may contribute to the development of their child's anxiety through a wide range of paths, including modelling of anxious behavior, overprotection of the child, and inadvertent reinforcement and encouragement of the child's anxious behavior and avoidance (see Dadds & Roth, this volume). Alternatively, by providing appropriate structure and expectations, parents may help protect their child against anxiety disorder (see Thompson, this volume).
Extent of experience with common conditioned stimuli for phobic anxiety	Evidence in both animals (Mineka & Cook, 1968) and children (e.g., Poser & King, 1975) suggests that experience with a stimulus that shows it to be safe or controllable can immunize against the effects of later traumatic conditioning. Such effects may stem from latent inhibition (see Dadds, Davey, & Field, this volume) or enhanced control or self-efficacy beliefs (Chorpita, this volume; Skinner, 1995).
Level of exposure to feared stimuli	Childhood fears may be more likely to persist and intensify to clinical levels if children's opportunities for exposure to feared stimuli is limited. Such limited exposure may stem from the influence of parents and others (see Dadds & Roth, this volume; Menzies & Harris, this volume), or may reflect children's own preferences.

A third example can be found in the potential transaction between the quality of a child's attachment relationship and his/her temperament. Nachmias, Gunnar, Mangelsdorf, Parritz, and Buss (1996) examined the interaction of behaviorally inhibited temperament and attachment status and found that only behaviorally inhibited children in insecure attachment relationships showed elevated levels of cortisol when exposed to the Strange Situation task.

A fourth example can be found in the possibility that the predisposing effects of uncontrollable environments may be mediated, in part, by biological changes. Gunnar (1980) reviewed evidence from studies of human infants that control experiences lead to changes in the endocrine systems associated with stress responses that may increase physiological reactivity to stressful events (see also Nachmias et al., 1996). Similarly, Insel, Scanlan, Champoux, & Suomi (1988) suggest that the anxiety-related effects of early exposure to controllable or uncontrollable environments may be mediated by changes in the benzodiazepine receptor system. However, such effects are also likely to be mediated by control-related cognitions (Bandura, 1989; Skinner, 1995). For example, Lopez and Little (1996) reported that higher levels of agency beliefs are related to lower levels of anxiety in 2nd–6th graders.

Many of these predisposing factors are likely to be enduring in nature, and thus they may play maintaining roles at later points on the pathway to the development and maintenance of an anxiety disorder. Similarly, enduring protective factors may contribute to the amelioration of anxiety disorders subsequent to their onset. These relations are depicted in fig. 1.1 by the arrows connecting predisposing and protective factors to maintaining and ameliorating factors, respectively. Of course, such factors may also have more transient effects and additional factors may appear subsequent to the onset of anxiety disorder that may play maintaining and protective roles.

Two Major Paths to the Onset of Anxiety Disorders

A variety of events may serve to precipitate the onset of anxiety disorders. As depicted in fig. 1.1, such precipitating influences are assumed to be unnecessary in the present model. Thus, the model describes two major pathways to the onset of anxiety disorders. Path 1 involves the influence of clear precipitating events; whereas in path 2, anxiety symptoms gradually intensify through transactional relations among predisposing factors until they reach clinical levels in the absence of any clear precipitant. These two paths are illustrated by the finding of Stemberger et al. (1995) of two paths to social phobia, one involving specific aversive experiences and the other lacking such experiences but instead involving more enduring risks such as temperament.

In path 1, the environmental events that precipitate the onset of anxiety disorder may be experienced either directly or indirectly. These may exert their influence through at least three subpaths: (1) direct and indirect (i.e., modeling and information transmission) respondent conditioning episodes (see Dadds et al., this volume); (2) operant conditioning experiences (see Ollendick et al., this volume); and (3) noncontingent exposure to stressful events.

Based on modern respondent conditioning theory (see Dadds et al., this volume), two types of events may precipitate onset of conditioned anxiety responses to previously neutral stimuli. First, events may produce an expectation that a previously neutral stimulus (i.e., the conditioned stimulus [CS]) predicts the occurrence of an aversive stimulus (i.e., the unconditioned stimulus [UCS]). This may occur through direct experience of such a predictive relation, or such an expectancy may be acquired through modeling or through verbal channels. Second, to the extent that a child has learned that a neutral stimulus predicts another neutral stimulus, a conditioned fear response to the first stimulus may appear if the second stimulus is revalued such that it acquires aversive properties (i.e., it becomes a UCS). Such stimulus revaluation may occur through direct experience or through indirect paths.

However, even severely traumatic episodes are not always sufficient to produce problematic anxiety responses. Many children exposed to traumatic events do not develop phobic responses (Lonigan et al , 1994; Vernberg et al., 1996). Similarly, traumatic conditioning episodes are also not necessary given that phobic anxiety may develop in their absence (Barlow, 1988). Instead, traumatic episodes appear to interact with predisposing factors such as temperament and prior learning history to produce heightened risk for phobic responses in vulnerable individuals (La Greca et al., 1998; Lonigan et al., 1994).

The operant conditioning subpath involves the onset or intensification of anxiety due to punishing experiences that follow approach responses, particularly incompetent approach responses that reflect deficient skills (e.g., social skills). In such a case, such situations may become discriminant stimuli signaling that punishment contingencies are in effect for the ineffective responses in the child's repertoire. As a result, the child may come to fear and avoid such situations.

With regard to the third subpath, evidence suggests that anxiety disorders may appear subsequent to exposure to unrelated stressful events (Barlow, 1988; Jacobs & Nadel, 1985). Several researchers have argued that stressful events may produce anxiety onset through dishabituation or return of previously mastered fears (e.g., normal childhood fears, Jacobs & Nadel, 1985; Menzies & Clarke, 1995). Consistent with this view, Gittelman-Klein and Klein (1980) reported that the onset of SAD in many of the cases they studied followed a major stressor that was unrelated to separation per se, such as an illness or a move to a new home or school. Alternatively, such events may exert their influence by virtue of their relation to the sudden removal of significant protective influences.

Figure 1.1 includes an arrow from cumulative risk to precipitating factors in recognition of the potential for such risks to operate, in part, by increasing the likelihood that children will encounter precipitating events. This is particularly apparent in the case of the operant conditioning subpath. To the extent that children have been sheltered from normal developmental challenges, they are likely to be deficient in important skills and thus may be at increased risk to experience punishing consequences owing to their deficient behavioral repertoires.

As depicted in fig. 1.1 by the arrow from cumulative risk to the arrow from precipitating influences to the onset of anxiety disorder, it is expected that the impact of potential precipitating influences may be moderated by cumulative risk. For example, as noted in the previous section, traumatic events are likely to lead to the onset of phobias or PTSD only among children who are at heightened risk due to anxiety-prone temperament and who lack significant protective factors.

The second path to the onset of anxiety disorder reflects the possibility that predisposing factors may, through repeated transactions over time, produce anxiety symptoms that gradually intensify until they reach clinical levels. One example of such a path can be found in the case of behaviorally inhibited children who are sheltered from exposure to contexts in which their normal fears may be mastered and who learn that their anxiety responses should be avoided because they are intense and uncontrollable. In such cases, an anxiety disorder may evolve gradually as children's temperamental biases and normal childhood fears intensify in transaction with various other risks.

Persistence and Desistance: The Influence of Maintaining and Ameliorating Factors

Once present, childhood anxiety disorders are likely to be maintained and intensified by a variety of influences. Similarly a wide range of influences may contribute to their amelioration. Factors that contribute to the maintenance and amelioration of anxiety disorders include both characteristics of the child and the environmental context the child experiences. As noted above, enduring risks and protective influences that initially influenced the onset of an anxiety disorder are likely to contribute to its maintenance or amelioration subsequent to onset. Figure 1.1 depicts these relations with arrows pointing from predisposing and protective factors forward in time to maintaining and ameliorating factors. These factors may be much the same as they were in the early stages of the pathway or they may have evolved by virtue of the child's experiences or development. For example, reflecting the view that early adaptation constrains later adaptation, the information-processing biases or emotion regulation deficits that initially predisposed to anxiety disorder may be significantly magnified by prolonged avoidance of critical developmental contexts. Of course, it is expected that some maintaining or ameliorating influences may arise subsequent to the onset of an anxiety disorder and have little or no direct relation to factors that predisposed to or protected against initial onset. Similarly, not all predisposing and protective factors are expected to exert persistent influence.

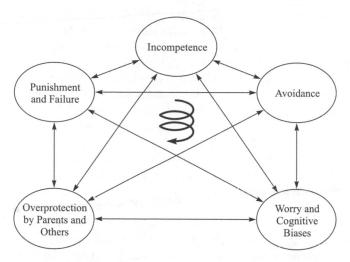

Figure 1.2. Possible contributors to the maintenance of anxiety disorders and potential transactional relations among them across time.

Although it is very likely that genetic and neurobiological factors may contribute to the maintenance of anxiety disorders, little is yet known about such influences or their relations to other possible maintaining or ameliorating factors. Thus, the present discussion will focus primarily on characteristics of anxious children and the environmental contexts in which they operate that may contribute to the persistence or desistance of developmental trajectories involving anxiety disorders.

Figure 1.2 depicts five main factors that are hypothesized to operate in dynamic transaction, with each having the potential to contribute to the maintenance and intensification of the others. Thus, together, these factors contribute to a cycle by which anxiety disorders may persist or desist. The five factors are: (1) excessive reliance on coping responses involving cognitive or behavioral avoidance; (2) incompetence with regard to social, emotion-regulation, and academic skills; (3) cognitive biases and distorted beliefs; (4) punishment and failure experiences including rejection and criticism by peers and parents; and (5) behaviors by parents and others that serve to protect the child from exposure to anxiety-provoking situations or reward the child for anxiety-related behaviors.

Once present, childhood anxiety disorders are likely to be maintained, in part, by the effects that anxious children have on their environments. This possibility is depicted in fig. 1.1 by the arrow pointing from the anxiety disorder onset oval to the maintaining influences oval. Just as antisocial children are architects of the coercive environments that foster their antisocial behavior (Patterson et al., 1992), anxious children may foster their own anxiety by virtue of their tendency to avoid anxiety-provoking situations and through their impact on the behavior of those around them.

To the extent that anxious children avoid contact with anxiety-provoking contexts, they are less likely to master the skills necessary for competent functioning in those contexts. Thus, when they do enter them, they are more likely to experience failure or other punishing consequences and less likely to encounter the contingencies that normally foster development in such contexts. As noted previously, this pathway is similar to the notion of "limited shopping" in Patterson's theory of antisocial behavior (Patterson et al., 1992). Because antisocial children become rejected by their peers and fail academically, their contact with important developmental contexts becomes increasingly limited, denying them opportunities to learn important skills. Such limited opportunities exacerbate their incompetence and make it increasingly likely that they will remain on deviant developmental pathways. Similarly, anxious children may also suffer the cumulative effects of limited contact with important developmental contexts owing to their tendency toward avoidant behavior and biased information processing. In turn, this increases the likelihood of punishing consequences, which in turn make avoidance even more likely in the future. Similarly, such experiences are likely to strengthen children's tendency toward anxiogenic cognitive biases and distortions.

Put another way, by virtue of their excessive reliance on cognitive and behavioral avoidance, anxious children reduce their exposure to corrective information so their anxiogenic maladaptive beliefs persist, deficits in their knowledge and skills increase, and their exposure to habituation or mastery contexts is further reduced (Foa & Kozak, 1986). For example, social avoidance may interfere with the correction of socially anxious children's distorted beliefs about social situations. Hauck, Martens, and Wetzel (1986) found that social avoidance interferes with the dissolution of the imaginary audience beliefs of adolescents, thereby contributing to persistent social anxiety. They studied imaginary audience awareness in adolescents and found that, "shyness of adolescents highly sensitive to an imaginary audience increased with age, possibly because they are unwilling to provide themselves with the social experiences necessary for decentering" (p. 529). In other words, these adolescents avoid social contact and thus never get exposed to information that might help them correct their distorted, anxiety-promoting beliefs or rules. Thus, they continue to experience an imaginary audience long after most others have corrected such adolescent cognitive distortions.

Avoiding challenges such as those in academic and social domains is also likely to lead to gradually broadening impairment and developmental delays due to lack of practice. Evans (1993) provided an excellent example of this in her discussion of the impaired discourse skills of socially withdrawn children. She noted: "Poorer communicative competence may be an outcome of a vicious cycle in which shy individuals have less experience through personal choice or the lack of opportunities afforded them to observe, try out, and practice interactional strategies" (p. 205). Without sufficient practice, such skills cannot become automatic in the manner required for competent discourse. Thus, the potential to fall behind peers in discourse skills owing to social avoidance seems high, and similar potential exists for falling behind in other skills.

Parents and teachers may also foster anxiety both because they are empathic and don't wish to cause children distress and because children's anxious responses can provide powerful consequences that punish those who impose anxiety-provoking demands and reinforce those who provide relief from such demands. Moreover, to the extent that anxious children become less competent at handling challenges over time, parents and teachers may become even more likely to protect them from such threats.

Although such avoidance by the child and avoidance-fostering behaviors by parents and others are likely to be effective at reducing anxiety in the short term, they are also likely to maintain and intensify vulnerability to anxiety in the long term. Kendall (1992) argued that short-term avoidance solutions can result in a habit that "forecloses on later adaptation." In other words, avoidance of anxiety-provoking situations is a coping strategy that has serious potential to impede future adaptation. Similarly, Thompson and Calkins (1996) suggested that vulnerable children's choices of anxiety regulating strategies may leave them vulnerable to problematic anxiety.

[handwritten margin note: coping strategy: stop driving to avoid panic attacks]

To the extent that children's avoidance is rewarded with short-term reductions in anxiety, it is likely to persist. Furthermore, because early avoidance typically require less effort than later avoidance (Stampfl, 1987), anxious children's avoidance responses, and their parents efforts to foster the child's avoidance, may gradually shift backward in time so that such children eventually do not even come close to feared situations. Such reductions in effort serve to reinforce avoidance in response to ever more distal cues that predict the ultimate encounter with the feared situation.

In summary, children's anxiety is likely to be maintained and intensified by virtue of: (a) its association with avoidance of important developmental contexts; (b) punishment and failure experiences; (c) cognitive biases and distortions; (d) growing incompetence in vital skill domains; and (e) responses by parents, teachers, and others which foster the child's avoidance or reward anxiety related behavior. In turn, each of these elements contributes to the maintenance and intensification of each of the others. Parents and teachers protect and compensate more as the child's incompetence grows. Growing incompetence fosters punishment and failure. Cognitive biases and distortions contribute to incompetence by sapping available attentional resources (Vasey & Daleiden, 1996). And so, in a worst-case scenario, the cycle can proceed on a downward spiral.

Finally, the cycle of persistence depicted in fig. 1.2 suggests the possibility of a complementary cycle of desistance. In such a cycle, each of the five elements would be replaced by its complement. Thus, avoidance becomes approach (i.e., exposure), incompetence becomes competence, cognitive biases and distortions adaptive cognitions (e.g., efficacy beliefs), punishment and failure is replaced by reward and success, and parental overprotection becomes parental support for approach and anxiety mastery. As in the cycle of persistence, transactional relations are expected among these influences that contribute to the child's gradual movement toward competence and remission of anxiety disorder. For example, as a child develops competence in various skills, success experiences should gradually replace failures. However, this will be, in part, a function of the extent to which the child approaches rather than avoids relevant contexts.

Although maintaining and intensifying factors may operate similarly regardless of the path by which the problematic anxiety is acquired, they may also operate differently in some paths than others depending on organismic variables such as temperament and developmental status. For example, a child who has a stable behaviorally inhibited temperament may respond to other maintaining factors more easily and strongly than most children (e.g., they may be more easily sensitized by even mildly punishing consequences). Similarly, they may respond to potentially corrective factors less rapidly and more weakly than most children (e.g., they may be poor habituators). Thus, it may take less to maintain anxiety in such children than it would in most others whereas it may take less to correct problematic anxiety in uninhibited children than most others. There may also be developmental differences in the operation of various factors. Some may operate only at particular ages (i.e., critical periods) or they may operate differently as various other skills or characteristics develop. For example, recent research on childhood depression suggests that cognitive variables such as attributional style do not serve to moderate the effects of negative life events on depression until preadolescence (Nolen-Hoeksema, Girgus, & Seligman, 1992; Turner & Cole, 1994).

Conclusion

The framework offered in this chapter is meant to foster conceptualization of the potentially diverse pathways by which childhood anxiety disorders may develop, persist, or remit. The elements discussed vary in the extent to which they are supported by empirical evidence. Because the upsurge of research activity in this area began only recently, most elements remain poorly understood and are in need of considerable attention by researchers. The potential for reciprocal relationships among these factors is a particularly important focus for future research. Because childhood anxiety disorders are likely to be consequences of multiple factors, it is unlikely that the role of any single factor can be understood if it is studied in isolation. Therefore, it is important that future research efforts concerning the etiology, prevention, and treatment of problematic childhood anxiety consider multiple factors and the potential transactional relationships among them. It is hoped that the framework offered in this chapter will foster such research efforts.

Acknowledgment and Note

Thanks are extended to Kelly Woolaway Bickel, Eric Daleiden, J. Michael Kendren, and Charles Wenar for their helpful feedback regarding this chapter. Please address correspondence to Michael W. Vasey, Department of Psychology, Ohio State University, 1885 Neil Avenue, Columbus, Ohio 43210-1222, USA. Email: Vasey.1@osu.edu.

References

American Psychiatric Association (1980). *Diagnostic and statistical manual of mental disorders* (3rd ed.). Washington, DC: American Psychiatric Association.

American Psychiatric Association (1994). *Diagnostic and statistical manual of mental disorders* (4th ed.). Washington, DC: American Psychiatric Association.

Anderson, J. C. (1994). Epidemiological issues. In T. H. Ollendick, N. J. King, & W. Yule (Eds.), *International handbook of phobic and anxiety disorders in children and adolescents* (pp. 43–66). New York: Plenum.

Anderson, J. C., Williams, S., McGee, R., & Silva, P. A. (1987). DSM-III disorders in preadolescent children: Prevalence in a large sample from the general population. *Archives of General Psychiatry, 44,* 69–76.

Bandura, A. (1989). Human agency in social cognitive theory. *American Psychologist, 44,* 1175–1184.

Barlow, D. A. (1988). *Anxiety and its disorders: The nature and treatment of anxiety and panic.* New York: Guilford.

Brady, E. U., & Kendall, P. C. (1992). Comorbidity of anxiety and depression in children and adolescents. *Psychological Bulletin, 111,* 244–255.

Burke, C. B., Burke, J. D., Regier, D. A., & Rae, D. S. (1990). Age at onset of selected mental disorders in five community populations. *Archives of General Psychiatry, 47,* 511–518.

Calkins, S. D. (1994). Origins and outcomes of individual differences in emotion regulation. In N. A. Fox (Ed.), *The development of emotion regulation: Biological and behavioral considerations* (pp. 53–72). *Monographs of the Society for Research in Child Development, 59* (2–3, Serial No. 240).

Chorpita, B., & Barlow, D. (1998). The development of anxiety: The role of control in the early environment. *Psychological Bulletin, 124,* 3–21.

Cicchetti, D., & Cohen, D. J. (1995). Perspectives on developmental psychopathology. In D. Cicchetti & D. Cohen (Eds.), *Developmental psychopathology: Vol. 1. Theory and methods* (pp. 3–20). New York: Wiley.

Cole, D. A., Peeke, L. G., Martin, J. M., Truglio, R., & Serocynski, A. D. (1998). A longitudinal look at the relation between depression and anxiety in children and adolescents. *Journal of Consulting and Clinical Psychology, 66,* 451–460.

Daleiden, E. L., Vasey, M. W., & Brown, L. M. (1999). Internalizing disorders. In W. K. Silverman & T. H. Ollendick (Eds.), *Developmental issues in the clinical treatment of children and adolescents* (pp. 261–278). New York: Allyn & Bacon.

Dweck, C., & Wortman, C. (1982). Learned helplessness, anxiety, and achievement. In H. Krohne & L. Laux (Eds.), *Achievement, stress, and anxiety.* New York: Hemisphere.

Evans, M. A. (1993). Communication competence as a dimension of shyness. In K. H. Rubin & J. B. Asendorpf (Eds.), *Social withdrawal, inhibition, and shyness in childhood* (pp. 189–212). Hillsdale, NJ: Erlbaum.

Foa, E. B., & Kozak, M. (1986). Emotional processing of fear: Exposure to corrective information. *Psychological Bulletin, 99,* 20–35.

Francis, G., Last, C. G., & Strauss, C. C. (1992). Avoidant disorder and social phobia in children and adolescents. *Journal of the American Academy of Child and Adolescent Psychiatry, 31,* 1086–1089.

Garber, J., & Strassberg, Z. (1991). Construct validity: History and applications to developmental psychopathology. In W. M. Grove & D. Cicchetti (Eds.), *Thinking clearly about psychology: Vol. 2. Personality and psychopathology* (pp. 219–258). Minneapolis: University of Minnesota Press.

Gittelman-Klein, R., & Klein, D. F. (1980). Separation anxiety in school refusal and its treatment with drugs. In L. Hersov & I. Berg (Eds.), *Out of school* (pp. 321–341). New York: Wiley.

Gunnar, M. (1980). Contingent stimulation: A review of its role in early development. In S. Levine & H. Ursin (Eds.), *Coping and health* (pp. 101–119). New York: Plenum.

Hayward, C., Killen, J. D., Kraemer, H. C., & Taylor, C. B. (1998). Linking self-reported childhood behavioral inhibition to adolescent social phobia. *Journal of the American Academy of Child and Adolescent Psychiatry, 37,* 1308–1316.

Hauck, W. E., Martens, M., & Wetzel, M. (1986). Shyness, group dependence and self-concept: Attributes of the imaginary audience. *Adolescence, 21,* 529–534.

Insel, T. R., Scanlan, J., Champoux, M., & Suomi, S. J. (1988). Rearing paradigm in a nonhuman primate affects response to β-CCE challenge. *Psychopharmacology, 96,* 81–86.

Jacobs, W. J., & Nadel, L. (1985). Stress-induced recovery of fears and phobias. *Psychological Review, 92,* 512–531.

Kagan, J. (1997). Temperament and the reactions to unfamiliarity. *Child Development, 68,* 139–143.

Kashani, J. H., & Orvaschel, H. (1990). A community study of anxiety in children and adolescents. *American Journal of Psychiatry, 147,* 313–318.

Kashani, J. H., Orvaschel, H., Rosenberg, T. K., & Reid, J. C. (1989). Psychopathology in a community sample of children and adolescents: A developmental perspective. *Journal of the American Academy of Child and Adolescent Psychiatry, 28,* 701–706.

Kazdin, A. E., & Kagan, J. (1994). Models of dysfunction in developmental psychopathology. *Clinical Psychology: Science and Practice, 1,* 35–52.

Keller, M. B., Lavori, P. W., Wunder, J., Beardslee, W. R., & Schwartz, C. E. (1992). Chronic course of anxiety disorders in children and adolescents. *Journal of the American Academy of Child and Adolescent Psychiatry, 31,* 595–599.

Kendall, P. C. (1992). Childhood coping: Avoiding a lifetime of anxiety. *Behaviour Change, 9,* 229–237.

Kendler, K. S., Neale, M. C., Kessler, R. C., Heath, A. C., & Eaves, L. J. (1992). The genetic epidemiology of phobias in women: The interrelationship of agoraphobia, social phobia, situational phobia, and simple phobia. *Archives of General Psychiatry, 49,* 273–281.

Kovacs, M., Feinberg, T. L., Crouse-Novak, M., Paulauskas, S. L., & Finkelstein, R. (1984). Depressive disorders in childhood: II. A longitudinal study of the risk for subsequent major depression. *Archives of General Psychiatry, 41,* 643–649.

La Greca, A. M., Silverman, W. K., Vernberg, E. M., & Prinstein, M. J. (1996). Symptoms of posttraumatic stress in children after hurricane Andrew: A prospective study. *Journal of Consulting and Clinical Psychology, 64,* 712–723.

La Greca, A. M., Silverman, W. K., & Wasserstein, S. B. (1998). Children's pre-disaster functioning as a predictor of posttraumatic stress following

Hurricane Andrew. *Journal of Consulting and Clinical Psychology*, *66*, 883–892.

Last, C. G., Hanson, C., & Franco, N. (1997). Anxious children in adulthood: A prospective study of adjustment. *Journal of the American Academy of Child and Adolescent Psychiatry*, *36*, 645–652.

Last, C. G., Perrin, S., Hersen, M., & Kazdin, A. E. (1996). A prospective study of childhood anxiety disorders. *Journal of the American Academy of Child and Adolescent Psychiatry*, *35*, 1502–1510.

Lewinsohn, P. M., Clarke, G. N., Seeley, J. R., & Rohde, P. (1994). Major depression in community adolescents: Age at onset, episode duration, and time to recurrence. *Journal of the American Academy of Child and Adolescent Psychiatry*, *33*, 809–818.

Lonigan, C. J., Shannon, M. P., Taylor, C. M., Finch, A. J., & Sallee, F. R. (1994). Children exposed to disaster: II. Risk factors for the development of post-traumatic symptomatology. *Journal of the American Academy of Child and Adolescent Psychiatry*, *33*, 94–105.

Lopez, D. F., & Little, T. D. (1996). Children's action-control beliefs and emotional regulation in the social domain. *Developmental Psychology*, *32*, 299–312.

Manassis, K., & Bradley, S. J. (1994). The development of childhood anxiety disorders: Toward an integrated model. *Journal of Applied Developmental Psychology*, *15*, 345–366.

Masten, A.S., & Braswell, L. (1991). Developmental psychopathology: An integrative framework. In P. R. Martin (Ed.), *Handbook of behavior therapy and psychological science. An integrative approach* (pp. 35–56). New York: Pergamon.

McGee, R. & Stanton, W. R. (1990). Parent reports of disability among 13-year-olds with DSM-III disorders. *Journal of Child Psychology & Psychiatry and Allied Disciplines*, *31*, 793–801.

Menzies, R. G., & Clark, J. C. (1995). The etiology of phobias: A non-associative account. *Clinical Psychology Review*, *15*, 23–48.

Merckelbach, H., de Jong, P. J. d., Muris, P., & Hout, M. A. v. d. (1996). The etiology of specific phobias: A review. *Clinical Psychology Review*, *16*, 337–361.

Mineka, S., & Cook, M. (1986). Immunization against observational conditioning of snake fear in rhesus monkeys. *Journal of Abnormal Psychology*, *95*, 307–318.

Moffitt, T. E. (1993). Adolescence-limited and life-course-persistent antisocial behavior: Developmental taxonomy. *Psychological Review*, *100*, 674–701.

Nachmias, M., Gunnar, M., Mangelsdorf, S., Parritz, R. H., & Buss, K. (1996). Behavioral inhibition and stress reactivity: The moderating role of attachment security. *Child Development*, *67*, 508–522.

Nolen-Hoeksema, S., & Girgus, J. S. (1994). The emergence of gender differences in depression during adolescence. *Psychological Bulletin*, *115*, 424–443.

Ollendick, T. H., & King, N. J. (1994). Diagnosis, assessment, and treatment of internalizing problems in children: The role of longitudinal data. *Journal of Consulting and Clinical Psychology*, *62*, 918–927.

Orvaschel, H., Lewinsohn, P. M., & Seeley, J. R. (1995). Continuity of psychopathology in a community sample of adolescents. *Journal of the American Academy of Child and Adolescent Psychiatry*, *34*, 1525–1535.

Öst, L.-G. (1987). Age of onset in different phobias. *Journal of Abnormal Psychology*, *96*, 223–229.

Patterson, G. R., Reid, J. B., & Dishion, T. J. (1992). *Antisocial boys*. Eugene, OR: Castalia Publishing.

Perrin, S., & Last, C. G. (1995). Dealing with comorbidity. In A. R. Eisen, C. A. Kearney, & C. A. Schaefer (Eds.), *Clinical handbook of anxiety disorders in children and adolescents* (pp. 412–435). Northvale, NJ: Jason Aronson.

Poser, E. G., & King, M. C. (1975). Strategies for the prevention of maladaptive fear responses. *Canadian Journal of Behavioural Science, 7*, 279–294.

Rothbart, M. K., Posner, M. I., & Hershey, K. L. (1995). Temperament, attention, and developmental psychopathology. In D. Cicchetti & D. J. Cohen (Eds.), *Developmental psychopathology: Vol. 1. Theory and methods* (pp. 315–340). New York: Wiley.

Silove, D., Manicavasagar, V., Curtis, J., & Blaszczynski, A. (1996). Is early separation anxiety a risk factor for adult panic disorder? A critical review. *Comprehensive Psychiatry, 37*, 167–179.

Skinner, E. A. (1995). *Perceived control, motivation, and coping*. Thousand Oaks, CA: Sage.

Spence, S. H. (1997). Structure of anxiety symptoms among children: A confirmatory factor-analytic study. *Journal of Abnormal Psychology, 106*, 280–297.

Stampfl, T. G. (1987). Theoretical implications of the neurotic paradox as a problem in behavior therapy: An experimental resolution. *Behavior Analyst, 10*, 161–173.

Stemberger, R. T., Turner, S. M., Beidel, D. C., & Calhoun, K. S. (1995). Social phobia: An analysis of possible developmental factors. *Journal of Abnormal Psychology, 104*, 526–531.

Strauss, C. C., Frame, C. L., & Forehand, R. (1987). Psychosocial impairment associated with anxiety in children. *Journal of Clinical Child Psychology, 16*, 235–239.

Thompson, R. A., & Calkins, S. D. (1996). The double-edged sword: Emotional regulation for children at risk. *Development and Psychopathology, 8*, 163–182.

Turner, J. E., & Cole, D. A. (1994). Developmental differences in cognitive diatheses for childhood depression. *Journal of Abnormal Child Psychology, 22*, 15–32.

Vasey, M. W. (1993). Development and cognition in childhood anxiety: The example of worry. In T. H. Ollendick & R. Prinz (Eds.), *Advances in clinical child psychology* (Vol. 15, pp. 1–39). New York: Plenum.

Vasey, M. W., & Daleiden, E. L. (1996). Information-processing pathways to cognitive interference in childhood. In I. G. Sarason, G. Pierce, & B. Sarason (Eds.), *Cognitive interference: Theory, methods, and findings* (pp. 117–138). Hillsdale, NJ: Lawrence Erlbaum.

Vasey, M. W., & Ollendick, T. H. (2000). Anxiety. In M. Lewis and A. Sameroff (Eds.), *Handbook of developmental psychopathology* (2nd ed.), pp. 511–529. New York: Plenum.

Vernberg, E. M., La Greca, A. M., Silverman, W. K., & Prinstein, M. J. (1996). Prediction of posttraumatic stress symptoms in children after Hurricane Andrew. *Journal of Abnormal Psychology, 105*, 237–248.

2

Developmental Variations in the Prevalence and Manifestation of Anxiety Disorders

DANIELLE D. WEISS and CYNTHIA G. LAST

Although there is growing interest in childhood anxiety disorders, there has been limited integrative discussion of factors that contribute to development of anxiety disorders across the lifespan. Examination of developmental patterns in prevalence rates and manifestations of anxiety disorders is fundamental to a clear understanding of the developmental psychopathology of anxiety. This is true for a number of reasons. First, research on anxiety disorders requires a clear understanding of the forms taken by the disorders throughout life. Second, theories on developmental psychopathology of anxiety need to first describe and then explain variations seen in the prevalence and manifestation of anxiety across ages and genders. Finally, information on developmental patterns of anxiety may offer clues regarding factors that contribute to the development and maintenance of anxiety disorders. This information may in turn inform treatment and prevention of anxiety disorders.

In this chapter we aim to provide a comprehensive, integrative review of current research on the manifestation and prevalence of anxiety disorders throughout childhood and across genders. First we discuss the overall prevalence of anxiety disorders in community samples. Next we address the overall prevalence of anxiety disorders in clinical samples. Then we consider the research on individual anxiety disorders to identify patterns for each disorder across age and gender. Finally, we suggest directions for future research.

Community Samples

Anxiety disorders represent one of the most common categories of child and adolescent psychopathology (e.g., Bernstein & Borchardt, 1991; Kashani & Orvaschel, 1990). Among nonreferred children and adolescents, prevalence rates for anxiety disorders have ranged from 10.7% (McGee et al., 1990) to 17.3% (Kashani & Orvaschel, 1988). Community sample studies find the most common disorders are separation anxiety disorder (Bird et al., 1988) and simple phobia (Anderson, Williams, McGee, & Silva, 1987).

27

In community samples, anxiety symptoms and disorders may be more common in girls (Costello, 1989; Kashani & Orvaschel, 1988, 1990) and younger children (Bell-Dolan, Last, & Strauss, 1990). Anxiety disorders have been associated with repetition of a grade in school, and family difficulties including parental stress about the child (Costello, 1989).

Results across studies may vary due to methodological differences, such as use of different diagnostic measures and criteria, and use of child versus parental report of symptoms. Kashani and Orvaschel (1990) and Benjamin, Costello, and Warren (1990) found that parents may report differently from children. Results between studies may also vary owing to differences in the diagnostic criteria used. Bell-Dolan et al. (1990) concluded that lower prevalence estimates are generally reported in studies utilizing more stringent criteria for identification of children as anxiety-disordered.

Despite these considerations, findings from community samples suggest that anxiety disorders are among the most common types of psychopathology present in children and adolescents. This indicates that research investigating the development and maintenance of childhood anxiety disorders is well justified.

Clinical Samples

Research indicates that anxiety disorders are more prevalent among clinical samples than among samples of nonreferred children. Last, Perrin, Hersen, and Kazdin (1992) reported that among clinic-referred youngsters (ages 5–18) lifetime prevalence rates for the more common anxiety disorders were 44.7% for separation anxiety disorder (SAD), 42.6% for simple phobia, 32.4% for social phobia, and 27.1% for overanxious disorder (OAD). Rates for the less common anxiety disorders were 14.9% for obsessive–compulsive disorder (OCD), 12.8% for panic disorder, 10.6% for avoidant disorder, and 3.7% for posttraumatic stress disorder (PTSD).

In a prospective study by Last, Perrin, Hersen, and Kazdin (1996), anxiety-disordered youngsters (5–18 years old) and peers who were never psychiatrically ill (NPI) were followed over 3–4 years. Prevalence rates for specific anxiety disorders among the anxious children were 31% for simple phobia, 29% for SAD, 27% for social phobia, 14% for OCD, 12% for panic disorder, 7% for avoidant disorder, 6% for PTSD, and 1% for anxiety disorder NOS. During follow-up, 30% of anxious children developed new psychiatric disorders while 11% of NPI children developed psychiatric disorders. Among children in the anxious group, 16% developed new anxiety disorders compared with 2% of NPI children. However, by the end of the follow-up period, 82% of the anxious children no longer met criteria for their intake anxiety disorders.

As would be expected, anxiety disorders appear to be more prevalent among clinical samples than among nonreferred samples. Furthermore, children referred for treatment of an anxiety disorder may be at greater risk than their never-psychiatrically-ill peers for developing new anxiety disorders.

Specific Anxiety Disorders

Separation Anxiety Disorder (SAD)

SAD is more prevalent among referred samples, including children referred specifically to an anxiety disorders clinic, than among community samples. Prevalence rates for SAD range from around 2% (Bowen, Offord, & Boyle, 1990) to 12% (Kashani & Orvaschel, 1990) in community samples and from around 29% (Last et al., 1992) to 45% (Last et al., 1996) among referred children.

Among a large general sample of 11-year-olds, SAD was one of the most prevalent DSM-III disorders with a 1-year prevalence rate of 3.5% and a female to male gender ratio equal to 1:0.4 (Anderson et al., 1987). Costello (1989) reported the weighted 1-year prevalence for SAD was 4.1% in a general pediatric sample (ages 7–11).This included 5% of girls and 3.1% of boys in the sample. In a general sample of 15-year-olds, the prevalence rate for SAD was 2.0% (McGee et al., 1990). Similar to younger samples, more females had SAD than males (F:M = 1.8:1.0).

Velez, Johnson, and Cohen (1989) followed nonreferred children (ages 1–10) over 8- and 10-year intervals. At 8-year follow-up, SAD was diagnosed in 25.6% of younger (ages 9–12) and 6.8% of older (ages 13–18) children. Two years later, prevalence decreased to 15.3% of children aged 11–14 years and 4.4% of children 15–20 years old. At both follow-ups, no gender differences were found within each age group.

In a community epidemiological study of children aged 12–16 years, there were close to equal numbers of males and females diagnosed with SAD (Bowen et al., 1990). Various ways of operationalizing DSM-III-R criteria for SAD yielded prevalence rates from 2.4% to 2.7%. Bird et al. (1988) reported that for SAD among nonreferred children (ages 4–16), 6-month-weighted prevalence rate for SAD with "definite maladjustment" was 4.7% compared with 2.1% for SAD with "possible maladjustment." Age-based comparisons revealed SAD was more common among children aged 6–11 years than among children 4–5 years or 12–16 years of age.

In a community sample (ages 8, 12, and 17), 12.4% of subjects met criteria for SAD (Kashani & Orvaschel, 1990). SAD affected 21% of females compared with 4.8% of males. Among 8-year-olds, 18.6% met criteria for SAD. The prevalence rate dropped to 8.6% among 12-year-olds and increased to 11.4% among 17-year-olds.

As would be expected, SAD is more common in clinical samples. Among youngsters with anxiety disorders (ages 5–18), SAD was the most common [can be a lifetime prevalence] anxiety diagnosis with a lifetime prevalence of 44.7% (Last et al., 1992). Of children with SAD, 47.6% were male. The mean age-at-onset for SAD was 7.5 years. However, the average age-at-intake was 10.3 years, suggesting some time lapse between onset and presentation for treatment.

In a 3- to 4-year prospective study, SAD was present among 29% of children (ages 5–18 years), and was the primary diagnosis for 21% of the sample (Last et al., 1996). By the end of follow-up, 22 of the 24 children

(92%) previously diagnosed with SAD no longer met criteria for the disorder. However, about 25% of SAD children developed a new psychiatric disorder by follow-up, most commonly a depressive disorder.

Last, Hersen, Kazdin, Finkelstein, and Strauss (1987) reported that among children aged 5–18 years with SAD, the mean age was 9.1 years and almost all SAD children (91%) were prepubertal. Of children with SAD, 64% were female. Another sample of children with SAD had a mean age at intake of 9.4 years. (Last, Francis, Hersen, Kazdin, & Strauss, 1987). More children were female (69%) than male.

SAD was the most common primary diagnosis in a sample of children and adolescents referred to the same anxiety disorder clinic with 32.9% meeting criteria for the disorder (Last, Strauss, & Francis, 1987). These children had an average age of 8.9 years at intake and included more girls (67%) than boys. Last and Strauss (1990) later examined school refusal in youngsters (aged 7–17) referred to the same anxiety clinic; of children with anxiety-based school refusal, 38% were diagnosed with SAD, and the average age at onset for SAD was 8.7 years.

A study by Francis, Last, and Strauss (1987) of outpatients with SAD revealed age differences, but no gender differences, in symptom constellation and number of symptoms. The most prevalent symptoms in young children (5–8 years) were "worry about harm befalling an attachment figure" and "reluctance or refusal to go to school." Middle children (9–12 years) most often reported excessive distress upon separation, while all adolescents (13–16 years) had physical complaints on school days. Young children presented with a greater number of symptoms than middle children.

Differences in findings obtained from these studies may be due, at least in part, to variations in the experimental designs. As discussed earlier, requiring clinically significant impairment may affect prevalence rates. Changes from DSM-III to DSM-III-R and DSM-IV may also contribute to the variability in the findings described. In addition, the different samples included, such as school children versus children receiving general pediatric care, may vary in terms of their characteristics and relative levels of functioning. Nonetheless, the studies reviewed illustrate a number of general patterns.

Overall, girls appear more likely to suffer from SAD than boys regardless of whether the samples are community- or clinic-based (e.g., Kashani & Orvaschel, 1990; Last, Hersen, et al., 1987). In addition, it seems that younger children are more likely to suffer from SAD than older children (e.g., Kashani & Orvaschel, 1990; Velez et al., 1989). The average age at onset among referred children ranged from 7.5 years to 8.7 years, suggesting that, for referred children, onset of the disorder seems to peak during the early grade school years. However, based on the literature, average age at intake varies from 8.9 years to 10.3 years, suggesting some delay between onset of the disorder and presentation for treatment.

In addition to being at greater risk for SAD, younger children may present with different symptom constellations than older children (Francis et al., 1987). Younger children with SAD may experience a greater number of symptoms than older children and adolescents diagnosed with SAD. The specific symptom presentation of SAD also seems to vary with developmental level.

Overanxious Disorder (OAD)

Overanxious disorder (OAD) is no longer included as an anxiety disorder in the DSM-IV. It has been replaced by generalized anxiety disorder (GAD) which previously was diagnosed only in adults.

Reported prevalence rates of OAD among nonreferred children and adolescents have ranged from around 3% (Anderson et al., 1987) to 12% (Kashani & Orvaschel, 1990). Among clinical samples, the disorder is more common with a prevalence rate ranging from about 24% (Last et al., 1996) to 27% (Last et al., 1992). Although Last and colleagues (1996) reported a relatively high recovery rate of 80% over 3 to 4 years, more severe cases have a greater likelihood of persisting over time (Cohen, Cohen, & Brook, 1993). Bowen et al. (1990) reported prevalence rates for OAD in nonreferred children (aged 4–16) ranged from 0% to 32.3% depending on how the diagnostic criteria were operationally defined.

An epidemiological study of community children aged 8, 12, and 17 years revealed that 12.4% of children suffered from OAD (Kashani & Orvaschel, 1990). More girls (15.2%) were affected by OAD than boys (9.5%). When age groups were compared, OAD was more common in 17-year-olds than in 8- or 12-year-olds. Costello (1989) examined DSM-III disorders in a primary-care pediatric sample of children aged 7–11 years. The 1-year prevalence rate for OAD was 4.6%, and more girls (6.4%) than boys (2.6%) were diagnosed with OAD.

Anderson et al. (1987) reported the 1-year prevalence rate for OAD was 2.9% among nonreferred 11-year-olds. OAD was more common among boys than girls with a M:F gender ratio of 1.7:1.0. In a nonclinical sample of 15-year-olds, OAD was present in 5.9% of adolescents with a M:F gender ratio of 1.9:1.0 (McGee et al., 1990). The most commonly reported symptoms related to school exams, sports performance, and others' opinions especially in social situations.

OAD was the most prevalent disorder in a community sample of 150 adolescents aged 14–16 years (Kashani & Orvaschel, 1988). Of 26 adolescents with anxiety disorders, 11 were identified as having OAD and functional impairment requiring treatment.

Velez et al. (1989) followed a nonclinical sample of children (aged 1–10 at intake) over 8- and 10-year intervals. Prevalence rates for OAD at 8-year follow-up were 19.1% in younger children (9–12 years) compared with 12.7% in older children (13–18 years). At 10-year follow-up, rates had decreased to 9.7% among younger children, and 8.6% in the older group. At both follow-up points there was no gender difference for the younger group, but prevalence was higher for females in the older group. Boys evidenced a gender-specific decline in prevalence of OAD with age, so that the gender ratio became weighted towards girls as children got older. This is consistent with a review of the literature by Werry (1991) who reported, that while OAD may begin at any age in childhood, the higher remission rate in males leads to an equal gender ratio until adolescence after which females predominate.

A $2\frac{1}{2}$-year longitudinal investigation of OAD in a general sample of youngsters (aged 9–18) indicated that greater severity was associated with greater likelihood that OAD would persist over time (Cohen et al., 1993). Diagnostic persistence did not appear to differ by age or gender. However, age did appear to interact with new onset of OAD at follow-up. For children in the younger group (aged 9–13), about one in five cases diagnosed at follow-up were new onset regardless of severity. Among the older group (aged 14–18), 56–60% of mild or moderate cases diagnosed at follow-up were new onset.

Last et al. (1996) followed anxiety-disordered children (aged 5–18) over a period of 3 to 4 years. OAD was present in 24% of subjects and was the primary diagnosis for 14% of the sample. OAD had one of the higher recovery rates in this partially treated sample, with 80% no longer meeting criteria for the disorder at follow-up.

Among 73 children and adolescents referred to an anxiety disorder clinic, 15.1% received a primary diagnosis of OAD (Last, Strauss, & Francis, 1987).The average age at intake for children with OAD was 10.8 years. More boys than girls had OAD as their primary diagnosis.

In another clinic sample of children and adolescents (aged 5–18) with anxiety disorders, OAD was one of the more common anxiety disorders with a lifetime prevalence of 27.1% (Last et al., 1992). OAD was the primary diagnosis at intake for 13.3% of participants. The mean age-at-onset for OAD was 8.8 years. Somewhat more females (52.9%) than males (47.1%) suffered from OAD.

In a sample of youngsters (5–18 years) referred to an outpatient anxiety clinic, children with OAD had a mean age at intake of 13.4 years and included equal numbers of boys and girls (Last, Hersen, et al., 1987). OAD was most likely to occur at or after puberty (69%).

From a sample of 106 anxiety-disordered children, Strauss, Lease, Last, and Francis (1988) identified 55 children with OAD. Fifty-five percent of the younger group (aged 5–11) was female compared with 62% of the older group (aged 12–19). Older children presented with a greater total number of OAD symptoms than younger children. The frequency of specific symptoms did not appear to differ based on age, and the most common symptom in both groups was "unrealistic worry about future events." Older children were more likely to have concurrent major depression or simple phobia, whereas younger children more often presented with comorbid SAD or attention deficit disorder (ADD). Older children also reported higher levels of anxiety and depression.

Overall, OAD appears to be more prevalent among older children than younger children (e.g., Cohen et al., 1993; Kashani & Orvaschel, 1990).

According to Last, Hersen, and colleagues (1987), the disorder is most likely to occur at or after puberty. In general, older children and adolescents experience more OAD symptoms than younger children (McGee et al., 1990) and are more likely to meet all or most criteria of the disorder (Strauss et al., 1988). However, the frequency of specific symptoms does not appear to differ by age, and unrealistic worry about future events is a key symptom among children of all ages (Strauss et al., 1988).

Patterns of comorbidity appear to vary by age. Younger children with OAD are most likely to receive a comorbid diagnosis of SAD or ADD whereas older children are more likely to suffer from concurrent depression or a specific phobia (Strauss et al., 1988). Based on self-report, older children may also endorse more severe anxiety and depression.

With regard to gender ratio, studies that report overall gender rates for samples including wide age ranges yield conflicting results. However, when younger versus older children are compared within studies, OAD appears to decline in prevalence among males as they age so that females predominate as children reach adolescence (Strauss et al., 1988; Velez et al., 1989).

Generalized Anxiety Disorder (GAD)

OAD was deleted from DSM-IV and has presumably been subsumed under generalized anxiety disorder (GAD). As a result of this relatively recent change, research on GAD in children is limited.

Whitaker and colleagues (1990) examined lifetime prevalence rates of selected DSM-III disorders in a school-based sample of adolescents in 9th through 12th grade. GAD was the most common of selected DSM-III disorders assessed, and had a weighted lifetime prevalence rate of 3.7% with gender rates of 4.6% of females and 1.8% of males.

Owing to the paucity of research on GAD in children, it is difficult to draw conclusions regarding the disorder in childhood. Research comparing GAD and OAD symptoms in children is needed in order to assess the appropriateness of replacing OAD with GAD.

Social Phobia

Majority of children with social phobia had additional anxiety disorder, including comorbid GAD, SAD, and avoidance disorder.

Based on a review of current literature, Beidel and Morris (1995) concluded that social phobia affects about 1% of the general child and adolescent population. Among nonreferred children and adolescents, social phobia *AS and NVLD %?* appears to have a prevalence close to 1% (e.g., Anderson et al., 1987; Kashani & Orvaschel, 1990; McGee et al., 1990). Among clinical samples, the prevalence ranges from about 27% (Last et al., 1996) to 32% (Last et al., 1992).

In a primary-care pediatric sample (aged 7–11) the weighted 1-year prevalence rate for social phobia was 1% (Costello, 1989). No boys received the diagnosis, while 2% of girls met criteria for social phobia. An epidemiological study of nonreferred children (aged 8, 12, & 17 years) yielded a prevalence rate of 0.95% for social phobia (Kashani & Orvaschel, 1990). The prevalence rate did not differ between boys and girls. While no 8-year-olds were diagnosed with social phobia, the prevalence rate among 12- and 17-year-olds was 1.4%.

Based on a large sample of nonreferred 11-year-olds, Anderson et al. (1987) reported a weighted 6-month prevalence rate of 0.9% for social phobia. Social phobia affected more girls than boys at a ratio of 1:0.2. In a general sample of 15-year-old adolescents, 1.1% had social phobia (McGee et al., 1990). The gender ratio was slightly higher for males than females (F:M = 0.7:1.0).

In a partially treated clinic sample of anxiety-disordered youngsters (aged 5–18), the lifetime prevalence for social phobia was 32.4% (Last et al., 1992). Social phobia was the primary diagnosis at intake for 14.9% of children and affected more females (56%) than males (44%). Mean onset for the disorder (11.3 years) was younger than mean age at intake (14.4 years), suggesting a delay of about three years between onset and presentation for treatment. An epidemiological study of social phobia among 13,000 adults indicated that the mean age at onset was 15.5 years (Schneier, Johnson, Hornig, Liebowitz, & Weissman, 1992).

Francis, Last, and Strauss (1992) examined demographic factors and patterns of comorbidity associated with social phobia among children (6–17 years) referred to an anxiety clinic. Fifty-eight percent of children with social phobia were female, and the mean age at intake was 14.2 years. Comorbid affective disorders were present in 24% of socially phobic youngsters.

Strauss and Last (1993) investigated characteristics of referred children with social phobia. All but one child presented with social phobia between ages 12 and 17 years. The mean age at onset was 12.3 years, while the mean age of children with the disorder was 14.9 years, indicating a mean duration of 2.6 years at the time of referral. Social phobia affected more females (59%) than males. Among children with the disorder, 64% exhibited a fear of school, and 57% reported a fear of public speaking. Other phobias included fear of blushing (25%), crowds (21%), eating or drinking in front of others (18%), and dressing in front of others (14%). Use of public bathrooms was a phobic stimulus for 7% of children. Socially phobic children were equally likely to have only one phobia or multiple phobias. The majority of children had an additional anxiety disorder including 41% with comorbid OAD, 17% with SAD, and 21% who met criteria for avoidant disorder. In addition, 17% of children had a comorbid affective disorder.

A study by Last and Strauss (1990) of youngsters (aged 7–17) with anxiety-based school refusal revealed that 30.2% had social phobia. The average age at onset was 12.4 years. Follow-up of referred youngsters (aged 5–18) over 3 to 4 years indicated that 27% of subjects met criteria for social phobia at intake, and 15% had social phobia as their primary diagnosis (Last et al., 1996). By the end of follow-up 86.4% no longer met criteria for the disorder.

Overall, social phobia appears to affect more females than males among nonreferred (Anderson et al., 1987; Costello, 1989) and clinical samples (Francis et al., 1992; Last et al., 1992; Strauss & Last, 1993). The disorder tends to have its onset around 11 to 12 years of age (Last & Strauss, 1990; Last et al., 1992; Strauss & Last, 1993). Although one study reported that mean onset was around 15 years of age (Schneier et al., 1992), the retrospective nature of the study may have reduced the accuracy of chronological information. There may be some delay between onset and presentation for treatment, as age at intake has tended to be around three years older than age of onset (e.g., Francis et al., 1992; Last et al., 1992).

Common phobic stimuli among children with social phobia include school and public speaking (Strauss & Last, 1993). Social phobia is a common diagnosis among children with anxiety-based school refusal (Last & Strauss, 1990). The majority of children referred for treatment of social phobia have comorbid anxiety disorders such as OAD, SAD, and avoidant disorder (Strauss & Last, 1993). In addition, these children may present with concurrent affective disorders.

Specific/Simple Phobia

In a general sample of 15-year-old adolescents, simple phobia was the third most prevalent DSM-III diagnosis with a prevalence rate of 3.6% (McGee et al., 1990). Females were about three times as likely as boys to have a simple phobia. The most common fears included speaking in front of the class, heights, flying, and water. In a community sample of 8-, 12-, and 17-year-olds, 3.3% of subjects had a simple phobia (Kashani & Orvaschel, 1990). Prevalence rates did not differ by age. However, phobias were more common among females (5.7%) than males (1.0%).

Based on an epidemiological study of general pediatric patients (aged 7–11), the weighted 1-year prevalence rate for simple phobia was 9.2% (Costello, 1989). Of these children, 11.9% of girls and 5.9% of boys had phobias. Anderson et al. (1987) reported a 1-year prevalence rate for simple phobia of 2.4%, and the ratio of girls to boys was 1:0.6 in a sample of nonreferred 11-year-olds.

Bird and colleagues (1988) reported simple phobia was among the more common disorders identified in a nonclinical sample of children aged 4–16 years. Six-month weighted prevalence rates were 2.6% for simple phobia with "definite maladjustment" and 1.3% with "possible maladjustment."

Last and colleagues (1992) investigated simple phobias in a partially treated sample of anxiety-disordered youngsters (aged 5–18). Results indicated a lifetime prevalence of 42.6% with equal gender rates. On average, simple phobia had its onset at 8.4 years of age. A prospective investigation over 3 to 4 years by the same researchers (1996) indicated that simple phobia was present in 31% of anxiety-disordered children (5–18 years old) and was the primary diagnosis for 17% of subjects. By follow-up, 69.2% of children previously diagnosed with a simple phobia no longer met criteria for the disorder.

In a sample of youngsters (aged 7–17) referred for treatment of anxiety-based school refusal, 22.2% had a primary diagnosis of school-related simple phobia (Last & Strauss, 1990). The average onset for simple phobia was at 12.4 years. In another sample of children and adolescents (aged 5–18) referred to an outpatient anxiety disorder clinic, 5.5% met DSM-III criteria for simple phobia (Last, Strauss, & Francis, 1987).

Another study explored demographic, clinical, and diagnostic correlates associated with simple phobia (Strauss & Last, 1993). Of 138 children (aged 4–17) referred to an outpatient anxiety clinic, 38 children had a simple phobia. Simple phobias were present in children throughout the 4–17 age range, with peaks at 10–11 and 12–13 years of age. The mean age of onset for a simple phobia was 7.8 years, and the mean duration at time of referral was 3.3 years. Of children with simple phobia, 55% were female and 82% presented with a single phobia. The most common phobic stimuli were the dark (29%), school (24%), and dogs (16%). Half of the phobic children presented with a concurrent anxiety disorder, and 5% of children suffered from a comorbid affective disorder.

In nonreferred samples, the prevalence rate ranges from about 2% (Anderson et al., 1987) to about 9% (Costello, 1989). However, most estimates were around 3% (e.g., Bird et al., 1988). Among clinic samples, prevalence rates tend to be about 30–40% (e.g., Last et al., 1992, 1996). It is possible that studies yielding lower rates have included self-selected samples of children tending to suffer from more severe disorders than specific phobias. The 5.5% prevalence rate in one study that included a wide age range (Last, Strauss, & Francis, 1987) may be related to the fact that phobias tend to begin around ages 10–11 and 12–13 (Strauss & Last, 1993) and resolve within a few years (Last et al., 1992), so that older participants may have been unlikely to suffer from a specific phobia at the time of the study. Finally, some of the variation in prevalence rates reported may be due to variation in the time periods covered as one would expect point prevalence rates to be lower than lifetime prevalence rates.

Across both community and clinic samples, more girls tend to have specific phobias than boys (e.g., Kashani & Orvaschel, 1990; McGee et al., 1990; Strauss & Last, 1993). Common fears among nonreferred children include speaking in class, heights, flying, and water (McGee et al., 1990). Common phobic stimuli among referred children include the dark, school, and dogs (Strauss & Last, 1993).

Panic Disorder

In a school-based community sample of adolescents in grades 9 through 12, panic disorder had prevalence rates of 0.7% and 0.6% in males and females, respectively (Whitaker et al., 1990). The estimated lifetime prevalence was 0.6%. Another study examined panic attack history in a large school-based sample of girls aged 10.3 to 15.6 years (Hayward et al., 1992). Among these girls, 5.3% had a history of one or more four-symptom panic attacks. After controlling for age, there appeared to be a significant relationship between pubertal stage and panic attack history. At any given age, the prevalence of panic attack history was higher in girls who were at more advanced stages of puberty.

Last and Strauss (1989a) examined panic disorder among children and adolescents (aged 5–18) at an outpatient anxiety disorders clinic. The incidence of panic disorder was 9.6% with a male to female ratio of 1 to 2. All but one of the 17 children with panic disorder were postpubertal at intake. Age of onset was 15.6 years on average and ranged from 13 to 18 years for all but one child whose onset was at age nine. While no fathers of these children reported having experienced panic attacks, one-third of the mothers received a lifetime diagnosis of panic disorder and each reported onset in late adolescence or early adulthood. In addition, among the 16 mothers who reported panic disorder, 15 reported onset in adolescence or adulthood. The authors suggested that younger children may lack the cognitive capacity to experience panic as spontaneous owing to the tendency to attribute internal sensations to external causes.

Among youngsters with anxiety disorders (aged 5–18), the lifetime prevalence was 12.8% for panic disorder (Last et al., 1992). Among children with panic disorder, 41.7% were male. The disorder had a mean age of 14.1 years at onset. A longitudinal study which followed youngsters with anxiety disorders (aged 5–18) over 3 to 4 years indicated that 12% of anxiety-disordered children had panic disorder, and 11% had it as their primary disorder (Last et al., 1996). Of those children with panic disorder, 70% no longer met criteria for the diagnosis by the end of follow-up.

Although panic disorder is uncommon before adolescence, some cases of panic may have their onset in childhood. Black and Robbins (1990) presented 6 cases of panic disorder (4 female, 2 male) with onset in childhood or adolescence. Although age at diagnosis ranged from 14 to 28 years, age at onset ranged from 4 to 15 years. Age at onset was 11 or 12 years for 2 males and 2 females.

Overall, panic attacks are uncommon in early childhood and tend to begin around adolescence. Last and Strauss (1989a) have suggested that this is due to children's tendency to attribute internal sensations to external stimuli which makes it unlikely that panic will be experienced as spontaneous. Generally, more females are affected by panic than males (e.g., Last & Strauss, 1989a; Last et al., 1992). Variations in reported prevalence rates may be related to differences in the ages included, and reporting of point versus period prevalence.

Obsessive–Compulsive Disorder (OCD)

In a sample of nonreferred children in 9th through 12th grade, obsessive–compulsive disorder (OCD) had a weighted lifetime prevalence of 1.9%

(Whitaker et al., 1990). More girls were affected than boys (weighted prevalence 1.8% and 0.6%, respectively). In a community sample of adolescents aged 14–16 years, no participants had OCD (Kashani & Orvaschel, 1988).

Last and Strauss (1989b) examined OCD in children and adolescents referred to an outpatient anxiety clinic. Among 190 consecutive referrals, 20 children met criteria for OCD, representing an incidence rate of 10.5%. Age at onset ranged from 5.6 to 17.5 years and had a mean of 10.7 years. Onset was between ages 10 and 14 years for most children (65%). There were more boys (60%) than girls (40%) with OCD and boys had an earlier mean age at onset (9.5 years) than girls (12.6 years). Gender and severity (symptoms or impairment) appeared to be unrelated. Obsessions in the absence of rituals were uncommon (20%). Multiple rituals were common (50%), and the most common ritual was washing. Among children with OCD, 60% suffered from a concurrent anxiety disorder and 20% had a past anxiety disorder.

Based on a clinic sample of children and adolescents (aged 5–18) with anxiety disorders, Last et al. (1992) reported that OCD, with a lifetime prevalence of 14.9%, was among the least common anxiety disorders. OCD had a relatively late onset with 10.8 years as the mean. Slightly more than half (53.6%) of youngsters with OCD were male. The same researchers (1996) conducted a follow-up investigation of anxiety-disordered children over 3 to 4 years. The partially treated sample of youngsters aged 5–18 years included 14% with OCD, and this was the primary diagnosis for 12% of participants. By the end of follow-up, 75% of children with OCD no longer met criteria for the disorder.

The prevalence rates reported are likely to vary based on whether they refer to incidence rates or period prevalence. Among nonreferred children, the lifetime prevalence has been estimated at around 2% (Whitaker et al., 1990). As would be expected, the disorder is more common among referred children with estimates ranging from about 10% incidence (Last & Strauss, 1989b) to 15% lifetime prevalence (Last et al., 1992). Onset tends to be between ages 10 and 14 years, although boys may have an earlier onset than girls (Last & Strauss, 1989b). Among referred children, more boys may be affected by OCD than girls (Last & Strauss, 1989b; Last et al., 1992); however, the opposite was observed among a school-based sample (Whitaker et al., 1990). There does not appear to be a relationship between gender and severity of the disorder (Last & Strauss, 1989b).

Posttraumatic Stress Disorder (PTSD)

Current research on posttraumatic stress disorder (PTSD) in children is limited. Last et al. (1992) studied a clinic sample of children (aged 5–18) with anxiety disorders. PTSD had a lifetime prevalence rate of 3.7%, and was the primary diagnosis for 3.2% of the sample. The same researchers (1996) conducted a 3 to 4 year prospective investigation of anxiety-disordered children (aged 5–18). At intake 6% of subjects had PTSD as their primary diagnosis.

Overall, there is limited information on the prevalence and manifestation of PTSD throughout childhood and across genders. Last and colleagues reported the point prevalence rate for PTSD among 188 children with anxiety disorders to be 6% (1992), whereas the lifetime prevalence rate for the disorder among 84 anxiety-disordered children and adolescents was reported to be 3.7% (1996).

Conclusions and Future Research

The research presented suggests that anxiety disorders affect a substantial number of referred and nonreferred children and adolescents. Among community samples, reported prevalence rates for anxiety disorders range from 10.7% (McGee et al., 1990) to 17.3% (Kashani & Orvaschel, 1988). As would be expected, anxiety disorders are more prevalent among clinical samples with rates ranging from 27.1% to 44.7% for the more common disorders (Last et al., 1992). Children referred for treatment of an anxiety disorder are more likely to develop new anxiety disorders than never-psychiatrically-ill peers (Last et al., 1996).

Although some research suggests that anxious children tend to remain anxious (see Craske, 1997, for a review), there exists contradictory evidence regarding stability of anxiety disorders. A study of clinic-referred children followed for 3–4 years after initial diagnosis revealed that 82% of children no longer met criteria for their initial anxiety disorder at follow-up (Last et al., 1996). However, 30% of children developed new psychiatric disorders, including 16% who developed new anxiety disorders. Thus stability of specific anxiety disorders may be lower than that of anxiety in general. According to Last et al., SAD had the highest recovery rate (92%); however, about 25% of children with SAD developed a new psychiatric disorder by follow-up, most commonly a depressive disorder. Velez et al. (1989) described decreasing rates of SAD in nonreferred children followed over 8–10 years. Last et al. (1996) described an 80% recovery rate for OAD, although Cohen et al. (1993) reported that greater severity of OAD is associated with increased likelihood of persistence over time. Velez et al. reported a gender-specific decline in boys with OAD over time. Last et al. also reported recovery rates of 86% for social phobia, 75% for OCD, 70% for panic disorder, and 69% for specific phobia.

Among nonreferred children and adolescents, more girls than boys suffer from anxiety disorders (Costello, 1989; Kashani & Orvaschel, 1990). Girls also tend to report different fears than boys (Bell-Dolan et al., 1990). The gender ratios differ for the specific anxiety disorders. Overall, girls are more likely than boys to suffer from SAD (e.g., Kashani & Orvaschel, 1990; Last, Francis, et al., 1987), social phobia (e.g., Anderson et al., 1987; Francis et al., 1992), avoidant disorder (e.g., Costello, 1989; Last et al., 1992), and specific phobias (e.g., Kashani & Orvaschel, 1990; Strauss & Last, 1993) regardless of whether children are selected from community or clinic samples. Generally, more females are affected by panic than males (e.g., Last & Strauss, 1989a; Last et al., 1992). However, OAD evidences a different gender pattern. The disorder appears to become less prevalent among males as they age so that females predominate as children reach adolescence (Strauss et al., 1988; Velez et al., 1989). Among referred children, OCD appears to affect more males than females (e.g., Last & Strauss, 1989b); however, the opposite was true among nonreferred school children (Whitaker et al., 1990).

Younger nonreferred children appear to be at a greater risk for anxiety disorders than older nonreferred children (Costello, 1989), and may report different fears than older children (Bell-Dolan et al., 1990). Developmental patterns differ among anxiety disorders. The research presented in this chapter suggests that younger children are at a greater risk for SAD (e.g., Kashani & Orvaschel, 1990; Velez et al., 1989), and may experience a greater number of SAD symptoms than older children (Francis et al., 1987). However, OAD appears to be more prevalent among older children (Cohen et al., 1993; Kashani & Orvaschel, 1990) and older children tend to experience more OAD symptoms than younger children (McGee et al., 1990). Panic disorder is uncommon in early childhood, and panic attacks tend to begin around adolescence (Last & Strauss, 1989a).

It is suggested that researchers further examine the manifestation of the specific anxiety disorders across age and gender given current DSM-IV diagnostic criteria. In particular, the research on GAD in childhood is quite limited as the disorder was formerly considered an adult disorder. In addition, it is strongly recommended that future research attempt to explain the developmental patterns described in this chapter. For instance, it would be useful to understand why girls tend to be at greater risk for developing anxiety disorders. This information could then be used to target preventive efforts and treatment. Future research should be aimed first at expanding the current understanding of developmental variations in anxiety, and then applying that information to treatment of anxiety disorders.

References

Anderson, J. C., Williams, S., McGee, R., & Silva, P. A. (1987). DSM-III disorders in preadolescent children: Prevalence in a large sample from a general population. *Archives of General Psychiatry, 44*, 69–76.

Beidel, D. C., & Morris, T. L. (1995). Social phobia. In J. S. March (Ed.), *Anxiety disorders in children and adolescents* (pp. 181–211). New York: Guilford.

Bell-Dolan, D. J., Last, C. G., & Strauss, C. C. (1990). Symptoms of anxiety disorders in normal children. *Journal of the American Academy of Child and Adolescent Psychiatry, 29*(5), 759–765.

Benjamin, R. S., Costello, E. J., & Warren, M. (1990). Anxiety disorders in a pediatric sample. *Journal of Anxiety Disorders, 4*, 293–316.

Bernstein, G. A., & Borchardt, C. M. (1991). Anxiety disorders of childhood and adolescence: A critical review. *Journal of the American Academy of Child and Adolescent Psychiatry, 30* (4), 519–532.

Bird, H. R., Canino, G., Rubio-Stipec, M., Gould, M. S., Ribera, J., Sesman, M., Woodbury, M., Huertas-Goldman, S., Pagan, A., Sanchez-Lacay, A., & Moscoso, M. (1988). Estimates of the prevalence of childhood maladjustment in a community survey in Puerto Rico: The use of combined measures. *Archives of General Psychiatry, 45,* 1120–1126.

Black, B., & Robbins, D. R. (1990). Panic disorder in children and adolescents. *Journal of the American Academy of Child and Adolescent Psychiatry, 29* (1), 36–44.

Bowen, R. C., Offord, D. R., & Boyle, M. H. (1990). The prevalence of overanxious disorder and separation anxiety disorder: Results from the Ontario child health study. *Journal of the American Academy of Child and Adolescent Psychiatry, 29* (5), 753–758.

Cohen, P., Cohen, J., & Brook, J. (1993). An epidemiological study of disorders in late childhood and adolescence: II. Persistence of disorders. *Journal of Child Psychology and Psychiatry, 34* (6), 869–877.

Costello, E. J. (1989). Child psychiatric disorders and their correlates: A primary care pediatric sample. *Journal of the American Academy of Child and Adolescent Psychiatry, 28* (6), 851–855.

Craske, M. (1997). Fear and anxiety in children and adolescents. *Bulletin of the Menninger Clinic, 61* (2, Suppl. A), A4–A36.

Francis, G., Last, C. G., & Strauss, C. C. (1987). Expression of separation anxiety disorder: The roles of age and gender. *Child Psychiatry and Human Development, 18,* 82–89.

Francis, G., Last, C. G., & Strauss, C. C. (1992). Avoidant disorder and social phobia in children and adolescents. *Journal of the American Academy of Child and Adolescent Psychiatry, 31* (6), 1086–1089.

Hayward, C., Killen, J. D., Hammer, L. D., Litt, I. F., Wilson, D. M., Simmonds, B., & Taylor, C. B. (1992). Pubertal stage and panic attack history in sixth- and seventh-grade girls. *American Journal of Psychiatry, 149,* 1239–1243.

Kashani, J. H., & Orvaschel, H. (1988). Anxiety disorders in mid-adolescence: A community sample. *American Journal of Psychiatry, 145,* 960–964.

Kashani, J. H., & Orvaschel, H. (1990). A community study of anxiety in children and adolescents. *American Journal of Psychiatry, 147,* 313–318.

Last, C. G., & Strauss, C. C. (1989a). Panic disorder in children and adolescents. *Journal of Anxiety Disorders, 3,* 87–95.

Last, C. G., & Strauss, C. C. (1989b). Obsessive-compulsive disorder in childhood. *Journal of Anxiety Disorders, 3,* 295–302.

Last, C. G., & Strauss, C. C. (1990). School refusal in anxiety-disordered children and adolescents. *Journal of the American Academy of Child and Adolescent Psychiatry, 29* (1), 31–35.

Last, C. G., Francis, G., Hersen, M., Kazdin, A. E., & Strauss, C. C. (1987). Separation anxiety and school phobia: A comparison using DSM-III criteria. *American Journal of Psychiatry, 144,* 653–657.

Last, C. G., Hersen, M., Kazdin, A. E., Finkelstein, R., & Strauss, C. C. (1987). Comparison of DSM-III separation anxiety and overanxious disorders: Demographic characteristics and patterns of comorbidity. *Journal of the American Academy of Child and Adolescent Psychiatry, 26* (4), 527–531.

Last, C. G., Perrin, S., Hersen, M., & Kazdin, A. E. (1992). DSM-III-R anxiety disorders in children: Sociodemographic and clinical characteristics. *Journal of the American Academy of Child and Adolescent Psychiatry, 31* (6), 1070–1076.

Last, C. G., Perrin, S., Hersen, M., & Kazdin, A. E. (1996). A prospective study of childhood anxiety disorders. *Journal of the American Academy of Child and Adolescent Psychiatry, 35* (11), 1502–1510.

Last, C. G., Strauss, C. C., & Francis, G. (1987). Comorbidity among childhood anxiety disorders. *Journal of Nervous and Mental Disease, 175* (12), 726–730.

McGee, R., Feehan, M., Williams, S., Partridge, F., Silva, P. A., & Kelly, J. (1990). DSM-III disorders in a large sample of adolescents. *Journal of the American Academy of Child and Adolescent Psychiatry, 29* (4), 611–619.

Schneier, F. R., Johnson, J., Hornig, C. D., Liebowitz, M. R., & Weissman, M. M. (1992). Social phobia: Comorbidity and morbidity in an epidemiological sample. *Archives of General Psychiatry, 49*, 282–288.

Strauss, C. C., & Last, C. G. (1993). Social and simple phobia in children. *Journal of Anxiety Disorders, 7*, 141–152.

Strauss, C. C., Lease, C. A., Last, C. G., & Francis, G. (1988). Overanxious disorder: An examination of developmental differences. *Journal of Abnormal Child Psychology, 16* (4), 433–443.

Velez, C. N., Johnson, J., & Cohen, P. (1989). A longitudinal analysis of selected risk factors for childhood psychopathology. *Journal of the American Academy of Child and Adolescent Psychiatry, 28* (6), 861–864.

Werry, J. S. (1991). Overanxious disorder: A review of its taxonomic properties. *Journal of the American Academy of Child and Adolescent Psychiatry, 30* (4), 533–544.

Whitaker, A., Johnson, J., Shaffer, D., Rapoport, J. L., Kalikow, K., Walsh, B. T., Davies, M., Braiman, S., & Dolinsky, A. (1990). Uncommon troubles in young people: Prevalence estimates of selected psychiatric disorders in a non-referred adolescent population. *Archives of General Psychiatry, 47*, 487–496.

II

PREDISPOSING, PROTECTIVE, MAINTAINING, AND AMELIORATING INFLUENCES

3

Contributions of Behavioral Genetics Research: Quantifying Genetic, Shared Environmental and Nonshared Environmental Influences

THALIA C. ELEY

The etiology of anxiety can be investigated using a number of behavioral genetic approaches. Early research focused on the use of the family study designs: the "top-down" design in which the children of anxiety-disordered adults are studied and the "bottom-up" design in which the adult relatives of child probands are studied. This approach is useful in ascertaining the extent to which symptoms or disorders aggregate in families; but it cannot identify whether it is environmental influences shared by family members, or shared genes, that account for any family resemblance found. In order to disentangle genetic and environmental influences, designs using groups of differentially related individuals are needed, such as the twin and adoption designs.

Twin studies make use of the natural experiment created by the existence of two types of twins in the human population: identical (monozygotic or MZ) who share all their genes, and fraternal (dizygotic or DZ) who share only half their segregating genes, as in any other sibling pair. Comparison of within-pair similarity for groups of MZ and DZ twins allows the estimation of the contribution of genetic and environmental influences to the phenotype being studied (Plomin, DeFries, McClearn, & Rutter, 1997). The environmental influences are divided into those which make family members resemble one another (shared environment), and those which are not shared by family members, making them differ from one another (nonshared environment). The adoption design follows similar principles: the comparison of biologically related and biologically unrelated siblings or parent–child pairs allows for the estimation of genetic and environmental influence on the phenotype of interest. In addition to the traditional twin and adoption designs there are a variety of possible sibling and family-based designs in which groups of differentially related dyads are compared for similarity of the trait of interest. For example, the use of half-siblings and full-siblings allows for the parameterization of genetic and environmental influences without the use of such unusual groups as families containing twins, or those where a child has been adopted.

Family Studies

Top-Down Studies

There have been several top-down family studies of anxiety, which all demonstrate considerable familiality of both symptoms and disorder. For example, in a study of 59 children (aged 7–12) from four groups (children of probands with anxiety disorders, children of probands with dysthymia, children of never-mentally-ill parents, and normal school children), the children of the anxiety probands were found to report higher levels of both anxiety and fear symptoms on self-report questionnaires than both the children of normal controls and the normal school children (Turner, Beidel, & Costello, 1987). The anxiety-disordered parents' children were seven times more likely to receive a diagnosis of an anxiety disorder than the control-group children, and twice as likely as the children of the dysthymic group. In a study of child and adolescent offspring (aged 4–20) of parents with panic disorder and agoraphobia, or with panic disorder, agoraphobia, *and* major depression, or with any psychiatric disorder, were more than twice as likely to have an anxiety disorder than children of normal controls (Biederman, Rosenbaum, Bolduc, Faraone, & Hirshfeld, 1991). The prevalence of anxiety disorder was four times as high in the group whose parents had a concurrent major depression than in the normal controls, indicating shared etiological influences on anxiety and depression. Furthermore, research by Weissman and colleagues has also demonstrated not only the familiality of anxiety disorders, but also the cross-generational nature of this familiality, and familiality of the association between anxiety and depressive disorders (e.g., Weissman, Leckman, Merikangas, Gammon, & Prusoff, 1984; Weissman, Warner, Wickramaratne, Moreau, & Olfson, 1997).

Bottom-Up Studies

Studies in which the child has been selected as the proband also demonstrate the high familiality of anxiety. Once again, this is seen to be relatively non-specific, with anxiety and depression found in relatively equal proportions in the adult relatives of anxious probands (e.g., Livingston, Nugent, Rader, & Smith, 1985). Although there is also considerable comorbidity between anxiety and disorders other than depression, there do not seem to be as high levels of shared familial influences for other disorders. For example, a family study of children with anxiety disorders, children with attention deficit hyperactivity disorder (ADHD), and never-psychiatrically-ill children (Last, Hersen, Kazdin, Orvaschel, & Perrin, 1991) found that relatives of the ADHD group had levels of anxiety disorders more similar to that in the relatives of the controls than the relatives of the anxiety group. The rates were 34.6% for the relatives of the anxiety group, compared with just 23.5% and 16.3% for the relatives of the ADHD group and the controls, respectively. The familiality appeared strongest for overanxious disorder, with these children being especially likely to have adult relatives with panic disorder. Contrary to expectation there was little specificity for separation anxiety disorder (SAD) and overanxious disorder (OAD), and no close relationships between OAD and generalized anxiety disorder (GAD). Overall the results from these family studies indicate a general familial element underlying all anxiety, which overlaps with the familial influences on depression.

Twin, Sibling, and Adoption Studies

Over the last decade there has been a proliferation of twin, sibling, and adoption studies of anxiety symptoms and disorders in children and adolescents. These studies have produced a wide variety of results, and their pattern is not entirely clear. These differences may be due to several factors associated with anxiety during childhood and adolescence. The first and most obvious is that several different phenotypes have been examined. It is possible that different types of anxiety may have very different origins. Second is the possibility that given changing prevalence of anxiety symptoms with age, there may be developmental changes in etiology. This would mean that samples with differing age groups might be more likely to produce discrepant results. Similarly, sex-effects on etiology could also cause differences between studies, especially if the sample is not large enough to analyze these specifically.

Another difficulty in the design of studies of anxiety during childhood is who should be used as the rater. Child-reported symptoms may differ in several ways from those reported by a parent. Specifically, parents appear to be relatively poor at distinguishing between anxiety and depression in their children (Achenbach, 1991), and as such their ratings of anxiety may not be of pure anxiety symptoms. If anxiety and depression symptoms differ considerably in their etiology, this could also lead to discrepancies between studies that have dealt with this issue to differing extents. In other words, parent-report measures may not tap as accurately into anxiety alone or depression alone as they appear to; and so, if there are differences in the etiology of the two types of symptom, this may lead to inaccurate results.

This leads on to another issue, the correlation between anxiety and depression, and the comorbidity seen between the two. Given the high correlation between these two types of symptom it is not surprising that distinguishing between them, particularly in parent-report, is hard. Bivariate genetic analyses address this issue by indicating whether it is predominantly genetic or environmental factors that influence both anxiety and depression that are responsible for their correlation.

Finally, there may be study design effects, but unfortunately there are too few studies using other designs such as the adoption design to consider each of these methodologies separately.

This review therefore begins by considering the different phenotypes that have been considered in this area: fear and phobia symptoms; anxiety symptoms as assessed by questionnaire; mixed anxiety/depression symptoms as assessed by a parent-report questionnaire; separation anxiety disorder (SAD); and overanxious disorder (OAD). This is followed by sections documenting results on age-related change, sex differences, rater effects, and the correlation between anxiety and depression.

Anxiety Phenotypes

Fear and Phobia Symptoms. The earliest twin study of anxiety used the Fear Survey Schedule for Children–Revised version (FSSC-R; Ollendick, 1983), a self-report measure of specific fear or phobia symptoms in 319 child same-sex twin-pairs aged 8–18 years (Stevenson, Batten, & Cherner, 1992). The total fear score was found to have moderate heritability ($h^2 = 0.29$), with some specific fear factors showing higher heritability, and some showing negligible heritability. The influence of shared environment was moderate and significant for all types of fear symptom ($c^2 = 0.23$ to 0.59). The nonshared environment factor was significant for all areas, but was particularly important for fear of medical procedures ($e^2 = 0.47$), and the authors suggest that this could be because such experiences are by their nature generally child-specific, so the environmental factors responsible for the fear they produce would be due in large part to nonshared environmental influences. Fear of failure, which as the authors note is the fear dimension most closely related to social fear, has a large shared environment factor ($c^2 = 0.51$), which suggests that such fears may be learned in the family setting. The authors also examined the influence of genetic and environmental factors on very high fear scores, and found that their influences were of very similar magnitude, for high levels of fear, to that found for individual differences in the normal range. This suggests that the same etiological influences may account for both normal and disorder levels of symptoms. A subsequent study of parent-rated levels of fear and phobia symptoms, that when high result in a diagnosis of DSM-IV specific phobia, also found a significant role for both genetic and shared-environment influences (Lichtenstein & Annas, 1997). Heritability estimates for animal, situational, and mutilation fears ranged from 16% to 55%, with shared environment accounting for between 31% and 60% of the variance. The finding of significant influence of shared environment is relatively rare in twin studies of psychopathology, and has been absent or minimal in studies of the etiology of adult phobias (Kendler, Neale, Kessler, Heath, & Eaves, 1992b; Kendler et al., 1995). This makes it particularly interesting that such influences are significant in predicting variance in the normal range of fear symptoms in children and adolescents.

Anxiety Symptoms. The first study of the full range of anxiety symptoms involved 376 pairs of twins aged 8–16 years (Thapar & McGuffin, 1994). In this study a parent-report anxiety questionnaire was completed for the whole sample, and the adolescents (aged 12–16) also completed a self-report version. The results from these two datasets were very different. The parent report of anxious symptomatology was found to have an estimated heritability of 59% with no age-effect, whereas the adolescent self-report measure had no significant genetic component. The shared environment showed the reverse pattern, being large and significant for the adolescent self-report measures only. Amongst the authors' hypothesized reasons for this discrepancy was the suggestion that the parents were rating an enduring trait, whereas self-report may reflect current state. This possibility could be tested by using the Spielberger State–Trait Anxiety Inventory for Children (STAIC; Spielberger, 1973) which specifically measures these two aspects of anxiety symptoms separately.

One of the largest studies in this area is the Virginia Twin Study of Adolescent Behavioral Development (VTSABD). This study is of 1412 same-sex twin pairs aged 8–16 years. There are two papers that present results on anxiety from this study, which give somewhat different results. The first paper presented child-reported data only (Topolski et al., 1997) and included results for the Revised Children's Manifest Anxiety Scale (RCMAS; Reynolds & Richmond, 1979), a measure of self-reported anxiety symptoms. The etiology of the questionnaire symptoms showed significant sex- and age-effects (described later), but overall this study indicated both shared-environment and genetic influence on anxiety symptoms. The second paper from the VTSABD (Eaves et al., 1997) included mother-, father-, and self-reported anxiety symptoms, as assessed by a factor-score created from questionnaire-rated anxiety symptoms. Overall these results indicated moderate genetic influence, with no significant influence of shared environment (except for child-reported questionnaire symptoms, for which the shared environment accounted for 33% of the variance in males).

Finally, a recent study of 395 same-sex child twin pairs aged 8–16 years found low heritability ($h^2 = 0.10$) and moderate shared-environment influence ($c^2 = 0.39$) on a factor score of anxiety that had been created specifically in order to reduce the level of depressive symptomatology included in the measure (Eley & Stevenson, 1999b).

In summary, as with the two studies of fear symptoms, these studies indicate a role for shared environment in anxiety symptoms, although this is greater in some studies than others. There are also indications of genetic influence, which varies rather more greatly across studies.

Anxiety/Depression Symptoms Ratings by Parents. The first adoption study to examine anxiety in children presented data from 111 adopted sibling pairs and 221 unrelated adopted sibling pairs aged 10–15 years (van den Oord, Boomsma, & Verhulst, 1994). The measure used was the Anxious/Depressed subscale of the Child Behavior Checklist (CBCL; Achenbach, 1991). The heritability of this measure was low ($h^2 = 0.13$), but the shared environment accounted for around one-third of the variance ($c^2 = 0.31$). More recently, the same measure was used in a twin study of 181 same-sex twin pairs aged 7–15 years (Edelbrock, Rende, Plomin, & Thompson, 1995). This study also found that the shared environment accounted for around one-third of the variance ($c^2 = 0.31$), but in addition, genetic factors accounted for a further third ($h^2 = 0.34$).

The third study to use this type of measure is a sibling–cousin study, which reported data on 436 pairs of full siblings, 119 pairs of half-siblings, and 122 pairs of first cousins (all pairs were same-sex), aged 4–10 years (van den Oord & Rowe, 1997). The measure used was the Anxious/Depressed subscale from the Behavior Problems Index (BPI; Peterson & Zill, 1986), a short form of the CBCL (Achenbach, 1991). This study found lower familiality than the other two studies, with genetic factors accounting for about one-quarter of the variance, and shared-environment factors around one-fifth. As with other questionnaire measures, there is a general picture of *both* genetic and shared environment being involved in anxiety symptoms, in addition to nonshared environment.

Finally, parent-reported anxiety symptoms as assessed by the Anxious/Depressed subscale of the CBCL were also collected on 395 same-sex twin pairs aged 8–16 years (Eley, 1996). Genetic factors accounted for almost half the variance in this measure, with negligible and nonsignificant shared-environment influence.

These four studies generally provide further evidence for shared-environment influence on anxiety in children, with genetic factors also playing a role.

Separation Anxiety Disorder (SAD). The two papers from the VTSABD also present data on SAD (Topolski et al., 1997; Eaves et al., 1997). In the first paper, which looked at the self-report measures only, variance in child-reported SAD was due to shared and nonshared environment with no significant influence of genes (Topolski et al., 1997). In contrast, in the second paper (Eaves et al., 1997), which reports on mother-, father-, and self-reported children's anxiety, child-reported SAD was influenced by additive genetic and nonshared environmental factors. Mother- and father-reported SAD showed very high nonshared-environment influence, with little genetic or shared-environmental variance. Thus in the latter paper shared environment was not significant in predicting SAD, for all three sources, including child-report in contrast to the child-reported results in the earlier paper. There are no clear reasons for this discrepancy, and one can only guess that different formulations of the diagnosis of SAD were used in the different analyses.

Another large study of 2043 same-sex twin pairs aged 3–18 years found both age- and sex-effects on maternally rated SAD (Feigon, Waldman, Levy, & Hay, 1997; in press). The results indicate both shared-environment and genetic influences on SAD. Similar results were found for retrospectively reported separation anxiety symptoms in a study of 200 same-sex twin pairs aged 17–66 years (Silove, Manicavasagar, O'Connell, & Morris-Yates, 1995). Although this study had a very biased sample (recruited from media advertising), it adds to the findings on sex differences in SAD which are discussed in more detail below.

The results for SAD generally indicate that both genetic and shared-environment influences play a role in SAD. These studies further demonstrate that anxiety in children and adolescents, unlike most other behavioral phenotypes, is influenced by the shared environment.

Overanxious Disorder (OAD). The last phenotype to have been considered is OAD, which was only looked at in the VTSABD (Topolski et al., 1997; Eaves et al., 1997). The results for OAD are rather more similar across the two papers than those for SAD, and indicate only additive genetic and nonshared environment as significant influences on OAD in children and adolescents, for mother-, father-, and self-reported data (Topolski et al., 1997; Eaves et al., 1997).

In summary, the etiology of anxiety in children appears to differ somewhat according to the definition. It is early days to draw clear distinctions between these phenotypes, but there are some indications that SAD may be more influenced by the family environment than OAD. This finding could perhaps be interpreted in the light of the role attachment may have for SAD (Warren, Huston, Egeland, & Sroufe, 1997). However, it should be noted that the questionnaire measures also revealed significant influence of shared environment, and these questionnaires are meant to tap the kinds of symptoms that would form the basis of a diagnosis such as OAD.

Rater Effects

Child-report. Several of the studies discussed above used the child as the reporter, sometimes with parent-report in addition (Stevenson et al., 1992; Thapar & McGuffin, 1995; Eaves et al., 1997; Topolski et al., 1997; Eley & Stevenson, 1999a). It is hard to conclude whether any differences between child-report and parent-report are due to the reporter, as they are confounded by age—child-report being used for children aged 8 years or older only. However, in general the child data indicate roughly equal contributions of genes and shared environment, although there are some indications that shared environment influences may account for slightly more variance. Between them the two account for around one-half of the variance, with the remainder due to nonshared environment and error.

Parent-report. Most of the studies cited have included parent-report, whether or not they also ascertained child report (van den Oord et al., 1994; Edelbrock et al., 1995; Thapar & McGuffin, 1995; Eaves et al., 1997; Feigon et al., 1997; in press; Lichtenstein & Annas, 1997; van den Oord & Rowe, 1997; Eley, 1996). The results for the whole group vary considerably; but overall, as with the child-report they suggest that genetic and shared-environment factors account between them for around one-half of the variance in anxiety. However, for the parent-reported data it looks as if genetic influences may be slightly greater than shared environment, which is particularly interesting given that rater effects due to one parent rating two children would inflate the shared environment rather than the genetic parameter (it would tend to inflate both MZ and DZ correlations). This suggests that parents and children may be rating somewhat different phenomena, a finding that has been demonstrated in several nongenetic studies of anxiety in children (e.g., Engel, Rodrigue, & Geffken, 1994).

Age-effects

Three studies directly tested for and demonstrated age-effects. The first paper from the VTSABD found both sex- and age-effects on the RCMAS (Reynolds & Richmond, 1979) (Topolski et al., 1997). The results indicated, for the girls, higher heritability of anxiety symptoms in early adolescence (ages 11–13) than in late childhood (8–10) or mid-adolescence (14–16), and decreasing familiality (both genetic and shared-environment influences) over time for the boys. The second study was of SAD in 2043 same-sex twin pairs aged 3–18 years (Feigon et al., 1997; in press). In this study heritability was found to increase with age. The third study also found *both* sex-effects and age-effects on child-reported anxiety symptoms (Eley & Stevenson, 1996). In this sample heritability was higher in adolescents (ages 12–16) than in children (8–11), particularly for the females. At least two other studies tested for, but did not find, age-effects (Eaves et al., 1997; Thapar & McGuffin, 1995).

It is clear from these results that there are age-related changes in the etiology of anxiety symptoms. It looks likely that heritability of anxiety increases with age, though this may be over a discrete period during adolescence. However, in order to clarify these age-related changes a more systematic approach to the issue is needed, as the three studies cited above used different methods, and notably, two used very different criteria for dividing their sample into age-groups (Eley & Stevenson, 1999b; Topolski et al., 1997). Longitudinal studies that are able to establish the causes of continuity and change in symptomatology over time will also be essential in understanding the developmental psychopathology of anxiety.

Sex-effects

Sex-effects have been addressed and identified in six of the studies reviewed here (Eaves et al., 1997; Topolski et al., 1997; Feigon et al., 1997; in press; Lichtenstein & Annas, 1997; Silove et al., 1995; Eley & Stevenson, 1999b). Of these, five found greater heritability estimates for girls than for boys (the exception was the study by Lichtenstein and Annas). This is the most consistent result yet to appear from the literature on behavioral genetic analyses of anxiety in children, and is one which may have implications for molecular genetic research in anxiety. For example, there may be greater successes in identifying genes for anxiety if a female sample is used. Furthermore, any genes found to influence anxiety may have a greater effect in females than they do in males.

Comorbidity

Anxiety and Depression. Two studies have addressed the origin of the correlation between anxiety and depression in children within a behavioral genetic design. The first investigated the causes of covariation between *maternally reported* anxiety and depression symptoms in 172 twin pairs aged 8–16 years (Thapar & McGuffin, 1997). This study found that most of the covariation between anxiety and depression symptoms could be explained by genetic factors that influenced both. There was some specific genetic influence on depression, but most of the genetic variance was shared. Some of the covariation was also accounted for by nonshared environmental influences relating to both measures, but this could have been correlated measurement error. Questionnaire measures of anxiety and depression in children tend to include some overlapping items which produces artificial inflation of the correlation between the scales.

A more recent study using data from a sample of 490 child twin pairs aged 8–16 years was designed specifically to reduce artifactual covariation between the measures of anxiety and depression (Eley, 1997; Eley & Stevenson, 1999a). A factor analytic procedure was used to produce relatively uncorrelated anxiety and depression scores ($r = 0.27$), compared with the high correlation found between the total scale scores for the two questionnaire measures used ($r = 0.67$). The production of these purer factors allowed for the identification of shared and specific etiological factors, having removed artifactual overlap between the measures. Bivariate genetic analyses indicated that all genetic variance was shared across the two measures, and this shared genetic factor accounted for 80% of the phenotypic correlation. In contrast, the environmental factors were almost entirely measure-specific. These results are in line with research in adults (Kendler, Heath, Martin, & Eaves, 1987; Kendler, Neale, Kessler, Heath, & Eaves, 1992a; Roy, Neale, Pedersen, Mathe, & Kendler, 1995; Kendler et al., 1992a; Roy et al., 1995), which has consistently found that the genetic influences on anxiety and depression, both as symptoms and disorders, are almost entirely shared, in contrast to the environmental influences which are largely specific.

Conclusions

Genes and Anxiety in Children

One clear finding from these studies is that there is genetic influence on anxiety in childhood, which accounts for around one-third of the variance in most cases. However, this contribution may differ for some definitions, and depending on the rater. It also appears that the genetic contribution may increase with age, and is greater for girls than boys. This suggests that molecular genetic research will need to consider carefully the group used in designing studies aimed at identifying specific genetic risk factors. It may be that adolescent girls, with the more highly genetic phenotypes, would be a good target for future genetic research, as this is the group for whom genetic factors appear to have the greatest influence on anxiety.

Another hypothesis relevant to molecular genetic research is that when genes are found for anxiety they will tend also to be associated with depression. In the child literature the high genetic correlation between anxiety and depression has been shown only with regard to questionnaire measures of symptoms, and needs to be extended to disorder. However, adult work suggests that the same situation will be found there, although in adults the genetic correlation varies by anxiety disorder type (Kendler et al., 1992a; Kendler, Neale, Kessler, Heath, & Eaves, 1993; Kendler et al., 1995; van den Oord & Rowe, 1997). Finally, the publication of an association between a marker in the promoter of the serotonin transporter gene and the emotional triad of anxiety, depression and neuroticism offers some support for this hypothesis (Lesch et al., 1996).

Shared Environment and Anxiety in Children

The clearest finding in this review of the literature is that there is significant shared-environment influence on most definitions of anxiety in children and adolescents. This is particularly exciting given the rarity with which this parameter has been found to be significant for most other behavioral disorders, in both childhood and adult disorders. In particular, adult studies of anxiety disorders have been notable in the lack of significant shared-environment influence (e.g., Kendler et al. 1992b). This emphasizes the need for separate research into anxiety disorders in *children and adolescents* where the shared environment has been demonstrated to be a significant influence. Shared-environment influences are defined as those that make family members resemble one another. It is therefore likely that a significant proportion of shared-environment influences will consist of shared family experiences during childhood, and that these will have greater effect during childhood than in later stages of life.

There are several published studies that investigate the role of environmental stressors in the development of anxiety during childhood. Perhaps the most obvious candidate for a shared environment factor is maternal psychopathology. The difficulty with this is that it is unclear from current research whether the high incidence of anxiety in children of anxious or depressed mothers is due to shared genes or shared environmental influences. Studies are needed of biological and adoptive mothers of children with high anxiety in order to unravel this relationship.

However, there is considerable evidence for relationships between several possible environmental mediators of parental psychopathology and anxiety in the child. For example, insecure attachment has shown to be more prevalent in infants of depressed mothers (Radke-Yarrow, Cummings, Kuczynski, & Chapman, 1985), and has also been demonstrated to be associated with anxiety and depression in the child (Armsden, McCauley,

Greenburg, Burke, & Mitchell, 1990). Furthermore, the absence of a good confiding relationship in a mother's life is associated with emotional disorders in her children (Goodyer, Wright, & Altham, 1988). Undesirable parenting, such as inconsistent or restrictive patterns of behavior, are also associated with anxiety in children (Kohlmann, Schumacher, & Streit, 1988; Krohne & Hock, 1991). There is also considerable evidence that early childhood bereavement predicts later anxiety (e.g., Kranzler, Shaffer, Wasserman, & Davies, 1989; Goodyer & Altham, 1991a; 1991b), an effect which may itself be mediated by parental psychopathology or altered parenting style. Divorce and other life-changing events, especially those involving separation from the mother (for example long-term hospitalization for illness), have also been associated with later anxiety (see Goodyer, 1990, for a review).

Finally, demographic factors such as poor housing or poverty may be relevant. It has been hypothesized that adverse physical environments may increase the chances of some types of life events that are known to be associated with anxiety (Goodyer, 1990).

Non-shared Environment and Anxiety in Children

The literature on environmental risk factors for anxiety also includes some candidates that would act as nonshared environmental factors. For example, recent stressful life events, which have been demonstrated to be associated with emotional disorders including anxiety, are likely to be child-specific (Goodyer, Kolvin, & Gatzanis, 1987). More specifically, friendships and the absence of school-based achievements have also been shown to be related to anxiety (Goodyer, Wright, & Altham, 1990).

One particularly interesting result described above is that the environmental influences on anxiety and depression are largely symptom-specific. Much of the research on environmental risks described above relates to depression as well as anxiety. However, one study of adults found a specific relationship between risks characterized by loss with depression as the outcome, and events characterized by threat, which were followed by an onset of anxiety (Finlay-Jones & Brown, 1981). A study of child and adolescent twin pairs in which at least one of the twins was highly anxious or highly depressed attempted to replicate this finding (Eley, 1996; Eley & Stevenson, in press). Threat and loss events were found to be associated with high levels of anxiety and depression, with some evidence of specificity of loss to depression and threat to anxiety.

In summary, the application of behavioral genetic designs to the study of anxiety in children and adolescents is beginning to provide some interesting insights into the relative importance of genetic and environmental influences. This approach is not limited merely to the identification of genetic influence on a phenotype, but is also able to clarify the role of environmental risk factors, some of which may act in conjunction with genetic influences. These methods will also be central to identifying how the influences on anxiety differ between the two sexes, and to exploring the etiology of continuity and change in symptoms over time. The combination of behavioral genetics and developmental psychopathology will in time lead to far greater understanding of the origin and development of anxiety in children and adolescents.

References

Achenbach, T. M. (1991). *Manual for the Child Behavior Checklist and 1991 profile.* Vermont: Burlington: University of Vermont, Department of Psychiatry.

Armsden, G. C., McCauley, E., Greenburg, M. T., Burke, P. M., & Mitchell, J. R. (1990). Parent and peer attachment in early adolescent depression. *Journal of Abnormal Child Psychology, 18*, 683–697.

Biederman, J., Rosenbaum, J. F., Bolduc, E. A., Faraone, S. V., & Hirshfeld, D. R. (1991). A high risk study of young children of parents with panic disorder and agoraphobia with and without comorbid major depression. *Psychiatry Research, 37*, 333–348.

Eaves, L. J., Silberg, J. L., Meyer, J. M., Maes, H. H., Simonoff, E., Pickles, A., Rutter, M., Neale, M. C., Reynolds, C. A., Erickson, M. T., Heath, A. C., Loeber, R., Truett, K. R., & Hewitt, J. K. (1997). Genetics and developmental psychopathology: 2. The main effects of genes and environment on behavioral problems in the Virginia Twin Study of Adolescent Behavioral Development. *Journal of Child Psychology and Psychiatry, 38*, 965–980.

Edelbrock, C., Rende, R. D., Plomin, R., & Thompson, L. A. (1995). A twin study of competence and problem behavior in childhood and early adolescence. *Journal of Child Psychology and Psychiatry, 36*, 775–785.

Eley, T. C. (1996). *The etiology of emotional symptoms in children and adolescents: Depression and anxiety in twins.* Unpublished doctoral thesis: University of London.

Eley, T. C. (1997). General genes: A new theme in developmental psychopathology. *Current Directions in Psychological Science, 6*, 90–95.

Eley, T. C., & Stevenson, J. (1999a). Using genetic analyses to clarify the distinction between depressive and anxious symptoms in children and adolescents. *Journal of Abnormal Child Psychology, 27*, 105–114.

Eley, T. C., & Stevenson, J. (1999b). Exploring the covariation between anxiety and depression symptoms: A genetic analysis of the effects of age and sex. *Journal of Child Psychology and Psychiatry, 40*, 1273–1284.

Eley, T. C., & Stevenson, J. (in press). Specific life events and chronic experiences differentially associated with depression and anxiety in young twins. *Journal of Abnormal Child Psychology.*

Engel, N. A., Rodrigue, J. R., & Geffken, G. R. (1994). Parent–child agreement on ratings of anxiety in children. *Psychological Reports, 75*, 1251–1256.

Feigon, S. A., Waldman, I. D., Levy, F., & Hay, D. A. (1997). Genetic and environmental influences on various anxiety disorder symptoms in children [Abstract]. *Behavior Genetics, 27*, 588.

Feigon, S. A., Waldman, I. D., Levy, F., & Hay, D. A. (in press). Genetic and environmental influences on separation anxiety disorder symptoms and their moderation by age and sex. *Behavior Genetics.*

Finlay-Jones, R., & Brown, G. W. (1981). Types of stressful life events and the onset of anxiety and depressive disorders. *Psychological Medicine, 11*, 803–815.

Goodyer, I. M. (1990). Family relationships, life events and childhood psychopathology. *Journal of Child Psychology and Psychiatry, 31,* 161–192.

Goodyer, I. M., & Altham, P. M. E. (1991a). Lifetime exit events and recent social and family adversities in anxious and depressed school-age children and adolescents: I. *Journal of Affective Disorders, 21,* 219–228.

Goodyer, I. M., & Altham, P. M. (1991b). Lifetime exit events and recent social and family adversities in anxious and depressed school-age children and adolescents: II. *Journal of Affective Disorders, 21,* 229–238.

Goodyer, I. M., Kolvin, I., & Gatzanis, S. (1987). The impact of recent undesirable life events on psychiatric disorders in childhood and adolescence. *British Journal of Psychiatry, 151,* 179–184.

Goodyer, I. M., Wright, C., & Altham, P. M. E. (1988). Maternal adversity and recent stressful life events in anxious and depressed children. *Journal of Child Psychology and Psychiatry, 29,* 651–667.

Goodyer, I. M., Wright, C., & Altham, P. M. E. (1990). Recent achievements and adversities in anxious and depressed school age children. *Journal of Child Psychology and Psychiatry, 31,* 1063–1077.

Kendler, K. S., Heath, A. C., Martin, N. G., & Eaves, L. J. (1987). Symptoms of anxiety and depression: Same genes, different environments? *Archives of General Psychiatry, 44,* 451–457.

Kendler, K. S., Neale, M. C., Kessler, R. C., Heath, A. C., & Eaves, L. J. (1992a). Major depression and generalized anxiety disorder. Same genes, (partly) different environments? *Archives of General Psychiatry, 49,* 716–722.

Kendler, K. S., Neale, M. C., Kessler, R. C., Heath, A. C., & Eaves, L. J. (1992b). The genetic epidemiology of phobias in women: The interrelationship of agoraphobia, social phobia, situational phobia, and simple phobia. *Archives of General Psychiatry, 49,* 273–281.

Kendler, K. S., Neale, M. C., Kessler, R. C., Heath, A. C., & Eaves, L. J. (1993). Major depression and phobias: The genetic and environmental sources of comorbidity. *Psychological Medicine, 23,* 361–371.

Kendler, K. S., Walters, E. E., Neale, M. C., Kessler, R. C., Heath, A. C., & Eaves, L. J. (1995). The structure of the genetic and environmental risk factors for six major psychiatric disorders in women: Phobia, generalized anxiety disorder, panic disorder, bulimia, major depression, and alcoholism. *Archives of General Psychiatry, 52,* 374–383.

Kohlmann, C. W., Schumacher, A., & Streit, R. (1988). Trait anxiety and parental child-rearing behavior: Support as a moderator variable? *Anxiety Research, 1,* 53–64.

Kranzler, E. M., Shaffer, D., Wasserman, G., & Davies, M. (1989). Early childhood bereavement. *Journal of the American Academy of Child and Adolescent Psychiatry, 29,* 513–520.

Krohne, H. W., & Hock, M. (1991). Relationships between restrictive mother–child interactions and anxiety of the child. *Anxiety Research, 4,* 109–124.

Last, C. G., Hersen, M., Kazdin, A. E., Orvaschel, H., & Perrin, S. (1991). Anxiety disorders in children and their families. *Archives of General Psychiatry, 48,* 928–934.

Lesch, K. P., Bengel, D., Heils, A., Zhang Sabol, S., Greenburg, B. D., Petri, S., Benjamin, J., Müller, C. R., Hamer, D. H., & Murphy, D. L. (1996). Association of anxiety-related traits with a polymorphism in the serotonin transporter gene regulatory region. *Science, 274,* 1527–1530.

Lichtenstein, P., & Annas, P. (1997). The heritability of specific fears and phobias in children [Abstract]. *Behavior Genetics, 27,* 598.

Livingston, R., Nugent, H., Rader, L., & Smith, G. R. (1985). Family histories of depressed and severely anxious children. *American Journal of Psychiatry, 142,* 1497–1499.

Ollendick, T. H. (1983). Reliability and validity of the Revised Fear Survey Schedule for Children (FSSC-R). *Behavior Research and Therapy, 21,* 685–692.

Peterson, J. L., & Zill, N. (1986). Marital disruption, parent–child relationship, and behavior problems in children. *Journal of Marriage and the Family, 48,* 295–307.

Plomin, R., DeFries, J. C., McClearn, G. E., & Rutter, M. (1997). *Behavioral Genetics* (3rd ed.). New York: W. H. Freeman.

Radke-Yarrow, M., Cummings, E. M., Kuczynski, L., & Chapman, M. (1985). Patterns of attachment in two- and three-year-olds in normal families and families with parental depression. *Child Development, 56,* 884–893.

Reynolds, C. R., & Richmond, B. O. (1979). Factor structure and construct validity of "What I Think and Feel": The Revised Children's Manifest Anxiety Scale. *Journal of Personality Assessment, 43,* 281–283.

Roy, M. A., Neale, M. C., Pedersen, N. L., Mathe, A. A., & Kendler, K. S. (1995). A twin study of generalized anxiety disorder and major depression. *Psychological Medicine, 25,* 1037–1049.

Silove, D., Manicavasagar, V., O'Connell, D., & Morris-Yates, A. (1995). Genetic factors in early separation anxiety: Implications for the genesis of adult anxiety disorders [Abstract]. *Acta Psychiatrica Scandinavica, 92,* 17–24.

Spielberger, C. (1973). *Preliminary test manual for the State–Trait Anxiety Inventory for Children.* Palo Alto: Consulting Psychologists Press.

Stevenson, J., Batten, N., & Cherner, M. (1992). Fears and fearfulness in children and adolescents: A genetic analysis of twin data. *Journal of Child Psychology and Psychiatry, 33,* 977–985.

Thapar, A., & McGuffin, P. (1994). A twin study of depressive symptoms in childhood. *British Journal of Psychiatry, 165,* 259–265.

Thapar, A., & McGuffin, P. (1995). Are anxiety symptoms in childhood heritable? *Journal of Child Psychology and Psychiatry, 36,* 439–447.

Thapar, A., & McGuffin, P. (1997). Anxiety and depressive symptoms in childhood a genetic study of comorbidity. *Journal of Child Psychology and Psychiatry, 38,* 651–656.

Topolski, T. D., Hewitt, J. K., Eaves, L. J., Silberg, J. L., Meyer, J. M., Rutter, M., Pickles, A., & Simonoff, E. (1997). Genetic and environmental influences on child reports of manifest anxiety and symptoms of separation anxiety and overanxious disorders: A community-based twin study. *Behavior Genetics, 27,* 15–28.

Turner, S. M., Beidel, D. C., & Costello, A. (1987). Psychopathology in the offspring of anxiety disordered patients. *Journal of Consulting and Clinical Psychology, 55,* 229–235.

Van den Oord, E. J. C. G., & Rowe, D. C. (1997). Continuity and change in children's social maladjustment: A developmental behavior genetic study. *Developmental Psychology, 33,* 319–332.

Van den Oord, E. J. C. G., Boomsma, D. I., & Verhulst, F. C. (1994). A study of problem behaviors in 10- to 15-year-old biologically related and unrelated international adoptees. *Behavior Genetics, 24,* 193–205.

Warren, S. L., Huston, L., Egeland, B., & Sroufe, A. (1997). Child and adolescent anxiety disorders and early attachment. *Journal of the American Academy of Child and Adolescent Psychiatry, 36,* 637–644.

Weissman, M. M., Leckman, J. F., Merikangas, K. R., Gammon, G. D., & Prusoff, B. A. (1984). Depression and anxiety disorders in parents and children: Results from the Yale Family Study. *Archives of General Psychiatry, 41,* 845–852.

Weissman, M. M., Warner, V., Wickramaratne, P., Moreau, D., & Olfson, M. (1997). Offspring of depressed parents: 10 years later. *Archives of General Psychiatry, 54,* 932–942.

4

Temperamental Influences on the Development of Anxiety Disorders

CHRISTOPHER J. LONIGAN and BETH M. PHILLIPS

The study of temperament has a long history dating to the early Greek and Greco-Roman physicians (Diamond, 1974). In more recent times, the components of contemporary theorists' ideas about temperament can be seen in Allport's classic delineation of the boundaries of personality: Temperament refers to

> the characteristic phenomenon of an individual's emotional nature, including his susceptibility to emotional stimulation, his customary speed and strength of response, the quality of his prevailing mood, and all the peculiarities of fluctuation and intensity of mood; these phenomenon being regarded as dependent on constitutional make-up. (1937, p. 54)

The study of temperament includes a rich descriptive literature of the static and changing nature of children's development. The concept of temperament holds much promise for understanding the development of psychopathology, including the development of anxiety disorders; however, much of this promise is only beginning to be realized. Only a limited number of studies have examined specific forms of psychopathology in the context of temperament, and the study of temperament has involved a large diversity of approaches, some with significant methodological shortcomings. Moreover, the low base rate of psychopathology makes such study difficult. In this chapter we begin with a definition of the key constructs of temperament. We then review the evidence and models for the relation between temperament and anxiety disorders and discuss factors that may affect this relation. Finally, we suggest a number of ways in which the field can be advanced.

What Is Temperament?

Whereas it appears that most people "understand" what temperament is generally, there is little agreement regarding the specific core dimensions and definitions of temperament. Among major temperament theorists, there are varying degrees of agreement and disagreement concerning the heritability of temperament, its relation to biological factors, and its stability across time and situations. Also debatable are its status as a personological versus interactional construct, the scope of temperamental behaviors, and appropriate dimensions of measurement (e.g., Goldsmith et al., 1987; Rothbart & Goldsmith, 1985). It is beyond the scope of this chapter to provide a comprehensive summary of all the major theories of temperament. The interested reader should consult other work for greater detail (e.g., Buss & Plomin, 1984; Goldsmith & Campos, 1986; Goldsmith et al., 1987; Rothbart, 1989; Thomas & Chess, 1985). In this section, we briefly highlight the areas of overlap and distinctiveness of theories of temperament and review a number of relevant measurement issues. We also offer an outline of one potential unifying approach to deal with these differences that we use as an organizational guide in much of this chapter.

Dimensions of Temperament

Thomas and Chess (e.g., 1985; Thomas, Chess, & Birch, 1968) developed their model of temperament based on an intensive analysis of frequent observations and parental interviews for a small group of infants. They conceptualize temperament as the stylistic component of behavior (i.e., the "how" of behavior), a view that distinguishes temperamental aspects of behaviors from aspects involving motivation, abilities, and personality. They established nine categories of temperamental behaviors: activity level, approach or withdrawal from novel stimuli, adaptability, sensory threshold, dominant quality of mood, intensity of mood expression, persistence/attention span, distractibility, and rhythmicity. In addition, they identified three temperamental patterns: easy temperament, difficult temperament (infants with extreme scores on approach/withdrawal, mood, intensity, adaptability, and rhythmicity), and slow-to-warm-up temperament.

Buss and Plomin (e.g., 1975, 1984) define temperament as a set of inherited personality traits that appear early in life (i.e., during the first year). Moreover, they see temperamental dimensions as reflecting stable and enduring qualities. Consequently, a trait like rhythmicity, which appears early in life but does not persist and thus has little developmental consequence, is not temperament. Buss and Plomin identify three dimensions of temperament: Emotionality (distress), Activity Level (tempo and vigor), and Sociability (preference for being with others). These three dimensions have been shown to be relatively stable within individuals across time (e.g., Rende, 1993). Emotionality, at first represented by general distress and autonomic arousal, is assumed to later differentiate into separate components of fear and anger (Buss, 1991). Positive aspects of emotionality were excluded from the model because their heritability had not been substantiated. Additionally, Buss (1991) suggested that even if positive emotions were found to be inherited, this may be attributed to interactions between Activity and Sociability (but see Tellegen et al., 1988). Their original theory also included impulsivity as a temperamental dimension, but later versions of the theory do not include this dimension because of questions concerning its heritability. Activity level, in that it reflects the style and intensity of behavior, is the dimension of this model that has most in common with Thomas and Chess' conceptualization of temperament.

Goldsmith and Campos (e.g., 1982, 1986) regard temperament as individual differences in the probability of experiencing and expressing the primary emotions (i.e., anger, sadness, fear, joy, pleasure, disgust, interest; e.g., Ekman, 1982; Izard, 1977). Goldsmith and Campos define emotion along four dimensions: (a) emotions are involved in the regulation of internal psychological processes; (b) emotions regulate social and interpersonal behavior; (c) emotions are specified by unique patterns of facial, vocal, or gestural expressions; and (d) emotions utilize a communication process that is innate. In this model, characterizations of temperament are restricted to the behavioral level. That is, observation of temperament consists of examining individual differences in behavioral tendencies to express the primary emotions. Motor activity also is assessed because it may reflect overall emotional arousal. Excluded from Goldsmith and Campos' definition of temperament are cognitive or perceptual factors.

The model of temperament developed by Rothbart (e.g., Derryberry & Rothbart, 1984; Rothbart, 1989) incorporates aspects of both Thomas and Chess' dimensions of temperament (i.e., behavioral style) as well as Goldsmith and Campos' (1982; i.e., emotional reactivity). Rothbart defines temperament as relatively stable, primarily biologically based individual differences in reactivity (i.e., arousability of behavioral, endocrine, autonomic, and central nervous system responses) and self-regulation (i.e., attention, approach, avoidance, inhibition). It appears that Rothbart's model of temperament can be viewed on two levels. At a higher level of organization, temperament consists of individual differences in negative reactivity, positive reactivity, behavioral inhibition to novel or intense stimuli, and effortful control/attention. At a lower level of organization, the dimensions of temperament consist of behaviors such as activity level, smiling and laughing, discomfort, fear, sadness, distress to limitations (frustration), soothability, attention focusing and shifting (orienting), autonomic reactivity, and high- and low-intensity pleasure. Rothbart has demonstrated cross-time and cross-method connections between behaviors within the higher- and lower-order dimensions (e.g., Rothbart, 1986, 1988; Rothbart, Ahadi, & Hershey, 1994).

Despite these seemingly disparate views of what constitutes temperament, we believe that there is actually more commonality between the positions than there are distinctions. Therefore, we tend to agree with McCall's synthesis of a roundtable discussion on temperament (Goldsmith et al., 1987, p. 524):

> Temperament consists of relatively consistent, basic dispositions inherent in the person that underlie and modulate the expression of activity, re-activity, emotionality, and sociability. Major elements of temperament are present early in life, and these elements are likely to be strongly influenced by biological factors. As development proceeds, the expression of temperament increasingly becomes more influenced by experience and context.

Consequently, although these four views of temperament differ with regard to aspects of the underlying definitions of temperament, there is quite a bit of overlap among the behaviors taken as indicators of the spectrum of temperamental influence. Moreover, within these views, with the exception of that of Thomas and Chess, temperament involves differences in motivational aspects of behavior.

Measurement Issues

Significant issues in defining the dimensions of temperament are the ability to demonstrate convergence of different measures of the same temperament dimension, discrimination between measures of different temperament dimensions, and stability in temperamental traits within an individual across time and situations in which stability is expected (but see Ahadi & Rothbart, 1994, for an alternative view). Many measures of temperament in infancy and early childhood have been rationally, rather than empirically, derived. Whereas most temperament measures have demonstrated moderate-to-high internal consistencies for separate scales, there is less evidence for the discriminant or construct validity of scales intended to reflect different dimensions of temperament.

Following the seminal work of Thomas et al. (1968) on difficult temperament, several measures designed to tap their nine dimensions of temperament have been constructed. In a review of large-sample factor analytic studies of these measures, Martin, Wisenbaker, and Huttunen (1994) concluded that only some of the original nine dimensions are recovered by factor analytic methods. Many studies have adopted the Thomas and Chess framework of temperament for studying the relations between temperament and psychopathology. Consequently, problems arise concerning how to relate dimensions and their attendant measures defined by this approach to empirical associations with external variables, like psychopathology. Also potentially problematic are studies using Thomas and Chess' temperamental patterns that create categorical classification from unique and relatively independent dimensions (e.g., Martin et al., 1994). When associations between "difficult" temperament and psychopathology are found, the unique or joint influences of the specific underlying dimensions are unknown. Moreover, the stability of difficult temperament may not extend beyond the preschool period (Lee & Bates, 1985; Maziade, Cote, Bernier, Boutin, & Thivierge, 1989).

The issue of the construct validity of temperament measures—and, by extension, the constructs themselves—is more general than questions concerning the scales designed to reflect the dimensions of Thomas and Chess. For example, Goldsmith, Rieser-Danner, and Briggs (1991) examined the overlap of reports of infant, toddler, and preschooler temperament on different measures completed by parents and teachers. Although they found evidence for convergence across measures for some similarly named scales, not all similarly named scales were correlated highly. More importantly, Goldsmith and colleagues found significant moderate correlations (i.e.,

0.40 to 0.50) between scales measuring nominally different dimensions of temperament. Thus, whereas there was some evidence of convergent validity across measures, a general absence of discriminant validity raises questions concerning the number and independence of different dimensions of temperament. This lack of clarity obfuscates issues concerning the relations between specific temperament dimensions and other aspects of development, like psychopathology.

Higher-order Models: Linking Temperament and the Big-Five Model of Personality

As noted earlier, Rothbart's conceptualization of temperament consists of higher- and lower-level dimensions. Similarly, Goldsmith and Campos' model, which follows closely research on basic emotions in humans, also may have higher-order dimensions. A second approach to the study of emotions emphasizes broad factors that are made up of the substantial and systematic relations among the basic emotions. Examination of self-report data from adults generally reveals two higher-order dimensions, namely negative affectivity and positive affectivity. These dimensions are consistently found across various descriptor sets, languages, populations, and response formats and account for roughly three-quarters of the variance among emotion-related terms (Watson & Tellegen, 1985; Zevon & Tellegen, 1982).

Higher-order models also are dominant within theories of adult personality. Most personality psychologists now agree that the domain of individual differences in adults, as measured by rating scales and questionnaire items, is almost completely described by five broad factors labeled Surgency/Extraversion, Agreeableness, Conscientiousness, Emotional Stability/Neuroticism, and Openness to Experience (i.e., the Big-Five model of personality). This five-factor structure of personality has been recovered using different groups of participants, different item pools, different instruments, different methods of analysis, and different languages (e.g., Digman, 1990; Goldberg, 1990; McCrae & Costa, 1987; Watson, Clark, & Harkness, 1994).

Several studies indicate substantial overlap between the dimensions of temperament and the factors of the Big-Five model of personality. For example, Ahadi, Rothbart, & Ye (1993) conducted a scale-level exploratory factor analysis of the Child Behavior Questionnaire (CBQ; Rothbart, 1988), a parent-report measure of child temperament, in 6- and 7-year-old children from the United States and the People's Republic of China. In both samples, three factors emerged; Ahadi and colleagues labeled these Surgency, Negative Affectivity, and Effortful Control. These three higher-order factors were conceptualized as being very similar to three of the higher-order adult personality factors described by the Big-Five model: Surgency/Extraversion, Emotional Stability/Neuroticism, and Conscientiousness. Ahadi et al.'s results suggest strong similarities between child temperament and adult personality factors that are relatively consistent cross-culturally. Results demonstrating overlap between temperament and the Big-Five model have been obtained with other samples of children and adults (e.g., Angleitner & Ostendorf, 1994; Digman, 1994).

Some of our own work has focused on establishing the similarity of components of temperament to two affective dimensions associated with the Big-Five model: Positive Affectivity (PA) and Negative Affectivity (NA; e.g., Watson et al., 1994). In a small pilot study of the overlap between measures of temperament and measures of affectivity (Dyer & Lonigan, 1997), parents of 104 2- to 5-year-old children (mean age 48.6 months, $SD = 10.85$) completed a shortened version of Rothbart's CBQ, the 20-item version of the EASI (Buss & Plomin, 1975), and a modified version of the Positive and Negative Affectivity Schedule (PANAS; Watson, Clark, & Tellegen, 1988). The EASI is the version of Buss and Plomin's temperament instrument that includes the dimension of Impulsivity. Similar to Ahadi et al 's (1993) results, scale-level principal-components analysis revealed three stable factors corresponding to Positive Affectivity/Surgency (hereinafter referred to as PA/S), Negative Affectivity/Neuroticism (NA/N), and Effortful Control (EC). Consistent with the theoretical goal of relating the two, the PA/S and NA/N factors represented blends of temperament dimensions with the higher-order affect factors. As in Rothbart's model, EC was defined as the self-regulation of affect through management of attention and other behaviors.

In a replication and extension of this work (Lonigan & Dyer, 2000), we asked parents of 215 children aged 3–8 years (mean age 68.9 months, $SD = 19.74$) to complete the full CBQ, the 20-item EASI, and the PANAS on their children. The results of a scale-level principal-components analysis are shown in table 4.1. Three distinct factors emerged from this analysis that accounted for 54.7% of the variance. The three factors corresponded to NA/N, PA/S, and (low) EC and were relatively independent from each other (i.e., $rs < 0.15$), consistent with theoretical models of the orthogonal nature of these dimensions.

Examination of how the individual scales loaded on the three factors revealed a number of scales with significant loadings on more than one factor. Notably, both the CBQ and the EASI scales measuring activity level had high loadings on both the PA/S and EC factors, indicating that activity level as measured by the CBQ and EASI is a blend of high PA/S and low EC. CBQ Approach had high loadings on both the PA/S and the NA/N factors, indicating that approach as measured by the CBQ involves a blend of surgency and inhibited approach. Interestingly, whereas the CBQ Impulsivity scale had high loadings on both the PA/S and the EC factors, the EASI Impulsivity scale was associated with the EC factor only. This result highlights the question of scale content and discriminant validity noted above, in that scales measuring nominally the same dimension have different patterns of association with other temperament dimensions. Several other CBQ scales (i.e., Anger/Frustration, Soothability, High Intensity Pleasure,

Table 4.1. Factor Loadings from Scale-level Principal-components Analysis of Temperament Measures with 3- to 8-Year-Old Children (Following Orthogonal Rotation)

	Factors		
Temperament scales	Negative Affectivity	Positive Affectivity/ Surgency	Effortful Control (low)
CBQ Discomfort	0.77		
CBQ Sadness	0.74		
CBQ Anger/Frustration	0.64		0.40
CBQ Fear	0.56		
CBQ Soothability	−0.49		−0.43
EASI Emotionality	0.64		
PANAS NA	0.49		
CBQ Smiling & Laughter		0.77	
CBQ Shyness		−0.63	
CBQ Impulsivity		0.63	0.60
CBQ High Intensity Pleasure	0.60	0.37	
CBQ Activity level		0.61	0.57
CBQ Approach	0.41	0.65	
CBQ Perceptual Sensitivity	0.43	0.44	−0.41
EASI Sociability		0.73	
PANAS PA		0.58	
CBQ Inhibitory Control			−0.84
CBQ Low Intensity Pleasure			−0.70
CBQ Attentional Focusing			−0.65
CBQ Attentional Shifting			−0.53
EASI Impulsivity			0.69
EASI Activity		0.53	0.55

Note. $N = 220$. CBQ = Children's Behavior Questionnaire; EASI = Emotionality, Sociability, Emotionality, Impulsivity Scale; PANAS = Positive and Negative Affect Scales. Only loadings greater than or equal to 0.30 are shown.

Perceptual Sensitivity) also had substantial associations with two or more of the three higher-order factors.

Separate analyses of data from the younger (3- to 5-year-old) and older (6- to 8-year-old) children revealed similar structure. Overall, the results of these two studies are largely consistent with the results obtained by Ahadi et al. (1993), and the results extend Ahadi et al.'s findings across different measures of temperament, to specific markers of two of the Big-Five factors, and to a broader age group. These results indicate that temperament in pre-school-age and early school-age children can be described adequately by three higher-order factors that directly correspond to similar higher-order factors found in adult personality.

We also have found a high degree of overlap between temperament constructs and PA and NA in older children. Hooe, Lonigan, and Anthony

(1997) had a group of 292 children in 5th to 11th grades complete the PANAS and a modified version of the adult self-report Emotionality, Activity, and Sociability Scales (EAS; Buss & Plomin, 1984). Principal-components analysis of the modified EAS revealed five lower-order factors, identical to those found with adults (i.e., Distress, Fear, Anger, Activity, and Sociability). Scale-level principal-components analysis of the modified EAS yielded two orthogonal (i.e., $r = 0.06$) higher-order factors. The first higher-order factor, Negative Temperament, consisted of the lower-order factors Distress, Fear, and Anger. The second higher-order factor, Positive Temperament, consisted of the lower-order factors Sociability and Activity. Correlations between the Negative Temperament factor and the NA scale of the PANAS ($r = 0.67$) and between the Positive Temperament factor and the PA scale of the PANAS ($r = 0.43$) indicated substantial overlap of the constructs.

Taken together, results across multiple measures and conceptualizations of temperament (e.g., Buss & Plomin, 1984; Rothbart, 1989), and varied ages, respondents, and cultures indicate that temperament can be conceptualized within the domain of several of the factors of the Big-Five model (i.e., NA/N, PA/S, and EC). Within this view, temperament can be seen as the nonintellectual component or developmental precursor of personality. The higher-order focus also accommodates the fact that different temperamental traits are likely to be expressed in unique behaviors at distinct points during development. For example, activity level in infancy is typically a sign of distress (Rothbart, 1989) characteristic of NA/N; whereas, later in development, activity is more associated with approach behavior (Digman & Inouye, 1986; Eaton, 1994) that would be characteristic of PA/S. Continuity within an individual may be at the higher order level, not at the behavioral level.

Behavioral Inhibition

The concept of behavioral inhibition (BI) as temperament is distinct from the theories of temperament outlined above because it is descriptive of *one* multi-faceted characteristic of children rather than being inclusive of the full range of possible temperamental behaviors. BI also is distinct from other theories of temperament because it is conceptualized as a discrete category, instead of a continuous distribution of behaviors (see Kagan, 1994, 1997; Kagan, Snidman, Arcus, & Reznick, 1994; Turner, Beidel, & Wolff, 1996, for reviews). This work grew out of an interest in investigating certain temperamental qualities in their extreme manifestations and as a follow-up to an earlier longitudinal study in which a small group of children were identified who were very fearful and inhibited. These children retained aspects of this fearfulness into adulthood.

BI is defined as an overt representation of a psychological and physiological state of uncertainty that results from exposure to unfamiliar objects, people, and stressful situations (Kagan, 1994, 1997). This restriction to novel contexts is an important one, as even the most inhibited children can demonstrate normal social skills when in familiar situations (Asendorpf, 1993; Kagan, 1994; Kagan et al., 1994). Behavioral criteria for BI include such variables as: latency to, and amount of unsolicited speech to, peers and adults; proximity to parent; verbal displays of distress; and cessation of activity. Also included in the criteria for BI are a set of eight physiological measurements: heart rate and heart rate variability; blood pressure; pupil dilation; muscle tension; levels of secreted cortisol; urinary norepinephrine levels; and vocal frequency (Kagan, Reznick, Snidman, Gibbons, & Johnson, 1988).

BI has been most thoroughly investigated in two cohorts of children studied longitudinally beginning in the mid 1980s. The first cohort included groups of children representing the top and bottom 20% of an initial sample of over 100 children. These children were preselected on the basis of parent reports of shyness and withdrawal behaviors at 21 months of age. The extreme groups were labeled behaviorally inhibited and behaviorally uninhibited, respectively. A second cohort was later established in a similar fashion, this one beginning at 31 months of age. Several other groups of children have been followed, with a few groups first assessed in early infancy (Kagan 1994; Kagan et al., 1988, 1994). On average, one-half to three-quarters of children originally classified as inhibited or uninhibited as toddlers maintained this classification across time intervals ranging between several months and several years (Kagan, 1994; Kagan et al., 1988; Turner et al., 1996). Of the two groups, the uninhibited children were those who showed the most stability of their classification status. Children were more likely to move from extreme inhibition into the normal range than to become more inhibited, suggesting a role for socialization pressures that reinforce active approach and socially engaged behavior (see below). Particularly noteworthy is evidence that the inhibited children who also had a consistently high and stable heart rate tended to be those who remained in the behaviorally inhibited category across time. Among the eight physiological markers, high and low heart-rate variability were the characteristics that best distinguished the two groups of children (Kagan et al., 1994; Turner et al., 1996).

Children who were categorized into one of the extreme groups at every age also showed the most extreme responses at most ages. In contrast, there was no demonstrable stability or predictive validity from behavioral inhibition indicators for children who fell in the mid-range between the extremes (Kagan, 1997; Turner et al., 1996). This pattern of results has been seen both in samples of children preselected for shyness or inhibition and in unselected samples, and has been interpreted as empirical support for the idea that the inhibited and uninhibited children have qualitative differences from each other and from those who fall between (e.g., Kagan, 1997; Kagan et al., 1988). Despite this categorical classification of BI, however, it is clear that the concept has strong similarities to the three higher-order factors outlined above. Children who are behaviorally inhibited exhibit behaviors consistent with high NA/N (i.e., distress, fear, inhibited approach), low EC (i.e., low attentional shifting), and perhaps low PA/S (i.e., low sociability).

Developmental and Neural Mechanisms and Models

A variety of models for explaining continuity and discontinuity in temperament systems have been developed. Within these models, temperament is
viewed as an organization of motivational systems. Recently, Derryberry
and Rothbart (1997; see also Derryberry & Reed, 1996) have outlined a
model of temperament as a self-organizing system involving what they
termed *reactive* and *effortful* processes. Reactive processes are motivational
influences involving both approach or activation systems and inhibitory
systems. Delineation of these two reactive motivational systems is often
related to Gray's (e.g., 1982, 1987; see also Fowles, 1988) model.
According to Gray, two neural systems serve to motivate behavior, the
Behavioral Activation System (BAS) and the Behavioral Inhibition System
(BIS). Activation of the BAS is associated with sensitivity to *signals* of both
reward and the absence of punishment. The behavioral effects of the BAS
include appetitive approach behavior. Although the BAS is sometimes said
to be associated with impulsivity (e.g., Derryberry & Reed, 1996), Tellegen
(1985) noted that impulsivity seems more associated with Conscientiousness/
Constraint (i.e., EC). Activation of the BIS is associated with *signals* of
punishment, signals of nonreward, and novelty. The behavioral effects of
the BIS include inhibition of ongoing behavior, increased attention, and
increased arousal (Gray, 1988).

Interactions and coordination between the BAS and BIS systems appear
not to be developed completely in early infancy. For instance, infants will
often display approach and grasp behavior toward a novel stimulus despite
displaying significant distress. In this case, novelty seems to activate both the
BAS (approach) and the distress component of the BIS with relatively little
influence of BIS on approach behavior. Across the first year of life, however,
inhibition of behavior develops, indexed, for example, by increased latency to
grasp high-intensity objects (Rothbart, 1988). Moreover, Rothbart (1988)
found that infants' tendencies to approach high-intensity toys were related
to their displays of positive and negative affect.

In contrast to the motivational influences of reactive processes, effortful
processes involve executive functions like the intentional allocation of attention. Such systems serve to modulate the effects of reactive motivational
systems. As a temperamental system, complex effortful processes are
relatively late developing (e.g., Reed, Pien, & Rothbart, 1984). Although
some evidence of these processes, such as orienting, can be seen during the
first few months of life, it appears that significant development occurs during
the toddler period with a relatively functional and stable system apparent by
18–24 months of age (Rothbart, Posner, & Hershey, 1995). The ability to
intentionally avoid or disengage attention from aversive stimuli that previously may have elicited an increase in NA/N represents the activity of
the newly developing EC system. Rothbart et al. (1995) suggested that EC
and attentional systems involve aspects of three neural networks: (a) a
posterior attentional network associated with orienting to sensory stimuli

in a spatial location; (b) an anterior attentional network associated with detection of events; and (c) a third network associated with vigilance (i.e., maintenance of attention). The influence of the anterior network appears after the other two, with much of its development occurring late in the first year (Rothbart et al., 1995).

As reviewed below, it appears that both NA/N reactive processes and EC processes are related to anxiety. For example, reactions to signals of novelty or punishment can increase NA/N and arousal, especially in individuals with a highly responsive BIS system. Conversely, EC processes, particularly through the activity of the anterior attention network, may allow an individual to more easily orient away from a novel or distressing stimulus. A variety of evidence indicates that children and adults with anxiety show attentional biases toward threatening stimuli (see Vasey & MacLeod, this volume), suggesting that anxiety disorders are associated with impaired or low levels of EC.

Owing to the potential moderating interaction of reactive and effortful systems, we believe that low EC is key to the development of anxiety disorders. Although anxiety is characterized by behaviors consistent with reactive control (e.g., inhibition of behavior) and are thus NA/N motivated, an individual with high EC is able to employ self-regulative processes in the form of attention and other coping behaviors, thus preventing or modulating the experience of distress in the presence of aversive stimulation. A failure of EC, either because of temperamentally low capacity, high situational demands, or a combination of both, leads to reactive control in highly aversive situations or in individuals with a low threshold for distress. Individuals high in NA/N have a greater need for EC because more stimuli are aversive, because they react more strongly to aversive stimulation, or both. Therefore, although high NA/N is a necessary condition for the development of anxiety, it is not sufficient. We believe that a dynamic combination of low EC and high NA/N is required (see Williams, Watts, MacLeod, & Mathews, 1997, for a similar conclusion).

Evidence for the Role of Temperamental Factors in Anxiety

Evidence for the role of temperament in anxiety spans a diverse literature, including studies of adults with anxiety or anxiety disorders, studies of factors associated with current anxiety or anxiety disorders in children, and longitudinal research on the relations between early temperament and the development of anxiety and internalizing psychopathology. A significant number of studies examining the relation between normative variation in temperament and psychopathology have employed the more global temperament categorization of Thomas and Chess. Only recently have studies looked more carefully at empirically derived temperamental dimensions and their relation to psychopathology. Finally, a number of studies have examined the link between BI and anxiety.

Studies of Concurrent Relations Between Temperament and Anxiety Disorders: Adults

In their tripartite model of depression and anxiety, Clark and Watson (1991) theorized that NA is a nonspecific factor that relates to both depression and anxiety. Depression is specifically characterized by low PA, whereas anxiety is specifically characterized by physiological hyperarousal. Watson, Clark, and Carey (1988) examined the overlap of anxiety and depressive disorders in adults and found that they could be discriminated by relatively pure measures of affect. Consistent with the tripartite model, individuals with either an anxiety or a depressive disorder reported high levels of NA, whereas only individuals with a depressive disorder reported low levels of PA. Using a large sample of adults diagnosed with anxiety disorders, Brown et al. (1998) demonstrated that NA was associated with all *Diagnostic and Statistical Manual of Mental Disorders* (DSM-IV; American Psychiatric Association, 1994) anxiety disorders and DSM-IV depression. In contrast, PA was associated with DSM-IV depression and DSM-IV Social Phobia but not other DSM-IV anxiety disorders. Finally, Brown and colleagues found that all DSM-IV anxiety disorders, but not depression, were associated with physiological hyperarousal, which might be related to anxiety sensitivity (e.g., Clark, Watson, & Mineka, 1994; Reiss, Silverman, & Weems, this volume) but appears not to be primarily temperament-based.

In their review of temperamental influences on adult psychopathology, Clark et al. (1994) noted that there were relatively few studies examining the influence of NA/N on anxiety disorders in adults, and they speculated that this was the result of the conceptual overlap of anxiety and NA/N. They concluded, however, that the small number of existing studies supported the notion that NA/N represented more than a state component of anxiety. For example, clinically anxious patients who show little improvement tend to have higher NA/N scores than patients who do improve. Stronger results for the influence of NA/N are found for depression, and evidence suggests that PA/S both represents a risk for and influences the course of depression. Subsequent studies have extended these results to include nonpatient samples and prospective studies (Krueger, Caspi, Moffitt, Silva & McGee, 1996; Trull & Sher, 1994). Together, these results indicate that, in adults, high NA/N serves as a general risk for psychopathology and that low PA/S, in combination with high NA/N, is a specific risk factor for depression.

Studies of Concurrent Relations Between Temperament and Anxiety: Children

Whereas there has been a significant amount of work examining the tripartite model in adults, there has been substantially less examination of the model in children. Lonigan, Carey, & Finch (1994) found support for the tripartite model in a group of children and adolescents hospitalized because of problems associated with anxiety or depression. Indices of NA were strongly related to both anxiety and depression, and NA did not distinguish between children diagnosed with anxiety disorders and children diagnosed with a depressive disorder. In contrast, indices of PA were uniquely related to depression; and, consistent with the tripartite model, PA distinguished children diagnosed with a depressive disorder from children diagnosed with an anxiety disorder. Similar results have been reported by others (e.g., Chorpita, Albano, & Barlow, 1998; Joiner, Catanzaro, & Laurent, 1996).

Other studies have found significant relations between temperamental factors and current anxiety in children. In the Hooe et al. (1997) study described above, both NA as assessed by the PANAS and the higher-order Negative Temperament factor strongly predicted children's concurrent reports of anxiety and depression. Similar results concerning NA/N have been obtained in other samples (Lonigan, Hooe, David, & Kistner, 1999; Wertlieb, Weigel, Springer, & Feldstein, 1987; Wolfe et al., 1987). For example, Wertlieb et al. (1987) found evidence for an association between temperament and problem behaviors, as well as an interaction between life stressors and temperament in a community sample of 6- and 9-year-old children. Temperamental traits of high activity, high distractibility, and low threshold were associated more with externalizing symptoms, whereas withdrawal was associated more with internalizing symptoms.

A number of recent studies have examined the conceptualization of Block and Block (1980) concerning ego-resiliency and ego-control as temperamental factors associated with the Big-Five model. For instance, Robins, John, Caspi, Moffitt, and Stouthamer-Loeber (1996) mapped the Blocks' typology of Ego Resilients, Unsettled Overcontrollers, and Vulnerable Overcontrollers on to the Big-Five model dimensions. They found that Vulnerable Overcontrolling (low ego-resilience and high ego-control) adolescent boys were characterized by factors corresponding to low PA/S, low EC, and high NA, compared with Ego Resilients (high ego-resilience and high ego-control). These boys were more likely than Ego Resilients or Unsettled Overcontrollers (low ego-resilience and low ego-control) to have internalizing problems, based on caregivers' reports. Similarly, John, Caspi, Robins, Moffitt, and Stouthamer-Loeber (1994) reported on the relation between Big-Five factors assessed using the mothers' Q-sorts on the California Child Q-Sort (CCQ) and teacher reports of problem behaviors in a group of 350 13-year-old boys who were participants in the Pittsburgh Youth Study. Significantly, John and colleagues found substantial differences between boys classified as having an internalizing disorder (i.e., those scoring above the 18th percentile on the internalizing scale of the Child Behavior Checklist, CBCL; Achenbach, 1991) and those without an internalizing disorder on both a neuroticism scale (i.e., NA/N) and a conscientiousness scale (i.e., EC). High NA/N and low EC were associated with internalizing disorders.

Longitudinal Studies of the Relation Between Temperament and Anxiety Symptoms

In addition to demonstrating concurrent associations between NA/N and anxiety, we found that scores on the NA scale of the PANAS predicted changes in 300 4th–11th grade children's self-reported levels of anxiety in a 7-month longitudinal study (Lonigan, Kistner, Hooe, & David, 1997). This finding indicates that NA/N, as measured by the PANAS, assesses more than the state component of anxiety, and that NA/N represents a temperamental risk for the development of anxiety. Similarly, Rende (1993) examined the longitudinal association between EAS temperamental traits and parental reports of internalizing and externalizing problems in middle childhood for a group of 164 children. When the children were between the ages of one and four years, mothers completed an EAS temperament measure. Temperament ratings from the year 1 and year 2 assessments were averaged to form an infancy rating, and temperament ratings from the year 3 and year 4 assessments were averaged to form an early childhood rating. For both boys and girls, higher levels of emotionality in infancy and early childhood were significantly related to mothers' reports of anxiety/depression on the CBCL when children were 7 years old. For girls only, lower levels of sociability in infancy and early childhood also were related to anxiety/depression on the CBCL.

In one of the more extensive studies to date, Caspi, Henry, McGee, Moffitt, and Silva (1995) reported the outcome of a 12-year longitudinal study of a group of over 800 children taking part in the Dunedin Multidisciplinary Health and Development Study. Temperament-related behavioral ratings of the children were made by trained examiners during psychological examinations when the children were 3 and 5 years of age. Parent and teacher reports of problem behaviors were collected when the children were 9, 11, 13, and 15 years of age. Analysis of the temperament ratings yielded three factors that were consistent across age and sex. Caspi and colleagues labeled these factors: (a) Lack of Control, consisting of behaviors indicating inability to modulate impulsive expression, lack of persistence, and sensitivity to challenge; (b) Approach, consisting of behaviors indicating a willingness to explore stimuli in novel situations; and (c) Sluggishness, consisting of behaviors indicating passivity and withdrawal from novelty. The Sluggishness factor also contained behaviors indicating shyness, fearfulness, and limited verbalizations.

For both boys and girls there was evidence of moderate stability of these three factors from age three to age nine (i.e., cross-time correlations ranged from 0.12 to 0.42). Parent and teacher ratings were combined, and the associations between the three temperament factors and various internalizing and externalizing problems were examined separately for boys and girls at 9, 11, 13, and 15 years of age. Although temperament at both age three and age five was associated consistently with externalizing problems, only temperament at age five was associated consistently with anxiety. For boys, anxiety was related to Lack of Control ($r = 0.12$ to 0.15), Inhibited Approach ($r = 0.12$ to 0.23), and more weakly with Sluggishness ($r = 0.02$ to 0.15). For girls, a similar pattern was obtained except that Inhibited Approach was less consistently related to anxiety ($r = 0.3$ to 0.15); both Lack of Control ($r = 0.10$ to 0.15) and Sluggishness ($r = 0.07$ to 0.15) were related to later anxiety in girls. Separate multiple regression analyses for boys and girls revealed that both Lack of Control and Inhibited Approach were independent predictors of anxiety in boys, whereas Lack of Control and Sluggishness were independent predictors of anxiety for girls.

These longitudinal relations between variables associated with NA/N and EC provide significant support for the role of temperament in anxiety. As noted above, the results of Lonigan et al. (1997) demonstrate that NA/A represents more than a state component of anxiety. These results converge with results concerning adults (e.g., Clark et al., 1994; Krueger et al., 1996; Trull & Sher, 1994) implicating NA/N as a causal factor in the development or maintenance of anxiety. Caspi et al.'s (1995) findings concerning the relation between their Lack of Control factor and internalizing problems on the CBCL provide similar evidence for EC as a causal factor in the development of children's internalizing symptoms.

Longitudinal Studies of the Relation Between Temperament and Anxiety Disorders

Virtually all research examining the longitudinal association between temperament and clinical cases of anxiety has involved studies of BI. These studies indicate that a child classified as behaviorally inhibited is more susceptible to anxiety and anxiety disorders than other children. Kagan and colleagues have investigated such longer-term sequelae with their own samples and have found support for this association. A study of the 31-month cohort at age $5\frac{1}{2}$ years showed that over 90% of the inhibited children who concurrently showed a high and stable heart rate had two or more significant fears during the previous year, according to maternal report. Three-quarters of the inhibited children had significantly more pervasive fears than did the uninhibited children (Turner et al., 1996). A number of researchers also have found striking similarities between the behavior of inhibited children and retrospective reports of the childhood behavior of adults with anxiety disorders (see Silove & Manicavasagar, this volume).

Biederman and colleagues explored some of these relations in a series of studies comparing one of Kagan's longitudinal cohorts with children whose parents were diagnosed as having panic disorder with agoraphobia (e.g., Rosenbaum et al., 1988; see Turner et al., 1996, for review). The three control groups included children of nondiagnosed parents, children whose parents had Major Depression, and those whose parents were diagnosed with both Depression and Panic Disorder. Relations were found in both directions, such that children of parents with Panic Disorder were more likely to be behaviorally inhibited than children in any other group. Secondly, the parents of inhibited children were significantly more likely to meet criteria for prior or current anxiety problems, and this was especially true for parents of children who were both inhibited and met concurrent criteria for one or more anxiety disorders.

Biederman and colleagues also found that rates of anxiety disorders were particularly high in those children consistently classified as inhibited across their development and that the parents of these children also were more likely to be affected by anxiety problems. A 3-year follow-up indicated that there were significantly more anxiety disorders diagnosed in the group of children who were behaviorally inhibited at baseline (Biederman, Rosenbaum, Chaloff, & Kagan, 1995). These children also were more likely to have multiple comorbid disorders. Again, the rates were the greatest in those children with a history of stable BI. Together, these results suggest that the children most at-risk for anxiety disorders are those with stable BI whose parents have a current anxiety disorder.

Most other longitudinal studies investigating temperament and anxiety disorders have employed the Thomas and Chess model (e.g., Maziade et al., 1985, 1990). These studies have found few significant relations between temperament characteristics as defined by this model and later anxiety or other internalizing disorders. The majority of children with difficult temperaments who later developed psychopathology were diagnosed with externalizing disorders such as Oppositional Defiant Disorder or Attention Deficit Hyperactivity Disorder (Maziade et al., 1985, 1990). Although these results do not demonstrate a clear connection between temperament and anxiety disorders, the use of the aggregated difficult temperament classification and a focus on extreme groups (i.e., easy versus difficult temperament) may have obscured a relation between the temperamental dimensions and internalizing disorders (cf., Wertlieb et al., 1987).

Models of the Relations Between Temperament and Psychopathology

Although the foregoing studies demonstrate a convincing link between components of temperament and anxious psychopathology across the developmental spectrum, there is little data that would allow a clear specification of the pathway through which temperament is related to a specific manifestation of psychopathology. That is, temperamental effects on anxiety disorders may be direct, indirect, or serve to moderate other causal factors. Four primary models of how temperament or personality may influence the development of psychopathology have been proposed (e.g., see Akiskal, Hirschfeld, & Yerevanian, 1983; Clark et al., 1994). First, temperament may serve as a *predisposition*, playing a direct causal role in the development of psychopathology. A common version of this predisposition model, the diathesis–stress model, suggests that a relevant stressor, in combination with a temperamental predisposition, is needed to trigger the onset of the disorder.

Second, temperament may serve to moderate the expression or course of a disorder without having a direct causal role in its onset. This *pathoplasticity* model also encompasses situations in which temperament plays a role in shaping the environment of the individual. Third, temperament may be altered or affected by the experience of a disorder. In this *complication* model, the experience of having a disorder may cause relatively enduring changes in temperamental factors by fundamentally altering them or because of residual symptoms of the disorder. Finally, a disorder may reflect the extreme of some dimension of temperament. In this *continuity* model, both temperament and disorder are seen as reflecting the same underlying process.

These models are not mutually exclusive across or within individuals. It is possible that temperament can predispose to a disorder, influence the symptoms and course of the disorder once present, and be modified by the experience of the disorder. Within the predisposition model, the vulnerability may be general, for a class of disorders (e.g., anxiety disorders, distress disorders including both mood and anxiety disorders), or for a specific subtype of a class of disorders (e.g., Panic Disorder, Unipolar Depression). The sections below outline a number of more specific hypothetical developmental pathways through which temperament may be related to anxiety disorders in children. Simplified versions of several of these models are shown in fig. 4.1.

Main-effects Model of Temperamental Predisposition to Anxiety

The simplest model of the role of temperament in the development of anxiety disorders is a main-effects model in which a child is predisposed to an anxiety disorder or disorders because of his or her temperament. Within the higher-order framework outlined above, temperamental characteristics representing either high NA/N or low EC would be associated with anxiety disorders. It is unlikely, however, that a main-effects model (i.e., continuity) accounts for a substantial proportion of children who develop anxiety disorders (see Vasey & Dadds, this volume). Only about one-third of behaviorally inhibited children will manifest anxiety disorders in late childhood or adolescence (Kagan et al., 1994; Turner et al., 1996). Biederman et al. (1990) noted that nearly 70% of the inhibited children they studied did not show symptoms of any anxiety disorders. Collectively, this preliminary body of research suggests that temperamental factors, including BI, although placing a child at an increased risk for an anxiety disorder, can be considered neither necessary nor sufficient in the development of this psychopathology. Psychopathology itself is a rare event; inhibited and temperamentally prone children are among those for whom such pathology is more likely.

Interactive-effects Models of Temperament on the Development of Anxiety Disorders

Evidence reviewed above suggests that combinations of temperamental factors are associated with psychopathology, and that these combinations

A. *Interactive Model of Temperamental Effects*

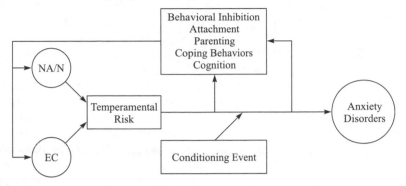

B. *Mediational Model of Temperamental Effects*

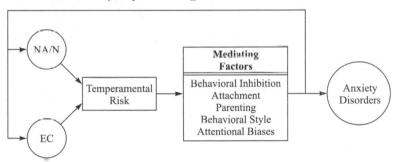

C. *Moderated Model of Temperamental Effects*

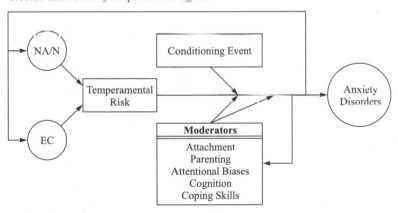

Figure 4.1. Three simplified hypothetical models of how temperament may be related to the development of anxiety disorders.

of temperamental factors discriminate individuals with anxiety from individuals with a different form of psychopathology (e.g., Caspi et al., 1995; John et al., 1994; Joiner & Lonigan, in press; Lonigan et al., 1994; Robins et al., 1996; Watson et al., 1988). With regard to anxiety, we propose that the *combination* of high NA/N and low EC predisposes children, either directly or indirectly (see below), to the development of anxiety. This combination distinguishes risk for anxiety (i.e., high NA/N and low EC) from risk for depression (i.e., high NA/N and low PA/S; Clark & Watson, 1991), and may distinguish risk for anxiety from risk for other forms of psychopathology like conduct problems (e.g., O'Brien & Frick, 1996).

As noted by Vasey and Dadds (this volume), existing research suggests that there are at least three main paths to the acquisition of problematic anxiety: respondent conditioning, failure of habituation of fears, and dishabituation of previously mastered fears. It is likely that temperament plays at least a partial role in some of these processes (see fig. 4.1A). Individual differences in temperamental reactivity influences the conditionability of individuals to both positive and negative events (e.g., see Gray, 1981; Mineka & Zinbarg, 1995). Consequently, a child with high NA/N exposed to an aversive conditioning event may be more likely to acquire a phobic response. For instance, Lonigan, Shannon, Finch, Daugherty, and Taylor (1991) found that among children exposed to Hurricane Hugo, those with high trait anxiety were more likely to meet criteria for a DSM diagnosis of Posttraumatic Stress Disorder. Moreover, level of trait anxiety interacted with level of exposure to predict severity of posttraumatic symptoms (Lonigan, 1993). Once a conditioning event has affected anxiety in a temperamentally prone individual, it may negatively affect other behaviors as well as temperamental expression (i.e., a complication model). Children high in NA/N or low in EC also may be less likely to habituate to normal childhood fears, be more likely to show disinhibition of previously mastered fears, or both, either because of high reactivity or a pattern of behavioral style and avoidance (see below) that prevents repeated or prolonged exposure to the feared situation.

Indirect-effects Models of Temperament on the Development of Anxiety Disorders

In addition to more direct and interactive ways that temperament can be related to the development of anxious psychopathology, temperament has an influence on other factors that may predispose children to anxiety. Hence, the influence of temperament may be indirect or mediated by external factors that are themselves partially the results of a child's temperamental characteristics (see fig. 4.1B).

Behavioral Style. BI, high NA/N, or low EC may lead to susceptibility to anxiety disorders indirectly by increasing the likelihood of avoidance behaviors. This is a pathway to anxiety that has been explored by a number of researchers (see Rubin & Burgess, this volume). Some easily distressed children may choose to cope with their heightened negative reactivity to novel or mildly aversive stimuli by engaging in passive avoidance, not allowing themselves to come in contact with stimuli that would upset them. An inhibited style of interaction in unfamiliar or challenging settings can have repercussions that extend far beyond the immediate behavior. Thompson and Calkins, for example, suggested that children who are temperamentally prone to experiencing heightened physiological responsiveness to novelty will as infants be easily distressed by such stimuli, and as the child develops, "global patterns of infancy evolve into the more sophisticated behavioral repertoire of the preschooler that fosters not just reactance to external stimuli, but also efforts to control exposure to arousing stimuli and to emotionally manage their impact" (1996, p. 174). This strategy has a number of costs that accrue from consistent use, including having fewer opportunities to learn more active self-regulatory skills.

Passive solitary play (versus solitary active play or more associative play) has been found to be related to the development of internalizing disorders (Rubin, Hymel, Mills, & Rose-Krasnor, 1991; Rubin, Coplan, Fox, & Calkins, 1995) and BI (Asendorpf, 1993). For instance, Asendorpf used latency to unsolicited speech to assess the stability of behavior in inhibited children when interacting with unfamiliar adults and found considerable stability of BI from ages 4 to 8 years. Across this same interval, the amount of solitary passive play actually increased for the most inhibited children, and Asendorpf attributed this to the increased impact of the children's lack of adaptive coping skills in peer settings. BI, high NA/N, and low EC can thus predispose children to behaviors that may lead to isolation and rejection. Both are significant risk factors for internalizing disorders, like depression and anxiety (e.g., Baker, Milich, & Manolis, 1996; Kupersmidt, & Patterson, 1991).

Attachment Relationships. There is considerable debate concerning the degree and directionality of temperamental influence on attachment. That is, does temperament partially cause particular types of attachment relationships or does temperament merely influence the behaviors manifest within an attachment relationship (e.g., level of distress upon separation)? It seems clear that at least a part of children's attachment with their primary caregiver is a function of their own temperamental characteristics (e.g., Goldsmith & Alansky, 1987). Fox and Calkins (1993) have suggested that a child's attachment relationships may mediate the role of temperament in later negative reactivity and inhibition. For example, Calkins and Fox (1992) measured infants' distress reactivity at 5 months, attachment classification at 14 months, and level of inhibition displayed in a laboratory session at 24 months. Infants' distress reactivity was related to later attachment. Highly reactive infants were classified as insecurely (avoidant and resistant) attached. High heart-rate stability and distress to novelty predicted resistant attachment at 14 months, whereas heart rate variability and easy frustration were related to avoidant attachment. Moreover the children's attachment classification at 14 months predicted inhibition at 24 months.

Attentional Biases. As noted above, there is substantial evidence that individuals with anxiety disorders show attentional biases toward threatening information (Vasey & MacLeod, this volume). To date, however, there is little data that would allow a determination of whether this robust finding is a cause or consequence of anxiety. Although attentional biases may act as a mediator of temperamental risk for anxiety, they may also moderate the effects of other factors in temperamentally prone individuals (e.g., see fig. 4.1C). As noted by Derryberry and Reed (1996), both reactive processes, like those associated with NA/N and PA/S, and effortful processes, like those associated with EC, may impact the development of children's internal cognitive representations of themselves, others, and the world. In the temperamentally high NA/N child, attention to threatening aspects of the world and developing representations of lack of competence (e.g., Hymel, Woody, & Bowker, 1993) may lead to a more generalized and more stable anxious response to threatening or ambiguous situations (e.g., Hock, Krohne, & Kaiser, 1996). However, the extent to which these cognitive features are causes or merely symptomatic of anxiety is largely an untested question.

Moderating Effects on Temperamental Influence

The finding that there is only a moderate degree of stability in extreme temperamental reactivity, like BI, and that early temperament is less related to psychopathology than is latter temperament (e.g., Biederman et al., 1995; Caspi et al., 1995) suggests that external and developmental factors may moderate the nature of children's development of temperament expression through the infant and toddler period. These variables may serve as risk or protective factors for temperamentally prone children (see fig. 4.1C).

Effects of Development. Much of the evidence for the effects of development come from the study of BI, which is not surprising given that these groups of children have been perhaps the most consistently followed across time. The results noted above demonstrate that BI is a robust temperament factor with well-documented stability in a small but significant percentage of children. Yet even in the most consistently inhibited children there is a clear influence of environmental and developmental variables that affect the expression of the temperament. As inhibited children develop, the triggers for an inhibited response change, although the construct of BI remains consistent across time. For example the situations used by Kagan and colleagues to categorize children were altered at each age to account for developmental changes (e.g., exposure to a single unfamiliar child vs. exposure to a group of unfamiliar children).

Similarly, the form of the behavioral response will be altered with development. During the first several months of life, distinct responses of fear, frustration and other forms of distress are not evident (e.g., Kagan et al., 1994; Rothbart, 1989). Rather, what can be seen is a generalized negative reaction to varied precipitating stimuli. As the child matures, the global distress response differentiates and it becomes possible to identify fear apart from frustration. The former is increasingly linked to withdrawal and inhibition whereas the latter is associated with an anger-motivated approach. Motor activity, at first associated with distress, becomes more and more linked to PA/S and frequent approach behaviors. Eventually, crying and retreat give way to indicators that are better defined as the absence of behavior (e.g., being on the periphery of a group of peers, speaking to a strange adult only in response to direct questions). Some developmental changes also may influence the degree of distress and associated behavioral responses experienced in challenging situations. That is, children who experience a great amount of distress and inhibition to novelty over a long period of time may actually lower their threshold to such stimuli so that eventually even mild discomforts generate the same pattern of inhibited behavior.

Effects of Parenting. Although children's temperament can impact parenting behaviors, parenting also can directly alter the expression of temperament (e.g., Lee & Bates, 1985; van den Boom, 1989). Parental behavior influences the level of behavioral inhibition, withdrawal, and distress that children display. Parents may help create and maintain an avoidant and inhibited behavioral style by modeling and encouraging its use. For instance, many parents of high reactive infants may choose to protect their children from such distress by reducing the frequency of exposure to unfamiliar stimuli and by quickly stepping in to soothe them when the experience of novelty is unavoidable (Thompson & Calkins, 1996). However, if avoidant or inhibited behavior remains unchallenged, novelty will stay novel and the child will have a limited, negative view of both the environment and her or his ability to cope with it. This can become a source for later distress that may itself reinforce withdrawal and avoidance.

Some evidence supports the idea that being too sensitive to a child's distress can actually be counterproductive. Kagan et al (1994) found that reactive infants whose mothers set limits and were more focused on teaching their child to cope than on just soothing them were more likely to show less fear and inhibition at subsequent observations. This type of parental decision had much less of an effect on low reactive infants because they were less often distressed. Conversely, inhibited children whose parents were not sensitive enough, and who imposed socialization demands on their children in an abrupt or overly negative way, were vulnerable to increased feelings of guilt and sensitivity to criticism. Other data also suggest that parental overprotectiveness increases the risk of problem behaviors in children temperamentally prone to anxiety (e.g., Rubin & Mills, 1991; but see Bowen, Vitaro, Kerr, & Pelletier, 1995).

A good balance between comforting and the teaching of coping skills seems to be what is most effective in moderating inhibited tendencies. Moreover, Fox and Calkins (1993) suggested that the amount of guidance that a parent gives with respect to the development of self-regulative skills (see below) can have a large effect on the child's long-term behavior and reactivity. van den Boom (1989) found that mothers of distress-prone infants became less attentive and less positive over time. She also demonstrated that a training procedure designed to teach mothers how to play with and soothe their infants led to increased positive and decreased negative behavior from the infants. One year later, infants whose mothers had taken part in the training program were less likely to be classified as avoidant and more likely to engage in exploratory play than infants whose mothers did not receive the training.

Self-regulatory Coping Behavior. In addition to positive self-regulative functions of EC, other forms of self-regulation may moderate the risk for the development of psychopathology in temperamentally prone children (see Thompson, this volume). For example, Eisenberg and Fabes (1992) outlined a model of how emotion regulation, including both temperamentally based processes and learned coping skills, can impact social competence and other socially relevant behaviors. Eisenberg and her colleagues have reported significant association between children's emotionality, self-regulation, and both positive and negative outcomes (e.g., Eisenberg et al., 1996). The use of coping and available social support by children who are temperamentally prone toward anxiety may buffer them against the negative effects of stress (e.g., Compas, 1987; La Greca, Silverman, Vernberg, & Prinstein, 1996).

Sex Differences and Age-effects. Ultimately, any theory of how temperament is related to psychopathology will need to deal with sex differences in the prevalence of different forms of psychopathology and with the increased frequency of psychopathology across development. Generally, anxiety and depressive disorders are more common in girls than boys, particularly from late childhood through adolescence and into adulthood (see Weiss & Last, this volume). In contrast, however, there are relatively few early temperamental differences between girls and boys (e.g., Rothbart, 1986). There is a slight tendency for girls to maintain status as behaviorally inhibited compared with boys (Kagan et al., 1994). One reason for differences between girls and boys in the stability of inhibition and the expression of distress disorders may be differential socialization processes. There is evidence of differential acceptability of shyness for girls versus boys (Engfer, 1993; Stevenson-Hinde & Hinde, 1986). Shyness in boys but not girls becomes less acceptable to parents as children get older (Stevenson-Hinde & Shouldice, 1993). Consequently, behaviors indicative of inhibition and fearfulness may become unacceptable to parents for boys, resulting in encouragement and the promotion of exposure to social situations for boys but not girls. Such a process might explain the differential findings between boys and girls of Rende (1993) and Caspi et al. (1995) for the relation of low sociability and withdrawal from novelty to anxiety problems.

Conclusions

In this chapter, we have outlined a skeletal framework and the evidence for how temperament may influence the development of anxiety and anxiety disorders. We believe that there is substantial evidence that individual differences in temperamental factors are related to risk for the development of anxiety and other forms of psychopathology. However, with a few noteworthy exceptions (e.g., Caspi et al., 1995) there is little strong empirical evidence demonstrating long-term longitudinal links between normative variation in temperament and the development of problematic anxiety. Most extant data demonstrate connections between early temperament and externalizing problems (e.g., Maziade et al., 1985, 1990), connections between children in extreme temperament groups and internalizing problems (e.g., Biederman et al., 1995), or concurrent associations between temperament and both internalizing and externalizing forms of psychopathology (e.g., John et al., 1994; Wertlieb et al., 1987). A number of steps are likely to result in greater progress in establishing clear links between early temperament and the development of psychopathology. We outline some of these steps below.

Need for Better Instrumentation

In the absence of psychometrically sound instruments that measure clearly defined and empirically distinct temperament constructs, there is little hope of demonstrating unambiguous connections between children's early temperament and the development of later internalizing disorders. It is reasonable to suggest that behaviors reflecting approach, activity, soothability and other temperamental dimensions reflect the joint influence of different factors (e.g., Ahadi & Rothbart, 1994); however, to the extent that these higher-order dimensions of temperament have been hypothesized to reflect individual differences in separate neural substrates (e.g., Ahadi & Rothbart, 1994; Derryberry & Rothbart, 1997), individual markers of the higher dimensions should be relatively independent of the other dimension— at least at the aggregate level. It is unclear at present whether results that fail to demonstrate discriminant validity of lower-order temperament dimensions reflect the joint influence of different temperament systems and of different neural substrates, or merely reflect content overlap between lower-order temperament scales.

Because the relative overlap and independence of the lower-order dimensions of temperament are not clear, a well-elaborated developmental model of how specific lower-order temperamental dimensions relate to psychopathology or other factors is not yet possible. We suggest that a potential starting place is at the higher-order factor level of temperamental constructs (i.e., NA/N, EC). As noted above, there are already several demonstrations that these higher-order dimensions are related to forms of internalizing psychopathology and that these higher-order dimensions are supported across early development through adulthood. We encourage the examination and refinement of temperament measures to demonstrate *both* convergent *and* discriminant validity to uncover the unique aspects of lower-order dimensions of temperament.

Given the low base rate of psychopathology, however, it likely will be difficult to demonstrate linkage between specific temperamental traits and specific anxiety disorders—particularly in samples representative of the range of normative temperamental development. This task will be complicated by the difficulty of measuring internalizing disorders in children because of inadequate instrumentation (e.g., see Lonigan et al., 1994, 1999; Chorpita et al., 1998). For instance, many measures of internalizing disorders in children fail to demonstrate discriminant validity. Moreover, although a longstanding issue in psychopathology research involves the issue of mono-methodism (e.g., see Lonigan et al., 1999, for discussion), a resolution to questions of the advantages and disadvantages of mono- versus multi-methodism is not clear-cut for internalizing problems like anxiety. We would argue that anxiety is uniquely an internal state that is best reported by the individual and that the degree to which the reports of an observer, such as a parent, teacher, or peer, would agree with a child's report of anxiety is likely to be moderated by opportunity for observation across contexts, the age of the child, the expressivity of the child, and the affect construct assessed. Consequently, the overlap between children and observers (i.e., multi-methodism) may underestimate anxiety.

Need for Longitudinal Studies

More longitudinal research is needed to clarify the risks that are faced by behaviorally inhibited and temperamentally reactive children. Although NA/N and BI may be relatively stable temperamental characteristics, they are subject to influence by numerous environmental factors, including the behavior of the children's parents and the frequency of exposure to the novel stimuli that precipitate the behavioral response. Additionally, other temperamental characteristics, like EC, may mitigate or exacerbate the expression of NA/N or behavioral inhibition. Investigation of the interactions between these and other variables, and the relation that they have to anxiety disorders, is needed before conclusive statements can be made about the specific role of BI, NA/N, and EC in the development of anxiety and other disorders.

Need for Multifaceted Measurement and Integration

In this chapter, we have noted just a few of the ways in which temperamental factors may be related to the development of anxiety disorders and other forms of psychopathology. Whereas it is clear that it would be impossible to consider all of these potential paths of influence in a single study, we encourage researchers to at least consider, if not investigate, how *some* of these alternative pathways may be involved in observed relations (e.g., Calkins & Fox, 1992; Wertlieb et al., 1987). This is true both for researchers working from a temperament perspective and for researchers working from interpersonal, environmental, cognitive, or biological perspectives. We suspect that a part of the lack of progress in this area to date reflects the predominance of univariate and unidimensional approaches.

The model we have proposed is largely an interactive one. Consequently, we believe that it is unlikely, except in extreme cases, that a single dimension of temperament would account for a large degree of explanatory variance in outcomes related to psychopathology, including anxiety. That is, even high levels of temperamental NA/N will be unlikely to lead to anxiety disorders in children with high levels of EC because they can modulate their distress in the face of aversive stimuli. Conversely, children with lower levels of temperamental EC will be unlikely to develop anxiety disorders unless they also have elevated temperamental NA/N because their distress to potentially aversive stimuli will be low. Additionally, factors such as parenting, including restricting or promoting exposure to distressing situations, teaching of effective coping responses, or preventing the development of avoidance, are likely to have a large influence on the probable expression of anxiety, even in children temperamentally prone to anxiety.

Acknowledgments and Note

Preparation of this chapter was supported, in part, by a grant from the National Institute of Child Health and Human Development (1 RO3 HD36067) to Christopher J. Lonigan. We wish to acknowledge the contributions of Sarah M. Dyer and Eric S. Hooe for their part in collecting some of the data reported in this chapter. Please address correspondence to Christopher J. Lonigan, Department of Psychology, Florida State University, Tallahassee, FL 32306-1270, USA. E-mail: lonigan@psy.fsu.edu.

References

Achenbach, T. (1991). *Child Behavior Checklist*. Burlington, VT: Author.

Ahadi, S. A., & Rothbart, M. K. (1994). Temperament, development, and the Big Five. In C. F. Halverson, Jr., G. A. Kohnstamm, & R. P. Martin (Eds.), *The developing structure of temperament and personality from infancy to adulthood* (pp. 189–207). Hillsdale, NJ: Erlbaum.

Ahadi, S. A., Rothbart, M. K., & Ye, R. (1993). Children's temperament in the US and China: similarities and differences. *European Journal of Personality*, 7, 359–377.

Akiskal, L. Y., Hirschfeld, R. M. A., & Yerevanian, B. J. (1983). The relationship of personality to affective disorders. *Archives of General Psychiatry*, 40, 801–810.

Allport, G. W. (1937). *Personality: A psychological interpretation*. New York: Holt.

American Psychiatric Association (1994). *Diagnostic and statistical manual of mental disorders* (4th ed.). Washington, DC: APA.

Angleitner, A., & Ostendorf, F. (1994). Temperament and the big five factors of personality. In C. F. Halverson, Jr, G. A. Kohnstamm, & R. P. Martin (Eds.), *The developing structure of temperament and personality from infancy to adulthood* (pp. 69–90). Hillsdale, NJ: Erlbaum.

Asendorpf, J. B. (1993). Beyond temperament: A two-factorial coping model of the development of inhibition during childhood. In K. H. Rubin & J. B. Asendorpf (Eds.), *Social withdrawal, inhibition, and shyness in childhood* (pp. 265–289). Hillsdale, NJ: Erlbaum.

Baker, M., Milich, R., & Manolis, M. B. (1996). Peer interactions of dysphoric adolescents. *Journal of Abnormal Child Psychology, 24,* 241–256.

Biederman, J., Rosenbaum, J. F., Chaloff, J. & Kagan, J. (1995). Behavioral inhibition as a risk factor for anxiety disorders. In J. S. March (Ed.), *Anxiety Disorders in Children and Adolescents.* New York: Guilford.

Biederman, J., Rosenbaum, J. F., Hirshfeld, D. R., & Faraone, S. V. (1990). Psychiatric correlates of behavioral inhibition in young children of parents with and without psychiatric disorders. *Archives of General Psychiatry, 47,* 21–26.

Block, J. H., & Block, J. (1980). The role of ego control and ego resiliency in the organization of behavior. In A. Collins (Ed.), *Minnesota symposium on child psychology,* (Vol. 11, pp. 39–101). Hillsdale, NJ: Erlbaum.

Bowen, F., Vitaro, F., Kerr, M., & Pelletier, D. (1995). Childhood internalizing problems: Prediction from kindergarten, effect of maternal overprotectiveness, and sex differences. *Development and Psychopathology, 7,* 481–498.

Brown, T. A., Chorpita, B. F., & Barlow, D. H. (1998). Structural relations among dimensions of the DSM-IV anxiety and mood disorders and dimensions of negative affect, positive affect, and autonomic arousal. *Journal of Abnormal Psychology, 107,* 179–192.

Buss, A. H. (1991). The EAS theory of temperament. In J. Strelau & A. Angleitner (Eds.), *Explorations in temperament: International perspectives on theory and temperament* (pp. 43–60). New York: Plenum.

Buss, A. H., & Plomin, R. (1975). *A temperament theory of personality development.* New York: Wiley.

Buss, A. H., & Plomin, R. (1984). *Temperament: Early developing personality traits.* Hillsdale, NJ: Erlbaum.

Calkins, S. D., & Fox, N. A. (1992). The relations among infant temperament, security of attachment, and behavioral inhibition at twenty-four months. *Child Development, 63,* 1456–1472.

Caspi, A., Henry, B., McGee, R. O., Moffitt, T. E., & Silva, P. A. (1995). Temperamental origins of child and adolescent behavior problems: From age three to age fifteen. *Child Development, 66,* 55–68.

Chorpita, B. F., Albano, A. M., & Barlow, D. H. (1998). The structure of negative emotions in a clinical sample of children and adolescents. *Journal of Abnormal Psychology, 107,* 74–85.

Clark, L. A., & Watson, D. (1991). Tripartite model of anxiety and depression: Psychometric evidence and taxonomic implications. *Journal of Abnormal Psychology, 100,* 316–336.

Clark, L. A., Watson, D., & Mineka, S. (1994). Temperament, personality, and the mood and anxiety disorders. *Journal of Abnormal Psychology, 103,* 103–116.

Compas, B. E. (1987). Coping with stress during childhood and adolescence. *Psychological Bulletin, 101,* 393–403.

Derryberry, D., & Reed, M. A. (1996). Regulatory processes and the development of cognitive representations. *Development and Psychopathology, 8,* 215–234.

Derryberry, D., & Rothbart, M. K. (1997). Reactive and effortful processes in the organization of temperament. *Development and Psychopathology, 9,* 633–652.

Derryberry, D., & Rothbart, M. K. (1984). Emotion, attention and temperament. In H. C. Izard, J. Kagan, & R. Zajonc (Eds.), *Emotion, cognition, and behavior* (pp. 132–166). Cambridge, England: Cambridge University Press.

Diamond, S. (1974). *The roots of psychology: A sourcebook in the history of ideas.* New York: Basic Books.

Digman, J. M. (1990). Personality structure: Emergence of the five factor model. *Annual Review of Psychology, 41,* 417–440.

Digman, J. M. (1994). Child personality and temperament: Does the five-factor model embrace both domains? In C. Halverson, G. Kohnstamn, & R. Martin (Eds.), *The developing structure of temperament and personality from infancy to adulthood* (pp. 323–338). Hillsdale, NJ: Erlbaum.

Digman, J. M., & Inouye, J. (1986). Further specification of the five robust factors of personality. *Journal of Personality and Social Psychology, 50,* 116–123.

Dyer, S. M., & Lonigan, C. J. (1997, April). *The hierarchical structure of temperament and affect in preschool children: A confirmatory factor analysis.* Paper presented at the Biennial Meeting of the Society for Research in Child Development, Washington, DC.

Eaton, W. O. (1994). Temperament, development, and the five-factor model: Lessons from activity level. In C. F. Halverson, Jr, G. A. Kohnstamm, & R. P. Martin (Eds.), *The developing structure of temperament and personality from infancy to adulthood* (pp. 157–172). Hillsdale, NJ: Erlbaum.

Eisenberg, N., & Fabes, R. A. (1992). Emotion, regulation, and the development of social competence. In M. S. Clark (Ed.), *Review of personality and social psychology: Vol. 14. Emotion and social behavior* (pp. 119–150). Newbury Park, CA: Sage.

Eisenberg, N., Fabes, R. A., Karbon, M., Murphy, B. C., Wosinski, M., Polazzi, L., Carlo, G., & Juhnke, C. (1996). The relations of children's dispositional prosocial behavior to emotionality, regulation, and social functioning. *Child Development, 67,* 974–992.

Ekman, P. (Ed.) (1982). *Emotion in the human face* (2nd ed.). Cambridge, England: Cambridge University Press.

Engfer, A. (1993). Antecedents and consequences of shyness in boys and girls: A 6-year longitudinal study. In K. H. Rubin & J. B. Asendorpf (Eds.), *Social withdrawal, inhibitions, and shyness in childhood* (pp. 49–79). Hillsdale, NJ: Erlbaum.

Fowles, D. C. (1988). Psychophysiology and psychopathology: A motivational approach. *Psychophysiology, 25,* 373–392.

Fox, N. A. & Calkins, S. D. (1993). Pathways to aggression and social withdrawal: Interactions among temperament, attachment, and regulation. In K. H. Rubin & J. B. Asendorpf (Eds.), *Social withdrawal, inhibition, and shyness in childhood* (pp. 81–100). Hillsdale, NJ: Erlbaum.

Goldberg, L. R. (1990). An alternative "description of personality": The Big-Five factor structure. *Journal of Personality and Social Psychology, 59,* 1216–1229.

Goldsmith, H. H., & Alansky, J. A. (1987). Maternal and infant temperament predictors of attachment: A meta-analytic review. *Journal of Consulting and Clinical Psychology, 55,* 805–816.

Goldsmith, H. H., & Campos, J. J. (1982). Toward a theory of infant temperament. In R. N. Emde & R. J. Harmon (Eds.), *The development of attachment and affiliative systems* (pp. 161–193). New York: Plenum.

Goldsmith, H. H., & Campos, J. J. (1986). Fundamental issues in the study of early temperament: The Denver Twin Temperament Study. In M. E. Lamb, A. L. Brown, & B. Rogoff (Eds.), *Advances in developmental psychology* (pp. 231–283). Hillsdale, NJ: Erlbaum.

Goldsmith H. H., Buss, A., Plomin, R., Rothbart, M. K., Thomas, A., Chess, S., Hinde, R. A., & McCall, R. B. (1987). Roundtable: What is temperament? Four approaches. *Child Development, 58*, 505–529.

Goldsmith, H. H., Rieser-Danner, L. A., and Briggs, S. (1991). Evaluating convergent and discriminant validity of temperament questionnaires for preschoolers, toddlers, and infants. *Developmental Psychology, 27*, 566–579.

Gray, J. A. (1981). A critique of Eysenck's theory of personality. In H. J Eysenck (Ed.), *A model for personality*. New York: Springer-Verlag.

Gray, J. A. (1982). *The neuropsychology of anxiety: An enquiry into the functions of the septo-hippocampal system*. New York: Oxford University Press.

Gray, J. A. (1987). *The psychology of fear and stress*. New York: Cambridge University Press.

Gray, J. A. (1988). Behavioural and neural-system analyses of the actions of anxiolytic drugs. *Pharmacology, Biochemistry & Behavior, 29*, 767–769.

Hock, M., Krohne, H. W., & Kaiser, J. (1996). Coping dispositions and the processing of ambiguous stimuli. *Journal of Personality and Social Psychology, 70*, 1052–1066.

Hooe, E. S., Lonigan, C. J., & Anthony, J. L. (1997). Negative and positive affectivity: Toward a hierarchical structure of temperament in school-age children. *Association for the Advancement of Behavior Therapy Abstracts, 4*, CD-ROM Version.

Hymel, S., Woody, E., & Bowker, A. (1993). Social withdrawal in childhood: Considering the child's perspective. In K. H. Rubin & J. B. Asendorpf (Eds.), *Social withdrawal, inhibitions, and shyness in childhood* (pp. 237–264). Hillsdale, NJ: Erlbaum.

Izard, C. E. (1977). *Human emotions*. New York: Plenum.

John, O. P., Caspi, A., Robins, R. W., Moffitt, T. E., & Stouthamer-Loeber, M. (1994). The "little five": Exploring the nomological network of the five-factor model of personality in adolescent boys. *Child Development, 65*, 160–178.

Joiner, T. E., Jr, Catanzaro, S., & Laurent, J. (1996). The tripartite structure of positive and negative affect, depression, and anxiety in child and adolescent psychiatric inpatients. *Journal of Abnormal Psychology, 105*, 401–409.

Joiner, T. A., Jr, & Lonigan, C. J. (in press). The tripartite model of depression and anxiety in youth psychiatric patients: Relation to diagnostic status and future symptoms. *Journal of Clinical Child Psychology*.

Kagan, J. (1994). Inhibited and uninhibited temperaments. In W. B. Carey & S. C. McDevitt (Eds.), *Prevention and Early Intervention: Individual Differences as Risk Factors for the Mental Health of Children*. New York: Brunner/Mazel.

Kagan, J. (1997). Temperament and the reactions to unfamiliarity. *Child Development, 68*, 139–143.

Kagan, J., Reznick, J. S., Snidman, N., Gibbons, J. & Johnson, M. O. (1988). Childhood derivatives of inhibition and lack of inhibition to the unfamiliar. *Child Development, 59*, 1580–1589.

Kagan, J., Snidman, N., Arcus, D., & Reznick, S. J. (1994). *Galen's prophecy: Temperament in human nature*. New York: Basic Books.

Krueger, R. F., Caspi, A., Moffitt, T. E., Silva, P. A., & McGee, R. (1996). Personality traits are differentially linked to mental disorders: A multitrait–multidiagnosis study of an adolescent birth cohort. *Journal of Abnormal Psychology*, *105*, 299–312.

Kupersmidt, J. B., & Patterson, C. J. (1991). Childhood peer rejection, aggression, withdrawal, and perceived competence as predictors of self-reported behavior problems in preadolescence. *Journal of Abnormal Child Psychology*, *19*, 427–449.

La Greca, A. M., Silverman, W. K., Vernberg, E. M., & Prinstein, M. J. (1996). Symptoms of posttraumatic stress in children after Hurricane Andrew: A prospective study. *Journal of Consulting and Clinical Psychology*, *64*, 712–723.

Lee, C. L., & Bates, J. E. (1985). Mother–child interaction at age two years and perceived difficult temperament. *Child Development*, *56*, 1314–1325.

Lonigan, C. J. (1993). Children's reactions to disaster: The role of negative affectivity. *Society for Research in Child Development Abstracts*, *9*, 469.

Lonigan, C. J. & Dyer, S. M. (2000). *Toward a hierarchical affective model of temperament in early childhood.* Manuscript in preparation.

Lonigan, C. J., Carey, M. P., & Finch, A. J., Jr. (1994). Anxiety and depression in children and adolescents: Negative affectivity and the utility of self-reports. *Journal of Consulting and Clinical Psychology*, *62*, 1000–1008.

Lonigan, C. J., Hooe, E. S., David, C. F., & Kistner, J. A. (1999). Positive and negative affectivity in children: Confirmatory factor analysis of a two-factor model and its relation to symptoms of anxiety and depression. *Journal of Consulting and Clinical Psychology*, *67*, 374–386.

Lonigan, C. J., Kistner, J. A., Hooe, E. S., & David, C. (1997). An affective model of anxiety and depression in children: Evidence from a longitudinal study. *Association for the Advancement of Behavior Therapy Abstracts*, *4*, CD-ROM Version.

Lonigan, C. J., Shannon, M. P., Finch, A. J, Jr., Daugherty, T. K , & Taylor, C. M. (1991). Children's reactions to a natural disaster: Symptom severity and degree of exposure. *Advances in Behaviour Research and Therapy*, *13*, 135–154.

Martin, R. P., Wisenbaker, J., & Huttunen, M. (1994). Review of factor analytic studies of temperament measures based on Thomas–Chess structural model: Implications for the Big Five. In C. F. Halverson, Jr, G. A. Kohnstamm, & R. P. Martin (Eds.), *The developing structure of temperament and personality from infancy to adulthood* (pp. 157–172). Hillsdale, NJ: Erlbaum.

Maziade, M., Caperaa, P., LaPlante, B., Boudreault, M., Thiverge, J., Cote, R., & Boutin, P. (1985). Value of difficult temperament among 7-year-olds in the general population for predicting psychiatric diagnosis at age 12. *American Journal of Psychiatry*, *142*, 943–946.

Maziade, M., Caron, C., Cote, R., Merette, C., Bernier, H., LaPlante, B., Boutin, P., & Thivierge, J. (1990). Psychiatric status of adolescents who had extreme temperaments at age 7. *American Journal of Psychiatry*, *147*, 1531–1536.

Maziade, M., Cote, R., Bernier, H., Boutin, P., & Thivierge, J. (1989). Significance of extreme temperament in infancy for clinical status in preschool years. II: Patterns of temperament and implications for the appearance of disorders. *British Journal of Psychiatry*, *154*, 544–551.

McCrae, R. R., & Costa, P. T. (1987). Validation of the five factor model across instruments and observers. *Journal of Personality and Social Psychology, 49,* 710–727.

Mineka, S., & Zinbarg, R. (1995). Conditioning and ethological models of social phobia. In R. G. Heimberg, M. R. Liebowitz, D. A. Hope, & F. R. Schneier (Eds.), *Social phobia: Diagnosis, assessment, and treatment* (pp. 134–162). New York: Guilford.

O'Brien, B. S., & Frick, P. J. (1996). Reward dominance: Associations with anxiety, conduct problems, and psychopathology in children. *Journal of Abnormal Child Psychology, 24,* 223–240.

Reed, M., Pien, D., & Rothbart, M. K. (1984). Inhibitory self-control in preschool children. *Merrill-Palmer Quarterly, 30,* 131–147.

Rende, R. D. (1993). Longitudinal relations between temperament traits and behavioral syndromes in middle childhood. *Journal of the American Academy of Child and Adolescent Psychiatry, 32,* 287–290.

Robins, R. W., John, O. P., Caspi, A., Moffitt. T. E., & Stouthamer-Loeber, M. (1996). Resilient, overcontrolled, and undercontrolled boys: Three replicable personality types. *Journal of Personality and Social Psychology, 70,* 157–171.

Rosenbaum, J. F., Biederman, J., Gersten, M., Hirshfield, D. R., Meminger, S. R., Herman, J. B., Kagan, J., Reznick, J. S., & Snidman, N. (1988). Behavioral inhibition in children of parents with panic disorder and agoraphobia: A controlled study. *Archives of General Psychiatry, 45,* 463–470.

Rothbart, M. K. (1986). Longitudinal observation of infant temperament. *Developmental Psychology, 22,* 356–365.

Rothbart, M. K. (1988). Temperament and the development of inhibited approach. *Child Development, 59,* 1241–1250.

Rothbart, M. K. (1989). Temperament and development. In G. A. Kohnstamm, J. E. Bates, & M. K. Rothbart (Eds.), *Temperament in childhood* (pp. 187–247). New York: Wiley.

Rothbart, M. K., & Goldsmith, H. H. (1985). Three approaches to the study of temperament. *Developmental Review, 5,* 237–260.

Rothbart, M. K., Ahadi, S. A., & Hershey, K. L. (1994). Temperament and social behavior. *Merrill-Palmer Quarterly, 40,* 21–39.

Rothbart, M. K., Posner, M. I., & Hershey, K. L. (1995). Temperament, attention, and developmental psychopathology. In D. Cicchetti & D. J. Cohen (Eds.), *Developmental Psychopathology: Vol. 1. Theory and Methods* (pp. 315–340). New York: Wiley.

Rubin, K. H., & Mills, R. S. L. (1991). Conceptualizing developmental pathways to internalizing disorders in childhood. *Canadian Journal of Behavioral Differences, 23,* 300–317.

Rubin, K. H., Coplan, R. J., Fox, N. A., & Calkins, S. D. (1995). Emotionality, emotion regulation, and preschoolers' social adaptation. *Development and Psychopathology, 7,* 49–62.

Rubin, K. H., Hymel, S., Mills, R. S. L., & Rose-Krasnor (1991). Conceptualizing different pathways to and from social isolation in childhood. In D. Cicchetti & S. Toth (Eds.), *The Rochester symposium on developmental psychopathology: Vol. 2. Internalizing and externalizing expressions of dysfunction* (pp. 91–122). New York: Cambridge University Press.

Stevenson-Hinde, J., & Hinde, R. A. (1986). Changes in associations between characteristics and interactions. In R. Plomin & J. Dunn (Eds.), *The study of temperament: Changes, continuities, and challenges* (pp. 115–129). Hillsdale, NJ: Erlbaum.

Stevenson-Hinde, J., & Shouldice, A. (1993). Wariness to strangers: A behavioral systems perspective revisited. In K. H. Rubin & J. B. Asendorpf (Eds.), *Social withdrawal, inhibitions, and shyness in childhood* (pp. 101–116). Hillsdale, NJ: Erlbaum.

Tellegen., A. (1985). Structures of mood and personality and their relevance to assessing anxiety with an emphasis on self-report. In A. H. Tuma & J. D. Maser (Eds.), *Anxiety and the anxiety disorders* (pp. 681–706). Hillsdale, NJ: Erlbaum.

Tellegen, A., Lykken, D. T., Bouchard, T. J., Wilcox, K. J., Segal, N. L., & Rich, S. (1988). Personality similarity in twins reared apart and together. *Journal of Personality and Social Psychology, 54,* 1031–1093.

Thomas, A., & Chess, S. (1985). The behavioral study of temperament. In J. Strelau and F. H. Farley (Eds.), *The biological bases of personality and behavior: Vol. 1. Theories, measurement techniques, and development* (pp. 213–225). Washington, DC: Harper & Row.

Thomas, A., Chess., S., & Birch, H. G. (1968). *Temperament and behavior disorders in children.* New York: New York University Press.

Thompson, R. A., & Calkins, S. D. (1996). The double-edged sword: Emotional regulation for children at risk. *Development and Psychopathology, 8,* 163–182.

Trull, T. J., & Sher, K. J. (1994). Relationship between the five-factor model of personality and axis I disorders in a nonclinical sample. *Journal of Abnormal Psychology, 103,* 350–360.

Turner, S. M., Beidel, D. C., & Wolff, P. L. (1996). Is behavioral inhibition related to the anxiety disorders? *Clinical Psychology Review, 16,* 157–172.

Van den Boom, D. C. (1989). Neonatal irritability and the development of attachment. In G. A. Kohnstamm, J E. Bates, & M. K. Rothbart (Eds.), *Temperament in childhood* (pp. 299–318). Chichester, England: Wiley.

Watson, D., & Tellegen, A. (1985). Toward a consensual structure of mood. *Psychological Bulletin, 98,* 219–235.

Watson, D., Clark, L. A., & Carey, G. (1988). Positive and negative affectivity and their relation to anxiety and depressive disorders. *Journal of Abnormal Psychology, 97,* 346–353.

Watson, D., Clark, L. A., & Harkness, A. R. (1994). Structures of personality and their relevance to psychopathology. *Journal of Abnormal Psychology, 103,* 18–31.

Watson, D., Clark, L. A., & Tellegen, A. (1988). Development and validation of brief measures of positive and negative affect: The PANAS scales. *Journal of Personality and Social Psychology, 54,* 1063–1070.

Wertlieb, D., Weigel, C., Springer, T., & Feldstein, M. (1987). Temperament as a moderator of children's stressful experiences. *American Journal of Orthopsychiatry, 57,* 234–245.

Williams, J. M. G., Watts, F. N., MacLeod, C., & Mathew, A. (1997). *Cognitive psychology and emotional disorders* (2nd ed.). New York: Wiley.

Wolfe, V. V., Finch, A. J., Jr, Saylor, C. F., Blount, R. L., Pallmeyer, T. P., & Carek, D. J. (1987). Negative affectivity in children: A multitrait–multimethod investigation. *Journal of Consulting and Clinical Psychology, 55,* 245–250.

Zevon, M. A., & Tellegen, A. (1982). The structure of mood change: An idiographic/nomothetic analysis. *Journal of Personality & Social Psychology, 43,* 111–122.

5

Anxiety Sensitivity

STEVEN REISS, WENDY K. SILVERMAN, and CARL F. WEEMS

The level of a child's anxiety sensitivity (AS) at ages 7 to 14 may predict the development of panic disorder at ages 16 to 30. AS may be a cause of spontaneous panic attacks or it may correlate with a causal factor. If researchers can show that AS is a childhood risk factor for adult panic disorder, clinicians will be able to evaluate vulnerability to panic disorder about 10–15 years before the age at which this disorder is usually first diagnosed. By identifying and treating AS in childhood, moreover, researchers may study ways to prevent panic disorder in late adolescence or early adulthood. Researchers may also clarify the etiology of panic disorder.

This chapter provides a summary of AS in children, showing that significant progress has been made toward demonstrating an early risk factor. The second and third authors are in the process of evaluating relations among childhood AS, adolescent AS, and the emergence of panic attacks. We already know that AS measured in late adolescence and in young adulthood predicts spontaneous panic attacks and panic disorder in adults (Maller & Reiss, 1992; Schmidt, Lerew, & Jackson, 1997). When it is shown that childhood AS predicts adolescent AS, an important step will have been taken in showing that childhood AS is an early risk factor for adult panic disorder.

Recently, Reiss (2000a) expanded sensitivity theory into a comprehensive account of human motivation. AS is only one of a number of early motivational risk factors that predict psychopathology (Reiss & Havercamp, 1996), according to Reiss's theory. Motivational traits may predict disorders such as major depression, schizophrenia, or autism (Reiss, 2000a; Reiss & Havercamp, 1997). If future research supports these theoretical predictions, sensitivity theory may lead to significant improvements in the assessment and early prediction of a wide range of disorders.

Researchers have also studied the assessment and clinical significance of AS. Generally, the consistency and magnitude of the findings were impressive—in many of the studies, the difference between criterion groups exceed a full standard deviation in AS and sometimes approach two standard deviations. Adult patients with panic disorder, for example, scored nearly *two* standard deviations above the norms for AS, as measured by the Reiss–Epstein–Gursky Anxiety Sensitivity Index (ASI; Reiss, Peterson, Gursky, &

McNally, 1986). Findings of this magnitude have established the ASI as one of the most accurate psychometric instruments ever devised. The Child Anxiety Sensitivity Index (CASI; Silverman, Fleisig, Rabian, & Peterson 1991) has psychometric properties paralleling the ASI.

Theoretical, measurement, and research issues on high AS are reviewed in this chapter. Our aim is to summarize existing knowledge and stimulate additional research on AS in children. What about low AS? It has not been studied very much, although it may predict recklessness or fearlessness.

Brief History of Theories of Anxiety Sensitivity

When the first author developed the ASI, a standardized questionnaire to assess AS, many colleagues questioned its significance. "You are asking people if they dislike anxiety," they said. "Since anxiety is aversive, doesn't everybody dislike it?" Our colleagues thought that individuals differed primarily in how much anxiety they experienced, not in their sensitivity to that anxiety. Because high AS is experienced by only a small percentage of the population, many colleagues found it difficult to appreciate the AS construct intuitively. Lacking themselves the experience of high AS, they argued that anxiety already implied sensitivity and that no additional constructs were needed. The results of many research studies, however, has established the AS construct (see Taylor, 1999).

According to Reiss's sensitivity theory (Reiss, 2000), the origins of AS reflect (a) individual variations in the genes that render anxiety a displeasure and (b) individual differences in beliefs about the personal consequences of anxiety experiences. Reiss and Havercamp (1998) put forth a genetic argument for AS that predicts that anxiety is a greater displeasure for some people than for others. These individual variations are called "sensitivity to anxiety." Stein, Jang, and Livesley (1999) provided evidence based on a twin study that AS is inherited. Moreover, Schmidt et al. (in press) showed genetic factors that interact with AS to produce panic attacks in response to 35% CO_2 challenge.

The development of AS is influenced by cognitive factors in addition to genetic ones. By the time children become 7–10 years old, they have formed beliefs about what will happen to them when they become nervous or experience stress. According to Reiss's sensitivity theory, these beliefs modify significantly the child's inherited sensitivity to anxiety. Children with high AS are easily frightened by the experience of a pounding heart or shaking body. These children acquire beliefs that anxiety sensations lead to illness, embarrassment, or loss of control. When they again become anxious, they worry about what is happening to their body, and this worry itself increases their stress. Thus a vicious circle can occur in which stress leads to anxiety sensitivity beliefs which leads to more stress. In contrast, children with average or low AS are less frightened by the experience of anxiety. They regard the bodily sensations of anxiety as a harmless nuisance that will dissipate when the source of the stress is removed.

A central idea of our work is that individual differences in sensitivity to anxiety predict vulnerability to panic disorder apart from the quantity of anxiety a person experiences. People with high sensitivity should experience panic attacks under conditions of moderately intense or persistent stress, whereas those with low sensitivity should not experience panic attacks even under conditions of intense or persistent stress.

The ASI asks adults, and the CASI asks adolescents and children, to rate the extent to which they agree with certain statements about the frightening nature of anxiety sensations and behavior. The greater the number of statements endorsed, and the more strongly each statement is endorsed, the higher is the level of AS. The various ASI items ask how motivating anxiety sensations are (e.g., "It scares me when my heart beats rapidly") or what will happen when anxiety is experienced ("When I notice that my heart is beating rapidly, I worry that I might have a heart attack").

Trait Anxiety Versus Anxiety Sensitivity

Lilienfeld and Jacob Turner (1989) put forth the idea that AS is trait anxiety, even though Watson and Clark (1984), had distinguished trait anxiety (negativity affectivity) from fearfulness (such as the fear of anxiety.) McNally (1989) and Taylor (1995) responded effectively to each specific criticism that was raised in Lilienfeld et al.'s controversial articles. Although Lilienfeld (1999) has acknowledged that his previous criticisms of AS in adults were invalid, similar issues have been put forth anew regarding AS in young children (Chorpita, Albano & Barlow, 1996). It is instructive, therefore, to revisit the issue and review the major conclusions.

McNally (1996) argued that trait anxiety and AS are distinct concepts. Whereas trait anxiety predicts a general proneness to respond anxiously to threatening stimuli, AS predicts a proneness specific to the symptoms of anxiety. The difference is similar to that of a general measure of fearfulness and a specific measure of fear of flying. Taylor (1996) further elaborated on this viewpoint, often citing supporting evidence.

Reiss (1997) discussed the conceptual differences between trait anxiety and AS. In trait anxiety, the feared stimulus is regarded as dangerous; for example, a person has a vague sense that leaving the home is dangerous. In AS, the feared stimulus is seen as harmless, so that what is feared is an uncontrollable reaction. For example, the person knows that leaving the home is not objectively dangerous because he/she recognizes that the feared stimulus is not dangerous to other people. However, the person is afraid by leaving home he/she will have a panic attack. This concern is rational because the person very well might have a panic attack. Only under the concept of AS are phobias and panic attacks the result of *rational* thought processes.

Further, Reiss (1997) argued that trait anxiety is not what people think it is. By definition, people with high trait anxiety are those who experienced a fair amount of anxiety in the past and who have a propensity to continue to do so. The simplest way to assess trait anxiety, therefore, would be to ask people how often they were anxious in the past. You might be surprised to learn, however, that the widely used measures of trait anxiety do not do this. What these measures assess is not specific to anxiety and is not focused on past frequency of symptoms.

The various measures of trait anxiety assess much more than anxiety because they have a common origin with the MMPI, which is a general measure of psychopathology. They were developed during an era when psychodynamic theorists thought that an underlying process, not symptoms, was the basis for diagnosis of mental disorders. Taylor (1953) distinguished between manifest and unconscious anxiety, and then developed a question-naire called the Taylor Manifest Anxiety Scale (TMAS). Manifest anxiety referred to those anxiety symptoms of neurosis and psychosis that could be observed. Taylor asked five clinicians to use Cameron's (1947) description of chronic anxiety reactions to rate 200 items from the Minnesota Multiphasic Personality Inventory (MMPI) for the purpose of identifying those items that refer to manifest anxiety. Since the MMPI items were intended to differ-entiate clinical from mentally healthy groups, and since Cameron's (1947) description of chronic anxiety reactions included symptoms of what today would be called panic disorder, the TMAS items have content overlap with symptoms seen in patient populations.

It may surprise you to learn also that Spielberger's trait anxiety scale, the State–Trait Anxiety Inventory, is the equivalent of the TMAS, (Spielberger, 1985) which is a measure of psychopathology symptoms seen in chronic anxiety reactions. As Spielberger himself wrote, the TMAS and the STAI-T "can be considered, essentially, as equivalent measures of trait anxiety" (Spielberger, 1985). Many of Spielberger's STAI items are equivalents of TMAS items; the TMAS was based on the MMPI; thus, measures of trait anxiety assess a broad range of psychopathology beyond anxiety symptoms.

Why is it important to note this brief history of the STAI and its similarities to the TMAS? If the goal is to develop a measure of persistent anxiety in a nonclinical population, we should construct a scale in which all items assess how often anxiety symptoms have been experienced in the past. The STAI does not do this. It lists a range of symptoms of negative affect, including anxiety, depression, guilt, and insecurity. In many ways, the STAI is a measure of Freud's old concept of "neurotic anxiety," which Spielberger (1985) cited favorably. The STAI may be more a measure of trait neurosis than of trait anxiety.

When Reiss, Peterson, Gursky, and McNally (1986) introduced the ASI, they were aware of the conceptual issues in the measurement of trait anxiety. On the one hand, trait anxiety referred to a persistent prone-ness to experience anxiety over a period of years. On the other hand, the conventional measures of trait anxiety, which originated from the MMPI, all measure something broader than anxiety, perhaps what Watson and Clark (1984) called "negative affectivity." In order to distinguish empirically between AS and trait anxiety, therefore, Reiss developed an Anxiety Frequency Questionnaire (AFQ). The AFQ items consistently measured the past frequency of anxiety. Compared with the TMAS and Spielberger's STAI-T, the AFQ may be much more of a direct measure of a person's proneness to experience anxiety. The AFQ, which is arguably the "true" measure of trait anxiety, and the ASI are correlated in the .4 range, which is much too low to support the idea that AS is trait anxiety. Thus, Reiss et al. (1986) showed that the ASI measures something distinct from the AFQ. However, the correlation between Spielberger's STAI and the ASI is higher than is the correlation between the AFQ and the ASI (Peterson & Reiss, 1991). But the higher correlation can be explained by the fact that Spielberger's measure assesses more than trait anxiety and, in fact, includes symptoms of panic disorder.

Numerous researchers have shown that AS is distinct even from Spielberger's measure of trait anxiety (see Peterson & Reiss, 1991; Taylor, 1999). The ASI has been empirically distinguished from STAI by showing that it predicts fearfulness even after the effects of STAI are controlled.

In conclusion, AS is theoretically and empirically distinct from trait anxiety, whether that construct is measured by the AFQ, the TMAS, or the STAI. The issue is no longer in dispute for adults—only the age at which the distinction can be validated is still disputed. Further, the AFQ may be a more "pure" or consistent measure of trait anxiety than are the more widely used measures.

Measurement of Anxiety Sensitivity

Reiss–Epstein–Gursky Anxiety Sensitivity Index

As noted, the most commonly used and extensively validated measure of anxiety sensitivity in adults is a 16-item questionnaire called the Reiss–Epstein–Gursky Anxiety Sensitivity Index (ASI). Each item consists of a statement about the motivational properties or personal consequences of anxiety. The respondent chooses the one phrase that best represents the extent to which he or she agrees with the item. Each item is scored on a 0 (very little) to 4 (very much) scale, and the total score is obtained by a simple sum of all items. The range of the total score is 0 to 64.

The ASI has sound psychometric properties (Peterson & Reiss, 1991). Various studies have estimated Cronbach's alpha coefficient of internal reliability at 0.85 (Peterson & Heilbronner, 1987), 0.82 (Telch, Shermis, & Lucas, 1989), 0.87 (Cox, Parker, & Swinson, 1996), and 0.91 and 0.84 (Taylor, Koch, McNally, & Crockett, 1992b). Reiss et al. (1986) calculated two-week test reliability for a sample of 127 college students at $r = 0.75$. These findings show that ASI scores are reliable.

Childhood Anxiety Sensitivity Index

The Childhood Anxiety Sensitivity Index (CASI) was developed by Silverman, Fleisig, Rabian, and Peterson (1991). Designed for use with school-aged children (6–17 years), the 18-item CASI requires children to rate their fear to the same types of anxiety-related sensations or experiences that are represented on the adult version. The main difference is in the simplicity of the items and ratings. The CASI uses the same 3-point scale that Ollendick (1983) found to be readily understood by children as young as 7 years on the revised Fear Survey Schedule for Children; that is, children rate each item on the CASI as either none (1), some (2), or a lot (3). Total scores on the CASI range from 18 to 54. A copy of the CASI items, including the instructions that are given to the children, are presented in fig. 5.1.

The CASI has sound psychometric properties similar to those reported for the adult ASI. Cronbach's alpha coefficient has been estimated at 0.87, and 2-week test–retest reliability at 0.76. Further, the CASI was validated by showing that it predicts fearfulness even after the effects of trait anxiety are controlled. Specifically, CASI scores account for 35–48% of the variance in children's scores on the Fear Survey Schedule for Children (FSSC-R; Ollendick, 1983) after controlling ("partial out") the variance explained by the child version of the AFQ.

Recently, a Spanish version of the CASI has been made available (see Sandin, 1997). This instrument has been shown to have similar psychometric properties as those demonstrated for the English-language version. The adult ASI has been translated into 11 languages thus far.

Factor Structure

AS was originally proposed as a unitary construct (Reiss & McNally, 1985). At the time, Reiss wanted to encourage the use of the total score on the ASI. Empirical evaluation of the factor structure of the ASI has yielded inconsistent findings. Several early factor analytic studies provided support for the unitary nature of AS (Reiss et al., 1986). Others found that the ASI is multifactorial (Telch, Shermis, & Lucas, 1989; Wardle, Ahmad, & Hayward, 1990).

Two studies using confirmatory factor analytic techniques have attempted to clarify the factor structure of the ASI. These techniques provide a method for evaluating competing factor solutions by examining goodness-of-fit indices for various models. Taylor, Kock, McNally, and Crockett (1992b) concluded that the ASI was best viewed as a single-factor measure even though an orthogonal four-factor model results in a similar goodness-of-fit (Telch et al., 1989). Taylor et al. (1992b) argued that the first four-factor solutions obtained by Telch et al. and Wardle et al. (1990) were artifacts of the orthogonality constraint because significant interfactor correlations resulted when this constraint was removed. The high level of interfactor association suggested that it was more appropriate to regard these four factors as facets

Directions: A number of statements which boys and girls use to describe themselves are given below. Read each statement carefully and put an X in the box in front of the words that describe you. There are no right or wrong answers. Remember, find the words that best describe you.

1. I don't want other people to know when I feel afraid.   ___None ___Some ___A lot
2. When I cannot keep my mind on my schoolwork I worry that I might be going crazy.   ___None ___Some ___A lot
3. It scares me when I feel "shaky."   ___None ___Some ___A lot
4. It scares me when I feel like I am going to faint.   ___None ___Some ___A lot
5. It is important for me to stay in control of my feelings.   ___None ___Some ___A lot
6. It scares me when my heart beats fast.   ___None ___Some ___A lot
7. It embarrasses me when my stomach growls (makes noise).   ___None ___Some ___A lot
8. It scares me when I feel like I am going to throw up.   ___None ___Some ___A lot
9. When I notice that my heart is beating fast, I worry that there might be something wrong with me.   ___None ___Some ___A lot
10. It scares me when I have trouble getting my breath.   ___None ___Some ___A lot
11. When my stomach hurts, I worry that I might be really sick.   ___None ___Some ___A lot
12. It scares me when I can't keep my mind on my schoolwork.   ___None ___Some ___A lot
13. Other kids can tell when I feel shaky.   ___None ___Some ___A lot
14. Unusual feelings in my body scare me.   ___None ___Some ___A lot
15. When I am afraid, I worry that I might be crazy.   ___None ___Some ___A lot
16. It scares me when I feel nervous.   ___None ___Some ___A lot
17. I don't like to let my feelings show.   ___None ___Some ___A lot
18. Funny feelings in my body scare me.   ___None ___Some ___A lot

Figure 5.1. Childhood Anxiety Sensitivity Index

of a single construct, and that it was the most parsimonious to view the ASI as a single-factor measure.

Cox, Parker, and Swinson (1996) evaluated both orthogonal and oblique rotations of several four-factor models to compare them with a unidimensional model of the ASI. Cox and associates found that the oblique solutions for the multidimensional models, in particular the Peterson and Heilbronner (1987) model, provided the better-fit indices than did the unidimensional model. In using oblique models, Cox et al. acknowledged that the correlations among the factors may compromise the view that the ASI is multidimensional. However, these authors felt that the factor intercorrelations were sufficiently low to support the position that the ASI was multidimensional.

Silverman, Ginsburg, and Goedhart (1999) evaluated the factor structure of the CASI using both clinic ($n = 258$) and nonclinic ($n = 249$) samples. The results supported a hierarchical, multidimensional model with either three or four first-order factors. The two most robust factors were called Physical Concerns and Mental Incapacitation Concerns. What remains unresolved is whether Control of anxiety symptoms and Social Concerns should be interpreted as two or one factor. Similar factor results were reported by Laurent, Schmidt, Catanzaro, Joiner, and Kelley (1998), who evaluated with an instrument called the Anxiety Sensitivity Index for Children (ASIC). Like the CASI, the ASIC is a modified version of the ASI.

Research Studies with Adults

Research on AS with adults can be organized into four categories of findings: (1) associations between AS and various types of anxiety disorders; (2) laboratory studies of the role of AS in biological challenge; (3) longitudinal studies of AS; (4) studies extending the construct of AS beyond anxiety disorders. Because the study of AS with children has been heavily influenced by the findings with adults, we shall summarize briefly the major findings in the adult literature. Readers who are interested in a more detailed account should consult Taylor's (1999) edited volume on AS.

AS and Anxiety Disorder

The 1993 revised ASI test manual reports normative data on 4,517 adults with no clinical diagnosis and 1,821 anxiety patients. Since 1993, data on thousands of additional patients have been reported supporting the norms in the test manual. Generally, women score higher than men on the ASI (Stewart, Samoluk, & MacDonald, 1999). Further, equivalent cross-cultural norms have been demonstrated for the Spanish ASI (Flavia, 1989) and Italian ASI (Saviotti et al., 1991).

The main findings are as follows. Patients with panic disorder score about two standard deviations (SD) above the ASI norm. Patients with post-traumatic stress disorder score about 1.5 s.d. above the ASI norm, and those with phobias scores about 1 SD above the ASI norm. Patients with alcoholism or chronic drinking problems score about one SD about the norm.

AS and Biological Challenge

McNally developed an innovative method for testing the validity of the ASI. If the ASI measures a tendency to misinterpret catastrophically the bodily sensations of anxiety, then the experimental induction of such sensations should cause anxiety or even panic in people with high ASI. The phrase "biological challenge" is used to refer to experimental methods of inducing autonomic arousal, including hyperventilation and inhalation of 35% CO_2.

A number of studies have shown that AS is related to the person's response to biological challenge (Holloway & McNally, 1987), even after the effects of trait anxiety are controlled (Donnell & McNally, 1990; Rapee & Medoro, 1994). Moreover, Telch & Harrington (1994) showed a dramatic videotape of college students with high AS who become frightened after inhaling 35% CO_2, and those students with low AS laughed off the autonomic arousal.

Longitudinal Studies of AS

AS scores at time-1 have been shown to predict panic and other anxiety disorders at time-2. Both prospective and retrospective studies have been reported. Maller and Reiss (1992) reported a 3-year follow-up study on college students who had scored either high ($n = 23$) or low ($n = 25$) on the ASI as assessed in 1984. High-AS students were five times more likely than low-AS students to have a DSM-III-R anxiety diagnosis three years later in 1987. Further, three of four students who experienced panic attacks for the first time during the follow-up period were in the high-AS group.

Schmidt et al. (1997) conducted a large-scale study of AS as a risk factor for spontaneous panic attacks in a prospective study of an entire entering class at the US Air Force Academy. They administered a battery of measures to 1,401 cadets about to start basic training, which is a highly stressful experience. Approximately 20% of the cadets with high AS experienced a panic attack during the 5-week follow-up period, compared with only 6% for all other cadets. The ASI also predicted anxiety symptomatology and functional impairment created by anxiety. These findings, which have been replicated in a subsequent study of another class of cadets starting basic training at the US Air Force Academy, provide strong evidence that AS is a risk factor for panic attacks and anxiety symptoms.

AS and Other Disorders

AS plays a role in chronic pain reactions (Asmundson, 1999). In adults with chronic back pain, high AS was found to be associated with greater use of medication after equating for severity of pain (Asmundson, 1999). The association between sensitivity to anxiety and sensitivity to pain is sufficiently high to form a single factor on the Reiss Profile of Fundamental Goals and Motivational Sensitivities (Reiss & Havercamp, 1998).

AS may be a risk factor for adolescent drinking problems (Stewart, Samoluk, & MacDonald, 1999) and women's drinking problems (Stewart, Knize, & Phil, 1992), especially when drinking is motivated to blunt the sensations of anxiety. AS may be the key factor in "dual diagnosis," or the joint occurrence of anxiety and drinking problems. Longitudinal research is needed to explore this possibility.

AS has been reported to be associated with depression (Otto, Pollack, Fava, Uccello, & Rosenbaum, 1995). However, Schmidt, Lerew, and Joiner (1998) believe that the association between AS and depression is largely or wholly a result of the overlap between anxiety and depressive symptoms in some clinical cases.

Research Studies with Children

Although the major findings from studies of AS in adults have been shown to occur with children, research with children poses certain challenges. We need to link the ASI scores from childhood, adolescence, and adulthood. This would connect the child and adult literatures on AS, so that all of the validity data on the adult AS would also accrue to the CASI. It would be possible to predict anxiety, fear, and panic in adults based on CASI scores measured at ages 7–10. Researchers could then study the origins of AS in order to understand better the causes of panic attacks and also to improve clinical management.

Trait Anxiety and AS in Children

Chorpita et al. (1996) tested the construct validity of AS in children. According to their interpretation of their own results, they showed that AS predicts trait anxiety in older children, aged 12–17, but not in younger children, aged 7–11. They concluded that AS may not be reliable with young children. This analysis, however, was flawed because it is based on a double-standard in which AS is critically evaluated but trait anxiety is uncritically accepted (Reiss, 1997). Suppose that the CASI is reliable at ages 7–11 but that childhood measures of trait anxiety are unreliable. Under these conditions, Chorpita et al. would show no correlation because it is impossible for a reliable measure to predict (or correlate with) an unreliable one. The research result showing that the CASI does not predict trait anxiety in young children may suggest that the CASI is unreliable, or it may suggest that the CASI is reliable and the measure of trait anxiety is unreliable. The Chorpita et al. research study is invalid.

Weems, Hammond-Laurence, Silverman and Ginsburg (1998) also tested the validity of the CASI in samples of young children (6–11 years old; $n = 202$) and adolescents (12–17 years old; $n = 78$) who were referred to an anxiety disorders clinic. They determined if the CASI could account for variance in children's fears beyond that accounted for by trait anxiety and anxiety frequency in both younger and older children. Using the established methodology of demonstrating incremental validity in the prediction of fearfulness (see Reiss et al., 1986), Weems and colleagues showed that the CASI exhibited incremental validity in both children and adolescents. In this study, the CASI was reliable at younger ages.

AS and Behavioral Challenge Tasks in Children

Unnewehr, Schneider, Margraf, Jenkins and Forin (1996) asked children to rate their fear of the physical symptoms of anxiety on a scale of one to five (the CASI was not available when they began their study). The participants were the offspring, aged 7–15, of parents who were receiving treatment for panic disorder ($n = 27$) or for animal phobia ($n = 21$), or of parents who were not in treatment (normal control; $n = 29$). The participants were presented with two fearful stimuli, exposure to a spider and a hyperventilation task. The children who initially reported at least moderate levels of fear of physical symptoms reacted to the hyperventilation task with higher levels of subjective anxiety and also were more likely to prematurely terminate the task. These results suggest that high AS may predispose children to react anxiously and negatively to autonomic arousal, as is the case for adults.

Rabian, Embry, and MacIntyre (1999) conducted a behavioral validation of the CASI. Elementary-school children ($N = 56$; aged 8–11 years) completed the CASI and three additional self-report measures (i.e., a 0–4 fear rating of how they felt at that moment and the state and trait versions of the STAIC). The children then performed a physically challenging, stair-stepping task designed to increase physiological arousal. The fear rating was administered during and after the task; the STAIC-State version was re-administered after the task. The results of hierarchical regression analyses indicated that the CASI significantly predicted the levels of state anxiety and subjective fear reported in response to the challenge task, even after controlling for trait anxiety and pre-task levels of state anxiety and fear. The CASI also predicted changes (pre- to post-task) in fear experienced in response to the challenge task. Such findings demonstrate that the CASI possesses unique incremental validity relative to measures of trait anxiety and also provided a behavioral validation of the CASI in pre-adolescent children. These results suggest that the CASI is reliable at younger ages.

Anxiety and Other Disorders

Children who experience panic attacks have the highest CASI scores, followed by children with nonpanic anxiety disorders, who have higher CASI scores than children with no anxiety disorder. For example, Rabian, Peterson, Richters, and Jensen (1993) found CASI scores of 30.6, 28.8, and 26.4, respectively, for 18 children with anxiety disorders, 31 children with externalizing disorders, and 62 children with no psychiatric diagnosis. The CASI scores were significantly higher for children with anxiety disorders versus the children with no disorders. The difference between the children with anxiety disorders and those with externalizing disorder was not statistically significant. However, this may be due to the presence of comorbid conditions in which some children with anxiety disorder also had externalizing disorders. It is also important to note that other children's anxiety measures, such as the RCMAS and STAIC, often fail to differentiate children with anxious disorder from those with externalizing disorder (Perrin & Last, 1992).

Vasey, Daleiden, Williams and Brown (1995) found significant differences in CASI scores between 12 children with anxiety disorders (mean CASI score = 32.4) and 12 control subjects matched on age, gender, and intellectual ability who did not meet diagnostic criteria for a psychiatric disorder (mean CASI score = 26.0). Interestingly, scores on the RCMAS and STAIC-T did not distinguish these two groups.

A number of studies evaluated the relation between CASI scores and anxiety disorders. Kearney, Albano, Eisen, Allan, & Barlow (1997) compared children meeting criteria for panic disorder ($n = 20$) with children meeting diagnostic criteria for other anxiety disorders ($n = 20$) on several self-report measures of fear and anxiety, including the CASI. Only CASI scores differed significantly between the two groups. Further, Lau, Calamari, and Waraczynski (1996) found a 0.42 correlation between CASI scores and total number of reported panic symptoms in a community sample of 77 high-school adolescents. The CASI was correlated with the number of panic attacks in the past year, with the distress the panic attacks caused, and with the judged seriousness of the attacks. Further, participants were categorized as "panickers" and "non-panickers" based on their responses on the Panic Attack Questionnaire (PAQ; Norton, Dorward, & Cox, 1986). The 30 panickers scored significantly higher on the CASI than the 47 non-panickers. More recently, Hayward et al. (1997) used the ASI to compare a large community sample of adolescent girls (aged 11–16; $N = 1013$) who were classified as having panic attacks (either interview-determined or questionnaire-determined). Results were similar using either method to determine panic: girls with panic attacks ($n = 233$) had significantly higher ASI scores than girls with no panic attacks ($n = 736$). In addition, girls with interview-determined panic disorder ($n = 17$) had significantly higher ASI scores than girls with interview-determined panic attacks ($n = 38$) and non-panickers ($n = 958$).

Mattis and Ollendick (1997) investigated children's cognitive responses to the physical symptoms of panic in a sample of nonreferred 3rd, 6th, and 9th graders. The children listened to a tape describing a panic attack and were told to imagine that they were experiencing the condition described on the tape. Only the children's CASI scores predicted their tendencies to make internal catastrophic attributions (e.g., thoughts of going crazy, losing control, or dying). Mattis and Ollendick concluded that the CASI predicted catastrophic attributions for children of all ages and speculated that "it is possible that high levels of AS and elevated internal attributions in response to negative outcomes set the stage for the development of panic attacks and subsequent panic disorder" (p. 55).

Recent research investigated the relation between AS and depression in children. In a sample of 209 children and adolescents referred for anxiety problems, Weems, Hammond-Laurence, Silverman, and Ferguson (1997) found a significant correlation between CASI scores and scores on the Children's Depression Inventory (CDI; Kovacs, 1981) ($r = 0.52$). The CASI and CDI had a partial $r = 0.52$ even after controlling for clinician severity ratings.

Silverman, La Greca and Wasserstein (1995) examined the relation between worry and various indices of anxiety. They found that CASI scores were significantly related to the number, frequency, and intensity of children's worries. It is possible that children who report worrying about "a lot" of things (e.g., school, performance, health) also are inclined to worry about their anxiety symptoms. Support for this hypothesis was reported by Weems et al. (1997) who found that the correlation between the CASI and CDI was lowest when controlling for the worry subscale of the RCMAS ($r = 0.21$), as compared with the physiological subscale ($r = 0.31$) and the concentration subscale ($r = 0.32$).

The CASI has been successfully used in a number of clinical studies. Ollendick (1995) used the CASI in a study of cognitive–behavioral treatment for panic disorder with agoraphobia in four adolescents aged 13, 14, 16, and 17. This study used a multiple-baseline design. Treatment involved progressive muscle relaxation and breathing training, *in vivo* exposure, and a fourth session devoted to cognitive coping procedures. The CASI was found to be a sensitive measure of change in the treatment of the four adolescents who had panic attacks.

In addition to using the CASI as a treatment outcome measure, the CASI has been used to prescribe treatment. Two single case studies addressed the potential use of the CASI in this manner (Eisen & Silverman, 1993, 1998). Although these two studies did not target AS per se, they showed that children showed greater improvement when they received a prescribed treatment in accordance with their specific response classes (or symptom patterns) of anxiety. For example, Eisen and Silverman (1998) used a multiple-baseline design across subjects to examine the efficacy of prescriptive versus nonprescriptive cognitive–behavioral intervention for four boys (ages 8, 11 and two 12-year-olds). The boys met DSM III-R criteria for a primary diagnosis of Overanxious Disorder as well as DSM IV criteria for Generalized Anxiety Disorder. Using the CASI in conjunction with other indices, the children were classified into either the Somatic Response Class (i.e., many somatic complaints, high physiological tension, elevated anxiety sensitivity) or into the Cognitive Response Class (i.e., a lot of worry, negative cognition—but not related to anxious symptoms). The results indicated that three of the four participants met high end-state functioning criteria by falling within normal limits on appropriate outcome measures, one of which was the CASI, following prescriptive treatment. These improvements were maintained at the 6-month follow-up assessment point. In contrast, nonprescriptive treatment failed to produce sufficient change for participants to satisfy high end-state functioning criteria. One case, for example, following nonprescriptive treatment deteriorated and experienced clinically significant levels of distress on the CASI (from 26 to 34).

New Directions

As already noted, longitudinal research is needed to evaluate how CASI scores assessed in childhood predict ASI scores, spontaneous panic attacks, and anxiety disorders in adulthood. With this goal in mind, the second and third authors have recently collected data on 44 children who were administered the CASI in 1991. The study examined: (a) the stability of CASI scores; (b) the relation of CASI to ASI scores in adolescents over time; and (c) the predictive relations between AS and panic, which was assessed by the PAQ. Based on the existing theoretical and empirical work on AS with both adults and children (Maller & Reiss, 1992; Reiss, 1991; Schmidt et al., 1997; Silverman & Weems, 1999), it was expected that CASI scores would be stable beyond ages 7–10 and that high scores would predict the occurrence of panic attacks and fears in adolescents. Childhood may be a time when AS is a risk factor for panic attacks, and full-intensity panic disorder may not be seen until later ages (Silverman & Weems, 1999).

Based on a preliminary analysis of our data from 44 children, we found that children whose CASI scores increased from time-1 (1991) to time-2 (1998) were significantly more likely to report experiencing panic attacks, as measured on the PAQ, than were children whose CASI scores decreased from time-1 to time-2 ($X^2 = 7.9$, $p = 0.005$). Specifically, 71% (10 of 14) whose CASI scores increased from time-1 to time-2 reported having one or more panic attack. In contrast, 27% (8 of 30) whose CASI scores decreased from time-1 to time-2 reported no panic attacks. The children were between the ages of 6.9 and 11 at time-1 versus 14 to 18 at time-2. We conducted a logistic regression analysis with panic attack status as the dependent variable and age, gender, CASI scores at time-1, CASI scores at time-2, family history of panic attacks, and CASI score change status (i.e., increase or decrease) as variables. We found that increases in CASI scores (Wald = 6.2, $p = 0.013$) predicted panic attacks beyond a family history of panic, and that the relation was not mediated by age or gender (model $X^2 = 26.3$, $p = 0.0002$, overall classification accuracy 91%).

These results suggest that it is not simply the level of CASI scores, but rather the developmental trajectory of CASI scores, which predict panic from childhood to adolescence. The results indicated that increases in CASI scores predicted panic attacks, such that childhood may be a time when AS is a risk factor for panic, and panic disorder is still in a developmental stage. Moreover, the results showing that decreases in CASI scores were associated with the absence of panic attacks may mean that reductions in AS protect against the development of panic disorder.

The notion that AS is still developing during childhood was supported by findings indicating that CASI scores at time-1 were not significantly correlated with CASI scores ($r = 0.15$), ASI scores ($r = 0.09$) or the number of panic attacks experienced in the last year ($r = -0.08$) at time-2. CASI scores at time-2 were, however, correlated with ASI scores ($r = 0.75$, $p < 0.001$) at time-2, and both CASI and ASI scores concurrently predicted the number of anxious symptoms reported at time-2 ($r = 0.46$, $p < 0.01$ and $r = 0.30$, $p < 0.05$, respectively). Finally, CASI scores at time-2 were significantly correlated with parent-reports of the child's internalizing symptoms on the Child Behavior Checklist ($r = 0.35$, $p < 0.05$). Future research is needed to determine the general validity of these findings in larger samples of children followed over time.

Future researchers also need to follow up on a recent finding concerning test anxiety. Park (1998) analyzed test anxiety in terms of Reiss's (1991) expectancy theory of fear, which was viewed as a fear of taking tests. She predicted that test anxiety is associated primarily with how much pressure a student puts on himself or herself to avoid failure, called "failure sensitivity," independent of past frequency of failure in taking examinations. Her study confirmed her prediction. She developed two new measures, a 45-item self-report measure called the Failure Sensitivity Index (FSI), and the Failure Frequency Checklist (FFC). She then demonstrated sound psychometric properties for each measure. For example, the Cronbach's alpha for the FSI was 0.96 ($n = 188$), and the 4-week test–retest reliability was estimated at 0.90 ($n = 74$). She showed a 0.72 correlation between self-report and parent ratings of the FFC. She then showed that test anxiety is much more strongly correlated with failure sensitivity ($r = 0.66$) than it is with frequency of failure ($r = 0.22$). Finally, she used test anxiety as the dependent measure, performed a multiple-regression analysis, and showed that the FSI predicted test anxiety even after the variance explained by failure frequency had been controlled.

Another area of promising research is the extent to which sensitivities other than anxiety and failure may be related to anxiety and other types of psychopathology. Reiss and his colleagues are developing a child rating version of the Reiss Profile of Fundamental Goals and Motivational Sensitivities. The Reiss Profile is the first standardized instrument that permits a comprehensive assessment of end ("intrinsic") motives (Reiss & Havercamp, 1998; Reiss, 2000b). By developing a child version of this instrument, it should be possible to test for risk factors for various psychiatric syndromes such as schizophrenia or depression (Reiss, 1999; Reiss & Havercamp, 1996). Using a version of the Reiss Profile specially adapted for use with adults with mental retardation, Dykkens and Risener (1999) showed that various developmental syndromes of genetic origin are associated with distinctive motivational profiles.

Researchers need to study how AS, as well as other sensitivities, develop in young children. How do the motives and sensitivities of parents affect those of their children? Reiss and Havercamp (1998) and Reiss (2000a) have discussed genetic factors. Silverman and Weems (1999) have discussed the possible influences of behavioral inhibition (e.g., Kagan, Reznick, & Snidman, 1987; Kagan, Reznick, & Gibbons, 1989) and attachment theory (see Manassis & Bradley, 1994). Further, social learning in the form of observation and instruction probably affects the development of AS in children. Researchers already have shown that such indirect pathways occur in the development of children's fears (e.g., Ollendick, King, & Hamilton 1991), and that mothers' cognitive triads are predictive of their children's cognitive triads and levels of depression (Stark, Schmidt & Joiner, 1996). We still need to study how these processes affect AS.

In conclusion, significant progress has been made in the study of AS in children, but much remains to be investigated. We have developed and validated a sound measure of anxiety sensitivity and shown that it is related to anxiety disorders, especially panic disorder. We have begun to study AS longitudinally and address theoretically questions of causation. The construct has been shown to have clinical applications. Further, AS may be just one part of an overall new, motivational approach to the study of psychopathology (Reiss, 2000a).

References

Asmundson, G. J. G. (1999). Anxiety sensitivity and chronic pain: Empirical findings, clinical implications, and future directions. In S. Taylor (Ed.), *Anxiety sensitivity: Theory, research, and treatment of the fear of anxiety* (pp. 269–288). Mahwah, NJ: Erlbaum.

Cameron, N. (1947). The psychology of behavior disorders: A biosocial interpretation. Boston: Houghton Mifflin.

Chorpita, B. F., Albano, A. M., & Barlow, D. H. (1996). Child anxiety sensitivity index: Considerations for children with anxiety disorders. *Journal of Clinical Child Psychology, 25,* 77–82.

Cox, B. J., Parker, J. D., & Swinson R. P. (1996). Anxiety sensitivity: Confirmatory evidence for a multidimensional construct. *Behaviour Research and Therapy, 34,* 591–589.

Donnell, C. D., & McNally, R. J. (1990). Anxiety sensitivity and panic attacks in a nonclinical population. *Behaviour Research and Therapy, 28,* 83–85.

Dykens, E. M., & Risener, B. A. (1999). Refining behavioral phenotypes: Personality-motivation in Williams and Prader-Willi Syndromes. *American Journal of Mental Retardation, 104,* 158–169.

Eisen, A. R., & Silverman, W. K. (1993). Should I relax or change my thoughts? A preliminary study of the treatment of Overanxious Disorder in children. *Cognitive Psychotherapy Research: An International Quarterly, 7,* 265–280.

Eisen, A. R., & Silverman, W. K., (1998). Prescriptive treatment for generalized anxiety disorder in children. *Behavior Therapy, 29,* 105–123.

Flavia, M. (personal communication, October 15, 1989).

Hayward, C., Killen, J. D., Kraemer, H. C., Blair-Greiner, A., Strachowski, D., Cunning, D., & Taylor, C. B. (1997). Assessment and phenomenology of nonclinical panic attacks in adolescent girls. *Journal of Anxiety Disorders, 11,* 17–32.

Holloway, W., & McNally, R. J. (1987). Effects of anxiety sensitivity on the response of hyperventilation. *Journal of Abnormal Psychology, 96,* 330–334.

Kagan, J., Reznick, J. S., & Gibbons, J. (1989). Inhibited and uninhibited types of children. *Child Development, 60,* 838–845.

Kagan, J., Reznick, J. S., & Snidman, N. (1987). The physiology and psychology of behavioral inhibition. *Child Development, 58,* 1459–1473.

Kearney, C. A., Albano, A. M., Eisen, A. R., Allan, W. D., & Barlow, D. H. (1997). The phenomenology of panic disorder in youngsters: An empirical study of a clinical sample. *Journal of Anxiety Disorders, 11,* 49–62.

Kovacs, M. (1981). Rating scales to assess depression in school aged children. *Acta Paedopsychiatrica, 46,* 305–315.

Lau, J. J., Calamari, J. E., & Waraczynski, M. (1996). Panic attack symptomatology and anxiety sensitivity in adolescents. *Journal of Anxiety Disorders, 10,* 355–364.

Laurent, J., Schmidt, N. B., Catanzaro, S. J., Joiner, T. E., & Kelley, A. M. (1998). Factor structure of a measure of anxiety sensitivity in children. *Journal of Anxiety Disorders, 12,* 307–331.

Lilienfeld, S. O. (1999). Anxiety sensitivity and the structure of personality. In S. Taylor (Ed.), *Anxiety sensitivity: Theory, research and the treatment of the fear of anxiety* (pp. 239–268). New Jersey: Laurence Erlbaum Associates.

Lilienfeld, S. O., Jacob, R. G., & Turner, S. M. (1989). Comment on Holloway and McNally's (1987) "Effects of anxiety sensitivity on the response to hyperventilation." *Journal of Abnormal Psychology, 98,* 100–102.

Maller, R. G. & Reiss, S. (1992). Anxiety sensitivity in 1984 and panic attacks in 1987. *Journal of Anxiety Disorders, 6,* 241–247.

Manassis, K., & Bradley, S. J. (1994). The development of childhood anxiety: Toward an integrated model. *Journal of Applied Developmental Psychology, 15,* 345–366.

Mattis, S. G. & Ollendick, T. H. (1997). Children's cognitive responses to the somatic symptoms of panic. *Journal of Abnormal Child Psychology, 25,* 47–57.

McNally, R. J. (1989). Is anxiety sensitivity distinguishable from trait anxiety? Reply to Lilienfeld, Jacob, and Turner (1989). *Journal of Abnormal Psychology, 98,* 193–194.

McNally, R. J. (1994). *Panic disorder: A critical analysis.* New York: Guilford.

McNally, R. J. (1996). Anxiety sensitivity is distinguishable from trait anxiety. In R. M. Rapee (Ed.), *Current controversies in the anxiety disorders* (pp. 214–227). New York: Guilford.

Norton, G. R., Dorward, J., & Cox, B. J. (1986). Factors associated with panic attacks in nonclinical subjects. *Behavior Therapy, 17,* 239–252.

Ollendick, T. H. (1983). Reliability and validity of the revised Fear Survey Schedule for Children (FSSC-R). *Behaviour Research and Therapy, 21,* 685–692.

Ollendick, T. H. (1995). Cognitive behavioral treatment of panic disorder with agoraphobia in adolescents: A multiple baseline design analysis. *Behavior Therapy, 26,* 517–531.

Ollendick, T. H., King, N. J., & Hamilton, D. I. (1991). Origins of childhood fears: An evaluation of Rachman's theory of fear acquisition. *Behaviour Research and Therapy, 29,* 117–123.

Otto, M. W., Pollack, M. H., Fava, M., Uccello, R., & Rosenbaum, J. F. (1995). Elevated Anxiety Sensitivity Index scores in patients with major depression: Correlates and changes with antidepressant treatment. *Journal of Anxiety Disorders, 9,* 117–123.

Park, L. (1998). Failure sensitivity, failure frequency, and test anxiety. Unpublished master's thesis, Department of Psychology, Ohio State University.

Perrin, S. & Last, C. G. (1992). Do childhood anxiety measures measure anxiety? *Journal of Abnormal Child Psychology, 20,* 567–587.

Peterson, R. A., & Heilbronner, R. L. (1987). The anxiety sensitivity index: Construct validity and factor analytic structure. *Journal of Anxiety Disorders, 1,* 117–121.

Peterson, R. A. & Reiss, S. (1991). *Anxiety Sensitivity Index manual (revised).* Orland Park, IL: International Diagnostic Systems Inc.

Rabian, B., Embry, L., & MacIntyre, D. (1999). Behavioral validation of the Childhood Anxiety Sensitivity Index in children. *Journal of Clinical Child Psychology, 28,* 105–112.

Rabian, B., Peterson, R. A., Richters, J., & Jensen, P. S. (1993). Anxiety sensitivity among anxious children. *Journal of Clinical Child Psychology, 22,* 441–446.

Rapee, R. M., & Medoro, L. (1994). Fear of physical sensations and trait anxiety as mediators of the response to hyperventilation in nonclinical subjects. *Journal of Abnormal Psychology, 103,* 693–699.

Reiss, S. (1991). Expectancy model of fear, anxiety, and panic. *Clinical Psychology Review, 11,* 141–153.

Reiss, S. (1997). Trait anxiety: It's not what you think It is. *Journal of Anxiety Disorders, 11,* 201–214.

Reiss, S. (1999). The sensitivity theory of aberrant motivation. In S. Taylor, (Ed.), *Anxiety sensitivity: Theory, research, and treatment* (pp. 35–58). Mahwah, NJ: Erlbaum.

Reiss, S. (2000a). *Who Am I: The 16 desires that motivate our actions and determine our personality.* New York: Tarcher/Putnam.

Reiss, S., (2000b). Why people turn to religion: A motivational analysis. *Journal for the Scientific Study of Region, 39,* 47–52.

Reiss, S., & Havercamp, S H (1996). The sensitivity theory of human motivation: Implications for psychopathology. *Behavior Research and Therapy, 34,* 621–632.

Reiss, S., & Havercamp, S. H. (1997). The sensitivity theory of aberrant motivation: Why functional analysis is not enough. *American Journal of Mental Retardation, 101,* 553–566.

Reiss, S., & Havercamp, S. H. (1998). Toward a comprehensive assessment of fundamental motivation: Factor structure of the Reiss Profiles. *Psychological Assessment, 10,* 97–106.

Reiss, S., Peterson, R. A., Gursky, D. M., & McNally, R. J. (1986). Anxiety sensitivity, anxiety frequency and the prediction of fearfulness. *Behaviour Research and Therapy, 24,* 1, 1–8.

Sandin, B. (1997). *Ansidad miedos y fobias en ninos y adolescents.* Madrid: Dykinson.

Saviotti, F. M., Grandi, S., Savron, G., Ermentini, R., Bartolucci, G., Conti, S., & Fava, G. A. (1991). Characterological traits of recovered patients with panic disorders and agoraphobia. *Journal of Affective Disorders, 23,* 113–117.

Schmidt, N. B., & Lerew, D. R. (1998). Prospective evaluation of psychological risk factors as predictors of functional impairment during acute stress. *Journal of Occupational Rehabilitation, 8,* 199–212.

Schmidt, N. B., Lerew, D. R., & Jackson, R. J. (1997). The role of anxiety sensitivity in the pathogenesis of panic: Prospective evaluation of spontaneous panic attacks during acute stress. *Journal of Abnormal Psychology, 106*, 355–364.

Schmidt, N. B., Lerew, D. R., & Joiner, T. E. (1998). Anxiety sensitivity and the pathogenesis of anxiety and depression: Evidence for symptoms specificity. *Behaviour Research and Therapy, 36*, 165–177.

Schmidt, N. B., Storey, J., Greenberg, B. D., Santiago, H. Y., Li, Q., & Murphy, D. L. (in press). Evaluating gene X psychological risk factor effects in the pathogenesis of anxiety: A new model approach. *Journal of Abnormal Psychology*.

Silverman, W. K., & Weems, C. F. (1999). Anxiety sensitivity in children. In S. Taylor (Ed.), *Anxiety sensitivity: Theory, research and the treatment of the fear of anxiety* (pp. 239–268) New Jersey: Laurence Erlbaum Associates.

Silverman, W. K., Fleisig, W., Rabian, B., & Peterson, R. (1991). Childhood anxiety sensitivity index. *Journal of Clinical Child Psychology, 20*, 162–168.

Silverman, W. K., La Greca, A. M., & Wasserstein, S. (1995). What do children worry about? Worry and its relation to anxiety. *Child Development, 66*, 671–686.

Silverman, W. K., Ginsburg, G. S., & Goedhart, A. W. (1999). Factor structure of the Childhood Anxiety Sensitivity Index. *Behaviour Research and Therapy, 37*, 903–917.

Spielberger, C. D. (1973). *Manual for the State–Trait Anxiety Inventory for Children*. Palo Alto, CA: Consulting Psychologists Press.

Spielberger, C. D. (1985). Assessment of state and trait anxiety: Conceptual and methodological issues. *Southern Psychologist, 2*, 6–16.

Stark, K. D., Schmidt, K. L., & Joiner, T. E., (1996). Cognitive triad: Relationship to depressive symptoms, parents' cognitive triad, and perceived parental messages. *Journal of Abnormal Child Psychology, 24*, 615–621.

Stein, M. B., Jang, K. L., & Livesley, J. (1999). Heritability of anxiety sensitivity: A twin study. *American Journal of Psychiatry, 156*, 246–251.

Stewart, S. H., Knize, K., & Phil, R. O. (1992). Anxiety sensitivity and dependency in clinical and nonclinical panickers and controls. *Journal of Anxiety Disorders, 7*, 119–131.

Stewart, S. H., Samoluk, S. B., & MacDonald, A. B. (1999). Anxiety sensitivity and substance use and abuse. In S. Taylor (Ed.), *Anxiety sensitivity: Theory, research, and treatment of the fear of anxiety*. Mahwah, NJ: Lawrence Erlbaum.

Taylor, J. A. (1953). A personality scale of manifest anxiety. *Journal of Abnormal and Social Psychology, 48*, 285–290.

Taylor, S. (1995). Anxiety sensitivity: Theoretical perspectives and recent findings. *Behaviour Research and Therapy, 33*, 243–258.

Taylor, S. (1996). Nature and measurement of anxiety sensitivity. Reply to Lilienfeld, Turner, and Jacob (1996). *Journal of Anxiety Disorders, 6*, 249–259.

Taylor, S. (Ed.) (1999). *Anxiety sensitivity: Theory, research, and treatment of the fear of anxiety*. Mahwah, NH: Lawrence.

Taylor, S. Koch, W. J., McNally, R. J., & Crockett, D. J. (1992a). How does anxiety sensitivity vary across the anxiety disorders. *Journal of Anxiety Disorders, 6*, 249–259.

Taylor, S. Koch, W. J., McNally, R. J., & Crockett, D. J. (1992b). Conceptualizations of anxiety sensitivity. *Psychological Assessment, 4*, 245–250.

Telch, M. J., & Harrington, P. J. (1994, November). Anxiety sensitivity and expectedness of arousal in mediating affective response to 35% carbon dioxide inhalation. Paper presented at the 28th meeting of the Association for the Advancement of Behavior Therapy, San Diego, CA.

Telch, M. J., Shermis, M. D., & Lucas, J. A. (1989). Anxiety sensitivity: Unitary construct or domain specific appraisals. *Journal of Anxiety Disorders, 3,* 25–32.

Unnewehr, S., Schneider, S., Margraf, J., Jenkins, M., & Forin, I. (1996). Exposure to internal and external stimuli: Reactions in children of patients with panic disorder or animal phobia. *Journal of Anxiety Disorders, 10,* 489–508.

Vasey, M. W., Daleiden, E. L., Williams, L. L., & Brown, L. (1995). Biased attention in childhood anxiety disorders: A preliminary study. *Journal of Abnormal Child Psychology, 23,* 267–279.

Wardle, J., Ahmad, T., & Haywood, P. (1990). Anxiety sensitivity in agoraphobia. *Journal of Anxiety Disorders, 4,* 325–333.

Watson, D., & Clark, L. A. (1984). Negative affectivity: The disposition to experience aversive emotional states. *Psychological Bulletin, 98,* 465–490.

Weems, C. F., Hammond-Laurence, K., Silverman, W. K., & Ferguson, C. (1997). The relation between anxiety sensitivity and depression in children referred for anxiety. *Behaviour Research and Therapy, 35,* 961–966.

Weems, C. F., Hammond-Laurence, K., Silverman, W. K., & Ginsburg, G. (1998). Testing the utility of the anxiety sensitivity construct in children and adolescents referred for anxiety disorders. *Journal of Clinical Child Psychology, 24,* 69–77.

6

Control and the Development of Negative Emotion

BRUCE F. CHORPITA

Over the past 15 years, an accumulation of evidence from a variety of areas has fostered some important theoretical advances in the understanding of negative emotions. A central theme, and one which necessitates the mention of depression in a book on anxiety, involves the notion that anxiety disorders and depression appear to be characterized by a shared temperamental risk factor (Barlow, Chorpita, & Turovsky, 1996; Brady & Kendall, 1992; Fowles, 1995; Kendler, Neale, Kessler, Heath, & Eaves, 1992; King, Ollendick, & Gullone, 1991; Watson & Clark, 1984). Consistent with this theme, a variety of models has been advanced concerning such potentially unifying constructs as behavioral inhibition (Gray, 1982; Kagan, Reznick, & Snidman, 1987), positive and negative affectivity (Clark & Watson, 1991; Watson & Clark, 1984), and helplessness–hopelessness (Alloy, Kelly, Mineka, & Clements, 1990). At the same time, additional work has focused on detailing possible mechanisms or processes that may establish or intensify risk for negative emotions, including coping strategies (Kendall, 1992), social–familial transmission (Barrett, Rapee, Dadds, & Ryan, 1996; Chorpita, Albano, & Barlow, 1996), information processing (Vasey, Daleiden, Williams, & Brown, 1995; McNally, 1996), and complex forms of conditioning (e.g., Mineka & Zinbarg, 1996). Given these major advances, the study of the development of risk for anxiety and depression may currently benefit at least as much from the integration of existing ideas as from the development of new ones. One recurrent and possibly organizing theme throughout much of this growing literature involves the role of perceptions of control in both the expression and the development of negative emotions (Barlow et al., 1996; Chorpita & Barlow, 1998). It is thus the purpose of the present chapter to examine the idea that experience with control plays an important role in the development of a psychological vulnerability for anxiety and depression. A number of ideas central to this theme have previously been outlined by Chorpita and Barlow (1998); however, for completeness major points are repeated and elaborated here, along with some significant new insights and developments.

Vulnerability for Negative Emotions

Before the definitions and mechanisms involving control and experience with control can be detailed, it is first necessary to draw together some of the diverse findings concerning the relation between anxious and depressed emotion and the vulnerability for these conditions. Perhaps the most appropriate foundation upon which to formulate an integrated model of vulnerability should begin with the extensive work of Jeffrey Gray (1982, 1987; Gray & McNaughton, 1996). Gray (1982) detailed the operations of a functional brain system that he termed the "behavioral inhibition system" (BIS), involving the septal area, the hippocampus, and the Papez circuit, as well as the neocortical inputs to the septohippocampal system, dopaminergic ascending input to the prefrontal cortex, cholinergic ascending input to the septohippocampal system, noradrenergic input to the hypothalamus, and the descending noradrenergic fibers of the locus coeruleus (Gray, 1982). According to Gray, this system is activated by signals for punishment, signals for nonreward, and novelty. The primary, short-term outputs of the BIS involve narrowing of attention, inhibition of gross motor behavior, increased stimulus analysis (e.g., vigilance or scanning), increased central nervous system arousal (e.g., alertness), and priming of hypothalamic motor systems for possible rapid action that may be required (i.e., possible activation of the fight/flight system [FFS]). It is important to note that BIS activity is distinct from some traditional notions of anxiety, in that it does not inherently involve peripheral physiological arousal (e.g., rapid heartbeat, dry mouth). Rather, its phenomenology is characterized mainly by increased caution, vigilance, and processing of threat relevant information. For this reason, the BIS has sometimes been referred to as the "stop, look, and listen" system.

It is remarkable that the outputs of the BIS, when defined in such a manner, are consistent with a number of constructs related to vulnerability for anxiety disorders and depressive disorders (Barlow et al., 1996; Brown, Chorpita, & Barlow, 1998; Clark & Watson, 1991; Gray & McNaughton, 1996). For example, Clark and Watson (1991; Watson & Clark, 1984) articulated a general temperamental factor, negative affectivity, thought to underlie the expression of the signs and symptoms of both anxious and depressive syndromes. Clark, Watson, and Mineka (1994) described negative affectivity as a "stable, highly heritable general trait dimension with a multiplicity of aspects ranging from mood to behavior" (p. 104). Evidence from a number of sources supports the validity of the negative affectivity construct in children (e.g., Chorpita, Albano, & Barlow, 1998; Joiner, Catanzaro, & Laurent, 1996; Lonigan, Carey, & Finch, 1994).

In Clark and Watson's (1991) model, this construct of negative affectivity bears a striking similarity to Gray's BIS outputs. However, to complicate matters, a difficult issue of semantics arises here in that Gray (1982, 1987), and to a degree Barlow et al. (1996), called these BIS outputs "anxiety," whereas Clark and Watson (1991) considered "anxiety" to involve both negative affectivity and physiological hyperarousal (activity of the autonomic nervous system). As noted above, BIS output does not explicitly involve autonomic arousal. Commenting on these taxonomic issues, Gray (1991) noted that this literature in general is "badly in need of a common vocabulary" (p. 78). Nevertheless, despite differences in terminology, the substantive arguments of these theorists are convergent regarding the idea of a general factor involving oversensitivity to negative stimuli associated with negative emotional and behavioral outputs.

Recent genetic evidence supports this notion of a general sensitivity or risk factor. For example, Kendler et al. (1992) demonstrated that heritability plays an important role in the development of a vulnerability for both generalized anxiety disorder (GAD) and major depression (MD). Analyses of models in a study involving 1,033 pairs of female twins demonstrated that genetic factors for MD and GAD were correlated at 1.0, suggesting that "the same genetic liability influences risk to both MD and GAD" (p. 720). This finding is strong support for the notion of shared vulnerability. However, little is known about the precise relation of negative affectivity or the BIS to the heritable risk identified by Kendler et al. (1992). This is clearly an important avenue for continued study.

A thorough explication of the taxonomy and structure of negative emotions is beyond the scope of the present chapter. Nevertheless, with certain assumptions one can accept the premise that a general emotional factor, consistent with Gray's BIS activity (and similar constructs from the related models discussed above), may function as a core component of anxiety disorders and depressive disorders (e.g., Brown, Chorpita, Korotitsch, and Barlow, 1997; Chorpita, Albano, et al., 1998; Joiner et al., 1996; Lovibond & Lovibond, 1995). In order to link the understanding of this biological system to psychological theories of experience with control, further details on the operation of the BIS are necessary.

Inputs to the BIS are negotiated by what Brooks (1986) and Gray and McNaughton (1996) call the comparator, a subsystem involving the Papez circuit, which runs from the subicular area, to the mammilary bodies, to the anteroventral hypothalamus, to the cingulate cortex, and back to the subicular area. The comparator analyzes information from a number of sources and, based on these analyses, regulates BIS activity. Principally, the information involves: (1) the current observed state of the world; (2) the next planned step in the organism's motor program; (3) stored regularities about the world (stimulus–stimulus associations as determined by Pavlovian conditioning); and (4) stored regularities about the behavior–outcome relations (stimulus–behavior–stimulus associations as determined by instrumental conditioning) (see fig. 6.1). According to Gray and McNaughton (1996, p. 75):

> [The comparator] has the task of predicting the next sensory event to which the animal will be exposed and checking whether it actually does occur; of operating the outputs of the BIS either if there is a mismatch between the actual and predicted events or if the predicted event is aversive; and of testing out alternative strategies (including alternative multi-dimensional descriptions of stimuli and/or responses) which may overcome the difficulty with which the animal is faced.

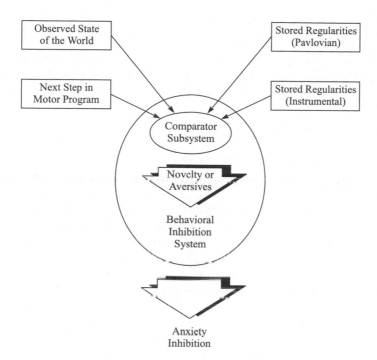

Figure 6.1. Schematic of Gray's model of the behavioral inhibition system, detailing the function and operation of the comparator subsystem. Copyright American Psychological Association. Reprinted by permission.

It is important to note here that BIS activity is very much a function of the stored regularities associated with conditioning history (i.e., experience), which may be largely established during early development. In more cognitive language, one could use the term "schemata" to describe these information banks of supposed laws about the operations and events in the world (e.g., Beck, Rush, Shaw, & Emery, 1979; Beck & Emery, 1985). Regardless of their name, these schemata, stored regularities, or records of experience are accessed by the comparator circuits every 100–200 ms, or 5–10 times per second, in a constant cycle quantized by the rhythmic theta activity of the hippocampus. In other words, such stored information is rich fuel for the constant firing of the engine of the BIS. Thus, even within this highly biological framework, the model articulated here is clearly biopsychosocial, with substantial room for theorizing about psychological influences on the operation of the BIS.

Theoretical Models of Control

Issues concerning control and experience with control are ubiquitous among the major theories of anxiety and depression, and thus it would not be surprising if these phenomena were somehow critically related to BIS operation. For example, Barlow (1988, pp. 71–72) defined anxiety as:

> [A] diffuse cognitive–affective structure consisting of a negative feedback cycle characterized to varying degrees by components of high negative affect; a sense of both internal and external events proceeding in an unpredictable, uncontrollable fashion; and maladaptive shifts in attention.

Thus, a sense for the individual that events are not under one's control is central to the emotion, according to Barlow.

Alloy, Kelly, Mineka, and Clements (1990), approaching some of the same theoretical issues from the perspective of depression, articulated a similar point of view (see also, Abramson, Metalsky, & Alloy, 1989). Alloy et al. (1990) asserted that one dimension on which anxiety and depressive disorders are said to vary involves the individual's degree of a sense of control. Specifically, when an individual experiences uncertainty about the ability to control outcomes (i.e., "uncertain helplessness"), the resulting affective state is one of "aroused anxiety." If the lack of control increases (i.e., "certain helplessness"), one experiences a state of "mixed anxiety–depression." Finally, when an individual's sense of control is entirely diminished (i.e., "hopelessness") and there is certainty of a negative outcome, one experiences a depressive state (Alloy et al., 1990, pp. 525–526). Where Alloy et al. differ from Barlow is in their commitment to the idea that helplessness or hopelessness are proximally causal variables, whereas Barlow (1988, 1991) considers uncontrollability as part of the definition of anxiety, which implicitly disallows a causal status (but see Chorpita & Barlow, 1998).

Control as a Causal Influence on Negative Emotion

Control and related constructs have been discussed and investigated so extensively that a central difficulty involves integrating the diversity of findings (e.g., Bandura, 1986; Biglan, 1987; Minor, Dess, & Overmier, 1991). Much as with the issues concerning negative affectivity and BIS activity discussed above, many of the controversial issues and arguments regarding control may be more semantic than substantive. In the hope of unifying and encompassing the widest range of these existing ideas, control is defined here rather broadly as the ability to influence directly or indirectly events or outcomes in one's environment, principally those related to positive or negative reinforcement. This definition is a slight revision of that offered by Chorpita and Barlow (1998), in that indirect avenues to control (e.g., soliciting the help of another to assist with coping) are given greater emphasis than before.

Given such a definition, there is an accumulation of evidence supporting the idea that an immediate sense of diminished control is commonly associated with the immediate expression of negative emotion (Barlow, 1988, 1991; Beck & Emery, 1985; Lazarus, 1966, 1968; Lazarus, Averill, & Opton, 1970; Mandler, 1972; Sanderson, Rapee, & Barlow, 1989). In terms of Gray's BIS, reduced control over a threatening stimulus would increase the expected probability of danger, given that fewer negative reinforcement behavior–consequence regularities (i.e., escape or avoidance strategies) could be accessed by the comparator. Likewise, reduced control over a reinforcing stimulus would increase the expected probability of experiencing nonreward, given that relevant positive reinforcement behavior–consequence regularities would not be available for the comparator. Finally, the degree of control over the environment should also be negatively related to the degree of novelty that the organism experiences (Gray, 1987, describes novelty as a mismatch in the comparator between the observed and predicted states of the world), given that total control would preclude the unexpected. Hence, the perception of low control at any given time could increase the flow of information along pathways to the comparator that would increase BIS activity.

Examples of this phenomenon abound. For example, Geer, Davison, and Gatchel (1970) found that autonomic responding was reduced in 40 male undergraduates participating in a reaction time task involving shock. In the test phase, those participants who were told that decreasing their reaction time would lessen the duration of shock showed fewer and smaller skin conductance responses relative to participants who were not told that their reaction time could reduce shock, yet all participants were given 3 s of shock, regardless of group assignment. Similar results have been found in panic disorder populations using a carbon dioxide (CO_2) inhalation paradigm (Sanderson et al., 1989). Participants who were told they could control inhaled CO_2 levels by turning a dial showed reduced panic responses, even though all participants received the same concentration of CO_2. Similar phenomena have been documented with children as young as 12 months (Gunnar, 1980).

Experience with Control as a Developmental Risk Factor

The evidence is considerable regarding the immediate effects of diminished control on negative emotion, and the model outlined in the present chapter is on one level intended to articulate possible mechanisms underlying these observations. Far more relevant to developmental theory, however, is the idea that a history of lack of control may put individuals at eventual risk to experience chronic negative emotional states through the development of a psychological vulnerability. Evidence from a variety of areas suggests that sufficient early experience with uncontrollable events may foster an increased generalized tendency to perceive or process events as not within one's control (see Chorpita & Barlow, 1998; Schneewind, 1995). This biased perception or processing would then have the effects of increasing negative emotion through some of the mechanisms outlined above. That is, an individual reared with control over events will have relatively greater access to stored information that predicts the possibility of limiting punishment or nonreward (through the so-called instrumental regularities; see fig. 6.1). Alternatively, experience with diminished control over events during development may establish stored regularities that more commonly result in the comparator predicting a punishing or frustrating outcome. Thus, assuming identical inputs from the environment and even identical biological properties of the BIS for two individuals, stored information would result in heightened BIS activity in one individual with a history of low control relative to another individual without such a history. Of course, environmental and biological differences among individuals are not only possible, but virtually unavoidable, and history with control is discussed here only as one of the many possible mechanisms for the establishment and intensification of risk for anxiety and depression.

Early experience with uncontrollable events may therefore be thought of as one primary pathway to the development of negative emotion in that such experience may foster an increased likelihood to process events as not within one's control (i.e., a psychological vulnerability). Much in the way that a cognitive set or schema might be self-perpetuating, it appears that early experience with diminished control can be disproportionately important in that it weights or colors all subsequent experience and often precludes incorporation of new information into the stored regularities (e.g., through avoidance). Of course, this suggestion is not meant to imply that later experience cannot modify the stored regularities, only that early experiences contribute most heavily to their formation (Rotter, 1966). Indeed, the modification of this maladaptive information is likely to be one of the mechanisms of action involved in cognitive behavior therapy.

Control in Animal Models of Emotion

Many of these ideas related to the developmental influences of diminished control stem from animal models of emotion, which have implicated experience with uncontrollable events as subsequently fostering anxious responding (e.g., Mowrer & Viek, 1948; Weiss, 1971a, 1971b). Perhaps the best known work in this regard involved the study of *learned helplessness* in animal models of depression (e.g., Overmier & Seligman 1967; Seligman & Maier, 1967). This classic experimental preparation involved repeatedly exposing dogs to inescapable shock and subsequently observing them when escape was made possible (Overmier & Seligman, 1967). It was found that the dogs did not attempt to escape in this second phase of the experiment, although escape was possible. By having an additional group that experienced escapable shock yoked to the inescapable shock group, it was further shown that escape deficits were not due to the amount of aversive stimulation, but rather were a result of the uncontrollability of the shock (e.g., Maier, 1970; Seligman & Maier, 1967). These behavioral deficits were seen as an analog for the type of withdrawal and disengagement noted in depressed humans.

Another classic study of control emerged within the context of animal models for anxiety. In an interesting and highly informative turn of these ideas, Mineka, Gunnar, and Champoux (1986) investigated the effects of control over appetitive, not aversive, events during rearing. This preparation involved the following three groups: (1) a "master" group of 8 infant rhesus monkeys raised in conditions allowing their control over delivery of food, water, and toys; (2) a "yoked" group of 8 monkeys receiving these same stimuli noncontingently, by having delivery of the reinforcers yoked to the first group; and (3) a "standard rearing" group of 4 monkeys, raised in typical lab conditions. The monkeys were raised in these environments for up to 12 months, and the testing phase began at approximately the eighth month. During the testing, members of the master group were noted to habituate more quickly than the yoked and standard rearing groups when confronted with a mechanical toy robot. Also, the master group demonstrated more exploratory behavior in a novel playroom situation, and showed enhanced active coping responses during selected trials of separation from peers. The work of Mineka et al. (1986) is noteworthy with respect to the finding that control over appetitive events mitigated behavior that appeared consistent with the emotions of anxiety or fear. By extending the developmental focus beyond the role of aversives and demonstrating the highly generalized results of these early experiences, Mineka et al. (1986) opened the possibility that nearly all aspects of rearing can have an impact on the development of a psychological vulnerability for negative emotions.

Control in the Child Literature

Naturally, these developments in the animal models accelerated the ongoing research regarding control and helplessness in humans. Many of these efforts were inspired by the work of Rotter (1954), who first sought to define and measure a sense of control in humans. Rotter's (1966) idea of *locus of control* involved a continuum from internal to external causality over events. According to Rotter's theory, the degree to which an individual is reinforced by a stimulus is mediated by the direction of one's belief about the response–stimulus relation. Thus, one might predict that contingent positives would not have as strong reinforcing properties if the individual believed that the positives were not due to the behavior. Locus of control in this sense has specific implications for learning. However, considered more broadly as the extent to which an individual perceives personal control over events in one's environment, the dimension also has important implications for emotional responding, particularly regarding the BIS, as noted above.

Measurement of this dimension in children was occasioned by the development of a scale by Nowicki and Strickland (Nowicki–Strickland Locus of Control Scale; NSLOC; 1973). Consistent with the present model of control and emotion, external control scores on the NSLOC have been found to correlate with anxiety scores in both clinical samples ($r = 0.31$; Finch & Nelson, 1974) and school samples ($r = 0.31$; Nunn, 1988). Because many of these early studies were conducted prior to the development of models implicating a shared risk factor for anxiety and depression, one can only speculate about whether the locus-of-control measures were correlated with anxiety measures because of the BIS-comparator mechanisms outlined above. These are important avenues for further investigation.

However, it is encouraging that similar findings have emerged using measures of childhood depression as well. For example, McCauley, Mitchell, Burke, and Moss (1988) evaluated 47 children with a current diagnosis of depression, 30 children whose depression had remitted within the past year, and 31 nondepressed psychiatric controls. Significant differences were noted in the expected order, with the depression group showing the highest, the remitted group showing the next highest, and the control group showing the lowest scores for external locus of control. Further, McCauley and colleagues (1988) found a correlation of 0.33 between the NSLOC and the Childhood Depression Inventory (CDI; Kovacs, 1981) across the three groups. Particularly given the uniformity of the magnitude of NSLOC correlations with anxiety and depression scores, it is possible to imagine that locus of control may be related to some higher-order factor common to both anxiety and depression. Similar findings regarding control and negative emotion have emerged from studies in adult populations as well (e.g., Hoehn-Saric & McLeod, 1985).

Towards a Developmental Model of Control and Negative Emotion

Again, the idea that negative emotion and low (external) perceptions of control are concurrently related has considerable support. What, then, about the idea that experience with low control establishes an enduring vulnerability for negative emotions in the future? With respect to such notions of timing and development, Cole and Turner (1993) pointed out the lack of specific attention in the literature to the differentiation of moderational and mediational processes that are implicitly part of any cognitive–developmental theory (Baron & Kenny, 1986). In the context of the present model, a mediational relation would suggest that environmental stimuli influence perceptions about control, which in turn contribute to increased BIS activity. On the other hand, a moderational model would describe the interaction of environmental stimuli with stored regularities regarding control to influence BIS activity (see fig. 6.2). An important distinction is that in the moderational model, the sense of control is no longer influenced by experience, but rather serves to weight or color the effects of experience on emotions. The diathesis–stress conceptualizations of most cognitive and cognitive–affective theories of depression and anxiety (e.g., Alloy et al., 1990; Barlow et al., 1996; Beck & Emery, 1985; Clark, 1986) are implicitly moderational, in that the effects of environmental events on emotion are moderated or amplified in this way by a cognitive vulnerability. The important question for developmental theorists thus concerns: (1) the establishment of this vulnerability (i.e., identifying a mediational model in early

A. *Mediational Model (Early Development)*

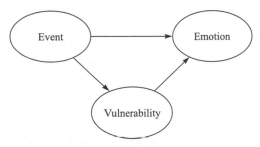

B. *Moderational Model (Later Development)*

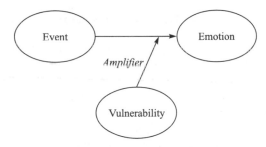

Figure 6.2. Mediational and moderational models of the influence of psychological factors on the expression of emotion. Copyright American Psychological Association. Reprinted by permission.

development); and (2) outlining the progression from a mediational to a moderational model over the course of development.

In light of the present model relating control and BIS activity, the general contrast between evidence for a mediational model in early childhood and a moderational model for late childhood and adulthood offers a useful conceptual framework (Cole & Turner, 1993; Hammen, Adrian, & Hiroto, 1988). That is, the environment may help to foster maladaptive stored regularities, with early uncontrollable experience contributing to the formation of a vulnerability (i.e., a mediational model). Later in development, this vulnerability may then begin to operate as an amplifier for the effects of environmental events on BIS activity (i.e., a moderational model), and as mentioned above, because of the associated outputs (e.g., avoidance, inhibition), these stored regularities may become relatively insulated and hence potentially maladaptive for the individual.

Implications for Family Environment

Before speculating further about structure in the present model of control cognitions and anxiety, it is necessary to review more fundamental relations regarding anxiety, control, and the environment. Given the idea that early experience plays a role in the formation of a vulnerability in the BIS, the relevance of family processes make them a natural point of inquiry. Addressing such issues is a considerable body of evidence suggesting that: (1) a particular set of family characteristics is associated with the development of control-related cognitions in children (e.g., Chorpita, Brown, & Barlow, 1998; Schneewind, 1995); and (2) a particular set of family characteristics is associated with the development of anxiety and its disorders (e.g., Turner, Beidel, & Costello, 1987). If the respective family characteristics are the same for both processes, then control cognitions and BIS activity may in fact be linked in a mediational structure in early development (see fig. 6.2).

Control of the Caregiver: The Role of Attachment

The notion that particular family characteristics are related to the development of a sense of control in children calls to mind the literature on attachment theory, in that attachment theory implicitly involves the development of a cognitive style characterized by security (Thompson, 1998) and has been implicated in the development of negative emotions and psychopathology in general (Campbell, 1989). Attachment theory (Bowlby, 1969, 1973, 1980) specifies that the caregiver serves an evolutionary and biological function of a protective and secure base (i.e., attachment object) from which the child operates. Critical to the child's healthy functioning is a secure and predictable relationship with the caregiver. If the child encounters novelty or threat of aversives, he or she can retreat safely to the caregiver. According to Bowlby, a child separated from the attachment object should therefore become anxious and protest, in a programmed attempt to elicit reunion. If this relationship is disrupted, however, one possible outcome may involve the child's exhibiting "anxious attachment," that is, becoming more chronically dependent or apprehensive. Further disruption in the relationship will be followed by the gradual dissolution of the anxious response pattern and will predispose a more withdrawn and depressive nature over time (e.g., Rutter, 1980).

Clearly, this is one of the earliest domains in which a child may experience control over events, and the possible role of the BIS in this process is apparent. Unlike later experience with control, however, the attachment domain is dyadic in nature—it involves another individual. Obviously, the child can never be fully in control of the world at this point (hence the emphasis on indirect control noted above), and development of a healthy attachment relationship depends as much on the sensitivity and effectiveness of the caregiver as on the infant's ability to influence the caregiver.

Rutter (1980) has elaborated on this reciprocal communicative nature of the attachment relationship. He suggested that to the extent that the infant and mother have a well-established repertoire of ways in which to interact, communicate, and influence each other (e.g., smiling, cooing, grabbing), the greater the potential for secure exploratory behavior by the infant.

According to Rutter, attachment has specific effects on the infant that are not characteristic of other social interactions. In particular: (1) threat or surprise will increase attachment or proximity seeking; (2) separation from the attachment figure will increase anxiety and withdrawal; and (3) presence of the attachment figure will promote exploration and lowers inhibition and anxiety.

Again, the possible role of the BIS in this process of negotiating novelty, threats, and the associated emotional and behavioral outputs is clear. Sroufe (1990) offered an excellent example of this process. Specifically, healthy infants who become overstimulated during interaction with the mother can signal the mother to de-escalate the interaction using subtle cues (e.g., head turning). Mothers who respond to these cues appropriately allow the child to return to a state of less arousal, and hence prevent crying or other negative emotion in the infant. According to Sroufe, this ability to negotiate the intensity of interaction is thought at some point to become internalized in the infant. Children who are unable to develop this particular skill are believed to be at risk for subsequent anxiety or depression (Sroufe, 1990).

In the context of the present model, the attachment figure can be thought of as signaling the availability of positive reinforcement (e.g., attention) or negative reinforcement (e.g., rescue). It makes sense, then, that if the observed state of the world involves separation from the attachment figure, there would be increased likelihood of punishment or nonreward predicted in the comparator subsystem, thus activating the BIS. The infant should, as Bowlby suggested, appear anxious upon separation and determined to elicit reunion as part of the naturally programmed response described by Bowlby. However, at some point the attachment relationship can become disrupted, raising a critical question. How does a sense of control over the caregiver progress from a mediator to a moderator? In other words, what are the relevant formative experiences, and how do they become encoded to color subsequent experience?

Classic attachment theory suggests that such variables as early separation or caregiver insensitivity can lead to subsequent disruptions in the attachment relationship. In terms of the present model, these early experiences are incorporated into the infant's memory as representing which actions produce successful outcomes (e.g., attention or rescue by the caregiver). If there is sufficient availability of instrumental regularities that associate the infant's behavior with this type of reinforcement, the infant should engage in a motor plan to reduce BIS activity (e.g., proximity seeking or verbal cueing to the caregiver). Without stored regularities that represent these behavior outcome relations (as one would expect with the disrupted attachment history), the infant should display simple inhibition of motor behavior (e.g., withdrawal) and anxious emotion. Within the framework of attachment theory, the former response is consistent with behaviors that represent "secure" attachment whereas the latter response is consistent with behaviors associated with "insecure" attachment.

These issues have been addressed indirectly in recent models of attachment theory, which emphasize the quality of the infant–child relationship as an antecedent of general sociopersonality development (see Thompson, 1998, for a review). For example, Thompson stated: "Another kind of expectation emerging from ... early interactive experiences concerns the infant's emerging sense of agency or effectance"; and further: "An awareness that [infants'] signals and actions can have predictable effects on others is fostered by the contingency inherent in the adult's responsiveness" (p. 29). In addition, research in the area of *attachment representations*—internal working models of the early attachment relationship carried forward into adulthood—have similar implications (e.g., Bretherton, 1992; van Ijzendoorn & Bakermans-Kranenburg, 1996). Thus, there is at least the hint that the child's sense of control of the attachment object becomes internalized or incorporated into the stored regularities. As alluded to earlier, the attachment relationship may be the primary domain in which the individual establishes a sense of control over reinforcement, and thus, the relationship may be one from which a sense of control over additional domains (e.g., the world, the self) may or may not generalize. When conceptualized in this manner, the study of attachment representations that carry forward into adulthood can be regarded as filling some of the conceptual gaps between early developmental models and cognitive models of negative emotion.

To complete this connection, it becomes important to ask how and whether these early socialization processes may be related to later psychopathology. Campbell (1989) reviewed a number of empirical investigations on the long-term outcome of attachment patterns. In a high-risk sample of children from impoverished and stressful environments, for example, Sroufe (1983) found anxious attachment (avoidant and resistant) at 1 year of age to be related to behavioral, school-related, and interpersonal problems in preschool. Similarly, in a sample of middle-class children, Lewis, Feirig, McGuffog, and Jaskir (1984) detected an association between anxious attachment at 1 year and level of psychopathology at age 6, but only for boys. Unfortunately, because of the lack of clinical measures, it is unclear the degree to which these behaviors were related to negative emotion. Other findings are less consistent. For example, Bates and Bayles (1988) followed a similar sample over five years and found no relation between security of attachment at infancy and subsequent behavior problems as reported by the mother.

In general, the evidence regarding long-term outcomes is difficult to interpret clearly. As stated earlier, it is frequently difficult to rule out the confounding effects of extensive biological and environmental factors that can act as common influences for attachment and outcome measures (e.g., Lewis, 1990), and Lewis et al. (1984) strongly emphasized the interplay of attachment with other variables (i.e., stressors, demographics) in predicting later child functioning. Continued efforts to evaluate the long-term outcome of attachment in terms of psychopathology and specific syndromes are greatly needed (Thompson, 1998).

Control of the World: The Role of Parenting

Parenting and Control-related Regularities

As infant becomes child, the domain in which to experience control expands considerably. Here it is likely that the family continues to play a formative role involving the establishment of a sense of control. Such ideas have inspired a growing amount of literature examining familial antecedents for a sense of diminished control in children. For example, children who have the opportunity for undivided attention from parents and who need not compete with siblings for the available reinforcers have been shown to be more likely to develop a sense of control over events. Numerous studies have demonstrated that firstborn children display more internal locus of control than later siblings (Crandall, Katkovsky, & Crandall, 1965; Hoffman & Teyber, 1979; Krampen, 1982) and that external locus of control beliefs increase as family size increases (Walter & Ziegler, 1980).

Particular dimensions of parenting style have also been found to be related to a diminished sense of control in children. For example, parents who are less consistently responsive provide their child with fewer occasions to experience the ability to solicit reinforcement, which may represent the earliest opportunities to experience control. Along those lines, Davis and Phares (1969) documented an association between inconsistent parental behavior during a family decision-making task and children's external locus of control. As expected, parents who are consistently and contingently responsive to their children have been shown to have children with a more internalized locus of control (Diethelm, 1991; Schneewind & Pfeiffer, 1978). Similarly, Skinner (1986) used observational methodology to assess parental contingency and found a tendency for high parental contingency to be positively associated with the child's internal locus of control. These findings are difficult to interpret at times, in that amount of attention from parents is often confounded with contingency of attention.

Other dimensions are important as well. For example, parents who are intrusive and protective and who do not provide the child with occasions to develop new skills or to explore the environment would help cultivate a diminished sense of control. Some findings support this idea. For example, it has been demonstrated that parents who provide more opportunity for autonomy and independence and who encourage the development of new skills are more likely to foster internal locus of control beliefs in their children (Chandler, Wolf, Cook, & Dugovics, 1980; Gordon, Nowicki, & Wichern, 1981). In a large review of the literature on parental protectiveness (e.g., Biocca, 1985) and intrusive governing (e.g., Washington, 1974), Carton and Nowicki (1994) emphasized the association between such parenting styles and external locus of control in children. Parents of children showing internal control beliefs were more likely to reward, value, or encourage independence (e.g., Gordon et al., 1981). In terms of the present model, it may be that such experiences over time become part of the child's stored regularities and contribute to a sense of diminished control that may generalize to additional domains of functioning (e.g., Bryant & Trockel, 1976; Carton & Nowicki, 1994).

Parenting and Psychopathology

Not surprisingly, some rather similar aspects of parenting have been strongly implicated in the development of psychopathology as well, supporting the possibility of a link from parenting style, to control beliefs, and to clinical disorders. Perris, Jacobsson, Lindstrom, von Knorring, and Perris (1980) conducted a number of studies to evaluate *overprotection* (i.e., the degree to which parents limit and constrain the behavior of the child, particularly in threatening or novel environments) and its relation to anxiety and mood disorders. Parker (1983; see also Silove, Parker, Hadzi-Pavlovic, Manicavasagar, & Blaszczynski, 1991), who has conducted perhaps the most extensive examination of such phenomena, also used the term "overprotection." Parker (1983) described overprotection as involving excessive parental involvement in controlling the child's environment in order to minimize aversive experiences for the child (Parker, 1983). Thus, the term "overprotection" implies behaviors that should limit the establishment of stimulus–behavior–outcome regularities which link threat or novelty to child's behavior to nonaversive outcome. In other words, the child will develop minimal history with successful coping, mastery, or resolution of threatening or novel events, owing to the limited exposure to such events and the narrow range of the child's independent responses to these events likely to be allowed or encouraged by the parent.

Across a number of studies, this type of parenting style appears to be related to later anxiety and depression. For example, scores on scales of parental overprotection were found to discriminate between clinically anxious samples and controls (e.g., Ehiobuche, 1988) and remitted depressives and controls (e.g., Gotlib, Mount, Cordie, & Whiffen, 1988). Parker, however, has suggested that overprotection alone may not be sufficient to predict anxious or depressive outcomes over the course of development. Rather, the combination of overprotection and low *care* (i.e., warmth or sensitivity) is likely to have the most negative influence. This formulation makes conceptual sense in terms of the present model. Although overprotective parents may foster a limited sense of control over events in the child's environment, they may nevertheless foster a sense of control over parental reinforcement (e.g., crying could elicit a [caring] parental response of attention or rescue). Here, the link back to attachment theory can be drawn as well, with the dimension of "care" being more relevant to that primary domain of control over the caretaker and the dimension of "overprotection" being more relevant to the secondary domain of events out in the world.

To assess these dimensions of care and overprotection, Parker, Tupling, and Brown (1979) developed the Parental Bonding Instrument (PBI). In a study of 125 depressed patients, 125 matched controls, and 125 controls with no history of depression, depressed patients were found to have a significantly higher frequency of classifying their parents as low in care and as overprotective relative to the other groups (Parker, 1979a). Parker (1979b) then examined the relation of PBI scores to various self-report measures in a nonclinical sample of 236 predominantly Australian participants, and found that overprotection scores for the primary parenting figure were significantly and moderately correlated with trait depression, the number of depressive episodes in the past year, low self-esteem, trait anxiety, and neuroticism scores. Care scores were also significantly negatively correlated with trait depression, the number of depressive episodes in the years, low self-esteem, and alienation. Replication of the research involving depression and parenting style has demonstrated that adults with Major Depression rate their parents higher on overprotection and lower on care than do nonclinical participants (Plantes, Prusoff, Brennan, & Parker, 1988).

Similar investigations have been conducted with anxiety disorder samples. Parker (1981) compared 50 outpatients having diagnoses of an anxiety disorder with a matched sample of controls (Parker et al., 1979) and found that anxious participants showed a significantly higher rate of classifying parents as overprotective and low in care. In a sample of 289 nonclinical adults, Parker (1979c) found that participants classifying their parents as overprotective and low on care demonstrated significantly higher trait anxiety scores than the others in the sample.

Similar dimensions have been looked at more recently in the larger context of heritability and other aspects of family environment. In a study of 708 families, Reiss et al. (1995) examined the effects of various dimensions of parenting on depression and antisocial behavior in adolescents. Adolescent-report, parent report, and behavioral observation measures were used to provide multivariate assessment of the variables, which were examined in terms of their relation to self- or parent-reported symptoms in the adolescent. Parenting style was classified into domains of Conflict/Negativity, Warmth/Support, and Monitoring/Control. Consistent with the parenting style literature, Warmth/Support (similar to Parker's construct of care) was found to have significant path coefficients (-0.26 and -0.37) to adolescent depressive symptoms, suggesting that low scores on this dimension predicted increased depressive symptoms in the adolescent. Monitoring/Control did not demonstrate a significant effect on depressive symptoms; however, one of this construct's lower-order factors, maternal "attempts at control" over the adolescent, was found to have a path coefficient of 0.22 on depression.

With the exception of Reiss et al. (1995), most studies of parenting style are limited by the fact that assessment has been conducted retrospectively, requiring individuals with anxiety or depression to describe their perceptions of early parenting experiences. Although some evidence exists that these retrospective accounts may not be biased (e.g., Parker, 1979d), there is a need to extend this line of work with an emphasis on cross-sectional or longitudinal designs. Furthermore, although all of these studies reviewed represent a major advance in linking parenting style to later psychopathology, they omit the evaluation of mediating cognitive links (e.g., control beliefs) in the chain from parenting to psychopathology.

One recent evaluation designed to investigate this link was conducted by Chorpita et al. (1998). In a mixed clinical and nonclinical sample of 93 families, the investigators evaluated a mediational model for the development of negative affect in children, positing controlling family environment as the principal influence on a sense of control. In light of the accumulated evidence in the parenting literature suggesting the formative role of controlling parenting style, it was hypothesized that the influence of high control in the family environment (assessed with parent and child measures; Family Environment Scale; Moos, 1986) on children's negative affect (assessed using the CDI, RCMAS, and Internalizing Scale of the Child Behavior Checklist; Achenbach, 1991) would be mediated by children's locus of control scores (NSLOC; Nowicki & Strickland). The best fitting model supported the hypothesized mediational structure, and further demonstrated a positive relation of negative affect scores with clinician rated severity of anxiety and depressive disorders in the sample. Effect sizes among latent variables were large, and the parameter estimates suggested that controlling family environment was associated with high external locus of control, which in turn had a positive influence on negative affect, which in turn influenced disorder severity (see fig. 6.3). Although preliminary, the results represent a noteworthy advance owing to the use of a cross-sectional design, measures of clinical disorders, and multimethod assessment of the relevant constructs. Continued investigations in this area would be strengthened by a more detailed investigation of the emergence of a moderational structure as a function of age (e.g., Turner & Cole, 1994).

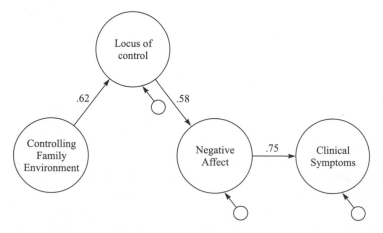

Figure 6.3. Structural model linking family environment, control beliefs, negative affect, and clinical symptoms.

Control of the Self: Internal Events and Attributes

Research related to mastery and control has moved beyond early correlational studies to investigate potential mechanisms underlying these phenomena. Dweck and her colleagues (e.g., Dweck, 1996; Dweck & Leggett, 1988) have examined cognitive risk factors related to persistence, mainly in the context of academic achievement. Dweck and Leggett's (1988) model specifies two critical dimensions: (1) *goal orientation* and (2) *ability theory*. Dweck (1991) posited that children who approach a task as an opportunity for self-evaluation (*performance goals*) would be less likely to persist on a challenging task than children who view a task as an opportunity for practice and improvement (*learning goals*). According to Dweck, this goal orientation is driven to some extent by children's ability theories, which reflect whether children perceive their abilities as fixed or malleable over time. Children who see their abilities as malleable are called *incremental theorists*, whereas those who see their abilities as inflexible are called *entity theorists*. In a number of studies, Dweck and colleagues demonstrated that children who see their abilities as malleable (*incremental theorists*) show a higher likelihood of a learning goal orientation; and children who see their abilities as inflexible (*entity theorists*) are more likely to demonstrate a performance goal orientation and thus to persist on challenging academic tasks (e.g., Dweck & Leggett, 1988). Developed within the context of academic achievement, Dweck's model has strong implications for motivation, and hence is likely to have theoretical connections with Gray's (1982, 1987) model involving the BIS.

Before examining those connections further, another important consideration of Dweck's model deserves attention—specifically, the age at which children may develop this capacity to form trait conceptions of their own academic abilities (i.e., entity theories). That is, if young children do not have the capacity for cognitive representation of trait stability, then the emergence of persistent maladaptive responses to challenge might be much less common before middle childhood. Along these lines, Dweck and Elliott (1983) argued that children younger than about 9 or 10 years in fact do not show the ability to form stable trait conceptions of their own intelligence and should therefore be more insulated against demonstrating nonpersistence in the face of failure experiences.

More recently, however, Burhans and Dweck (1995) updated this model in light of accumulating evidence for nonpersistence found in children as young as preschoolers (see also Dweck, 1991, 1996). This more recent model now suggests that a child need only possess a sense that a task reflects on his or her general self-worth to demonstrate a nonpersisting style in the face of a challenge. Thus, although holding an entity theory may predispose a performance-goal orientation, an entity theory is not necessary for such an orientation. When these ideas are viewed together with Dweck and Leggett's (1988) prior formulation, one would predict that the greatest likelihood for helplessness should arise when the child views a negative outcome as both

(a) an indication of general self-worth and (b) attributable to an invariant aspect of the self. This formulation allows for some critical variables to arise early in development (i.e., a sense of contingent self-worth) and for additional intensifying factors to arise later in development (i.e., conceptions of trait invariance).

Exactly how do these ideas relate to the present biopsychosocial model of control? To begin with, a sense of conditional self-worth and goal orientation appear to be related to negative emotion and performance, but not necessarily to issues of control. Specifically, a child who possesses a sense of self-worth conditional on outcomes may (but does not have to) experience anxious emotion when involved in tasks that determine those outcomes. In other words, such a child would struggle to achieve a result that did not reflect badly on himself or herself. A performance orientation serves to strengthen the aversive stimulus, in that an outcome that reflects on self-worth will be more intense than one that does not. The stakes are simply higher, which should increase anxious emotion and non-persistence—a finding that has been observed in younger children (Dweck, 1991).

In contrast, the development of an entity theory is relevant not only to the idea of a sense of diminished control; it may also be a critical generalization of a sense of diminished control, in that an entity theory implies lack of control over the self and that one's abilities cannot be changed. Such a child would give up quickly in the face of initial failure, owing to the belief that any struggle to achieve an outcome that reflects positively about the self would be useless, not only because the outcome is difficult to achieve, but also because a positive outcome could not change one's initial view of one's own ability, which is thought by entity theorists to be fixed.

A central premise of the present model is that a sense of diminished control increases BIS activity. However, the work of Dweck and others highlights the potential importance of the various domains in which this sense may develop. It is possible that generalization of a sense of diminished control can occur along the boundary of features within and not within the self. In other words, it is bad to perceive that aspects of the world are not within one's control, but perhaps even worse to believe further that aspects the self are not within one's control, which can occur as the child develops the capacity for an entity theory. This implies that the stored regularities informing the BIS could become more influential at some point in development, as a function of the child's increased capacity to comprehend or represent notions of permanence about the self.

Interestingly, the evidence for late emergence of the capacity for an entity theory may help to explain the well-known pattern that many anxiety disorders are common in children, yet such disorders as depression and panic do not become common until adolescence (Albano, Chorpita, & Barlow, 1996; Hammen & Rudolph, 1996; Mattis & Ollendick, 1997). Anxiety disorders in youth frequently involve external stimuli (e.g., animals, bullies, caretaker), and it is the theme of this chapter that the severity of these disorders can be amplified or attenuated by the child's sense of control over these stimuli. For example, children who feel secure that they can control access to their caretaker should be less likely to develop separation anxiety. In later childhood and adolescence, such emerging disorders as panic and depression are characterized in contrast by a greater involvement with internal stimuli (e.g., interoceptive cues, beliefs about the self). A sense of control over these internal stimuli is similarly likely to influence the severity of the disorder. A sense of diminished control plays a role in disorders of emotion at all ages, but an important distinction concerns the domains to which this applies. Control over internal events is of much greater relevance to such disorders as panic disorder, generalized anxiety disorder, and major depressive disorder. Individuals with these syndromes are likely to be concerned that something is unalterably wrong with them, that they cannot calm down, feel better, or stop worrying. Thus, it could be that the capacity for representations of trait invariance (i.e., entity theories) is prerequisite to a sense of diminished control over aspects of the self, and that such a developmental progression is one factor underlying the marked change in phenomenology of negative emotional disorders observed at the beginning of adolescence. These ideas are of course speculative and warrant further research.

In summary, the present model suggests that development of a sense of control or diminished control may be specific to particular domains and that these domains may be linked in a developmental sequence, as the child comes to terms with the caregiver, the world, and the self. Thus, articulation of this possible sequence of control within specific domains may necessitate investigation of more complex dimensions than can be represented by a generalized locus of control. Again, confirmation of many of these ideas awaits considerable investigation.

The Neuroendocrine Pathway

So far, the present model has suggested that nearly all of the operations relevant to control are based in the stored regularities and the comparator subsystem of the BIS. However, there is considerable evidence that there exists another pathway from experience with low control to negative emotions, specifically involving neuroendocrine responding and biological self-regulation of the BIS and related brain systems. The understanding of these principles is best derived from a closer examination of the physiology associated with exposure to stress (see also Gunnar, 1994; Gunnar, this volume). Dienstbier (1989), arguing that there are two separate short-term physiological responses to stress, described these as: (1) a catecholamine response, involving the sympathetic nervous system and adrenal medulla; and (2) a cortisol response, involving the hypothalamic–pituitary–adrenocortical (HPA) axis. Reviewing a great number of studies from both human and nonhuman populations, Dienstbier concluded that the long-term ill-effects of stress involve either catecholamine depletion or chronic cortisol secretion.

At the heart of Dienstbier's model is the idea that appropriate activation of these systems increases their efficiency, a process Dienstbier labeled "toughening." In one sense, the healthy development of these stress systems are akin to exercising muscle tissue. Small amounts of moderate exercise will increase the capacity of a muscle, whereas insufficient restorative periods or overstraining can lead to breakdown of the muscle. Dienstbier (1989) described how intermittent stressors activate the catecholamine response; and in predictable situations or those allowing coping action, the cortisol response will be minimized and hence more efficient (cf. "toughening up"; Miller, 1980). An organism experiencing these types of stressors will actually undergo an increase in catecholamine responding potential, ultimately leading to improvements in performance and functioning under later stress (e.g., O'Hanlon & Beatty, 1976). So long as there are sufficient intervals between stressful events to allow catecholamine restoration, and there is enough control to inhibit excessive HPA activity, the organism will benefit from this exposure. In this manner, Dienstbier has identified possible biological substrates of the development of mastery, which represents the other end of the control dimension.

Other important details emerge from examination of the operation of the HPA system. Research in adult humans has demonstrated that individuals with negative emotional disorders appear to be insensitive to the amount of cortisol in their system. The *dexamethasone suppression* test indirectly assesses pituitary feedback sensitivity to cortisol by introducing dexamethasone (an agent indistinguishable from cortisol by the pituitary gland) into the individual. Under normal circumstances, the pituitary gland should respond to the presence of dexamethasone by decreasing (i.e., suppressing) the release of adrenocorticotropic releasing hormone (ACTH), a hormone which precedes cortisol secretion in the neurohormonal sequence of the HPA system. It has been shown, however, that some adults with anxiety or depression do not show these normal rates of suppression (e.g., Carroll, 1985; Schweizer, Swenson, Winokur, Rickels, & Maislin, 1986).

Inspired by these ideas, Sapolsky (1989) attempted to ascertain the physiological source of excessive cortisol secretion. In multiple investigations using wild olive baboons, hypercortisolism was found disproportionately among those who were lower in social rank. These baboons were frequent targets of displaced and unpredictable aggression and more disruption in attempted consortships with females. One might infer that glucocorticoid dysregulation might be the cause of impaired social functioning; however, other data do not fully support this contention. For example, it has been found that as animals' social ranks change over time, changes in psychophysiological profiles of these animals will follow (Rose, Bernstein, Gordon, & Catlin, 1974). Reviewing observations that hypercortisolism was high not only among the displaced males but also among the high-ranking males in unstable hierarchies, Sapolsky (1989) concluded that it was not subordinance per se, but the experience of low control or instability of rank, that was responsible for hypercortisolism (Sapolsky and Ray, 1989).

A common theme, then, of both Dienstbier and Sapolsky is that the degree to which the organism can control the stimuli with which it is confronted appears to be responsible for the differential long-term effects of stress on neuroendocrine functioning. According to Dienstbier (1989, pp. 86–87), "in a range of subjects from rats to mice to primates, exposure to stressors with minimal predictability, control, or feedback ... results in heightened cortisol responses"; and "when stressful situations are sufficiently extended, they also lead to catecholamine depletion." It has been shown that the effects of such events can lead to damage to the systems themselves, involving a feedforward cycle that likely contributes further to increased negative bias (Sapolsky, 1992). Thus, it is possible that a history of low control may operate not only through establishing maladaptive stored regularities, but also through damage to, and dysregulation of, the systems that underlie negative emotion.

Conceptual Model

The collective evidence reviewed suggests a number of important points. First, it appears that experience with lack of control may lead to the subsequent processing of events as not in one's control. This sense may over time become fixed and begin to play an important role in the development of negative affect and its pathological manifestations, such as anxiety disorders and depression. In other words, a sense of diminished control is possibly a mediator between stressful events and negative affect early in development, and over time this sense of diminished control becomes a moderator of the expression of negative affect (see fig. 6.2).

The model depicts further that the establishment of a sense of high or low control occurs in a sequence of domains, speculated here as minimally including aspects of the caregiver, the environment, and the self. If such a sequence were to exist, it is likely that the establishment of a sense of diminished control within an earlier domain influences the likelihood of developing that same cognitive pattern within the subsequent domain. Such a model is detailed in fig. 6.4. Note that within the first column, the relation between events and emotion are purely mediational. If a low sense of control is established within this first domain, this sense is posited to moderate or color the nature of events encountered in the second domain (diagonal arrow). In the second domain, this sequence is played out again, and so on until early adulthood. By this time it is possible that the cumulative developmental effects have established a fixed cognitive vulnerability that amplifies the BIS activity in response to events. It is clear from the figure that if a child begins in the first column with high temperamental BIS activity and the events are frequently uncontrollable, the child is likely to enter the next domain processing events as uncontrollable, even when they are not. Thus, over the course of development, the actual nature of the events for the

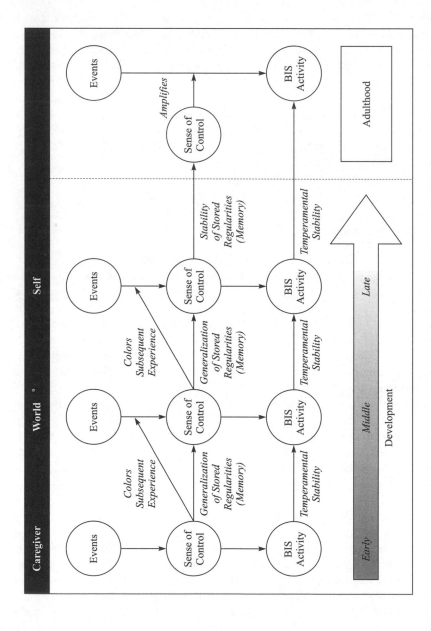

Figure 6.4. Control-based model of the development of vulnerability for anxiety and depression.

child become less influential as cognitive factors begin to color experience to a greater and greater degree.

Clearly, the evidence for such a detailed network is far from complete. Nevertheless, a diversity of research supports one or another section of the model. For example, it is well known that the moderational structure in the rightmost part of fig. 6.4 is operative with anxiety and mood disorders (e.g., Sanderson et al., 1989). A number of studies support the idea of temperamental stability (Hirshfeld et al., 1992) and of memory as a mechanism for the stability of cognitive vulnerabilities (e.g., Daleiden, 1998). Finally, new evidence supports the mediational structure in the second column of the figure as well (see fig. 3; Chorpita, Brown, et al., 1998). As mentioned at the outset of the chapter, the main task facing researchers may be largely one of integration. One hopes that the accumulation of detailed evidence over the next 15 years will bring the overall picture into even sharper focus.

Note

Prease address correspondence Bruce F. Chorpita, Department of Psychology, University of Hawaii at Manoa, 2430 Campus Road, Honolulu, HI 96822, USA. E-mail: chorpita@hawaii.edu.

References

Abramson, L. Y., Metalsky, G. I., & Alloy, L. B. (1989). Hopelessness and depression: A theory based subtype of depression. *Psychological Review, 96*, 358–392.

Achenbach, T. M. (1991). *Manual for the Child Behavior Checklist/4–18 and 1991 Profile*. Burlington, VT: University of Vermont Department of Psychiatry.

Albano, A. M., Chorpita, B. F., & Barlow, D. H. (1996). Childhood anxiety disorders. In E. J. Mash and R. A. Barkley (Eds.), *Child psychopathology* (pp. 196–241). New York: Guilford.

Alloy, L. B., Kelly, K. A., Mineka, S., & Clements, C. M. (1990). Comorbidity of anxiety and depressive disorders: A helplessness–hopelessness perspective. In J. D. Maser & C. R. Cloninger (Eds.), *Comorbidity of mood and anxiety disorders* (pp. 499–543). Washington, DC: American Psychiatric Press.

Bandura, A. (1986). *Social foundations of thought and action*. Englewood Cliffs, NJ: Prentice-Hall.

Barlow, D. H. (1988). *Anxiety and its disorders: The nature and treatment of anxiety and panic*. New York: Guilford.

Barlow, D. H. (1991). Disorders of emotion. *Psychological Inquiry, 2*, 58–71.

Barlow, D. H., Chorpita, B. F., & Turovsky, J. (1996). Fear, panic, anxiety, and the disorders of emotion. In D. A. Hope (Ed.), *Nebraska symposium on motivation: Perspectives on anxiety, panic, and fear: Vol. 43*, (pp. 251–328). Lincoln, NE: University of Nebraska Press.

Baron, R. M., & Kenny, D. A. (1986). The moderator–mediator variable distinction in social psychological research: Conceptual, strategic, and statistical considerations. *Journal of Personality and Social Psychology, 51*, 1173–1182.

Barrett, P. M., Rapee, R. M., Dadds, M. R., & Ryan, S. M. (1996). Family enhancement of cognitive style in anxious and aggressive children: Threat bias and the FEAR effect. *Journal of Abnormal Child Psychology, 24,* 187–203.

Bates, J. E., & Bales, K. (1988). The role of attachment in the development of behavior problems. In J. Belsky & T. Nezworski (Eds.), *Clinical implications of early attachment* (pp. 253–259). Hillsdale, NJ: Erlbaum.

Beck, A. T., & Emery, G. (1985). *Anxiety disorders and phobias: A cognitive perspective.* New York: Basic Books.

Beck, A. T., Rush, A. J., Shaw, B. F., & Emery, G. (1979). *Cognitive therapy of depression.* New York: Guilford.

Biglan, A. (1987). A behavior–analytic critique of Bandura's self-efficacy theory. *The Behavior Analyst, 10,* 1–15.

Biocca, L. J. (1985). The relationship among locus of control, perceived parenting, and sex-role attributes in adolescence. *Dissertation Abstracts International, 47,* 2193B.

Bowlby, J. (1969). *Attachment and loss: Vol. 1. Attachment.* New York: Basic Books.

Bowlby, J. (1973). *Attachment and loss: Vol. 2. Separation.* New York: Basic Books.

Bowlby, J. (1980). *Attachment and loss: Vol. 3. Loss, sadness, and depression.* New York: Basic Books.

Brady, E., & Kendall, P. C. (1992). Comorbidity of anxiety and depression in children and adolescents. *Psychological Bulletin, 111,* 244–255.

Bretherton, I. (1992). The origins of attachment theory: John Bowlby and Mary Ainsworth. *Developmental Psychology, 28,* 759–775.

Brooks, V. B. (1986). How does the limbic system assist motor learning? A limbic comparator hypothesis. *Brain, Behavior, and Evolution, 29,* 29–53.

Brown, T. A., Chorpita, B. F., & Barlow, D. H. (1998). Structural relationships among dimensions of the DSM-IV anxiety and mood disorders and dimensions of negative affect, positive affect, and autonomic arousal. *Journal of Abnormal Psychology, 107,* 179–192.

Brown, T. A., Chorpita, B. F., Korotitsch, W., & Barlow, D. H. (1997). Psychometric properties of the Depression Anxiety Stress Scales (DASS) in clinical samples. *Behaviour Research and Therapy, 35,* 79–89.

Bryant, B. K., & Trockel, J. F., (1976). Personal history of control of psychological stress related to locus of control orientation among college women. *Journal of Consulting and Clinical Psychology, 44,* 266–271.

Burhans, K. K., & Dweck, C. S. (1995). Helplessness in early childhood: The role of contingent worth. *Child Development, 66,* 1719–1738.

Campbell, S. B. (1989). Developmental perspectives. In T. H. Ollendick & M. Hersen (Eds.), *Handbook of child psychopathology* (2nd ed.). New York: Plenum.

Carroll, B. J. (1985). Dexamethasone suppression test: A review of contemporary confusion. *Journal of Clinical Psychiatry, 46,* 13–24.

Carton, J. S., & Nowicki, S. (1994). Antecedents of individual differences in locus of control of reinforcement: A critical review. *Genetic, Social, and General Psychology Monographs, 120,* 31–81.

Chandler, T. A., Wolf, F. M., Cook, B., & Dugovics, D. A. (1980). Parental correlates of locus of control in fifth graders: An attempt at experimentation in the home. *Merrill–Palmer Quarterly, 26,* 183–195.

Chorpita, B. F., & Barlow, D. H. (1998). The development of anxiety: The role of control in the early environment. *Psychological Bulletin, 124,* 3–21.

Chorpita, B. F., Albano, A. M., & Barlow, D. H. (1996). Cognitive processing in children: Relationship to anxiety and family influences. *Journal of Clinical Child Psychology*, 25, 170–176.

Chorpita, B. F., Albano, A. M., & Barlow, D. H. (1998). The structure of negative emotions in a clinical sample of children and adolescents. *Journal of Abnormal Psychology*, 107, 74–85.

Chorpita, B. F., Brown, T. A., & Barlow, D. H. (1998). Perceived control as a mediator of family environment in etiological models of childhood anxiety. *Behavior Therapy*, 29, 457–476.

Clark, D. M. (1986). A cognitive approach to panic. *Behaviour Research and Therapy*, 24, 461–470.

Clark, L. A., & Watson, D. (1991). Tripartite model of anxiety and depression: Psychometric evidence and taxonomic implications. *Journal of Abnormal Psychology*, 100, 316–336.

Clark, L. A., Watson, D., & Mineka, S. (1994). Temperament, personality, and the mood and anxiety disorders. *Journal of Abnormal Psychology*, 103, 103–116.

Cole, D. A., & Turner, J. E. (1993). Models of cognitive mediation and moderation in child depression. *Journal of Abnormal Psychology*, 102, 271–281.

Crandall, V. C., Katkovsky, W., & Crandall, V. J. (1965). Children's belief in their own control of reinforcements in intellectual–academic achievement situations. *Child Development*, 36, 91–109.

Daleiden, E. (1998). Childhood anxiety and memory functioning: A comparison of systemic and processing accounts. *Journal of Experimental Child Psychology*, 68, 216–235.

Davis, W. L., & Phares, E. J. (1969). Parental antecedents of internal–external control of reinforcement. *Psychological Reports*, 24, 427–436.

Dienstbier, R. A. (1989). Arousal and physiological toughness: Implications for mental and physical health. *Psychological Review*, 96, 84–100.

Diethelm, K. (1991) Mutter–Kind Interaktion: Entwicklung von ersten Kontrollüberzeugungen [Mother–child interaction: Development of early control beliefs]. Bern, Switzerland. Huber.

Dweck, C. S. (1991). Self-theories and goals: Their role in motivation, personality, and development. In R. Dienstbier (Ed.), *Nebraska symposium on motivation and emotion: Vol. 36* (pp. 199–235). Lincoln, NE: University of Nebraska Press.

Dweck, C. S. (1996). Implicit theories as organizers of goals and behavior. In P. M. Gollwitzer & J. A. Bargh (Eds.), *The psychology of action: Linking cognition and motivation to behavior* (pp. 69–90). New York: Guilford.

Dweck, C. S., & Elliott, E. S. (1983). Achievement motivation. In E. M. Hetherington (Ed.), *Socialization, personality, and social development* (pp. 643–691). New York: Wiley.

Dweck, C. S., & Leggett, E. L. (1988). A social-cognitive approach to motivation and personality. *Psychological Review*, 95, 256–273.

Ehiobuche, I. (1988). Obsessive–compulsive neurosis in relation to parental child rearing patterns amongst Greek, Italian, and Anglo-Australian subjects. *Acta Psychiatrica Scandinavica*, 78, 115–120.

Finch, A. J., & Nelson, W. M. (1974). Locus of control and anxiety in emotionally disturbed children. *Psychological Reports*, 35, 469–470.

Fowles, D. C. (1995). A motivational theory of psychopathology. In W. Spaulding (Ed.), *Nebraska symposium on motivation: Integrated views of motivation, cognition, and emotion: Vol. 41.* Lincoln, NE: University of Nebraska Press.

Geer, J. H., Davison, G. C., & Gatchel, R. I. (1970). Reduction of stress in humans through nonveridical perceived control of aversive stimulation. *Journal of Personality and Social Psychology, 16*, 731–738.

Gordon, D. A., Nowicki, S., & Wichern, F. (1981). Observed maternal and child behaviors in a dependency-producing task as a function of children's locus of control orientation. *Merrill–Palmer Quarterly, 27*, 43–51.

Gotlib, I. H., Mount, J. H., Cordie, N. I., & Whiffen, V. E. (1988). Depression and perception of early parenting: A longitudinal investigation. *British Journal of Psychiatry, 152*, 24–27.

Gray, J. A. (1982). *The neuropsychology of anxiety.* New York: Oxford University Press.

Gray, J. A. (1987). *The psychology of fear and stress* (2nd ed.). Cambridge: Cambridge University Press.

Gray, J. A., & McNaughton, N. (1996). The neuropsychology of anxiety: A reprise. In D. A. Hope (Ed.), *Nebraska symposium on motivation: Perspectives on anxiety, panic, and fear: Vol. 43* (pp. 61–134). Lincoln, NE: University of Nebraska Press.

Gunnar, M. R. (1980). Control, warning signals, and distress in infancy. *Developmental Psychology, 16*, 281–289.

Gunnar, M. R. (1994). Psychoendocrine studies of temperament and stress in early childhood: Expanding current models. In J. E. Bates & T. D. Wachs (Eds.), *Temperament: Individual differences at the interface of biology and behavior* (pp. 175–198). Washington, DC: American Psychological Association.

Hammen, C., & Rudolph, K. D. (1996). Childhood depression. In E. J. Mash and R. A. Barkley (Eds.), *Child psychopathology* (pp. 153–195). New York: Guilford.

Hammen, C., Adrian, C., & Hiroto, D. (1988). A longitudinal test of the attributional vulnerability model in children at risk for depression. *British Journal of Clinical Psychology, 27*, 37–46.

Hirshfeld, D. R., Rosenbaum, J. F., Biederman, J., Bolduc, E. A., Faraone, S. V., Snidman, N., Reznick, J. S., & Kagan, J. (1992). Stable behavioral inhibition and its association with anxiety disorder. *Journal of the American Academy of Child and Adolescent Psychiatry, 31*, 103–111.

Hoehn-Saric, R., & McLeod, D. R. (1985). Locus of control in chronic anxiety disorders. *Acta Psychiatrica Scandinavia, 72*, 529–535.

Hoffman, J. A., & Teyber, E. C., (1979). Some relationships between sibling age, space, and personality. *Merrill–Palmer Quarterly, 25*, 77–80.

Joiner, T. E., Jr, Catanzaro, S. J., & Laurent, J. (1996). Tripartite structure of positive and negative affect, depression, and anxiety, in child psychiatric inpatients. *Journal of Abnormal Psychology, 105*, 401–409.

Kagan, J., Reznick, J. S., & Snidman, N. (1987). The physiology and psychology of behavioral inhibition. *Child Development, 58*, 1459–1473.

Kendall, P. C. (1992). Childhood coping: Avoiding a lifetime of anxiety. *Behavioural Change, 9*, 1–8.

Kendler, K. S., Neale, M. C., Kessler, R. C., Heath, A. C., & Eaves, L. J. (1992). Major depression and generalized anxiety disorder: Same genes, (partly) different environments? *Archives of General Psychiatry, 49*, 716–722.

King, N. J., Ollendick, T. H, & Gullone, E. (1991). Negative affectivity in children and adolescents: Relations between anxiety and depression. *Clinical Psychology Review, 11*, 441–459.

Kovacs, M. (1981). Rating scales to assess depression in preschool children. *Acta Paedopsychiatry, 46*, 305–315.

Krampen, G. (1982). Schulische und familiäre Entwicklungsbedingungen von Kontrollüberzeugungen [School and familial conditions for developing control beliefs]. *Schweizerische Zeitschrift für Psychologie und ihre Andwendugen, 41*, 16–35.

Lazarus, R. S. (1966). Behaviour reversal vs. non-directive therapy vs. advice in effecting behaviour change. *Behaviour Research and Therapy, 4*, 209–212.

Lazarus, R. S. (1968). Emotions and adaptation: Conceptual and empirical relations. In W. J. Arnold (Ed.), *Nebraska symposium on motivation: Vol. 16*. Lincoln, NE: University of Nebraska Press.

Lazarus, R. S., Averill, J. R., & Opton, E. M., Jr (1970). Towards a cognitive theory of emotion. In M. Arnold (Ed.), *Feelings and emotion*. New York: Academic Press.

Lewis, M. (1990). Challenges to the study of developmental psychopathology. In M. Lewis & S. M. Miller (Eds.), *Handbook of developmental psychopathology*. New York: Plenum.

Lewis, M., Feirig, C., McGuffog, C., & Jaskir, J. (1984). Predicting psychopathology in six-year-olds from early social relations. *Child Development, 55*, 123–136.

Lonigan, C., Carey, M., & Finch, A. J. (1994). Anxiety and depression in children: Negative affectivity and the utility of self-reports. *Journal of Consulting and Clinical Psychology, 62*, 1000–1008.

Lovibond, P. F., & Lovibond, S. H. (1995). The structure of negative emotional states: Comparison of the Depression Anxiety Stress Scales (DASS) with the Beck Depression and Anxiety Inventories. *Behavior Research and Therapy, 33*, 335–342.

Maier, S. F. (1970). Failure to escape traumatic shock: Incompatible skeletal motor response or learned helplessness? *Learning and Motivation, 1*, 157–170.

Mandler, G. (1972). Helplessness: Theory and research in anxiety. In C. Spielberger (Ed.), *Anxiety: Current trends in theory and research: Vol. 1* (pp. 359–374). New York: Academic Press.

Mattis, S. G., & Ollendick, T. H. (1997). Panic in children and adolescents: A developmental analysis. In T. H. Ollendick & R. J. Prinz (Eds.), *Advances in clinical child psychology: Vol. 19* (pp. 27–74). New York: Plenum.

McCauley, E., Mitchell, J. R., Burke, P., & Moss, S. (1988). Cognitive attributes of depression in children and adolescents. *Journal of Consulting and Clinical Psychology, 56*, 903–908.

McNally, R. J. (1996). Cognitive bias in the anxiety disorders. In D. A. Hope (Ed.), *Nebraska symposium on motivation: Perspectives on anxiety, panic, and fear: Vol. 43* (pp. 211–250). Lincoln, NE: University of Nebraska Press.

Miller, N. E. (1980). A perspective on the effects of stress and coping on disease and health. In S. Levine & H. Ursin (Eds.), *Coping and health* (pp. 323–354). New York: Plenum.

Mineka, S., & Zinbarg, R. (1996). Conditioning and ethological models of anxiety disorders. In D. A. Hope (Ed.), *Nebraska symposium on motivation: Perspectives on anxiety, panic, and fear: Vol. 43* (pp. 135–210). Lincoln, NE: University of Nebraska Press.

Mineka, S., Gunnar, M., & Champoux, M. (1986). Control and early socioemotional development: Infant rhesus monkeys reared in controllable versus uncontrollable environments. *Child Development, 57,* 1241–1256.

Minor, T. R., Dess, N. K., & Overmier, J. B. (1991). Inverting the traditional view of "learned helplessness." In M. R. Denny (Ed.), *Fear, avoidance and phobias* (pp. 87–133). Hillsdale, NJ: Lawrence Erlbaum Associates.

Moos, R. H. (1986). *Family Environment Scale manual* (2nd ed.). Palo Alto, CA: Consulting Psychologist Press.

Mowrer, O. H., & Viek, P. (1948). An experimental analogue of fear from a sense of helplessness. *Journal of Abnormal Social Psychology, 83,* 193–200.

Nowicki, S., & Strickland, B. R. (1973). A locus of control scale for children. *Journal of Consulting and Clinical Psychology, 40,* 148–154.

Nunn, G. D. (1988). Concurrent validity between the Nowicki–Strickland Locus of Control Scale and the State-Trait Anxiety Inventory for Children. *Educational and Psychological Measurement, 48,* 435–438.

O'Hanlon, J. F., & Beatty, J. (1976). Catecholamine correlates of radar monitoring performance. *Biological Psychology, 4,* 293–304.

Overmier, J. B., & Seligman, M. E. P. (1967). Effects of inescapable shock upon subsequent escape and avoidance behavior. *Journal of Comparative and Physiological Psychology, 63,* 23–33.

Parker, G. (1979a). Parental characteristics in relation to depressive disorders. *British Journal of Psychiatry, 134,* 138–147.

Parker, G. (1979b). Parental deprivation and depression in a non-clinical group. *Australian and New Zealand Journal of Psychiatry, 13,* 51–56.

Parker, G. (1979c). Reported parental characteristics in relation to trait depression and anxiety levels in a non-clinical group. *Australian and New Zealand Journal of Psychiatry, 13,* 260–264.

Parker, G. (1979d). Reported parental characteristics of agoraphobics and social phobics. *British Journal of Psychiatry, 135,* 555–560.

Parker, G. (1981). Parental representation of patients with anxiety neurosis. *Acta Psychiatrica Scandinavica, 63,* 33–36.

Parker, G. (1983). *Parental overprotection: A risk factor in psychosocial development.* New York: Grune & Stratton.

Parker, G., Tupling, H., & Brown, L. B. (1979). A parental bonding instrument. *British Journal of Psychiatry, 52,* 1–11.

Perris, C., Jacobsson, L., Lindstrom, H., von Knorring, L., & Perris, H. (1980). Development of a new inventory for assessing memories of parental rearing behavior. *Acta Psychiatrica Scandinavica, 61,* 265–274.

Plantes, M. M., Prusoff, B. A., Brennan, J., & Parker, G. (1988). Parental representations of depressed outpatients from a USA sample. *Journal of Affective Disorders, 15,* 149–155.

Reiss, D., Hetherington, E. M., Plomin, R., Howe, G. W., Simmens, S. J., Henderson, S. H., O'Connor, T. J., Bussell, D. A., Anderson, E. R., & Law, T. (1995). Genetic questions for environmental studies: Differential parenting and psychopathology in adolescence. *Archives of General Psychiatry, 52,* 925–936.

Rose, R., Bernstein, I., Gordon, T., & Catlin, S. (1974). Androgen and aggression: A review and recent findings in primates. In R. Holloway (Ed.), *Primate aggression, territoriality, and xenophobia* (pp. 271–293). New York: Academic Press.

Rotter, J. B. (1954). *Social learning and clinical psychology.* Englewood Cliffs, NJ: Prentice-Hall.

Rotter, J. B. (1966). Generalized expectancies for internal versus external control of reinforcement. *Psychological Monographs, 80,* No. 609.

Rutter, M. (1980). Attachment and the development of social relationships. In M. Rutter (Ed.), *Scientific foundation of developmental psychiatry.* London: Heinemann.

Sanderson, W. C., Rapee, R. M., & Barlow, D. H. (1989). The influence of an illusion of control on panic attacks induced via the inhalation of 5.5% carbon dioxide enriched air. *Archives of General Psychiatry, 46,* 157–164.

Sapolsky, R. M. (1989). Hypercortisolism among socially subordinate wild baboons originates at the CNS level. *Archives of General Psychiatry, 46,* 1047–1051.

Sapolsky, R. M. (1992). Stress, the aging brain, and the mechanisms of neuron death. Cambridge, MA: MIT Press.

Sapolsky, R. M., & Ray, J. C. (1989). Styles of dominance and their endocrine correlates among wild olive baboons (*papio anubis*). *American Journal of Primatology, 18,* 1–13

Schneewind, K. A. (1995). Impact of family processes on control beliefs. In A. Bandura (Ed.), *Self-efficacy in changing societies* (pp. 114–148). New York: Cambridge University Press.

Schneewind, K. A., & Pfeiffer, P. (1978). Elteriches Erziehungsverhalten und kindliche Selbsverstandwortlichkeit [Parenting and children's self-responsibility]. In K. A. Schneewind & H. Lukesch (Eds.), *Familiäre Sozialisation [Family socialization]* (pp. 190–205). Stuttgart: Klett–Cotta.

Schweizer, E. E., Swenson, C. M. Winokur, A., Rickels, K., & Maislin, G. (1986). The dexamethasone suppression test in generalized anxiety disorder. *Archives of General Psychiatry, 149,* 320–322.

Seligman, M. E. P., & Maier, S. F. (1967). Failure to escape traumatic shock. *Journal of Experimental Psychology, 74,* 1–9.

Silove, D., Parker, G., Hadzi-Pavlovic, D., Manicavasagar, V, & Blaszczynski, A. (1991). Parental representations of patients with panic disorder and generalized anxiety disorder. *British Journal of Psychiatry, 159,* 835–841.

Skinner, E. A. (1986). The origins of young children's perceived control: Mother contingent and sensitive behavior. *International Journal of Behavioral Development, 9,* 359–382.

Sroufe, L. A. (1983). Infant–caregiver attachment and patterns of adaptation in preschool: The roots of maladaptation and competence. In M. Perlmutter (Ed.), *Minnesota symposium on child psychology: Vol. 16* (pp. 41–83). Hillsdale, NJ: Erlbaum.

Sroufe, L. A. (1990). Considering the normal and abnormal together: The essence of developmental psychopathology. *Development and Psychopathology, 2,* 335–347.

Thompson, R. A. (1998). Early sociopersonality development. In W. Damon (Series Ed.) & N. Eisenberg (Vol. Ed.), *Handbook of child psychology: Vol. 3. Social, emotional, and personality development* (pp. 25–104). New York: Wiley.

Turner, J. E., & Cole D. A. (1994). Developmental differences in cognitive diatheses for child depression. *Journal of Abnormal Child Psychology, 22,* 15–32.

Turner, S. M., Beidel, D. C., & Costello, A. (1987). Psychopathology in the offspring of anxiety disorders patients. *Journal of Consulting and Clinical Psychology, 55,* 229–235.

van Ijzendoorn, M. H., & Bakermans-Kranenburg, M. J. (1996). Attachment representations in mothers, fathers, adolescents, and clinical group: A meta-analytic search for normative data. *Journal of Consulting and Clinical Psychology, 64,* 8–21.

Vasey, M. W., Daleiden, E. L., Williams, L. L., & Brown, L. M. (1995). Biased attention in childhood anxiety disorders: A preliminary study. *Journal of Abnormal Child Psychology, 23,* 267–279.

Walter, D. A., & Ziegler, C. A. (1980). The effects of birth order on locus of control. *Bulletin of the Psychonomic Society, 15,* 293–294.

Washington, R. A. (1974). The relationship between children's school performances and parent participation as a function of the movement toward community control of the schools. *Dissertation Abstracts International, 35,* 4202B.

Watson, D., & Clark, L. A. (1984). Negative affectivity: The disposition to experience negative emotional states. *Psychological Bulletin, 96,* 465–490.

Weiss, J. M. (1971a). Effects of coping behavior in different warning signal conditions on stress pathology in rats. *Journal of Comparative and Physiological Psychology, 77,* 1–13.

Weiss, J. M. (1971b). Effects of punishing the coping response (conflict) on stress pathology in rats. *Journal of Comparative and Physiological Psychology, 77,* 14–21.

7

The Role of Glucocorticoids in Anxiety Disorders: A Critical Analysis

MEGAN R. GUNNAR

A recent theory of the etiology of anxiety disorders and depression (Rosen & Schulkin, 1998) argues that increased release of glucocorticoids and neuro-peptides (in particular, corticotropin-releasing hormone) during fear increases the excitability of fear circuits and plays a role in the organization of pathological anxiety in humans and animals. This theory builds on related models of the role of the HPA (hypothalamic–pituitary–adrenocortical) axis in the pathophysiology of anxiety and depression (e.g., Gold, Goodwin, & Chrousos, 1988; Schulkin, McEwen, & Gold, 1994; Schulkin, Gold, & McEwen, 1998). According to this theory, pathological anxiety reflects an exaggeration of normal anticipatory anxiety or anxious apprehension. Anticipatory anxiety occurs when danger is first encountered and is still distal, and can be distinguished from defensive behaviors (fight/flight) that occur when the danger is proximal or has already been encountered (Blanchard & Blanchard, 1988, Fanselow, 1994). Anxious apprehension involves phasic immobility or freezing, autonomic changes (e.g., increased sympathetic discharge), increased neuroendocrine activity (e g., elevated levels of glucocorticoids), heightened reflexive responses to sensory stimuli (e.g., fear-potentiated startle), hypoalgesia, and increased urination and defecation (Rosen & Schulkin, 1998). According to the theory, the amygdala and its connections play a central role in anxious apprehension (see also LeDoux, 1996).

Associative processes are expected to be critical in producing the neural sensitization or kindling that leads to enhanced perception and response to later threat and danger (LeDoux, 1996). Nonetheless, it is argued that in the presence of increased glucocorticoids and corticotropin releasing hormone (CRH), these processes are enhanced through a cascade of biomolecular events that includes increased gene expression of immediate–early genes (Makino, Gold & Schulkin, 1994; Watts & Sanchez-Watts, 1995). Accordingly, hyperexcitability of the CRH–HPA system forms an important biological diathesis for the development of anxiety and depressive disorders.

This is a potentially important approach to the biological bases of anxiety disorders and depression. As a researcher who has spent about 20 years studying responsivity of the HPA system in infants and children, I am gratified to find a theory suggesting that what I have been studying may provide clues to the etiology of affective pathology. However, my familiarity with the area also gives me pause. How firmly do the existing data in humans support the theory? If there are failures to find the expected associations, do these failures reflect a flaw in the theory or flaws in the methods used to examine the relations between anxiety and cortisol responsivity in human development? What alterations in the theory and/or improvement in methods are suggested by the answers to these questions?

Pathological Anxiety

For a variety of reasons, assessment of CRH–HPA activity in individuals with anxiety disorders does not allow an adequate test of the Rosen and Schulkin (1998) theory. Pathological anxiety is not one disorder but many, each of which displays different neurobiological patterns (Cameron & Nesse, 1988; Heniger & Charney, 1988). It is not clear, nor does the theory claim, that hyperexcitability of the CRH–HPA system plays a similar role in the etiology and maintenance of the different forms of pathological anxiety. However, elevated basal levels of ACTH and cortisol are rarely noted in studies of pathological anxiety, regardless of type. Indeed, for some forms of anxiety disorder, basal activity of the axis appears to be suppressed. This has been noted particularly for PTSD in studies of adults (e.g., Yehuda et al., 1995b) and children (e.g., Goenjian et al., 1996).

The dynamics of the HPA system in response to chronic stress have been used to explain these findings. Specifically, while emotional trauma may produce high levels of glucocorticoids initially, under conditions of chronic stress, regulatory mechanisms within the system operate to return glucocorticoids to normal or even suppressed basal levels (Henry, 1992). Indeed, although prolonged infusion of corticoids in animal models produce up-regulation of CRH activity in the amygdala, the same infusion produces down-regulation of CRH activity in the hypothalamus (Makino et al., 1994). These findings support the argument that hyperactivity of the axis may sensitize central fear circuits without producing a concomitant elevation in basal glucocorticoid levels.

Rosen and Schulkin (1998) argue that, although hyperactivity of the HPA axis in anxiety disordered patients should not be expected under basal conditions, this should be noted under conditions of challenge by fear-eliciting stimuli. This hypothesis seems to be consistent with the data from work on PTSD. Although chronic low basal levels of cortisol have been found in holocaust survivors and combat veterans with PTSD, in some instances an increased sensitivity of the axis has been noted to stressful challenges (Yehuda, Boisoneau, Lowry, & Giller, 1995a). It also appears consistent with data on clinic referred children. Children with increasingly severe anxiety disorders at follow-up have been shown to exhibit greater cortisol responses to psychosocial challenges (Granger, Weisz, McCracken,

Ikeda, & Douglas, 1996). Similar findings have also been noted for oppositional defiant and conduct disordered children who are comorbid for anxiety
disorder (McBurnett et al., 1991; van Goozen et al., 1998).

While these results appear consistent with the theory, it is remarkably
easy to identify counter examples. In a study of maltreated preschool-aged
children, Hart, Gunnar, and Cicchetti (1995) found that social conflict
produced elevations in cortisol among control children, but a lowering of
cortisol levels below baseline in maltreated children. This was the case even
though previous work had shown that maltreated children are more likely
than control children to become anxious and distressed by social conflict
(Cummings, Hennessy, Rabideau, & Cicchetti, 1994). Similarly, there are
now several studies showing that anxiety may be associated with a lowering
of cortisol below baseline when subjects come into the laboratory or clinic for
testing. Coming into the laboratory for evaluation should elevate cortisol
and often does for normally developing, emotionally stable children and
adults (e.g., Susman, Dorn, & Chousos, 1991; Susman, Dorn, Inoff-
Germain, Nottelman, & Chrousos, 1997). Several studies, however, have
shown that highly anxious subjects and/or those with anxiety disorders
decrease cortisol levels below home baselines when they first come in for
testing (Borchardt, Walters, Perwien, Bernstein, & Gunnar, 1996; Adam,
1998).

Thus, both hypo- and hyper-responding of the HPA axis has been noted
for clinically anxious individuals. While this does suggest alterations of HPA
axis functioning in this population, our current inability to predict whether
pathological anxiety will be associated with elevated, normal, or suppressed
activity of the HPA axis is disconcerting. It allows almost any pattern of
corticoid activity to be interpreted as support for the theory. Given the
difficulty of predicting HPA axis activity in pathological anxiety, examination of cortisol responsivity in normally functioning individuals and those
presumed to be genetically predisposed to anxiety disorders would seem
critical for evaluation of the theory.

Anxious Anticipation and HPA Axis Activity

Numerous studies have shown that cortisol elevations are larger the first
time individuals confront a challenging or threatening event and diminish
markedly with repetition (Kirschbaum & Hellhammer, 1989; Mason, 1968;
Rose, 1980). Similarly, cortisol levels that begin to rise during anticipation of
a stressful event often reach their peak prior to the onset of the event
(Kirschbaum & Hellhammer, 1994). This is one reason why successful stress
paradigms (e.g., those that tend most reliably to produce elevations in
cortisol) build in fairly prolonged periods of preparation or anticipation
(see Kirschbaum, Pirke, & Hellhammer, 1993). Not only laboratory studies
demonstrate the potency of anticipation of threat for activation of the HPA
axis. Researchers who use examinations as real-life stressors report elevated

levels of cortisol before the exam begin with levels often falling to baseline by the end of the exam period (Amario, Marti, Molina, de Pablo, & Valdes, 1996; Nicolson, 1992; Spangler, 1997). State anxiety also often reaches a peak prior to the exam, with exams that elicit more anxiety producing higher cortisol levels (Amario et al., 1996). Surgery has also been used as a real-life stressor in many studies. Again, cortisol levels typically rise prior to the surgery, as do self-reports of anxiety and this has been observed in children as well as adults (Aono, Ueda, Kataoda, & Manabe, 1997). Finally, despite concerns about self-selection, skydiving or parachute jumping has been used as a life-threatening stressor in several studies (Chatterton, Vogelsong, Lu, & Hudgens, 1997; Ursin, Baade, & Levine, 1978). Interestingly, in these studies there is evidence of suppressed baseline levels of cortisol on the morning prior to the jump, with levels of cortisol and adrenaline increasing just subsequent to the rise in self-reported anxiety in the minutes prior to the jump. Thus, the evidence that anticipation of threat is a potent stimulator of the adrenocortical system is quite strong. Cortisol elevates in anticipation of threat, and is often more strongly stimulated by anticipation of the stressor than in response to the onset of the stressful event. Furthermore, the cortisol response tends to diminish with repeated exposures to similar stressors.

These facets of glucocorticoid response appear consistent with requirements of the Rosen and Schulkin theory. However, for this theory to truly hold, we would expect that individuals prone to anxiety should be the ones who show the largest elevations in cortisol in anticipation of a stressor. This should be true especially on first exposure to a stressor when anxious apprehension and glucocorticoid elevations should be at their peak. However, this is where the theory may need adjustment.

Personality, Temperament, and Responsivity of the HPA Axis

In both laboratory and field studies, it is rarely the trait anxious individuals who show the greatest HPA axis responding in anticipation of a novel stressor. We have examined this in children using entry into new social groups as the stressor. Our work has included 2-year-olds embarking on their first group care experience, 3- and 4-year olds starting a new year of nursery school, and 1st through 5th grade children during the first week of school in the fall. These new social situations should be quite anxiety-provoking for shy or socially inhibited children, and parent report and observations indicate that shy children show anxious behavior, reticence, and sometimes intense behavioral distress when entering these new social situations. However, shy, anxious children are not the ones to show the largest increases in cortisol over home baseline levels, nor are they the ones who most frequently produce high cortisol levels during the initial weeks of school. Instead, high responders in these new social situations tend to be the most outgoing, active, impulsive or surgent, extroverted children

(Davis, Donzella, Krueger & Gunnar, 1999; de Haan, Gunnar, Tout, Hart, & Stansbury, 1998; Gunnar, Tout, de Haan, Pierce, & Stansbury, 1997). Indeed, when compared with home baseline levels of cortisol, a slight suppression from home levels is more typical of shy, socially inhibited children.

This type of finding is not peculiar to children. Studies of group formation in both nonhuman primates and in human adults have shown that elevations in cortisol are normative during these times. Furthermore, it is often the most dominant, assertive individuals who show the largest increases (Golub, Sassenrath, & Goo, 1979). This was strikingly demonstrated in a recent study of army recruits (Hellhammer, Buchtal, Ingmar, & Kirschbaum, 1997). Dominant and subordinate status was determined during 6 weeks of boot camp by weekly peer nomination. Stable patterns emerged quickly among the groups of 9 men housed together. Personality tests revealed no significant associations between status and anxiety or neuroticism. Each participant was subjected to two trials each of a psychological and a physical stressor. Consistent with the novelty or first-time effect described earlier, cortisol responses were larger on the first trials of each type of stressor. In addition, for both types of stressors, dominant subjects showed significantly more marked elevations in cortisol on these initial trials than did subordinates. Indeed, compared with the average status subjects, subordinates showed a blunted response to the psychological stressor and failed to respond at all, even on the first trial, to the physical stressor. Evidence of blunted responding was already apparent in the subordinates in the first week of boot camp training. Thus, this did not appear to be a result of the chronic stress of training.

Thus, although conditions that normatively increase anxiety also increase cortisol levels, it is often not the highly anxious individuals who produce the highest responses. Indeed, trait anxious individuals and those who tend to fall to low dominance status often exhibit blunted responding. These types of data seem highly inconsistent with the commonly held belief among stress researchers that elevations in cortisol reflect high anxiety and a failure in coping (Henry, 1992; Spangler & Schieche, 1994). Because they are found in nonclinic populations, even among normally developing toddlers, it is difficult to argue that the blunted or lower responding reflects adaptation of the axis to earlier intense or chronic elevations. Instead, these data suggest that individuals prone to more anxious apprehension may be somewhat protected from elevated cortisol levels during initial encounters with situations that stimulate anticipatory anxiety. While this doesn't invalidate the Rosen and Schulkin theory, it does raise at least two questions. First, if even the outgoing, extroverted, or dominant individuals are experiencing the anticipatory anxiety necessary to stimulate first-time exposure elevations in glucocorticoids, why don't they develop more sensitized fear circuits over time? Second, do trait anxious individuals or those at greater risk for depression ever show evidence of greater HPA axis responsivity? If so, what are the relevant conditions?

Cortisol Increases and Adaptive Functioning

There are many reasons why a rise in cortisol may not lead to deleterious consequences (Henry, 1992). Although the bad things glucocorticoids do have been emphasized, stress researchers also note that the capacity to mount an adrenocortical response to threat is essential to survival (Sapolsky, 1992). Only if cortisol rises too high, too often, or for too long are negative effects on physical and emotional health expected. Containment is usually described as the key to determining whether individual differences in responsivity pose a potential risk. As long as the response can be terminated quickly once the threat has passed and is reduced with repeated exposure to the stressor, then risk is expected to be minimal. Nonetheless, even under these circumstances, a life replete with the need to frequently activate even a well-organized, well-contained glucocorticoid response system is expected to enhance risk of affective disorder and impaired physical health (Schulkin et al., 1994). Activation of the HPA axis is almost always cast in a risk framework. In the case of frequent activation to help manage uncertain, frequently threatening life circumstances, the risk or *allostatic load* is expected to result in poorer psychological and physical health in the future, as the costs accumulate over a lifetime. While this may be true, must we always cast activation of the HPA axis as a potential risk, unless adequately contained?

The framing of glucocorticoid elevations solely as potential risks to health makes it very difficult to explain why lack of response sometimes appears to be the maladaptive pattern. The paradoxical nature of glucocorticoids, of course, has been long noted (McEwen et al., 1992). Basal levels of the hormone are necessary to maintain adequate functioning of many systems, including the health of the dentate area of the hippocampus. But this does not help us explain why, given adequate basal levels, lack of a response is sometimes associated with poor behavioral and cognitive functioning, while a moderate response is sometimes associated with more adequate functioning. It also does not help explain the increasing evidence of an inverted U-shape association between levels of glucocorticoids and performance, particularly cognitive performance (Sapolsky, 1997). Clearly, it is not just that too high, too frequent, and too prolonged a response is a risk for physical and emotional health. Small increases seem, at times, to support functioning. We need a better understanding of the potential positive impact of glucocorticoids to make sense of such findings. We also need to understand and to be able to predict, a priori, what we mean by "too high, too frequent, and too prolonged". Otherwise, we will remain in the uncomfortable position of always writing introduction sections that emphasize the risk of glucocorticoid elevations, and discussion sections that attempt to explain why the failure to elevate cortisol in this case co-occurred with seemingly more maladaptive behavior.

Although we are still far from being able to specify, a priori, what levels or increases can be considered small and potentially beneficial versus large and potentially deleterious, attempts are being made to explain the inverted U function. Sapolsky (1997) has recently argued that this may reflect the often opposing actions of the two glucocorticoid receptors. MRs are largely occupied under basal conditions, and the physiological actions mediated by these receptors tend to have generally positive effects, and are the first to be occupied when cortisol increases above basal levels. The processes mediated by GRs, on the other hand, tend to be catabolic. GRs become occupied in significant numbers when cortisol elevations are large. DeKloet (1991) among others has argued that the impact of glucocorticoids on functioning depends, in part, on the balance between MR and GR occupation. Only as MR/GR balance shifts towards high GR ratios should we expect elevations in cortisol to have deleterious effects.

Unfortunately this argument means that to predict the impact of glucocorticoid elevations it would be helpful to know something about the number of MRs and GRs receptors activated in relation to a given increase in glucocorticoids. However, a variety of factors, such as circadian, genetic, developmental (age of organism), and experiential, can affect MR and GR availability in different regions of the brain (Bohus, DeKloet, & Veldhuis, 1982; Dong et al., 1997; Meaney et al., 1993). Thus, the same increase in glucocorticoids may produce different patterns of MR/GR activation as these factors vary. Furthermore, there is now good evidence that not only the balance of receptor occupancy, but also the duration of time GRs are occupied, may be important in linking elevations in glucocorticoids to their behavioral and neural effects (Oitz, van Haarst, & DeKloet, 1997). Brief exposures to elevated glucocorticoids, even when GRs are targeted, tend to increase perceptions of vigor and heighten attentional focus. Prolonged occupancy of GRs, however, tends to heighten negative affect, including anxiety and depression, impair attention regulation, and produce a sense of exhaustion and fatigue.

The work on early experiences and their impact on regulation and reactivity of the HPA axis also points to the importance of analyzing receptor populations. Early handling of rat pups increases GR numbers, while early maternal separation reduces these numbers (Dong et al., 1997; Meaney et al., 1996). These changes are associated with numerous other changes in central stress and fear circuit activity. They are also associated with altered fear behavior in response to novel and strange events. Thus, it is highly likely that some of the diathesis in individuals prone to anxiety disorders is related to receptors, their balance in different brain regions, and the duration of GR occupation. How this plays out in the etiology of human anxiety disorders has not been fully explored, although Yehuda's group (Yehuda, Boisoneau et al., 1995) has begun to examine GR numbers in relation to PTSD.

Another issue may be the availability of what are being called anti-glucocorticoids. These are neuroactive steroids formed in the adrenals and gonads along enzyme pathways leading to sex steroid production. The two most studied have been dehydroepiandrosterone (DHEA) and its sulfate (DHEAS). These steroids often oppose corticoid mediated receptor actions, and thus reduce potential catabolic neuronal effects of corticoids. Ratios of cortisol to DHEA(S) change with development, with more cortisol relative to DHEA being reported for prepubertal children and aging adults (Guazzo, Kirkpatrick, Goodyer, Shiers, & Herbert, 1996). These steroids are produced in large amounts by the fetal adrenal, decrease as the fetal adrenal zone involutes in the first 6 months after birth, remain low until age 5 years, and then begin to rise with the onset of adrenarche, or the awaking of the adrenals in the first stages of puberty. They tend to increase with activation of the adrenals, but because they are also produced in high quantities by the gonads, they are suppressed under conditions that dampen activity of the hypothalamic–pituitary–gonadal axis. It is becoming increasingly clear that predicting the impact of glucocorticoids on functioning is enhanced when levels of DHEA(S) are also known (Kimonides, Khatibi, Svendsen, Sofroniew, & Herbert, 1998). This may also be true of attempts to understand the role of glucocorticoids in the development of anxiety and affective disorders.

In sum, we are handicapped in understanding the role of glucocorticoids in the etiology of affective disorders by the dearth of research and theory on small increases in corticoids within the ranges typically observed for normally functioning individuals in response to normative challenges and stressors. In many cases, small increases in corticoids appear to coincide with better, more competent functioning, while lack of a response or a blunted response is associated with higher anxiety or less competent, effective coping. We need to understand more about how high, how frequent, and how prolonged glucocorticoid increases need to be before deleterious effects are observed. In addressing this question, it may be important to include information about "anti-glucocorticoids" as they may moderate or modify the effects of cortisol and related glucocorticoids. We may also need to consider the balance between MRs and GRs. These changes or modifications in theory, however, will not solve our problem if we do not also address some of the methodological challenges in assessing cortisol and its relation to behavior.

Methodological Challenges

It has often been lamented that the typical correlation between behavioral and physiological measures, such as cortisol, is around 0.2 to 0.3, at best. Correlations are constrained by the reliability of the measures being correlated. Test–retest analyses are rarely reported for studies of cortisol responses to stressors. In part, this is because of the large "first-time" effect reported earlier. Because the HPA axis rapidly adapts to repetitions of a stressor, finding ways of assessing stability of first-time responses is challenging. However, unless we can determine reliability, it is hard to estimate whether the low correlations between HPA activity and anxiety or any other disposition reflect the true degree of association or poor reliability of our measures of axis responsivity.

Over a decade ago, Epstein and O'Brien (1985) argued for the need to aggregate behavioral measures across trials in studies of personality. They showed that, with aggregation, the trait component of behavior was revealed. They also demonstrated a similar need to aggregate when the trait component of physiological measures was of interest. Unfortunately, measures of HPA axis functioning were not among those they examined. Epstein and O'Brien showed that correlations between behavioral observations and paper-and-pencil tests of personality increased with aggregation of observations. Recently, this has also been demonstrated rather dramatically for measures of HPA axis responsivity. Pruessner et al. (1997) invited subjects into the laboratory on five occasions during which they performed the Trier Social Stress Test (TSST). Salivary cortisol was sampled 6 times at 10 min intervals during each test session, and the area under the curve (AUC) was calculated. As expected, the first test session produced the largest response or AUC, with a marked reduction in response by the second test session. The response to the first session, however, was not predictive of cortisol responses to the second through fifth test sessions. More importantly, the average correlation between the test-1 AUC and the measures that ultimately proved to be related to cortisol responsivity was the ubiquitous 0.30. This was not significant in this small sample. Likewise, for test days 2–5, correlations with personality measures were low. However, when the researchers began to aggregate over tests 2–5, the magnitude of the associations increased. With 3 days aggregated, the average correlation was 0.56. With 4 days aggregated the average correlation with personality characteristics increased to 0.62.

This study revealed two factors that may be critical to our understanding of the role of the HPA axis in the etiology of anxiety and affective disorders. First, it demonstrated the obvious, but typically overlooked point, that the trait component of HPA axis functioning is revealed only when our measures of axis functioning are reliable. Second, the results suggested that it is not glucocorticoid responsivity to the first encounter with a stressor that is associated with risk-related aspects of personality. Rather, continued responding to repeated instances of similar or identical stressors is what characterizes the linkages between glucocorticoid elevations and risks for affective psychopathology. In the Pruessner study (1997), continued HPA axis responding on the second through fifth trials of the TSST was significantly and highly correlated with core risk factors in the etiology of affective disorders: low self-esteem and external locus of control.

Failure to Adapt and Trait-anxious Personality

A similar set of results has been reported by van Eck and colleagues (van Eck, Berkhof, Nicolson, & Sulon, 1996; van Eck, Nicolson, Berkhof, & Sulon, 1996). They used experience sampling to assess cortisol and events in ambulatory subjects over 5 days with 10 event samples obtained each day. They also examined cortisol responses during one trial of a stress-inducing speech task in the laboratory. Trait anxiety and depression were associated with small, but statistically significant, cortisol elevations using the data from the 5 days of event sampling. No significant associations were found for the personality measures with cortisol responses to the laboratory speech stressor. Likewise, the cortisol response to the laboratory speech stressor did not predict cortisol responses during daily event sampling. Importantly, for the event sampling data, anxiety and depression were primarily associated with evidence of reduced habituation to recurrent events. Thus these two studies suggest we should expect the cortisol response to a one-shot laboratory stressor to be a poor predictor of both ambulatory cortisol responding and responses to repetitions of the same laboratory stressor. And, once reliable measures of responding to continued or repeated instances of similar stressors are obtained, the association between glucocorticoid elevations and trait anxiety and depressive dispositions is revealed.

Everyday Contexts, Ambulatory Sampling, and Behavioral Inhibition in Children

Few researchers have the luxury of bringing people into the laboratory multiple times to examine adaptation to repeated stressors and to aggregate measures. Even if budgets would allow it, in most cases research participants would not. Salivary sampling allows ambulatory measurement as participants go about their normal lives. Ambulatory sampling, while it loses some rigor, has the advantage of revealing what is typical for the individual. By their nature, ambulatory studies tend to reveal how the individual responds to typical or familiar stressors. As noted in the van Eck study described above, trait anxious adults show greater cortisol responses when studied in their familiar environments as they go about their everyday lives. Importantly, it is also the case that, when aggregation is used, ambulatory studies of children also reveal an association between more anxious, inhibited temperament and cortisol levels.

Two studies of extremely inhibited, shy, anxious preschoolers have shown that, compared with extremely uninhibited children, they have higher morning cortisol levels (Schmidt et al., 1997; Kagan, Reznick, & Snidman, 1987). In both of these studies, samples were aggregated across three mornings of sampling. Even then, my students and I (unpublished data) have found generally low Cronbach alphas (e.g., around 0.4 to 0.45) for morning cortisol levels. Rapid changes in levels in the hour or so after awakening probably makes it difficult to reliably assess the axis at this time (Pruessner et al., 1997). Our evidence suggests that evening samples are more reliable, with Cronbach alphas around 0.7, when samples taken on 3 evenings before bed are aggregated. Thus, the results reported for morning sampling and shy, inhibited temperament may under-represent the true association.

Extreme group analyses are not necessary to reveal a link between cortisol concentrations and shyness or internalizing dispositions when ambulatory sampling in familiar contexts is performed. Using only two days of mid-morning sampling, de Haan et al. (1998) found a significant positive correlation between teacher-reported internalizing behavior and home cortisol concentrations for normally developing 2-year-old children. Likewise, in two studies of children attending full-day childcare, shyness and sadness were found to be positively correlated with elevations in cortisol from morning to afternoon, particularly for boys (Dettling, Gunnar, & Donzella, 1999; Tout, de Haan, Kipp-Campbell, & Gunnar, 1998). Again, two or three days of sampling tend to yield only modestly reliable aggregate cortisol measures. The true association between HPA axis activity and behavioral dispositions probably requires aggregation across more days. Unfortunately, no studies are available (especially with children) to help the researcher determine, a priori, how many days of sampling are needed.

There are datasets, however, that may be helpful in attempting to address this question. Some of these reside in the hands of biological anthropologists who have incorporated salivary cortisol sampling into their research on the social economics and health of children in developing areas of the world. Flinn (Flinn & England, 1995), for example, has been studying the development of children for several years in a small village in the Caribbean. Each morning and afternoon he walks the village obtaining saliva samples for cortisol analysis. Over the course of several months each year, and repeated at yearly intervals, he has collected literally thousands of samples from these children. His work clearly shows associations between shy, anxious, internalizing trait characteristics and higher cortisol concentrations. It also demonstrates the impact of family stressors, such as parent–child conflicts, divorce, remarriage, and separation, on HPA axis responsivity in children Case studies within his sample reveal the heights to which cortisol can and does rise in response to real-life stressors, in particular, abusive treatment by parents and other caregivers. Similar work is being conducted on another Caribbean island by Durbrow, a researcher trained by Flinn. Durbrow's work (Durbrow, Gunnar, Bozoky, Adam, & Jimerson, 2000) also reveals associations between frequent elevations in cortisol and children's anxiety and attention regulation. In this case, for some children going to school regularly produces marked (3- to 4-fold) increases in cortisol. These children tend to be the ones who are both more anxious and who fail at their schoolwork. The combination of doing poorly at school and the use of caning and other harsh disciplinary practices by the teachers may explain why going to school each morning elevates cortisol so markedly in these children. When viewed in combination, these biological anthropologists' data clearly provide the necessary ingredients for the Rosen and Schulkin (1998) theory: associations between anxious, depressive traits and cortisol responsivity, and evidence that in their everyday lives some children clearly experience frequent and marked elevations in this stress hormone. However, it remains to be determined whether these elevations actually lead to anxiety.

Conclusions

The Rosen and Schulkin (1998) theory is only one of several related models that propose a key role for the HPA axis in the etiology of anxiety and depressive disorders. At first pass, support for this model seems fragile. Studies of clinic populations yield mixed findings. The dynamics of the system in response to chronic high stress have been used to explain why clinically anxious individuals might have normal-to-low cortisol concentrations (Henry, 1992). However, the capacity to interpret high, low, and normal concentrations of cortisol as consistent with the model is disconcerting. Turning to nonclinical populations, mixed findings continue to be observed. Indeed, it is in this body of data that we see evidence that the theory may need revision. Anticipatory anxiety does appear to be associated with the situations that elevate cortisol. Cortisol elevates more sharply the first time a stressor is encountered, and habituates upon repeated exposures. However, it is not necessarily the more anxious, depressed individuals who show the greatest first-time responses. Instead, low or blunted responding is more characteristic of anxious individuals and those with poor self-esteem and external loci of control. The Rosen and Schulkin theory, or any model that posits an important etiological role for cortisol responsivity in anxiety and depression, stumbles at this point. These kinds of findings will remain a significant problem for these models until we gain a better handle on the role of glucocorticoids in positive or enhanced cognitive and emotional responding to challenge. Indeed, it may well turn out that it is the lack of adequate HPA axis responding to novel stressors of normative magnitude that forms part of the etiology of more chronic trait anxiety and anxiety disorders.

In contrast to the rather dismal and challenging nature of the data examined to this point, the review of studies of repeated exposure and ambulatory cortisol sampling yielded evidence strongly supportive of the Rosen and Schulkin theory. Trait anxious, depressive, internalizing dispositions do appear to be associated with greater responsivity of the HPA axis. But this seems especially the case in familiar contexts where individuals are attempting to manage repeated instances of similar stressors. This suggests that the diathesis we are searching for is one that promotes continued responding, failure to habituate, and perhaps even the likelihood of sensitizing to the kinds of stresses and challenges that confront us repeatedly in roughly similar form. If so, then to understand this diathesis we may need to leave the laboratory and follow children and adults as they manage the challenges of their everyday lives (see also de Vries, 1992). In doing so we can also attend to a critical failing in much of the human research on this neuroendocrine axis: specifically, a failure to attend to the basics of good research, the need to obtain reliable measures. Only when the reliability of our physiological measures rises to a respectable level can we hope adequately to assess and understand the role of the CRH–HPA axis in the development of psychopathology.

Acknowledgment and Note

Work on this manuscript was supported by a National Institute of Mental Health Research Science Award (MH00946). The author would like to thank Bonny Donzella for her help in manuscript preparation. Please address correspondence to Megan R. Gunnar, Institute of Child Development, 51 East River Rd, University of Minnesota, Minneapolis, MN 55455, USA.

References

Adam, E. K. (1998). *Emotional and physiological stress in mothers of toddlers: An adult attachment model.* Unpublished dissertation, University of Minnesota, Minneapolis, MN.

Amario, A., Marti, O., Molina, T., de Pablo, J., & Valdes, M. (1996). Acute stress markers in humans: response of plasma glucose, cortisol and prolactin to two examinations differing in the anxiety they provoke. *Psychoneuroendocrinology, 21*, 17–24.

Aono, J., Ueda, W., Kataoda, Y., & Manabe, M. (1997). Differences in hormonal responses to preoperative emotional stress between preschool and school children. *Acta Anaesthesiologica Scandinavica, 41*, 229–31.

Blanchard, D. C., & Blanchard, R. J. (1988). Ethoexperimental approaches to the biology of emotion. *Annual Review of Psychology, 39*, 43–68.

Bohus, B., DeKloet, E. R., & Veldhuis, H. D. (1982). Adrenal steroids and behavioral adaptation: Relationship to brain corticoid receptors. In D. Granten & D. W. Pfaff (Eds.), *Current topics in neuroendocrinology* (pp. 107–148). Berlin: Springer Verlag.

Borchardt, C. M., Walters, N., Perwien, A., Bernstein, G. A., & Gunnar, M. R. (October, 1996). *Salivary cortisol during the treatment of adolescents with school refusal.* Poster presented at the annual meeting of the American Academy of Child and Adolescent Psychiatry, Philadelphia.

Cameron, O. G., & Nesse, R. M. (1988). Systematic hormonal and physiological abnormalities in anxiety disorders. *Psychoneuroendocrinology, 13*, 287–307.

Chatterton, R. T., Vogelsong, K. M., Lu, Y. C., & Hudgens, G. A. (1997). Hormonal responses to psychological stress in men preparing for skydiving. *Journal of Clinical Endocrinology and Metabolism, 82*, 2503–2509.

Cummings, E. M., Hennessy, K., Rabideau, G., & Cicchetti, D. (1994). Responses of physically abused boys to interadult anger involving their mothers. *Development and Psychopathology, 6*, 31–41.

Davis, E. P., Donzella, B., Krueger, W. K. & Gunnar, M. R. (1999). The start of a new school year: Individual differences in salivary cortisol response in relation to child temperament. *Developmental Psychobiology, 35*, 188–196.

de Haan, M., Gunnar, M., Tout, K., Hart, J., & Stansbury, K. (1998). Familiar and novel contexts yield different associations between cortisol and behavior among 2-year-olds. *Developmental Psychobiology, 31*, 93–101.

DeKloet, E. R. (1991). Brain corticosteroid receptor balance and homeostatic control. *Frontiers in Neuroendocrinology, 12*, 95–164.

Dettling, A., Gunnar, M. R., & Donzella, B. (1999). Cortisol levels of young children in full-day childcare centers: Relations with age and temperament. *Psychoneuroendocrinology, 24*, 519–536.

de Vries, M. W. (1992). *The experiences of psychopathology: Investigating mental disorders in their natural settings.* Cambridge, England: Cambridge University Press.

Dong, L., Diorio, J., Tannenbaum, B., Caldji, C., Francis, D., Freedman, A., Sharma, S., Pearson, D., Plotsky, P. M., & Meaney, M. J. (1997). Maternal care, hippocampal glucocorticoid receptors, and hypothalamic–pituitary–adrenal responses to stress. *Science, 277,* 1659–1662.

Durbrow, E. H., Gunnar, M. R., Bozoky, I., Adam, E., & Jimerson, S. (2000). Unwillingly to school: The contribution of attention problems and adrenocortical reactivity to the academic problems of Caribbean village children. Manuscript submitted for publication.

Epstein, S., & O'Brien, E. (1985). The person–situation debate in historical and current perspective. *Psychological Bulletin, 98,* 513–537.

Faneslow, M. S. (1994). Neural organization of the defensive behavior system responsible for fear. *Psychonomic Bulletin and Review, 1,* 429–438.

Flinn, M. V., & England, B. G. (1995). Childhood stress and family environment. *Current Anthropology, 36,* 854–866.

Goenjian, A. K., Yehuda, R., Pynoos, R. S., Steinberg, A., Tashjian, M., Yang, R., Najarian, L. & Fairbanks, L. (1996). Basal cortisol, dexamethasone suppression of cortisol, and MHPG in adolescents after the 1988 earthquake in Armenia. *American Journal of Psychiatry, 153,* 929–934.

Gold, P. W., Goodwin, F. K., & Chrousos, G. P. (1988). Clinical and biochemical manifestations of depression: Relations to the neurobiology of stress. *New England Journal of Medicine, 319,* 348–353.

Golub, M. S., Sassenrath, E. N., & Goo, G. P. (1979). Plasma cortisol levels and dominance in peer groups of rhesus monkey weanlings. *Hormones and Behavior, 12,* 50–59.

Granger, D., Weisz, J. R., McCracken, J. T., Ikeda, S. C., & Douglas, P. (1996). Reciprocal influences among adrenocortical activation, psychosocial processes, and the behavioral adjustment of clinic-referred children. *Child Development, 67,* 3250–3262.

Guazzo, E. P., Kirkpatrick, P. J., Goodyer, I. M., Shiers, H. M., & Herbert, J. (1996). Cortisol, dehydroepiandrosterone (DHEA), and the DHEA sulfate in the cerebrospinal fluid of man: Relations to blood levels and the effects of age. *Journal of Clinical Endocrinology and Metabolism, 81,* 3951–3960.

Gunnar, M. R., Tout, K., de Haan, M., Pierce, S., & Stansbury, K. (1997). Temperament, social competence, and adrenocortical activity in preschoolers. *Developmental Psychobiology, 31,* 65–85.

Hart, J., Gunnar, M., & Cicchetti, D. (1995). Salivary cortisol in maltreated children: Evidence of relations between neuroendocrine activity and social competence. *Development and Psychopathology, 7,* 11–26.

Hellhammer, D. H., Buchtal, J., Ingmar, G., & Kirschbaum, C. (1997). Social hierarchy and adrenocortical stress reactivity in men. *Psychoneuroendocrinology, 22,* 643–650.

Heniger, G. R., & Charney, D. S. (1988). Monoamine receptor systems and anxiety disorders. *Psychiatric Clinics of North America, 11,* 309–326.

Henry, J. P. (1992). Biological basis of the stress response. *Integrative Physiological and Behavioral Science, 27,* 66–68.

Kagan, J., Reznick, J. S., & Snidman, N. (1987). The physiology and psychology of behavioral inhibition in children. *Child Development, 58,* 1459–1473.

Kimonides, V. G., Khatibi, N. H., Svendsen, C. N., Sofroniew, M. V., & Herbert J. (1998). Dehydroepiandrosterone (DHEA) and DHEA-sulfate (DHEAS) protect hippocampal neurons against excitatory amino acid-induced neurotoxicity. *Proceedings of the National Academy of Sciences of the United States of America*, 95, 1852–1857.

Kirschbaum, C., & Hellhammer, D. H. (1989). Salivary cortisol in psychobiological research: An overview. *Neuropsychobiology*, 22, 150–169.

Kirschbaum, C., & Hellhammer, D. H. (1994). Salivary cortisol in psychoneuroendocrine research: Recent developments and applications. *Psychoneuroendocrinology*, 19, 313–333.

Kirschbaum, C., Pirke, K., & Hellhammer, D. H. (1993). The "Trier Social Stress Test"—A tool for investigating psychobiological stress responses in a laboratory setting. *Neuropsychobiology*, 28, 76–81.

LeDoux, J. E. (1996). *The emotional brain*. New York: Simon & Schuster.

Makino, S., Gold, P.W., Schulkin, J. (1994). Effects of corticosterone on CRH mRNA and content in the bed nucleus of the stria terminals; comparison with the effects in the central nucleus of the amygdala and the paraventricular nucleus of the hypothalamus. *Brain Research*, 657, 141–149.

Mason, J. W. (1968). A review of psychoendocrine research on the pituitary–adrenal cortical system. *Psychosomatic Medicine*, 30, 576–605.

McBurnett, K., Lahey, B. B., Frick, P. J., Risch, C., Loeber, R., Hart, E. L., Christ, M. G., & Hanson, K. S. (1991). Anxiety, inhibition, and conduct disorder in children: II. Relation to salivary cortisol. *Journal of the American Academy of Child and Adolescent Psychiatry*, 30, 192–196.

McEwen, B. S., Angulo, J., Cameron, H., Chao, H. M., Daniels, D., Gannon, M. N., Gould, E., Mendelson, S., Sakai, R., Spencer, R., & Woolley, C. (1992). Paradoxical effects of adrenal steroids on the brain: Protection versus degeneration. *Biological Psychiatry*, 31, 177–199.

Meaney, M. J., Diorio, J., Francis, D., Widdowson, J., La Plante, P, Caldui, C., Sharma, S., Seckl, J., & Plotsky, P. (1996). Early environmental regulation of forebrain glucocorticoid receptor gene expression. Implications for adrenocortical responses to stress. *Developmental Neuroscience*, 18, 49 72.

Meaney, M. J., O'Donnell, D., Viau, V., Bhatnagar, S., Sarrieau, A., Smythe, J., Shanks, N., & Walker, C. D. (1993). Corticosteroid receptors in the rat brain and pituitary during development and hypothalamic–pituitary–adrenal function. In I. S. Zagon & P. J. McLaughlin (Eds.), *Receptors in the developing nervous system: Growth factors and hormones: Vol. 1* (pp. 163–201). London: Chapman & Hall.

Nicolson, N. A. (1992). Stress, coping and cortisol dynamics in daily life. In M. W. de Vries (Ed.), *The experience of psychopathology: Investigating mental disorders in their natural settings* (pp. 219–232). Cambridge, England: Cambridge University Press.

Oitz, M. S., van Haarst, A. D., & DeKloet, E. R. (1997). Behavioral and neuroendocrine responses controlled by the concerted action of central mineralocorticoid (MRs) and glucocortocoid receptors (GRs). *Psychoneuroendocrinology*, 22 (Suppl. 1), S87–S94.

Pruessner, J. C., Gaab, J., Hellhammer, D. H., Lintz, D., Schommer, N., & Kirschbaum, C. (1997). Increasing correlations between personality traits and cortisol stress responses obtained by data aggregation. *Psychoneuroendocrinology*, 22, 615–625.

Pruessner, J. C., Wolf, O. T., Hellhammer, D. H., Buske-Kirschbaum, A., von Auer, K., Jobst, S., Kaspers, F., & Kirschbaum, C. (1997). Free cortisol levels after awakening: A reliable biological marker for the assessment of adrenocortical activity. *Life Sciences*, 61, 2539–2549.

Rose, R. M. (1980). Endocrine responses to stressful psychological events. *Psychiatric Clinics of North America*, 3, 251–275.

Rosen, J. B., & Schulkin, J. (1998). From normal fear to pathological anxiety. *Psychological Review*, 105, 325–350.

Sapolsky, R. M. (1992). Neuroendocrinology of the stress-response: Hormonal influence on nonsexual behavior. In J. B. Becker & S. M. Breedlove & D. Crews (Eds.), *Behavioral Endocrinology* (pp. 287–324). Cambridge, MA: MIT Press.

Sapolsky, R. M. (1997). McEwen-induced modulation of endocrine history: A partial review. *Stress*, 2, 1–12.

Schmidt, L. A., Fox, N. A., Rubin, K. H., Sternberg, E. M., Gold, P. W., Smith, C. C., & Schulkin, J. (1997). Behavioral and neuroendocrine responses in shy children. *Developmental Psychobiology*, 30, 127–140.

Schulkin, J., Gold, P. W., & McEwen, B. S. (1998). Induction of corticotropin-releasing hormone gene expression by glucocorticoids: implication for understanding the states of fear and anxiety and allostatic load. *Psychoneuroendocrinology*, 23, 219–243.

Schulkin, J., McEwen, B. S., & Gold, P. S. (1994). Allostasis, amygdala, and anticipatory angst. *Neuroscience and Behavioral Reviews*, 18, 385–396.

Spangler, G. (1997). Psychological and physiological responses during an exam and their relation to personality characteristics. *Psychoneuroendocrinology*, 22, 423–441.

Spangler, G., & Schieche, M. (1994, July). The role of maternal sensitivity and the quality of infant–mother attachment for infant biobehavioral organization. Paper presented at the 9th international conference on Infant Studies, Paris, France.

Susman, E. J., Dorn, L. D., & Chousos, P. (1991). Negative affect and hormone levels in young adolescents: Concurrent and predictive perspectives. *Journal of Youth and Adolescence*, 20, 167–190.

Susman, E. J., Dorn, L. D., Inoff-Germain, G., Nottelman, E. D., & Chrousos, G. P. (1997). Cortisol reactivity, distress behavior, and behavioral and psychological problems in young adolescents: A longitudinal perspective. *Journal of Research on Adolescence*, 70, 81–105.

Tout, K., de Haan, M., Kipp-Campbell, E., & Gunnar, M. R.(1998). Social behavior correlates of adrenocortical activity in daycare: Gender differences and time-of-day effects. *Child Development*, 69, 1247–1262.

Ursin, H., Baade, E., & Levine, S. (1978). *Psychobiology of stress: A Study of Coping Men*. New York: Academic Press.

van Eck, M., Berkhof, H., Nicolson, N., & Sulon, J. (1996). The effects of perceived stress, traits, mood states, and stressful daily events on salivary cortisol. *Psychosomatic Medicine*, 58, 447–458.

van Eck, M., Nicolson, N. A., Berkhof, H., & Sulon, J. (1996). Individual differences in cortisol responses to a laboratory speech task and their relationship to responses to stressful daily events. *Biological Psychology*, 43, 69–84.

van Goozen, S. H., Matthys, W., Cohen-Kettenis, P. T., Gispen-de Wied, C., Wiegant, V. M., & van Engeland, H. (1998). Salivary cortisol and cardiovascular activity during stress in oppositional-defiant disordered boys and normal controls. *Biological Psychiatry, 43,* 531–539.

Watts, A. G., & Sanchez-Watts, G. (1995). Region-specific regulation of neuropeptide mRNAs in rat limbic forebrain neurons by aldosterone and corticosterone. *Journal of Physiology, 484,* 721–736.

Yehuda, R., Boisoneau, D., Lowry, M. T., & Giller, E. L. J. (1995). Dose–response changes in plasma cortisol and lymphocyte glucocorticoid receptors following dexamethasone administration in combat veterans with and without post-traumatic stress disorder. *Archives of General Psychiatry, 52,* 583–593.

Yehuda, R., Kahana, B., Biner-Brynes, K., Southwick, S. M., Mason, J. W., & Giller, E. L. (1995). Low urinary cortisol excretion in Holocaust survivors with post-traumatic stress disorder. *American Journal of Psychiatry, 152,* 982–986.

8

Childhood Anxiety Disorders from the Perspective of Emotion Regulation and Attachment

ROSS A. THOMPSON

The field of developmental psychopathology offers potentially powerful conceptual tools for understanding childhood anxiety disorders. Several principles are especially relevant. First, developmental psychopathologists believe that a child's behavior should be understood in relation to the challenges and changes characteristic of each stage of development, not merely as a prototype of adult behavior (Cicchetti, 1990). Childhood anxiety disorders should be studied, for example, in the context of the normative fears of childhood, children's growing capacities to manage emotional arousal, and the importance of close relationships for regulating emotion, especially early in life (Izard & Youngstrom, 1996; Reed, Carter, & Miller, 1992). Moreover, the influence of certain risk factors for the development of anxiety disorders (such as a sudden or unexpected loss of a family member) may be contingent on the child's current stage of personality development and emotional growth. Because of this, the origins and outcomes of risk factors contributing to anxiety disorders are often developmentally contingent.

Second, by emphasizing the complex, interactive influences contributing to the growth of childhood disorders, developmental psychopathologists caution against searching for single, direct causes of pathology (Cicchetti & Cohen, 1995). "The action is in the interaction" over time among multiple internal and external influences that may contribute to childhood anxiety disorders. Any one of these influences (such as temperamental vulnerability) will not necessarily determine the course of subsequent adjustment but, taken collectively, their combined contribution to the development of anxiety disorders is likely to be more than additive (see Vasey & Dadds, this volume). Moreover, risk factors are transactionally influential over time, which adds to their cumulative impact on the growth and management of children's fears and anxiety. Temperamental inhibition may, for instance, sensitize children to fear-provoking stimuli in a manner that children with different temperamental profiles do not experience, heightening their aversive response to situations associated with fearful stimuli, and thus contributing to a cumulation of psychosocial risk over time.

Third, developmental psychopathologists also attend to protective as well as risk factors in the etiology of childhood disorders (Sroufe & Rutter, 1984). This means that influences within and outside the child can buffer the impact of pathogenic influences in the growth of childhood anxiety disorders, and any child's life history is likely to include both risks and protections. Occasionally, protections and risks may be afforded by the same source (e.g., a caregiving relationship in which a parent is both nurturantly concerned but also overprotective with respect to managing a child's fears). Fourth, developmental psychopathologists believe that there are multiple pathways leading to the development of childhood disorders (the principle of equifinality), and that any risk factor can lead to diverse outcomes depending on other influences on the child (the principle of multifinality) (Cicchetti & Rogosh, 1997). With respect to childhood anxiety disorders, this means that clinical researchers must seek to understand not only how pathogenic agents (such as traumatic conditioning experiences) contribute to the growth of disorder, but why these agents may be present in the life histories of children who are free of anxiety disorders, and why anxiety disorders can develop independently of these pathogens (Vasey & Ollendick, 2000).

Finally, developmental psychopathologists emphasize a broad range of influences on typical and atypical development, spanning the variety of ontogenetic, biogenetic, and neurophysiological processes characterizing individual growth, and also various levels of the social ecology (including the family, peer environment, socioeconomic system, and cultural values) in which the individual is embedded (Cicchetti & Toth, 1991). Thus understanding the origins of childhood anxiety disorders requires a broadly based assessment of intrinsic and contextual influences, and their interaction over time, in a manner that requires applying a broad lens to the child's life experience.

At root, a developmental psychopathology perspective to childhood anxiety disorders views typically developing children and children with clinical disorders *in common as developing persons*. This means that developmental studies of emotional ontogenesis and the growth of emotion regulation, attachment and family relationships, temperament, social cognition, and other features of typical development can be usefully applied to understanding how children with anxiety disorders incorporate these developmental processes into their efforts to cope with overwhelming fear and anxiety. Moreover, clinical studies of the developmental psychopathology of anxiety can highlight the adaptive (as well as maladaptive) developmental processes that emerge in individuals under stress, yielding insights that may not be revealed in research on typical populations alone. A developmental psychopathology of childhood anxiety disorders contributes complexity to clinical thinking because development is complex, especially as it is observed in individuals who are faced with atypical demands and stresses. But it is likely also to provide valuable heuristic insights that can helpfully inform developmental and clinical science.

Consistent with a developmental psychopathology view, this chapter considers childhood anxiety disorders in light of developmental research on emotion regulation and the security of attachment. Attachment and emotion regulation have been topics of considerable interest to developmental psychologists, and research in these areas can potentially offer new perspectives and raise new questions concerning the origins, maintenance, and treatment of childhood anxiety. Moreover, these developmental literatures may also help child psychopathologists regard childhood anxiety disorders in a different light: not as straightforward problems of emotion dysregulation or insecure attachment, but as complex adaptations to the psychological trade-offs that are required in children's striving to cope with intrinsic vulnerability, difficult environmental demands, and/or conflicting emotional goals that may contribute to the growth of fear and anxiety (Thompson & Calkins, 1996).

The chapter discusses the various avenues by which emotion becomes regulated in increasingly sophisticated ways as children mature, including the roles of temperamental individuality, attachment relationships, construals of emotionally arousing circumstances and of the cues of internal arousal, and other factors (see Thompson, 1990, 1994, and Thompson, Flood, & Lundquist, 1995, for further details concerning these constituents of emotion regulation). In each case, the formulations of developmental research are applied to the more limited research on childhood anxiety disorders to consider whether new insight into these disorders is achieved when they are viewed from an emotional regulatory and attachment perspective.

What Is Emotion Regulation?

Defining emotion regulation is essential to understanding the multidimensional features of this apparently straightforward phenomenon, and to appreciating how the management of emotion may entail psychological tradeoffs for children under stress. The following definition illustrates this: "*Emotion regulation consists of the extrinsic and intrinsic processes responsible for monitoring, evaluating, and modifying emotional reactions, especially their intensive and temporal features, to accomplish one's goals*" (Thompson, 1994, pp. 27–28). Several features of this definition merit further consideration.

First, emotion regulation incorporates the efforts of other people to manage one's emotions, as well as self-regulatory strategies. Both are important. External influences on emotion regulation are most apparent early in life, when caregivers devote considerable effort to interpreting and managing the emotions of young children. But the influences of other people remain a constant source of emotion regulation throughout life, whether they appear in the supportive assistance of family members and friends, the advice and counseling that alter emotion-relevant appraisals, or efforts to induce guilt, pity, or sympathy to spur necessary action in another person.

Usually these external influences on emotion regulation are consistent with an individual's self-initiated efforts to regulate emotion: others help an individual manage distress and improve a sense of emotional well-being. At times, however, a person's emotional self-regulatory efforts and the emotional influences of others may be out of sync, such as when children with insecure attachments seek secure comfort from an inconsistently responsive caregiver (Cassidy, 1994; Sroufe, 1998). In conditions of psychosocial risk, more significant dyssynchrony between extrinsic and intrinsic influences on emotion regulation can occur, such as with young children who are physically abused by their caregivers (Cicchetti, 1990; Gaensbauer & Sands, 1979; Kolko, 1996). In these instances, when a parent transitions unexpectedly and erratically between being a necessary emotional resource and a threat to the child, a young child's efforts to manage emotion in the context of strikingly inconsistent emotional needs (for nurturance and self-protection) may result in emotion that is shallow or disorganized, or the child's withdrawn demeanor. These emotional characteristics may be necessary adaptations to a pathogenic caregiving environment, even though they are also dysfunctional in other contexts (Thompson & Calkins, 1996; Thompson et al., 1995).

A second feature of this definition is that emotion regulation is portrayed as multicomponential: it entails *monitoring* ongoing emotional state, *evaluating* it (in terms of emotional goals), and *modifying* it if necessary. Developing skills of emotion regulation thus involve many things, including self-awareness of emotion (including its physiological and subjective components), an appreciation of the origins of emotional experience, an understanding of the potential consequences of emotional expression in different circumstances, and strategies for modifying emotion. Not all of these skills are controlled or deliberative, since automatic processing is also enlisted in emotion regulation. Because these skills function in concert to enable the effective management of emotion, emergent capabilities associated with each of these components are central features of emotional competence (Saarni, 1998).

In conditions of psychosocial risk, however, these components of emotional regulation may require psychological tradeoffs. Many children growing up in homes with serious domestic conflict, for example, must so carefully monitor parental behavior that children become hypervigilent to cues of impending parental dispute, and consequently they tend to overreact emotionally to the onset of conflict (Cummings & Davies, 1994; Katz & Gottman, 1991). Their capacities to manage the emotions evoked by parental arguments are undermined by their heightened monitoring of the circumstances signaling conflict and their heightened emotional responsiveness to those signals. But their monitoring is necessary because of the importance of anticipating domestic disputes before they erupt, and preparing for their emotional consequences. In a sense, these different components of emotion regulation simultaneously heighten both the child's resiliency and vulnerability to adult arguments at home (Thompson & Calkins, 1996).

Finally, this definition portrays emotion regulation *functionally*: its efficacy is evaluated in relation to the individual's emotional goals for the situation. Children and adults have various emotional goals for the circumstances in which they seek to manage emotion: to feel good, deter harm, create or restore positive relationships, enlist the assistance of others, and so forth. Different goals can lead to different kinds of emotional management efforts, so it is important to understand the purposes for which emotion is managed in studying emotion regulatory processes.

For children in difficult circumstances, however, there may be multiple goals relevant to emotion regulation. Furthermore, emotional goals may be mutually inconsistent, or their accomplishment may still leave the child vulnerable to other harms. Consider the dilemma of a child growing up with a depressed caregiver, whose sad affect, irritability, helplessness, criticism, and guilt-induction present young children with formidable emotional demands (Garber, Braafladt, & Zeman, 1991; Zahn-Waxler & Kochanska, 1990). The child's emotional goals may be oriented toward accomplishing any of several outcomes: maintaining feelings of well-being, avoiding critical reactions or rejection from the caregiver, self-defense against unfair accusations or unreasonable expectations, anticipating the next difficult encounter with the parent, or managing the parent's emotional state in order to protect one's own. Selecting among these goals involves necessary tradeoffs. Avoiding or confronting a depressed parent may contribute to preserving feelings of personal well-being, for example, but may do little to improve the emotional environment of the home and may thus exacerbate feelings of guilt and responsibility for the adult's emotional condition (Thompson & Calkins, 1996). Moreover, children may experience conflict between immediate emotional goals (such as ending a distressing encounter with an angry caregiver) and longer-term goals (such as improving the affective climate of the home).

Likewise, children with anxiety disorders may also experience conflicting goals: vigilantly avoiding situations that evoke overwhelming fear conflicts with child's efforts to act competently and in a manner that enhances self-esteem and peer sociability. But confronting fears may be emotionally intolerable without the guided assistance and support of caregivers that is often unavailable. The difficulty is that, in seeking to manage emotion effectively in the context of these formidable and conflicting emotional demands, children may reduce certain risks to their psychosocial well-being but, perhaps as a consequence, enhance others.

All of these definitional considerations are relevant to viewing childhood anxiety disorders from an emotion regulatory perspective. Parental efforts to assist offspring in managing feelings of fear and anxiety may result in overprotection, overcontrol, or enmeshment in children's dysfunctional behavioral patterns, and thus exacerbate rather than reduce the child's difficulties in managing anxious emotion. In this respect, consideration of extrinsic and intrinsic influences on competent emotional regulation is necessary to understanding the origins and maintenance of anxious fearfulness, as considered in greater detail below. Moreover, one of the characteristics of children with anxiety disorders is their hypervigilance for cues that signal anxiety-provoking situations. Because it also contributes to their hyperresponsiveness to those cues, this monitoring may undermine competent emotional management even as it enables children to anticipate anxiety-provoking situations before they occur. This is also considered in greater detail in the next section.

Finally, but perhaps most importantly, it is crucial to understand the goals that children with anxiety disorders have for the circumstances in which they anticipate confronting fearful stimuli. For many children, the psychological tradeoffs they accept in seeking to predict and avoid anxiety-provoking circumstances (even at a cost of competent functioning) may be the only satisfying responses they have to overwhelming and unpredictable emotional demands. If they cannot manage the fear they experience in certain circumstances, these children seem committed to regulating their potential exposure to those circumstances even though the strategies they use heighten their vulnerability to anxious pathology. Understanding that these children are not simply deficient in emotional regulation but enlist strategies that provide short-term benefits but long-term costs may contribute to a more multidimensional portrayal of the emotional dilemmas they face.

In the next section, these issues are considered in greater depth in the context of exploring the various avenues to emotion regulation in children with and without anxiety disorders.

Constituents of Emotion Regulation

Because emotion regulation is multicomponential, the skills of emotion regulation are multifaceted. There are various ways in which children and adults seek to manage their emotional experience, and a developmental account of the growth of emotion regulatory capacities explores the emergence of these diverse constituents of emotion regulation (Thompson, 1990, 1994; Thompson et al., 1995). To developmental psychopathologists, furthermore, considering the alternative ways in which children seek to manage emotion can highlight different ways in which emotion management can become impaired in children who are prone to anxiety disorders.

This discussion begins by considering briefly the neurophysiological bases for the growth of emotion regulation and the relevance of temperamental individuality to emotion management skills. Other constituents of emotion regulation are then considered, including how people encode their internal, visceral cues of emotional arousal, reinterpret the situations that evoke emotion, and shift attention away from (or toward) emotionally arousing events. In each case, children with anxiety disorders are faced with unique difficulties and challenges in managing their emotional experience. In the section that follows, emotion regulation is considered from the perspective of the attachment relationships that contribute significantly to emotional well-being, and anxiety disorders are viewed from the perspective of attachment theory and research.

Neurophysiological and Temperamental Influences

Psychological strategies for managing emotion are based on complex nervous system and endocrine system processes governing emotion. Throughout the first year of life, the excitatory processes associated with emotional arousal begin to stabilize and decline in lability owing to maturational changes in neuroendocrine and parasympathetic systems (Porges, Doussard-Roosevelt, & Maiti, 1994; Stansbury & Gunnar, 1994). Although these early developmental changes are important to the growth of emotion regulation because they enable the infant to be more effectively self-soothing and soothable in response to the nurturance of others, they are only the beginning. Further advances in emotion self-regulation in the years that follow are based on the maturation of cortical inhibitory processes, particularly in the prefrontal cortex, which begins in infancy but continues throughout childhood (Dawson, 1994; Fox, 1994; Thompson, in press). Indeed, it is partly because of the growing maturity of different regions of the prefrontal cortex that children become more deliberate, reflective, and self-inhibiting in intellectual and emotional functioning throughout early and middle childhood (Thompson, in press). There are other maturational changes in neuroendocrine functioning and parasympathetic regulation in the years after infancy that add further to the growth of emotion regulation capabilities.

In light of these neurophysiological constituents of emotion regulation, we might expect to find important differences in the self-regulatory capacities of children who differ in these physiological systems. And we do. Two research groups have studied young children who are behaviorally inhibited, as reflected in their fear, negative affect, and withdrawal when confronted with novelty and challenge. Kagan and his colleagues offer evidence suggesting that these children have a generally lower threshold of reactivity in limbic system structures mediating fear and defense, particularly in the amygdala and the hypothalamus (Kagan, 1998; Kagan, Reznick, & Snidman, 1987, 1988). Calkins, Fox, and their colleagues conclude instead from their studies that inhibited and uninhibited children differ primarily in parasympathetic and cortical regulation of emotion (Calkins, Fox, & Marshall, 1994; Fox, 1989). In either case, behaviorally inhibited children may be more vulnerable to the arousal of fear and distress, especially in challenging or novel situations, because of neuroendocrinological characteristics of their behavioral functioning that are moderately heritable (Robinson, Kagan, Reznick, & Corley, 1992). Their inhibited behavioral response to novel, challenging situations (especially social situations) may be viewed as an effort to cope emotionally with the heightened physiological arousal they experience in these circumstances.

These findings are important to the developmental psychopathology of anxiety disorders because of the association between early behavioral inhibition and the development of anxious pathology. Turner, Beidel, and Wolff (1996) conclude from their careful review of research that young children with behavioral inhibition who remain so into childhood are at risk to develop anxiety disorders, especially disorders involving social or social-evaluative anxiety. This may occur as inhibited young children experience heightened distress in social situations and, as a consequence, respond apprehensively, cautiously, and inappropriately when interacting with others. The rejection they experience from social partners, and the isolation that results from avoiding future social encounters, are together likely to exacerabate social anxiety and create further apprehension. In a sense, the inhibited child's behavioral response manages dispositionally heightened arousal in social situations, but at a cost to developing social competence and self-confidence, and with a risk for the growth of anxious pathology (Thompson & Calkins, 1996).

The conclusion that a small proportion of children may be temperamentally predisposed to the development of anxiety disorders is consistent with other research suggesting that genetic factors may contribute risk for anxiety disorders, although not in a disorder-specific fashion (see Eley, this volume; Kendler, Neale, Kessler, Heath, & Eaves, 1992; also see Albano, Chorpita, & Barlow, 1996, and Torgerson, 1993, for reviews). As Eley (this volume) notes, genetic influence can account for an important share of the variance in childhood anxiety, although genetic vulnerability for anxiety disorders also heightens risk for depression. However, not all behaviorally inhibited children remain so and most do not develop anxious pathology, and many children with anxiety disorders do not have a history of behavioral inhibition (Turner et al., 1996). This underscores the importance of appreciating the multiple developmental pathways leading from behavioral inhibition to later outcomes, and the multiple pathways contributing to child psychopathology. Genetic vulnerability is part of a complex developmental story.

Encoding Internal Emotional Cues

One way in which emotional arousal is managed is by how a person encodes and interprets the visceral cues of emotion. Increased heart rate, shortness of breath, queasy stomach, shakiness, sweaty palms and other cues of physiological arousal are common accompaniments to emotional arousal. In some circumstances they are experienced as performance facilitators (such as when an actor, athlete, or speaker prepares for the public), but in other situations they can be experienced as overwhelming and disorganizing. One of the skills of managing emotion is learning to anticipate these visceral cues of emotional arousal and encode them in a manner that contributes to effective functioning rather than undermining it. Indeed, this is one of the skills that capable public speakers or performance artists, and professional athletes, commonly describe. At present, however, little is known about the development of these interpretive processes, how children's understanding of their physiological arousal is socialized by caregivers, or the growth of individual differences in how children construe their internal experience of emotional arousal. It is an important topic for developmental research.

Children who regularly experience heightened emotion in ordinary situations (owing to temperamental vulnerability, traumatic conditioning, or for other reasons) may face special challenges in how they encode these cues of physiological arousal. Children with anxiety disorders, like their adult counterparts, become overly concerned with the physical manifestations of their anxiety, such as the shaking, sweating, stomach upset, dizziness, or tension that occurs, especially in social situations (Albano et al., 1996; Livingston, 1996). Complaints about other physical symptoms, such as stomach-aches, headaches, and illnesses, are also commonly reported in children with social phobias, generalized anxiety (or overanxious) disorder, and other anxiety disorders. Because of the intensity of their distress, young children with panic disorders become acutely concerned with the bodily manifestations of their fearful response, expressing worry about suddenly becoming ill, vomiting, or otherwise losing control, and describing their experience as like a physical illness (Albano et al., 1998; Moreau & Follett, 1993). In short, because these visceral signs are so often associated with overwhelming distress, children become acutely sensitive to their physical state because cues of internal arousal are difficult to encode as anything other than signs of impending disorganization. This is why children are so concerned about them. Children's acute sensitivity to these visceral sensations contributes to their hyperresponsiveness to them.

Children thus become hypersensitive and hyperresponsive to the bodily cues that anticipate and accompany heightened negative emotion. It may take relatively little actual disturbance (e.g., slight exposure to a fear-provoking event or mild interoceptive cues of anxiety) to trigger an intense emotional reaction because of how even these minor experiences have become associated with subsequent strong arousal (e.g., Katz & Gottman, 1991). Children in these circumstances are likely, according to Ekman (1984), to experience emotional "flooding" characterized by: (a) the onset of emotion in circumstances that would not be disturbing to most people; (b) rapid escalation of emotion to heightened intensity; (c) perseveration or "recycling" of emotional arousal with little regard to changes in elicitors; and (d) a lack of emotion regulation. These characteristics of "flooded" emotion closely approximate many of the characteristics of panic disorder. Indeed, emotional flooding seems to be a common experience of children and adults with several forms of anxiety disorder provoked, in part, by their heightened vigilance and responsiveness to the physiological cues signaling emotional arousal. It may therefore be extremely difficult for children to manage these feelings appropriately.

The construct of anxiety sensitivity, which is a well-established risk factor for adult anxiety disorders (particularly panic attacks and agoraphobia), captures this quality of hyperresponsiveness to internal cues signaling fearful arousal (see Reiss, Silverman, & Weems, this volume). Anxiety sensitivity is the fear of anxiety-related sensations and the belief that they have harmful psychological and social consequences and, indeed, signal a potentially catastrophic loss of self-control (Reiss, 1991; Taylor, 1995). Individuals high on anxiety sensitivity (especially as it is indexed on the Anxiety Sensitivity Index; see Reiss, 1991) are thus acutely vigilant for the physiological and cognitive sensations associated with anxiety and are likely to be hyperresponsive to these cues for the reasons described above (see, e.g., Rapee & Medoro, 1994; Schmidt, Lerew, & Jackson, 1997). This suggests that anxiety sensitivity, which is indexed partly by the respondent's acute sensitivity to the physiological cues of anxiety and fear and their cognitive concomitants (e.g., distraction), may merit exploration as a developmental component of childhood anxiety disorders also (Mattis & Ollendick, 1997), as well as its association with broader problems of emotion regulation (Cox, Borger, & Enns, 1998).

Interpreting Emotionally Arousing Events

Emotional arousal can also be managed by reinterpreting the circumstances that evoke emotion. Young children can be observed altering their constructions of reality for emotional management purposes, such as when they reinterpret a scary account ("He didn't *really* die, he just got frightened and ran away" or affirming "It's just a story!"), or conclude that a friend probably didn't *mean* to ruin a block tower when she ran past (Meerum Terwogt, Schene, & Harris, 1986), or substitute a different goal for one whose attainment has been frustrated. Adults also engage in similar reinterpretations, when they encounter anxiety-provoking events like a medical exam or a performance review, by minimizing its importance or emphasizing their likelihood of success. Parents commonly try to alter a child's construal of stressful but benign experiences by describing dental procedures as "tooth tickling," or by behaving supportively when a shy child encounters a new person for the first time (Miller & Green, 1985). In each case, emotion is managed by altering one's interpretation of the circumstances that evoke emotion to yield less distressed, more positive affect and to facilitate coping.

Children with anxiety disorders, however, are characterized by fixed, persistent, and biased threat-related interpretations of the benign situations that evoke fear for them. They construct a world that is more threatening than the one experienced by nonanxious children (Daleiden & Vasey, 1997; Vasey & Daleiden, 1996). Children with separation anxiety disorder (SAD) experience intense and unrealistic fears of getting lost or of harm occurring to attachment figures. The thoughts of phobic children are filled with anticipations of disastrous consequences to them from encounters with feared events. Children with generalized anxiety (overanxious) disorder similarly forecast catastrophic situations in the near future, including worries about competent performance. Anxious children also have distorted self-perceptions, and are especially prone to negative, denigrating self-regard that emphasizes their helplessness and incompetence in surmounting their fears. Moreover, the social responses that children often receive from parents and teachers may consolidate rather than alter these threat-enhancing interpretations of emotionally evocative events, especially when caregivers themselves become

anxious by the child's distress or try to behave supportively and sympathe-
tically with the child's unrealistic fears. Indeed, there is evidence that parents
tend to reinforce children's avoidance of fear-provoking situations and their
threat appraisals (Dadds, Barrett, Rapee, & Ryan, 1996).

As a consequence of this fixed and persistent interpretive focus that
exaggerates (rather than reduces) the threat they perceive in benign situations, children with anxiety disorders are likely to have considerable difficulty
reinterpreting these situations in less threatening ways. This is especially so if
social partners do not foster alternative interpretations because, as children
avoid the benign circumstances they fear, their limited exposure to these
situations makes it unlikely that they will begin to regard them in more
realistic, appropriate ways. Moreover, the cognitive interference produced
by their preoccupation with anticipated and perceived threat may undermine
children's capacities to function effectively at home and school (Vasey &
Daleiden, 1996). Consequently, children with anxiety disorders are likely
to suffer other academic and social difficulties because of their fearful avoidance (Kendall, 1992; Thompson & Calkins, 1996).

Attentional Processes

Another avenue to emotion regulation is through the management of attentional processes. From a very young age, children appreciate that emotion
can be managed by directing attention toward or away from emotionally
arousing stimuli: looking away from sad or upsetting events, and attending
to pleasant stimuli (Bretherton, Fritz, Zahn-Waxler, & Ridgeway, 1986;
Cummings, 1987; Altschuler & Ruble, 1989). Children know that one way
to tolerate situations involving delayed rewards is to redirect attention away
from the desired event and distracting oneself with alternative activity
(Vaughn, Kopp, Krakow, Johnson, & Schwartz, 1986). Parents assist
children by distraction during upsetting events, limiting the child's awareness
of potentially distressing information, or focusing the attention of offspring
on positive features of difficult circumstances (Miller & Green, 1985). By
middle childhood, children have become aware of the *inward* redirection of
attention to regulate emotion: even when one cannot escape difficult
circumstances, distracting ideation (e.g., thinking pleasant thoughts during
a distressing experience) and self-coaching can be helpful (Altschuler &
Ruble, 1989; Band & Weisz, 1988; Harris & Lipian, 1989). Knowledge of
these internal attention management strategies is especially valuable because
they provide a means of regulating emotion even when escape or avoidance
of emotionally arousing stimuli is impossible.

One of the hallmarks of anxiety (and affective) disorders, unfortunately,
is that the individual is preoccupied with negative emotion (Barlow, 1988).
This is easy to understand in light of the foregoing considerations, because
children with anxiety disorders are likely to remain focused on events that
signal threat or danger because of the interpretive biases and fear-related
encoding of internal arousal discussed above. Their effort to be hypervigilant

for fear-provoking events means that these children tend to construe even ambiguous or uncertain situations as threatening (Barrett, Rapee, Dadds, & Ryan, 1996; Miller, Boyer, & Rodoletz, 1990). They are attentionally focused on threat. Clinically anxious and high-test-anxious children, for example, selectively shift their attention *toward* threat-related stimuli, by contrast with non-test-anxious children who redirect attention *away* from threat (Vasey, Daleiden, Williams, & Brown, 1995; Vasey, El-Hag, & Daleiden, 1996). Test-anxious children also become attentionally focused on emotionally arousing self-critical self-talk and performance concerns that heighten their arousal, interfere with their attention to cognitive tasks, and thus impair their performance (Wigfield & Eccles, 1990). Children with other anxiety disorders are often preoccupied by the "what if ...?" concerns that cause them to ruminate on the catastrophic results that would occur if the events they fear were actually to occur. Because of this, it may be very difficult for these children to manage emotion by the inward direction of attention to more positive, less anxiety-ridden thoughts, or the outward direction of attention to more positive, less threatening stimuli.

Conclusion

If one of the lessons that typically developing children learn is that their emotions can be managed (and how to do so) (Thompson, 1990), there are many reasons to conclude that children with anxiety disorders do not learn the same lesson. The adaptive, flexible network of interpretive biases, emotional construals, internal encoding procedures, and attentional processes that typically developing children can enlist to smoothly manage emotional experience is instead, for children with overwhelming fear and anxiety, an inflexible, maladaptive network of constraints on their capacities to regulate their negative arousal effectively. For some anxious children, moreover, a temperamental bias lowers their physiological threshold for negative arousal and heightens their proneness to distress, rendering them even more vulnerable to fear and anxiety in circumstances that would not ordinarily perturb most children. The problem is not fundamentally that these children lack capacities for emotion management, because their anxious symptomatology reveals heightened efforts to anticipate fearful arousal through strategies such as hypervigilance for fear-provoking stimuli, active (and sometimes aggressive) avoidance of these stimuli, and overattention to physiological conditions that may anticipate or accompany distressed emotion. Rather, their problems with emotion regulation derive from the fact that their efforts to anticipate fearful situations provide immediate benefits but long-term costs that render them vulnerable to continued pathology. These double-edged strategies, in other words, enable them immediate relief from the turmoil of encountering fear-provoking events but, at the same time, consolidate and perpetuate their pathology and undermine developmentally appropriate functioning (Thompson & Calkins, 1996). The lesson that children with anxiety disorders learn is that if their negative emotion cannot be directly controlled it can at least be anticipated, and the perceived uncontrollability of their emotional experience contributes to the development of their anxious attentional focus, hypervigilance for fear-provoking events, threat-related interpretive biases, and anxious encoding of internal cues that heighten risk for emotional flooding in stressful circumstances. Children may be especially vulnerable to the psychological consequences of their perceived inability to control anxiety because of the importance of early experiences in shaping the cognitive expectancies contributing to anxious pathology, and to emotion regulation difficulties (Chorpita & Barlow, 1998).

The Importance of Attachment Relationships

Children do not manage their emotions alone. As illustrated above, caregivers promote the effective management of children's emotions in many ways (Thompson, 1990). They urge, coach, and reinforce strategies of emotion regulation appropriate for the circumstances. They model effective approaches to emotion regulation. Caregivers seek to structure children's lives to ensure that children encounter situations that are within their capacities to cope, and are protected from overwhelming or traumatizing events. They offer compassionate soothing, nurturant support, advice, and other forms of guidance to directly intervene into the distress of children. They help children manage their emotions in indirect ways also, such as by redirecting attention to more positive circumstances, altering how children interpret emotionally arousing situations by fostering more benign construals, and suggesting alternative modes of coping. Caregivers also socialize children's understanding of emotion in ways that incorporate an expanding awareness of emotion regulation into children's knowledge of emotion, its causes and consequences, and the social conditions governing emotional displays.

The emotional management efforts of caregivers are usually seamlessly integrated into the child's expanding repertoire of self-regulatory strategies because both partners are advancing the same emotional goals for the child. In concert with children, in other words, caregivers try to reduce distress, improve feelings of well-being, and constructively channel a child's feelings of anger, fear, and other emotions to accomplish positive outcomes. In most instances, there is synchrony in how caregivers and children seek to manage children's emotional lives. When there is dyssynchrony between the emotion goals underlying the emotional management efforts of a caregiver and child—such as when the adult ridicules a child's genuine fear or anger—there can be conflict between them and, if it is chronic over time, emotional difficulty for children. This is, unfortunately, more likely to be true in certain conditions of developmental psychopathology, such as when the emotional demands imposed by a depressed or abusive caregiver are inconsistent with the efforts of the child to manage emotion in a self-protective and developmentally appropriate manner (Thompson & Calkins, 1996).

In other conditions of developmental psychopathology, such as childhood anxiety disorders, the caregiver's management of emotion in accord with the child's emotional goals may actually exacerbate the child's underlying emotional difficulties. When an adult cooperates with the child's effort to avoid fear-provoking events, despite an awareness of how it contributes to dysfunctional behavior (or without any such realization), the caregiver inadvertently helps to perpetuate the child's pathology. It is easier to understand why an adult would do so in light of studies showing an intergenerational family history for anxiety disorders to which hereditary influences but also family learning processes make contributions (see Eley, this volume; Last, 1989; Silverman, Cerny, & Nelles, 1988). Anxiety is learned in families as part of the shared environment of the family system (Eley, this volume). A child who expresses intense fear or anxiety is likely to foster accommodating responses from caregivers, for example, especially if the child's distress or the fear-evoking circumstances also make the adult anxious. By responding overprotectively and overcontrollingly, and permitting the child to avoid confronting the fear-provoking event, caregivers provide little or no opportunity to master the anxiety (Gerlsma, Emmelkamp, & Arrindell, 1990; Vasey & Dadds, this volume; Vasey & Ollendick, 2000). In doing so, parents may be inadvertently reinforcing and also modeling anxious behavior and poor self-regulatory strategies. At the same time, they may be worried about the effects of anxious pathology on the child's capacities to function in a socially and developmentally appropriate manner, and thus parental overprotectiveness may be coupled with criticism and a lack of warmth and support (Gerlsma et al., 1990).

There are other ways in which parents may reinforce and consolidate a child's anxious pathology. A child who responds to an anticipated encounter with a fear-evoking event with screaming, tantrums, hiding, and aggressive resistance offers powerful incentives to adults to accede, and if the adult gives in, the child's subsequent settling down provides potent negative reinforcement for the caregiver to accede to the child's wishes in the future (Vasey & Ollendick, 2000). At the same time, the adult's acquiescence reinforces the child's future resistance, and the result are coercive family processes resembling those observed in other difficult families (cf. Patterson, 1982). Taken together, childhood anxiety disorders are likely to be acompanied by troubled parent–child relationships. They are troubled by a history of aversive encounters focused on a child's anxious efforts to avoid events that provoke irrational fear, but also by a more general emotional tone of uncertainty and insecurity.

Attachment theory is relevant to an understanding of the family dynamics of childhood anxiety because attachment theorists seek to characterize the underlying quality of parent–child relationships in terms of the security or trust that children derive from their caregivers (Ainsworth, Blehar, Waters, & Wall, 1978; Bowlby, 1969; Thompson, 1998). Infants and young children are considered to be securely attached or insecurely attached based on the extent to which their relationships with their caregivers confer a sense of security and confidence in the child's transactions with the environment, especially in uncertain, threatening, or difficult circumstances. Children with secure attachments confidently explore and investigate with the assurance that the caregiver will be available, when needed, for assistance. Insecurely attached children (especially those regarded as insecure-resistant) tend to be more hesitant, anxious or fearful because they are uncertain about the adult's availability or assistance (Cassidy & Berlin, 1994; Thompson, 1998). Differences in the security of attachment in young children are believed to derive primarily from the adult's sensitivity to the child, because prompt and helpful responding fosters the trust on which a secure attachment is based. These differences in attachment security in very young children are believed to lead to broader representations (or "internal working models") of relationships, the self, and the caregiver in the years that follow that are either secure or insecure in their underlying affective tone. Children with secure attachment representations are believed to be more self-confident, trusting in their relationships with close partners, and competent in social understanding than are children with insecure internal representations, and there is some limited empirical support for these formulations (Thompson, 1998; 1999).

Childhood anxiety disorders may be associated with insecure parent–child attachment relationships. Indeed, Bowlby (1973) himself argued that many common forms of anxiety disorders, including school phobia and other forms of phobic disorders (including "agoraphobia"), separation anxiety, and other kinds of anxious pathology could ultimately be traced to insecurity over the availability of an attachment figure. These insecure (or, in Bowlby's phrase, *anxious*) attachments could sometimes emerge in response to actual events (e.g., a major illness or death of a caregiver, or prolonged separations) or threats of abandonment by the attachment figure. Such real or even imagined events directly threaten the sense of security that should be intrinsic to the parent–child relationship and render the child vulnerable to feelings of helplessness and lack of control over important perceived dangers in the world. Others have argued that insecure attachment in the caregiver as well as the child can contribute to the development of anxious pathology in offspring (Manassis & Bradley, 1994). Taken together, an intergenerational family history of anxious pathology and the parent–child conflict associated with a child's anxious fearfulness can be understood in terms of the development of relational insecurity in the family system that contributes to the maintenance and consolidation of anxiety disorders in children.

To the same extent that insecure attachment is a risk factor for the development of anxious pathology, a secure attachment may be a protective factor. The parental sensitivity that is believed to lead to attachment security is likely also to foster a child's reassurance that, even in threatening or fearful circumstances, the adult will be available to provide reassurance even if the source of the threat cannot be avoided. Moreover, the self-confidence inspired by the internal working models associated with a secure attachment may also enable a fearful child to confront perceived threats, with the parent's assistance, more ably than would a comparably anxious child who is insecure.

In an important analysis, Cassidy (1995) has argued that childhood insecurity may be one basis for the development of adult generalized anxiety disorder, although her argument applies also to the development of childhood generalized anxiety. In the early years of life, insecure attachments (especially insecure-resistant attachments) are associated with heightened wariness, anxiety, and fear owing to the child's uncertainty concerning the availability of the attachment figure (Cassidy & Berlin, 1994). In the years that follow, the internal representations associated with attachment insecurity in older children resemble some of the interpretive processes described above that make the management of fearful anxiety so problematic for children with anxiety disorders. According to Cassidy, for example, insecurely attached (especially insecure-resistant) children vigilantly monitor the environment for cues of threat, becoming especially sensitive to the availability or absence of the attachment figure, and their play and exploration can be impaired because of this attentional focus. Moreover, like children with generalized anxiety (overanxious) disorder, children with insecure attachments tend to have interpretive biases that enhance their perception of threat in the broader world, even to the extent of interpreting ambiguous stimuli as potentially hostile. Children with anxiety disorders feel helpless and incompetent in coping with their fearfulness in a manner resembling the self-denigrating working models that one would expect to find in insecurely attached children. And while children with anxiety disorders seem to conclude that if their emotional experience cannot be controlled then distress can at least be anticipated through hypervigilance for threat, children with insecure attachments seem to conclude that if their attachment figures do not provide security then they, too, need to be overattentive to potential danger. In each case, as Cassidy (1994, 1995) has argued, insecure attachment and anxious pathology have common roots in the problems with emotion regulation that are related, at least in part, to problems in parent–child relationships.

Empirical evidence for these provocative conclusions is limited, owing largely to the fact that research on the representational features of attachment security is in its early stages, and little work has been completed examining the connections between insecure attachment and anxious pathology in children. There are some suggestive findings, however. Kirsh and Cassidy (1997) found that securely and insecurely attached preschoolers responded differently in laboratory tasks assessing attention and memory for positive parent–child interaction, with insecurely attached children exhibiting greater avoidance and cognitive interference. More substantive evidence comes from a study by Warren, Huston, Egeland, and Sroufe (1997), who studied a sample of 172 adolescents at age 17 on a variety of clinical measures. The same adolescents had been earlier studied in infancy, at which time measures of the security of infant–parent attachment, infant temperament, and maternal anxiety (as a marker of possible genetic contributions) were indexed. These researchers found that 28% of the teenagers who had been earlier deemed insecurely-resistantly-attached had, at age 17, either current or past problems with anxiety disorders. This compared with only 13% of the rest of the sample. More importantly, an early insecure-resistant attachment predicted later anxiety disorders over and above the influence of both maternal anxiety and temperament in infancy.

These findings suggest that early attachment insecurity can provide a foundation for the later growth of psychopathology, but caution is warranted in interpreting results such as these. As Greenberg (1999) has noted in his review of research on attachment and psychopathology in childhood, the relations between early attachment security and later child psychopathology are complex. Aspects of the parent–child relationship and of family circumstances after infancy and early childhood can assume a significant role in determining later risk for pathology, sometimes confirming the tendencies created by an initially insecure attachment and on other occasions redirecting developmental pathways. Often a secure or insecure attachment in infancy is an early marker for the overall quality of parent–child interaction that, as it continues to influence development in subsequent years, has broader and more significant influences on a child's sociopersonality functioning (Thompson, 1999). Sometimes attachment security is most influential in interaction with other variables: in one study, for example, toddlers in insecure attachment relationships who were also behaviorally inhibited were most likely to be stressed by novel challenges (Nachmias, Gunnar, Mangelsdorf, Parritz, & Buss, 1996). And it is also important to recognize that the outcomes of early attachment insecurity can be diverse—not only internalizing disorders like anxious pathology but also a variety of externalizing disorders are predicted by early insecure attachment (Greenberg, 1999). As Greenberg urges, therefore, the importance of attachment relationships must be viewed within the overall context of the broader developmental influences that also contribute to risk, or protection, for child psychopathology.

Conclusion

Greenberg's cautionary comments provide a reminder about the importance of the developmental psychopathology perspective to understanding childhood anxiety disorders. Rarely is complex psychopathology well-explained with reference to single predictors like early insecure attachment or behavioral inhibition. Instead, the developmental pathways leading to anxiety disorders are complex and multidimensional, entailing a combination of risk and protective factors that, as they emerge throughout a child's life, yield multiple avenues to a common diagnostic outcome. Moreover, the developmental pathways inaugurated by early risk factors like attachment insecurity or behavioral inhibition can lead to various outcomes, among which anxious pathology is one of several possible destinations. As developmental psychopathologists argue, these complex considerations are necessary constituents of understanding children with anxious pathology as developing persons who must confront the same challenges and opportunities of growth as do children in more typical circumstances.

By viewing childhood anxiety disorders from the perspective of emotion regulation and attachment, the common developmental experiences of typically developing children and those with anxiety disorders are affirmed. But it is also clear that children with overwhelming fear and anxiety have unique challenges to overcome. The attachment relationships with caregivers who are typically expected to be secure, "safe havens" may be, for these children, troubled relationships of uncertain insecurity in which their anxiety is paradoxically reinforced and criticized. The strategies of emotion self-regulation that provide, in typical circumstances, opportunities to smoothly manage feelings of distress, fear, or anxiety are instead, for these children, constraints that channel their attention and cognitions toward fear even while they enable the immediate anticipation and avoidance of fear-provoking events. From a developmental psychopathology perspective, these children do not lack skills in emotion regulation, but instead these skills are maladaptively oriented toward enhancing vigilance for the elicitors of emotional experiences that have become uncontrollable to the child. By contrast with the experience of typically developing children, strategies of emotion management have become, for children with anxious pathology, double-edged swords that purchase immediate relief from confrontations with fearful stimuli at a cost of longer-term developmental dysfunction and emotional pathology (Thompson & Calkins, 1996).

Viewed from an emotion-regulation and attachment perspective, children with anxiety disorders need guidance in coping with the challenges of emotional competence (Saarni, 1998). Developing emotional competence involves, among other things, the capacities to understand one's own emotional experience, to communicate openly and effectively about those emotions with others, and to cope successfully with aversive emotions and distressing circumstances. It includes also the capacity to enlist the psychological resources provided by close relationships in the management of emotion and the development of self-regulatory strategies. Viewed in this manner, children with anxiety disorders share in common with all other children the need to find security and satisfaction in their emotional lives with the assistance of the adults who care for them.

Note

Please address correspondence to Ross A. Thompson, Department of Psychology, University of Nebraska, 238 Burnett Hall, Lincoln, NE 68588-0308, USA. E-mail: rthompson1@unl.edu.

References

Ainsworth, M. D. S., Blehar, M. C., Waters, E., & Wall, S. (1978). *Patterns of attachment*. Hillsdale, NJ: Erlbaum.

Albano, A. M., Chorpita, B. F., & Barlow, D. H. (1996). Childhood anxiety disorders. In E. J. Mash & R. A. Barkley (Eds.), *Child psychopathology* (pp. 196–241). New York: Guilford.

Altschuler, J. L., & Ruble, D. N. (1989). Developmental changes in children's awareness of strategies for coping with uncontrollable stress. *Child Development, 60,* 1337–1349.

Band, E., & Weisz, J. R. (1988). How to feel better when it feels bad: Children's perspectives on coping with everyday stress. *Developmental Psychology, 24,* 247–253.

Barlow, D. H. (1988). *Anxiety and its disorders.* New York: Guilford.

Barrett, P. M., Rapee, R. M., Dadds, M. R., & Ryan, S. M. (1996). Family enhancement of cognitive style in anxious and aggressive children: Threat bias and the FEAR effect. *Journal of Abnormal Child Psychology, 24,* 187–203.

Bowlby, J. (1969). *Attachment and loss: Vol. I. Attachment.* New York: Basic Books.

Bowlby, J. (1973). *Attachment and loss: Vol. II. Separation.* New York: Basic Books.

Bretherton, I., Fritz, J., Zahn-Waxler, C., & Ridgeway, D. (1986). Learning to talk about emotions: A functionalist perspective. *Child Development, 57,* 529–548.

Calkins, S. D., Fox, N. A., & Marshall, T. R. (1994). Behavioral and physiological antecedents of inhibited and uninhibited behavior. *Child Development, 67,* 523–540.

Cassidy, J. (1994). Emotion regulation: Influences of attachment relationships. In N. A. Fox (Ed.), The development of emotion regulation and dysregulation: Biological and behavioral aspects. *Monographs of the Society for Research in Child Development, 59,* 228–249.

Cassidy, J. (1995). Attachment and generalized anxiety disorder. In D. Cicchetti & S. Toth (Eds.), *Rochester symposium on developmental psychopathology: Vol. 6. Emotion, cognition, and representation* (pp. 343–370). Rochester, NY: University of Rochester Press.

Cassidy, J., & Berlin, L. J. (1994). The insecure/ambivalent pattern of attachment: Theory and research. *Child Development, 65,* 971–991.

Chorpita, B. F., & Barlow, D. H. (1998). The development of anxiety: The role of control in the early environment. *Psychological Bulletin, 124,* 3–21.

Cicchetti, D. (1990). The organization and coherence of socioemotional, cognitive, and representational development: Illustrations through a developmental psychopathology perspective on Down syndrome and child maltreatment. In R. Thompson (Ed.), *Nebraska symposium on motivation: Socioemotional development. Vol. 36* (pp. 259–366). Lincoln, NE: University of Nebraska Press.

Cicchetti, D., & Cohen, D. J. (1995). Perspectives on developmental psychopathology. In D. Cicchetti & D. J. Cohen (Eds.), *Developmental psychopathology: Vol. 1. Theory and methods* (pp. 3–20). New York: Wiley.

Cicchetti, D., & Rogosh, F. A. (1997). Equifinality and multifinality in developmental psychopathology. *Development and Psychopathology, 8,* 597–600.

Cicchetti, D., & Toth, S. (1991). The making of a developmental psychopathologist. In J. H. Cantor, C. C. Spiker, & L. P. Lipsitt (Eds.), *Child behavior and development: Training for diversity* (pp. 34–72). Norwood, NJ: Ablex.

Cox, B. J., Borger, S. C., & Enns, M. W. (1998). Anxiety sensitivity and emotional disorders: Psychometric studies and their theoretical implications. In S. Taylor (Ed.), *Anxiety sensitivity: Theory, research, and treatment of the fear of anxiety* (pp. 115–148). Mahwah, NJ: Erlbaum.

Cummings, E. M. (1987). Coping with background anger in early childhood. *Child Development, 58*, 976–984.

Cummings, E. M., & Davies, P. (1994). *Children and marital conflict: The impact of family dispute and resolution.* New York: Guilford.

Dadds, M. R., Barrett, P. M., Rapee, R. M., & Ryan, S. (1996). Family process and child psychopathology: An observational analysis of the FEAR effect. *Journal of Abnormal Child Psychology, 24*, 715–734.

Daleiden, E. L., & Vasey, M. W. (1997). An information-processing perspective on childhood anxiety. *Clinical Psychology Review, 17*, 407–429.

Dawson, G. (1994). Frontal electroencephalographic correlates of individual differences in emotion expression in infants: A brain systems perspective on emotion. In N. A. Fox (Ed.), The development of emotion regulation and dysregulation: Biological and behavioral aspects. *Monographs of the Society for Research in Child Development, 59*, 135–151.

Ekman, P. (1984). Expression and the nature of emotion. In K. R. Scherer & P. Ekman (Eds.), *Approaches to emotion* (pp. 319–343). Hillsdale, NJ: Erlbaum.

Fox, N. A. (1989). Heart-rate variability and behavioral reactivity: Individual differences in autonomic patterning and their relation to infant and child temperament. In J. S. Reznick (Ed.), *Perspectives on behavioral inhibition* (pp. 177–185). Chicago: University of Chicago Press.

Fox, N. A. (1994). Dynamic cerebral processes underlying emotion regulation. In N. A. Fox (Ed.), The development of emotion regulation and dysregulation: Biological and behavioral aspects. *Monographs of the Society for Research in Child Development, 59*, 152–166.

Gaensbauer, T. J., & Sands, K. (1979). Distorted affective communications in abused/ neglected infants and their potential impact on caregivers. *Journal of the American Academy of Child Psychiatry, 18*, 238–250.

Garber, J., Braafladt, N., & Zeman, J. (1991). The regulation of sad affect: An information-processing perspective. In J. Garber & K. A. Dodge (Eds.), *The development of emotional regulation and dysregulation* (pp. 208–240). New York: Cambridge University Press.

Gerlsma, C., Emmelkamp, P. M. G., & Arrindell, W. A. (1990). Anxiety, depression, and perception of early parenting: A meta-analysis. *Clinical Psychology Review, 10*, 251–277.

Greenberg, M. T. (1999). Attachment and psychopathology in childhood. In J. Cassidy & P. Shaver (Eds.), *Handbook of attachment* (pp. 469–496). New York: Guilford.

Harris, P. L., & Lipian, M. S. (1989). Understanding emotion and experiencing emotion. In C. Saarni & P. L. Harris (Eds.), *Children's understanding of emotion* (pp. 241–258). New York: Cambridge University Press.

Izard, C. E., & Youngstrom, E. A. (1996). The activation and regulation of fear and anxiety. In D. Hope (Ed.), *Nebraska symposium on motivation: Perspectives on anxiety, panic, and fear: Vol. 43* (pp. 1–59). Lincoln, NE: University of Nebraska Press.

Kagan, J. (1998). Biology and the child. In N. Eisenberg (Ed.), *Handbook of child psychology: Vol. 3. Social, emotional and personality development* (5th ed., pp. 177–235). New York: Wiley.

Kagan, J., Reznick, J. S., & Snidman, N. (1987). The physiology and psychology of behavioral inhibition in children. *Child Development, 58*, 1459–1473.

Kagan, J., Reznick, J. S., & Snidman, N. (1988). Biological bases of childhood shyness. *Science, 240*, 167–171.

Katz, L. F., & Gottman, J. M. (1991). Marital discord and child outcomes: A social psychophysiological approach. In J. Garber & K. A. Dodge (Eds.), *The development of emotional regulation and dysregulation* (pp. 129–155). New York: Cambridge University Press.

Kendall, P. C. (1992). Childhood coping: Avoiding a lifetime of anxiety. *Behaviour Change, 9*, 229–237.

Kendler, K. S., Neale, M. C., Kessler, R. C., Heath, A. C., & Eaves, L. J. (1992). Major depression and generalized anxiety disorder: Same genes, (partly) different environments? *Archives of General Psychiatry, 49*, 716–722.

Kirsch, S. J., & Cassidy, J. (1997). Preschoolers' attention to and memory for attachment-relevant information. *Child Development, 68*, 1143–1153.

Kolko, D. J. (1996). Child physical abuse. In J. Briere, L. Berliner, J. A. Bulkey, C. Jenny, & T. Reid (Eds.), *The APSAC handbook of child maltreatment* (pp. 21–50). Thousand Oaks, CA: Sage.

Last, C. G. (1989). Anxiety disorders. In T. H. Ollendick & M. Herson (Eds.), *Handbook of child psychopathology* (2nd ed., pp. 219–227). New York: Plenum.

Livingston, R. (1996). Anxiety disorders. In M. Lewis (Ed.), *Child and adolescent psychiatry: A comprehensive textbook* (2nd ed., pp. 674–684). Baltimore, MD: Williams & Wilkins.

Manassis, K., & Bradley, S. J. (1994). The development of childhood anxiety disorders: Toward an integrated model. *Journal of Applied Developmental Psychology, 15*, 345–366.

Mattis, S. G., & Ollendick, T. H. (1997). Children's cognitive responses to the somatic symptoms of panic. *Journal of Abnormal Child Psychology, 25*, 47–57.

Meerum Terwogt, M., Schene, J., & Harris, P. L. (1986). Self-control of emotional reactions by young children. *Journal of Child Psychology and Psychiatry, 27*, 357–366.

Miller, S. M., & Green, M. L. (1985). Coping with stress and frustration: Origins, nature, and development. In M. Lewis & C. Saarni (Eds.), *The socialization of emotions* (pp. 263–314). New York: Plenum.

Miller, S. M., Boyer, B. A., & Rodoletz, M. (1990). Anxiety in children: Nature and development. In M. Lewis & S. M. Miller (Eds.), *Handbook of developmental psychopathology* (pp. 191–207). New York: Plenum.

Moreau, D., & Follett, C. (1993). Panic disorder in children and adolescents. *Child and Adolescent Psychiatric Clinics of North America, 2*, 581–602.

Nachmias, M., Gunnar, M., Mangelsdorf, S., Parritz, R. H., & Buss, K. (1996). Behavioral inhibition and stress reactivity: The moderating role of attachment security. *Child Development, 67*, 508–522.

Patterson, G. R. (1982). *Coercive family processes.* Eugene, OR: Castalia.

Porges, S. W., Doussard-Roosevelt, J. A., & Maiti, A. K. (1994). Vagal tone and the physiological regulation of emotion. In N. A. Fox (Ed.), The development of emotion regulation and dysregulation: Biological and behavioral aspects. Monographs of the Society for Research in Child Development, *59*, 167–186.

Rapee, R. M., & Medoro, L. (1994). Fear of physical sensations and trait anxiety as mediators of the response to hyperventilation in nonclinical subjects. *Journal of Abnormal Psychology, 103*, 693–699.

Reed, L. J., Carter, B. D., & Miller, L. C. (1992). Fear and anxiety in children. In C. E. Walker & M. C. Roberts (Eds.), *Handbook of clinical child psychology* (2nd ed., pp. 237–260). New York: Wiley.

Reiss, S. (1991). Expectancy model of fear, anxiety, and panic. *Clinical Psychology Review, 11*, 141–153.

Robinson, J. L., Kagan, J., Reznick. J. S., & Corley, R. (1992). The heritability of inhibited and uninhibited behavior: A twin study. *Developmental Psychology, 28*, 1030–1037.

Saarni, C. (1998). *Developing emotional competence.* New York: Guilford.

Schmidt, N. B., Lerew, D. R., & Jackson, R. J. (1997). The role of anxiety sensitivity in the pathogenesis of panic: Prospective evaluation of spontaneous panic attacks during acute stress. *Journal of Abnormal Psychology, 106*, 355–364.

Silverman, W. K., Cerny, J. A., & Nelles, W. B. (1988). The familial influence in anxiety disorders: Studies on the offspring of patients with anxiety disorders. In B. B. Lahey & A. E. Kazdin (Eds.), *Advances in Clinical Child Psychology: Vol. 11* (pp. 223–248). New York: Plenum.

Sroufe, L. A. (1998). *Emotional development.* New York: Cambridge University Press.

Sroufe, L. A., & Rutter, M. (1984). The domain of developmental psychopathology. *Child Development, 55*, 17–29.

Stansbury, K., & Gunnar, M. R. (1994). Adrenocortical activity and emotion regulation. In N. A. Fox (Ed.), The development of emotion regulation and dysregulation: Biological and behavioral aspects. *Monographs of the Society for Research in Child Development, 59*, 108–134.

Taylor, S. (1995). Anxiety sensitivity: Theoretical perspectives and recent findings. *Behaviour Research and Therapy, 33*, 243–258.

Thompson, R. A. (1990). Emotion and self-regulation. In R. A. Thompson (Ed.), *Nebraska symposium on motivation: Socioemotional development: Vol. 36* (pp. 383–483). Lincoln, NE: University of Nebraska Press.

Thompson, R. A. (1994). Emotion regulation: A theme in search of definition. In N. A. Fox (Ed.), The development of emotion regulation and dysregulation: Biological and behavioral aspects. *Monographs of the Society for Research in Child Development, 59*, 25–52.

Thompson, R. A. (1998). Early sociopersonality development. In N. Eisenberg (Ed.), *Handbook of child psychology: Vol. 3. Social, emotional, and personality development* (5th ed., pp. 25–104). New York: Wiley.

Thompson, R. A. (1999). Early attachment and later development. In J. Cassidy & P. Shaver (Eds.), *Handbook of attachment* (pp. 265–286). New York: Guilford.

Thompson, R. A. (in press). *Early brain development and public policy.* Lincoln, NE: University of Nebraska Press.

Thompson, R. A., & Calkins, S. (1996). The double-edged sword: Emotional regulation for children at risk. *Development and Psychopathology* [Special Issue on Regulatory Processes], *8*, 163–182.

Thompson, R. A., Flood, M. F., & Lundquist, L. (1995). Emotional regulation and developmental psychopathology. In D. Cicchetti & S. Toth (Eds.), *Rochester symposium on developmental psychopathology: Vol. 6. Emotion, cognition, and representation* (pp. 261–299). Rochester, NY: University of Rochester Press.

Torgersen, S. (1993). Relationship between adult and childhood anxiety disorders: Genetic hypothesis. In C. J. Last (Ed.), *Anxiety across the lifespan: A developmental perspective* (pp. 113–127). New York: Springer.

Turner, S. M., Beidel, D. C., & Wolff, P. L. (1996). Is behavioral inhibition related to the anxiety disorders? *Clinical Psychology Review, 16*, 157–172.

Vasey, M. W., & Daleiden, E. L. (1996). Information-processing pathways to cognitive interference in childhood. In I. G. Sarason, G. Pierce, & B. Sarason (Eds.), *Cognitive interference: Theory, methods, and findings* (pp. 117–138). Hillsdale, NJ: Erlbaum.

Vasey, M. W., & Ollendick, T. H. (2000). Anxiety. In M. Lewis & A. Sameroff (Eds.), *Handbook of developmental psychopathology* (2nd ed., pp. 511–529). New York: Plenum.

Vasey, M. W., Daleiden, E. L., Williams, L. L., & Brown, L. (1995). Biased attention in childhood anxiety disorders: A preliminary study. *Journal of Abnormal Child Psychology, 23*, 267–279.

Vasey, M. W., El-Hag, N., & Daleiden, E. L. (1996). Anxiety and the processing of emotionally threatening stimuli: Distinctive patterns of selective attention among high- and low-test-anxious children. *Child Development, 67*, 1173–1185.

Vaughn, B. E., Kopp, C. B., Krakow, J. B., Johnson, B., & Schwartz, S. S. (1986). Process analyses of the behavior of very young children in delay tasks. *Developmental Psychology, 22*, 752–759.

Warren, S. L., Huston, L., Egeland, B., & Sroufe, L. A. (1997). Child and adolescent anxiety disorders and early attachment. *Journal of the American Academy of Child and Adolescent Psychiatry, 36*, 637–641.

Wigfield, A., & Eccles, J. S. (1990). Test anxiety in the school setting. In M. Lewis & S. M. Miller (Eds.), *Handbook of developmental psychopathology* (pp. 237–250). New York: Plenum.

Zahn-Waxler, C., & Kochanska, G. (1990). The origins of guilt. In R. A. Thompson (Ed.), *Nebraska Symposium on Motivation: Socioemotional development: Vol. 36* (pp. 183–258). Lincoln, NE: University of Nebraska Press.

9

Nonassociative Factors in the Development of Phobias

ROSS G. MENZIES and LYNNE M. HARRIS

During the approximately eighty years since the case study of Little Albert was published by Watson and Rayner (1920) it has been widely accepted that fears and phobias may develop through associative learning. It is also widely understood that fears and phobias are not acquired arbitrarily. Rather, fears of some objectively dangerous stimuli, such as snakes, and spiders, are readily learned (e.g., Mineka, Davidson, Cook, & Weir, 1984; Öhman, Dimberg, & Öst, 1985), compared with fears of other, equally dangerous stimuli, such as automobiles. A number of models explaining the nonarbitrary acquisition of fears through associative learning processes have been developed (for reviews, see Dadds, Davey, & Field, this volume; Muris & Merckelbach, this volume). Recently, neoconditioning models have proposed a variety of associative processes, apart from Pavlovian conditioning, through which fears may be learned. These processes include the verbal and cultural transmission of information about a CS UCS contingency, pre-existing beliefs and expectancies about the covariation between a CS and UCS, pre-existing emotional reactions to a CS, and UCS revaluation, where subsequent information about the significance of a UCS causes a change in the response to a CS previously paired with the revalued UCS (for more detail, see Davey, 1997 and Dadds et al., this volume). The inclusion of these processes greatly increases the explanatory power of associative accounts of fear acquisition.

In the last couple of decades, however, nonassociative accounts of fear acquisition have attracted theorists from a variety of backgrounds (e.g., Bowlby, 1975; Clarke & Jackson, 1983; Marks, 1969, 1987; Menzies & Clarke, 1995a; Rachman, 1977). Nonassociative models assert that most members of a species will show fear to a set of biologically relevant stimuli on their first encounter, given normal maturational processes and normal background experiences (Menzies & Clarke, 1995a). These approaches suggest that some fears associated with these stimuli may appear without any aversive associative learning experiences, either direct (pairings of feared objects with stimuli producing pain or distress), or indirect (vicarious conditioning or information/instruction). It is argued that the "evolutionary-relevant" stimuli that support nonassociative fear reactions have been threatening throughout the evolutionary history of the species; and that while other stimuli of more recent importance to the success of the species may support fear reactions, nonassociative mechanisms will not underlie the development of fear associated with these "evolutionary-neutral" stimuli. In short, nonassociative accounts, such as that of Menzies and Clarke (1995a), propose that Darwinian natural selection has favored individuals who displayed some level of fear on their first encounter with a dangerous object or situation, rather than individuals who readily acquire fears given appropriate learning experiences, as suggested by Seligman (1971).

The possibility that some evolutionary-relevant fears may not require associative learning experiences was first suggested by Rachman (1977, p. 255):

> Rather than assume that a significant proportion of the population *acquires identical fears*, we can entertain the view that the predisposition to develop the most common fears is innate and universal, or nearly so, and that what we learn is how to overcome our existing predispositions.

A large body of evidence points to the onset of fear reactions among infants of a variety of species without traumatic conditioning episodes apparently preceding their acquisition. For example, in many species, visual looming, eyespot patterns, odors, and novelty can elicit fear in the first days of life without any prior aversive CS–UCS pairing being observed (Marks, 1987). Not only does this seem to support the case for the nonassociative acquisition of fear, but also the "unlearned" account appears a more plausible explanation of these phenomena than its major Darwinian opponent, Seligman's (1971) preparedness theory. In Seligman's account, at least one painful associative-learning trial is required for fear acquisition. One trial, given the dangers to the individual that it may bring, is regarded as one trial too many by modern Darwinian models (e.g., Bowlby, 1975; Clarke & Jackson, 1983; Menzies & Clarke, 1995a).

This chapter continues by reviewing evidence for the nonassociative account of fear acquisition by examining four of the most widely claimed exemplars of nonassociative fear, namely stranger fear, separation anxiety, height fear, and water fear. The chapter concludes with an examination of common criticisms of the nonassociative position.

Nonassociative Fears

Stranger Fear

Fear of unfamiliar members of the species is one of the most universal fears across a number of species. It has been documented in birds (Gray, 1971), chimpanzees (Hebb, 1946), and many other species including humans (Marks, 1987). Fear of strangers appears to develop in virtually all members of some species, lasting for time-limited periods and following virtually the same pattern. For example, human infants display stranger fear at similar ages in American samples, British samples, Guatemalan samples, and samples of !Kung Bushmen and Hopi Indians, in spite of dramatically different child-rearing practices (Dennis, 1940; Smith, 1979). Stranger fear develops from ages four to nine months, peaking around 12.5 months, before declining in the second year of life. Twin studies have demonstrated greater concordance of onset age (e.g., Freedman, 1965), and a greater similarity in expression of stranger fear (e.g., Plomin & Rowe, 1979) between identical than fraternal twins, further supporting the notion of a genetic basis for stranger fear.

The universality of stranger fear, both within and across species, makes it difficult to conceive of this fear arising primarily as a result of associative processes. To explain this phenomenon, traditional associative models would need to assume that virtually all children experience direct traumatic conditioning trials involving strangers within a 5-month period in the first year of life, despite differences in rearing habits, family structure, culture, presence of caregivers, and socioeconomic status. The existence of such universal traumatic pairing is not consistent with parental reports.

Neoconditioning associative models do not assume temporal CS–UCS contiguity, and it is conceivable that sensory preconditioning and UCS revaluation may explain both the apparent universality of stranger fear and the failure of parents to consistently report traumatic CS–UCS pairings. An infant who has frequent non-noxious encounters with large adult males may witness violence perpetrated by an adult male model and may, through sensory preconditioning and UCS revaluation, come to revalue the strangers from their earlier safe encounters so that fear may grow. Both of these explanations, however, require us to accept that these episodes are universal in child development. Further, it may be appropriate to question whether children in the first year of life possess the memory capacity to allow such revaluation processes.

Infantile amnesia is well known in children under 2 years of age. While conditioning and habituation procedures can be used to demonstrate a form of "memory" in very young infants, whether stable, long-lasting, conscious "explicit" memory is functional in children under 1 year of age has been the subject of debate. Infants at 8–10 months fail at Piaget's hidden object task, a finding interpreted as suggesting that at this age they do not have a symbolic representation of events and objects independent of the perceptuomotor procedures used in interacting with them (Moscovitch, 1985). However, Goubet and Clifton (1998) report evidence that infants as young as $6\frac{1}{2}$ months show evidence of an ability to retain information about objects and events that they cannot see, and, further, that they can use this knowledge to guide their behavior. The length of time that very young infants can retain information is also subject to speculation. It appears that the duration of retention increases monotonically between 2 and 18 months of age (e.g., Hartshorn et al., 1998), but the length of retention clearly depends on the nature of the task. Parkin and Streete (1988) found that children 3 years of age performed poorly on an explicit recognition memory test for a set of simple pictures after a delay of 7 days. However, Fagen et al. (1997) report that infants at 3 months demonstrate some retention of a simple motor response after 7 days, but only when the context present at encoding is reinstated. In humans, successful fear conditioning resulting from UCS revaluation has been demonstrated only in individuals who are able to describe consciously the relationship between the original UCS and the inflated UCS (e.g., White & Davey, 1989). This suggests that UCS revaluation depends on a conscious awareness of the contingency between the revalued UCS and the previously encountered CS that requires explicit memory, a capacity that arguably occurs in a range of species other than humans (Wynne, 1998). Given that explicit memory appears to be immature in young infants, it is questionable whether children less than 12 months old will be capable of UCS revaluation.

Thus, associative models of the development of stranger fear require that infants at an apparently set period in the first year of life, directly or indirectly, form associations between strangers and pain. This in itself seems very unlikely. In addition, as Marks (1987) reminds us, the killing of conspecifics is commonplace in many species, and it is usually directed towards unknown conspecifics, especially infants. Menzies and Clarke (1995a) have therefore argued that fear of strangers may have evolved to protect against this abuse. Of course, this argument relies largely on guesswork about the level of risk to our infant ancestors from conspecifics, and about the protective value of a fear display in the face of a stranger. Clearly, the best evidence that stranger fear does not require associative learning is not the survival value of stranger fear to our ancestors, but rather the fact that it has a uniform pattern across cultural and geographical groups; and across a wide range of species.

Before leaving stranger fear it is worth stating that the severity of the fear displayed during development will vary from child to child (Plomin & Rowe, 1979). It seems to be a common misperception that nonassociative models propose that *all* individuals will display the same level of response in their initial encounters with relevant fear stimuli. This is obviously not the case. Genetic variability will ensure that a range of fear levels will be present in infants. While it is an axiom of the nonassociative position that fear levels will be higher to evolutionary-relevant fear stimuli than to evolutionary-neutral fear stimuli across the species, this does not negate the role of genetic variability. Put simply, some infants should (and do) display relatively minor and transient stranger fear responses in the first year of life. As has been argued elsewhere, the critical feature of nonassociative fears is that, at some measurable level and for some period during an individuals' development, one would expect to see the fear evidenced in virtually all members of this species. This certainly appears to be true in the case of stranger fear.

Separation Anxiety

Separation fear occurs in many species, including a host of mammals and nearly all primate species studied (Kraemer, 1985; McKinney, 1985; Mineka,

1982). Human infants are likely to cry at their parent's departure at between 8 and 24 months of age (Kagan, Kearsley & Zelazo, 1978; Smith, 1979). As with stranger fear, this appears to occur despite widely varying child-rearing practices and across various cultural and geographic areas, including the United States, Guatemala and Israel (Kagan et al., 1978). It is also seen in children with a range of intellectual and sensory abilities, including children with Down's syndrome and children who are blind, who recognize the absence of their guardian by sound. Separation fear is the same regardless of whether the guardian is male or female, and of whether the child was reared at home or in daycare (Marks, 1987). Separation fear is unrelated to the amount of previous time spent with the guardian and, more importantly, is unrelated to past aversive experiences during separation (Bowlby, 1975; Clarke & Jackson, 1983; Marks, 1987). Again, it is easy to speculate on the adaptive value of the fear. Bowlby and Marks have both argued persuasively that separation from a caretaker increases the likelihood of coming to grief from a number of causes and in a number of species.

This nonassociative fear is of particular interest because of its potential link to two significant psychiatric disorders, namely Separation Anxiety Disorder in childhood, and Panic Disorder with Agoraphobia. Some have argued that separation fear in infancy is a nonassociative, normal developmental fear that, in extreme cases, may continue as school phobia and later agoraphobia (see Silove & Manicavasagar, this volume). Clarke and Wardman (1985) have noted the similarities between adult agoraphobia and childhood separation fears. Both conditions involve: (1) fear of leaving secure places; (2) fear of leaving secure people; (3) reduction of anxiety in the presence of safety signals (e.g., talismans, toys, pills); and (4) association with school phobia. Clarke and Wardman (1985) appear to suggest that agoraphobia, separation anxiety disorders and extreme displays of infantile separation anxiety are in fact one condition observed at different periods during the life of an individual.

Several studies have reported a link between adult agoraphobia and a history of child separation anxiety. In one of the more well-constructed reports, Silove et al. (1995) found adult agoraphobic women to have higher scores on a retrospective measure of childhood separation anxiety than women with other anxiety disorders. Importantly the effect was not simply due to elevated neuroticism scores. Coming at the problem in a different way, Tearnan, Telch, & Keefe (1984) described a definable subgroup with agoraphobia whose initial onset was directly preceded by a separation experience. It is well established that separation anxiety and school phobia are closely linked. In a Swedish sample, all 35 cases who met DSM-III diagnostic criteria for school phobia also met criteria for separation anxiety (Flakierska-Praquin, Lindstroem, & Gillberg, 1997). Consistent with Clarke and Wardman's (1985) suggestion that separation anxiety and agoraphobia are faces of the same disorder seen at different stages of the lifespan, there is also evidence that school phobia may be linked to agoraphobia, implying that the three conditions—separation anxiety, school phobia, and agoraphobia—

may reflect the same underlying cause. Gittelman-Klein and Klein (1984) reported that 50% of a sample with agoraphobia had a history of school phobia, almost double the rate observed in a comparison group with specific phobias. Similarly, Deltito, Perugi, Maremmani, Mignani, and Cassano (1986) reported that 60% of a sample with agoraphobia had a documented history of school phobia.

Several researchers mistakenly appear to believe that nonassociative models of agoraphobia consider excessive separation experiences, rather than excessive separation anxiety, to be precursors of the adult syndrome. Thyer, Hilme, and Fischer (1988) found that loss of a parent in childhood occurred no more frequently for those with agoraphobia than for control subjects. Similarly, Margraf, Ehlers and Roth (1986), in a review of the literature, reported no increase in the number of actual separations from parents in the childhood of those with agoraphobia. It appears to be largely on the grounds of such data that reviewers such as Margraf et al. (1986) and Salkovskis and Hackmann (1997) reject the literature on the relationship between childhood separation anxiety and adult agoraphobia as equivocal. However, supporters of nonassociative models do not argue that separation experiences per se would be increased in those who later develop agoraphobia, but rather that such individuals would experience higher levels of separation anxiety during childhood (Clarke & Jackson, 1983; Clarke & Wardman, 1985). Indeed, the former interpretation is more in line with an associative account of fear onset. Given the available data, a link between separation fear and adult agoraphobia is not firmly established. However, the claim that separation fear, like stranger fear, arises from nonassociative processes is supported.

Height Fear

Height fear provides one of the clearest examples of a fear that may arise in the absence of associative learning processes. Evidence of the nonassociative nature of the fear comes from retrospective studies of human adults as well as from longitudinal, prospective studies beginning in childhood. In addition, animal research has established the fear as one of the most widely experienced by land-dwelling animals. For these reasons, height fear will be given particular attention in the present chapter.

The earliest evidence for the nonassociative account of height fear comes from animal and infant studies beginning with the work of Gibson and Walk and the now-famous "visual cliff." The visual cliff was a thin board laid across a large sheet of glass supported at varying heights above the floor. On one side of the board a sheet of patterned material is placed flush against the underside of the glass. On the other side, a sheet of the same material is laid upon the floor, creating the visual cliff.

In their original work with human subjects, Gibson and Walk (1960) tested 36 infants of between 6 and 14 months of age and found that only 3 ever willingly crawled on to the deep side of the cliff, despite their mother standing at that side and calling to them. Many actually crawled away from their mother when she called to them from the deep side; others would pat the glass but refuse to cross it; and others simply cried (Gibson & Walk, 1960).

Findings with other terrestrial species were largely consistent and equally dramatic. Owing to their early self-produced locomotion, chicks, kids, and lambs were tested on the first day of life as soon as they could stand. *No* chick, goat, or lamb ever stepped on to the glass on the deep side, even at one day of age (Gibson & Walk, 1960); and when lowered on to the deep side, kids and lambs would refuse to put their feet down, and would adopt a defensive posture. The experience of finding themselves on the deep side of the cliff was so aversive that many would attempt to leap to the apparent safety of the center board rather than walk on the glass. Similar findings were obtained with cats, and other researchers have extended the list to include dogs, pigs, and neonatal monkeys to name but a few. Indeed, there are few fears that appear more consistently in terrestrial animals. Water birds such as ducks may be regarded as having little reason to fear a perceived drop, and these, unlike land-dwelling animals, readily cross on to the deep side of the cliff (Emlen, 1963; Routtenberg & Glickman, 1964).

Walk and Gibson (1961) concluded that fear and avoidance of heights is innate in a variety of terrestrial species, and that it appears by the time an infant is locomotive. However, to deny the role of experience and the environment in the development of fear is fraught with danger, and subsequent research has shown that certain background experiences may be necessary for the development of avoidance of the visual cliff. The most notable of these is self-produced locomotion. Despite some controversy (cf. Bertenthal & Campos, 1984; Campos, Hiatt, Ramsay, Henderson, & Svejda, 1978; Richards & Rader, 1983), it now appears clear that previous experience of self-produced locomotion may be necessary for avoidance and fear of the visual cliff to be consistently observed. Bertenthal, Campos and Barrett (1984) refer to various findings supporting this conclusion, including that prelocomotive infants at 7.5 months showed little cardiac change indicative of fear when placed on the deep side of the cliff, whereas locomotive infants of the same age displayed heart rate acceleration. Also, prelocomotive infants given locomotor experience via 40 hours in an infant walker showed heart rate acceleration when placed on the deep side, whereas prelocomotive infants of the same age without such experience did not.

While self-produced locomotion appears to be important in the development of avoidance of the visual cliff, previous falls have been found to be unrelated and unnecessary for avoidance to occur (e.g., Scarr & Salapatek, 1970). That is, while experience seems to play a role in the emergence of this fear, it need not take the form of aversive classical conditioning. Crawling may be important for expanding an infant's perspective by increasing encounters with new experiences, and seems to speed the emergence of spatial cognition, form extraction, and social communication, along with fear of heights (Marks, 1987).

Retrospective research with human phobic and analog samples further demonstrates the nonassociative nature of height fear. Menzies and Clarke (1993a) investigated the acquisition of fear of heights in an undergraduate student sample. Their 16-page Origins Questionnaire (OQ) was designed to avoid methodological pitfalls of earlier retrospective questionnaires (see Menzies, Kirkby, & Harris, 1998) and to give a comprehensive picture of an individual's history in relation to the phobic object or situation prior to the onset of their concerns. Unlike previous popular measures, such as Öst & Hugdahl's (1981) Phobic Origin Questionnaire, the OQ does not require the respondent to make causal attributions about fear onset, but rather to simply indicate and describe any informational, vicarious, direct conditioning, or other events that had occurred prior to onset. The questionnaire distinguishes between subjects who claim to have always been fearful and those who, while failing to recall the onset of their concerns, recognize an earlier nonphobic period in their lives. In addition, the questions are open-ended and allow a distinction to be made between classical conditioning events and traumatic events in which no identifiable UCS can be found. Height-fearful and nonfearful groups were formed on the basis of extreme scores to the heights item on the FSS-III (Wolpe & Lang, 1964). Subjects were then assessed with a battery of measures including: (1) the Origins Questionnaire (OQ); (2) the Acrophobia Questionnaire (AQ; Cohen, 1977); (3) Global Assessment of Severity; (4) Self-Rating of Severity; and (5) an Origins Interview. Results obtained questioned the significance of simple associative-learning events in the acquisition of height phobia. Only 18% of fearful subjects were classified as directly conditioned cases. No differences between groups were found in either the proportion of subjects who knew others who were fearful of heights, the proportion of subjects who had experienced relevant associative-learning events, or in the ages at which these events had occurred. In addition, no relationships between mode of acquisition and either severity or individual response patterns were obtained. In support of the psychometric properties of the new instrument, both the interrater reliability and construct validity of the new Origins Questionnaire (OQ) were found to be high, with significant agreement between raters (98%) and a strong relationship between the OQ and the Origins Interview (95%) being obtained.

In a second study with a clinical sample, Menzies and Clarke (1995b) sought to replicate these findings with a group of acrophobia sufferers who had sought treatment. This replication was particularly important given Rachman's (1977) hypothesis regarding the possible relationship between onset and response patterns, whereby he speculated that severe clinical phobias may be more likely to result from direct, traumatic conditioning episodes. This latter study included a behavioral test and physiological data. All of the measures used in the earlier study were administered to 148 subjects who sought treatment at a height phobia clinic. In addition, subjects completed a Behavioural Avoidance Test (BAT) that allowed for the assessment of subjective distress, negative thoughts, heart rate, systolic blood pressure, diastolic blood pressure, and avoidance. Menzies & Clarke (1995b) found that more people with acrophobia claimed that their fear had always been present, or had arisen in a nonassociative traumatic event, than were classified as directly conditioned cases. In fact, nonassociative categories accounted for 56% of subjects, compared with only 11.5% of subjects who were classified as cases of direct conditioning, and 20% classified as indirect conditioning onsets. Despite the inclusion of physiological and avoidance data, no relationships between onset, severity, and individual response patterns could be found. When height phobics were compared with age- and sex-matched controls, no differences were found in the proportion of subjects who knew others who were fearful of heights, the proportion of subjects who had experienced relevant associative-learning events, or in the ages at which these events had occurred.

Both of the reports on the origins of height fear by Menzies and Clarke are subject to errors inherent in research using the retrospective method. In both studies adult subjects were asked to recall events from early childhood. It must be acknowledged that subjects may have simply forgotten critical events (or critical aspects of the events), and this may have biased the results against conditioning explanations. For this reason, the recent longitudinal study of the origins of height fear by Poulton, Davies, Menzies, Langley and Silva (1998) has become a pivotal paper in understanding how height fear develops. The sample described in this report were members of the Dunedin Multidisciplinary Health and Development Study, a longitudinal investigation of young people's health, development, and behavior from birth to adulthood. The sample had been assessed with a diverse array of psychological, medical, and sociological measures with high rates of participation at the following ages: 3 years (n 1037); 5 years ($n - 991$); 7 years ($n = 955$); 11 years ($n = 925$); 13 years ($n = 850$); 15 years ($n = 976$); 18 years ($n - 1008$); and 21 years ($n = 992$). In the report on height fear, data from assessments conducted at ages 3, 5, 7, 9, 11, and 18 years were used. Poulton et al. (1998) looked at the relationship between serious falls before age 9 and height fear at ages 11 and 18. Only serious falls resulting in a fracture, dislocation, laccration, or intracranial injury were included in the study. Despite falls being the most common accident occurring to children up to 9 years (Gafford, Silva, & Langley, 1996), no positive relationship between putative aversive events and height fear at age 11 or phobia at age 18 could be found. In contrast, falls resulting in serious injury between 5 and 9 years occurred with greater frequency in those *without* a fear at age 18. Most importantly, no individuals who had a height phobia at age 18 had a history of a serious fall before the age of nine.

The report of Poulton et al. (1998) provides strong evidence that adult height phobia, like height fear demonstrated in infants on the visual cliff, appears to be independent of aversive conditioning processes. In the absence of data concerning height fear in childhood for this sample, the study cannot directly speak to the continuity between childhood and adult height fear. However, it should be noted that 57 of 148 adult height phobics in

Menzies and Clarke's (1995b) study reported that they had "always been this way," suggesting that for a large proportion of height phobics the fear remains from childhood to adulthood. Poulton et al. (1998) also provide support for Marks and Nesse's (1994) concept of "hypophobia." Marks and Nesse argue that the absence of "normal" levels of developmental fears represents a serious disorder that places the individual at increased risk of injury or death. They state (p. 254):

> Anxiety, too, is beneficial . . . too little anxiety leads to behavior that makes us more likely to fall off a cliff . . . people with too little anxiety do not come to psychiatrists complaining of deficient fear, so their disorders, the "hypophobias," still await formal description.

In perhaps the first clear evidence for hypophobia, Poulton et al. (1998) have shown that the absence of adult height fear is associated with an elevated history of serious falls in childhood. It is suggested that children without sufficient fear are likely to fall when in high, vulnerable positions. Further, directly opposed to a conditioning position, such children do not go on to develop height fear in adulthood. Instead, they continue with less fear than those individuals who have never fallen (Poulton et al., 1998).

A further feature of height fear that suggests a nonassociative onset is the timing of its appearance. Marks and Nesse (1994) argue that evolutionary-relevant fears should manifest at the age when they become adaptive. Height fear, as Marks and Nesse recognize, seems to exemplify this principle. In humans, height fear emerges at around 6 months, soon after the onset of self-locomotion. Prior to this point the fear would clearly be useless in human infants. Of course, as stated, in animals that are locomotive on the first day of life, the fear appears to be present from birth. Marks (1987) and others regard this feature as a clear pointer to the evolutionary-relevance of the fear and its independence from associative learning.

Finally, some comment should be made on the role of neoconditioning models in accounting for height fear. Davey (1997) has argued cogently that traumatic pairings of CSs and aversive UCSs are not needed in contemporary fear-conditioning models. Rather, cultural transmission, information and instruction, sensory preconditioning, and UCS revaluation can all effect fear level in individuals at any point in time. However, in the case of height fear in lambs on the first day of life it is difficult to see the relevance of any of these factors. Thus, traditional conditioning and neoconditioning models alike seem unable to account for this fear. Given all of the available data, it is not surprising that height fear continues to be regarded as a clear exemplar of nonassociative fears by many theorists (see Menzies & Clarke, 1995a, 1995b).

Water Fear

Given its early onset, it would seem appropriate to investigate the origins of water fear and phobia in early childhood. However, as with many other specific phobias this strategy has rarely been employed. Ollendick and King (1991) point out that, despite the fact that the majority of specific phobias are acquired in childhood, few researchers have investigated etiological formulations with child subjects. Instead, studies of the origins of phobias have tended to rely on the retrospective reports of adult patients who are asked to recall events that often occurred long ago. Not surprisingly, many adult patients appear unable to recall the events surrounding the early onset of their fears (McNally & Steketee, 1985). To the present authors' knowledge, there is only a single published study investigating the origins of a clinical group of childhood phobic cases, that of Menzies and Clarke (1993b). The focus of this study was nonassociative explanations of water phobia, and therefore its findings and conclusions will be examined closely.

Menzies and Clarke's study used parental reports of the events surrounding onset to investigate the origins of water phobia in young children. The sample comprised 50 subjects (20 female) with a mean age of 5.5 years, who were taking part in a water phobia treatment study at the University of New South Wales on the east coast of Sydney, Australia. This sample was selected from 200 initial respondents to announcements of the availability of treatment for water phobia at 55 infant and primary schools. All children who could spontaneously place their heads underwater were excluded from the study because of the low levels of their fear. The authors developed an instrument to measure phobic origin, which consisted of a list of previously identified causes of water phobia. These covered all of Rachman's (1977) pathways to fear (i.e., direct classical conditioning, vicarious conditioning, and information/instruction). From the list, parents were asked to indicate which option they believed to have been the most influential factor in the development of their child's water phobia.

Menzies and Clarke reported that the majority of parents (56%) believed that their child's phobic concern had been present from their very first contact with water. None of these parents chose any of the associative alternatives as being influential in the development of their child's phobia. That is, they believed their child's concern to be unrelated to either direct experience or information/observation. While a substantial proportion of parents (26%) did report indirect conditioning episodes, only 2% of parents attributed their child's phobic concern to a direct conditioning episode. That is, only one parent surveyed could recall such an event in the development of her child's fear. The remaining parents (16%) had no explanation of onset, recalling no traumatic experience, but also reporting that their child had not always displayed a fear of water.

The findings of this investigation include one of the lowest rates of classical conditioning ever reported in a retrospective study of the origins of human fear. In only two studies have lower rates of conditioning been observed, in a sample with spider fear (Jones & Menzies, 1995), and in a sample of people with a range of fears classified as having an evolutionary-relevant focus (Harris & Menzies, 1996). The 2% rate of conditioning is much lower than has typically been found with clinical cases of phobia, particularly in the extensive work on the origins of phobias conducted by Öst and his colleagues. Across a variety of phobic conditions, Öst and Hugdahl have found direct conditioning to account for between 45.5% and 81.3% of clinical cases (Öst and Hugdahl, 1981, 1983, 1985).

Several explanations of the marked differences in the rate of reported conditioning onsets between Menzies and Clarke's report and those of Öst and Hugdahl have previously been examined in detail (Menzies and Clarke, 1994). Firstly, Menzies and Clarke were the first to examine children. Adult memories of early childhood in Öst and Hugdahl's studies may have been subject to greater error than in Menzies and Clarke's study. Alternatively, the fact that Menzies and Clarke relied on parental reports rather than on the recall of those with phobia may have led to an underestimate of the rate of conditioning. Menzies and Clarke argued that the water-related experiences of young children are likely to have been closely monitored by parents. Still, it is difficult to rule out the possibility that associative, traumatic events occurred in the presence of other carers of which the reporting parent was unaware. It is perhaps significant that Menzies and Clarke did not ask both parents to complete the origins instrument, but simply the attending parent. Thirdly, differences between the origins instruments used across studies may account for some differences. It has been previously argued that the use of Öst and Hugdahl's (1981) Phobic Origin Questionnaire may lead to a significant overestimate of the frequency of classically conditioned cases (Marks, 1987; Menzies & Clarke, 1994). Menzies and Clarke (1993b, 1994) have suggested that the two classical conditioning questions on Öst and Hugdahl's scale fail to identify the essential ingredients of a Pavlovian conditioning procedure (e.g., presence of an independent UCS, pairing of the CS and the UCS, prior affective neutrality of the CS). Finally, differences across studies may be partly due to the nature of the different specific phobias examined in these reports. Fears of water may simply not require associative-learning events for their acquisition. This is the interpretation of the data offered by Menzies and Clarke (1993b). In line with the nonassociative account, they suggest that fear of water can develop in the absence of any previous negative experience with the feared stimulus. No direct or indirect traumatic pairing is required, and neither is negative information. Though some background experiences may be necessary, relevant aversive associative learning is not.

Some comment should be made about the high rate of indirect learning present in Menzies and Clarke's sample. In each of Öst and Hugdahl's examinations of phobic origins, direct conditioning episodes were reported more frequently than observational conditioning episodes. In Menzies and Clarke's water phobic sample, 26% reported vicarious learning experiences while only 2% reported direct conditioning. The strong presence of indirect learning in these young children might suggest that other family members had experienced fearful encounters with water and that a familial link exists. Menzies (1985) examined this possibility by comparing the level of the children's and parent's fears of water. Children's scores on a 7-item water phobia schedule were correlated with parent's reports of their own fears on a modified version of the instrument. A small-to-moderate relationship between the fear intensity of mother's and their children ($r = 0.39$) was observed, whereas no relationship between father's and children's fear levels was found ($r = 0.05$). Since many young children spend more time in their mothers' care than in their fathers', the opportunity for vicarious learning from fathers may be reduced. Of course, vicarious conditioning is only one of the many possible explanations for a relationship between the water fear level of mother and child. Other explanations include genetic influences, similar direct traumatic experiences, and a lack of opportunity to receive repeated nontraumatic exposure to water so that habituation may occur. This latter possibility seems particularly plausible from the perspective of the nonassociative model of water fear described previously. If a mother is water-fearful it is unlikely that she will frequent beaches or swimming pools with her young children. If they spend the majority of time in their mothers care, young children may selectively fail to habituate to fears that their mothers' also share.

Unfortunately, few data are available on the histories of adults with water phobia. Whether or not the fear can persist into adulthood in the absence of water-related trauma is simply not known at this point. Little has been published on the natural history of the fear and it is possible that adults with water phobia seen in clinical practice come from an essentially different population from the childhood subjects of Menzies and Clarke (1993b). Certainly the fear appears to be less frequent in adulthood, suggesting that in most individuals fear declines during the early years of life. This is not surprising from either an associative or a nonassociative perspective. Whether due to extinction or habituation, the constant exposure to water from regular bathing should eliminate the fear in most individuals, and the sheer frequency of such exposure should lead to generalization to other contexts involving water. Anecdotally, it is often observed that persistent cases of water fear have been associated with a marked avoidance of bathing from the earliest years of life.

One recent study does attempt to trace water experiences in childhood and their relationship to water fear in early adulthood. Using the Dunedin cohort described earlier, Poulton, Menzies, Craske, Langley and Silva (1999) examined water trauma and confidence up to the age of 9 years and water fear at age 18 years. Again, no evidence of a relationship between water trauma (i.e., conditioning events) and later water fear could be found, suggesting that water phobia does not require direct associative learning for its appearance. Unfortunately, although information about the presence of childhood water fear at age 9 years would provide better support for the nonassociative account, measures of water fear were not taken at that age.

Common Criticisms of the Nonassociative Account

This section briefly examines the two major criticisms of the nonassociative account of fear acquisition.

The Model Is Intrinsically Post Hoc

Merckelbach and de Jong (1997) and Muris and Merckelbach (see this volume) argue that the nonassociative account assumes that researchers can reconstruct the challenges faced by our long-past ancestors. That is, they claim that the model rests on the ability of the theorist to "guess" which stimuli represented dangers in the distant past, and which did not. Menzies, Clarke, Jones, Harris and their colleagues do not claim that heights, water etc. are nonassociative fear stimuli simply because their relevance to our ancestors' survival appears obvious. Rather, these researchers claim that such stimuli may elicit fears of a nonassociative origin because there is little evidence that associative learning is required for fear acquisition to these stimuli in current samples. In fact, contrary to the suggestion that the allocation of stimuli to the nonassociative group is arbitrary and based on theorists' individual insights, these authors have sought to directly verify which stimuli appear to support nonassociative fears. Menzies and Harris have conducted two retrospective studies concerning the onset of fear using the OQ, one examining a mixed group of nonclinical, highly fearful people (Harris & Menzies, 1996), and the second examining a mixed clinical sample with specific phobias (Menzies & Harris, 1997). In both studies, independent raters divided stimuli into those that appeared to be evolutionary-relevant, thereby suggesting a nonassociative mode of onset, and those that appeared to be evolutionary-neutral, suggesting an associative onset may be likely, on an a priori basis. This division enabled a comparison of reported modes of onset between the two groups. In both samples, reports of fear onset associated with conditioning episodes, vicarious learning, or information transmission were rare among those whose fears were classified as evolutionary-relevant and more common for the group whose fears were classified as evolutionary-neutral. The findings were thus consistent with the notion that some fears may be primarily acquired through associative processes, while for others nonassociative modes of acquisition are more common. This approach appears the most appropriate way to proceed, as attempting to establish independently the relevance of stimuli to our ancestors' likelihood of sexual dominance is unlikely to be a fruitful method of enquiry. However, establishing whether any evidence exists that an individual case of fear onset involved an independent UCS should be a simpler matter, and this is what human retrospective research in the area has sought to accomplish.

Even critics of the nonassociative model seem to accept that some stimuli seem likely to have provided a long-term threat to the species. Merkelbach and de Jong (1997), note that "it is reasonable to assume that fear of heights and fear of strangers are relevant to fitness" (p. 336). Arguably, however, rather than attempting to speculate on the severity of danger posed by a particular stimulus, research needs to focus on evidence that associative learning does not appear to be required for fear acquisition. Thus, fear of heights should be regarded as a nonassociative fear, not because it is reasonable to assume its relevance to fitness, but because: (1) fewer than 20% of those with acrophobia can report conditioning events in their histories, and a large percentage report having always had a fear of heights; (2) fewer than 15% of undergraduate height-fearfuls can report on conditioning events in their history, and a large percentage report having always had a fear of heights; (3) fear of heights appears as early as the onset of crawling in children; (4) fear of heights is evident in land-dwelling animals as early as the first day of locomotion, which in the case of infant lambs and goats, is the first day of life; and (5) prospective human research suggests that adult height fear is associated with a *reduced* likelihood of having fallen in childhood. Taken together, these findings indicate (a) the early onset and apparent universality of height fear in infants, and (b) the absence of reported learning experiences in the history of adult height phobics. Both phenomena are difficult to reconcile with learning accounts of fear acquisition. Given these findings it is clear that one does not need to rely on simple guesswork in rebuilding threats to our ancestors to establish nonassociative fears.

Not All People Suffer from Nonassociative Fears

Proponents of the nonassociative account first considered this issue. Commenting on an early version of the Menzies and Clarke model, Clarke and Jackson (1983, pp. 181–182) stated:

> The reader who accepts the argument up to this point would, understandably, wonder why we are all not phobic to all of these "natural clues" to threat? If phobias are a form of "survival instinct," why don't they emerge at birth and remain in force for evermore?

Merckelbach and de Jong (1997) and Muris and Merckelbach (see this volume) raise similar questions. We now explore three explanations of this phenomenon.

Genetic Variability. Clearly, the most obvious reason for the apparent absence of fear in some individuals lies in genetic variability. To ask why it is that not all people suffer from phobias is closely akin to asking why we don't all have the same metabolic rate or the same muscle length. The answer is each case appears to be the same: genetic variability that allows differences within a species to exist in order to allow for the species to adapt to changes in the environment.

To demonstrate this further, the nonassociative model would explain elevated snake fear as particularly adaptive for a species living in an environment shared with snakes, without floors in homes, without cement and paths covering areas where snakes may potentially live. However, as the human environment has changed so that humans seldom find themselves in environments where they are threatened by snakes, elevated snake fear becomes maladaptive, leading those with concerns about snakes to seek help to deal with their fears.

The nonassociative model emphatically does not suggest that all individuals of a given species will display the same level of fear to a given nonassociative stimulus. Rather, the distribution of fear responses to each nonassociative stimulus may be expected to follow a normal curve. Admittedly, the nonassociative model does suggest that, owing to evolutionary pressures, fear to particular evolutionary-relevant stimuli will have increased across the population over time, such that a measurable level of fear response will be present in most individuals. This appears to be true for fear of heights, as virtually all members of nearly all land-dwelling species tested to date display some level of fear on the visual cliff at some point in early development. However, the level of nonassociative fear to some stimuli will be less depending on the effect on the gene pool of the danger across time. In essence, the nonassociative model suggests that the average level of fear in the population has increased for some stimuli.

Support for the position that genetic variability affects fear level can be drawn from data showing similarities between the levels of fear in children and their parents. (Of course, such data are also consistent with indirect associative transmission through vicarious learning and information transmission.) Such support is available for some nonassociative fears. For example, Menzies (1985) reported a small-to-moderate relationship ($r = 0.39$) between level of water fear in parents and fear level in water phobic children. Better evidence for the genetic transmission of fear comes from twin studies. From a sample of 2163 adult female twins, Kendler et al. (1992) found that the best explanation of the familial aggregation of agoraphobia, social phobia, and situational phobia was additive genetic factors, and not the similarity of adult and childhood environments.

Opportunities for Exposure. Menzies and Clarke (1995a) suggest that the majority of individuals will gain sufficient exposure in the naturalistic environment to nonassociative fears so as to lead to habituation of the fear response, and this is the principle means by which individuals are assumed to eliminate nonassociative fears. While all human infants appear to fear height on the visual cliff, all adults do not report height fear and the majority of human adults are able to encounter extreme heights in controlled environments, such as office towers, without distress. Menzies and Clarke (1995a), and Clarke and Jackson (1983) before them, argue that this reduction of fear occurs through habituation. Naturalistic and gradual encounters with height across the life course leads to ever-declining levels of fear through habituation. From this perspective, the question to be asked is not why is it that only some individuals have adult fears of nonassociative stimuli, but rather, why do any? Why do some adults fail to habituate to the feared stimuli?

Clearly, a lack of opportunity for safe exposure with the feared stimulus will not allow habituation to occur. Clarke and Jackson (1983) first raised this as an explanation of the absence of adult fear. For example, individuals living in rural farm areas on low-lying plains may have infrequent encounters with substantial heights. Menzies (1997) suggests that water fearful parents may systematically fail to take their children to swimming pools and other places where encounters with deep water are possible, leading to similar failures to habituate in these children. Anecdotally, the majority of persistent cases of adult water fear have been associated with a marked avoidance of bathing from the earliest years of life (Menzies, 1997).

Differences in the Speed of Habituation. Finally, Menzies and Clarke (1995a) suggest that nonassociative fears can remain in individuals who habituate at a slower pace than is usual. Again, Merkelbach and de Jong (1997) and Muris and Merckelbach (see this volume) argue that this account begs a more fundamental question: Why do some individuals habituate rapidly and others slowly? Again, the answer must lie with genetic variability. It is surely of no surprise that there will be variability in the rate of habituation to these or any other stimuli. Some individuals will require fewer and others will require additional exposures to nonassociative stimuli in order for habituation to occur. It goes without saying that the same is true for any other learning phenomenon—as any primary school teacher will attest, variability in rate of learning is the norm rather than the exception.

Summary and Conclusions

This chapter has presented evidence that some common fears, such as fear of strangers, separation, heights, and water, may develop without the need for associative learning episodes. It is argued that the nonassociative model provides the most parsimonious explanation for the frequent appearance of these fears across a wide range of cultural groups living in diverse environments.

It should be noted that there is evidence to support the development of fear by nonassociative means in a range of other "evolutionary-relevant" fears not discussed in detail here. For example, Kleinknecht (1982) investigated the origin of spider fear among a group with concerns about tarantulas. Kleinknecht reports that the description of any experience consistent with a direct associative learning episode was "salient by its omission" in his sample (Kleinknecht, 1982, p. 440), a finding supported by Davey (1992) and by Jones and Menzies (1995). These retrospective reports converge despite the use of quite different instruments for evaluating onset. In claustrophobia, the evidence for the role of associative learning in the development of the fear is strong (for a review, see Rachman, 1997). Recently, however, Rachman has proposed that some cases of claustrophobia may have a nonassociative onset, and the wide distribution and early onset of the fear are consistent with this explanation (Rachman, 1997). The notion that some cases of "nonassociative" fears may appear to have been acquired associatively is entirely consistent with the nonassociative model, although the model would predict higher rates of associative learning for "evolutionary-neutral" fears than for "evolutionary-relevant" fears (e.g., Harris & Menzies, 1996; Menzies & Harris, 1997).

While the present chapter reviews evidence for the role of nonassociative acquisition in the development of some specific fears, it is important to note that the model aims to explain only the origins of a limited number of fears. Clearly, as noted above, fears of situations and stimuli that have existed only recently in our evolutionary history as a species, such as those concerned with driving and dentistry, should not be acquired nonassociatively, and they do not appear to be (e.g., Munjack, 1984; Moore, Brodsgaard, & Birn, 1991). That is, nonassociative processes are only one means by which fears may be acquired. Other modes of fear acquisition are discussed elsewhere in this volume (e.g., Dadds et al., this volume). However, it is the phobias that begin in early childhood, such as fear of strangers, separation, heights, and water, that will be most likely candidates for a nonassociative mode of onset.

Most of the research concerning the origins of specific phobia uses a retrospective methodology. Despite attempts to control for forgetting and possible response biases, such methodologies will always be open to criticism. However, large-scale, prospective, longitudinal studies like those of Poulton et al. (1998, 1999) avoid the pitfalls of retrospective research. Further studies using prospective methodologies of this kind are needed to evaluate the utility of associative and nonassociative accounts in explaining the development of fear to a range of stimuli and situations.

Notes

Please address correspondence to Dr Ross G. Menzies, Department of Behavioural Sciences, University of Sydney, PO Box 170 Lidcombe, NSW 2141, Australia. E-mail: R.Menzies@cchs.usyd.edu.au.

References

Bertenthal, B. I., & Campos, J. J. (1984). A reexamination of fear and its determinants on the visual cliff. *Psychophysiology, 21*, 413–417.

Bertenthal, B. I., Campos, J. J., & Barrett, K. C. (1984). Self-produced locomotion: An organizer of emotional, cognitive, and social development in infancy. In R. Emde & R. Harmon (Eds.), *Continuities and discontinuities in development* (pp. 175–210). New York: Plenum.

Bowlby, J. (1975). *Attachment and loss: Vol. 2*. London: Penguin.

Campos, J. J., Hiatt, S., Ramsay, D., Henderson, C., & Svejda, M. (1978). The emergence of fear on the visual cliff. In M. Lewis & L. A. Rosenblum (Eds.), *The development of affect* (pp. 149–181). New York: Plenum.

Clarke, J. C., & Jackson, J. A. (1983). *Hypnosis and behavior therapy: The treatment of anxiety and phobias*. New York: Springer.

Clarke, J. C., & Wardman, W. (1985). *Agoraphobia: A clinical and personal account*. Sydney: Pergamon.

Cohen, D. C. (1977). Comparisons of self-report and overt-behavioral procedures for assessing acrophobia. *Behavior Therapy, 18*, 17–23.

Davey, G. C. L. (1992). Classical conditioning and the acquisition of human fears and phobias: A review and synthesis of the literature. *Advances in Behaviour Research and Therapy, 14*, 29–66.

Davey, G. C. L. (1997). A conditioning model of phobias. In G. C. L. Davey (Ed.), *Phobias: A handbook of theory, research and treatment*. Chichester, England: Wiley.

Deltito, J. A., Perugi, G., Maremmani, I., Mignani, V., & Cassano, G. B. (1986). The importance of separation anxiety in the differentiation of panic disorder from agoraphobia. *Psychiatric Developments, 3*, 227–236.

Dennis, W. (1940). Does culture appreciably affect patterns of infant behavior? *Journal of Social Psychology, 12*, 305–317.

Emlen, J. T. (1963). Determinants of cliff edge and escape responses in herring gull chicks. *Behaviour, 22*, 1–15.

Fagen, J., Prigot, J., Carroll, M., Pioli, L., Stein, A., & Franco, A. (1997). Auditory context and memory retrieval in young infants. *Child Development, 68*, 1057–1066.

Flakierska-Praquin, N., Lindstroem, M., & Gillberg, C. (1997). School phobia with separation anxiety disorder: A comparative 20 to 29 year follow-up study of 35 school refusers. *Comprehensive Psychiatry, 38*, 17–22.

Freedman, D. (1965). Hereditary control of early social behavior. In B. M. Foss (Ed.), *Determinants of infant behavior: Vol. III* (pp. 149–155). London: Methuen.

Gafford, J. E., Silva, P. A., & Langley, J. D. (1996). Injuries. In P. A. Silva and W. R. Stanton (Eds.), *From child to adult: The Dunedin Multidisciplinary Health and Development Study*. Auckland: Oxford University Press.

Gibson, E. J., & Walk, R. D. (1960). The "visual cliff." *Scientific American, 202*, 64–71.

Gittelman-Klein, R., & Klein, D. (1984). Relationship between separation anxiety and panic and agoraphobic disorders. *Psychopathology (supplement), 17*, 56–65.

Goubet, N., & Clifton, R. K. (1998). Object and event representation in 6½ month old infants. *Developmental Psychology, 34*, 63–76.

Gray, J. A. (1971). *The psychology of fear and stress*. London: Weidenfeld & Nicholson.

Harris, L. M., & Menzies, R. G. (1996). Origins of specific fears: A comparison of associative and nonassociative accounts. *Anxiety, 2*, 5–9.

Hartshorn, K., Rovee-Collier, C., Gerhardstein, P., Bhatt, R. S., Wondoloski, T. L., Klein, P., Gilch, J., Wurtzel, N., & Campos, M. (1998). The ontogeny of long-term memory over the first year-and-a-half of life. *Developmental Psychobiology, 32*, 69–89.

Hebb, D. O. (1946). On the nature of fear. *Psychological Review, 53*, 259–276.

Jones, M. K., & Menzies, R. G. (1995). The etiology of fear of spiders. *Anxiety, Stress, & Coping, 8*, 227–234.

Kagan, J., Kearsley, R. B., & Zelazo, P. R. (1978). *Infancy: Its place in human development*. Cambridge, MA: Harvard University Press.

Kendler, K. S., Neale, M. C., Kessler, R. C., Heath, A. C., & Eaves, L. J. (1992). The genetic epidemiology of phobias in women: The interrelationship of agoraphobia, social phobia, situational phobia, and simple phobia. *Archives of General Psychiatry, 49*, 273–281.

Kleinknecht, R. D. (1982). The origins and remission of fear in a group of tarantula enthusiasts. *Behaviour Research and Therapy, 20*, 437–443.

Kraemer, G. W. (1985). Effects of differences in early social experience on primate neurobiological–behavioral development. In M. Reite & T. Field (Eds.), *The psychobiology of attachment* (pp. 135–161). New York: Academic Press.

Margraf, J., Ehlers, A., & Roth, W. (1986). Biological models of panic disorder and agoraphobia. *Behaviour, Research, & Therapy, 24,* 553–567.

Marks, I. M. (1969). *Fears and phobias.* London: Heinemann.

Marks, I. M. (1987). *Fears, phobias and rituals: Panic, anxiety and their disorders.* New York: Oxford University Press.

Marks, I. M., & Nesse, R. M. (1994). Fear and fitness: An evolutionary analysis of anxiety disorders. *Ethology and Sociobiology, 15,* 247–261.

McKinney, W. T. (1985). Separation and depression: Biological markers. In M. Reite & T. Field (Eds.), *The psychobiology of attachment* (pp. 201–222). New York: Wiley.

McNally, R. J., & Steketee, G. S. (1985). The etiology and maintenance of severe animal phobias. *Behaviour Research and Therapy, 23,* 431–435.

Menzies, R. G. (1985). The etiology and treatment of children's water phobia. Unpublished honors thesis.

Menzies, R. G. (1997). Water Phobia. In G. C. L. Davey (Ed.), *Phobias: A handbook of theory, research and treatment.* Chichester, England: Wiley.

Menzies, R. G., & Clarke, J. C. (1993a). The etiology of fear of heights and its relationship to severity and individual response patterns. *Behaviour Research and Therapy, 31,* 355–365.

Menzies, R. G., & Clarke, J. C. (1993b). The etiology of childhood water phobia. *Behaviour Research and Therapy, 31,* 499–501.

Menzies, R. G., & Clarke, J. C. (1994). Retrospective studies of the origins of phobias: A review. *Anxiety, Stress, & Coping, 7,* 305–318.

Menzies, R. G., & Clarke, J. C. (1995a). The etiology of phobias: A nonassociative account. *Clinical Psychology Review, 15,* 23–48.

Menzies, R. G., & Clarke, J. C. (1995b). The etiology of acrophobia and its relationship to severity and individual response patterns. *Behaviour Research and Therapy, 33,* 795–803.

Menzies, R. G., & Harris, L. M. (1997). Mode of onset in evolutionary-relevant and evolutionary-neutral phobias: Evidence from a clinical sample. *Depression and Anxiety, 5,* 134–136.

Menzies, R. G., Kirkby, K., & Harris, L. M. (1998). The convergent validity of the Phobia Origins Questionnaire (POQ): A review of the evidence. *Behaviour Research and Therapy, 36,* 1081–1089.

Merckelbach, H., & de Jong, P. J. (1997). Evolutionary models of phobias. In G. C. L. Davey (Ed.), *Phobias: A handbook of theory, research and treatment.* Chichester, England: Wiley.

Mineka, S. (1982). Depression and helplessness in primates. In H. E. Fitzgerald, J. A. Mullins, & P. Gaze (Eds.), *Child nurturance: Vol. 3* (pp. 197–242). New York: Plenum.

Mineka, S., Davidson, M., Cook, M., & Weir, R. (1984). Observational conditioning of snake fear in rhesus monkeys. *Journal of Abnormal Psychology, 93,* 355–372.

Moore, R., Brodsgaard, I., & Birn, H. (1991). Manifestations, acquisition and diagnostic categories of dental fear in a self-referred population. *Behaviour Research and Therapy, 29,* 51–60.

Moscovitch, M. (1985). Memory from infancy to old age: Implications for theories of normal and pathological memory. *Annals of the New York Academy of Science*, *444*, 78–96.

Munjack, D. J. (1984). The onset of driving phobias. *Journal of Behavior Therapy and Experimental Psychiatry*, *15*, 305–308.

Öhman, A., Dimberg, U., & Öst, L.-G. (1985). Animal and social phobia: Biological constraints on learned fear responses. In S. Reiss & R.R. Bootzin (Eds.), *Theoretical issues in behavior therapy* (pp. 123–175). New York: Academic Press.

Ollendick, T. H., & King, N. J. (1991). Origins of childhood fears: An evaluation of Rachman's theory of fear acquisition. *Behaviour Research and Therapy*, *29*, 117–123.

Öst, L.-G., & Hugdahl, K. (1981). Acquisition of phobias and anxiety response patterns in clinical patients. *Behaviour Research and Therapy*, *19*, 439–447.

Öst, L.-G., & Hugdahl, K. (1983). Acquisition of agoraphobia, mode of onset and anxiety response patterns. *Behaviour Research and Therapy*, *21*, 623–632.

Öst, I.-G., & Hugdahl, K. (1985). Acquisition of blood and dental phobia and anxiety response patterns in clinical patients. *Behaviour Research and Therapy*, *23*, 27–34.

Parkin, A. J., & Streete, S. (1988). Implicit and explicit memory in young children and adults. *British Journal of Psychology*, *79*, 361–369.

Plomin, R., & Rowe, D. C. (1979). Genetic and environmental etiology of social behavior in infancy. *Developmental Psychology*, *15*, 62–72.

Poulton, R., Davies, S., Menzies, R. G., Langley, J. D., & Silva, P. A. (1998). Falls in childhood and height fear in adolescence: Evidence for a nonassociative model of fear acquisition in a longitudinal study. *Behaviour Research and Therapy*, *36*, 537–544.

Poulton, R., Menzies, R. G., Craske, M. G., Langley, J. D., & Silva, P. A. (1999). Water trauma and swimming experiences up to age 9 and fear of water at age 18: A longitudinal study. *Behaviour Research and Therapy*, *37*, 39–48.

Rachman, S. (1977). The conditioning theory of fear acquisition: A critical examination. *Behaviour Research and Therapy*, *15*, 375–387.

Rachman, S. J. (1997). Claustrophobia. In G. C. L. Davey (Ed.), *Phobias: A handbook of theory, research and treatment*. Chichester, England: Wiley.

Richards, J., & Rader, N. (1983). Affective, behavioral, and avoidance responses on the visual cliff: effects of crawling onset age, crawling experience, and testing age. *Psychophysiology*, *20*, 633–642.

Routtenberg, G. A., & Glickman, S. E. (1964). Visual cliff behavior in undomesticated rodents, land and aquatic turtles and cats. *Journal of Comparative and Physiological Psychology*, *58*, 143–146.

Salkovskis, P. M., & Hackmann, A. (1997). Agoraphobia. In G.C.L. Davey (Ed.), *Phobias: A handbook of theory, research and treatment*. Chichester, England: Wiley.

Scarr, S., & Salapatek, P. (1970). Patterns of fear development during infancy. *Merrill–Palmer Quarterly*, *16*, 53–90.

Seligman, M. E. P. (1971). Phobias and preparedness. *Behavior Therapy*, *2*, 307–320.

Silove, D., Harris, M., Morgan, A., Boyce, P., Manicavasagar, V., Hadzi-Pavlovic, D., & Wilhelm, K. (1995). Is separation anxiety a specific precursor of panic-disorder agoraphobia? *Psychological Medicine*, *25*, 405–411.

Smith, P. K. (1979). The ontogeny of fear in children. In W. Slukin (Ed.), *Fear in animals and man* (pp. 164–168). London: Van Nostrand.

Tearnan, B., Telch, M., & Keefe, P. (1984). Etiology and onset of agoraphobia: a critical review. *Comprehensive Psychiatry, 25,* 51–62.

Thyer, B., Hilme, J., & Fischer, D. (1988). Is parental death a selective precursor to either panic disorder or agoraphobia? A test of the separation anxiety hypothesis. *Journal of Anxiety Disorders, 2,* 333–338.

Walk, R., & Gibson, E. J. (1961). A comparative and analytic study of visual depth perception. *Psychological Monographs, 75* (15, Whole No. 519), 1–44.

Watson, J. B., & Rayner, R. (1920). Conditioned emotional reactions. *Journal of Experimental Psychology, 3,* 1–14.

White, K., & Davey, G. C. L. (1989). Sensory preconditioning and UCS inflation in human fear conditioning. *Behaviour Research and Therapy, 27,* 161–166.

Wolpe, J., & Lang, P. J. (1964). A fear schedule for use in behavior therapy. *Behaviour Research and Therapy, 2,* 27–30.

Wynne, C. D. L. (1998). A natural history of explicit learning and memory. In K. Kirsner & C. Speelman (Eds.), *Implicit and explicit mental processes* (pp. 255–269). Erlbaum: New Jersey.

10

Developmental Aspects of Conditioning Processes in Anxiety Disorders

MARK R. DADDS, GRAHAM C. L. DAVEY, and ANDY P. FIELD

Can conditioning theory aid our understanding of developmental progressions of clinically significant fear and anxiety? In this chapter, we describe contemporary models of conditioning and their application to anxiety disorders. The aim is not to present an evaluation or comprehensive review of conditioning models of fear and anxiety; a number of other authors have done this and the reader is referred to Davey (1992a, 1997), Muris and Merckelbach (this volume), Rachman (1977), and Menzies and Clarke (1995). These previous reviews deal comprehensively with the application of conditioning theory to specific fears in particular and present the range of contemporary theoretical and methodological issues. However, they have not addressed how conditioning might be related to predictable changes in fear across the lifespan, and are relatively silent on the more diffuse forms of anxiety such as generalized anxiety disorder.

To tackle developmental issues, we will have to be somewhat speculative but hopefully creative, as very little has been written about developmental changes in conditioning phenomena for us to draw upon. The idea we embrace is not that the conditioning process per se changes across development, but rather that the characteristics the organism brings to conditioning change in important and predictable ways.

Early behaviorists were eager to avoid intraorganism explanations of behavior, the preference being for externally observable aspects of learning. Stimuli were held to be observable over and above their meaning or salience to the organism. Thus, the effects of a stimulus on an organism was thought to be explainable in terms of the organism's prior history of learning with respect to that stimulus, rather than any intrinsic characteristic of the organism. Specifically, the strength of conditioning was argued to be based solely on the number of contiguous pairings of the conditioned stimulus (CS) and unconditioned stimulus (UCS). Animal studies were the primary method used that tended to support this conceptualization. Given this primary focus on stimuli themselves, it is understandable that classical conditioning has not typically been discussed within a developmental framework. By our reckoning the omission of developmental factors thus represents a serious omission from the conditioning literature and has limited its potential to contribute to the understanding of human learning. Contemporary models of classical conditioning have focused much more on *human* learning and now emphasize the importance of cognition in the learning process. As we will see, two of the most important shifts in conditioning theory have been the recognition of the importance of cognitive variables in the nature and strength of association learned between the CS and the UCS, and in the evaluation of the UCS itself. The inclusion of these cognitive factors clearly necessitates a move to more serious consideration of the developmental state of the organism, and, in particular, how the organism's developing cognitive capacities interact with conditioning processes to generate learned anxieties.

In the next section, we describe some of the main features of contemporary human conditioning models. The chapter then continues by discussing how the special features of contemporary conditioning models might be applied to the understanding of the development of fears and anxieties across the lifespan.

Contemporary Models of Human Conditioning

Contemporary models of human classical conditioning differ from their contiguity-based predecessors in a number of important ways. First, it is now well accepted that many factors other than the experienced pairings of CS and UCS can affect the strength of the association between these events. In the case of humans, these include verbally and culturally transmitted information about the CS–UCS contingency (e.g., Dawson & Grings, 1968; Wilson, 1968), existing beliefs and expectancies about the possible consequence associated with a particular CS (Davey, 1992b; Honeybourne, Matchett, & Davey, 1993), and emotional reactions currently associated with the CS (Davey & Dixon, 1996; Diamond, Matchett, & Davey, 1995). This means: (1) CS–UCS associations can be formed without direct experience of the CS paired with the UCS (cf. Rachman, 1977); and (2) the strength of the CS–UCS association can be influenced by a number of factors other than the number of pairings of CS and UCS.

Second, and arguably of most importance in this context, is the finding that the strength of a CR can be radically influenced, not just by the strength of the CS–UCS association, but also by the way in which the individual evaluates the UCS (Davey, 1989, 1992a). In humans there are a variety of processes that can influence the evaluation of a traumatic UCS, and some of these are discussed below.

Figure 10.1 provides a schematic representation of a contemporary model of human classical conditioning. This illustrates the kinds of factors that may influence the strength of an association between a CS and the UCS representation (Expectancy Evaluations), and also how the UCS representation's evocation of a CR will be influenced by how the UCS has been evaluated or revalued (UCS Revaluation Processes). The next subsections will discuss these expectancy evaluation and UCS-revaluation processes in more detail.

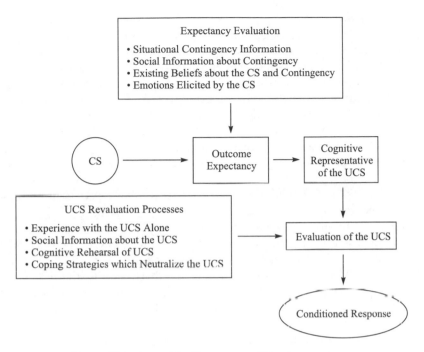

Figure 10.1. A model of human conditioning processes.

Expectancy Evaluation

Traditional incremental–decremental models of conditioning claim that the strength of an association between CS and UCS is dependent on the number of experienced pairings of the CS and UCS. It is now clear that many other factors than this can influence the strength of the learnt association.

First, people do not have to experience pairings of CS and UCS in order to learn the association, they can simply be told what the relationship is between these stimuli. In laboratory conditioning experiments, merely informing the subjects of the CS–UCS contingency can generate a CR prior to any pairings of CS and UCS (e.g., Dawson & Grings, 1968; Katz, Webb, & Stotland, 1971; McComb, 1969; Wilson, 1968). Often, even when subjects are given false information about the contingencies, their conditioned responding complies with this false information rather than the situational contingencies (Deane, 1969; Epstein & Clarke, 1970). An implication of this is that an association between a stimulus and a traumatic outcome can be learned as a result of information about the contingency, or through observing someone else experiencing the contingency (vicarious learning). In terms of contemporary conditioning models, this is still conditioning.

Second, when individuals enter a conditioning episode they are not *tabula rasa* but hold existing beliefs and expectancies about what is likely to happen in that episode. Often these prior expectancies are based on previous experiences with the events in the episode, or they are based on ad hoc judgements about those events. An example of the associative biases that influence the formation of learned associations can be found in covariation assessment studies. Studies of covariation have pointed out that assessing the relationship or covariation between events appears to be influenced by both situational information (i.e., current information about the contingency) and prior expectations or beliefs about the covariation (e.g., Crocker, 1981; Nisbett & Ross, 1980; Alloy & Tabachnik, 1984). For example, in circumstances where situational information is unambiguous and prior expectations are low, human subjects can detect event contingencies fairly accurately (e.g., Beach & Scopp, 1966; Erlick & Mills, 1967; Peterson, 1980). However, there are a variety of circumstances in which the combination of situational information and prior expectancies give rise to what is called a "covariation bias" which generates a distorted perception of the covariation—usually in the direction of the prior expectation (Crocker, 1981; Nisbett & Ross, 1980). Covariation biases can be found in exactly those circumstances which might generate CS–UCS associations. For instance, Tomarken, Mineka, and Cook (1989) exposed subjects to slides of fear-relevant stimuli (snakes, spiders) and fear-irrelevant stimuli (flowers, houses) that were followed by electric shock, a tone, or nothing. Although the relationship between the slides and outcomes was completely random, subjects consistently overestimated the contingency between slides of fear-relevant stimuli and shock (see also Davey, 1992b).

What studies such as these show is that prior outcome expectancies can influence the speed with which a CS–UCS association is learnt. These expectancy biases tend to be associated especially with fear-relevant stimuli and appear to be based on judgments about the nature of the CS and the features that the CS shares in common with the potential UCS (cf. Davey & Dixon, 1996; Davey & Craigie, 1997).

Third, one other important factor that influences UCS expectancy is the degree to which the CS already elicits prior fear or anxiety. Tomarken et al. (1989) found that initial fear of a stimulus was an important determinant of covariation bias with phylogenetic fear-relevant stimuli when the number of stimulus–shock pairings was relatively small (33%), but not when it was increased to 50% (see also de Jong & Merckelbach, 1991; de Jong, Merckelbach, Arntz, & Nijman, 1992; Diamond et al., 1995). One implication of this role of prior fear, of course, is that prior fear to a CS will hasten its association with an aversive UCS, and is also likely to retard extinction of the association (cf. Diamond et al., 1995).

UCS Revaluation Processes

Davey (1989, 1992a, 1997) has argued that contemporary human conditioning models are basically incomplete without a performance factor which describes processes by which the subject's evaluation of the UCS may be changed. Figure 10.1 shows that the learned fear CR is mediated through a representation of the UCS which is activated through the CS–UCS association; this implies that changes in the strength or nature of the fear CR will be affected by any factor which changes knowledge about the UCS contained in the UCS representation. For example, if the subject acquires information which suggests that the UCS is now less traumatic or aversive than had previously been conceived, then this will result in the UCS representation mediating a significantly weaker fear CR when the CS is next encountered.

There are two important points to make about UCS revaluation processes in relation to conditioning models of anxiety. First, UCS revaluation can occur independently of any changes in the strength of the association between CS and UCS. Thus, changes in the strength of the anxiety CR can be caused without the individual having any experiences which might affect the strength of the CS–UCS association (e.g., without any further CS–UCS pairings). Second, although the animal conditioning literature has identified a few processes by which a UCS can be revalued (see Davey, 1992a), the ability to represent information symbolically and to communicate complex information between individuals opens up the possibility for many more modes of UCS revaluation in humans than in animals. Some of these modes are represented under UCS Revaluation Processes in fig. 10.1.

First, post-conditioning experiences with the UCS alone (i.e., in the absence of the CS) can lead to revaluation of the UCS—especially if these experiences lead to the individual perceiving the UCS as either more or less aversive than it was during the conditioning episode. For example, an individual may reassess a UCS more favorably if he or she experiences a number of UCS-alone trials which allow the fear to the UCS to habituate (Davey & McKenna, 1983). The next presentation of the CS then evokes a much weaker CR. Similarly, the perceived aversiveness of the UCS may be inflated by experiences with a similar UCS of greater intensity (e.g., White & Davey, 1989). In this latter example, an individual may learn to associate a CS and UCS while the UCS is perceived as being relatively unaversive (i.e., there will be little or no conditioned fear to the CS). Some time later that individual may have an experience with the UCS which inflates the aversive evaluation of it. Subsequent encounters with the CS will then evoke a much stronger and perceivable anxiety response (see White & Davey, 1989, and Davey, de Jong, & Tallis, 1993, for examples). This type of UCS inflation scenario means that a contemporary conditioning model of phobias is not bound by the need to discover contiguous stimulus(CS)–trauma(UCS) experiences in the histories of anxiety problems in order to verify the conditioning account.

Second, a further method of UCS revaluation involves socially or verbally transmitted information about the UCS. For example, in a laboratory conditioning experiment participants can simply be told that on future presentations the UCS will be more or less intense than before. If the person believes this information, then the evaluation of the UCS is changed, and this affects the strength of the CR on subsequent CS presentations (Davey, 1983; Davey & McKenna, 1983).

Third, many anxious people attend to their own bodily sensations and use these stimuli as information about possible threatening events or as a means of assessing the aversive nature of potentially threatening consequences (cf. Valins, 1966; Parkinson, 1985; Davey, 1988). As a result, the individual's reaction to either the CS or UCS can act as an important source of information for evaluating the UCS. Studies of the effects of interoception in aversive conditioning studies have revealed that, when participants *believe* they are emitting a strong fear CR even when they are not (e.g., in a false feedback study), they emit a stronger differential CR and exhibit a resistance to extinction compared with attentional controls, and compared with participants who believe they are emitting only a weak CR (Davey, 1987; Russell & Davey, 1991).

Davey (1988, 1992a, 1995) has argued that CR and UCR interoception influences CR magnitude by influencing the person's evaluation of the UCS. That is, an individual may perceive what is believed to be a strong CR and attribute this to the fact that he or she must still be anxious or frightened at the forthcoming UCS; this inflates the aversive evaluation of the UCS which in turn activates a higher magnitude CR on subsequent trials. Two experiments by Davey and Matchett (1996) support this interpretation. The first experiment found that participants receiving false feedback indicating high levels of responding gave significantly higher UCS aversiveness ratings than other participants. The second experiment indicated that response feedback influenced CRs by changing the participant's evaluation of the UCS rather than the CS. More direct evidence that phobics use information from emotional responding to evaluate potentially threatening consequences (UCSs) comes from a study by Arntz, Rauner, and van den Hout (1995). They asked anxiety patients and normal controls to rate the danger they perceived in a hypothetical scenario when information about objective safety–danger or anxious–nonanxious responding was varied systematically. The results showed that anxiety patients inferred danger on the basis of information regarding anxious responding significantly more than non-anxious controls. Such findings suggest that phobics use interoceptive cues as an important source of information in inferring and defining the threatening or aversive nature of a consequence.

Fourth, it is clear that individuals who suffer anxiety disorders do have a tendency to focus on and rehearse the possible aversive outcomes of phobic encounters (Marks, 1987), and this ruminative tendency may act to inflate their aversive evaluation of the aversive outcome (UCS). Davey (1992a) argued that, while UCS rehearsal appeared to maintain differential fear CRs, there may be circumstances in which persistent UCS rehearsal might enhance fear responding to the aversive CS in a way that is characteristic of incubation. One such factor that might facilitate the effects of UCS rehearsal is a high level of trait anxiety. High levels of anxiety have been shown to be associated with the selective processing of threatening information (Mathews & MacLeod, 1994), and this might elaborate and define the threatening features of the UCS during UCS rehearsal—thus inflating the aversive evaluation of the UCS. Davey and Matchett (1994) conducted two experiments using a cued-UCS rehearsal procedure devised by Jones and Davey

(1990). The first experiment compared the effects of UCS rehearsal in high and low trait-anxious individuals. This study found that participants with high levels of trait anxiety exhibited significantly greater CRs following UCS rehearsal than did participants who were low in trait anxiety, and these higher magnitude CRs were associated with significantly higher levels of self-reported aversiveness of the rehearsal process. High trait-anxious subjects also exhibited a significant increase in CR strength following UCS rehearsal. In the second experiment, Davey and Matchett found that post-rehearsal enhancement of the CR could be found in normal participants who, just prior to UCS rehearsal, had experienced an anxious mood induction procedure. Thus, CR enhancement following UCS rehearsal is not confined to people who report high levels of trait anxiety, but can also be found in individuals who report experimentally induced increases in levels of state anxiety. These results are consistent with the hypothesis that increases in CR magnitude following UCS rehearsal are a result of the rehearsal process inflating the aversive evaluation of the UCS.

Fifth, many individuals who have traumatic experiences fail to develop phobic reactions. One reason for this failure may be the ability of some individuals to devalue the trauma immediately following the experience, and they may do this by adopting coping strategies which allow them to effectively devalue the stressful meaning of the trauma. In an early survey of methods of coping with marriage, parenting, household economics, and occupation, Pearlin and Schooler (1978) described three major types of coping with stressors. The first two types closely resembled the problem- and emotion focused coping outlined in most traditional accounts of coping (cf. Lazarus & Folkman, 1984). However, the third type of coping dealt with strategies that functioned to control the meaning of the stressor or trauma (appraisal strategies). Pearlin and Schooler reported that this could be achieved in at least three ways: by positive comparisons (e.g., "Lots of people experience similar stressful experiences"), by selective ignoring (e.g., "I'll try and forget this problem and look at the good things in life"), or by devaluing the importance of the stressful event (e.g., "This problem isn't worth getting upset about").

In a preliminary investigation of the kinds of stressor devaluing strategies described by Pearlin and Schooler, Davey (1993) used a factor analysis pro-cedure to identify a coherent neutralizing strategy labeled "threat devalua-tion." This construct was derived from the coping strategies categorized by Pearlin and Schooler as ones which functioned to control the traumatic meaning of the stressor. Clearly, the use of such threat devaluation strategies has implications for the development of phobic responding following trau-matic experiences: If individuals are able to actively devalue the impact of trauma by deploying threat devaluation strategies, then they should be sig-nificantly less likely to develop anxious reactions to stimuli associated with the trauma. There is some evidence that this is the case. Davey, Burgess, and Rashes (1995) compared the coping strategies of simple phobics, panic dis-order patients and normal controls. They found that both simple phobics and panic disorder patients differed from normal controls by reporting greater use of avoidance coping strategies and reduced use of threat devaluation strategies in dealing with stressors. In a second study, they also found that use of threat devaluation strategies was inversely related to levels of some specific fears as measured by the Fear Survey Schedule (Wolpe & Lang, 1964). Both studies imply that the use of threat devaluation strategies is associated with a significantly reduced incidence of anxious or phobic responding.

In a more recent study, Davey and McDonald (2000) have refined the threat devaluation construct and identified seven factorially independent constructs all of which contribute to trauma or UCS devaluation. These are downward comparison (e.g., "Other people are worse off than me") (Wills, 1981; Gibbons & Gerrard, 1991), positive reappraisal (e.g., "In every problem there is something good") (Davey, 1993), cognitive disengagement (e.g., "The problems involved in this situation simply aren't important enough to get upset about"), optimism (e.g., "Everything will work itself out in the end") (Scheier & Carver, 1992), faith in social support (e.g., "I have others who can help me through this"), denial (e.g., "I refuse to believe this is happening") (Breznitz, 1983), and life perspective (e.g., "I can put up with these problems as long as everything else in my life is okay"). Davey et al. (1998) found that use of all of these strategies (except for denial) was positively correlated with measures of psychological health and inversely correlated with a variety of measures of psychopathology. In addition, a prospective study discovered that the use of these devaluing strategies was not simply an inverse function of existing psychopathology, but predicted future psychological health even when existing levels of psychological health were controlled for.

Studies such as these imply that the use of coping strategies which effectively devalue the aversive meaning of a trauma will have a beneficial effect across a broad range of psychological health measures. From the point of view of a conditioning model of anxiety, they also imply that use of such strategies will help to insulate the individual against the development of pathological anxiety following traumatic experiences, and may help to explain at least some of the instances when experienced trauma does not result in pathological anxiety.

Summary

The main developments in contemporary human conditioning theory have been to incorporate into the basic conditioning model cognitive processes which are primarily restricted to humans and which can modify the strength and nature of the conditioned response. UCS revaluation processes represent a particularly central feature of this development. From the point of view of the application of these models to anxiety and anxiety disorders, they have far broader predictive value and do not rely on experienced pairings of anxiety-provoking stimuli (CSs) with traumatic outcomes (UCSs) as the sole determinant of response strength. More importantly, the model provides a flexible conceptual framework for understanding how anxiety-provoking stimuli become associated with representations of threatening outcomes, and describes a variety of processes that can modulate the anxious responding that is generated by this association.

With this increasing emphasis on the cognitively and emotionally mediated evaluation of stimuli has come the identification of a host of other organismic variables that impact upon evaluative processes to stimuli. These include information from others, the information processing style of the individual, and both trait and state affectivity. It is in relation to these that developmental changes in the organism may alter the input, throughput processing, and output responses that make up a conditioned response and affect the progress of fear and anxiety. Before considering developmental changes in these, we will next briefly discuss some characteristics of fear and anxiety across the lifespan as a general context for the following discussion.

Conditioning Processes and Developmental Features of Anxiety

What are the developmental characteristics of clinically significant fear and anxiety that demand explanation? There are a number of these in the literature, and no doubt many more than researchers have as yet identified; but for the sake of this analysis there are four characteristics of anxiety through development that have been observed consistently.

First, different forms of anxiety and fear switch in and out at reasonably predictable phases of the lifecycle. As Vasey and Dadds (this volume) have pointed out, the emergence of problematic fears can be associated with any one or more of the following: (1) new conditioned learning; (2) a failure of the growing child to overcome normal developmental fears; and (3) dishabituation of previously mastered fears, say following exposure to stress or new learning. Many specific fears typically have an early age of onset whereas more generalized forms of anxiety appear to emerge in late childhood/early adolescence. Pain, loud noises, and loss of physical support (i.e., falling) reliably elicit the first signs of fear in humans. Retrospective reports by sufferers indicate that environmental fears such as of water and heights have always been present (Menzies & Clarke, 1993). By contrast, blood-injury, most social and some animal fears have onset in late childhood and learning factors associated with onset can be more easily identified (see Muris & Merckelbach, this volume). Claustrophobia and agoraphobia (and the underlying panic problems) appear to emerge most commonly in early adulthood and, again, conditioning experiences can usually be identified with onset. Further, fears are very common in young children and tend to lessen in frequency with age; the modal fear in a child is thus transitory and will disappear spontaneously. For a minority of children, fears persist and become problematic.

Second, the mechanisms associated with the development of fear and anxiety appear to vary according to the nature of the fear and the phase of life during which it typically occurs. Fears that originate in late childhood (animal, blood-injury) are more likely associated with modeling and information input from intimates, while fears that originate in adulthood are more likely associated with direct conditioning experiences (e.g., claustrophobia). A subject's identification of modeling and negative information (rather than direct conditioning experiences) as a cause of fear onset is associated with earlier age of onset (Öst, 1987).

Third, there are reliable individual differences in vulnerability to anxiety problems that show some trait stability, but also change across the lifespan and across settings, and in response to environmental stress. For example, gender differences in specific phobias occur throughout the lifespan; but for more generalized worry, gender differences emerge after adolescence such that females report more problems. The strength and number of fears in children is related to temperamental factors such as behavioral inhibition (BI: an overt display of psychological and physiological distress in response to novel people, objects, and situations; Kagan, Reznick & Snidman, 1988; also see Lonigan & Phillips, this volume) and disgust sensitivity (Davey, 1994).

Fourth, the development and expression of problematic anxiety takes place in an interpersonal context. Sole reliance on the psychological and biological aspects of an individual's fear will be incomplete given that individuals learn to detect, interpret, and respond to threat through exposure to the behavior of other people. In the case of children, much of this learning comes from early caregiving relationships.

Taking these characteristics as an axiomatic starting point, the next section looks at how the elements of contemporary conditioning theory identified above might help us to understand some of these phenomena.

UCS Evaluation Processes: Developmental Changes in the Salience and Impact of Unconditioned Stimuli

A UCS is defined as a stimulus that provokes an automatic response that is independent of learning. Those commonly identified include pain, loud noises, sexual stimuli, falling or loss of support, and movement toward the eyes. As an organism matures and accumulates learning it becomes increasingly difficult to separate UCSs from CSs as more and more of the latter will function to produce responses by previous association with a UCS. Leaving this problem aside, it is still clear that the salience and impact of UCSs can and will switch in and out at different points in development. For example, certain sexual stimuli may only function as UCSs (that is, produce sexual arousal) after adolescence and sexual maturity. Early UCSs such as darkness and strange people generally lose their potential to elicit fear as people grow out of childhood. These changes in the salience and impact of UCSs may in part explain the common developmental changes seen in the anxiety disorders.

With regard to early signs of vulnerability to anxiety disorders, the stimuli that reliably elicit markers of behavioral inhibition (BI) in children change across the early years. Thus, researchers (Kagan, Reznick, Snidman, Gibbons, & Johnson, 1988; Rothbart, 1986) have demonstrated that stability in BI in children can be demonstrated as long as the stimuli used to elicit it are chosen for the child's developmental level. Loud noises and the presence of even one stranger provoke distress in the BI infant but have little impact of the older child, who may show a BI response to a large group of strangers.

Apart from the impact that UCS revaluation processes might have on UCS salience, we are not aware of attempts in the literature to develop a model of developmental changes in the salience and impact of various stimuli underlying associative learning. If such a model were to be useful, it would have to be more than an empirically driven "shopping list" of important UCSs and the developmental times at which they usually begin and cease to have impact on humans. Rather, stimuli would have to be grouped in ways that meaningfully relate to parallel developmental changes in the organism so that the mechanisms responsible for their onset and offset as UCSs could be identified.

For example, some attention to natural changes in the salience (that is, the perceivability) of various categories of UCSs seems warranted. This variation may in part explain the natural developmental variation in fears that humans exhibit. Typically fears begin with highly salient threatening stimuli such as loud noises, pain, loss of support, and separation from caregivers. As the individual develops, more abstract threats such as social embarrassment, loss of control, illness and injury, and threats to self-esteem, and even death, become highly salient.

UCSs are reasonably universal within species and can be grouped into categories on the basis of their physical, semantic, or other characteristics. For example, work with both children (King, Hamilton, & Ollendick, 1988) and adults (Kenardy, Evans, & Oei, 1992) have shown that human fears are structured into a small number of semantic categories (social, death and injury, medical). The salience of semantic groupings to the developing individual can be studied empirically. The developmental literature has a number of examples of such an approach. For example, children's understanding of death (e.g., Lazar & Torney-Purta, 1991) and contagion and illness (Occhipinti & Siegal, 1994; Seigal & Share, 1990) has received considerable attention, and shows predictable progression in parallel with the child's cognitive maturity. However, the implications of this type of work for conditioning have not been explored. It is conceivable that developmental maps for the salience of the major groups of putative UCSs for anxiety learning—such as rejection, loss of control, abandonment, injury—could be studied as a means of understanding their changing role as UCSs across the lifespan.

The salience of a stimulus is only one of a number of variables that predict an organism's responsiveness to it. In our review of contemporary models of conditioning, we saw that sources of information other than direct experience with CS–UCS pairings can produce conditioned learning. One of these is information about the UCS. Clearly, the exposure and responsiveness (or susceptibility) of the individual to a range of information about the valence and likely impact of a UCS (and CS–UCS associations) will be dependent upon a number of factors that vary developmentally, and thus, may in part explain the normal variations observed in the modes of acquisition of various fears across the lifespan.

First, children's level of cognitive sophistication will determine their receptiveness to increasingly abstract forms of information input. Thus, as the child grows, he or she will become increasingly able to be influenced by a range of input, including other people's talk, media information, and direct observations of other people's reactions to stimuli. Intuitively, it appears that the susceptibility of individuals to this sort of vicarious learning may show an asymptotic distribution across the lifespan. The newborn infant may be relatively immune to all but the most physically salient fear reactions in caregivers. Through childhood and adolescence, the individual probably reaches a peak of susceptibility to vicarious learning, and this susceptibility may decrease through adulthood as new learning in general decreases, exposure to new sources of information becomes increasingly restricted, and prior experience limiting CS–UCS expectancies and UCS evaluations.

Indirect evidence for this may be found in the age of onset of different specific fears. Fears that originate in late childhood (animals, blood-injury) are more likely associated with modeling and information, while fears that originate in adulthood are more likely associated with direct conditioning experiences rather than social information (e.g., claustrophobia). Further, a subject's identification of modeling and negative information (rather than direct conditioning experiences) as a cause of fear onset is associated with earlier age of onset (see Öst, 1987, for information on different ages of onset of specific fears). Our argument is that these findings are consistent with contemporary models of conditioning such that learning about UCSs can occur through a variety of means over and above direct experience and, early in life, the individual will be more susceptible to information about UCSs from the social environment.

This argument paves the way for a more serious consideration of social transmission of information about threat and safety. As an example, it is disappointing that the findings of research into autobiographical memory have had little impact on conditioning theory. It has been shown that parents vary greatly in the ways they teach children to construct, represent and retrieve autobiographical data. For example, clear gender differences have been noted in which females are treated to more emotionally elaborated recall of events that emphasizes interpersonal relationships and feeling states, and males are treated to more instrumental interpretations (e.g., Fivush, 1995). In experimental tests of autobiographical memory, males and females perform quite differently, with males typically recalling fewer memories with emotional content (Davis, 1999). Thus, our second and third axioms above may be in part explained via these processes. That is, reliable differences in modes of acquisition may be associated with different types of anxiety and fear as well as demographic traits such as age and gender. This emphasis on the social aspects of learning about UCSs could be usefully incorporated into anxiety research. A number of authors are beginning to explore the way families of anxious children communicate about threat (e.g., Barrett, Rapee, Dadds, & Ryan, 1996). However, this work generally focuses on hypothetical or laboratory-based threat material. It is interesting to consider the enormous potential for the learning of fear versus courage, in particular UCS evaluation and revaluation, which can occur in the construction of autobiographical memories.

Thus, we have argued that UCS evaluation is an important part of contemporary models of conditioning. Several mechanisms affecting UCS evaluation vary developmentally and could in part explain changes in the onset and course of normal and problematic anxiety. Specifically, developmental changes in the salience and impact of various UCSs may help explain normal variations in fear and anxiety across the lifespan. Further, the processes by which learning about UCSs occurs will vary with the social–cognitive sophistication of the individual and may in part explain observed differences in modes of acquisition of fears across the lifespan, and the susceptibility of various demographic groups to anxiety problems. Examples of methods for studying these processes include mapping the developmental changes in the salience and impact of the main classes of UCSs that drive fear and anxiety in humans, exposure and vulnerability to vicarious information about UCSs, and the processes whereby UCSs are incorporated into stable autobiographical memories about threat.

Developmental Changes in CS and UCS Representations

Classical and contemporary models of conditioning posit that the CS produces a cognitive representation (interpreted loosely to mean a verbal or sensory representation) of the UCS that then produces the conditioned response. Thus, for a lift-phobic person, the lift (CS) may evoke images of falling or being trapped, suffocating and so on (UCS) that produces an anxiety response (CR). A recent review of experimental evidence by Dadds, Bovbjerg, Redd, and Cutmore (1997) supported the view that mental representations of stimuli can produce and sustain conditioned responses over and above, or in conjunction with, experience with external stimuli, especially for people who score highly on trait measures of imagery ability. Thus, some forms of conditioning may occur in part or fully at the mental representative level, in the absence of direct experience. For example, the lift-phobic person may rehearse the scenario in which he or she falls to their death in a lift, or is trapped in a lift and the phobia may develop or incubate, in the absence of real-world experiences.

Indeed, studies carried out by Davey, Peerbhoy and Field (2000) suggest that cognitively rehearsing (i.e., imagining) the consequences of interaction with a phobic stimulus or event can increase levels of self-reported fear and anxiety to the phobic stimulus. This effect of the ruminative rehearsal of outcomes on incubation of fear appears to be quite specific: incubation occurs only when the individual includes in his or her ruminations components which relate to personal fear or anxiety. Asking a spider-phobic to imagine interaction with a spider does not result in the incubation of spider fear unless rehearsal includes the phobic thinking about the negative or aversive aspects of their own reactions. The more a person is capable of cognitively representing an UCS, the more likely that representation may influence the development and maintenance of conditioned responses.

The studies reviewed by Dadds et al. (1997) typically employed the idea of imagery ability; that is, the ability to generate and manipulate mental images in various sensory modalities. Apart from the ability to produce a clear mental representation of stimuli, at least two other factors have been shown to influence the power of a representation to influence behavior. First, the literature on PTSD has shown that controllability of images is an important predictor of the persistence of anxiety symptoms. Specifically, high imagery ability in conjunction with low controllability of images is predictive of vulnerability to persistence of PTSD symptomatology (Dadds et al., 1997). Second, there are reliable individual differences in people's tendency to respond to mental representations as if they were real. The most common operationalization of this "as if" trait is Tellegen's measure of absorption (Tellegen & Atkinson, 1974), which is positively correlated with hypnotizability and defined as the tendency to become fully engaged in one's mental contents and respond as if they were real.

Thus, the question of developmental changes in people's ability to represent, regenerate, control, and respond to the "reality" of cognitive representations of stimuli may be important to developmental changes in vulnerability to conditioning. So far, very little research has attempted to map any putative developmental changes. However, the existing literature provides some ideas about what researchers should look at. These include developmental changes in image clarity, controllability, and its impact on physiological and behavioral systems, as well demographic maps of the content of imagery people naturally experience. Intuitively, it may be argued that increasing age might be associated with an increase in the number, type, and linked associations of various cognitive representations of unconditioned and conditioned stimuli available to the individual. However, this sort of research has not been conducted. Similarly, little is known about developmental changes in absorption. If younger children are more susceptible to responding to mental representations as if they were real, this may explain in part the increased role of vicarious experiences observed in many early-onset fears.

Borkovec's ideas on the role of imagery in maintaining the uncontrollable worry that characterizes generalized anxiety disorder (GAD) is a useful case in point. He (e.g., Borkovec & Roemer, 1995) argues that GAD worry is primarily verbal–propositional activity (i.e., if A, then B; or using an example relevant to anxiety—if my children go out at night, they may be harmed) that is not only ineffective as a problem-solving strategy, but functions to protect the worrier from the negative affect associated with imagery of frightening events. If one thinks of these images (e.g., of accidents and harm to loved ones, of personal failure and other tragedy) as UCSs, and the worry as protecting the worrier from experience of these images, the whole process parallels the conditioning–avoidance trap that has repeatedly been shown to maintain and even incubate clinical fears. That is, the worry is reinforced by reduction it brings in unpleasant affect from images; and until the worrier actively engages the images and re-evaluates them as relatively harmless, they will maintain their threatening potential and the worry will continue to be reinforced by its ability to block the images.

This effect was noted in the studies on imagery in conditioned chemotherapy nausea and vomiting by Redd, Dadds, Bovbjerg, and Taylor (1994). Interviews were conducted with women who, after having received chemotherapy for breast cancer, continued to show conditioned responses (e.g., nausea) to previously neutral hospital stimuli. During the interviews, they spoke at length about their susceptibility to feeling nauseous even when thinking about the chemotherapy setting. However, none actually showed any unpleasant sensations despite talking about it. In contrast, asking the women to stop "thinking" about the chemotherapy and instead generate imagery of the setting led to immediate nausea responses.

As with Borkovec's work, these phenomena indicate that conditioned responses can be elicited when the person engages in imagery of stimuli using the relevant sensory systems. However, as noted by Dadds et al. (1997), it is difficult to separate imagery of UCSs and CSs from imagery of the person's reaction to these stimuli. Thus, the women in the Redd et al. (1994) study may have been imagining their nausea, as well as the setting in which it occurred, making these findings consistent with those of Davey, Peerbhoy and Field (2000) that rehearsal of the CR is needed for incubation of the conditioned response.

The above processes have theoretical and applied significance. Theoretically, processes of stimulus representation and rehearsal are important in conditioned phenomena and may aid explanations of the acquisition and maintenance of fear above that afforded by consideration of people's real-world experiences. We know very little about developmental changes in these phenomena. However, this analysis indicates that further attention to the development of various attributes of cognitive representation (clarity, controllability, responsiveness to) has the potential to refine our understanding of fear acquisition and maintenance. In applied terms, a wealth of research has documented the importance and clinical usefulness of incorporating imagery into exposure programs for fearful children (King et al., 1988) and adults (see Dadds et al., 1997). Treatments that aim to overcome fear by imaginal exposure to threat stimuli are clearly dependent upon the patient engaging the threat image until habituation or extinction occurs. Experimental evidence supports the notion that nontraumatic exposure to mental images does function to decrease fear responses as predicted by conditioning theory (see Dadds et al., 1997).

The above evidence indicates that representation, retrieval, control, and responsiveness to images of threat stimuli are important in fear and anxiety. Further, the way these representations function in fear and anxiety appears to be highly consistent with conditioning models. However, little is known about developmental changes in image representation in humans. Clearly, some careful mapping of developmental changes in imagery ability, susceptibility, and function may yield some important benefits for understanding conditioned effects in clinical fear and anxiety.

The Role of Relationships in Influencing Significant Features of the Conditioning Process

It is axiomatic and empirically clear that much early learning about threat and safety takes place in the context of the family. The most commonly acknowledged mechanisms whereby the family influences anxiety in children are: (1) social learning processes whereby children learn fear versus courage via imitation, information, and reinforcement; and (2) attachment processes whereby the development of confidence to explore novel stimuli and emotion regulation skills are compromised by insecure attachments to caregivers (see Dadds & Roth, this volume). Contemporary models of conditioning emphasize at least two related processes that should be considered in relation to conditioning learning of fear.

First, the increasing emphasis on UCS evaluation in contemporary conditioning alerts us to consider the impact of models on specific learning about UCSs; i.e., threat and safety in the environment. The content of this learning is probably fairly clear; that is, anxious parents will be more likely to facilitate learning that a range of UCSs are threatening and should be avoided. In this regard, the individual's repertoire of fear and anxiety versus courage will be reflective of the fear and anxiety versus courage that exists in his or her family unit. Evidence has shown clearly that anxiety does show familial loading that includes a significant shared environment component (see Eley, this volume), that parental reactions to threat stimuli (e.g., separation, dental procedures, injections) are a major source of learning of fear in young children (e.g., Lumley, Melamed, & Abeles, 1993), and that attention to threat and avoidance is enhanced in anxious children when they are exposed to family processes compared to when they are asked to process information alone (Barrett, Rapee et al., 1996; Dadds, Barrett, Rapee, & Ryan; 1996).

Further, individual family member's reports of their anxiety are not independent of other family members' anxiety. Rosenbaum and Ronen (1997) showed that, in threat situations, children's ratings of their parents' anxiety were primarily associated with their own anxiety levels (projected information). Parents' ratings of their partner's anxiety was based on their partner's behavior (emitted information); but parents' ratings of their child's anxiety was predicted from their partner's evaluations (shared information) more accurately than from the child's actual behavior. This highlights that families participate in reciprocal information exchange about important emotions such as anxiety, and that each individuals' experience of anxiety is not independent from other members. This alerts us to consider that conditioning could, in this sense, be conceptualized as occurring at a systemic level. A child who witnesses another family member being bitten by a dog may develop a fear of dogs; but when asked later for recall of any aversive experiences with dogs may fail to report on such a vicarious experience through to an assumption that the question referred to them personally. Further, enmeshment in a close family system which is characterized by anxiety will expose individual members to more information about threat stimuli and their associations and more modeling of anxious responses.

Beyond this, the relative salience of information provided by anxious parents may be greater for anxious children. Support for this comes from three sources. First, retrospective reports of anxious adults indicate that anxious children may be isolated from other social contacts (Bruch, 1989). Second, a longitudinal study of BI children found that they were less likely than their non-BI peers to have left the family home by early adulthood. Third, studies of the interactional processes in anxious families have shown repeatedly that parents of anxious children are relatively high on controlling and restrictive parenting styles (see Dadds & Roth, this volume). Thus, in anxious families, the parents may be the main source of information about threat, and exposure to more courageous models may be lacking.

A wealth of research has shown that the strength of interpersonal learning is in part predicted by the nature of the relationship between the model and the learner (Bandura, 1989). Generally, the closer the relationship, the more interpersonal learning. Thus, we would expect that susceptibility to learning about the valence of various stimuli, and their associative connections, will vary across the lifespan according to the types and strengths of intimate relationships that are formed. Early relationships with caregivers will provide the context for most early vicarious learning. A theme that emerged through the above studies was that enmeshment in a close family system may facilitate the exchange of fear learning where problematic anxiety exists in one or more members.

However, the other extreme of lack of intimate relationships must be considered. Emerging research from an attachment perspective indicates that a lack of predictable, nurturing relationships with caregivers can predispose the child to anxiety problems. According to the original model developed by Bowlby (1969), development of secure attachments allows the individual to develop an internal model of soothing and reassurance that promotes coping and effective emotion regulation in the face of adversity. If one knows what it feels like to feel good, to feel safe, to feel protected, these resources can be used to buffer against challenges to one's well-being. Research has shown that individuals with poor attachment histories are more likely to be anxious and have poor emotion regulation skills (Warren, Huston, Egeland, & Sroufe, 1997).

In our review of contemporary conditioning models, it was noted several times that high levels of state and trait anxiety increase individual's susceptibility to learn conditioned fear responses. This appears to occur both by magnifying conditioned responses and by predisposing anxious persons to use information about their own reactions to attribute threat to irrelevant, external stimuli. Given that individuals who have not experienced secure attachments are low on emotional regulation skills and thus experience higher and more variable levels of negative affectivity, these individuals should be more susceptible to learning conditioned fear responses. Theories of both adult panic sufferers (Clark & Ehlers, 1993) and childhood BI (Kagan et al., 1988) emphasize sensitivity to internal distress signals and its role in the learning to fear novel external stimuli. By this analysis, the experience of insecure attachment, to the extent it is associated with high negative affectivity and poor emotion-regulation skills, will thus increase susceptibility to the formation of threat interpretations and uncontrollable aversive responses to CS and UCS, which underlie fear learning.

An integration of the above two points about enmeshed social learning processes and insecure attachments together points to a healthy middle ground in protection against anxiety problems. Minimization of anxiety problems will be achieved for the individual who grows up with caregivers that (1) promotes the internalization of effective emotion regulation skills that protect against susceptibility to fear conditioning, and (2) allows the individual to develop confidence with a range of social stimuli through early nonaversive exposure to novelty, modeling of courage, and information facilitative of confidence.

We hope this brief discussion shows that conditioning theory can provide a useful framework for analyzing relationships between attachment and the learning of fear. Others have made related arguments. Perhaps the model that best elucidates this integration was the seminal but now largely ignored work of the Harlows (Harlow & Harlow, 1962). They described patterns of insecure attachment and "approach–avoidance" conditioning using infant-monkey/mechanical-mother-monkey dyads in which both food and comfort, as well aversive stimuli, were delivered via the mechanical mother. The delivery of aversive stimuli originating from the mother monkey led to increases in clinging rather than avoidance behavior, as well as anxiety, and distress, in the infant monkeys. A more specific analysis of the relationship between attachment and social learning processes in anxiety can be found elsewhere in this book (see Dadds & Roth, this volume).

In summary to this section, relationships throughout the lifespan: (1) are important sources of information about the valence and interconnections of various unconditioned and conditioned stimuli; (2) provide models for strategies for responding to fearful stimuli (coping versus fear and avoidance); (3) are providers of secure versus insecure attachments that influence the child's ability to regulate emotional responsivity, and thus, conditionability to aversive stimuli; (4) themselves function as conditioned stimuli for a range of important unconditioned stimuli from food, comfort, and safety, to physical abuse; and (5) as shown in Harlow's work, can directly produce anxious responses in children via "approach–avoidance" conflicts (i.e., being the source of both comforting and aversive stimuli to a child who is dependent of them).

Development as an Accumulation of Prior Learning: The Contribution of Specific Conditioning Processes

Studying development as an accumulation of prior learning seems almost tautologically simplistic and warranting little attention. However, with the discovery of conditioning phenomena such as latent inhibition and sensory preconditioning, the accumulation of prior learning can have important implications for clinical phenomena such as anxiety. Latent inhibition (e.g., Lipp, Siddle, & Vaitl, 1992) refers to the phenomenon where previous non-reinforced or non-paired exposure to a stimulus inhibits its future potential to develop the properties of a conditioned stimulus. Conversely, a lack of previous experience with a stimulus (such as social gatherings, large animals, water) can facilitate their potential to be established as CSs for fear responses. Sensory preconditioning refers to the process by which "silent learning," in which an organism learns to associate two *neutral* stimuli (i.e., one predicts the other), affects later conditioning.

It is quite likely that latent inhibition was involved in the failure of studies to replicate Watson and Rayner's (1920) work with Little Albert and show fear conditioning in laboratory experiments. That is, the children failed to show conditioning to various ordinary objects, such as the wooden duck in the study by English (1929), but showed accidental conditioning to unintended objects in the laboratory. Previous experience with the ordinary objects would inhibit their potential as CSs, whereas lack of previous experience, or more importantly previous conditioning experiences with other objects, could potentiate their establishment as CSs. This idea is complementary to that presented by Menzies and Clark (1995) who emphasize that the failure of parents to expose children to habituation experiences with normally feared situations (e.g., swimming pools) can facilitate the expression of phobias of related stimuli (see Menzies & Harris, this volume).

Similarly, sensory preconditioning can lead to learning effects that are very difficult to observe in any but tightly controlled experimental conditions (cf. White & Davey, 1989). Davey, de Jong and Tallis (1993) report a number of anxiety disorder case histories that appear to include an element of sensory preconditioning and UCS incubation in their etiology. This combination of processes begins with the individual first associating a stimulus or situation with a particular benign consequence. However, as a result of a subsequent experience the valence of the consequence changes to become aversive. This sequence of events then means that negative affect comes to be elicited by the cue that had become associated with the consequence—even though the cue itself had never been explicitly paired with trauma or aversive events. One example quoted by Davey et al. (1993) is of a young girl who is in bed when a spider crawls over her. She does not find this in any way frightening and relates the story to her parents at a later time. Her parents react to the story with shock and horror. From that point in time the girl developed a severe spider phobia that subsequently required treatment. Lying in bed at night then becomes a fearful activity—even though lying in bed itself had never *explicitly* occurred in conjunction with a traumatic experience.

This type of silent learning may underlie the development of many phobic and traumatic reactions that previously were inexplicable in terms of classical conditioning theory. For a developing organism, experience with a particular stimulus could establish it in connections with other UCs that will only be potentiated later in life. As another hypothetical example, consider separation fears. Most children have their first experience of separation in public places such as shopping centers and public transport. In most instances, this does not lead to the development of problematic fears, but the experience could be considered as a sensory preconditioning. Later in life, separation may be re-evaluated as a significant UCS, for example during early adulthood when one separates from family or later in life when one's children are leaving home. Owing to the early sensory preconditioning, public places could then (seemingly out of the blue) take on CS properties eliciting fear of separation and abandonment, or perhaps even a fear of losing control in public, and acting as many children do when they first find themselves alone in a public place. Thus, the previously mastered fear of separation is elicited in the same situations that first signaled separation. The above is highly speculative but is finding increasing support in the research of clinicians who argue that panic/agoraphobia is a later manifestation of separation anxiety disorder (see Silove & Manicavasagar, this volume).

It is interesting to consider the possible interactions of latent inhibition and sensory preconditioning phenomena. In one person, repeated nondistressing experience early in life with public places may inhibit their potential as CSs, and fear reactions may not be establishable in these contexts, as appears to be the case in persons who can identify no environmental triggers for their panic. In others, early trauma experiences and, less dramatically, early sensory preconditioning could set up their potential to take on CS properties.

These processes may help explain our axiom 2 that modes of acquisition of anxiety problems vary across the lifespan. Given that a young child will have relatively little experience with many stimuli (i.e., they are novel), they will be easily established as CSs, and thus susceptible to social information as well as direct experience. For adults, by way of contrast, relatively few stimuli will be novel and it may take direct contact with a strong UCS to produce conditioning to a CS. Previous experience with CSs will make them relatively immune to conditioning via social information.

Latent inhibition and sensory preconditioning may also be involved in the observation that females show more anxiety problems after adolescence. It is likely that this may be in part due to males being exposed to a larger range of potentially threatening stimuli throughout early development. Differences in parents' differential encouragement of boys and girls with regard to risky activities has been repeatedly documented in the developmental literature (e.g., Spence, Deax, & Helmreich, 1985). Further, the growing literature on autobiographical memories has shown that parents engage in very different behaviors with girls and boys in this regard. That is, parents tend to talk to boys about the instrumental aspects of events in contrast to higher levels of analyses of feeling states with girls (e.g., Fivush, 1989). Boys may be exposed to a wider range of stimuli in a way that promotes instrumental responses and thus (latently) inhibits their potential as CSs; whereas girls may be exposed to fewer stimuli and in a way that promotes emotional rather than instrumental processing.

In this section, we have argued that contemporary conditioning phenomena can provide a framework for understanding how accumulated learning can influence the acquisition of conditioned fear responses. In particular, latent inhibition and sensory preconditioning are two mechanisms that add to the explanatory power of conditioning processes in fear learning. Prior to the informed consideration of these processes, many clinical aspects of anxiety appeared to be inconsistent with conditioning theory, in particular the absence of obvious conditioning experiences associated with the onset of fears, and the failure of stimuli to take on fear-eliciting properties despite being associated with a UCS.

Final Comments

We have attempted to provide a brief overview of contemporary aspects of conditioning theory and then apply these to developmental aspects of anxiety and fear in young people. The analysis has been decidedly post hoc and highly speculative. However, we have tried to show that various developmental characteristics, reliably observed of anxiety and fear, have a good deal of consistency with predictions coming from recent models of conditioning.

Many lines of research have been suggested through our analysis, in particular, the study of developmental changes in (1) the salience and impact of various unconditioned stimuli, (2) people's ability to represent, control, and respond to mental images of stimuli, (3) access and vulnerability to different sources and types of information about threat, (4) temperamental characteristics which predispose individuals to conditioning such as anxiety, disgust sensitivity, emotional regulation, and behavioral inhibition, and (5) people's ability to re-evaluate, and thus alter responsivity, to stimuli through information alone.

These conditioning phenomena have important clinical implications as well. This has been shown by recent developments in the treatment of anxiety disorders in adults. Many well-established treatments for anxiety disorders have been based on classical conditioning theory. Lately, these treatments have been updated in line with contemporary models of conditioning that emphasize information processing of stimuli and their associations, resulting in highly efficacious treatments which can be delivered in relatively short time-frames (e.g., Clark & Fairburn, 1997). These treatments are based on a growing body of research literature that has painstakingly tested its underlying theoretically assumptions.

While a number of treatments have been shown to be effective with anxious children and adolescence (Barrett, Dadds, & Rapee, 1996; Kendall, 1994), relatively little work has been undertaken to test the theoretical models underlying their development. As with their adult parallels, these treatments typically involve an exposure component. However, our current lack of knowledge about developmental aspects of the conditioning processes by which fear is learned and overcome may be severely restricting the efficiency with which these treatments can be delivered to children of different ages, as well as the adaptability of these treatments for use as preventative strategies that are programmed to produce maximum prophylactic effects at various developmental stages.

References

Alloy, L. B., & Tabachnik N. (1984). Assessment of variation by humans and animals: The joint influence of prior expectations and current situational information. *Psychological Review*, *91*, 441–485.

Arntz, A., Rauner, M., & van den Hout, M. (1995). "If I feel anxious, there must be danger": ex consequentia reasoning in inferring danger in anxiety disorders. *Behaviour Research and Therapy*, *33*, 917–925.

Bandura, A. (1989). Human agency in social cognitive theory. *American Psychologist*, *44*, 1175–1184.

Barrett, P. M., Dadds, M. R., & Rapee, R. M. (1996). Family treatment of childhood anxiety: A controlled trial. *Journal of Consulting and Clinical Psychology*, *64*, 333–342.

Barrett, P. M., Rapee, R. M., Dadds, M. R., & Ryan, S. (1996). Family enhancement of cognitive styles in anxious and aggressive children: The FEAR effect. *Journal of Abnormal Child Psychology*, *24*, 187–203.

Beach, L. R., & Scopp, T. S. (1966). Inferences about correlations. *Psychonomic Science*, *6*, 253–254.

Borkovec, T. D., & Roemer, L. (1995). Perceived functions of worry among generalized anxiety disorder subjects: Distraction from more emotionally distressing topics? *Journal of Behavior Therapy and Experimental Psychiatry*, *26*, 25–30.

Bowlby, J. (1969). *Attachment and loss: Vol. 2. Separation, anxiety and anger*. New York: Basic Books.

Breznitz, S. (1983). *The denial of stress*. New York: International Universities Press.

Bruch, M. A. (1989). Familial and developmental antecedents of social phobia: Issues and findings. *Clinical Psychology Review*, *9*, 37–47.

Clark, D., & Ehlers, A. (1993). An overview of the cognitive theory and treatment of panic disorder. *Applied and Preventive Psychology*, *2*, 131–139.

Clark, D. M., & Fairburn, C. G. (1997). *Science and practice of cognitive behaviour therapy*. Oxford, England: Oxford University Press.

Crocker, J. (1981). Judgements of covariation by social perceivers. *Psychological Bulletin, 90,* 272–292.

Dadds, M. R., Barrett, P. M., Rapee, R. M., & Ryan, S. (1996). Family process and child anxiety and aggression: An observational analysis. *Journal of Abnormal Child Psychology, 24,* 715–734.

Dadds, M. R., Bovbjerg, D., Redd, W. H., & Cutmore, T. H. (1997). Imagery and human classical conditioning. *Psychological Bulletin, 122,* 89–103.

Davey, G. C. L. (1983). An associative view of human classical conditioning. In G. C. L. Davey (Ed.), *Animal models of human behaviour: Conceptual, evolutionary, and neurobiological perspectives* (pp. 95–114). Chichester, England: Wiley.

Davey, G. C. L. (1987). An integration of human and animal models of Pavlovian conditioning: Associations, cognitions and attributions. In G. C. L. Davey (Ed.), *Cognitive processes and Pavlovian conditioning in humans* (pp. 83–114). Chichester, England: Wiley.

Davey, G. C. L. (1988). Pavlovian conditioning in humans: UCS revaluation and self-observation of conditioned responding. *Medical Science Research, 16,* 957–961.

Davey, G. C. L. (1989). UCS revaluation and conditioning models of acquired fears. *Behaviour Research and Therapy, 27,* 521–528.

Davey, G. C. L. (1992a). Classical conditioning and the acquisition of human fears and phobias: A review and synthesis of the literature. *Advances in Behaviour Research and Therapy, 14,* 29–66.

Davey, G. C. L. (1992b). An expectancy model of laboratory preparedness effects. *Journal of Experimental Psychology: General, 121,* 24–40.

Davey, G. C. L. (1993). A comparison of three cognitive appraisal strategies: The role of threat devaluation in problem-focused coping. *Personality & Individual Differences, 14,* 535–546.

Davey, G. C. L. (1994). Self-reported fears to common indigenous animals in an adult UK population: The role of disgust sensitivity. *British Journal of Psychology, 85,* 541–554.

Davey, G. C. L. (1995). Preparedness and phobias: Specific evolved associations or a generalized expectancy bias? *Behavioral & Brain Sciences, 18,* 289–325.

Davey, G. C. L. (1997). A conditioning model of phobias. In G. C. L. Davey (Ed.), *Phobias: A handbook of theory, research and treatment.* Chichester, England: Wiley.

Davey, G. C. L., & Craigie, P. (1997). Manipulation of dangerousness judgements to fear relevant stimuli: Effects of *a priori* UCS expectancy and *a posteriori* covariation assessment. *Behaviour Research and Therapy, 35,* 607–617.

Davey, G. C. L., & Dixon, A. (1996). The expectancy bias model of selective associations: The relationship of judgements of CS dangerousness, CS–UCS similarity and prior fear to *a priori* and *a posteriori* covariation assessments. *Behaviour Research and Therapy, 34,* 235–252.

Davey, G. C. L., & Matchett, G. (1994). UCS rehearsal and the retention and enhancement of differential "fear" conditioning: Effects of trait and state anxiety. *Journal of Abnormal Psychology, 103,* 708–718.

Davey, G. C. L., & Matchett, G. (1996). The effects of response feedback on conditioned responding during extinction: Implications for the role of interoception in anxiety-based disorders. *Journal of Psychophysiology, 10,* 291–302.

Davey, G. C. L., & McDonald, A. S. (2000). Cognitive neutralizing strategies and their use across different stressor types. *Anxiety, Stress & Coping, 13,* 115–141.

Davey, G. C. L., & McKenna, I. (1983). The effects of postconditioning revaluation of CS and UCS following Pavlovian second-order electrodermal conditioning in humans. *Quarterly Journal of Experimental Psychology, 35B*, 125–133.

Davey, G. C. L., Burgess, I., & Rashes, R. (1995). Coping strategies and phobias: The relationship between fears, phobias and methods of coping with stressors. *British Journal of Clinical Psychology, 34*, 423–434.

Davey, G. C. L., de Jong, P. J., & Tallis, F. (1993). UCS inflation in the etiology of a variety of anxiety disorders: Some case histories. *Behaviour Research and Therapy, 31*, 495–498.

Davey, G. C. L., McDonald, A. S., Ferguson, C. E., O'Neill, A-M., Shepherd, J. & Band, D. (1998). Cognitive neutralizing strategies, coping and psychological health. Unpublished manuscript.

Davey, G. C. L., Peerbhoy, D., & Field, A. P. (2000). UCS rehearsal and the enhancement of self-reported fear in spider-fearful and nonfearful individuals. Manuscript submitted for publication.

Davis, P. (1999). Sex differences in auto memory. *Journal of Personality and Social Psychology, 76*, 498–510.

Dawson, M. E., & Grings, W. W. (1968). Comparison of classical conditioning and relational learning. *Journal of Experimental Psychology, 76*, 227–231.

De Jong, P. J., & Merckelbach, H. (1991). Co-variation bias and electrodermal responding in spider phobics before and after behavioural treatment. *Behaviour Research and Therapy, 29*, 307–314.

De Jong, P. J., Merkelbach, H., Arntz, A., & Nijman, H. (1992). Co-variation detection in treated and untreated spider phobics. *Journal of Abnormal Psychology, 101*, 724–727.

Deane, G. E. (1969). Cardiac activity during experimentally induced anxiety. *Psychophysiology, 6*, 17–30.

Diamond D., Matchett, G., & Davey, G. C. L. (1995). The effect of prior fear levels on UCS-expectancy ratings to a fear-relevant stimulus. *Quarterly Journal of Experimental Psychology, 48A*, 237–247.

English, H. B. (1929). Three cases of the "conditioned fear response." *Journal of Abnormal & Social Psychology, 34*, 221–225.

Epstein, S., & Clarke, S. (1970). Heart rate and skin conductance during experimentally induced anxiety: Effect of anticipated intensity of noxious stimulation and experience. *Journal of Experimental Psychology, 73*, 9–14.

Erlick, D. E., & Mills, R. G. (1967). perceptual quantification of conditional dependency. *Journal of Experimental Psychology, 73*, 9–14.

Fivush, R. (1995). Language, narrative, and autobiography. *Consciousness and Cognition: An International Journal, 4*, 100–103.

Gibbons, F. X., & Gerrard, M. (1991). Downward comparison and coping with threat. In J. Suls & T. A. Wills (Eds.), *Social comparison: Contemporary theory and research* (pp. 317–345). Hillsdale, NJ: Erlbaum.

Harlow, H. F., & Harlow, M. (1962). Social deprivation in monkeys. *Scientific American, 207*, 136–146.

Honeybourne, C., Matchett, G., & Davey, G. C. L. (1993). Expectancy models of laboratory preparedness effects: A UCS-expectancy bias in phylogenetic and ontogenetic fear-relevant stimuli. *Behavior Therapy, 24*, 253–264.

Jones, T., & Davey, G. C. L. (1990). The effects of cued UCS rehearsal on the retention of differential "fear" conditioning: An experimental analogue of the worry process. *Behaviour Research and Therapy, 28*, 159–164.

Kagan, J., Reznick, J. S., & Snidman, N. (1988). Biological bases of childhood shyness. *Science, 240,* 167–171.

Kagan, J., Reznick, J. S., Snidman, N., Gibbons, J., & Johnson, M. O. (1988). Childhood derivatives of inhibition and lack of inhibition to the unfamiliar. *Child Development, 59,* 1580–1589.

Katz, A., Webb, L., & Stotland, E. (1971). Cognitive influences on the rate of GSR extinction. *Journal of Experimental Research in Personality, 5,* 208–215.

Kenardy, J., Evans, L., & Oei, T. P (1992). The latent structure of anxiety symptoms in anxiety disorders. *American Journal of Psychiatry, 149,* 1058–1061.

Kendall, P. C. (1994). Treating anxiety disorders in youth: Results of a randomized clinical trial. *Journal of Consulting and Clinical Psychology, 62,* 100–110.

King, N. J., Hamilton, D. J., & Ollendick, T. H. (1988). *Children's phobias: A behavioural perspective.* Chichester, England: Wiley.

Lazar, A., & Torney-Purta, J. (1991). The development of the subconcepts of death in young children: A short-term longitudinal study. *Child Development, 62,* 1321–1333.

Lazarus, R. S., & Folkman, S. (1984). *Stress, appraisal and coping.* New York: Springer.

Lipp, O. V., Siddle, D, A , & Vaitl, D. (1992). Latent inhibition in humans: Single-cue conditioning revisited. *Journal of Experimental Psychology, 18,* 115–125.

Lumley, M. A., Melamed, B. G., & Abeles, L. A (1993). Predicting children's presurgical anxiety and subsequent behavior changes. *Journal of Pediatric Psychology, 18,* 481–497.

Marks, I. M. (1987). *Fears, phobias and rituals.* New York: Oxford University Press.

Mathews, A., & MacLeod, C. (1994). Emotional processing biases. *Annual Review of Psychology, 45,* 25–50.

McComb, D. (1969). Cognitive and learning effects in the production of GSR conditioning data. *Psychonomic Science, 16,* 96.

Menzies, R. G., & Clarke, F. C. (1995). The etiology of phobias: A non-associative account. *Clinical Psychology Review, 15, 23–48.*

Nisbett, R. E., & Ross, L. (1980). *Human inference: Strategies and shortcomings of social judgement.* Englewood Cliffs, NJ: Prentice-Hall.

Occhipinti, S., & Siegal, M. (1994). Reasoning and food and contamination. *Journal of Personality and Social Psychology, 66,* 243–253.

Öst, L.-G. (1987). Age of onset in different phobias. *Journal of Abnormal Psychology, 96,* 223–229.

Parkinson, B. (1985). Emotional effects of false autonomic feedback. *Psychological Bulletin, 98,* 471–494.

Pearlin, L. I., & Schooler, C. (1978). The structure of coping. *Journal of Health & Social Behaviour, 19,* 2–21.

Peterson, C. R. (1980). Recognition of non-contingency. *Journal of Personality & Social Psychology, 38,* 727–734.

Rachman, S. J. (1977). The conditioning theory of fear acquisition: A critical examination. *Behaviour Research and Therapy, 15,* 375–387.

Redd, W. H., Dadds, M. R., Bovberg, D. H., & Taylor, K. (1994). Nausea induced by mental images of chemotherapy. *Cancer, 73,* 756.

Rosenbaum, M., & Ronen, T. (1997). Parents' and children's appraisals of each other's anxiety while facing a common threat. *Journal of Clinical Child Psychology, 26,* 43–52.

Rothbart, M. K. (1986). Longitudinal observation of infant temperament. *Developmental Psychology, 22*, 356–365.

Russell, C., & Davey, G. C. L. (1991). The effects of false response feedback on human "fear" conditioning. *Behaviour Research and Therapy, 29*, 191–196.

Scheier, M. F., & Carver C. S. (1992). Effects of optimism on psychological and physical well-being: Theoretical overview and empirical update. *Cognitive Therapy and Research, 16*, 201–228.

Siegal, M., & Share, D. L. (1990). Contamination sensitivity in young children. *Developmental Psychology, 26*, 455–458.

Spence, J. T., Deax, K., & Helmreich, R. L. (1985). Sex roles in contemporary American society. In G. Lindsey & E. Aronson (Eds.), *Handbook of social psychology: Vol. 2* (pp. 149–178). New York: Random House.

Tellegen, A., & Atkinson, G. (1974). Openness to absorbing and self-altering experiences ("absorption"): A trait related to hypnotic susceptibility. *Journal of Abnormal Psychology, 83*, 268–277.

Tomarken, A. J., Mineka, S., & Cook, M. (1989). Fear-relevant selective associations and co-variation bias. *Journal of Abnormal Psychology, 98*, 381–394.

Valins, S. (1966). Cognitive effects of false-heart-rate feedback. *Journal of Personality & Social Psychology, 4*, 400–408.

Warren, S. L., Huston, L., Egeland, B., & Sroufe, L. A (1997). Child and adolescent anxiety disorders and early attachment. *Journal of the American Academy of Child and Adolescent Psychiatry, 36*, 637–644.

Watson, J. B., & Rayner, R. (1920). Conditioned emotional reactions. *Journal of Experimental Psychology, 3*, 1–14.

White, K., & Davey, G. C. L. (1989). Sensory preconditioning and UCS inflation in human "fear" conditioning. *Behaviour Research and Therapy, 27*, 161–166.

Wills, T. A. (1981). Downward comparison principles in social psychology. *Psychological Bulletin, 90*, 245–271.

Wilson, G. T. (1968). Reversal of differential GSR conditioning by instructions. *Journal of Experimental Psychology, 76*, 491–493.

Wolpe, J., & Lang, P. J. (1964). A fear survey schedule for use in behavior therapy. *Behaviour Research and Therapy, 2*, 27.

11

Operant Conditioning Influences in Childhood Anxiety

THOMAS H. OLLENDICK, MICHAEL W. VASEY,
and NEVILLE J. KING

Childhood phobic and anxiety disorders are likely to be determined by multiple factors, none of which alone is necessary or sufficient to produce and maintain these disorders. Indeed, in an early review of phobic and anxiety disorders in children, we asserted that many childhood phobias and anxiety disorders are multiply determined and, in most instances, over-determined (see Ollendick, 1979) As discussed by Vasey and Dadds (this volume), multiple pathways to these disorders are possible if not probable and a host of factors may serve to predispose to, precipitate, and maintain them. Similarly, a wide range of factors may serve to protect or insulate children from development of these disorders or contribute to their amelioration subsequent to their onset. As noted by Rutter (1990), such risk and protective factors neither cause nor protect against pathological outcomes per se; instead, they are indicators of mechanisms that impact on individual adaptation. Given this, specification of the mechanisms involved is imperative (Cicchetti & Cohen, 1995). To that end, we will examine the role of operant conditioning influences in the onset, maintenance, and amelioration of childhood anxiety disorders. We argue that operant conditioning processes are among the major mechanisms through which various external risk and protective factors impact on the etiology and course of childhood anxiety disorders. We recognize the potential importance of other mechanisms as well (e.g., direct and indirect respondent conditioning, biological changes, etc.), but here we simply emphasize the role of operant conditioning mechanisms.

We first review basic principles and premises of operant conditioning. Second, we explore the utility of these principles in understanding the onset and maintenance of phobic and anxiety disorders. Third, we examine these principles and their utility in the treatment of these disorders. Finally, we explore developmental issues associated with operant factors in the onset, maintenance, and treatment of these disorders.

Principles of Operant Conditioning

The operant conditioning model is also referred to as Skinnerian conditioning after B.F. Skinner, the person most responsible for its paradigmatic

development. The operant conditioning model, however, was based originally upon Thorndike's Law of Effect (1911, p. 244):

> Of several responses made to the same situation, those which are accom-
> panied or closely followed by satisfaction to the animal will, other things
> being equal, be more firmly connected with the situation, so that, when it
> reoccurs, they will be more likely to reoccur; those which are accom-
> panied or closely followed by discomfort to the animal will, other things
> being equal, have their connections with the situation weakened, so that,
> when it reoccurs, they will be less likely to occur. The greater the satis-
> faction or discomfort, the greater the strengthening or weakening of the
> bond.

As such, the operant conditioning model emphasizes the active role the
organism plays in obtaining rewards or avoiding punishments for itself.
Skinner (1953) distinguished two types of responses, respondents and
operants. Respondents are those behaviors that are elicited by specific stimuli
and in which the organism plays a more or less passive role; that is, the
presentation of the eliciting stimulus is not under the control of the organism
(see Dadds, Davey, & Fields, this volume). Salivation in response to food in
the mouth and constriction of the pupil in response to a bright light are
examples of respondent behavior. Operant behaviors, on the other hand,
are not elicited from an organism in response to a specific stimulus. Rather,
operant responses are emitted by an organism seemingly "spontaneously";
thus, the organism takes an active role in producing the behaviors, and the
behavior in some fashion operates on the environment to generate some consequence. Pressing a lever because doing so has produced food in the past, or
crying because it has been successful in gaining someone's attention in the
past, are examples of operantly conditioned behaviors. In general, an operant
may be defined as any behavior that is affected by its consequences (Ollendick
& Cerny, 1981).

Two types of learning are relevant to understanding operant conditioning
influences. A given operant may be either contingency-governed, rule-
governed, or both (Hayes & Hayes, 1992). Contingency-governed behavior
describes operants which have been influenced by directly experienced contingencies. In contrast, rule-governed behavior refers to operants that are
controlled by verbal (or imaginal) descriptions of contingencies rather than
by a history of directly experienced contingencies. Thus, in human beings,
behavior is potentially influenced by two sets of contingencies, one involving
those related directly to the behavior in similar circumstances in the past (i.e.,
contingency-governance), and the second to verbally described contingencies
that may be completely different from the direct contingencies which have
been historically associated with the behavior in question (Zettle & Hayes,
1982). Thus, in seeking to understand the role of operant conditioning processes in the development and maintenance of childhood anxiety disorders, it
is important to consider both direct contingencies and rules. In other words,
it is important to consider not only what response- contingent consequences

anxious children have experienced directly but also the beliefs they have about the likely outcomes of such responses.

Whether directly experienced or described in a rule, there are two general classes of contingent stimulus events that determine changes in operant responses: reinforcers and punishers. Reinforcers increase the probability of the response occurring in the future whereas punishers decrease the likelihood of its occurrence in the future. Within each of these, two subclasses can be defined based on whether the consequence involves presentation or withdrawal of a stimulus. Positive reinforcers are those stimulus events that are contingent on a response and increase the probability of the response occurring in the future. Negative reinforcers are those stimulus events whose contingent withdrawal *increases* the probability of the response occurring in the future. In both cases, the consequence that follows the response increases the probability that the response will be repeated in the future under similar stimulus conditions. However, in the case of a positive reinforcer a stimulus event (e.g., praise) is added to the organism's environment, whereas in the case of a negative reinforcer a stimulus event (e.g., nagging) is removed from the organism's environment. Thus, the functional consequence of any reinforcer is to increase the probability of future occurrences of a behavior. Procedurally, this objective may be accomplished by adding something to the environment (positive reinforcer) or removing something from the environment (negative reinforcer). In either case, the only way to determine the reinforcing properties of a stimulus event is to directly test its effects on behavior.

The class of contingent events known as punishers can similarly be divided into two subcategories. That type which involves the contingent presentation of an aversive stimulus is typically (and confusingly) labeled punishment. In contrast, response cost or penalty involves the removal of a positive stimulus contingent on the response in question. In both cases, the consequence that follows the response *decreases* the probability that the response will be repeated in the future under similar stimulus conditions. As with reinforcers, punishers are defined functionally and thus must be empirically determined. In other words, although a stimulus may be generally perceived as aversive, unless it decreases the probability of a response when it is contingently presented, it is not a punisher. Similarly, it is important to note that a reinforcer does not need to be a "pleasant" event or a punisher an unpleasant or "aversive" event. An event that is a reinforcer for one child in one situation may be a punisher for the same child in another situation. Similarly, what is determined to be reinforcing for one child might be found punishing for another, and vice versa.

The operant model also entails procedures for the development of specific responses (through a process called "shaping") and the maintenance of behaviors by careful and selective use of schedules of reinforcement and contingency contracting procedures. In addition, the model allows for use of discrimination and generalization learning in order to bring operant responses under the selective control of specified stimuli (referred to as "discriminant" stimuli); that is, it delineates procedures that can be used to establish cues or signals for behaviors. As such, the operant model has much to offer in understanding the onset and maintenance of phobic and anxiety disorders and their subsequent treatment.

Onset and Maintenance of Disorders

Just how children acquire phobias and anxiety disorders from a learning perspective is an intriguing question, about which there has been much controversy but little empirical data (King, Hamilton, & Ollendick, 1988; Morris & Kratochwill, 1993). Conditioning theory, one of the earliest and foremost theories, is based on the assumption that phobias and related anxiety disorders have traumatic and sub-traumatic origins. However, conditioning theory is more elaborate than direct aversive classical conditioning theory alone (see Dadds, Davey, & Field, this volume). Limitations in conditioning theory in accounting for the onset and course of anxiety and phobic disorders led Rachman (1977) to propose three "major" pathways to the acquisition of fear and anxiety. In addition to direct aversive conditioning, Rachman emphasized the importance of indirect, vicarious acquisition of fears through observational learning (i.e., modeling) and the transmission of information (e.g., verbal instruction) as pathways by which a previously neutral stimulus can come to be associated with a fear response. Somewhat surprisingly, he did not comment upon the role of operant factors as a potential causal pathway. We believe this to be a serious omission in his otherwise seminal treatise on the origin of fears and anxiety. Elsewhere, we have proposed the inclusion of operant factors as a "fourth" major pathway (King et al., 1988). Below, we discuss the potential roles of operant conditioning processes in the onset and maintenance of phobic and anxiety disorders. Because operant conditioning processes may be relevant to understanding critical aspects of Rachman's two indirect conditioning paths, our discussion begins with a brief introduction of each.

The vicarious acquisition of fears and anxieties involves what is commonly referred to as "observational learning" or "modeling." For example, having been exposed to the fearful or phobic behavior of parents, siblings, or friends at the sight of a spider, a child may imitate or "model" these reactions on future occasions when the child is confronted with the relevant stimulus. The precise manner by which children acquire such fears or anxieties in the natural environment is currently unknown, although arousal level, attention to the model, identification with the model, and possible consequences of such behavior to the model all seem to play critical roles (Bandura, 1969, 1977, 1986). Mineka and Zinbarg (1995) reviewed the experimental evidence for observational learning of fear in human beings and concluded that it is suggestive but limited by the fact that only very mild and short-lived fears have been produced owing to ethical limitations. However, they point to much stronger animal research showing that modeling can create intense and persistent fears. For example, Mineka and colleagues (e.g., Mineka, Davidson, Cook, & Keir, 1984) showed that lab-reared rhesus monkeys with no fear of snakes learned to fear them after only briefly observing their parents reacting fearfully to snakes. Although indirect, evidence supports the influence of modeling in the acquisition of children's fears. For example, children with fears and phobias often have anxious parents who possess similar fears (e.g., Bandura & Menlove, 1968; Hagman, 1932; Windheuser, 1977). Although this relation could stem from genetic factors, the fact that behavior genetics studies of childhood anxiety consistently show significant influence of the shared environment is consistent with modeling influences (see Eley, this volume).

Although a child could observe a family member or friend display fearful or anxious behavior in the presence of fear-producing stimuli, it is equally probable that the family member or friend's distress would be conveyed to the child at other times through conversation, stories, jokes, and the like. Opportunities for direct and immediate observation are far more limited than are exposures to experiences and attitudes communicated indirectly by friends, family members, and others. As Rachman (1977, p. 384) noted:

> Although I am unaware of any conventionally acceptable evidence that fear can be acquired through the transmission of information (and particularly, by instruction), it seems to be undeniable. Information-giving is an inherent part of child-rearing and is carried on by parents and peers in an almost unceasing fashion, particularly in the child's earliest years. It is probable that informational and instructional processes provide the basis for most of our commonly encountered fears in everyday life.

Operant Factors in the Onset of Anxiety Disorders

Another way in which operant conditioning mechanisms may contribute to the onset of anxiety disorders involves the vicarious paths of operant conditioning. For example, in addition to learning to associate a situation with fear by observing parents' responses, children may similarly learn to cope with anxiety through avoidance by observing that their anxious parents' avoidance responses are reinforced by reductions in anxiety. In this fashion they may also derive maladaptive rules to govern their future behavior in the face of anxiety. For example, it may be that one pathway to the development of anxiety sensitivity may be through observation of an anxious parent's reactions to anxiety or through hearing the anxious parent's verbal rules concerning methods for coping with anxiety.

To the extent that some aspects of anxiety are operants, it becomes possible for such behavior to be selectively reinforced. Such anxiety-relevant operants may include verbalizations concerning subjective fear, statements about inability to cope, and beliefs regarding the uncontrollability of anxiety and fear. As noted early on by Miller, Barrett, and Hampe (1974, p. 115):

> Parents and significant persons teach children to be afraid by selectively attending and rewarding fearful and avoidant behaviors. Thus, children are taught fear of the dark, dogs, separation, school, and such, by parents' and age mates' responding with affection, anger, or reassurance to the child's fear, cautious approaches, and avoidance of these situations. The child, in turn, learns that parents are sensitive to such behaviors and respond with much attention and preoccupation so that a little fear evokes intense and frequent responses from significant others.

In such instances, the child may fail to develop adaptive responses to aversive stimuli. Rather, since fear and avoidance are rewarded by significant others, these responses may persist and intensify. Thus, phobic behavior in children may be established on a gradual basis through inadvertent or deliberate reinforcement (shaping) on the part of parents and significant others. Intermittent reinforcement would be expected to be very powerful in the maintenance of such behavior once acquired in this manner.

In a recent review of Rachman's three pathways theory, in addition to reporting considerable support for each of Rachman's three pathways and for operant factors, King, Gullone, and Ollendick (1998) noted emerging support for a nonassociative perspective on the origin of phobias (see Menzies & Clark, 1993a, 1994, and Menzies & Harris, this volume). According to nonassociative theory, many children who have undergone normal maturational development will show fear on their first contact with evolutionarily relevant stimuli regardless of their associative learning experiences (e.g., conditioning history). For most children, this initial fearful response will diminish across time owing to repeated nontraumatic exposure to the feared object or situation (i.e., habituation). On the other hand, some children will remain fearful of such stimuli from their first encounter, often appearing for treatment at a later age.

According to the nonassociative theory, one of the primary reasons why some children's fears persist is that their opportunities for normal habituation experiences with fearful stimuli are limited owing to parental fear of the very same stimuli (Menzies & Clarke, 1995; Menzies & Harris, this volume). Limited evidence exists in support of this hypothesis. For example, Hagman (1932) found that children were less likely to get over fears that they shared with their mothers. Given that Hagman also found that exposure was the most successful method used by mothers to reduce their children's fears, one explanation for this association is that fearful mothers were less likely to or less effective than nonfearful mothers in exposing their children to their mutually shared fear stimuli. Similar findings have been reported by Windheuser (1977). Further, based on their study of the offspring of agoraphobic mothers, Silverman, Cerny, and Nelles (1988) argued that such mothers' avoidance behavior is, in part, likely to limit their children's experiences with feared situations.

Like the nonassociative model, the operant perspective assumes that, although there are wide individual differences in intensity, many children show fear to some stimuli. It would seem that the ideas advanced by nonassociative theory can be considerably expanded through consideration of operant conditioning influences. First, more may occur during normative exposure to fearful stimuli than habituation. Such experiences also provide important contexts for learning emotion regulation strategies and coping responses. Thus, to the extent that such skills are learned owing to their consequences, operant conditioning influences have clear potential to contribute to mastery of typical and atypical fears.

Second, as noted by Vasey and Ollendick (2000), parents need not be anxious themselves to contribute to their child's anxiety by inadvertently fostering limited exposure to fear mastery situations. Parents' responses to their child's anxiety are likely to shape and be shaped by their child's anxiety through operant conditioning influences.

The processes through which operant factors operate in the learning of fear and avoidance in a family context are nicely illustrated in a recent study by Barrett, Rapee, Dadds, and Ryan (1996). Based on clinical observations, Barrett et al. reasoned that anxious children and their parents would be more likely to make threat interpretations of ambiguous situations than their nonanxious counterparts, and that parents of these anxious children would be more likely to approve and reinforce such solutions than would parents of nonanxious children. Twelve ambiguous situations that could be interpreted as either threats or non-threats were presented to the children and parents separately. Then, two of these situations were selected to be the focus of brief family discussions. Each family discussion included parents and child and the child was instructed to present a final solution at the end of the family discussion. The content of the final solution was subsequently compared with the solution previously provided by the child alone. Children were between 7 and 14 years of age. Children and their parents in the anxious group independently perceived more of the ambiguous situations as possessing threat than did children and parents in the nonanxious group. Moreover, independent solutions of children, mothers, and fathers in the anxious group were characterized by higher levels of avoidance (actions that allowed escape from or avoidance of potentially harmful or embarrassing situations) than that found in the non-anxious group. Finally, the family discussion was associated with a large increase in the percentage of anxious children choosing an avoidant solution—far in excess of that chosen by any family member prior to the family discussion. Thus, avoidant solutions greatly increased following family discussions for the anxious children. It seems that the family may play an important role in a child's choice of problem-solving strategies, and that avoidance may be reinforced in families with anxious children. Barrett and associates label this effect the "family enhancement of avoidant response" effect (FEAR effect). In a subsequent study, this group of clinical researchers provided direct behavioral observation of this effect, illustrating the reinforcement process through which more avoidant solutions were generated (Dadds, Barrett, Rapee, & Ryan, 1996). Siqueland, Kendall, and Steinberg (1996), as well as Chorpita, Albano, and Barlow (1996), have reported similar findings. Collectively, these findings illustrate information/ instruction, modeling, and positive reinforcement pathways of fear acquisition and behavioral avoidance.

Operant Factors in the Maintenance of Anxiety Symptoms and Disorders

Regardless of the pathway by which children acquire anxious responses, there are several ways in which operant conditioning influences may foster their maintenance and intensification. First, a significant problem that had to be overcome in the development of conditioning theory centered around the fact that extinction (i.e., presentation of conditioned stimuli in the absence of unconditioned stimuli, resulting in the eventual disappearance of the conditioned response) did not always occur in the natural environment. Very often, anxious and phobic children engage in escape or avoidance behavior in the presence of conditioned stimuli, preventing extinction from occurring. Consequently, conditioning theory evolved as a "two-factor" or "two-stage" theory that was then able to address both the acquisition and maintenance of these disorders. The two-factor theory had its origins in the writings of Mowrer (1939). Mowrer's first factor addressed the origin of the phobia and was consistent with the classical aversive conditioning model. Mowrer wrote "anxiety is a learned response, occurring to signals' (conditioned stimuli) that are premonitory of (i.e., have in the past been followed by) situations of injury or pain (unconditioned stimuli)" (p. 563). The second factor of his theory addressed the maintenance of escape/avoidance behavior that Mowrer conceptualized in terms of anxiety reduction. According to Mowrer, "reduction of anxiety may serve powerfully to reinforce behavior that brings about such a state of relief' or security'" (p. 564). Escape or avoidance of the unpleasant state associated with anxiety serves as a negative reinforcer, increasing avoidant behaviors in turn. Removal of the aversive event (i.e., anxiety) serves to reinforce avoidant behaviors.

A second path to maintenance and intensification of anxiety that involves operant conditioning mechanisms reflects the consequences of avoidance. As noted by Vasey and Ollendick (2000), to the extent that anxiety interferes with opportunities to enter important developmental contexts, it is likely to persist. Avoidance can prevent mastery of normal developmental challenges and thereby increase the likelihood of its persistence or increase risk for related problems in the future. This pathway is similar to the notion of "limited shopping" in Patterson's theory of antisocial behavior (Patterson, Reid, & Dishion, 1992). Because antisocial children become rejected by their peers and fail academically, their contact with important developmental contexts becomes increasingly limited, denying them opportunities to learn important skills. Such limited opportunities exacerbate their incompetence and make it increasingly likely that they will remain on deviant developmental pathways. Similarly, anxious children may also suffer the cumulative effects of limited contact with important developmental contexts owing to their tendency toward avoidant behavior and biased information processing.

Thus, anxiety should lead to incompetence owing to limited contact with important developmental contexts. Indeed, substantial evidence shows that anxiety is associated with incompetence in academic contexts (Dweck & Wortman, 1982) and social contexts (Rubin, 1993; Strauss, Frame, & Forehand, 1987; Vernberg, Abwender, Ewell, & Beery, 1992). In addition, it appears to be associated with biases and deficits in information-processing and emotion regulation that may also be viewed as examples of incompetence. Because of their failure to acquire important skills and because anxiety may interfere with performance, anxious children face increased risk of failure or other punishing outcomes when they encounter threatening situations. As noted in the previous section, these consequences should increase the anxiety associated with such situations and increase the likelihood of avoidance in the future.

The social consequences of withdrawal exemplify the potential for punishing outcomes faced by anxious children. Rubin's Waterloo Longitidunal Project has yielded substantial evidence that social anxiety and withdrawal lead to peer rejection and unpopularity by mid- to late-childhood (see Rubin, 1993, and Rubin & Burgess this volume). Withdrawn children's peers begin to recognize them as being sensitive, shy, fearful and withdrawn by second grade. At about the same age, withdrawn children begin to experience elevated levels of social rejection when they attempt to direct their dyadic interactions with peers (Rubin, 1993). Finally, by early adolescence, withdrawn children are more rejected by their peers, more likely to view themselves as socially incompetent, and more lonely and depressed than normal peers (Rubin, Chen, & Hymel, 1993). The rejection and social failure experienced by such children is likely to be at least partly due to deficiencies in their social skills stemming from lack of practice. For example, Evans (1993) concluded that the impairment in discourse skills shown by socially withdrawn children reflects an actual skill deficit because these children did not show similar performance decrements on nonverbal tasks.

Another aspect of operant factors that must be addressed is the operant conditioning by anxious children of parental behaviors that may maintain or intensify the child's anxiety. For example, how is it that parents of anxious children come to behave as they did in the Barrett et al. (1996) study? Anxious children and their parents influence one another in a complex dance of shifting contingencies and consequences with each shaping the other in ways that may increase or decrease the child's anxiety in the future. Anxious children, through the reinforcing (primarily negative) and punishing aspects of their responses may shape the behavior of those around them in ways that makes their anxiety and avoidance more likely in the future. In this manner, the anxious child, like Patterson's prototypic conduct disordered child, is architect and victim of an environment (made up of parents, teachers, peers) that offers contingencies and consequences that interfere with competence and foster anxiety and avoidance. Similarly, parents, in an effort to reduce their child's anxiety (particularly in the short term), may inadvertently contribute to its maintenance and intensification. Can operant processes help us to understand why parents of anxious children tend to be both overprotective and emotionally unsupportive?

Summary

Operant factors appear to play an important role in the acquisition and maintenance of fears and anxieties in children, largely through family processes (see Dadds & Roth, this volume). In addition, operant factors are frequently evident in other contexts as well. Not infrequently, children receive considerable reinforcement for anxiety related behaviors. The young child who whines or fusses upon separation from the caregiver, for example, is frequently reinforced by attention and comfort from well-meaning teachers and peers. The child who worries excessively about how she or he will do on a test is offered encouragement and consolation by teachers and peers alike. In such instances, positive reinforcement principles may be at work. Similarly, the "anxious" child in these situations is frequently allowed to escape or avoid the unpleasant aspects of the situation and, in turn, may be negatively reinforced. As a result, positive and negative reinforcement may serve as powerful factors in the development and maintenance of anxiety in situations such as these. Operant factors also play an important role in the treatment of phobic and anxiety disorders, a topic to which we now turn our attention.

Operant Factors and the Treatment of Phobic/Anxiety Disorders

There is a sizeable literature concerning the use of operant conditioning techniques in the treatment of childhood anxiety disorders. To the extent that such techniques are effective, they may provide clues regarding naturally occurring protective and ameliorative influences that help to explain why some high-risk children fail to develop anxiety disorders, and why some of those who do, are successfully able to return to a normal developmental pathway. There may be important parallels between the operant conditioning procedures used in treatment and the factors that operate in normal children's development to foster approach and decrease anxiety and avoidance.

Derived from principles of operant conditioning, contingency management procedures attempt to change phobic and anxious behaviors by manipulating their consequences (Ollendick & Cerny, 1981; King & Ollendick, 1997). Inasmuch as these procedures have been used somewhat differently with phobic and anxiety disorders, the utility of these procedures for treating phobic and anxiety disorders will be reviewed separately. The treatment of phobic disorders will be examined first. Operant-based procedures rest on the assumption that acquisition of approach responses to the fear-provoking situation is sufficient for behavior change to occur and that anxiety reduction, per se, is not necessary. Shaping, positive reinforcement and extinction are the most frequently used contingency management procedures to reduce phobic behaviors and increase approach behaviors. Basically, approach behaviors are shaped and subsequently reinforced whereas associated behaviors such as crying and complaining are placed on extinction schedules (i.e., reinforcement is withheld for these behaviors).

In the first systematic application of these principles to the reduction of phobic avoidance, Obler and Terwilliger (1970) randomly assigned 30 emotionally disturbed, neurologically impaired children (7–12 years of age) to a reinforced practice condition or to a no-treatment control condition. The children all presented clinically with severe monophobic disorders of either riding on a school bus or interacting with a dog. In the reinforced practice condition, children obtained graduated and repeated practice in approaching the actual feared stimulus and were reinforced profusely for doing so. Complaints and crying were systematically ignored. Results indicated that treated children were less phobic and avoidant than untreated children, and the treated children, but not the untreated ones, were able to perform approach tasks (i.e., get on the bus, pet a dog) that they were unable to do prior to treatment.

In a second examination of this procedure, Leitenberg and Callahan (1973) randomly assigned 14 nursery and kindergarten children who showed extreme fear and avoidance of the dark to a reinforced practice condition or to a no-treatment condition. As in the Obler and Terwilliger study, significant changes in dark tolerance were evinced for the reinforced practice group only; changes were not evident in the control group.

Sheslow, Bondy, and Nelson (1983) provided yet another demonstration of the efficacy of reinforced practice. This study compared reinforced practice, verbal coping skills, and their combination in treating fear of the dark in young children (4–5 years of age). Thirty-two children were randomly assigned to one of the three treatment conditions or a control group condition. Reinforced practice consisted of graduated and repeated exposure to dark stimuli accompanied by verbal and tangible reinforcement. Verbal coping skills consisted of teaching children a set of self-instructions designed to assist them in coping with, and handling, their fears while in the dark. In the combined group, verbal coping skills were practiced while the children spent increasingly greater time in the dark and were reinforced for doing so. Results indicated that the reinforced practice group and the combined verbal self-instruction plus reinforced practice group demonstrated significant changes on the behavioral avoidance task; such changes were not evinced for the verbal coping-only group or the control group. Moreover, the addition of coping statements did not enhance the effects of the reinforced practice-alone group.

Similarly, positive support for the efficacy of reinforced practice was found by Menzies and Clarke (1993b). They examined the relative efficacy of reinforced practice and modeling in reducing children's phobic anxiety and avoidance of water. Forty-eight water-phobic children between the ages of 3 and 8 years were randomly assigned to one of four groups: (a) reinforced practice, (b) live modeling, (c) reinforced practice plus live modeling, and (d) an assessment-only control group. At the end of treatment, the reinforced practice condition had produced statistically and clinically significant gains that had generalized to other water-related activities. In contrast, the live modeling condition did not lead to greater treatment benefits than those observed in the control children. Moreover, modeling did not appear to enhance the effects of reinforced practice, as was anticipated by the authors. The combined treatment condition was no more effective than the reinforced practice-alone condition.

On the basis of these four treatment outcome studies, Ollendick and King (1998) concluded that reinforced practice—based firmly in principles of operant conditioning—had strong empirical support for its clinical use. In these studies, reinforced practice was shown to be more effective than no-treatment in two studies (Leitenberg & Callahan, 1973; Obler & Terwilliger, 1970) and to be superior to two other treatments that have been shown to be more effective than no treatment—verbal coping skills (Sheslow et al., 1983) and live modeling (Menzies & Clarke, 1993b). It is evident, however, that these positive treatment outcomes have been obtained with young children, for the most part, and that its efficacy with older children and adolescents has not been examined. Furthermore, it is evident that these effects have been obtained in clinical settings, with little or no parental or family involvement. The treatment has been implemented by clinicians with individual children, and the child has been the sole target of intervention in these investigations. That is, even though parents have been shown to prompt and reinforce avoidant behaviors in their children (Barrett, Rapee et al., 1996; Dadds et al., 1996), reinforced practice has not been designed to target such patterns that likely serve to maintain phobic avoidance.

One notable exception to this development was a pilot study undertaken by Heard, Dadds, and Conrad (1992). In this study, three adolescent girls meeting criteria for simple (i.e., specific) phobia were treated. Penny, 15 years of age, displayed extreme fear and anxiety when faced with medical procedures or even just being near medical settings. She tried to avoid these settings at all times and whenever medical attention had been necessary she reacted by struggling, screaming, and fleeing. Melissa, 13 years of age, was referred for fear of the dark. She also reported extreme anxiety when having to separate from her mother when left at school or when her parents went out at night. Melissa called out every night, displayed excessive need for reassurance, and needed to have someone awake in the house before going to sleep each night. Sandra, 12 years of age, refused to go to school. Her parents reported that she would not get out of bed in the mornings, would complain of stomach and headaches, and, if forced to get up, would vomit. They also reported that she had been very tearful and withdrawn since the new school year had begun.

Treatment in this single case design study was multifaceted, using relaxation training, *in vivo* exposure, and cognitive restructuring in addition to a home-based contingency management program. The contingency management program consisted of *in vivo* exposure and instructing the family to minimize attention to fear reactions and to positively reinforce approach behavior to the phobic stimuli. All three adolescents were successfully treated. Although the nature of this multifaceted treatment precluded isolating its effective ingredients, the authors indicated that the home-based contingency management program was of great importance. They concluded: "parents and other care providers need to be actively involved in therapy as agents of behavior change" (p. 81).

A similar home-based contingency management approach has been used with anxious children by Barrett, Dadds, and Rapee (1996). This comprehensive intervention included training parents in skills for managing the child's anxiety and avoidance, helping parents deal with anxiety that they themselves experienced, and improving family problem-solving, as well as working with the child using cognitive–behavioral procedures. Seventy-nine children aged 7–14 years were randomly assigned to a cognitive–behavioral treatment aimed solely at the child (CBT), cognitive–behavioral treatment plus family anxiety management condition, and a waiting-list control condition. Of particular importance here is the family anxiety management condition. Three specific components were included. First, parents were provided training in how to reward "courageous" behavior and extinguish excessive anxiety in their child. Specifically, parents were trained in reinforcement strategies including use of verbal praise, privileges, and tangible rewards made contingent on facing up to feared situations. Planned ignoring (i.e., extinction) was used as a method for dealing with excessive complaining and anxious behavior; that is, parents were trained to listen empathically to their child's complaints the first time they occurred. However, repetitious complaints were followed by the parent's prompting the child to engage in a coping strategy (learned in the parallel CBT intervention) and then withdrawing their attention until the anxious or complaining behaviors ceased. Thus, parents were taught how to use contingency management strategies such as descriptive praise, natural consequences, and planned ignoring. In addition, parents were taught how to deal with their own emotional upsets, gain awareness of their own anxiety responses in stressful situations, and model problem-solving and proactive responses to feared situations. Finally, they were provided brief training in communication and problem-solving skills so that they could become better able to work with their children. At post-treatment, 57.1% of the children receiving CBT alone and 84% of the children receiving the combined treatment were diagnosis-free. In contrast, only 26% of the children in the waiting-list condition were free of anxiety disorder diagnoses upon completion of treatment. At 1-year follow-up, 70.3% of children in CBT remained diagnosis-free, whereas

95.6% of children in the combined treatment remained so. At both post-treatment and follow-up, the combined treatment was superior to the CBT-alone treatment. (Children in the waiting list were assigned to treatment following post-treatment.)

Again, it is difficult to determine which components in the combined treatment were responsible for the superior treatment effects. Quite obviously, the family intervention consisted of three relatively distinct, albeit interrelated, components. Any one of the components might be responsible for the enhanced effects obtained. However, in post-hoc analyses conducted to determine the effects of child age on outcome, the authors reported that the combined treatment was more effective than CBT alone for younger children (aged 7–10) but not for older ones (aged 11–14). Specifically, at post-treatment, 100% of younger children in the combined treatment were diagnosis-free compared with 55.6% of younger children in the CBT-alone treatment. In contrast, 60% of the older children in both active treatment conditions were diagnosis-free. At follow-up, the same effect was observed for both groups with only the younger group showing a significantly higher proportion of children diagnosis-free in the combined group (exact percentages not reported).

As noted by the authors, it may be more important to enhance parenting skills for younger children than older ones; for older children, individual child cognitive work and exposure to the feared stimuli may be sufficient to produce improvements. Conversely, they note, cognitive interventions and exposure may not be sufficient for younger children. However, further consideration of this pattern of results suggests a different interpretation. The fact that the efficacy of CBT was similar in younger and older children (55.6% vs. 60%) is inconsistent with the conclusion that individual cognitive work may be sufficient to produce improvement in older but not younger children. The fact that the efficacy of the program among younger but not older children was greatly enhanced by the addition of the family component suggests that anxiety-related behaviors of young children are under significant control by parental contingencies and consequences whereas those of adolescents are not. Thus, among adolescents it would appear that responses by parents do not function as reinforcers or punishers for anxiety-relevant behavior. Apparently, the anxiety-related behavior of adolescents is sufficiently under the control of other contingencies and consequences that modifying parental behavior is insufficient to change it. What these other contingencies and consequences are is an interesting and important question; as is the question of what developmental factors contribute to this reduced parental influence and increase of other influences.

Further indication that cognitive self-instructions and exposure alone may not be sufficient can be found in work conducted by Kendall and colleagues (Kendall et al., 1997) and Ollendick and his colleagues (Hagopian, Weist, & Ollendick, 1990; Ollendick, Hagopian, & Huntzinger, 1991). For example, Ollendick et al. (1991) examined the efficacy of cognitive–behavioral treatment in reducing nighttime fears in two separation-anxious girls. Mary, a

10-year-old, expressed concerns about her mother's well-being and evidenced nighttime problems as she refused to sleep in her own bed. She began requesting that she sleep with her mother about three months prior to her first clinic appointment. During that period, mother allowed her to sleep with her intermittently in order to reassure her and to help reduce her emerging fears. Ten days prior to her first appointment, her fears worsened rapidly. Mary woke up after midnight to the sound of sirens and became very concerned that her mother was not yet home from a party (Mary was home alone at the time). After that incident, Mary began sleeping with her mother every night. She stated that she had lost her dad (her parents divorced a year earlier) and older brother (who went away to college) and was afraid "of losing mom, too." Lucy, an 8-year-old girl, also presented with excessive concerns about her mother's well-being, nighttime problems including refusal to sleep in her own bed, and self-disparaging comments. Concerns about her mother reportedly began a few weeks before her mother had back surgery (about seven months prior to her first clinic visit). Over the ensuing months, her concerns became more exaggerated, and Lucy began refusing to sleep in her own bed, often sleeping with her parents. Self-disparaging statements such as "Maybe I just don't belong on this earth" and "I can't be happy ... I used to be happy ... even my friends don't like me now" began shortly before her parents brought her to treatment.

A multiple baseline design across girls was used to demonstrate the controlling effects of treatment. Following completion of a baseline phase, Self-Control Training (SCT: relaxation, self-monitoring, and verbal self-instructions) was implemented. Following this second phase, contingency management procedures were systematically added to the program. In this third phase, parents were provided a brief overview of how phobic behaviors are learned and maintained (from an operant perspective), and a specific illustration of how these processes worked in relation to their children's nighttime behaviors was described. The principles of positive reinforcement and extinction were discussed in detail. Role-plays and didactic instruction were used to train the mothers to make clear and firm commands for their children to go to bed in their own beds; to ignore whining, crying, and similar behaviors; to ignore their children if they insisted on getting in bed with them; and to provide positive rewards the morning after their children slept alone in their own beds throughout the night. Both Mary and Lucy were actively involved in setting up and enacting the contingency management program.

Results showed little change following implementation of the self-control phase of the program. Both girls remained acutely anxious in the evenings and refused to sleep in their own beds. Considerable strife ensued. Only when the contingency management phase was added to the treatment program did nighttime problems cease. Moreover, their anxiety was greatly reduced and the girls no longer met criteria for separation anxiety disorder. Use of the multiple baseline design and the systematic institution of self-control training and reinforcement contingencies in an additive fashion suggested that the addition of contingency management was the critical factor in the reduction of nighttime problems and separation anxiety in these two young girls. Very similar results were obtained in the treatment of an 11-year-old girl fearful of AIDS, infections, and other diseases (Hagopian et al., 1990). She presented with extreme worries and fears of a one-year duration. As in the Ollendick et al. (1991) demonstration, self-control procedures were initially implemented, followed by a home-based contingency management program. Only when contingency management procedures were added to the treatment program did significant change result. When the home-based reinforcement system was added, the anxious episodes subsided completely. In both studies, enduring effects were obtained.

The significance of *in vivo* exposure and contingency management procedures was also demonstrated in a recent randomized clinical trial by Kendall and his associates (1997). In this study, 94 anxious children (aged 9–13 years) were randomly assigned to CBT or waiting-list control conditions. CBT was divided into two phases. In the first phase, treatment was aimed at the recognition and analysis of anxious cognition and the development of management strategies to cope with anxiety-provoking situations. It was largely educational in scope. In the second phase, children were encouraged to practice the skills in anxiety-provoking situations at home and school and were rewarded for successfully completing weekly homework assignments. It was largely enactive in scope. Overall, the treatment was highly successful, a finding similar to that obtained in an earlier randomized clinical trial reported by Kendall (1994). When changes due to waiting list and due to the first phase of treatment were compared, however, the results were insignificant, indicating that the first half of treatment, by itself, was not responsible for the beneficial gains that were produced by the overall treatment package. Analyses conducted on the second phase of treatment clearly revealed that changes occurred during this phase. Such findings are similar to those reported by Ollendick and colleagues and recently by King et al.'s (1998) treatment of school-refusing children with CBT plus home- and school-based reinforcement systems. However, although this pattern suggests the importance of behavioral practice, it must be noted that, in the absence of the appropriate control group, it cannot be firmly concluded that the skills taught in the first half of the program would not have produced similar progress given the passage of additional time.

Implications of the Findings

First, it appears that operant factors play an important role in the onset, maintenance, and treatment of phobic and anxiety disorders in children. Of course, this is not to suggest that these factors operate in a vacuum or that they are the only factors worthy of consideration. Nor, for that matter, do they suggest that operant factors represent necessary conditions for development and maintenance of these disorders. Consistent with a developmental psychopathological perspective, they represent one set of factors, among many, that contribute to the onset of these disorders. Multiple pathways undoubtedly exist. However, once on a developmental pathway involving serious anxiety, it is difficult to imagine that such factors do not play a role in the maintenance and intensification of childhood anxiety disorders. For example, it seems unlikely that most parents would not slowly change their behavior in response to their child's anxiety in such ways that they come to play a role in the maintenance and intensification of the child's anxiety.

Second, it is interesting to speculate about possible developmental processes and how they might interact with operant factors in occasioning, maintaining, and treating phobic and anxiety disorders. As evident in our review, much of the support for operant factors has been obtained with young children and, to a lesser extent, with middle-school-aged children; rarely has strong support been shown for the influence of these factors with adolescents. For example, young children and parents frequently report that fears and worries are acquired through modeling of significant or important others and reinforcement processes (both positive and negative reinforcement), less so through direct conditioning processes (King et al., 1998). On the other hand, direct conditioning events are more frequently associated with phobias having their onset in adolescence or adulthood. Phobic and anxious parents may contribute to their children's fears and anxieties in a variety of ways. In addition to modeling of avoidance responses, they may be reluctant to allow their child to be exposed to fear-producing stimuli and thereby interfere with the normal process of fear habituation or mastery (see Menzies & Clarke, 1994; Windheuser, 1977). Reduced demand for contact with such challenging situations has long been thought to contribute to the development of childhood phobic and anxiety disorders. In addition, once young children exhibit fearful behavior, numerous opportunities exist for such behavior to be influenced by its consequences and, in turn, to shape the behavior of parents (and others). For example, by virtue of the extreme distress shown in the presence of the feared stimulus, children are likely to be effective at punishing their caregivers and others for not accommodating their desires for avoidance of the feared stimuli. Simultaneously, relief from their children's intense negative reactions is likely to be a potent source of negative reinforcement for parents and others when they allow the child to escape or avoid the feared situation. Thus the behavior of parents and others may come to be controlled by its short-term reduction of the child's fear, at the expense of the child's ultimate mastery of fear or anxiety and the demands of anxiety-producing situations. In addition, parents may supply various tangible rewards to make up for the child's inability to attend the avoided situation. Hence, a dynamic transaction between the child, parent, and significant others may become evident (Vasey & Ollendick, 2000). Here, we suggest that these processes are more likely to be present in young children than older ones. In keeping with recent behavioral genetics findings, among older children, it seems likely that parental influences are largely replaced by unshared environmental influences—that is, peers and teachers.

Furthermore, greater support for the role of operant factors in the onset and maintenance of disorder has been shown for phobic disorders than anxiety disorders, with the possible exception of separation anxiety disorder. It is interesting to speculate on these observations and the typical onset of such disorders, as revealed in epidemiological studies and retrospective reports of adults. For example, separation anxiety disorder is found to be most common in early childhood, with a mean age of onset between 4 and 8 years of age, and to decline in prevalence across age (Lease & Ollendick, 1993; Ollendick, King, & Yule, 1994). Similarly, according to retrospective reports of adults, specific phobias tend to have their onset in early childhood, with a mean age of onset between 6 and 8 years of age (Ollendick et al., 1998). In contrast, generalized anxiety disorder, social phobia, and panic disorder all tend to occur with, or following, the onset of puberty and adolescence. Thus, it appears that the various disorders for which operant factors, especially those influences related to parents and other significant adults, play the most critical roles in terms of onset and maintenance occur prior to adolescence. However, when the distinction between contingency-governed and rule-governed behavior is considered, another interpretation of this pattern is suggested. Specifically, directly experienced or observed contingencies may be more likely to play roles in anxiety disorder onset and maintenance prior to adolescence. In contrast, to the extent that operant conditioning influences play a role in the onset and maintenance of anxiety disorders having their typical onset in adolescence or even adulthood, it is likely to be through the operation of maladaptive rules (e.g., faulty beliefs or assumptions about contingencies). If so, this may reflect paths to new disorders that are opened up by the development of cognitive capacities related to rule-governance of behavior.

Similarly, it is tempting to speculate on the relations among operant factors, treatment outcome, and development. Again, much of our review suggests strong support for the utility of contingency management procedures with younger children, less so with older ones and adolescents. For example, evidence for the efficacy of individually oriented reinforced practice was found exclusively with younger children, typically those between 4 and 10 years of age (with one exception; see Obler and Terwilliger, 1970). Moreover, in the only study to examine home-based contingency management procedures with children and adolescents (Barrett, Rapee et al., 1996), it was reported that the treatment was effective for 100% of children between 7 and 10 years of age but for only 60% of children between 11 and 14 years of age. This pattern suggests several possibilities.

First, it suggests that parental sources of reinforcement are an important factor in maintaining anxiety disorders in childhood but their importance fades in adolescence. It may be that the contingencies controlled by parents are more relevant for children than adolescents. Sources of reinforcing and punishing consequences are likely to shift as children develop into adolescents. For example, as Barrett (this volume) suggests, peers may replace parents to a substantial degree as sources of influential consequences in adolescence. Another possibility is that this pattern may reflect the increasing role of maladaptive rules in the maintenance of anxiety disorders in adolescence. One of the hallmarks of rule-governed behavior is that it persists in the face of changes in the immediate contingencies (Zettle & Hayes, 1982). To the extent that adolescents have developed a complex set of verbal rules related to their anxiety disorder, their disorders are likely to be resistant to change by manipulating the immediate contingencies experienced.

Finally, and perhaps most likely, as suggested by Vasey and Dadds (this volume), incompetence stemming from prolonged reliance on avoidance as a primary means of coping with anxiety-provoking situations may become harder to overcome with age. As a function of avoidance, children are likely to acquire increasingly serious deficits in social and other skills with age. Aside from reducing inadvertent parental reinforcement for anxiety-relevant behaviors, parental interventions to date have largely focused on encouraging the child to enter feared situations (i e , increased exposure). This may be ineffective and possibly even harmful in the case of a child who lacks skills necessary to contact reinforcement contingencies and avoid punishment contingencies operating in previously avoided situations. For example, it may be ineffective at best and harmful at worst for parents to encourage their socially anxious adolescent to enter social situations if he/she has acquired serious social skill deficits that may decrease chances of success and increase the chances of punishing failure experiences. Based on this interpretation, it is not adolescence per se that is associated with the decreased effectiveness of parental interventions, but rather the duration of the child's limited contact with normative developmental contexts. The longer the child has excessively avoided the context in question, the less likely to be effective are parent interventions that encourage exposure in the absence of significant skills training.

In sum, it seems probable to us that operant factors play an important role in the development, maintenance, and treatment of phobic and anxiety disorders, especially so in children. Although much research remains to be conducted to ferret out the processes by which these influences make their mark, we already know much. In all probability, operant factors will be found to interact with a host of other important determinants, many of which are examined thoroughly in other chapters in this volume.

References

Bandura, A. (1969). *Principles of behavior modification.* New York: Holt, Rinehart, & Winston.

Bandura, A. (1977). Self-efficacy: Towards a unifying theory of behavior change. *Psychological Review, 84,* 191–215.

Bandura, A. (1986). *Social foundations of thought and action: A social cognitive theory.* Englewood Cliffs, NJ: Prentice-Hall.

Bandura, A., & Menlove, F. L. (1968). Factors determining vicarious extinction of avoidance behavior through symbolic modeling. *Journal of Personality & Social Psychology, 8,* 99–108.

Barrett, P. M., Dadds, M. R., & Rapee, R. M. (1996). Family treatment of childhood anxiety: A controlled trial. *Journal of Consulting and Clinical Psychology, 64,* 333–342.

Barrett, P. M., Rapee, R. M., Dadds, M. R., & Ryan, S. M. (1996). Family enhancement of cognitive style in anxious and aggressive children: The FEAR effect. *Journal of Abnormal Child Psychology, 24,* 187–203.

Chorpita, B. F., Albano, A. M., & Barlow, D. H. (1996). Cognitive processing in children: Relation to anxiety and family influences. *Journal of Clinical Child Psychology, 25,* 170–176.

Cicchetti, D., & Cohen, D. (1995). Perspectives on developmental psychopathology. In D. Cicchetti & D. Cohen (Eds.), *Developmental psychopathology: Vol. 1. Theory and methods* (pp. 3–20). New York: Wiley.

Dadds, M. R., Barrett, P. M., Rapee, R. M., & Ryan, S. (1996). Family process and child anxiety and aggression: An observational analysis. *Journal of Abnormal Child Psychology, 24,* 715–734.

Dweck, C., & Wortman, C. (1982). Learned helplessness, anxiety, and achievement. In H. Krohne & L. Laux (Eds.), *Achievement, stress, and anxiety.* New York: Hemisphere.

Evans, M. A. (1993). Communication competence as a dimension of shyness. In K. H. Rubin & J. B. Asendorpf (Eds.), *Social withdrawal, inhibition, and shyness in childhood* (pp. 189–212). Hillsdale, NJ: Erlbaum.

Hagman, E. R. (1932). A study of fears of children of preschool age. *Journal of Experimental Education, 1,* 110–130.

Hagopian, L. P., Weist, M. D., & Ollendick, T. H. (1990). Cognitive–behavior therapy with an 11-year-old girl fearful of AIDS infection, other diseases, and poisoning: A case study. *Journal of Anxiety Disorders, 4,* 257–265.

Hayes, S. C., & Hayes, L. J. (1992). Some clinical implications of contextualistic behaviorism: The example of cognition. *Behavior Therapy, 23,* 225–249.

Heard, P. M., Dadds, M. R., & Conrad, P. (1992). Assessment and treatment of simple phobias in children: Effects on family and marital relationships. *Behaviour Change, 9,* 73–82.

Kendall, P.C. (1994). Treating anxiety disorders in children: Results of a randomized clinical trial. *Journal of Consulting and Clinical Psychology, 62,* 100–110.

Kendall, P. C., Flannery-Schroeder, E., Panichelli-Mindel, S. M., Southam-Gerow, M., Henin, A., & Warman, M. (1997). Therapy for youths with anxiety disorders: A second randomized clinical trial. *Journal of Consulting and Clinical Psychology, 65,* 366–380.

King, N. J., & Ollendick, T. H. (1997). Annotation: Treatment of childhood phobias. *Journal of Child Psychology and Psychiatry, 38,* 389–400.

King, N. J., Gullone, E., & Ollendick, T. H. (1998). Etiology of childhood phobias: Current status of Rachman's three pathways theory. *Behaviour Research and Therapy, 36,* 297–309.

King, N. J., Hamilton, D. I., & Ollendick, T. H. (1988). *Children's phobias: A behavioural perspective.* Chichester, England: Wiley.

King, N. J., Tonge, B. J., Heyne, D., Pritchard, M., Rollings, S., Young, D., Myerson, N., & Ollendick, T. H. (1998). Cognitive–behavioral treatment of school-refusing children: A controlled evaluation. *Journal of the American Academy of Child and Adolescent Psychiatry, 37,* 395–403.

Lease, C. A., Ollendick, T. H. (1993). Development and psychopathology. In A. S. Bellack & M. Hersen (Eds.), *Psychopathology in adulthood* (pp. 89–103). Boston: Allyn & Bacon.

Leitenberg, H., & Callahan, E. J. (1973). Reinforced practice and reduction of different kinds of fear in adults and children. *Behaviour Research and Therapy, 11,* 19–30.

Menzies, R. G., & Clarke, J. C. (1993a). The etiology of childhood water phobia. *Behaviour Research and Therapy, 31,* 499–501.

Menzies, R. G., & Clarke, J. C. (1993b). A comparison of *in vivo* and vicarious exposure in the treatment of childhood water phobia. *Behaviour Research and Therapy, 31,* 9–15.

Menzies, R. G., & Clarke, J. C. (1994). Retrospective studies of the origins of phobias: A review. *Anxiety Stress and Coping, 7,* 305–318.

Menzies, R. G., & Clarke, J. C. (1995). The etiology of phobias: A non-associative account. *Clinical Psychology Review, 15,* 23–48.

Miller, L. C., Barrett, C. L., & Hampe, E. (1974). Phobias of childhood in a pre-scientific era. In A. Davids (Ed.), *Child personality and psychopathology. Current topics.* New York: Wiley.

Mineka, S., & Zinbarg, R. (1995). Conditioning and ethological models of social phobia. In R. G. Heimberg, M. R. Liebowitz, D. A. Hope, & F. R. Schneier (Eds.), *Social phobia: Diagnosis, assessment, and treatment.* New York: Guilford.

Mineka, S., Davidson, M., Cook, M., & Keir, R. (1984). Observational conditioning of snake fear in rhesus monkeys. *Journal of Abnormal Psychology, 93,* 355–372.

Morris, R. J., & Kratochwill, T. R. (1993). *Treating children's fears and phobias: A behavioral approach.* New York: Pergamon.

Mowrer, O. H. (1939). A stimulus–response theory of anxiety and its role as a reinforcing agent. *Psychological Review, 46,* 553–565.

Obler, M., & Terwilliger, R. F. (1970). Pilot study on the effectiveness of systematic desensitization with neurologically impaired children with phobic disorders. *Journal of Consulting and Clinical Psychology, 34,* 314–318.

Ollendick, T. H. (1979). Fear reduction techniques with children. In M. Hersen, R. M. Eisler, & P. M. Miller (Eds.), *Progress in behavior modification: Vol. 8* (pp. 127–168). New York: Academic Press.

Ollendick, T. H., & Cerny, J. A. (1981). *Clinical behavior therapy with children.* New York: Plenum.

Ollendick, T. H., & King, N. J. (1998). Empirically supported treatments for children with phobic and anxiety disorders: Current status. *Journal of Clinical Child Psychology, 27,* 156–167.

Ollendick, T. H., Hagopian, L. P., & Huntzinger, R. M. (1991). Cognitive–behavior therapy with nighttime fearful children. *Journal of Behavior Therapy and Experimental Psychiatry, 22,* 113–121.

Ollendick, T. H., Hagopian, L. P., & King, N. J. (1998). Specific phobias in children. In G. L. C. Davey (Ed.), *Phobias: A handbook of theory, research and treatment* (pp. 201–226). Chichester, England: Wiley.

Ollendick, T. H., King, N. J, & Yule, W. (Eds.) (1994). *International handbook of phobic and anxiety disorders in children and adolescents.* New York: Plenum.

Patterson, G. R., Reid, J. B., & Dishion, T. J. (1992). *Antisocial boys.* Eugene, OR: Castalia Publishing.

Rachman, S. (1977). The conditioning theory of fear acquisition: A critical examination. *Behaviour Research and Therapy, 15,* 375–387.

Rubin, K. H. (1993). The Waterloo longitudinal project: Correlates and consequences of social withdrawal from childhood to adolescence. In K. H. Rubin & J. B. Asendorpf (Eds.), *Social withdrawal, inhibition, and shyness* (pp. 291–314). Hillsdale, NJ: Erlbaum.

Rubin, K. H., Chen, X., & Hymel, S. (1993). The socio-emotional characteristics of extremely aggressive and extremely withdrawn children. *Merrill–Palmer Quarterly, 39,* 518–534.

Rutter, M. (1990). Psychosocial resilience and protective mechanisms. In J. Rolf, A. S. Masten, D. Cicchetti, K. H. Nuechterlein, & S. Weintraub (Eds.), *Risk and protective factors in the development of psychopathology* (pp. 181–214). New York: Cambridge University Press.

Sheslow, D. V., Bondy, A. S., & Nelson, R. O. (1983). A comparison of graduated exposure, verbal coping skills, and their combination in the treatment of children's fear of the dark. *Child and Family Behavior Therapy, 4,* 33–45.

Silverman, W. K., Cerny, J. A., & Nelles, W. B. (1988). The familial influence in anxiety disorders: Studies on the offspring of patients with anxiety disorders. In B. B. Lahey & A. E. Kazdin (Eds.), *Advances in Clinical Child Psychology: Vol. 11* (pp. 223–248). New York: Plenum.

Siqueland, L., Kendall, P. C., & Steinberg, L. (1996). Anxiety in children: Perceived family environments and observed family interaction. *Journal of Consulting and Clinical Psychology, 25,* 225–237.

Skinner, B. F. (1953). *Science and human behavior.* New York: Macmillan.

Skinner, B. F. (1969). *Contingencies of reinforcement: A theoretical analysis.* New York: Appleton–Century–Crofts.

Strauss, C. C., Frame, C. L., & Forehand, R. (1987). Psychosocial impairment associated with anxiety in children. *Journal of Clinical Child Psychology, 16,* 235–239.

Thorndike, E. L. (1911). *Animal intelligence: Experimental studies.* New York: Macmillan.

Vasey, M. W., & Ollendick, T. H. (2000). Anxiety. In M. Lewis & A. Sameroff (Eds.), *Handbook of developmental psychopathology* (2nd ed, pp. 511–529). New York: Plenum.

Vernberg, E. M., Abwender, D. A., Ewell, K. K., & Beery, S. H. (1992). Social anxiety and peer relationships in early adolescence: A prospective analysis. *Journal of Clinical Child Psychology, 21,* 189–196.

Windheuser, H. J. (1977). Anxious mothers as models for coping with anxiety. *Behavioral Analysis and Modification, 2,* 39–58.

Zettle, R. D., & Hayes, S. C. (1982). Rule-governed behavior: A potential theoretical framework for cognitive–behavioral therapy. In P. C. Kendall (Ed.), *Advances in cognitive–behavioral therapy: Vol. 1* (pp. 73–118). New York: Academic Press.

12

Information-processing Factors in Childhood Anxiety: A Review and Developmental Perspective

MICHAEL W. VASEY and COLIN MACLEOD

In contrast to the impressive body of research on information-processing factors in adult anxiety disorders that has accumulated across the past 15 years or so, studies of cognitive processing in anxious children have, until recently, been all too rare. This is not only unfortunate, but also surprising, given that studies of adults have offered substantial evidence to suggest the importance of such factors in both the etiology and maintenance of anxiety disorders (Mathews & MacLeod, 1994; Mogg & Bradley, 1998; Williams, Watts, MacLeod, & Mathews, 1997). Nevertheless, the late 1990s saw an upsurge of interest in information processing among childhood anxiety researchers that holds the promise of rapid expansion of knowledge regarding the roles played by such factors in childhood anxiety. The present chapter examines this expanding research literature with two main goals. First, because many studies have appeared since the last published reviews of this literature (Daleiden & Vasey, 1997, Gotlib & MacLeod, 1997), the chapter provides an overview of these recent research findings and considers what conclusions can be drawn thus far. Within the context of this review, the second goal is to consider how the adoption of a developmental perspective can illuminate our understanding of the association between information-processing variables and childhood anxiety. Several alternative models concerning the development of attentional biases in anxious children are evaluated, and the implications for future research direction are highlighted.

An Overview of Information-processing Models

The information-processing paradigm provides a useful framework for modeling the diverse cognitive biases and distortions that appear to be operative in childhood anxiety, and for explaining the relationships among them (Daleiden & Vasey, 1997; Gotlib & MacLeod, 1997; Vasey & Daleiden, 1996). Information-processing accounts are based upon the structural and functional properties of the cognitive system. Taking a variety of forms, information-processing models typically implicate a sequence of steps in the manipulation and modification of information as it progresses through the cognitive system (Massaro & Cowan, 1993). For example, the social information-processing model offered by Dodge and colleagues to account for aggression in childhood (see Crick & Dodge, 1994) distinguishes six inter-related stages: (1) encoding, (2) interpretation, (3) goal selection, (4) response access or construction, (5) response selection, and (6) behavioral enactment. Processing activity within each of these stages is considered to be a function of activity within other stages and, more generally, is influenced also by memory processes and by the content and organization of memory stores.

An influential dichotomy was introduced to the information-processing paradigm by Shiffrin and Schneider (1977), who distinguished two primary modes of information-processing, which they labeled automatic and con-trolled processing. The term *automatic* describes processing that is uninten-tional, effortless, relatively fast, and occurring without awareness. In contrast the term *controlled* is used to describe processing that is intentional, effortful, relatively slow, and mediated by conscious awareness. Although this dichot-omy has proven useful, it is not the case that any given process must be exclusively automatic or controlled in nature. Rather, processes may best be characterized by the relative degrees to which they display certain qualities—such as intentionality, awareness, effort, and speed—that deline-ate automatic and controlled processing (Bargh, 1989).

Often, it is important to maintain a distinction between automatic and controlled processing when considering the cognitive biases associated with childhood anxiety. Both classes of cognitive operations certainly can be observed in children, and it is possible that each may be differentially impli-cated in the mediation of alternative patterns of processing selectivity. For example, an automatic bias favoring the processing of certain stimuli may precede a controlled bias that operates to attenuate the processing of such stimuli. It has been common for automatic and controlled aspects of infor-mation processing to have been distinguished within many studies that have investigated the cognitive correlates of anxiety within adult populations. For example, Mogg & Bradley (1998) review many studies that have manipulated the degrees to which experimental stimuli could be consciously apprehended, in order to investigate the automaticity of various anxiety-linked processing biases displayed by adults. However, few empirical studies of childhood anxiety have attempted to discriminate these two classes of mental operation. Instead, research on childhood anxiety more typically has assessed informa-tion processing using tasks that permit the influence of both controlled and automatic processes. In such research, for instance, the stimulus materials have been presented in a manner that has permitted conscious awareness of their identity, and sufficient time for an effortful cognitive response. Though this certainly would enable controlled processing to influence task perfor-mance, it would not prevent automatic processes from also exerting an effect (Bargh & Chartrand, 1999).

This chapter will provide an overview of those studies that have investi-gated patterns of selective information processing in anxious children. It will be seen that, although some of this research has examined interpretation, judgment and memory, the great bulk of the work has focused on attentional selectivity. Consequently, we will draw most heavily on these attentional studies when, towards the end of the chapter, we endeavor to construct a developmental account of the information-processing biases now known to be associated with childhood anxiety.

Biased Information Processing in Childhood Anxiety

Across the past few years, several experiments have provided consistent evidence to suggest that anxious children may display an interpretative bias that serves to impose disproportionately negative interpretations upon ambiguous stimuli or situations. For example, Hadwin, Frost, French, and Richards (1997) examined the relationship between self-reported levels of trait anxiety and the interpretation of ambiguous stimuli among children aged 7–9 years. Those authors used a pictorial homophone task in which each homophone had a threatening and a neutral meaning. Children first heard a homophone and were then shown pictures of two objects, each of which corresponded to one possible meaning of the word. For example, the homophone "hanging" was followed by pictures of a gallows and of clothes on a line. Children were asked to point to the picture that went with the word they had heard. Consistent with findings among anxious adults, trait anxiety scores were positively correlated with the number of threatening interpretations chosen.

Taghavi, Moradi, Neshat Doost, Yule, and Dalgleish (in press) used a homograph task to compare the interpretative processing of clinically anxious and normal children, aged 9–16 years. The homographs each had a threatening and a neutral meaning, and were presented on cards to the children, who were instructed to use each word to construct a sentence. As predicted, the clinically anxious children showed a significantly elevated tendency to produce sentences based upon the more threatening interpretations of these homographs, compared with control children.

Barrett, Rapee, Dadds, and Ryan (1996) examined the interpretation of ambiguous information by presenting children with ambiguous vignettes, and asking them to explain what was happening in each. Clinically anxious children's accounts revealed that they imposed threatening interpretations on these vignettes significantly more often than did controls. Using this same task, Chorpita, Albano, and Barlow (1996) also found that anxious children made significantly more threatening interpretations than nonanxious controls. Bell-Dolan (1995) employed a slight variant of this approach to compare the interpretations made by high- and low-anxious children in grades four and five. These children heard a series of vignettes that varied in their degree of ambiguity regarding the hostile or neutral intent of a peer towards another child. When asked to interpret these vignettes with regard to the peer's intent, high-anxious children were more likely than their low-anxious counterparts to interpret neutral situations as hostile.

In summary, therefore, a growing body of evidence now indicates that anxious children, like their adult counterparts, demonstrate a biased pattern of interpretative processing, favoring the more threatening interpretations of currently available ambiguous information. It also appears to be the case that anxious children may display biases in the ways they anticipate the future, cope with the present and remember the past.

Concerning anticipation of the future, Spence, Donovan, and Brechman-Toussaint (1999) found that children with social phobia, aged 7–14 years, significantly underestimate the future likelihood of positive social events, relative to control children. These researchers also observed a strong trend for the phobic children to overestimate the future likelihood of experiencing negative social events. These effects were not attributable to group differences in the perceived likelihood of *all* positive or negative events, being evident only for events that involved some level of social interaction.

With respect to coping styles, Barrett et al. (1996) found that clinically anxious children selected significantly more avoidant solutions to situations they perceived as threatening than did children with ODD or controls. Similarly, Chorpita et al. (1996) found that elevated trait anxiety was associated with increased likelihood of selecting avoidant coping responses. Consistent with this pattern, Bell-Dolan (1995) examined children's proposed reactions to threatening circumstances conveyed by vignettes and found that high-anxious children tended to propose more maladaptive coping strategies (e.g., appeal to authority) than adaptive coping strategies (e.g., approach-based solutions). The reverse was true of low-anxious children. Vasey, Daleiden, and Williams (1992) also used a vignette-based approach to compare the coping responses preferred by clinically anxious and control children, aged 9–14 years. Once again, the anxious children selected significantly more distraction and avoidance responses than did the controls, even though both groups of children displayed equivalent knowledge of alternative possible coping responses.

Surprisingly, little research has investigated the possibility that anxious children might display biased patterns of memory. In what appears to be the only published study that has addressed this issue, Daleiden (1998) found evidence of a memory bias, favoring negative information, among high-trait-anxious children in grades 6–8. Despite these encouraging results, it should be noted that the reliability of this effect was dependent upon the specific nature of the memory task. Consequently, it would be prudent to await the results of further research before drawing firm conclusions concerning the possible association between anxiety and selective memory in children.

In contrast, when one turns to the study of selective *attention* in anxious children, one encounters a far more extensive experimental literature. The remainder of this section will focus on providing a fairly detailed appraisal of this burgeoning attentional literature. The experimental emphasis that seems to have been placed upon the study of attentional processing in anxious children may stem from a realization that biased attentional processes potentially could have a very broad impact across all other aspects of information processing (Bugental, 1992). It also might reflect the fact that considerable evidence exists to suggest that attentional processes may be integrally involved in emotional regulation. For example, reactive and effortful attentional processes appear to play a central role in mediating the relationship between temperament, dysregulation of negative affect, and psychopathology (Derryberry & Reed, 1996; Lonigan & Phillips, this volume; Rothbart, Posner, & Hershey, 1995). As stated by Wilson and Gottman (1996), "Attentional processes provide a 'shuttle' between the cognitive and emotional realms, and ... the abilities involved in being able to attend and to shift attentional focus are fundamental to emotional regulatory processes" (p. 189). This view is supported by research on infants, children, and adults showing that individual differences in the selective encoding of stressful or negative emotional stimuli are related to variations in emotion regulation and dysregulation and, among children and adults, psychopathology (see Lonigan & Phillips, this volume).

A substantial body of empirical evidence suggests that high-trait-anxious and clinically anxious adults attend selectively to threatening stimuli when such stimuli compete with neutral stimuli for processing priority (for reviews, see Mathews & MacLeod, 1994; Mogg & Bradley, 1998; Williams et al., 1997). In addition to this bias towards threatening information characteristic of high-trait-anxious subjects, at least one adult cognitive theory (Williams et al., 1988, 1997) proposes that low-trait-anxious individuals should display an attentional bias *away* from threat-relevant information and that this bias should intensify as state anxiety is elevated. Several studies have revealed evidence of this attentional bias away from threat cues in low-trait-anxious adults (Fox, 1993; MacLeod, Mathews, & Tata, 1986). Some studies have shown also that the attentional avoidance of threat shown by low-trait-anxious individuals is increased when state anxiety is elevated (MacLeod & Mathews, 1988), although contrary results have been reported (e.g., Mogg, Mathews, Bird, & MacGregor-Morris, 1990).

As will become clear below, evidence now exists to suggest both the presence of an attentional bias towards threat cues among high-anxious children and an attentional bias away from threat cues among low-anxious children. However, several puzzling contradictions within this general pattern of findings have been reported that require explanation. It appears possible that some of these discrepancies may reflect important differences between the two experimental methodologies that have been used most commonly to assess attentional processing. Virtually all studies have employed, for this purpose, some variant of either the modified Stroop color-naming task, or of the probe detection task. Findings revealed by experiments that have adopted each type of task are reviewed separately below.

Studies Using Modified Stroop Tasks

By comparing a person's average latency to name the color in which threat-relevant and non-threatening words are written, modified Stroop color-naming tasks provide a measure of the cognitive interference caused by threatening words. Although alternative explanations exist (see Williams et al., 1997, pp. 107–108), longer color-naming latencies on threatening words relative to neutral words commonly are interpreted as evidence that these threat words have captured attention to a greater degree than the neutral words. Two variants of this modified Stroop task have been employed to assess attentional bias in children and adolescents. In the first variant, which here will be termed the "card format," many words of a given emotional valence are presented simultaneously, usually written on a single card, and the total time required to color-name the entire set of threat-relevant or neutral words is recorded, most often manually. In the second variant, which here will be termed the "single trial" format, each word appears individually on a computer screen and the latencies to color-name individual stimuli are recorded to millisecond accuracy by the computer, using a voice key.

The earliest study to have used a modified Stroop task with children (Martin, Horder, & Jones, 1992) employed a card-format variant to assess attentional bias in 6–7 year olds, 9–10 year olds, and 12–13 year olds, who were either high or low in self-reported fear of spiders. These researchers found that, across all children, color-naming latencies were generally longer on the spider-relevant words than on the spider-irrelevant words. However, this effect was modified by subject group. The spider-fearful children showed a more pronounced slowing to color-name spider-relevant words relative to the spider-irrelevant words. Indeed, for children not fearful of spiders, color-naming times did not differ significantly between these two classes of stimulus words.

Although the older children displayed significantly shorter color-naming latencies than did the younger children, age did not modify the observed group difference in interference effects across word types. Because the interference produced by the spider-relevant words in the spider-fearful children did not increase with age, despite the likelihood that older children would have endured their fears for longer, Martin and associates argued that the observed processing bias is likely to represent an integral feature of anxiety status, rather than a gradually acquired consequence of a longstanding fear.

In a more recent study that also used a card-format variant of the modified Stroop task, Martin and Jones (1995) more directly assessed whether either the duration of spider fear, or its manner of acquisition, influenced observed patterns of interference effects. This study employed pictorial stimuli, and tested boys and girls aged 4–5, 6–7, and 8–9 years. Again, there was a general tendency for all children to be slower to color-name spider stimuli than neutral stimuli, regardless of their level of spider fear. However, once more, high-fearful children were slowed to a greater extent when color-naming such stimuli than were low-fearful children. The pattern of observed effects did not differ between the sexes, and the magnitude of interference due to spider stimuli did not vary significantly across the age range studied. Furthermore this effect was not modified by either the length of time since fear onset, or the mode of fear acquisition. Thus, these authors again concluded that increased interference on fear-relevant stimuli does not develop as a subsequent response to fear, but instead represents an integral characteristic of fear.

Somewhat different findings have been reported by Kindt, Brosschot, and Everaerd (1997) who, instead of a card format, employed a single-trial variant of the modified Stroop task in two studies that compared 8–9 year old children, who were either high or low on both trait anxiety and injection fear. In both studies, four categories of words were used, resulting from the crossing of two factors representing concern-relatedness (i.e., related vs. unrelated to the injection context) and valence (i.e., threatening vs. neutral). This produced four word conditions: concern-related/threat (e.g., injection), concern-related/non-threat (e.g., salve), concern-unrelated/threat (e.g., suffocate), and concern-unrelated/non-threat (e.g., baker). (Although English translations are provided here, Dutch words were used in all the studies by Kindt and colleagues.)

In the first of these studies, children were tested in a hospital setting immediately prior to receiving an injection. Contrary to expectations, no differences were found between the high- and low-anxiety/injection fear groups, with stimulus valence having no effect on color-naming latencies for either group of children. However, all children displayed greater interference on concern-related words than on concern-unrelated words, regardless of whether these words were threatening or neutral in nature. Kindt and coworkers note that this apparent attentional orientation towards concern-related words, shown by all of these children awaiting this stressful event, has been observed also in at least one adult study. Specifically, Mogg et al. (1990) found that both high-trait-anxious adults and low-trait-anxious adults showed an attentional bias towards stress-relevant stimuli when exposed to an acute stressor. Like Mogg and colleagues, Kindt, Brosschot and Everaerd (1997) suggested that it may have been the presence of the acute stressor, in the form of the imminent injection, that led all the children to display an attentional bias towards the injection-relevant stimuli. Furthermore, these researchers suggested that the presence of this stressor may have served to obscure the predicted attentional difference between the high- and low-anxious children, which they had expected to be revealed by a disproportionately large interference effect on threatening words within the high-anxious group. Consistent with this possibility, several adult studies have shown that anxious subjects may display suppression of color-naming interference on threatening words when exposed to stressful situations (e.g., MacLeod & Rutherford, 1992; Mathews & Sebastian, 1993). Thus, Kindt and colleagues speculated that the stress of the impending injection may not only have enhanced the processing of all concern-relevant information among both groups of children, but also may have suppressed the normally heightened tendency of highly-anxious children to process the more threatening information selectively.

To test this hypothesis, Kindt's group conducted a second study which was identical to the first except that the children were tested in a nonstressful school context, rather than while awaiting injection at a hospital. Despite the removal of the stressor, however, all children again displayed elevated color-naming interference on the injection-related words. On this occasion, a significant main effect of valence was obtained also, with all children showing greater color-naming interference on threatening than on neutral words. However, this effect was not modified by anxiety status, indicating that both the high- and low-anxious children displayed this threat interference effect to an equivalent degree.

Based on these results, Kindt and colleagues dismiss the possibility that the increased color-naming interference shown by all children on the injection-related words in their initial study could have represented a response to the stress of the imminent injection. They do note that the presence of increased interference on threatening relative to neutral words in study two, but not study one, is consistent with the possibility that the processing of threat stimuli may have been generally suppressed by the presence of this stressor. However, Kindt and colleagues concluded that their data provide no evidence that elevated anxiety in children 8–9 years of age is associated with any increase in the selective processing of threatening stimuli. They consider that this "throws some doubt on the suggestion that such biases form a causal link between trait anxiety and the development of anxiety disorders" (p. 94). Instead, they argue, all children may process threatening stimuli selectively, but this tendency may be suppressed by the presence of acute stress.

The apparent contradiction between the findings obtained by Martin and colleagues (Martin et al., 1992; Martin & Jones, 1995) and those reported by Kindt's group requires explanation. Two possible accounts of this discrepancy invite particular empirical scrutiny. First, it is possible that the divergent patterns of effects may reflect differences between spider-fear and injection-fear. Second, it is possible that the discrepancy between the findings may result from the fact that Martin and colleagues employed a card-format variant of the modified Stroop task, while Kindt's group adopted a single-trial format. This latter account is lent plausibility by the findings of McNally, Amir, and Lipke (1996) who, in a study of adult patients with posttraumatic stress disorder (PTSD), observed greater evidence of an anxiety-linked attentional bias using a card-format variant, compared with a single-trial variant.

Each of these possibilities was addressed by Kindt, Bierman, and Brosschot (1997). Both formats of the modified Stroop task were employed to assess the patterns of cognitive interference shown by children reporting high or low levels of spider-fear. Regardless of the format of the task, both groups demonstrated greater interference on spider words than on control words. However, only on the single-trial variant of the task was it found that this effect was modified by subject group, though to a differing degree depending on age. Based on their visual examination of the mean interference scores for each group across age, Kindt and colleagues concluded that interference on spider words increased with age in the spider-fearful group, whereas it decreased with age in the low-fearful group. Because they did not report follow-up tests of this interaction, it remains unclear whether either or both of these effects, observed in this single-trial variant of the modified Stroop task, were statistically reliable. What does seem certain, however, is that on their card variant of this task, Kindt's group failed to replicate the earlier findings of an anxiety-linked attentional bias towards threatening stimuli in the youngest children that had been observed by Martin and her colleagues within their card-format version of the modified Stroop.

It is difficult to avoid the conclusion that, despite occasionally supportive findings, the modified Stroop task has proven to be a fairly unreliable method of demonstrating attentional bias to feared stimuli in children suffering from specific fears. The sensitivity of the experimental paradigm to this putative effect seems to be dependent on as yet poorly understood methodological parameters. This has been well illustrated in a study by Kindt and Brosschot (1999), who compared spider-fearful and control girls aged 8–12 years, using word and pictorial versions of a single-trial Stroop task. When word stimuli were used, on half the trials these words were presented using colored letters (i.e., integrated format), while on the remaining trials the letters were mono-chrome but were superimposed on a colored circle (i.e., nonintegrated format). Spider-fearful children, but not control children, displayed dispro-portionately long color-naming latencies on spider words, but only when trials were presented in the nonintegrated format. No differences were found between groups on trials presented in the integrated format. On these trials, as in previous studies, both groups showed greater interference on spider-related relative to neutral words. When pictorial stimuli were employed, even though these always appeared in the nonintegrated format, no group differences were observed. Clearly, children with specific fears dis-play increased color-naming latencies on the feared stimuli only under very particular experimental conditions.

Inconsistent findings have not been restricted to studies that have con-trasted children differing in levels of specific fears. For example, two studies have employed modified Stroop tasks to compare the patterns of selective attention shown by behaviorally inhibited and uninhibited children. These studies are relevant to the present discussion given the established relation between behavioral inhibition and childhood anxiety disorders (see Lonigan & Phillips, this volume). In the first of these experiments, Schwartz, Snidman, and Kagan (1996) used a single-trial Stroop task to compare adolescents (with a mean age of 13 years) who had been classified as either inhibited or uninhibited at either 21 or 31 months of age. The Stroop task included threatening, neutral, and positive words. Contrary to expectations, inhibited children displayed no disproportionate slowing to color-name the threat words. Instead, all children were slower to color-name both the threatening and the positive words than the neutral words. Nevertheless, an additional analysis of extremely long latencies revealed that adolescents who had been inhibited as toddlers did display significantly more of these long latencies on threatening words than did adolescents who had been uninhibited toddlers.

A related study by Kagan, Snidman, Zentner, and Peterson (1999) compared 7-year-olds who had been classified as high- or low-reactive in infancy. These researchers also divided this sample based on children's level of anxiety symptoms at 7 years of age to permit a contrast between high- and low-anxious children. Owing to the limited reading ability of these children, a pictorial version of the modified Stroop task was adopted. Using a single-trial format, this task presented neutral, threatening, aggressive, and positive pictures in various colors. No differential patterns of color-naming latencies were found, either between inhibited and uninhibited children or between high- and low-anxious children. Instead, as observed in a number of previous studies, all children were significantly slower to color-name the threatening stimuli than to color-name the other classes of stimuli.

More encouraging findings have been obtained from recent studies that have employed the modified Stroop task to assess selective attention in children suffering from PTSD, or who have a parent suffering from this anxiety disorder. Moradi, Taghavi, Neshat Doost, Yule, and Dalgleish (1999) compared the color-naming latencies shown by children aged 9–17 years, with and without PTSD, on a range of emotional stimulus words. Children with PTSD were significantly slower to color-name trauma-related words than neutral words, suggesting attentional orientation towards such stimuli, whereas the color-naming latencies shown by the control children did not differ as a function of word type.

Using this same task, Moradi, Neshat Doost, Taghavi, Yule, & Dalgleish (1999) compared children who had a parent suffering from PTSD and children whose parents had no history of anxiety disorder. As in the Moradi, Taghavi et al. (1999) study, these children ranged in age from 9 to 17 years. Offspring of PTSD patients showed significantly elevated color-naming latencies on threat-relevant words compared with neutral words. In contrast, offspring of normal controls did not show heightened interference on these threat-relevant words.

Moradi, Neshat Doost et al. (1999) discuss two possible reasons why the children of PTSD patients may show an attentional bias towards generally threatening words, despite the fact that they themselves have not been traumatized. First, it could be that such children have higher levels of anxiety symptoms than children of controls. However, not only was it the case that none of the children of PTSD patients had any diagnosable mental disorder, but also they did not differ from children of controls with regard to self-report symptom measures of anxiety; so this account would appear implausible. The second possibility considered by Moradi, Neshat Doost et al. is that children of PTSD patients, although not more anxious than children of controls, may have developed greater expertise in the processing of threat-related information owing to their having lived with a traumatized parent suffering from PTSD. Certainly, there is evidence to suggest that expertise with a particular domain of processing can produce Stroop interference on stimuli falling within this domain. For example, Dalgleish (1995) showed that ornithologists displayed heightened color-naming interference on bird-related words. Perhaps the most interesting account of Moradi, Neshat Doost et al.'s findings, however, is that the children of PTSD parents may share with these parents an inherited or learned disposition to process threatening information selectively. Such a disposition may increase the risk of developing PTSD following exposure to a traumatic event.

While studies that have employed the modified Stroop task to assess processing selectivity in anxious children have yielded some encouraging findings, firm conclusions are rendered difficult by the often contradictory nature of the results obtained. Whereas at least four studies have found the predicted exaggeration of color-naming latencies on threatening stimuli among highly anxious children, a similar number have failed to reveal such an effect. Often, such studies have found a general tendency for threat-related or concern-related words to produce heightened color-naming latencies in all children, regardless of their level of anxiety or fear. The possible theoretical implications of this pattern of conflicting findings will be considered, in some detail, following a review of those studies that have used probe detection tasks to assess attentional bias in anxious children.

Studies Using Probe Detection Tasks

In contrast to modified Stroop tasks, variants of the probe detection task developed by MacLeod et al. (1986) to assess attentional responses to emotional stimuli consistently have produced evidence of an attentional bias towards threat stimuli among anxious children. In this type of task, on each trial, two words are presented briefly on a computer screen, one above the other. On critical trials, one word is threat-relevant whereas the other is emotionally neutral and, subsequent to the disappearance of the words, a small dot probe appears in the position previously occupied by either word. The latency to detect this probe provides a measure of the extent to which a child's attention was directed towards the word that had just appeared within the probed screen location. Thus, faster latencies to detect probes in a given screen location, when a threat word rather than a neutral word had just appeared within this location, would indicate an attentional bias towards this threat word. The opposite pattern would indicate a tendency to direct attention away from the threat stimuli.

In the first study to use this probe detection methodology with children, Vasey, Daleiden, Williams, & Brown (1995) compared clinically anxious and control children, aged 9–14 years. Consistent with expectations, clinically anxious children displayed evidence of an attentional bias towards threatening words. Detection latencies for probes in the lower screen location were significantly faster, for these anxious children, when threatening words rather than neutral words had just been presented to this same screen location. Among the younger anxious children, this effect fell short of significance for probes presented to the upper screen location, but older anxious children were more likely to display the effect for upper probes also. Control children showed no evidence of any attentional bias either towards or away from threatening words, detecting probes with equal speed regardless of their spatial proximity to either class of emotional words.

Recent research using this dot probe paradigm to assess nonclinical children suggests that individual differences in this attentional response to emotional stimuli are associated with variations in trait anxiety. This issue was investigated, for example, by Bijttebier (1998), who employed a dot probe task to compare high- and low-trait-anxious children in grades 3–8 (mean age = 10.8 years). Bijttebier found that high-trait-anxious children alone showed the pattern of speeding to detect probes in the vicinity of threat words that indicates an attentional bias towards these threatening stimuli. Low-trait-anxious children actually displayed a slowing to detect probes in the vicinity of the threat words, suggesting that these children are characterized by an attentional bias away from such stimuli.

Schippell, Vasey, Cravens-Brown, and Bretveld (2000) report further evidence to suggest the importance of trait anxiety in moderating the patterns of attentional bias observed on this dot probe task. These researchers employed a regression approach to examine the emotional correlates of performance on the dot probe task among nonclinical children aged 12–14 years. They found that trait anxiety was positively correlated with speeding to detect probes in the vicinity of threatening words, indicating that the attentional bias towards threat words was more pronounced in high-trait-anxious subjects.

In contrast to this positive association between trait anxiety and attentional bias towards threat, there is little evidence to suggest that elevated levels of state anxiety serve to increase selective attention to threat in children. Indeed, a negative association between state anxiety and attention to threat among children has been reported in at least two studies. For example, in a dot probe study that compared high- and low-test-anxious children, aged 12–14 years, Vasey, El-Hag, and Daleiden (1996) observed that high-test-anxious children showed the predicted attentional bias towards threatening words. Low-test-anxious children showed no such attentional bias and, at least for boys, there was evidence that attention was directed away from the threatening stimuli. Importantly, it was found that elevated state anxiety did not serve to increase attentional bias towards threat. Instead, surprisingly, a marginal tendency was found for state anxiety to be negatively related to this attentional bias across all subjects.

Although the negative relation between state anxiety and threat bias reported by Vasey et al. (1996) was unexpected, a similar finding reported by Vasey and Schippell (1999) suggests that it is replicable. Using a regression approach to study a sample of adolescents 14–18 years of age, Vasey and Schippell confirmed that trait anxiety was, as expected, positively correlated with the pattern of probe detection latencies indicating an attentional bias towards threat. Again, however, these researchers found state anxiety to be negatively correlated with this effect. Thus, once more, elevated state anxiety was observed to be associated with reduced attention to threatening information.

Finally, it is interesting to consider the possible role that may be played by depression in mediating the patterns of attentional bias displayed by anxious children. In Vasey and Schippell's (2000) study, the association between trait anxiety and speeding to detect probes in the vicinity of threat stimuli became nonsignificant when depression scores were entered into the regression model. Further analyses suggested that depression scores may have been related primarily to an attentional bias towards social threat words whereas anxiety scores were primarily related to bias for physical threat words. It is noteworthy that this same pattern was reported among adults by Mathews, Ridgeway, and Williamson (1996).

A study by Taghavi, Neshat Doost, Moradi, Yule, and Dalgleish (1999), using the probe detection task to study children and adolescents aged 8–18 years, found less evidence to indicate any association between depression and attentional bias to threatening stimuli. These children suffered from either clinical anxiety or mixed anxiety–depression. Findings for the clinically anxious group replicated those of Vasey et al. (1995), revealing an attentional bias towards threat among these children. However, children in the anxiety–depression group displayed no evidence of any such bias towards negative stimuli. These researchers concluded that this result is consistent with find-ings among adults, which suggest that depression is not associated with an attentional bias towards negative information. It is somewhat curious, though, that the anxiety–depression group did not show such an attentional bias, given not only that they were subclinically depressed, but also that they displayed fairly high levels of anxiety. Given that children high in trait anxiety consistently appear to display such a bias, the failure to find this bias in the anxiety–depression sample is surprising. One possibility, that Taghavi and colleagues acknowledge, is that individuals in the anxiety–depression group may not have had sufficiently serious levels of either depres-sion or anxiety to show such a bias. Another intriguing possibility worthy of future research is that, under some conditions, depression may be associated with suppression of the attentional bias towards threat cues that is normally related to high levels of trait anxiety.

To summarize, in contrast to the inconsistent results yielded by studies that have attempted to find evidence of an anxiety-linked attentional bias in children using modified Stroop tasks, research programs operating within three independent laboratories have consistently confirmed the presence of such an effect using dot probe tasks. Anxious children have shown evidence of the same attentional bias towards threat cues as is displayed by their adult counterparts on this task (Vasey et al., 1995). Also, as in adults, it appears that low levels of anxiety in childhood can be associated with an attentional bias away from threat cues (Bijttebier, 1998; Schippell et al., 2000; Vasey et al., 1996). This pattern of attentional bias appears to be a direct function of trait anxiety. There is less evidence that any general tendency to orient attention towards threatening stimuli is associated with elevated depression in children (Taghavi et al., 1999). Nor is there evidence that this attentional bias is increased by elevated levels of state anxiety among this population. Indeed, the results of some studies suggest that elevated state anxiety in children actually may serve to inhibit the selective allocation of attention towards threatening material (Vasey et al., 1996; Vasey & Schippell, 2000).

Resolving Conflicting Results

The above review indicates that differential support for the presence of an attentional bias among anxious children has been obtained from experiments that have employed variants of the probe detection task and from those that have used variants of the modified Stroop task. Despite the consistently supportive findings yielded by probe detection studies, results have been far more variable across modified Stroop studies. There is a need, therefore, to examine the similarities and differences between these studies, in order to account for their discrepant findings. The two most obvious classes of explanation that might serve to resolve these observed inconsistencies implicate, respectively, differences in task details and differences in the samples studied. Each of these possibilities will be considered in turn.

Task Characteristics

Given that probe detection task studies have obtained evidence of an attentional bias towards threat in anxious children more consistently than have modified Stroop studies, it might simply be argued that the probe detection measure could provide the more sensitive index of attentional bias. Indeed, Stroop interference may not be due to selective attention at all. For example, it could be the case that anxious and nonanxious individuals each pay equivalent attention to the content of the threatening and neutral words in the modified Stroop task, but that the threatening words slow color-naming more in anxious subjects because they produce a more intense emotional reaction in these individuals. It should be noted that, when reviewing this possibility, Williams et al. (1997, pp. 107–108) conclude that, at least in some cases, Stroop interference probably can be attributed to attentional effects. However, no studies have directly compared the sensitivity of the modified Stroop approach and the probe detection approach to the assessment of attentional bias, either in children or adults, and this may be a profitable focus for future research. Even if it proves to be the case that that the modified Stroop task does represent a sensitive measure of attentional bias, it seems likely that variants of the experimental approach may differ in their sensitivity to this effect. Thus, perhaps the reason why some Stroop studies have found evidence of an attentional bias in anxious children, while others have not, can be attributed to variations in procedural detail.

Some support for the hypothesis that anxious children should show increased color-naming latencies on threatening words has been provided by studies that have used card-format variants of the modified Stroop task (Martin et al., 1992; Martin & Jones, 1995). Kindt, Bierman et al. (1997) proposed that it may be easier to obtain evidence of attentional bias using the card format than the single-trial format version of this task. The notion that these two variants of the modified Stroop task may not be equivalent in their capacity to measure the same attentional effects is supported by Kindt et al.'s observation that the patterns of color-naming interference displayed by the same subjects across these two task formats are uncorrelated.

Kindt, Bierman et al. suggest that greater levels of color-naming interference may result from the more distracting contextual stimuli present only in the card format of the Stroop task. In this presentation format, color-naming interference may reflect not only the processing of the target-word meaning, but may result also from the processing of the other words that flank this target word. No such distracting stimuli are present in the single-trial format of this task. Kindt and colleagues argue that younger children are likely to be more distracted by these contextual stimuli than are older children. They cite evidence provided by Lane and Pearson (1982), who have reported the presence of a curvilinear relation between age and distraction due to irrelevant stimuli, with increases seen from 7 to 11 years of age and decreases from 11 to 20 years of age.

Kindt, Bierman et al. (1997) also consider a rather different possible reason why card-format variants may reveal effects more readily than single-trial variants. Specifically, they draw attention to the fact that, while color-naming latencies are timed objectively by computer in single-trial tasks, often to millisecond accuracy, these latencies typically are timed manually by an experimenter using a stopwatch in card-format tasks. Thus, there is more room for error, or systematic experimenter bias, in studies that use the card format. Kindt and colleagues note that, in many card-format studies, such as those conducted by Martin and her colleagues, the experimenters have been aware of each subject's anxiety status when manually recording their color-naming latencies. This may cast some doubt upon the veracity of the findings. Indeed, Kindt's group failed to find any evidence of an anxiety-linked elevation of threat interference in a card-format version of the modified Stroop task when they kept experimenters "blind" to subjects' group status. Certainly, the observations of Kindt and her colleagues do suggest that it may be appropriate to place more weight on findings obtained using single-trial versions of the modified Stroop task. However, subsequent research has shown that, under certain circumstances, single-trial variants of this task also can reveal evidence of increased threat interference in anxious children (Kindt & Brosschot, 1999; Moradi, Neshat Doost et al., 1999; Moradi, Taghavi et al., 1999). Therefore, it seems unlikely that the difference between these task variations alone can account for the observed pattern of inconsistencies in the results obtained across the studies reviewed.

Sample Characteristics

There are two primary dimensions of variation in terms of subjects' characteristics across these studies that can provide possible explanations for the discrepant findings. First, it may be that an attentional bias towards threat is displayed more consistently by clinically anxious children than by children who are merely high in trait anxiety or fear of specific stimuli (e.g., spiders). Such a pattern would be consistent with findings among adults. However, as only three of the ten experiments to have reported evidence of such an attentional bias in anxious children have examined clinically disordered samples, it is clear that this account cannot accommodate the observed pattern of discrepant findings.

A more promising possibility is that such inconsistencies might represent some systematic function of children's age. Studies that have failed to find evidence of an anxiety-linked attentional bias typically have assessed younger children, ranging in age from 7 to 12 years. In contrast, most supportive findings come from studies that have assessed older children, ranging in age from 9 to 17 years.

The major exceptions to this pattern of findings are the studies of Martin and colleagues, who reported exaggerated threat interference in anxious children as young as 4–5 years of age. However, as already has been discussed, these studies employed a card-format variant of the Stroop and used manual timing, making them susceptible to potential experimenter bias. When only those studies that have used computer-controlled timing are considered, then there appears to be a clear age-related pattern. Younger children do not show any anxiety-linked elevation in their color-naming latencies for threatening words, whereas older children consistently do so. Within studies that have employed a broader age range, it has been the case that older children have shown more evidence of this anxiety-linked attentional bias than has been demonstrated by younger children. For example, Kindt, Bierman et al. (1997) reported that this effect was not evident among their youngest 8-year-old children, but that it became more evident as age increased.

Thus, in summary, there is reason to believe that younger anxious children may be less likely to display increased attentional orientation towards threat than is the case for older anxious children. As will be discussed below, it appears to be a more common finding among younger anxious children that, regardless of anxiety level, attention is allocated towards threatening information by everyone.

Is There a General Attentional Bias Toward Threat-related or Concern-relevant Information in Children?

Across the range of experiments reviewed within this chapter, a general tendency has been reported for children to display longer color-naming latencies on threatening or concern-relevant words, relative to neutral words. The finding that all children, regardless of their anxiety levels, display exaggerated interference effects on threat-related words has been observed in at least seven Stroop studies to date. This effect has been obtained in studies that have used the card format and the single-trial format versions of the task. Furthermore, it has been reported in studies assessing children of widely differing ages, between 4 and 13 years. This pattern of results suggests that all children may show a general attentional bias towards threatening information.

Despite the reliability of this effect, possible explanations for it have yet to be fully evaluated. However, given that no parallel finding has emerged with similar consistency from the adult literature, it is tempting to entertain a developmental account of the phenomenon. Kindt, Bierman et al. (1997) have offered such a developmental explanation. These researchers argue that the effect reflects limitations in younger children's ability to inhibit the processing of threatening stimuli, whereas older children have greater capacity to suppress the processing of threatening material. Kindt and colleagues suggest that their account is similar to nonassociative theory, which postulates that some phobias may reflect a failure to unlearn or master childhood fears (see Menzies & Harris, this volume). However, whereas non-associative theory assumes that children who develop phobias were fearful of the phobic stimulus in early childhood and never learned to master that fear, the model offered by Kindt and colleagues does not pertain only to children who are fearful and who fail to master their fear. Rather, they propose that all children show deficiencies in their ability to inhibit the processing of threat-related information.

Across experiments, the degree to which stimuli have been threatening for subjects commonly has been confounded with the degree to which these stimuli have been concern-relevant for these individuals. It is of interest to note that, in the two studies (by Kindt's group) to have empirically discriminated the threat-relatedness and concern-relatedness of stimulus materials, the general attentional bias displayed by all children was found to favor concern-relevant material, rather than threat-related material. Perhaps it is simply because concern-related content is primed within the cognitive system that such materials are associated with greater levels of color-naming interference across all children.

It remains for future research to determine whether, and under what conditions, it is threat-relatedness or concern-relatedness that recruits selective attention across all children. For the present, however, we will conclude this chapter by considering how the overall pattern of reviewed findings might be accommodated within a developmental framework.

A Developmental Perspective

The weight of accumulated evidence indicates that, under particular circumstances, anxious children display a similar attentional bias towards threat as is shown by their anxious adult counterparts. To the extent that this attentional bias is evident at the earliest ages when elevated anxiety can be detected, so it becomes more probable that this cognitive style could predate, and potentially predispose to, the anxiety elevation. As has been indicated earlier in this chapter, however, evidence to suggest that the attentional bias accompanies elevated anxiety in very young children has been somewhat mixed. An anxiety-linked attentional bias has not commonly been observed in children below the age of 8 years. Single-trial variants of the modified Stroop task consistently have failed to reveal such an effect in these younger children. Only in the two studies reported by Martin and colleagues, which employed the card-format Stroop task, has it been observed that anxious children as young as 4–5 years display inflated color-naming latencies on threatening stimuli.

If one accepts the validity of Martin's group's finding, then this would permit the possibility that an attentional bias to threat may contribute to the early development of anxiety disorders in young children. Indeed, Martin and her colleagues themselves conclude, on the basis of their own experimental results, that this attentional bias is an integral component of anxious or fearful emotion rather than a subsequently acquired cognitive consequence of this emotional condition. In contrast, if one accepts the results of those other researchers, such as Kindt and her colleagues, who have failed to obtain evidence of an anxiety-linked attentional bias in younger children, then this would cast doubt on the hypothesis that such a bias could play a functional role in mediating the development of elevated anxiety. On the basis of her findings, Kindt argues against the possibility that such an attentional bias could serve as a risk factor for the development of anxiety disorders, at least in children younger than about 10 years.

Given that theories concerning the role played by attentional bias in the development of anxiety disorders depend so critically upon the age at which the association between attentional bias and elevated trait anxiety becomes evident, it would seem to be of particular importance that future research should endeavor to resolve this issue. As has been noted, it is possible that single-trial versions of the Stroop task may have failed to find an attentional difference between young "high-anxious" and "low-anxious" children because this type of task places particularly heavy demands upon children's limited capacity for inhibitory control of attention. Kindt and Brosschot (1999) have suggested that it may be more difficult for children to ignore distracting information when the distractor and target information are integrated into a single stimulus, as they are in most Stroop tasks, than when distractor and target information are represented by discrete stimuli, as is the case in probe detection tasks. This account leads to the prediction that probe detection tasks should reveal evidence of an anxiety-linked attentional bias even in very young children. The confirmation of such a prediction must await the outcome of further research. However, Kindt and Brosschot do provide some empirical support for their position, by comparing performance across integrated and nonintegrated versions of the Stroop task. Consistent with their proposal, spider-fearful children showed more evidence of an attentional bias towards threat than did non-fearful children only on the nonintegrated version of the task. On integrated trials, both groups showed a general attentional bias towards threat cues. Thus, it does appear possible that an anxiety-linked attentional bias may be reliably observed in young children under conditions that do not overtax these children's limited capacity to inhibit attention to distracting stimuli.

It should be recognized that Martin et al.'s success in detecting increased color-naming interference on threatening words in anxious 4-year-olds, using the card version of the modified Stroop, itself might be explained by Kindt and Brosschot's proposal. Within this card format of the task, although the distractor and target information will be integrated within each stimulus word, the subject must color-name the target word while attempting to ignore the nonintegrated information provided by the distracting stimuli that flank this target. Therefore, the card-format variant of the Stroop might be considered to represent a less integrated version of this task than does the single-trial variant. This may be what renders this format of the task unusually sensitive to anxiety-linked attentional bias in younger children. Future research could usefully address, in a more systematic fashion, the hypothesis that tasks within which the distracting emotional information is somewhat distal from the target stimulus, or within which separate stimuli compete for processing priority, may consistently reveal an anxiety-linked bias towards threatening information even in very young children.

Another important topic for future research concerns the possible emotional impact of children's ability to effortfully modify their attentional responses to threatening information. Lonigan and Phillips (this volume), have suggested that measures of trait anxiety confound the two temperamental dimensions of negative affectivity/neuroticism (NA/N) and effortful control (EC). They argue that the relation between high levels of NA/N and anxiety disorders may be mediated by an attentional bias towards threat-related cues and, further, that the elevated risk for anxiety disorders associated with high levels of NA/N may be moderated by high levels of EC, which permit the inhibition of this attentional bias.

Lonigan and Vasey (1999) have articulated this theory further. Specifically, they hypothesize that NA/N should be associated with a pre-conscious automatically mediated attentional bias towards threat cues. However, they also propose that the extent to which this bias is observed on those tasks that permit conscious awareness of the stimuli and provide sufficient time for effortful processing will be dependent on a child's level of EC. According to this position, only children who are high in NA/N but low in EC should continue to display an attentional bias towards threat under such experimental conditions.

While the idea that it could be important to distinguish automatically mediated from strategically mediated patterns of selective attention has received little scrutiny within the child anxiety literature, evidence consistent with this view has been provided by research on anxiety in adults. For example, in keeping with Lonigan and Vasey's hypothesis, Derryberry (1998) found that high-trait-anxious adults displayed an attentional bias toward signals of punishment at a presentation interval too brief to permit the effortful control of attention (i.e., 250 ms). However, when the presentation interval was extended to enable the effortful control of attention (i.e., 500 ms) this attentional orientation towards these negative stimulus cues remained present only among those high-trait-anxious individuals who were low in attentional control (i.e., low in EC). Under this latter presentation condition, high-trait-anxious participants who were high in attentional control now shifted attention away from the negative stimuli, to the same degree as did the low-trait-anxious subjects.

It will be recalled that, in two of the child anxiety studies reviewed earlier in this chapter, it was observed that elevated state anxiety served to reduce attentional bias towards threatening information (Vasey et al., 1996; Vasey & Schippell, 2000). A possible explanation for this finding could be that high-EC individuals are most likely to effortfully inhibit the processing of threat cues under conditions of heightened state anxiety. A direct test of this proposal could be provided by future studies that measure EC and manipulate state anxiety, in order to determine the validity of the prediction that state anxiety increases will decrease attention to threat only among subjects with high levels of EC.

Distinguishing automatic from effortful patterns of attention, as suggested by Lonigan and Vasey (1999), also may serve to resolve conflicting findings within the adult literature. For example, although some studies have found that heightened state anxiety or stress is related to increased attentional bias towards threat cues, especially in high-trait-anxious individuals (MacLeod & Mathews, 1988; Mogg, Kentish, & Bradley, 1993; Mogg, Bradley, & Hallowell, 1994; Mogg, Bradley, De Bono, & Painter, 1997), others have found that elevated state anxiety or stress is associated with shifts of attention away from negative stimuli, regardless of trait anxiety level (Mathews & Sebastian, 1993; Mogg et al., 1993). It seems likely that these conflicting patterns of findings may reflect differences in the manner of stimulus presentation across these studies. Some presentation conditions permit effortful control of attention, while under other presentation conditions the opportunity to effortfully control attention is minimized. It is principally when the former class of methodologies have been employed that state anxiety elevations have elicited the general attentional avoidance of threat, suggesting that subjects can, and do, effortfully direct attention away from threat when they feel state anxious. In contrast, it is when studies have used methodologies that minimize the potential for effortful attentional control that state anxiety elevations have been found to increase attention to threat, particularly among high-trait-anxious individuals. MacLeod and Rutherford (1992) manipulated exposure conditions within a single study, in a manner designed to either permit or preclude the effortful control of attention. They observed that their high-trait-anxious subjects responded to elevated state anxiety with decreased attentional orientation towards threat when effortful control of attention was permitted, but with increased attentional orientation towards threat when it was precluded.

In the light of this observation, that effortful biases in selective attention can operate to oppose automatically mediated attentional responses to threatening information, it becomes of interest to explore the possibility of individual differences in the development of each category of attentional bias across childhood. Mathews and MacLeod (1994) have noted that clinical anxiety patients, unlike nonclinical subjects who report high levels of trait anxiety, commonly fail to display effortful attentional avoidance of threatening information, even under experimental circumstances that should readily enable this. In view of this, these researchers suggest that the absence of such controlled attentional avoidance of threat may represent a hallmark of clinical status. If this is true, then it may transpire that individual differences in the degree to which children succeed in developing the ability to effortfully direct attention away from threatening information may prove to be the most important determinant of their future clinical status. Consistent with this possibility, Lonigan and Vasey (1999) have argued that the inability to acquire such a strategically mediated pattern of attentional avoidance may reflect a pre-existing deficit in attentional control, and may heighten risk for the future development of anxiety pathology.

Summary and Conclusions

Available space has permitted no more than a brief introduction to this exciting new domain of clinical investigation. Following upon recent advances in our understanding of the cognitive idiosyncrasies displayed by anxious adults, the studies reviewed within this chapter have commenced the important task of charting the developmental origins of those processing biases most firmly associated with adult clinical anxiety disorders. Although still in its infancy, this work already has generated a number of extremely interesting findings, and has identified a variety of intriguing questions for future researchers.

It now stands beyond doubt that anxious children do display many of the information-processing biases that characterize anxious adults. Anxious children disproportionately favor the more threatening interpretations of ambiguity. They show a selective preference for maladaptive coping responses. They overestimate the likelihood of experiencing threatening events in the future, and may perhaps demonstrate enhanced memory for threatening information. Also, it is clear that anxious children display an attentional bias towards threatening stimulus materials. Now that the presence of such processing biases among anxious children has been firmly established, our research efforts can begin to address the two major questions that remain to be answered: At what stage of development does this association between anxiety and selective information processing become established? And what role, if any, does the development of such cognitive biases play in determining a child's future risk of anxiety pathology?

It does appear that the association between anxiety and processing selectivity becomes more difficult to detect as the age of the population reduces, though evidence of this association has been reported in children as young as 4 years. One of the challenges now facing investigators is to determine whether anxiety-linked processing biases are less easy to detect among very young children because such cognitive biases have not yet developed, or because available experimental techniques fail to overcome the methodological difficulties associated with the assessment of selective cognition in this population. The particular ways in which childhood variations in selective information processing ultimately may be incorporated into developmental models of psychopathology will depend, in part, upon the outcome of research that overcomes these methodological limitations. However, it seems likely that, in the fullness of time, such theoretical accounts will receive their most stringent empirical appraisal within longitudinal research programs, designed to investigate directly the earliest childhood predictors of subsequent individual differences in anxiety vulnerability. We feel confident that such research programs will be much enriched by the body of knowledge concerning emotional processing biases in children that is certain to grow from the foundational work that we have reviewed within this chapter.

Notes

Please address correspondence to Michael W. Vasey, Department of Psychology, Ohio State University, 1885 Neil Avenue, Columbus, OH 43210-1222, USA. E-mail: vasey.1@osu.edu.

References

Bargh, J. A. (1989). Conditional automaticity: Varieties of automatic influence in social perception and cognition. In J. S. Uleman & J. A. Bargh (Eds.), *Unintended thought* (pp. 3–51). New York: Guilford.

Bargh, J. A., & Chartrand, T. L. (1999). The unbearable automaticity of being. *American Psychologist, 54,* 462–479.

Barrett, P. M., Rapee, R. M., Dadds, M. R., & Ryan, S. M. (1996). Family enhancement of cognitive style in anxious and aggressive children: Threat bias and the FEAR effect. *Journal of Abnormal Child Psychology, 24,* 187–203.

Bell-Dolan, D. J. (1995). Social cue interpretation of anxious children. *Journal of Clinical Child Psychology, 24,* 1–10.

Bijttebier, P. (1998). Monitoring and blunting coping styles in children. Unpublished doctoral thesis. Catholic University of Leuven, Belgium.

Bugental, D. B. (1992). Affective and cognitive processes within threat-oriented family systems. In I. E. Sigel, J. Goodnow, & A. McGillicudy-deLisi (Eds.), *Parental belief systems: The psychological consequences for children* (pp. 219–248). Hillsdale, NJ: Erlbaum.

Chorpita, B. F., Albano, A. M., & Barlow, D. H. (1996). Cognitive processing in children: Relationship to anxiety and family influences. *Journal of Clinical Child Psychology*, *25*, 170–176.

Crick, N. R., & Dodge, K. A. (1994). A review and reformulation of social information-processing mechanisms in children's social adjustment. *Psychological Bulletin*, *115*, 74–101.

Daleiden, E. L. (1998). Childhood anxiety and memory functioning: A comparison of systemic and processing accounts. *Journal of Experimental Child Psychology*, *68*, 216–235.

Daleiden, E. L., & Vasey, M. W. (1997). An information-processing perspective on childhood anxiety. *Clinical Psychology Review*, *17*, 407–429.

Dalgleish, T. (1995). Performance on the emotional Stroop task in groups of anxious, experts and control subjects: A comparison of computer and card presentation formats. *Cognition and Emotion*, *9*, 341–362.

Derryberry, D. (1998). Attention and the control of anxiety. Paper presented at the Developmental Psychobiology of Stress Consortium Meeting, Pittsburgh, Pennsylvania, May 1998.

Derryberry, D., & Reed, M. A. (1996). Regulatory processes and the development of cognitive representations. *Development and Psychopathology*, *8*, 215–234.

Fox, E. (1993). Allocation of visual attention and anxiety. *Cognition and Emotion*, *7*, 207–215.

Gotlib, I., & MacLeod, C. (1997). Information processing in anxiety and depression: A cognitive developmental perspective. In J. A. Burack & J. T. Enns (Eds.), *Attention, development, and psychopathology* (pp. 350–378). New York: Guilford.

Hadwin, J., Frost, S., French, C. C., & Richards, A. (1997). Cognitive processing and trait anxiety in typically developing children: Evidence for an interpretation bias. *Journal of Abnormal Psychology*, *106*, 486–490.

Kagan, J., Snidman, N., Zentner, M., & Peterson, E. (1999). Infant temperament and anxious symptoms in school age children. *Development and Psychopathology*, *11*, 209–224.

Kindt, M., & Brosschot, J. F. (1999). Cognitive bias in spider phobic children: Comparison of a pictorial and a linguistic spider Stroop. *Journal of Psychopathology and Behavioral Assessment*, *21*, 207–220.

Kindt, M., Bierman, D., & Brosschot, J. S. (1997). Cognitive bias in spider fear and control children: Assessment of emotional interference by a card format and a single-trial format of the Stroop. *Journal of Experimental Child Psychology*, *66*, 163–179.

Kindt, M., Brosschot, J. S., & Everaerd, W. (1997). Cognitive processing bias of children in a real life stress situation and a neutral situation. *Journal of Experimental Child Psychology*, *64*, 79–97.

Lane, D. M., & Pearson, D. A. (1982). The development of selective attention. *Merrill–Palmer Quarterly*, *28*, 317–337.

Lonigan, C. J., & Vasey, M. W. (1999). Temperament, psychopathology, and the processing of emotion-relevant stimuli. Manuscript submitted for review.

MacLeod, C., & Mathews, A. (1988). Anxiety and the allocation of attention to threat. *Quarterly Journal of Experimental Psychology*, *40A*, 653–670.

MacLeod, C., & Rutherford, E.M. (1992). Anxiety and the selective processing of emotional information: Mediating roles of awareness trait and state variables, and personal relevance of stimulus materials. *Behavioural Research and Therapy, 30,* 479–491.

MacLeod, C., Mathews, A., & Tata, P. (1986). Attentional bias in emotional disorders. *Journal of Abnormal Psychology, 95,* 15–20.

Martin, M., & Jones, G. V. (1995). Integral bias in the cognitive processing of emotionally linked pictures. *British Journal of Psychology, 86,* 419–435.

Martin, M, Horder, P., & Jones, G. V. (1992). Integral bias in naming of phobia-related words. *Cognition and Emotion, 6,* 479–486.

Massaro, D. W., & Cowan, N. (1993). Information processing models: Microscopes of the mind. *Annual Review of Psychology, 45,* 25–50.

Mathews, A., & MacLeod, C. (1994). Cognitive approaches to emotion and emotional disorders. *Annual Review of Psychology, 45,* 25–50.

Mathews, A. M. & Sebastian, S. (1993). Suppression of emotional Stroop effects by fear arousal. *Cognition and Emotion, 7,* 517–530.

Mathews, A., Ridgeway, V., & Williamson, D. A. (1996). Evidence for attention to threatening stimuli in depression. *Behaviour Research and Therapy, 34,* 695–705.

McNally, R. J., Amir, N., & Lipke, H. J. (1996). Subliminal processing of threat cues in posttraumatic stress disorder? *Journal of Anxiety Disorders, 10,* 115–128.

Mogg, K., & Bradley, B. P. (1998). A cognitive–motivational analysis of anxiety. *Behaviour Research and Therapy, 36,* 809–848.

Mogg, K., Bradley, B. P., De Bono, J., & Painter, M. (1997). Time course of attentional bias for threat information in non-clinical anxiety. *Behaviour Research and Therapy, 35,* 297–303.

Mogg, K., Bradley, B. P., & Hallowell, N. (1994). Attentional bias to threat: Roles of trait anxiety, stressful events, and awareness. *Quarterly Journal of Experimental Psychology, 47A,* 841–864.

Mogg, K., Kentish, J., & Bradley, B. P. (1993). Effects of anxiety and awareness on color identification latencies for emotional words. *Behaviour Research and Therapy, 31,* 559–567.

Mogg, K., Mathews, A. M., Bird, C., & MacGregor-Morris, R. (1990). Effects of stress and anxiety on the processing of threat stimuli. *Journal of Personality and Social Psychology, 59,* 1230–1237.

Moradi, A. R., Neshat Doost, H. T., Taghavi, R., Yule, W., & Dalgleish, T. (1999). Performance of children of adults with PTSD on the Stroop color-naming task: A preliminary study. *Journal of Traumatic Stress, 12,* 663–672.

Moradi, A. R., Taghavi, M. R., Neshat Doost, H. T., Yule, W., & Dalgleish, T. (1999). Performance of children and adolescents with PTSD on the Stroop colour-naming task. *Psychological Medicine, 29,* 415–419.

Rothbart, M. K., Posner, M., I., & Hershey, K. L. (1995). Temperament, attention, and developmental psychology. In D. Cicchetti & D. J. Cohen (Eds.), *Developmental psychopathology: Vol. 1. Theory and methods* (pp. 315–340). New York: Wiley.

Schippell, P., Vasey, M. W., Cravens-Brown, L., & Bretveld, R. (1999). Suppressed attention to social rejection, ridicule and failure cues: A specific correlate of reactive but not proactive aggression in youth. Manuscript submitted for publication.

Schwartz, C. E., Snidman, N., & Kagan, J. (1996). Early temperamental predictors of Stroop interference to threatening information in adolescence. *Journal of Anxiety Disorders, 10,* 89–96.

Shiffrin, R. M., & Schneider, W. (1977). Controlled and automatic human information processing: II. Perceptual learning, automatic attending, and a general theory. *Psychological Review, 84*, 127–190.

Spence, S. H., Donovan, C., & Brechman-Toussaint, M. (1999). Social skills, social outcomes, and cognitive features of childhood social phobia. *Journal of Abnormal Psychology, 108*, 211–221.

Taghavi, M. R., Moradi, A. R., Neshat Doost, H. T., Yule, W., & Dalgleish, T. (in press). Interpretation of ambiguous emotional information in clinically-anxious children and adolescents. *Cognition and Emotion.*

Taghavi, M. R., Neshat Doost, H. T., Moradi, A. R., Yule, W., & Dalgleish, T. (1999). Biases in visual attention in children and adolescents with clinical anxiety and mixed anxiety-depression. *Journal of Abnormal Child Psychology, 27*, 215–223.

Vasey, M. W., & Daleiden, E. L. (1996). Information-processing pathways to cognitive interference in childhood. In I. G. Sarason, G. Pierce, & B. Sarason (Eds.), *Cognitive interference: Theory, methods, and findings* (pp. 117–138). Hillsdale, NJ: Lawrence Erlbaum.

Vasey, M. W., & Schippell, P. (2000). Beyond anxiety: Coping preferences and depression as correlates of threat-relevant attentional bias in adolescence. Manuscript in preparation.

Vasey, M. W., Daleiden, E., & Williams, L. L. (1992, November). Coping with worrisome thoughts: Strategies of anxiety-disordered and normal children. Poster presented at the twenty-sixth annual convention of the Association for the Advancement of Behavior Therapy, Boston.

Vasey, M. W., Daleiden, E. L., Williams, L. L., & Brown, L. M. (1995). Biased attention in childhood anxiety disorders: A preliminary study. *Journal of Abnormal Child Psychology, 23*, 267–279.

Vasey, M. W., El-Hag, N., & Daleiden, E. L. (1996). Anxiety and the processing of emotionally-threatening stimuli: Distinctive patterns of selective attention among high- and low-test-anxious children. *Child Development, 67*, 1173–1185.

Williams, J. M. G., Watts, F. N., MacLeod, C., & Mathews, A. (1988). *Cognitive psychology and emotional disorders.* New York: Wiley.

Williams, J. M. G., Watts, F. N., MacLeod, C., & Mathews, A. (1997). *Cognitive psychology and emotional disorders* (2nd ed.). New York: Wiley.

Wilson, B. J., & Gottman, J. M. (1996). Attention—the shuttle between emotion and cognition: Risk, resiliency, and physiological bases. In E. M. Hetherington and E. A. Blechman (Eds.), *Stress, coping, and resiliency in children and families.* Mahwah, NJ: Lawrence Erlbaum.

13

Family Processes in the Development of Anxiety Problems

MARK R. DADDS and JANET H. ROTH

The twentieth century saw the development of a range of theoretical and methodological tools for studying interpersonal determinants of human behavior. Within this approach, the experiences and behavior of an individual are seen, in part, as a simultaneous product and a determinant of his or her interpersonal context. Having developed within this context, interpersonal models of psychopathology emphasize etiological, assessment, and treatment formulations that incorporate a focus on the functional relationships between problematic behavior and the interpersonal contexts in which they occur. Although anxiety and fear have traditionally been thought of as very personal experiences, the last few decades have seen a rise in emphasis on research into how interpersonal systems (e.g., families, couples, large groups) process information about threat and select strategies for coping with it. As a result, there are now clear indications that the early development of anxiety problems in children is linked to more general anxiety in the family, through mechanisms of inherited temperament, learning that emphasizes threat and avoidance, and high parental control and low levels of secure attachment. The aim of this chapter is to review family processes with regard to development and maintenance of anxiety disorders in young people. We will not present comprehensive reviews of genetic aspects of familial transmission, attachment, or basic learning processes. While these mechanisms are central to familial models of anxiety in young people, and thus we will be incorporating them as necessry into our review, specialist chapters in this book focus specifically on these topics.

Preliminary Notes on the Family as a Causal Pathway to Anxiety

Several theoretical and methodological difficulties complicate analysis of the role of the family in the development of childhood psychopathology. The family is in itself a complex system that takes on various forms. For the present purposes we will define a family as any system of people that includes a parental (adult) system that is responsible for the care of one or more children. Most family-focused research has concerned itself with parent–child relationships and hence the literature is richest in this area. In keeping with this, much of our consideration of "family" processes will focus on parent–child relationships.

Research has only recently begun to identify and test characteristics of families that are hypothesized to be important in the development of anxiety problems. However, theoretical models are numerous, especially within the psychodynamic and family systems movements. For the sake of parsimony, we will focus on those family characteristics that have both been put forward theoretically and have been subject to empirical scrutiny. Thus we focus mainly on two explanatory models, social learning theory (SLT) and attachment theory (AT), as they apply to parent–child processes, and present some novel thoughts on the value of integrating these approaches.

Families are not static and undergo normal and disrupted changes both in structure and function, in parallel with changes in their constituent members. Similarly, anxiety problems in children follow a developmental progression that will involve both change and stability. Yet only recently has attention been paid to the early developmental trajectory of anxiety problems. Early signs of anxiety problems attract different labels (e.g., shyness, behavioral inhibition), and so to be developmentally comprehensive we will review associations between family variables and these early precursors to anxiety. Thus, in terms of formal causal analysis, difficulties are inherent in finding and testing links between two systems that are in a state of flux. Longitudinal studies that measure family factors and child anxiety at repeated points in time are one of the best existing designs, but these are rare in the child anxiety literature. Thus, we are constricted to making the best of cross-sectional studies, and the reader must be alert to the common and tempting error of concluding that a family characteristic facilitates (or causes) anxiety problems in children simply because the two are found to be associated in cross sectional studies.

A number of writers in the area of developmental psychopathology have tried to make explicit the assumptions inherent in the specification of causal pathways leading through and to psychopathology (e.g., Carlson & Sroufe, 1995). Unfortunately, these tend to make us acutely aware of how little we know, rather how much. Current developmental models of psychopathology acknowledge diverse and multifaceted influences across time on either adaptation or maladaptation. Genetic, biological, and psychological factors interact with each other and in relation to changing environmental contexts. From this highly inclusive and interactive approach have evolved concepts of multifinality and equifinality. Multifinality refers to the process by which the same path does not necessarily lead to the same outcome. Organismic and environmental factors interact with varying degrees of influence, unique to each individual. For example, while maternal depression appears to be predictive of psychopathology, not all children of depressed mothers develop psychopathology. Alternatively, equifinality suggests that individuals can arrive at the same outcome through a range of different pathways. A phobia may develop through a direct traumatic experience, or through vicarious modeling of a significant member of the family. There are, nevertheless, certain developmental pathways which exert a strong influence in the direction of psychopathology and increase the likelihood of a maladaptive course.

Sroufe (1990) and Carlson and Sroufe (1995) proposed six broad axioms that summarize this approach:

1. Even prior to the onset of psychopathology, certain developmental pathways represent adaptational failures that probabilistically forecast later pathology.
2. Not all outcomes of a given pathway need be pathological (or nonpathological).
3. Diverse, but conceptually related, patterns of pathological outcomes may emerge from a given early pathway.
4. Alternative early pathways may lead to the same outcome (principle of equifinality).
5. Change is possible at each phase of development. However, change is constrained by prior adaptation, and alterations in some forms of adaptation may be more likely for certain individuals.
6. Following change, prior adaptations may still be reactivated in certain circumstances.

While these axioms might be taken to suggest that developmental psychologists have arrived at a point of definitive uncertainty, a more generous interpretation would emphasize an openness and flexibility with regard to the multifaceted nature of causality. With regard to the current analysis, it is thus important to remember that the constellation of family variables we review represents only one set among a number of factors which bear upon a child's development. Further, it is still premature to conclude that the family variables reviewed, by themselves, are definitive causes of child anxiety problems. For the sake of parsimony, it will be necessary to analyze family variables largely in isolation, with the hope that the reader can integrate this analysis within the larger context of the book.

Family Transmission

Eley (this volume) provides a comprehensive review of the literature on the genetic transmission of anxiety. However, as a context to the following review, some comments are warranted here. Anxiety problems tend to run in families, with support coming from both studies of parents of children with anxiety/depression disorders, and children of parents with anxiety/depression disorders. However, it should be noted that behavioral genetic studies of childhood anxiety also show a significant influence of shared environment, and thus set the context for models of parental or other family behavioral influence (see Eley, this volume). Further, there is little evidence that transmission is specific to individual disorder categories, and a number of other clinical conditions may be associated with increased risk for anxiety and depression. For example, a comparison of nonclinic families and families with a member diagnosed with antisocial disorder found that children from these latter families had higher rates of ADHD, major depression, anxiety disorders, and substance-use disorder (Faraone et al., 1995). In a comparison of children with major depressive disorder (MDD) and psychiatric controls, it was found that the MDD children's families also had symptomatology of MDD, any mood disorder, antisocial personality disorder, and anxiety disorders (Weller et al., 1994).

Thus, the literature supports the familial transmission of affective and anxiety disorders, but only in quite broad terms, and consequently a biological–environmental interaction model is usually invoked (e.g., Rosenbaum, Biederman, Hirschfeld, Bolduc, & Chaloff, 1991). The reasons for the lack of specificity of transmission may be due in part to the nature of the research designs used to test family transmission models. Temperamental factors, parental attachment and child-rearing styles, peer interaction, and sociodemographic and cultural variables, are all likely to interact and impinge to different degrees on the developing child and his or her ability to cope within a variety of contexts. Thus, future studies need to consider transmission of disorder in the context of other environmental variables that have predictive power. Further, most transmission studies use the presence or absence of psychological disorders as the dependent variable. The use of categorical diagnostic systems has advantages but is marred by a lack of precision and unclear theoretical foundations. More productive outcomes may be achieved by studying transmission of underlying vulnerabilities hypothesized to predispose individuals to various forms of psychopathology. Thus, for anxiety disorders, future research might benefit from studying family transmission of vulnerabilities such as behavioral inhibition (Kagan, 1997; Kagan, Reznick, & Snidman, 1988), reticence (Mills & Rubin, 1990), disgust sensitivity (Davey, 1994), high negative affectivity and neuroticism (Lonigan & Philips, this volume), and anxiety sensitivity (Reiss, Silverman, & Weems this volume)—rather than simply focus on the presence or absence of disorder. Such an approach is exemplified by the Daniels and Plomin (1985) study of family transmission of shyness and sociability: low levels of parental sociability were predictive of infant shyness in both biological and adoptive mothers.

Some Issues in Directly Measuring Anxiety in Children and Families

Dadds, Rapee, and Barrett (1994) argued that the adoption of an observational methodology with anxious children is a way of embracing a more comprehensive view of anxiety itself. This is especially important for understanding anxiety in terms of its social context. People, especially children, find it very difficult accurately to identify and describe the influential characteristics of social fields in which they are immersed. A child cannot report on the role of his or her anxiety in the functioning of the family, the fears he or she has seen expressed by parents during critical developmental moments, the reactions his or her fear has brought from others, and the meanings that fear has been assigned by the group. Thus one task of the behavioral scientist interested in family factors is to develop measures that will allow us to assess these contextual influences on anxiety.

Anxiety is a very difficult phenomenon to measure in ecologically meaningful ways. To operationalize a person's ability to approach a snake in a laboratory is reasonably simple. However, to operationalize more complex forms of anxiety, such as generalized anxiety and panic, and then measure them using observations in real-world situations is a challenge to current knowledge and technology. The development of observational strategies for measuring child anxiety mostly took place in the 1960s and 1970s, and since that initial burst of activity little has occurred in terms of the development and refinement of these methodologies and most existing observational strategies focus solely on the child. Creative attempts to operationalize the social context of the child's anxiety and examine its functional relationship to the development of anxiety are sorely needed.

Dadds et al. (1994) argued that as well as developing methods to measure children's anxiety in terms of its social context, observations need to be designed and used in a way that allows for conceptual integration with other aspects of anxiety, such as cognitive processing style, family interaction, and physiological reactivity. For example, much progress is currently being made in understanding the way anxious people process information about threat in their environment (e.g., Butler & Matthews, 1983). That is, anxious people show an exaggerated tendency to perceive, attend to, and respond to threat in their environments. An important question then is whether this processing style is learned or intensified through interaction with significant others, namely anxious parents. A methodology that integrates information processing and direct observation of the child in interaction with others may yield important insights into this process. Work by Krohne and colleagues (e.g., Krohne & Hock, 1991) and by our group (Barrett, Rapee, Dadds & Ryan, 1996; Dadds, Barrett, Rapee, & Ryan, 1996), reviewed below, are examples of fruitful attempts in this direction. The work by Nachmias, Gunnar, Mangelsdorf, Parritz, and Buss (1996) and by Fox and Calkins (1993) integrating direct observations of parent–child interactions with temperamental, attachment, and biological indices are other innovative examples in this direction.

A consistent finding from studies of anxiety in families is that individual member's reports are influenced by their own and other family members' anxiety. This is well exemplified by a recent study by Rosenbaum and Ronen (1997) into family reports of anxiety during missile attacks on Israel in the 1991 Gulf war. Family members were asked to rate each others' levels of anxiety without directly consulting that particular member. Parents were strongly influenced in both their ratings of their own and their spouse's anxiety, by their spouse's actual expressions of anxiety. Further, parents' ratings of their child's anxiety were not independent but rather appeared to be co-constructed, shared in the natural process of communicating about their children. On the other hand, children's ratings of their parents' anxiety was primarily projected from the child's own anxiousness. Families who were closer physically, and therefore shared more information about their emotional states, showed a higher degree of agreement on ratings. Similarly, Steele, Tripp, Kotchick, Summers, and Forehand (1997) showed that family experiences of illness uncertainty were overlapping and predictive of anxiety in children. Studying families in which the father had chronic illness, they demonstrated that levels of child anxiety could be predicted from the mother's level of uncertainty about her partner's prognosis, over and above the child's own uncertainty.

This highlights that families participate in reciprocal information exchange about important emotions such as anxiety, and that each individuals' experience of anxiety is not independent from other members'. In practical terms, clinical reports of anxiety in children and parents will be somewhat infected by anxiety elsewhere in the family. While this may be problematic when attempting to accurately specify the extent of anxiety in an individual, it is theoretically important, alerting us to the socially constructed nature of anxiety in intimate groups.

Early childhood poses extra problems with regard to assessment of anxiety, especially in terms of child self-reports. Parent–child agreement is typically low, and none of the established self-report measures of childhood anxiety has been shown to be valid when used with children younger than middle childhood. Thus, we are reliant on assessing related constructs that are hypothesized to be early risk factors for anxiety problems. Measures have been developed for related constructs such as behavioral inhibition (e.g., Kagan et al., 1988; Nachmias et al., 1996), reticence (Rubin & Burgess, this volume), and other temperamental factors (Buss & Plomin, 1984) such as emotionality, sociability and shyness that may lead to social withdrawal and eventual peer problems (Lonigan & Phillips, this volume; Parker, Rubin, Price & DeRosier, 1995). We will begin our review of family factors by considering the relationship of these to the early concomitants of anxiety.

Pre-anxious Risk Factors and Family Process

Several temperamental traits of infants have been identified as early signs of internalizing problems in later life. Of these, behavioral inhibition in the toddler years onward has received the most empirical support as a specific precursor to later anxiety problems. Biederman et al. (1993) showed that extremes of behavioral inhibition in infants predicted anxiety problems later in childhood, and Gest (1997) showed that behavioral inhibition-like traits measured at 8–12 years were predictive of social and emotional problems in adulthood. Operationalized as approach and interaction versus avoidance and distress in response to novel stimuli, the construct of behavioral inhibition is readily amenable to direct observation, with measurable physiological correlates. Several teams of researchers are beginning to explore links between behavioral inhibition and other familial and physiological constructs.

In order to examine the associations between temperament, attachment, and inhibition over time, Fox and Calkins (1993) assessed children's behavioral and physiological responses to novelty and restraint, attachment styles, and maternal ratings of child temperament, from birth to 24 months. As is common in this area, the infants could be reliably grouped according to two distinct patterns of observed behavior and physiological reactivity. Even in the first days of life, some infants were frustrated by the imposition of limits to their behavior (e.g., arm restraint) and remained undistressed by novelty (peek-a-boo with a stranger, novel visual stimuli). Other infants reacted by accepting the imposition of limits but were clearly distressed by novelty. Similar to Kagan's (e.g., 1988) measures, the autonomic responses of fearful infants reflected an inability to respond adaptively to changes and novelty in the environment. Fox and Calkins suggest that this group of infants is showing temperamental features that logically appear to be early signs of behavioral inhibition.

However, no relationship was found between the early measures of infant reactivity and behavioral inhibition measured at 24 months, suggesting that early temperament alone is not sufficiently able to account for the development of behavioral inhibition. However, a stable, consistent pattern emerged from the maternal reports of infant behavior across the 24-month period in association with later signs of behavioral inhibition. Maternal ratings of low positive affect and activity subscales at 5 months, and social fear at 14 months and 24 months, correlated positively with inhibition in toddlerhood. Thus, mothers were able to report on characteristics of their infants that were predictive of later inhibition, even though the independent measures of early behavioral reactivity did not.

Further, there were clear relationships between the early reactivity measures and the style of attachments that the mother–child dyads formed. The freedom/novelty-seeking infants tend to elicit negative responses from their parents, and actually avoid the controlling parent in an attempt to maintain their freedom. They were termed "insecure–avoidant" according to attachment classifications. In contrast to this group, the infants who were easily distressed by novelty (insecure-resistant) placed high demands upon parents for proximity and soothing, which parents were likely to meet with variable consistency.

Fox and Calkins found that attachment style interacted with the early behavioral measures in predicting behavioral inhibition in toddlerhood. In particular, those infants who were behaviorally and physiologically distressed by novelty and had high insecure-anxious attachments tended to move into higher levels of behavioral inhibition.

Both of the above groups elicited negative responses from parents, either bids for control which the child avoided, or frustration at the child's excessive proximity and soothing demands, which ironically increased the child's stress and demanding behavior. This interaction between insecure-anxious attachment styles and behavioral processes in which the child's demanding leads to a coercive cycle of parental frustration and rejection, and thus, increasing child demands, emerges from several diverse theoretical and empirical approaches to understanding families and anxiety. Further discussion of these processes will be presented at the end of this chapter.

Nachmias et al. (1996) studied a group of 78 eighteen-month-old toddlers in another attempt to integrate attachment theory and physiological correlates of behavioral inhibition. In this study children were presented with three novel events: an exuberant live clown, a robot clown, and some lively puppets. Behavioral inhibition was rated as "ease of approach." Physiological stress reactions were operationalized as the activation of neuroendocrine responses in the hypothalamic–pituitary–adrenocortical (HPA) system, which is measured through cortisol secretions in the child's saliva. To reduce confounding the influence of inhibition with attachment, the measurement of attachment via the Strange Situation (see Ainsworth, 1989) occurred at least one week apart from the inhibition session. The results indicated that variance in children's physiological signs of anxiety/stress problems were accounted for by the interaction of the child's temperament and the quality of the parent–child relationship. Specifically, only children who were both insecurely attached and behaviorally inhibited were unsuccessful at reducing the activation of their neuroendocrine response to stress. No other group, neither securely attached, inhibited children, nor secure/insecure-noninhibited children, showed similar elevations in cortisol levels after exposure to the novel, arousing events. When inhibition extremes were used in a subsequent analysis, this inhibition by attachment interaction was reduced to a trend and no longer achieved significance. This could have been due to the reduced statistical power that is commonly associated with using split rather than whole/continuous samples.

However, an earlier study (Calkins & Fox, 1992), which tested both attachment and inhibition in the same experimental session, showed a different pattern of results in support of links between high inhibition and resistant attachment, and low inhibition and avoidant attachment (Kagan, Resnick, Clarke, & Garcia-Coll, 1984). Nachmias and her colleagues have argued that Calkins and Fox's testing of inhibition immediately prior to testing attachment may have increased resistant behavior in children, who under different circumstances would not have been observed to have a resistant (insecure) attachment style. Secondly, fussing and crying are often considered behavioral indicators of behavioral inhibition (Calkins & Fox, 1992; Kagan et al., 1988). In the Nachmias et al. study, fussing and crying were measured as a separate aspect of children's behavior, reflecting irritability, and not included in the definition of inhibition. Nachmias et al. (1996) cite studies (Belsky & Rovine, 1987; Goldsmith & Alansky, 1987) which point to irritability as a distinguishing feature of resistant attachment style. The disentanglement of observations of fussing and crying with constructs of resistant attachment, inhibition, and irritability provides avenues for future research.

Children's and parents' behaviors were also extensively coded and then factor analyzed by Nachmias et al. (1996). Children's behavior was factor analyzed into comfort-seeking (including fussing), coping-competence, and distraction. Mothers' behaviors were categorized into encourage-approach, comfort-giving, or demand-approach factors. Overall, there was no significant interaction between attachment and inhibition. However, inhibited toddlers received more maternal comforting and encouragement to approach than did less inhibited toddlers. Inhibited toddlers also sought more comfort from the mother, suggesting a reciprocal cycle as discussed in Patterson (1982), an important point which will be expanded upon later in the chapter. As would be expected, securely attached toddlers demonstrated significantly more coping competence than did insecurely attached toddlers.

When average pre- and post-cortisol levels were examined, inhibition accounted for a large portion of the variance in both measures. Children who were able to cope competently with the novel situations showed significantly lower elevations of cortisol. Additionally, when mothers of insecurely attached children intruded upon their child's coping efforts by overly encouraging their children to interact or approach an arousing stimulus, high posttest cortisol levels resulted. This maternal style is hypothesized to have interfered with the toddler's tendency to cautiously regulate their own proximity and contact with the stimulus, which could have increased the child's perception of imminent threat. Thus behavioral inhibition, hypothesized to be the child's preferred coping mechanism in the face of arousing stimuli, was not allowed to operate owing to maternal intrusiveness. In these cases cortisol levels were atypically elevated, a sign of stress. Additionally, and less clear, was the association observed between comfort-giving and higher cortisol levels. It is possible that mothers' increased efforts to calm their children may actually extend beyond the immediate needs of the child for comforting, and indirectly convey messages of increased threat, simultaneously undermining the child's own coping strategies.

In summary, the above studies show important interactions between infant temperament and parent–child interactional style in the prediction of anxious outcomes for young children. A recent study, to be reviewed later, has shown that the interaction of early temperament and insecure attachment patterns may be predictive of longer-term anxiety problems (Warren, Huston, Egeland, & Sroufe, 1997). These studies also highlight the difficulties of parenting a child with high levels of inhibition and fear of novelty. Pushing such children too forcefully toward challenge, or alternatively being overly protective, both appear to enhance fearful responding, prevent anxious children from developing a sense of their own ability to cope, and reduce opportunities for them to experience and become familiar with novel challenges.

Another study of familial aspects of behavioral inhibition employed the construct of expressed emotion (EE). Used extensively in research with adult psychiatric patients and their families, EE is a measure of criticism and/or emotional overinvolvement in relatives, usually parents. EE in relatives is a risk factor for poor prognosis in the developmental course of a number of psychiatric disorders; and more specifically, high maternal emotional over-involvement has shown some association with anxiety disorders.

Hirshfeld, Biederman, Brody, Faraone, & Rosenbaum (1997a) examined maternal EE and child behavioral inhibition in a pilot study with at-risk children aged between 4 and 10 years. Children of parents with panic disorder and agoraphobia or major depression or other disorders, or at-risk as siblings of children with ADD, comprised their at-risk sample. Comparison children were either high or low on behavioral inhibition, but without other familial mental health problems. Structured interviews with mothers determined the children's diagnostic status. Videos of the Five-Minute Speech Sample (Magana et al., 1986), in which mothers describe the parent–child relationship, were coded for EE, specifically criticism and emotional over-involvement (EOI). In the at-risk sample, maternal criticism was associated with higher incidence of child behavioral inhibition, and maternal EOI was associated with higher incidence of separation anxiety problems independently of the children's other behavior and mood disorders. Sample sizes were limited, and only four children in the sample had mothers who were high EOI. However, in an epidemiological sample, Stubbe, Zahner, Goldstein, and Leckman (1993) observed a similar association between high EOI and child anxiety disorders.

To summarize, preliminary investigations of maternal EE point towards an association between maternal criticism and behavioral inhibition, irrespective of comorbid psychiatric diagnoses. High maternal EOI appears to be connected with separation anxiety in at-risk children.

In a continuing study (Hirshfeld et al., 1997b), maternal criticism was positively associated with a lifetime history of maternal anxiety disorder, with or without comorbidity. Especially relevant to our discussion of family process is the observed interaction between maternal anxiety disorder and child behavioral inhibition, which predicted the rate of maternal criticism. On the other hand, maternal criticism showed no relationship to children with or without behavioral inhibition in families where mothers were non-anxious. This suggests a reciprocal interaction between maternal anxiety and child inhibition. Child inhibition would be challenging for parents, as they could be expected to be easily frustrated and upset by their difficult child, as well as finding it difficult to calm themselves or their child once aroused. Anxious parents may therefore be more likely to respond irritably to their child, as well as overestimating the degree of threat to themselves or their child, and underestimating their own coping resources. Parents with a history of anxiety, quite possibly "perfectionists," may be more likely to respond critically to their child's difficult behavior, which is likely to encourage continued inhibition (Hirshfeld et al., 1997b).

Child psychopathology (operationalized as number of diagnosable disorders) was significantly higher in families with anxious mothers who also expressed high levels of criticism, even controlling for age, sex, and behavioral inhibition of the child. In families with nonanxious mothers, the level of maternal criticism did not appear to influence the children's number of disorders. When maternal age, SES, size, and cohesion of family were considered, no significant relationships were found between these environmental variables and EE, although a negative trend was observed between family cohesion and criticism. This suggests that the mother's voicing of dissatisfaction with her child may be restricted to a dyadic interaction and not necessarily general family environmental influences. Further research is needed to see whether this interaction holds with noninhibited siblings.

Maternal criticism was not severe in these two studies (Hirshfeld, 1997a, 1997b), but closer to dissatisfaction ("borderline high criticism"). Criticism seemed to be significant in anxious-mother/BI-child dyads, whereas this association was not observed in nonanxious-mother/BI-child or anxious-mother/non-BI-child dyads. Also, maternal EOI was associated with separation anxiety only in a sample of children deemed at-risk.

Thus a growing body of evidence suggests associations of behavioral inhibition (a potential marker for future anxiousness), maternal criticism, maternal overprotectiveness or self-sacrificing behaviors, and maternal control. The paternal role is glaringly absent within this literature on infants, and has not yet been examined adequately. Causal connections between maternal overprotective/self-sacrificing behavior (EOI) and separation anxiety, or between maternal criticism and behavioral inhibition, have not been examined, but the correlations indicating associations are consistent with previous research and clinical reports as discussed by Nachmias et al. (1996), albeit with methodological limitations, such as small sample sizes, lack of control groups, and lack of longitudinal EE measurement (Hirshfeld et al., 1997a, 1997b).

Empirical Findings: Anxious Children and Family Processes

In the middle-childhood to adolescent years, many of the common anxiety disorders emerge, and these problems can be reliably identified on the basis of caregiver and child reports. Thus, a growing literature on children with identifiable anxiety disorders and their families is available. In this section, we review studies of family process associated with clinical presentations of anxiety problems in children and adolescents.

It should be noted at the outset that the relationship between family factors and anxiety problems may reside not only in the style of interactions that take place, but also in terms of the amount of reciprocal influence the family and the anxious individual afford each other. In the longest study thus far of inhibited children, Gest (1997) has shown that inhibited children are less likely than their more confident peers to have moved out of the family home by adulthood. Further, adult social phobics consistently report that their families isolated them in terms of social contact (Bruch & Heimberg, 1994). Thus, it is likely that socially anxious children experience relatively high levels of exposure to family influences and low levels of exposure to alternative social systems.

Most evidence supporting family factors in child anxiety pertains to child-rearing styles, and there is little evidence that more systemic or structural aspects of the family are causally related to child anxiety problems. For example, while marital conflict is a correlate of anxiety in nonclinic children (e.g., Dadds & Powell, 1991), there is no evidence that it is a specific risk factor for clinically significant anxiety. The samples of anxious children described by Barrett and associates in 1996 were not different from other groups on marital conflict or dimensions of family functioning measured by the FACES scale (enmeshment, adaptability). Green, Loeber, and Lahey (1992) found no evidence for the presence of deviant family hierarchies, as predicted by family systems theory (Haley, 1976; Minuchin, 1974), in the families of overanxious boys. A study by Stark, Humphrey, Crook, and Lewis (1990) showed that anxious children saw their families as less supportive, less sociable, more conflictual and enmeshed than nonclinic children. However, the results were even more striking for depressed and mixed depressed/anxious children, and so these factors are unlikely to be specific correlates of childhood anxiety. Similarly, Bernstein and Borchardt (1996) found that anxious children refusing school reported normal family functioning on the Family Assessment Measure.

The work by Bruch and colleagues (Bruch, 1989; Bruch & Heimberg, 1994) has shown that adult social phobics recall their families as seeking to isolate them from social experiences, and placing undue importance on the opinions of others. Further research is needed to show that these characteristics actually exist during childhood and are not just a product of biased memories. Given that many anxious children will have been raised by anxious parents, it is highly plausible that low sociability would characterize at least a subset of families of anxious children. Studies show that shyness in infants is positively related to low sociability in both biological and adoptive parents (Daniels & Plomin, 1985), and so it is likely that low sociability in parents may be an important environmental variable associated with the early development of anxiety.

The above evidence, taken as a whole, provides little support for the view that systemic aspects of families are reliable or specific risk factors for anxiety problems in children. This may in part reflect the more difficult methodological problems of measuring systemic factors compared with individual and dyadic factors. Thus, we now turn our attention to research into more specific parental characteristics and parent–child relationships associated with anxiety.

Historically, clinical literature has stereotyped mothers of anxious children as domineering, overprotective, and overinvolved with the child. However, as Hetherington and Martin (1979) also noted, this image of the overprotective mother and the highly structured family system were based on "rather indirect sources of data" (p. 61). Empirical studies are more limited in the support they provided for many of these stereotypes, but links have begun to emerge between elevated levels of anxiety in the parents of anxious children and high levels of parental control.

A recent review of child-rearing styles (Rapee, 1997) points to a strong association between maternal control and anxiety, and between maternal rejection and depression. Rapee suggests that maternal overprotection not only conveys the perception to the child of the continual presence of threat and danger, but also restricts the child's opportunities to develop successful coping mechanisms, and may prevent the child from developing more optimistic and realistic cognitive appraisals of the world (see also, Barrett et al., 1996; Cobham, Dadds, & Spence, 1999).

Supportive data have come from direct observational studies of social learning processes. Krohne and Hock (1993; see also LaFreniere & Capuano, 1997) argued that a child's competencies are related to the parents' tendency to help the child develop problem-solving and coping skills, and inversely, to overly control the child (restriction). The idea of parental overcontrol has often been related to anxiety problems in children. Solyom, Silberfeld, and Solyom (1976) reported that mothers of agoraphobic patients scored significantly higher on measures of maternal control than did mothers of normals. Krohne and Hock (1991) found that the mothers of highly anxious girls were judged by independent observers to be more restrictive than mothers of less-anxious girls during a common problem-solving task. Similarly, Dumas, LaFreniere, and Serketich (1995) observed parent–child interactions between aggressive, anxious, and nondistressed dyads: the anxious dyads were characterized by relatively high parental control and aversiveness.

In our research clinic, the emphasis has been on using an integrative theoretical and methodological approach. Using observational strategies of family processes, we have focused on the ways in which parents influence the child's problem-solving in courageous versus avoidant directions. Thus, we emphasize the importance of parental control and restriction (Khrone & Hock, 1991; Dumas et al., 1995), most readily measured via parent–child contingencies (Patterson, 1982), in reinforcing a bias toward high levels of threat interpretation (Butler & Matthews, 1983; Clark, 1991), thus increasing the child's susceptibility to avoidance and aversive conditioning experiences (Dadds, Bovbjerg, Redd, & Cutmore, 1997; Davey, 1992). This process is thought not to occur for all children in the family, but rather becomes focused on the child or children who show early signs of an anxious/inhibited temperament.

A recent study demonstrated this approach. Barrett, Rapee et al. (1996) asked samples of anxious, aggressive, and nonclinic children to interpret various ambiguous social and physical scenarios and plan what they would do in response to the scenario. (For example: (1) You want to join in with some children playing ball at school. As you approach you notice they are all laughing. (2) You are on your way to school and you notice that your tummy feels a little sick.) Parents were also asked to interpret the scenarios as they though their child would. Interpretations were coded into threatening and non-threatening categories, and plans were coded into avoiding, proactive, and aggressive response categories. Results demonstrated that both anxious and aggressive children and their parents make relatively high numbers of threat interpretations in response to ambiguous situations. However, in response to those interpretations, anxious children and their families predominantly chose avoidant solutions, whereas the aggressive children and parents chose aggressive solutions when faced with ambiguous hypothetical social problems.

In the second part of the experimental procedure, the families of anxious, aggressive, and nonclinic children were brought together for 10 minutes to discuss how the child should deal with these ambiguous situations. They were told that while all could express their opinions during the discussion, the final plan was to be decided by the child. For anxious children only, the likelihood that the child would devise an avoidant solution increased dramatically after the family discussion. For aggressive children, the likelihood of aggressive solutions showed a similar increase, whereas the nonclinic children stayed with a preference for prosocial solutions throughout. These data show that family processes can facilitate expression of the child's vulnerabilities even in a brief experimental task such as this.

In a follow-up paper, Dadds et al. (1996) analyzed the contingent stream of family behaviors that had been videotaped in these family discussions. Parent and child behaviors were coded using the Family Anxiety Coding System and conditional probabilities were calculated using the methods developed and described by John Gottman (1980). Results showed that parents of anxious children were more likely than parents of nonclinic and aggressive children to reciprocate the child's proposals of avoidant solutions, and were less likely to encourage prosocial solutions to ambiguous social situations. In a final test of the influence of these parent–child sequences, it was found that the more likely the parents were to reciprocate avoidance and fail to reinforce prosocial behavior, the more likely the child was to choose a final avoidant solution.

Chorpita, Albano, and Barlow (1996) observed similar parental influences in four children aged 9–13 years with a clinical diagnosis of anxiety disorder, although the low numbers prohibit generalization. In this study, low and high anxious children exhibited high threat interpretation, but only the highly anxious children also included avoidance as the method of dealing with the perceived threat. This supports contentions that avoidance is a learned phenomenon. Reinforcement for avoidance may come not only from the removal of the distressing stimuli (negative reinforcement), but also through parental positive reinforcement of avoidant solutions. One possible explanation is that this cognitive bias could arise as a result of maternal overprotectiveness, which conveys not only a threat bias, but also the need to avoid, rather than take action against, perceived threat (Hirshfeld et al., 1997a, 1997b). Examination of anxious child–mother dyads (Dumas et al., 1995) also showed mothers of anxious children as demonstrating high levels of aversive control, using such strategies as criticism, intrusiveness, and punishment. Studies including paternal influences are rare, yet Chorpita et al. (1996), found that paternal verbalizations were more influential in children's post-family discussion threat interpretations and avoidant plans. This is certainly an area that deserves further investigation.

Chorpita, Brown, Albano, and Barlow (1996) pursued the idea of cognitive biases further through path analysis in an attempt to understand the relationship between children's attributional style, locus of control, and the degree of control within the family environment. Sixty-three clinically referred anxious children and their parents, and 31 controls, were assessed. The Family Environment Scale (FES) and the Child Behavior Checklist (CBCL) were used for parents. The children were assessed with the Revised Children's Manifest Anxiety Scale (RCMAS), the Children's Depression Inventory (CDI), the Children's Attributional Style Questionnaire (CASQ), and the Nowicki–Strickland Locus of Control Scale (LOC). Unfortunately the child cognitive measures (CASQ and LOC) were found to be unreliable. Notwithstanding that, two of their structural models offer preliminary support for a model in which the influence of parental control on children's negative affect is mediated by variations in children's locus of control. In agreement with the review by Rapee (1997), Chorpita and Barlow (1998) suggest a growing body of support for the role of control in a child's early development. Specifically, when a child's sense of control is compromised either through uncontrollable and unpredictable environmental influences, or through parental overcontrol, the child may be at greater risk of problems of helplessness (anxiety) or hopelessness (depression: see Chorpita, this volume).

Early experience of the world as uncontrollable may later foster the sense of helplessness and anxious responding, regardless of the actual controllability of events. Recent research and theorizing (Chorpita & Barlow, 1998) indicates that early experiences of uncontrollability increase activation of the behavioral inhibition system (BIS; see Gray, 1982), as well as increasing the probability of exposure to perceived novel stimuli. The work reviewed earlier by Fox and Calkins (1993) and Nachmias et al. (1996) shows that behavioral inhibition in infants is associated with clinging to parents, and this can result in a parental style that pushes the child towards novelty; which in turn activates their inhibition system. Clearly, this line of research is highly consistent with ideas of uncontrollability discussed by Chorpita with reference to Gray's BIS, and demonstrates that learning about novelty and control, and their implications for self-confidence versus anxiety, begin early in life within the parent–child system.

Cobham et al. (1999) elaborated on the Barrett, Rapee et al. (1996) and Dadds et al. (1997) studies by substituting a real threat task for the ambiguous scenarios used by Barrett et al. Using similar samples of anxious, aggressive, and nonclinic children, the methodology invited the children to give a short talk about themselves in front of a small audience and a videotaping camera. Parent–child discussions were held before and after the talks and ratings of the child's confidence and anxiety were made by the child and parents at various points in the procedure. Contrary to Barrett, Rapee et al.

(1996), the parent–child discussions did not increase the child's anxiety or avoidance of the task. Rather, they tended to lessen. Our surprise at these results was heightened by analysis of the actual content of the parent–child discussions. Similar to Barrett et al., the parents of anxious children were consistently observed to use an openly domineering and controlling style with their children, directing the children what to talk about and giving very little room for them to direct their own behavior.

Cobham et al. (1999) presented a rationale for how to account for these discrepant results. They hypothesized that the differences were due to differences in the timing of the tasks. In the Barrett, Rapee et al. (1996) study, the threat and family discussion tasks were part of the intake assessment, and parents were not informed of the decision about the eligibility for the (free) treatment until after the experimental procedure. Thus parents were motivated to emphasize their child's anxiety for the researchers to see, and in the discussion they tended to push the child to admit to their anxiety. In the Cobham and Dadds study, the experimental procedure was inadvertently presented after parents were accepted into the program, and thus parents were more likely to see the task as part of the treatment. Thus, they were more likely to push the child to participate and be confident. However, in both cases we clearly observed a highly controlling style in the parents of anxious children.

These studies highlight the gains that can be made by studying anxiety in its social context using direct observational procedures and integrative theoretical models. Clearly, the task discussion method is particularly useful for examining the relationships between individual factors such as child cognitions and behavior, and family factors such as threat emphasis and contingent responses to those individual variables.

Studies of Attachment Processes in Anxious Children

One aspect of research using a social learning and direct observation emphasis that receives little attention from social learning theorists is that the contextual relationships we are studying are the most basic of our intimate and long-term relationships. Bandura pointed to the importance of close ties in the functioning of effective models, and a wealth of data has shown how susceptible young children and other primates are to behavioral contagion when exposed to fear displays in conspecifics, especially caregivers. Given this, it is worthwhile looking more deeply at the nature of close relationships and context they provide for the learning of fear versus courage. The primary model addressing these intimate relationships has been attachment theory, and with regard to anxiety comes from recent empirical work into attachment processes. (See Thompson, this volume, for a comprehensive review of attachment processes.)

"Attachment" refers to the establishment of early intimate relationships and the internalization of these relationships as stable cognitive representations of the relation of the self to intimates throughout the lifespan (Bowlby, 1971). Over the last few decades a number of strategies for operationalizing attachment processes have been developed, including observational measures of parent–infant bonds (Ainsworth, 1989), and self-report and structured interview measures of current adult relationships and past relationships to parents (Main, 1996). A number of manifestations of insecure attachment have been described and empirically verified, including dismissive (or avoidant; e.g., avoiding or failing to seek out intimate contact) and preoccupied (or anxious/ambivalent styles; e.g., showing distress at separation, clinging, failure to show independent exploration). Using various methods of categorizing attachment, numerous studies have been published showing that different attachment processes characterize psychologically healthy versus distressed adults and children. Clinic-referred samples of children and adults show relatively low rates of secure attachment (that is, intimate relationships marked by predictable, stable, and generous levels of care and support) compared with nonclinic samples (Main, 1996).

Earlier in this chapter we reviewed studies showing that attachment styles interact with infant temperament in predicting early markers of anxiety problems such as behavioral inhibition. In this section we review literature on attachment patterns in older children and adolescents with anxiety problems.

In general, it has been difficult to find specific relationships between particular forms of psychopathology and specific types of insecure attachment. (See van Ijzendoorn & Bakermans-Kranenburg, 1996, for a meta-analytic review.) Recent improvements in the design of studies may overcome this lack of specificity. As an example of the most replicated finding to date, Rosenstein and Horowitz (1996) found that clinically referred adolescents with a "preoccupied" or "anxious ambivalent" attachment style were much more likely to have anxiety and depression problems than those with a dismissive style, who tended to show conduct problems.

In perhaps the most comprehensive study to date, Warren et al. (1997) examined whether infants who were anxiously/resistantly attached in infancy developed more anxiety disorders during childhood and adolescence than did infants who were securely attached. To test different theories of anxiety disorders, newborn temperament and maternal anxiety were included in multiple regression analyses. Infants participated in Ainsworth's Strange Situation Procedure at one year of age. The Schedule for Affective Disorders and Schizophrenia for School-Age Children was administered to the 172 children when they reached 17.5 years. Maternal anxiety and infant temperament were assessed near the time of birth. The hypothesized relation between anxious/resistant attachment and later anxiety disorders was confirmed. Anxious/resistant attachment continued to predict child/adolescent anxiety disorders significantly, even when entered last, after maternal anxiety and temperament, in multiple regression analyses.

Clearly these results are intuitively appealing and careful research is worth pursuing in this area. If valid they indicate that relationships marked by high involvement but low security may be associated with internalizing profiles. It should be noted, however, that the attachment area still tends be characterized by reliance on global typology categories and absence of specific descriptions of behavioral processes mediating attachment and psychopathology. This is highlighted by the DeKlyen (1996) study which showed that maternal attachment added no predictive power to the child's behavioral problems once direct observational measures of parent–child interactions were considered. Gender effects also need to be considered and more effort is needed to include fathers in this area. Cowan, Cohn, Pape-Cowan, and Pearson (1996), for example, found that mother's and father's attachment styles were differentially related to internalizing versus externalizing problems in their children. They assessed attachment history, family interaction, and children's externalizing/internalizing behaviors over a 2-year period. With respect to the internalizing behaviors of anxiety disorder, they found that the mother's attachment history and family interaction accounted for 60% of the variance in children's internalizing behavior, with positive marital relationships functioning as a buffer between a mother's history of insecure attachment and subsequent ineffective parenting style. The father's profile was associated with children's externalizing behaviors. In effect, by examining parental attachment styles researchers are afforded a view of three generations of interaction in examining children's adaptive and dysfunctional patterns.

Integrating Social Learning and Attachment Processes

Dadds and Barrett (1996) have argued that some aspects of attachment models of anxiety are highly consistent and complementary with the coercive operant model of parenting (Patterson, 1982; Dumas et al., 1995) that has been utilized so effectively with family conflict. Taken together, they have enormous potential to contribute to our understanding of familial aspects of anxiety problems. That is, attachment patterns and coercive operant cycles can work together to lock children into a pattern of anxiety and dependency with parents. Children who are temperamentally difficult (e.g., insecure, behaviorally inhibited, anxious) may repeatedly seek closeness and reassurance which is beyond the comfort level of the parent. Proximity and reassurance-seeking will often, in the short term, be rewarded with protection, proximity, talk, contact, and so on.

However, when the parent's tolerance levels are exceeded, the parent will be propelled, now and then, into a rejecting stance in which the child is pushed to be more independent. The research by Fox and Calkins (1993) showed how the parent's attempts to push the child away results in further stress in the child and an increase in demanding. The rejection, although it may be very temporary and mild, will reinforce the child's construction that high levels of coercive or fearful, dependent behavior are needed to regain and then maintain closeness. If the child escalates his or her fearful behavior and/or demands for nurturance, the parent is likely to acquiesce, at which point the child's escalation is reinforced by the parental attention associated with the acquiescence, and the parent's acquiescence is simultaneously reinforced by the termination of the child's demands. Under such operant circumstances, we would expect an increase in cycles of the child's fearfulness and demanding, and in the parent's rejection and acquiescence. As such cycles repeat, the more the relationship could be characterized as insecure and the more operant factors will ensure these cycles continued existence and strength. Such cycles have been eloquently described by Patterson (1982) with respect to aggression in families, but clinical observations and the above studies lead us to believe they also contribute to the development of anxiety problems early in life. The studies by Fox and Calkins (1993) and Nachmias et al. (1996) provide some very elegant demonstrations of the interplay between attachment and interactional cycles.

A model that provided a working integration of learning theory and attachment processes was the seminal but now largely ignored work of the Harlows (Harlow & Harlow, 1962). As will be recalled, they described patterns of insecure attachment and "approach–avoidance" conflicts using infant-monkey/mechanical-mother-monkey dyads in which both food and comfort, as well as aversive stimuli, were delivered via the mechanical mother. The delivery of aversive stimuli originating from the mother monkey led to increases in clinging rather than avoidance behavior, as well as anxiety and distress in the infant monkeys. Both a strength and limitation of the Harlows' research was that the mother's behavior was controlled by the experimenter and could not be shaped by the infant. In the real world, the increased clinging behavior by the infant monkey would have powerful effects on the mother. In some cases the mother would react with displeasure to the clinging and thus would increase rejecting behaviors. This would lead to increases in the likelihood of further aversive clinging behavior from the infant, thus setting up an escalating cycle into anxiety and insecurity. The parent may also try to comfort the clinging infant; if this were done consistently, the clinging might be reduced as the infant gained confidence. However, parents are only human (well, not the Harlows'). It is most likely that the parent would fluctuate between comforting and rejection according to variations in a host of factors, including the infant's behavior, the parent's mood, the quality of the parent's own adult relationships, and so on. Thus, intermittent patterns of reinforcement would be established which would strengthen the infant's demonstrations of anxiety and insecurity.

These attachment processes as described by the Harlows and others are clearly quite consistent and complementary with the learning processes that characterize troubled families, so eloquently described by Patterson and colleagues. Perhaps more exciting and scientifically useful is that the two models actually make predictions that are contradictory and can be pitted against each other in empirical tests. Rarely do the mental health sciences have the opportunity to test critical differences in theoretical predictions, because our models are lacking in specificity. For example, SLT would predict that contingent parental soothing should reinforce fear displays, and punishment of fear responses should suppress them. By contrast, AT predicts that parental soothing will facilitate the child's skills in self-soothing, leading to a decrease in future fear displays, whereas punishment of fear responses will lead to an insecure attachment and an increase in fear behavior. Both of these have received indirect empirical support (e.g., King, Hamilton, & Ollendick, 1988, and Dadds et al., 1996, for SLT; and Harlow & Harlow, 1962, for AT). This raises the exciting possibility that critical experiments could be designed to compare and contrast these predictions.

These last two points can be elaborated using a clinical example presented by Dadds (1998). Consider that common in anxious children is their insistence on sleeping with their parents. This can be a difficult behavior for parents to cope with because it often elicits conflicting responses. On the one hand, there is the desire to comfort the distressed child and allow his or her the closeness and security of the parental bed. On the other hand, parents are often aware that doing this can prevent the child from learning other more mature ways of coping with fear. A purely operant approach would specify that coming into the parental bed should not be reinforced; the child should be returned to her or his own bed and rewarded for staying there. Attachment theory specifies that the promotion of independence in the child is achieved when the child is able to take to bed a secure (cognitive) representation of the parent's support. Interestingly, most parents integrate these two approaches when they learn to deal effectively with this phase in the child's development. That is, they return the child to his or her own bed, but also communicate liberal doses of parental support and consistency ("I am just in the other room," "Daddy is here," and so on). Clearly, maturity demands, appropriately supported with sound social learning principles and the promotion of a secure model of attachment for the child, can inform optimum parental and clinical strategies.

Another example stems directly from the work of Calkins and Fox (1993) and Nachmias et al. (1996). The reader is also referred to Thompson (this volume) for a discussion of these types of parent–child interactions from an emotion regulation perspective. Consider the inhibited infant who shows a stress reaction to new people, manifested as distress and clinging to parents. Most parents when faced with this scenario alternate between attempts to soothe the child and allow him or her to remain close and comfortable, and attempts to encourage the child to explore the novelty. AT predicts the former would be the best response, allowing the child to feel secure with the parent before feeling comfortable to explore the novelty. SLT would predict this would reinforce the child's avoidance and prevent the child from learning to cope with novelty. Clearly, a parenting response that would be consistent with both models is one that allowed the child to remain proximal and comfortable but would take opportunities to encourage the child to explore without exceeding the child's comfort level and thus pushing her or him into a stress response.

Summary

The literature reviewed here indicates that three models of the development of anxiety problems, when taken together, have established explanatory power and empirical support, and lead to several practical implications for clinical prevention and treatment. These are: models of infant temperament, social learning theory (SLT) as applied to parent–child interactions, and attachment theory (AT). Figure 13.1 presents a diagrammatical representation of a model of the development of anxiety problems: an interaction of attachment and social learning processes that is hypothesized to take place against a background of behavioral and temperamental characteristics of both the parent and child.

In many senses, the theoretical elements of this model provide complementary strengths in each other's weak areas. For example, SLT suffers from its lack of emphasis on the individual differences in temperament, and the importance of the quality of intimate relationships in the developing child's life. In its purest forms, SLT takes all individuals and stimuli as potentially equal and has little to say about the biological and developmental relevance of various stimulus settings and intimate relationships. By contrast, AT correctly recognizes that particular settings may be very potent for learning fear versus courage, such as the parents' and child's first experiences of separation and reunion. Conversely, AT places little emphasis of the microprocesses that establish and maintain behaviors, or the methodologies by which these microprocesses can be examined under controlled conditions. SLT has a rich and successful history in these domains.

Theoretically, we propose that attachment processes and social learning processes, when operating with a severely inhibited or anxious child, can

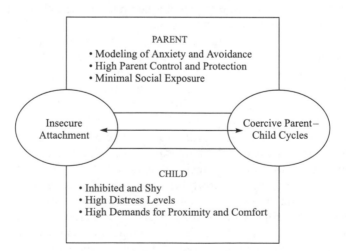

Figure 13.1. The anxious-coercive cycle: A representation of parent-child processes hypothesised to form an escalating path to anxiety problems.

become locked together in a vicious circle that may maintain and magnify anxious responding. Insecure attachments can drive a pattern of clinging and dependency that becomes self-perpetuating through the reinforcement processes described by Patterson (1982). These reinforcement patterns in turn maintain the sense of insecurity in the intimate relationship. Alternatively, parenting that balances attachment needs with encouragement to explore, and the minimization of anxious avoidance, would appear to promote the healthiest outcomes for vulnerable children.

Within this integrative model of temperament, attachment, and parent–child learning processes, recent studies of developmental pathways to problems with anxiety draw attention to the interconnectedness of child temperament, family process, and challenging situations. Infants who are easily distressed in novel situations, difficult to soothe, and form insecure–anxious attachments with caregivers, may reach extremes of behavioral inhibition in the toddler years and anxiety problems in later life. These children tend to be demanding of parental attention, eventually surpassing parental tolerance levels. In their natural efforts to manage this difficult temperamental style, parents tend to either protect their children from novel situations and people; or alternatively push their child to interact with the novel stimuli in challenging situations. Recent empirical work indicates that for behaviorally inhibited children both of these responses maintain or even exacerbate the physiological (elevated cortisol levels) and behavioral (withdrawal, distress) indices of anxiety. These family processes can prevent the child from developing competence or confidence in their own ability to cope with stress. Furthermore, the child learns to avoid situations which could provide opportunities for development of coping strategies and more realistic appraisal of threat. Insecure attachment may develop between the child and the parent, as the child's demands for soothing extend beyond the parental limits of availability. Thus, a cyclic and escalating pattern of interaction between parents leading towards insecurely attached, behaviorally inhibited children emerges which reinforces hyperattention to threat, underestimation of coping resources, and avoidance of potentially threatening situations.

Note

Please address correspondence to Mark Dadds, School of Applied Psychology, Griffith University, Mt. Gravatt Campus, Queensland 4111, Australia. E-mail: m.dadds@hbs.gu.edu.au.

References

Ainsworth, M. (1989). Attachments beyond infancy. *American Psychologist, 44,* 709–716.
Barrett, P. M., Dadds, M. R. & Rapee, R. M. (1996). Family treatment of childhood anxiety: A controlled trial. *Journal of Consulting and Clinical Psychology, 64,* 333–342.

Barrett, P. M., Rapee, R. M., Dadds, M. R., & Ryan, S. (1996). Family enhancement of cognitive styles in anxious and aggressive children: The FEAR effect. *Journal of Abnormal Child Psychology, 24,* 187–203.

Belsky, J., & Rovine, M. (1987). Temperament and attachment security in the Strange Situation: An empirical rapprochement. *Child Development, 58,* 787–795.

Bernstein, G. A., & Borchardt, C. M. (1996). School refusal: Family constellation and family functioning. *Journal of Anxiety Disorders, 10,* 1–19.

Biederman, J., Rosenbaum, J. F., Bolduc-Murphy, E. A., Faraone, S. V., Chaloff, J., Hirshfeld, D. R., & Kagan, J. (1993). A 3-year follow-up of children with and without behavioral inhibition. *Journal of the American Academy of Child and Adolescent Psychiatry, 32,* 814–821.

Bowlby, J. (1971). *Attachment and loss.* (Vol. 1, Attachment). Harmondsworth, UK: Penguin.

Bruch, M. A. (1989). Familial and developmental antecedents of social phobia: Issues and findings. *Clinical Psychology Review, 9,* 37–47.

Bruch, M. A., & Heimberg, R. G. (1994). Differences in perceptions of parental and personal characteristics between generalized and nongeneralized social phobics. *Journal of Anxiety Disorders, 8,* 155–168.

Buss, A. H., & Plomin, R. (1984). *Temperament: Early developing personality traits.* Hillsdale, NJ: Erlbaum.

Butler, G., & Mathews, A. (1983). Cognitive processes in anxiety. *Advances in Behaviour Research Therapy, 5,* 51–62.

Calkins, S., & Fox, N. (1992). The relations among infant temperament, security of attachment, and behavioral inhibition at twenty-four months. *Child Development, 63,* 1456–1472.

Carlson, E. A., & Sroufe, L. A. (1995). Contribution of attachment theory to developmental psychopathology. In D. Cicchetti & D. J. Cohen (Eds.), *Developmental psychopathology: Vol. 1. Theory and methods* (pp. 581–617). New York: Wiley.

Chorpita, B. F., & Barlow, D. H. (1998). The development of anxiety: The role of control in the early environment. *Psychological Bulletin, 124,* 3–21.

Chorpita, B. F., Albano, A. M., & Barlow, D. H. (1996). Cognitive processing in children: Relation to anxiety and family influences. *Journal of Clinical Child Psychology, 25,* 170–176.

Chorpita, B. F., Brown, T. A., Albano, A. M., & Barlow, D. H. (1996). *The Influence of Parenting Style on Psychological Vulnerability for the Development of Anxiety Disorders.* New York: Association for Advancement of Behavior Therapy.

Clark, D. M. (1986). Cognitive therapy for anxiety. *Behavioural Psychotherapy, 14,* 283–294.

Cobham, V. E., Dadds, M. R., & Spence, S. H. (1999). Anxious children and their parents: What do they expect? *Journal of Clinical Child Psychology, 28,* 220–231.

Cowan, P. A., Cohn, D. A., Pape-Cowan, C. P., & Pearson, J. L. (1996) Parents' attachment histories and children's externalizing and internalizing behaviors. *Journal of Consulting and Clinical Psychology, 64,* 53–63.

Dadds, M. R. (1998, February). Learning and intimacy in the families of anxious children. Paper presented at the 30th Conference on Behavioural Science, Banff, Canada.

Dadds, M. R., & Barrett, P. M. (1996). Family process in childhood anxiety and depression. *Behaviour Change, 13,* 231–239.

Dadds, M. R., & Powell, M. B. (1991). The relationship of interparental conflict and marital adjustment to aggression, anxiety and immaturity in aggressive and nonclinic children. *Journal of Abnormal Child Psychology, 19,* 553–567.

Dadds, M. R., Barrett, P. M., Rapee, R. M., & Ryan, S. (1996). Family process and child anxiety and aggression: An observational analysis. *Journal of Abnormal Child Psychology, 24,* 715–734.

Dadds, M. R., Bovbjerg, D., Redd, W. H., & Cutmore, T. H. (1997). Imagery and human classical conditioning. *Psychological Bulletin, 122,* 89–103.

Dadds, M. R., Rapee, R. M., & Barrett, P. M. (1994). Behavioral observation. In T. H. Ollendick, N. J. King, & W. Yule (Eds.), *International handbook of phobic and anxiety disorders in children and adolescents* (pp. 349–364). New York: Plenum.

Daniels, D., & Plomin, R. (1985). Origins of individual differences in infant shyness. *Developmental Psychology, 21,* 118–121.

Davey, G. C. L. (1992). Classical conditioning and the acquisition of human fears and phobias: A review and synthesis of the literature. *Advances in Behaviour Research and Therapy, 14,* 29–66.

Davey, G. C. L. (1994). Self-reported fears to common indigenous animals in an adult UK population: The role of disgust sensitivity. *British Journal of Psychology, 85,* 541–554.

DeKlyen, M. (1996). Disruptive behavior disorder and intergenerational attachment patterns. *Journal of Consulting and Clinical Psychology, 64,* 357–365.

Dumas, J. E., LaFreniere, P. J., & Serketich, W. J. (1995). "Balance of power": A transactional analysis of control in mother–child dyads involving socially competent, aggressive, and anxious children. *Journal of Abnormal Psychology, 104,* 104–113.

Faraone, S., Chen, W., Warburton, R., Biederman, J., Milberger, S., & Tsuang, M. (1995). Genetic heterogeneity in attention deficit hyperactivity disorder: Gender, psychiatric comorbidity and maternal ADHD. *Journal of Abnormal Psychology, 104,* 334–345.

Fox, N. A., & Calkins, S. D. (1993). Social withdrawal: Interactions among temperament, attachment, and regulation. In K. H. Rubin & J. B. Asendorph (Eds.), *Social withdrawal, inhibition and shyness in childhood* (pp. 81–100). Hillsdale, NJ: Erlbaum.

Gest, S. D. (1997). Behavioral inhibition: Stability and associations with adaptation from childhood to early adulthood. *Journal of Personality and Social Psychology, 72,* 467–475.

Goldsmith, H. H., & Alansky, J. A. (1987). Maternal and infant temperamental predictors of attachment: A meta-analytic review. *Journal of Consulting and Clinical Psychology, 55,* 805–816.

Gottman, J. M. (1980). Analyzing for sequential connection and assessing interobserver reliability for the sequential analysis of observational data. *Behavioral Assessment, 2,* 361–368.

Gray, J. A. (1982). *The neuropsychology of anxiety.* NH: Oxford University Press.

Green, S. M., Loeber, R., & Lahey, B. B. (1992). Child psychopathology and deviant family hierarchies. *Journal of Child and Family Studies, 1,* 341–350.

Harlow, H. F., & Harlow, M. (1962). Social deprivation in monkeys. *Scientific American, 207,* 136–146.

Haley, J. (1976). *Problem-solving therapy.* San Francisco: Jossey-Bass.

Hetherington, E. M., & Martin, B. (1979). Family interaction. In H. C. Quay & J. S. Werry (Eds.), *Psychopathological disorders of childhood* (pp. 30–82). New York: Wiley.

Hirshfeld, D. R., Biederman, J., Brody, L., Faraone, S. V., & Rosenbaum, J. F. (1997a). Associations between expressed emotion and child behavioral inhibition and psychopathology: A pilot study. *Journal of the American Academy of Child and Adolescent Psychiatry, 36*, 205–213.

Hirshfeld, D. R., Biederman, J., Brody, L., Faraone, S. V., & Rosenbaum, J. F. (1997b). Expressed emotion toward children with behavioral inhibition: Associations with maternal anxiety disorder. *Journal of the American Academy of Child and Adolescent Psychiatry, 36*, 910–917.

Kagan, J. (1997). Temperament and the reactions to unfamiliarity. *Child Development, 68*, 139–143.

Kagan, J., Resnick, J. S., Clarke, C. S., & Garcia-Coll, C. (1984). Behavioral inhibition to the unfamiliar. *Child Development, 55*, 2212–2225.

Kagan, J., Reznick, J. S., & Snidman, N. (1988). Biological bases of childhood shyness. *Science, 240*, 167–171.

King, N. J., Hamilton, D. J., & Ollendick, T. H. (1988). *Children's phobias: A behavioural perspective.* Chichester, England: Wiley.

Krohne, H. W., & Hock, M. (1991). Relationships between restrictive mother–child interactions and anxiety of the child. *Anxiety Research, 4*, 109–124.

Krohne, H. W., & Hock, M. (1993). Coping dispositions, actual anxiety, and the incidental learning of success- and failure-related stimuli. *Personality and Individual Differences, 15*, 33–41.

LaFreniere, P. J., & Capuano, F. (1997). Preventive intervention as a means of clarifying direction of effects in socialization: Anxious–withdrawn preschoolers case. *Development and Psychopathology, 9*, 551–564.

Magana, A. B., Goldstein, M. J., Karno, M., Kiklowitz, D. J., Jenkins, J., & Falloon, I. R. H. (1986). A brief method for assessing expressed emotion in relatives of psychiatric patients. *Psychiatry Research, 17*, 203–212.

Main, M. (1996). Overview of the field of attachment. *Journal of Consulting and Clinical Psychology, 64*, 237–243.

Mills, R. S., & Rubin, K. H. (1990). Parental beliefs about problematic social behaviors in early childhood. *Child-Development, 61*, 138–151.

Minuchin, S. (1974). *Families and family therapy.* Cambridge, MA: Harvard University Press.

Nachmias, M, Gunnar, M., Mangelsdorf, S., Parritz, R. H., & Buss, K. (1996). Behavioral inhibition and stress reactivity: The moderating role of attachment security. *Child Development, 67*, 508–522.

Parker, J. G., Rubin, K. H., Price, J. M., & DeRosier, M. E. (1995). Peer relationships, child development, and adjustment: A developmental psychopathology perspective. In D. Cicchetti & D. J. Cohen (Eds.), *Developmental psychopathology: Vol. 2: Risk, disorder, and adaptation* (pp. 96–161). NY: John Wiley.

Patterson, G. R. (1982). *Coercive family process.* Eugene, OR: Castalia Press.

Rapee, R. M. (1997). Potential role of childrearing practices in the development of anxiety and depression. *Clinical Psychology Review, 17*, 47–67.

Rosenbaum, J. F., Biederman, J., Hirschfeld, D. R., Bolduc, E. A., & Chaloff, J. (1991). Behavioural inhibition in children: A possible precursor to panic disorder or social phobia. *Journal of Clinical Psychiatry, 52*, 5–9.

Rosenbaum, M., & Ronen, T. (1997). Parents' and children's appraisals of each other's anxiety while facing a common threat. *Journal of Clinical Child Psychology, 26,* 43–52.

Rosenstein, D. S., & Horowitz, H. A. (1996). Adolescent attachment and psychopathology. *Journal of Consulting and Clinical Psychology, 64,* 244–253.

Solyom, L., Silberfeld, M., & Solyom, C. (1976). Maternal overprotection in the etiology of agoraphobia. *Canadian Psychiatric Association Journal, 21,* 109–113.

Sroufe, L. A. (1990). Considering normal and abnormal together: The essence of developmental psychopathology. *Development and Psychopathology, 2,* 335–347.

Stark, K. D., Humphrey, L. L., Crook, K., & Lewis, K. (1990). Perceived family environments of depressed and anxious children. *Journal of Abnormal Child Psychology, 18,* 527–548.

Steele, R. G., Tripp, G., Kotchick, B. A., Summers, P., & Forehand, R. (1997). Family members' uncertainty about parental chronic illness: The relationship of hemophilia and HIV infection to child functioning. *Journal of Pediatric Psychology, 22,* 577–591.

Stubbe, D. E., Zahner, G. E. P., Goldstein, M. J., & Leckman, J. F. (1993). Diagnostic specificity of a brief measure of expressed emotion: A community study of children. *Journal of Child Psychology and Psychiatry, 34,* 139–154.

Van Ijzendoorn, M. H., & Bakermans-Kranenburg, M. J. (1996). Attachment representations in mothers, fathers, adolescents and children: A meta-analytic search for normative data. *Journal of Consulting and Clinical Psychology, 64,* 8–21.

Warren, S. I., Huston, L., Egeland, B., & Sroufe, L. A. (1997). Child and adolescent anxiety disorders and early attachment. *Journal of the American Academy of Child and Adolescent Psychiatry, 36,* 637–644.

Weller, R. A., Kapadia, P., Weller, E. B., Fristad, M., Lazaroff, C., & Preskorn, S. (1994). Psychopathology in families of children with major depressive disorders. *Journal of Affective Disorders, 31,* 247–252.

14

Current Issues in the Treatment of Childhood Anxiety

PAULA BARRETT

Early approaches to the treatment of childhood anxiety used techniques and processes from adult treatment models, derived from adult-based theories, with terminology adapted for a youth population. More recently, however, there has been a growing recognition of the need to consider developmental factors as they relate to the etiology, assessment, and treatment of various childhood disorders. Given the potential for anxiety problems to occur across the lifespan (see Weiss and Last, this volume), as well as the emerging links between childhood anxiety disorders and psychological disorder later in life, the application of a developmental perspective in the treatment of childhood anxiety seems warranted.

The aim of the current chapter is to examine the relevance of developmental factors to the treatment of childhood anxiety, and in so doing to argue for their consideration and inclusion in future clinical research and practice. A brief review of treatment literature currently existing in the child and adolescent anxiety field is included, as is a discussion of various issues related to treatment design and implementation that are linked either directly or indirectly to developmental themes.

Historically, literature addressing the treatment of anxiety in children has been scarce. At the beginning of the century some individual case studies that employed traditional psychodynamic frameworks were reported (see Barrios & O'Dell, 1989, for a review). However, descriptions of treatment components were vague and studies lacked procedures for evaluating clinical effectiveness. The acquisition of specific fears by children was dealt with by the early behavioral schools, who mainly invoked conditioning mechanisms (Harris, 1979; Watson & Rayner, 1920). Relatively little attention was allocated to the treatment of anxiety problems in children, as these were considered rare in comparison with the externalizing problems which were more salient and disruptive for families and educators. Hence, as recently as the late 1970s, research regarding the treatment of childhood anxiety consisted of a handful of single case studies examining specific fears (e.g., Jones, 1924a; 1924b).

It appears that the major classification changes that appeared in the third edition of the *Diagnostic and Statistical Manual of Mental Disorders*

(DSM-III) in 1980 were responsible in part for spurring widespread interest in the treatment of anxious children and adolescents (Last, 1992). At that time, a new diagnostic category was introduced that specifically focused on anxiety disorders in childhood and adolescence, and treatment studies have become a major research focus since 1980. While this focus has led to the development of a number of systematic, controlled treatment trials, there is still much to be learned about what works and how best to apply it in real-life settings.

The next section presents a brief review of studies that have evaluated currently available treatments for childhood anxiety. Later discussion relates specifically to how these studies have addressed, or failed to address, some major developmental and methodological issues. The studies reviewed in the current chapter focus on psychological interventions only. Readers interested in a review of psychopharmacological interventions for childhood anxiety problems are referred to Bernstein (1994).

Evaluation of Treatments for Generalized Anxiety Problems

The few randomized controlled studies in the area of childhood anxiety have mainly evaluated cognitive–behavioral techniques—in particular, education about the nature of anxiety, cognitive restructuring, and behavioral exposure (e.g., Albano, Chorpita & Barlow, 1996; Kendall, 1994; Ollendick & King, 1994).

Kendall (1994) examined the effectiveness of an individualized 16-session cognitive–behavioral therapy program for children with overanxious, separation, or social anxiety problems. The main focus of treatment was the child's development of a "FEAR" plan: F for feeling frightened and learning to recognize the physiological symptoms of anxiety; E for expecting good versus bad things to happen, using positive self talk; A for approaching actions to take in the face of fear; and R for results and rewards, evaluating performance and utilizing self-reinforcement. The results showed that at the end of treatment 64% of treated children, compared with 5% of the waiting-list control group, did not meet diagnostic criteria for an anxiety disorder. These clinically significant gains were maintained at 12 months and 3 years follow-up (Kendall & Southam-Gerow, 1996).

Kendall and colleagues later replicated and extended the original study with a sample of 94 youths (aged 9–13 years) diagnosed with adjustment disorder, overanxious disorder, or separation-anxiety disorder (Kendall et al., 1997). Participants again received an individualized 16-session cognitive–behavioral intervention. Results supported the first trial, with over 50% of treated children free from their diagnosed anxiety disorder at post-treatment assessment. For those cases in which the primary diagnosis remained, analyses showed significant reductions in severity scores. Maintenance of gains were evident at 1-year follow-up.

These pioneering, randomized treatment trials demonstrated the efficacy and potential of individualized cognitive–behavioral treatments in helping children overcome anxiety disorders. However, the studies also raised the question of whether these results could be improved if the treatment intervention was modified to consider the role of the family. Barrett, Dadds, and Rapee (1996) conducted individualized CBT interventions with 79 children aged 7–14 years who fulfilled the diagnostic criteria for separation anxiety, overanxious disorder, or social phobia. The children were allocated randomly to one of three treatment conditions: cognitive–behavioral therapy (CBT); CBT plus family anxiety management (CBT + FAM); and waiting list. The Family Anxiety Management (FAM) component was administered in parallel with the CBT condition, and included training in child management, parental anxiety management, and communication and problem-solving skills.

The effectiveness of the interventions was evaluated at immediately after treatment and at 6- and 12-month follow-ups. The results indicated that, across treatment conditions, 69.8% of children no longer met diagnostic criteria for an anxiety disorder. The results at 12-month follow-up indicated ongoing improvements, with 70.3% of the children in the CBT group and 95.6% of those in the CBT + FAM group no longer meeting diagnostic criteria. Barrett (1998) and Cobham, Dadds, and Spence (1999; see below) replicated these results with group-based treatments, indicating that CBT interventions for childhood anxiety disorders can be administered effectively in a group format.

Barrett, Dadds, et al. (1996) conducted additional analyses in order to examine age effects. Participants were divided into groups of younger children (7–10 years) and adolescents (11–14 years). Younger children had significantly higher rates of diagnosis-free participants after treatment (100%) in the CBT + FAM condition in comparison with the CBT condition (55.6%). Older children did not show significant differences across treatment conditions (60% for both CBT and CBT + FAM). These results suggest that, for some children, family plays an important role in the treatment of childhood anxiety disorders. However, additional research is required to determine which children would benefit most from the inclusion of family elements in treatment.

The literature has shown that parents of anxious children are more likely than parents of nonanxious children to themselves meet criteria for an anxiety diagnosis (Last, Hersen, Kazdin, Francis & Grubb, 1987), and that such parents play a role in the maintenance of childhood anxiety (Rapee, 1997). Therefore, it would seem reasonable to conclude that children with an anxious parent would benefit more from a CBT + FAM intervention than children with a nonanxious parent. However, the Family Anxiety Management program discussed above included three active treatment strategies. In an effort to evaluate the effectiveness of the individual strategies, Cobham et al. (1999) incorporated only the parental anxiety management (PAM) component into their research. They therefore sought to investigate (a) the role of parental anxiety as a moderator of outcome in the treatment of childhood anxiety, and (b) whether parental anxiety management is more beneficial for anxious children with an anxious parent, compared with anxious children whose parents are not anxious. Sixty-seven anxious children (aged 7–14 years) and their families were assigned to treatment groups according to parental anxiety level. Within these groups, children were assigned randomly to one of two treatment conditions: child-focused CBT (CBT) or child-focused CBT plus parental anxiety management (CBT + PAM). Immediately after treatment, results indicated that, within the child-anxiety-only group, 82.4% of children in the CBT and 80% of children in the CBT + PAM condition no longer met criteria for an anxiety disorder. Within the child-plus-parent anxiety group, 38.9% of children in the CBT condition no longer met diagnostic criteria, compared with 76.5% of children in the CBT + PAM condition. These results suggest that children with one or more anxious parent(s) responded less favorably to child-focused CBT that did children whose parents were both nonanxious. However, the provision of a PAM component significantly enhanced the efficacy of child-focused CBT for children with one or more anxious parent(s). This was not the case for children with nonanxious parents. While additional age analyses were conducted, there were few significant findings. A greater percentage of older children (11–14 years) were diagnosis-free in the CBT-only condition (85.7%) than in the CBT + PAM condition (20.0%). No other age effects were found. While this finding is somewhat supportive of the age differences found in the Barrett, Dadds et al. (1996) study, there is clearly a need for further research on age factors and developmental differences to treatment interventions.

Despite the somewhat ambiguous findings related to age, in combination, the results of the Barrett et al. and Cobham et al. studies suggest that the family may play an important role in the treatment of anxiety disorders in some children. However, these findings are in need of replication if the inclusion of family elements in treatment are to be optimized. In addition, long-term follow-up must be implemented in order to establish maintenance effects.

The literature outlined above illustrates that CBT treatments for childhood anxiety have been extended from an individualized intervention to include family treatment models (via the inclusion of parenting and child management skills, parental anxiety management skills, and family cognitive techniques) and peer learning via group interventions. The effectiveness of CBT treatments (individual, family, and group) for childhood anxiety has been demonstrated up to 4 years follow-up, for children aged 7–14 years.

Many of the treatment trials reviewed above excluded children with comorbid diagnoses (except perhaps a comorbid anxiety disorder). However, comorbid diagnoses are extremely common in anxious children. Referral bias may be one reason for the high rates of comorbidity seen among clinical populations, in that the more severe disorders may also be more highly comorbid or comorbidity may increase the probability of referral. However, the rates in the general population are not insignificant, indicating levels of comorbidity of around 40% in preadolescent anxiety disorders and 35% in adolescent anxiety disorders (Anderson, 1994). Therefore, treatment research that takes account of comorbidity is vital. For example, younger anxious children frequently present with the additional complaints of social withdrawal and isolation, and/or behavior problems; school-age children with behavior problems and ADHD; adolescents with depression and substance abuse. If we are to claim that we can treat anxiety disorders successfully in children and adolescents, we can no longer ignore the patterns of comorbidity that exist across the lifespan.

Treatment of Specific Disorders

The fact that comorbidity of anxiety disorders is very high amongst children (Rapee, Barrett, Dadds, & Evans, 1994) means that it is not known which aspects of treatment are most effective for which particular disorder. In an effort to overcome this, some studies have applied cognitive–behavioral principles to the treatment of specific anxiety disorders, using the primary diagnosis as their target in most cases.

Obsessive–Compulsive Disorder

Unfortunately, little is known with respect to treatment of childhood obsessive–compulsive disorder (OCD), which is currently considered a form of anxiety disorder both in children and adults. Some single case studies and uncontrolled trials have been published, but only one systematic assessment or treatment protocol has been evaluated (March, Mulle, & Herbel, 1994). In the most recent randomized clinical trial of childhood OCD treatment available, three main comparisons were evaluated: (1) cognitive–behavior therapy (CBT; exposure and response prevention) was compared to anxiety management training (AMT); (2) a daily/intensive course of CBT was compared to a weekly/standard schedule; and (3) CBT alone was compared to CBT plus medication (Franklin et al., 1998). Owing to the small size of the sample (14 children, aged 10–17 years), conclusions made about the relative merit of each of the approaches described above must be interpreted with caution. The study found that for all participants who received CBT, the mean ratings of OCD symptomatology had reduced by 67% immediately after treatment, and by 62% at 9-month follow-up. Results from the study tended to indicate that exposure and response prevention were the key ingredients of therapy, with neither of the added components of medication or anxiety management adding advantage to CBT alone. Furthermore, standard weekly sessions were found to be as effective as intensive daily sessions. About this finding the authors themselves speculate that intensive, daily sessions may be of most benefit to severe cases of OCD, whereas all cases involved in their study were of moderate severity. Further randomized-controlled studies of childhood

OCD treatment, which involve a larger number of participants of various ages, are sorely needed.

There are many developmental issues yet to be addressed by the childhood OCD literature. In terms of the components of childhood OCD treatment, those presently described seem to use cognitive–behavioral techniques parallel to the ones developed for OCD in adults (Salkovskis, 1996). As with other forms of anxiety disorders in children, no theoretical framework has yet been developed to explain the etiology and maintenance of this severe disorder, nor have the common and distinct features of childhood OCD in relation to other forms of childhood anxiety disorders been investigated. In conclusion, clinicians and researchers appear generally unclear about the nature of childhood OCD; sometimes conceptualized as a more serious anxiety problem—at the extreme end of the anxiety spectrum—and at other times considered a markedly different phenomenon.

School Refusal and Social Phobia

Blagg and Yule (1984) report an exposure-based treatment study dealing exclusively with anxiety-based school phobia. A treatment series of 30 cases (10–16 year olds) were employed to compare outcome for three treatment conditions: (1) a behavioral approach centered around an immediate return to school; (2) inpatient hospitalization; and (3) individualized psychotherapy plus home tutoring. Results revealed that 93% of the behavioral group returned to school. This contrasted with similar improvements in only 38% of the hospitalized group and only 10% of the home-tutored group. Moreover, children in the behavioral group took an average of 2 weeks to treat, compared with 45 weeks and 72 weeks, respectively, for the hospitalized and home-tutored groups.

King et al. (1998) developed and evaluated the efficacy of a 4-week cognitive–behavioral treatment involving children, teachers, and parents. Outcome measures indicated that, relative to waiting-list controls, children in the active condition improved in school attendance, emotional coping, reports of fear and anxiety, and clinician ratings of global functioning. Parent and teacher reports on children's behavior corroborated the improvements, immediately after treatment and at 3-month follow-up.

Last, Hansen, and Franco (1998) reported a randomized cognitive–behavioral treatment study, this time for children and adolescents with social phobia and school refusal. Fifty-six children were assigned randomly to CBT or an attention–placebo control condition consisting of educational and supportive group therapy. Results showed that the attention–placebo condition was as effective as standard group CBT treatment. Parents and children were involved in assessments before and after treatment, but only the children participated in treatment sessions. Outcome measures included self-reported anxiety and depression, diagnostic status (60–70% children were diagnosis-free at the end of treatment), and school attendance rates.

Recent research with childhood social phobia (Spence, Donovan, & Brechman-Toussaint, 1999) suggests that these children (aged 7–14 years) tend to have expectations of poor performance in social-evaluation situations. In addition, they typically demonstrate anticipation of negative outcomes from such situations, and poor self-appraisal of performance. This valuable study, investigating cognitive and interpersonal characteristics of children with social phobia, indicates specific deficits that should be addressed when clinicians design and evaluate future treatment programs for this disorder.

Specific Phobias

As with other anxiety disorders, early treatment studies for specific phobias focused upon single-case experimental designs, typically employing cognitive–behavioral approaches. Giebenhain and O'Dell (1984) developed a parent training manual for treatment of phobia of the dark that integrated coping self-statements, desensitization, and reinforcement procedures. Using a multiple baseline design with fear measures reported by children, substantial gains were achieved and maintained at 1-year follow-up. Similarly, Graziano, Mooney, and Ignasiak (1979) used cognitive-behavioral strategies with 7 children presenting with severe nighttime fears. Techniques included relaxation training, imagery, token reinforcements implemented by parents, and self-control instructions. Within 19 weeks, all children had achieved 10 consecutive fearless nights.

Heard, Dadds, and Conrad (1992) evaluated a cognitive–behavioral treatment package for simple phobias in children using a multiple baseline design across subjects. The participants were three girls aged 12–15 years presenting with a principal DSM-III-R diagnosis of Simple Phobia. Therapy involved the construction of fear hierarchies for *in vivo* exposure, with cognitive restructuring and the application of previously rehearsed relaxation and breathing retraining techniques. Concurrently, home contingency management of phobic behaviors by parents was also undertaken. Results show marked improvement (at the end of treatment and at 3-month follow-up) in anxiety symptoms for all three adolescents, both at overt-behavioral and cognitive levels, with no negative effects on family and dyadic adjustment.

Muris and colleagues conducted a series of studies examining the efficacy of EMDR for the treatment of spider phobia. In the first trial, spider phobia was examined and treated in 22 girls aged 9–14 years (de Jong, Andrea, & Muris, 1997). All children were treated individually, and treatment consisted of $1\frac{1}{2}$ hours of eye-movement desensitization and reprocessing, and $1\frac{1}{2}$ hours of *in vivo* exposure. While significant differences were obtained on the Spider Phobia Questionnaire for Children before and after treatment, the study unfortunately did not examine the changes in self-report after each treatment condition. Consequently, it could not be determined which component of the treatment was most successful.

In a second study, 26 spider-phobic girls aged 8–16 years were treated in two phases (Muris, Merckelbach, Holdrinet, & Sijsenaar, 1998). During the first phase ($2\frac{1}{2}$ hours), children were randomly assigned to either (a) an EMDR group ($n = 9$), (b) an exposure *in vivo* group ($n = 9$), or (c) a computerized exposure (control) group ($n = 8$). During the second phase, all groups received a $1\frac{1}{2}$-hour session of *in vivo* exposure. Therapy outcome measures included self-reported fear and behavioral avoidance tests. Results indicated that the first-phase *in vivo* exposure session produced significant improvement on all outcome measures. In contrast, EMDR yielded a significant improvement only on self-reported spider fear. Computerized exposure produced nonsignificant improvement. No evidence was found to suggest that EMDR potentiates the efficacy of a subsequent *in vivo* exposure treatment. The authors concluded that *in vivo* exposure remains as the treatment of choice for childhood spider (specific) phobia.

Panic Disorder

Despite advances in understanding the phenomenology of panic disorder and its treatment in adults, little is known about these disorders or their treatment in children and adolescents. Although cognitive and cognitive–behavioral techniques have been shown to be effective in the treatment of adults (e.g., Barlow, Brown, Craske, Rapee, & Anthony, 1991), only one study examining treatment efficacy with children and adolescents could be found (Ollendick, 1995). A multiple-baseline across-subjects design was employed in the treatment of four adolescents aged 13–17 years with Panic Disorder with Agoraphobia (PDAG). Treatment combined information with cognitive–behavioral strategies such as relaxation, breathing retraining, positive self-statements, cognitive coping procedures, and *in vivo* exposure. In these subjects, attacks were eliminated, agoraphobic avoidance was reduced, and self-efficacy for coping with future panic attacks was enhanced as a result of treatment, the effects of which were maintained at 6-month follow-up.

Although the studies reviewed above indicate that cognitive–behavioral strategies can be effective for reducing symptoms of phobia and panic in children and adolescents, the treatments and assessment strategies were all drawn from outcome studies conducted with adults. If these disorders are phenomenologically different in children, as suggested by some (e.g., Abelson & Alessi, 1992; Nelles & Barlow, 1988), then considerable work remains to be done.

General Developmental Issues

The majority of the standardized clinical interventions for childhood anxiety have developed from CBT models of adult anxiety (Ollendick & King, 1998) that are "downloaded" on the implicit assumptions that: (a) children are little adults; (b) children at all stages of development will have their needs met with a single treatment approach; and (c) all children respond equally to treatment, independently of cultural background. By regarding children as "little adults," we may be failing to adjust our vocabulary to the child's level of comprehension. Very little work has been undertaken to map out the lexicon children use at various developmental stages to talk about fear and anxiety, or the cognitive strategies that are used to manage these emotions. Protocols are typically written using the vocabulary we use to communicate with adult clients or even fellow psychologists. A further concern is the implicit dependence upon intrapsychic or individualistic models of treatment that may be applicable to adult patients seen in clinical settings. As children are heavily dependent upon their immediate family and peer environment, a better model of treatment may be one founded on interpersonal and systemic factors (see Dadds & Roth, this volume, for a discussion of family factors), and which aims to implement interventions at social rather than individual levels.

Children at different stages of development are unlikely to have their needs addressed adequately by a single treatment approach. Many of the existing CBT assessment and intervention protocols do not explicitly allow for variations in children's ability to understand self and other's emotional states, regulate their own behavior, and engage in metacognition (i.e., think about their own thinking). We know from the developmental literature that these abilities are usually fully developed only in late childhood (Hergenhahn & Olson, 1997). While young adolescents (11–14 years) should possess these skills, it is less likely that younger children (e.g., 5 or 6 years) will. This latter age thus becomes a cutoff below which the child-focused CBT model could not be expected to work without some significant modification. For example, children of 7–8 years would require much more of an emphasis upon behavioral conditioning, such as reinforcement principles, than on intrinsically motivated cognitive techniques.

Similarly, the importance of including broader systems in treatment varies with age. In the Barrett, Dadds et al. (1996) study, children aged 7–10 years received great benefit from an adjunctive family component (FAM) that was added to the standard CBT intervention. No such benefit was found for young adolescents (11–14 years) who did equally well in the CBT and CBT + FAM condition. In fact, in the Cobham et al. (1999) study, adolescents benefited more from the individual CBT condition than the CBT + PAM (parental anxiety management) condition. It is therefore possible that a CBT-alone intervention, with its reliance upon cognitive skill development, is more appropriate for adolescents than for children. Children may require the addition of a family intervention in order to assist them fully to understand the treatment elements. Alternatively, it is possible some children in middle childhood have already developed sufficient cognitive skills for the CBT treatment to work, while others have not. Further research is required to address these issues.

The call to acknowledge developmental issues in the conceptualization of childhood psychological disorders is not new. However, the impact of this call has been slow to filter down to the treatment literature, especially with regard to anxiety. Examination of common developmental pathways gives insight into potential vulnerabilities, limitations, and windows of opportunity for intervention that exist as a function of developmental stage.

Developmental Guidelines for Treatment

It is now recognized that some antecedents of problematic anxiety are evident from soon after birth. Temperamental factors, such as the characteristics of behavioral inhibition, are thought to bear the risk of future anxiety problems. (See Lonigan & Phillips, this volume, for a detailed account of temperamental influences on anxiety.) Where these temperamental factors are placed in a context of insecure attachment to the primary caregiver, this risk is heightened (Fox & Calkins, 1993). However, treatment research has been slow to incorporate these recent developments, and temperament and attachment should become the focus of future research attention. Given the current reliance of CBT interventions on self-regulatory and metacognitive skills in the child, early interventions (whereby "early" is defined as early in the child's life) need to be geared primarily towards parents and major parental support systems (e.g., grandparents, relevant community services). Such programs could, for example, present specific strategies that help caregivers promote the positive exposure of behaviorally inhibited, sensitive young children to a variety of social interactions, as well as facilitate the acquisition of skills pertinent to the development of healthy child/caregiver attachment patterns. In the light of research linking the maintenance of childhood anxiety to family interaction variables (Barrett, Rapee, Dadds, & Ryan, 1996), and given the growing emphasis on preventative and early intervention models (Spence, 1994), the evaluation of these type of interventions should be a research priority.

However, the feasibility of mounting interventions at early stages of development presents a number of practical problems. These include the costs and time involved in mounting accurate and nonstigmatizing identification, assessment, and recruitment, as well as the challenge of trying to devise programs that are relevant to parents and thus able to compete for commitment with the many demands of early parenthood. Moreover, infancy-based intervention may often prove unnecessary, as we know that many children who demonstrate behavioral inhibition do not necessarily develop anxiety disorders. Indeed, to imply to families that a sure relationship exists between early temperament and attachment problems and later anxiety problems may have negative effects on parental expectations.

It is important here to note that many forms of anxiety experienced in childhood are in fact adaptive and necessary for normal development. Spence (1994) states that part of children's development is the acquisition of control over their fears. This includes learning to discriminate dangerous from neutral situations or stimuli, thereby learning when it is appropriate to be afraid and to avoid; developing appropriate avoidance procedures to deal effectively with threatening stimuli; and learning to cope with aversive situations that may be necessary or unavoidable (see Thompson, this volume). The accumulation of these skills is vital for the development of normal, everyday functioning in human beings. As is recognized by any diagnostic system, anxiety ceases to be adaptive when it is out of proportion to the threat posed and when it significantly interferes with, rather than aids, normal activities.

During early childhood, problematic anxiety is more commonly manifested as fear of separation from a familiar caregiver or environment, or as a fear of novel objects or situations. Because of the limitations in their cognitive development, young children typically express their anxiety through behavior, and the difficulties of working at a cognitive level with children have been noted. The most logical starting point for designing treatment of early childhood anxiety would seem, therefore, to be the application of a behavioral skills development approach that includes a strong familial focus. However, the validity of this approach remains untested because, to the present time, relatively little attention has been paid to early childhood interventions for anxiety.

As noted, most childhood anxiety treatments currently available are designed for children in middle childhood (7 years and beyond). The problem behaviors exhibited by children of this age begin to impact significantly beyond the family sphere (e.g., at school, with peers), such that they are open to the attention of caregivers and observers outside of the home. Fears during this period tend to be more generalized than in earlier childhood, and a growing awareness of others' thoughts and motivations leads to the beginnings of socially based concerns. With regards to treatment, the predominance of protocols designed for this age group suggests that it is an opportune developmental stage for intervention. Certainly there are practical benefits to working with those in middle childhood, as opposed to adolescents for example. Primary-school children tend to be more amenable to treatment; it is usually easier to engage their parents; and school or community-based interventions are more easily implemented. Yet, as illustrated in the review of treatment research, even in this comparatively well-researched age stratum, new and arguably better approaches to anxiety treatment are still being proposed. For example, cognitive–behavioral techniques have been found effective (Kendall, 1994), and the inclusion of a parental component has been demonstrated to add to this effectiveness (Barrett, Dadds et al., 1996; Barrett, Rapee et al., 1996). In addition, the value of school- and peer-based interventions are only beginning to emerge (e.g., Barrett, 1998). Hence, the refinement of anxiety treatments directed at middle childhood is by no means complete.

Compared with middle childhood, treatments designed specifically for older adolescents are sparse. This is in spite of the fact that adolescence is a period of particular vulnerability to anxiety and comorbid disorders. During this period of development, young people become more capable of abstract cognitive reasoning, the peer group replaces the family as the dominant sphere of influence, and interpersonal issues become paramount. The impact of these developments can be seen in the types of fears reported by adolescents: fear of negative evaluation, fear about the future, and anxiety about existential and broader social issues. Furthermore, the patterns of anxious and avoidant behavior that are established in adolescence serve as powerful precursors to adult anxiety. The difficulty in providing developmentally appropriate treatments specifically for adolescence is compounded by the reluctance of teenagers to report their problem anxiety, for the very reason that it may expose them to negative evaluation from peers. Yet it is important that researchers and clinicians endeavor to overcome these obstacles as there is a marked need for anxiety treatment programs aimed at this age group.

Although it may be argued that some of the extant empirically supported treatment programs have demonstrated success in treating adolescent anxiety (e.g., Kendall, 1994), these programs were administered individually, and therefore did not take into account the very powerful influence of the peer group. Indeed, CBT is no more effective for adolescents than for children. Consequently, there is significant room for improvement in terms of treatment efficacy and effectiveness. The need therefore remains for the development of treatment protocols that are administered in a setting relevant to the adolescent (e.g., at school, with peers), and that focuses specifically upon many of the fears commonly expressed by this age group (e.g., fear of negative evaluation and social anxieties). In addition, the treatment protocols need to be examined with respect to their social validity. Do the adolescent's themselves find the intervention to be helpful and rewarding? Perhaps when such peer-based interventions are evaluated, we will find that treatment effectiveness increases beyond 60%. The elevated risk of comorbid depression and substance abuse that exists within adolescence only adds to the urgency for developmentally specific interventions to be tested.

In short, many differences between child and adult anxiety are now commonly acknowledged, with the result that those involved in treatment design and application have recognized the desirability of child-focused approaches. Less recognized, or at least less acted upon however, have been the developmental variations associated within different stages of childhood and adolescence. The utility of applying a similar treatment template to children and youth of all ages is arguably as ineffectual as employing a blanket adult-based approach. The adaptation and shaping of treatment protocols for various age strata should, therefore, be a continuing process.

Issues and Limitations Arising from Treatment Research

The aim of the present section is to discuss in broader terms some of the methodological issues in need of consideration when conducting treatment research in the field of child and adolescent anxiety.

Issues of Assessment

An aspect of assessment that has been the subject of much debate, and which relates directly to the selection of individuals for participation in anxiety treatment programs, is that of cross-informant consistency. An excellent meta-analytic review of informant-dependent information was conducted by Achenbach, McConaughy, and Howell (1987). Articles included in this review spanned the period from 1967 to 1985, and detailed cross-informant analyses of inappropriate behavior of children. Among different informants, correlations were found to be in the range of 0.20 to 0.30. More specifically, the correlation between parent and teacher reports was 0.27; teacher and child, 0.20; and parent and child, 0.25. Whilst no significant gender differences were found, there was significantly higher cross-informant consistency for children than for adolescents, and for externalizing versus internalizing problems.

McCombs-Thomas, Forehand, Armistead, Wierson, and Fauber (1990) suggest that a lack of consistency across informants does not necessarily equate to error; it is more likely a product of the informant's environment and perspective. The authors reached this conclusion based on research conducted with 52 young adolescents where the adolescents themselves, as well as their mothers, fathers, and teachers, served as informants. The results showed that informants did not agree on the measure of externalizing problems, but did agree on internalizing problems.

It is clear that informant reports about a child's behavior are likely to differ. Parents seem to be better informants for younger children, but adolescents tend to give better information about their own anxiety problems (Rapee et al., 1994). Overall, research supports the position that children are better informants of internalizing behavior, or behavior unknown to parents, and parents are better informants for externalizing behavior, particularly for children under 10 years of age (McCombs-Thomas et al., 1990).

A key issue that emerges from this literature is how to aggregate discrepant reports to form meaningful and useful information about the child's problem. Based on the cross-informant research conducted to date, it appears that the development of a weighting system, for information obtained from various sources, may be beneficial in the diagnosis and assessment of the anxious child. More research is evidently needed in this area.

One possible means of overcoming some of the problems associated with self-report instruments is to include behavioral observation tasks in both the assessment and treatment evaluation protocol. As a technique for use with anxious children and their families, this type of methodology is increasing in popularity owing to the advantage of observing problems in the social context in which they occur. Behavioral observation techniques for anxiety can be grouped into two broad categories (Dadds, Rapee, & Barrett, 1994). The first is behavioral avoidance tests, where anxious behaviors are observed under controlled and artificial conditions. The second is direct observation, whereby behaviors are observed under more naturalistic conditions. The relative advantages and disadvantages of both categories have been discussed elsewhere by Dadds et al. (1994). In terms of discriminant validity, there is evidence suggesting that behavioral observation measures effectively differentiate anxious children from nonclinical samples, and from children with other disorders (Barrett, Dadds et al., 1996). Moreover, direct observation measures conducted with families of anxious children prior to and following treatment interventions have proven sensitive to clinical change (Barrett, Dadds et al., 1996).

There are two particularly appealing aspects to behavioral observation assessments. The first is that they can be developed creatively to be sensitive to the developmental age of the child; and the second is that they are representative of the real-life situations that children face within their family and peer environments. Consequently, a behavioral observation suitable for a very young child (5–6 years) may be with respect to his fear of separation from a parent; whereas for an adolescent we may instead design an observation that assesses the adolescents public speaking anxiety.

The usefulness of a diagnosis in informing treatment is controversial and in part limited by the quality of the classification system and assessment tools from which the diagnosis was made. Silverman (1991) examined the reliability of structured interviews for diagnosing childhood anxiety disorders. It was concluded that the methodological differences between the studies make it difficult to report with confidence that the anxiety diagnoses assigned to children and adolescents using structured interviews are reliable. Some of the methodological variables making comparability between studies difficult included: confusion as to how to combine discrepant information obtained from children and parents; the use of different methods to control for reliability in various studies (e.g., videotapes, audiotapes, and interviewer–observer); and different sample characteristics between studies. Given their popularity, further research is clearly needed to clarify the extent to which structured interviews can provide reliable anxiety diagnoses in children and adolescents.

However, the reliability of diagnostic structured interviews may be improved through more careful consideration of developmental limitations. Specifically, while various questionnaires are applicable to a wide range of age groups, it is uncertain how accurate they are in assessing the problems of children under the age of 10 years. It is conceivable that a child's concept of a problem will be different from that of a clinician, and this discrepancy may, in itself, lead to invalidation of information provided by the child.

Evaluation of Treatment Effectiveness

Carefully designed longitudinal studies that could potentially identify variables related to the maintenance of therapeutic change over time are very scarce in the childhood anxiety area. Long-term follow-up is needed to highlight the influence, and relationship to treatment outcome, of variables such as age of onset, gender, duration of disorder, comorbidity, family dysfunction, and socioeconomic status (Kovacs & Devlin, 1998; Ollendick & King, 1994). Despite the long-term efficacy of treatment being well documented, treatment outcomes are usually followed only for a period of one to two years, revealing little about the mechanisms or predictors of individual or family change (Ollendick & King, 1994).

One also has to consider the relevance and applicability of the current clinical research designs and derived protocols to mental health professionals working with anxious children in community settings, where the large majority of cases may be severe and have multiple parenting and family problems. Usually, these families need assistance and support in a variety of ways, therefore necessitating inclusion of a variety of factors into the treatment of childhood anxiety. Suggestions include: (a) parenting skill level; (b) parental anxiety and stress; (c) marital adjustment; (d) severity and pervasiveness across different settings of child anxiety; and (e) the nature of life events in the parents' and child's life.

Whilst children and adolescents with anxiety disorders are often seen in clinical practice, and many research studies have derived samples from such populations, other large groups of children are treated through schools and community groups. Research has not yet examined the effectiveness of treatment in these alternative settings, nor in others such as home, special after-school care, and residential settings. There is a notable lack of information regarding the effect of setting on treatment and of the influence of those providing treatment in alternative settings. Given that treatment is occurring in these contexts, and has the potential to occur more often in the future, there is a clear need to attend to these unknowns.

Kazdin (1995) suggests that the treatment outcomes obtained in clinical settings often do not approach those achieved in research. These findings are clearly difficult to verify as few controlled studies are available that draw these comparisons. Future identification of factors associated with treatment effectiveness across settings is therefore important. The opportunity to compare the cost efficacy and treatment effectiveness of various interventions, such as those conducted in group and school settings, is a further motivation for research in this area (Barrett, 1998; Dadds, Spence, Holland, Barrett & Laurens, 1997).

Issues of Individual Differences in Treatment

Most of the focus until now has been on group norms, yet we are all well aware that individual differences play a large role in treatment outcome. In terms of clinical practice, individual differences are often addressed within the therapy process; however, we currently lack a formal system of knowledge about the way in which child variables may interact with different types of childhood anxiety interventions (Kazdin & Weisz, 1998). Variables such as learning history, gender, age, ethnicity, and culture can impact on how and when children are identified for treatment, on the association with risk and protective factors, and on help-seeking behavior.

Some investigation of gender variations in childhood anxiety has been carried out. Epidemiological research with the general population indicates that girls report a greater number of fears than boys, although the content of the fears does not differ significantly (King et al., 1989; Ollendick and King, 1991). The same gender pattern has been reflected in retrospective studies of clinical samples where, at age 6 years, females are already twice as likely to have experienced an anxiety disorder than males (Lewinsohn, Gotlib, Lewinsohn, Seeley, & Allen, 1998). However, contradictory results obtained from direct clinical interviews with children and adolescents failed to find any gender differences in terms of anxiety diagnoses (Treadwell, Flannery-Schroeder, & Kendall, 1995). These discrepancies may well be a consequence of referral bias and problem severity. This is reflected in the finding that disturbed boys receive treatment more often than similarly afflicted girls (Costello & Janiszewski, 1990). Nonetheless, gender remains an important issue. It could be that treatment conducted in a clinical setting, which assumes that children of different gender respond to the same treatment, may be erroneous. Therein lies the possibility that children of different gender may respond differently to different treatments.

For boys with overanxious disorder, a strong linear decline in symptomatology has been noted from ages 10 to 20 (Cohen et al., 1993). However, while a small decline was evident for girls, the presence of the disorder remained relatively stable within the same age range. The longitudinal nature of this research leads to the conclusion that, for girls, the course of overanxious disorder may be more chronic, whilst for boys it would appear that the greatest vulnerability is in late childhood. In terms of treatment for boys, this indicates a possible window of opportunity for implementation of preventative programs.

Individual ethnic and cultural differences are also important for diagnostic assessment and treatment. Ethnic, cultural, or racial identity has the potential to impact on the time and method by which children are referred for treatment, on risk and resilience factors, on age of onset, and on help-seeking behaviors and use of treatment facilities (Kazdin, 1995). For example, Portuguese research on parent–child relationships indicates that it is culturally appropriate for children as old as 7 years to sleep in their parents' bedroom; a behavior that would likely indicate nighttime fears or separation anxiety within Anglo-Saxon-based cultures.

On a more personal level, cultural customs, religious beliefs, and attitudes impact on the attributed causation of symptomatology, on the meaning ascribed to the behavior, and on how information relating to the problem is conveyed (Bird, 1996). Because of potential communication difficulties, the risk of "category fallacy" becomes relevant. This refers to a situation where a child may be misclassified owing to the use of a diagnostic instrumentation developed for another, specific cultural population. For example, variation in mean scores on the CBCL have been noted between cultures such as the United States, Jamaica, the Netherlands, Puerto Rico, Thailand, and China, although it must be added that the effects due to culture were minimal

(Bird, 1996). How other instruments and diagnosis/assessment techniques fare in light of such comparisons is an area in need of future research. Bird argues that "we need to develop culturally sensitive translations of instruments into different languages, or use interviewers from the same cultural and linguistic background as the study subjects" to overcome cross-cultural barriers in the therapy process.

With regard to the impact of cross-cultural identity on treatment responsiveness, very little research has been completed. Last and Perrin (1992) explored the similarities and differences between African–American and white children seeking treatment for anxiety in an outpatient mental health facility. In terms of epidemiology, it was found that the two groups were more similar than different in relation to sociodemographics, clinical features, and diagnosis. These similarities may, conceivably, be a consequence of referral bias, so more studies are needed to explore whether the findings are reflected in the community. It stands to reason, however, that if they are similar in clinical characteristics, these two groups may also respond similarly to treatment. Research has in fact found that cognitive–behavioral therapy is equally effective for African–American and white children with anxiety disorders (Treadwell et al., 1995). Research to determine if a similar response to treatment exists between other cultural groups would be valuable.

Conclusions

A number of standardized treatment programs for childhood and adolescent anxiety have been designed and evaluated using increasingly sophisticated research designs. Efficacy trials indicate that we have developed clinically beneficial interventions for children and adolescents (7–14 years) who present with anxiety disorders, and that the demonstrated treatment effects can be maintained for at least four years. Most of the interventions employ a CBT paradigm with demonstrated efficacy for at least 60% of participants, and these treatment effects remain independent of whether the intervention is administered individually or in groups.

Despite the advances that have been made, several conceptual and methodological limitations remain. The current chapter has sought to highlight some of these, with particular emphasis on the developmental domain. First, while treatment interventions have internal validity, their external validity remains questionable. Most studies were conducted with relatively "pure" samples of anxious children. Participants with comorbid disorders were generally excluded, and the generalizability of findings across populations and settings remains unclear. Consequently, while the efficacy of treatments for childhood anxiety seems to be well demonstrated, demonstrations of effectiveness or clinical utility are still needed.

Second, most studies have failed to accommodate developmental differences in children's competencies and did not assess the benefits of various interventions for youth at different ages and different developmental levels.

The interventions often appeared to be downward extensions of adult anxiety interventions, and failed to incorporate the pertinent developmental psychology literature on cognitive and affective development. Researchers need to remain cognizant of the developmental psychology literature and integrate this research when devising and implementing therapies for anxious children and adolescents. Given that children are embedded within a family context, a developmental perspective also highlights the importance of active family involvement.

A third problem is the lack of a culturally sensitive perspective. Most studies were conducted with middle-class Caucasian youth, and little attention has been paid to the cultural relevance of the materials used and the intervention strategies incorporated. Future research needs to focus upon culturally diverse groups of children, and therapists must remain aware of the child's sociocultural context. In addition, culturally sensitive assessments and interventions should be incorporated.

Finally, there is little data to indicate which components of treatment are most effective for different groups of anxious children and adolescents. Research would be more informative if it examined which children benefited most from which intervention components, as clinicians could then target specific components.

Note

Please address correspondence to Dr Paula Barrett, School of Applied Psychology, Mt. Gravatt Campus, Griffith University, Messines Ridge Rd, Mt. Gravatt, QLD, 4122, Australia. E-mail: p.barrett@mailbox.gu.edu.au.

References

Abelson, J. L., & Alessi, N. E. (1992). Discussion of "child panic revisited." *Journal of the American Academy of Child and Adolescent Psychiatry, 31*, 114–116.

Achenbach, T. M., McConaughy, S. H., & Howell, C. T. (1987). Child/adolescent behavioral and emotional problems: Implications of cross- informant correlations for situational specificity. *Psychological Bulletin, 101*, 213–232.

Albano, A. M., Chorpita, B. F., & Barlow, D. H. (1996). Childhood anxiety disorders. In E. J. Mash & R. A. Barkley (Eds.), *Child psychopathology* (pp.196–241). New York: Guilford.

Anderson, J. C. (1994). Epidemiological issues. In T. H. Ollendick, N. J. King, & W. Yule (Eds.), *International handbook of phobic and anxiety disorders in children and adolescents* (pp. 43–66). New York: Plenum.

Barlow, D. H., Brown, T. A., Craske, M. G., Rapee, R. M., & Anthony, M. (1991). Treatment of panic disorder: Follow-up and mechanisms of change. Paper presented at the 25th annual meeting of the Association for the Advancement of Behavior Therapy, New York.

Barrett, P. M. (1998). Evaluation of cognitive–behavioral group treatments for childhood anxiety disorders. *Journal of Clinical Child Psychology, 27*, 459–468.

Barrett, P. M., Dadds, M. R., & Rapee, R. M. (1996). Family treatment of childhood anxiety: A controlled trial. *Journal of Consulting and Clinical Psychology, 64,* 333–342.

Barrett, P. M., Rapee, R. M., Dadds, M. R., & Ryan, S.(1996). Family enhancement of cognitive styles in anxious and aggressive children: The FEAR effect. *Journal of Abnormal Child Psychology, 24,* 187–203.

Barrios, B. A., & O'Dell, S. L. (1989). Fears and anxieties. In E. J. Mash & R. A. Barkley (Eds.), *Treatment of childhood disorders* (pp. 167–221). New York: Guilford.

Bernstein, G. A. (1994). Psychopharmacological interventions. In T. H. Ollendick, N. J. King, & W. Yule (Eds.), *International handbook of phobic and anxiety disorders in children and adolescents* (pp. 439–452). Plenum: New York.

Bird, H. R. (1996). Epidemiology of childhood anxiety disorders in a cross-cultural context. *Journal of Child Psychology and Psychiatry, 37,* 35–49.

Blagg, N. R., & Yule, W. (1984). The behavioral treatment of school refusal: A comparative study. *Behavior Research and Therapy, 22,* 119–127.

Cobham, V. E., Dadds, M. R., & Spence, S. H. (1999). The role of parental anxiety in the treatment of child anxiety. *Journal of Consulting and Clinical Psychology, 66,* 893–905.

Cohen, P., Cohen, J., Kasen, S., Noemi Velez, C., Hartmark, C., Johnson, J., Rojas, M., Brook, J., & Streuning, E. L. (1993). An epidemiological study of disorders in late childhood and adolescence: 1. Age- and gender-specific prevalence. *Journal of Child Psychology and Psychiatry, 34,* 851–867.

Costello, E. J., & Janiszewski, S. (1990). Who gets treated? Factors associated with referral in children with psychiatric disorders. *Acta Psychiatrica Scandinavica, 81,* 523–529.

Dadds, M. R., Rapee, R. M., & Barrett, P. M. (1994). Behavioral observation. In T. H. Ollendick, N. J. King, & W. Yule (Eds.), *International handbook of phobic and anxiety disorders in children and adolescents* (pp. 349–364). New York: Plenum.

Dadds, M. R., Spence, S. H., Holland, D. E., Barrett, P. M., & Laurens, K. R. (1997). Prevention and early intervention for anxiety disorders: A controlled trial. *Journal of Consulting and Clinical Psychology, 65,* 627–635.

De Jong, P. J., Andrea, H., & Muris, P. (1997). Spider phobia in children: Disgust and fear before and after treatment. *Behavior Research and Therapy, 35,* 559–562.

Fox, N. A., & Calkins, S. D. (1993). Pathways to aggression and social withdrawal: Interactions among temperament, attachment and regulation. In K. H. Rubin & J. B. Asendorpf (Eds.), *Social withdrawal, inhibition, and shyness in childhood,* (pp. 81–100). Hillsdale, NJ: Lawrence Erlbaum.

Franklin, M. E., Kozak, M. J., Cashman, L. A., Coles, M. E., Rheighold, A. A., & Foa, E. B. (1998). Cognitive behavioural treatment of pediaric obsessive–compulsive disorder. An open clinical trial *Journal of the Americal Academy of Child and Adolescent Psychiatry, 37,* (4), 412–419.

Giebenhain, J. E., & O'Dell, S. L. (1984). Evaluation of a parent training manual for reducing children's fears of the dark. *Journal of Applied Behavioral Analysis, 17,* 121–125.

Graziano, A. M., Mooney, K. C., & Ignasiak, D. (1979). Self-control instructions for children's fear reduction. *Journal of Behavior Therapy and Experimental Psychiatry, 10,* 221–227.

Harris, B. (1979). What ever happened to Little Albert? *American Psychologist, 34,* 151–160.

Heard, P. M., Dadds, M. R., & Conrad, P. (1992). Assessment and treatment of simple phobias in children: Effects on family and marital relationships. *Behaviour Change, 9,* 73–82.

Hergenhahn, B. R., & Olson, M. H. (1997). *An introduction to theories of learning* (5th ed). Englewood Cliffs, NJ: Prentice-Hall.

Jones, M. C. (1924a). The elimination of children's fears. *Journal of Experimental Psychology, 1,* 383–390.

Jones, M. C. (1924b). A laboratory study of fear: The case of Peter. *Pedagogical Seminar, 31,* 308–315.

Kazdin, A. E. (1995). Scope of child and adolescent psychotherapy research: Limited sampling of dysfunctions, treatments, and client characteristics. *Journal of Clinical Child Psychology, 24,* 125–140.

Kendall, P. C. (1994). Treating anxiety disorders in youth: Results of a randomized clinical trial. *Journal of Consulting and Clinical Psychology, 62,* 100–110.

Kendall, P. C., & Southam-Gerow, M. A. (1996). Long-term follow-up of a cognitive–behavioral therapy for anxiety disordered youth. *Journal of Consulting and Clinical Psychology, 64,* 724–730.

Kendall, P. C., Flannery-Schroeder, E., Panichelli-Mindel, S. M., Southam-Gerow, M., Henin, A., & Warman, M. (1997). Therapy for youths with anxiety disorders: A second randomized clinical trial. *Journal of Consulting and Clinical Psychology, 65,* 366–380.

King, N. J., Ollier, K., Iacuone, R., Schuster, S., Bays, K., Gullone, E., & Ollendick, T. H. (1989). Fears of children and adolescents: A cross-cultural study using the Revised-Fear survey Schedule for Children. *Journal of Child Psychiatry and Psychology, 30,* 775–784.

King, N. J., Tonge, B. J., Heyne, D., Pritchard, M., Rollings, S., Young, D., Myerson, N., & Ollendick, T. H. (1998). Cognitive–behavioral treatment of school-refusing children: A controlled evaluation. *Journal of the American Academy of Child and Adolescent Psychiatry, 37,* 394–403.

Kovacs, M., & Devlin, B. (1998). Internalizing disorders in childhood. *Journal of Child Psychology and Psychiatry, 39,* 47–63.

Last, C. G. (1992). Anxiety disorders in childhood and adolescence. In W. M. Reynolds (Ed.), *Internalizing disorders in children and adolescents.* New York: Wiley.

Last, C. G., & Perrin, S. (1992). Anxiety disorders in African–American and White children. *Journal of Abnormal Child Psychology, 21,* 153–164.

Last, C. G., Hansen, C., & Franco, N. (1998). Cognitive–behavioral treatment of school phobia. *Journal of the American Academy of Child and Adolescent Psychiatry, 37,* 404–411.

Last, C. G., Hersen, M., Kazdin, A. E., Francis, G., & Grubb, H. J. (1987). Psychiatric illness in the mothers of anxious children. *American Journal of Psychiatry, 144,* 1580–1583.

Last, C. G., Hersen. M., Kazdin, A., Orvaschel, H., & Perrin, S. (1991). Anxiety disorders in children and their families. *Archives of General Psychiatry, 48,* 769–773.

Lewinsohn, P. M., Gotlib, I. H., Lewinsohn, M., Seeley, J. R., & Allen, N. B. (1998). Gender differences in anxiety disorders and anxiety symptoms in adolescents. *Journal of Abnormal Psychology, 107,* 109–117.

March, J. S., Mulle, K., & Herbel, B. (1994). Behavioral psychotherapy for children and adolescents with obsessive–compulsive disorder: An open trial of a new protocol-driven treatment package. *Journal of the American Academy of Child and Adolescent Psychiatry, 33,* 333–341.

McCombs-Thomas, A., Forehand, R., Armistead, L., Wierson, M., & Fauber, R. (1990). Cross-informant consistency in externalizing and internalizing problems in early adolescence. *Journal of Psychopathology and Behavioral Assessment, 12,* 255–262.

Muris, P., Merckelbach, H., Holdrinet, I., & Sijsenaar, M. (1998). Treating spider phobic children: Effects of EMDR versus exposure. *Journal of Consulting and Clinical Psychology, 66,* 193–198.

Nelles, W. B., & Barlow, D. H. (1988). Do children panic? *Clinical Psychology Review, 8,* 359–372.

Ollendick, T. H. (1995). Cognitive–behavioral treatment of panic disorder with agoraphobia in adolescents: A multiple baseline design analysis. *Behavior Therapy, 26,* 517–531.

Ollendick, T. H., & King, N. J. (1991). Origins of childhood fears: An evaluation of Rachman's theory of fear acquisition. *Behaviour Research and Therapy, 29,* 117–123.

Ollendick, T. H., & King, N. J. (1994). Diagnosis, assessment, and treatment of internalizing problems in children: The role of longitudinal data. *Journal of Consulting and Clinical Psychology, 62,* 918–927.

Ollendick, T. H., & King, N. J. (1998). Empirically supported treatments for children with phobic and anxiety disorders: Current status. *Journal of Clinical Child Psychology, 27,* 156–167.

Rapee, R. M. (1997). The potential role of child-rearing practices in the development of anxiety and depression. *Clinical Psychology Review, 17,* 47–67.

Rapee, R. M., Barrett, P. M., Dadds, M. R., & Evans, L. (1994). Reliability of the DSM-III-R childhood anxiety disorders using structured interview: Interrater and parent–child agreement. *Journal of the American Academy of Child and Adolescent Psychiatry, 33,* 984–992.

Salkovskis, P. M. (1996). The cognitive approach to anxiety: Threat beliefs, safety seeking behaviour, and the special case of health anxiety and obsessions. In P. M. Salkovskis (Ed.). *Frontiers of cognitive therapy* (pp. 48–74). New York: Guilford.

Silverman, W. K. (1991). Diagnostic reliability of anxiety disorders in children using structured interviews. *Journal of Anxiety Disorders, 5,* 105–124.

Spence, S. H. (1994). Preventative strategies. In T. H. Ollendick, N. J. King, & W. Yule (Eds.), *International handbook of phobic and anxiety disorders in children and adolescents* (pp. 453–474). New York: Plenum.

Spence, S. H., Donovan, C., & Brechman-Tousaint, M. (1999). Social skills, social outcomes and cognitive features of childhood social phobia. *Journal of Abnormal Psychology, 108,* 211–221.

Treadwell, K. R. H., Flannery-Schroeder, E. C., & Kendall, P. C. (1995). Ethnicity and gender in relation to adaptive functioning, diagnostic status, and treatment outcome in children from an anxiety clinic. *Journal of Anxiety Disorders, 9,* 373–384.

Watson, J. B., & Rayner, P. (1920). Conditional emotional reactions. *Journal of Experimental Psychology, 3,* 1–14.

15

Prevention Strategies

SUSAN H. SPENCE

It is clear from the previous chapters that anxiety disorders represent one of the most common forms of psychopathology among children. Such problems are associated with a range of debilitating social, emotional, and academic consequences. In addition, recent evidence has emerged to suggest that child anxiety may play a causal role in the development of depression among young people (Cole, Peeke, Martin, Truglio, & Serocynski, 1998). Of further concern are findings that child anxiety disorders tend to persist if left untreated. For example, Dadds et al. (1999) demonstrated that approximately 50% of children in a community sample of 8–12 year olds who met diagnostic criteria for an anxiety disorder at a moderate to severe level still exhibited an anxiety disorder 2 years later. Cantwell and Baker (1989) found similar results in a 4-year follow-up of children aged 2–11 years. Not all studies, however, have confirmed the stability of children's anxiety disorders (Poulton, Trainor, Stanton, & McGee, 1997; Last, Perrin, Hersen, & Kazdin, 1996). The differing results may reflect the age group of the sample, the measures used to assess the presence of anxiety problems, and the extent to which children were also receiving treatment for their problems during the follow-up period.

A further reason for regarding child anxiety disorders as an issue for concern is the considerable evidence that the many adult anxiety disorders have their origins in childhood and adolescence (Keller et al., 1992; Mattison, 1992; Öst, 1987; Turner & Beidel, 1989; Stemberger, Turner, Beidel, & Calhoun, 1995). It is also clear that the majority of children with anxiety disorders do not attend any agency for treatment (Zubrick et al., 1997), perhaps because anxiety in children does not generally present as a major behavioral management problem for parents and teachers.

Significant progress has been made in the development of effective treatment approaches to child anxiety (Barrett, Dadds, & Rapee, 1996; Cobham, Dadds, & Spence, 1998; Kendall, 1994). Although such treatments are highly effective for the majority of children, there are several reasons why it would be preferable to prevent the development of child anxiety disorders before they become well established. The costs of child anxiety disorders are manifold. In addition to a great deal of personal suffering by children and their families, we must consider the cost of treatment by mental health professionals. Clinic-based interventions are expensive, even when conducted on a group basis. By the time children are referred for treatment, the disorder is often well established and many of the adverse effects upon school performance and peer relationships have already occurred and are hard to reverse. Also, current treatments have also been found to be ineffective for a significant proportion of anxious children, with approximately 30–40% still meeting diagnostic criteria for a clinically significant anxiety disorder at the end of treatment (Barrett, Dadds et al., 1996; Kendall, 1994). If anxiety disorders persist to adulthood a range of expenses are incurred, such as the cost of unemployment, days lost from work, hospitalization, medication, and pension payments. Interestingly, estimates from the recent Burden of Disease Project (Murray & Lopez, 1996) suggest that anxiety disorders represent one of the most significant health problems in terms of global burden of disease, exceeding the vast majority of physical health problems.

This same project noted that mental disorders generally account for around 20% of the total global burden of disease. It is not surprising, therefore, that the policies of governments and mental health agencies have started to emphasize the prevention of mental health problems. This interest has been reflected in the growing number of papers in academic journals describing conceptual frameworks, theoretical models, debates, and perspectives relating to prevention of mental health problems (e.g., Albee, 1996; Coie et al., 1993; Pelosi, 1996; Reiss & Price, 1996). Despite the encouraging policy statements from government bodies and attention from theorists, only a relatively small proportion of expenditure on mental health is directed towards prevention, with the vast majority of funding going towards treatment of established conditions. The neglect of prevention is also reflected in the activities of mental health professionals who typically spend only a negligible proportion of their time upon preventive functions (Peterson, Hartmann, & Gelfand, 1980). Despite increasing emphasis upon prevention within mental health policy and planning documents, there is little evidence to suggest that this focus has changed the work patterns of practitioners.

Practitioners are not, however, the only group of professionals to neglect the implementation of prevention programs. Academics and researchers are similarly neglectful. The vast majority of literature in academic journals relating to prevention focuses upon theoretical discussion rather than reporting the results of controlled evaluative studies.

Definitions and Conceptual Frameworks for Prevention

Prevention can be defined as intervention that occurs before the onset of a clinically diagnosable disorder and that aims to reduce the number of new cases of that disorder (Munoz, Mrazek, & Haggerty, 1996). Underlying many approaches to prevention is the assumption that mental health problems typically develop along a trajectory. Prevention can therefore be viewed as any attempt to prevent entry to, or progression along, the pathway from mild symptoms to a severe, debilitating psychological disorder. Empirical evidence suggests that a developmental trajectory exists for many mental disorders and childhood anxiety is no exception. For example, Dadds, Spence, Holland, Barrett, & Laurens (1997) found that approximately 50% of children who showed symptoms of anxiety, but did not yet meet diagnostic criteria, were diagnosed as meeting the criteria for an anxiety disorder 6 months later if they were left untreated. Thus, early symptoms of anxiety predicted the onset of full-blown anxiety disorders.

Much of the recent literature in the area of prevention distinguishes three levels of prevention—namely universal, selective, and indicated—based on the position of the target sample along the developmental continuum.

Universal/generic prevention is provided to entire populations that have not been identified on the basis of any risk factor. Selective prevention is targeted to subgroups or individuals who are assumed to have a high lifetime or imminent risk of developing a problem as the result of exposure to some biological, psychological, or social risk factor(s). Indicated prevention focuses on high-risk individuals who show minimal but detectable symptoms of a mental disorder, or biological markers suggestive of a predisposition towards the development of a full-blown mental disorder (Mrazck & Haggerty, 1994). Many researchers and practitioners also use the term "early intervention" to refer to a form of indicated prevention that targets those with symptoms of a disorder but who do not yet meet criteria for a clinically diagnosable problem.

Another recent development in the prevention literature has been the increased focus on identifying risk and protective factors for the development of specific disorders. Risk factors refer to biological, environmental, and psychological factors that increase the probability of development of a psychological problem. Protective factors, on the other hand, produce resilience to the development of psychological difficulties in the presence of adverse risk factors. The identification of protective variables is important, as there are many risk factors that cannot be easily altered. An alternative or additional strategy for prevention therefore is to build up protective factors to counteract the impact of risk variables.

There are several prerequisites for effective prevention (Spence, 1994, 1996b) including (a) an empirically based, tested model of the etiology of the problem which identifies risk and protective factors; (b) a reliable and valid method of identifying children at risk; (c) effective methods for reducing risk and enhancing protective factors; and (c) the opportunity to apply these methods in practice. If one applies these prerequisites to the prevention of child anxiety disorders, it is clear that the research evidence goes a long way towards fulfilling these requirements. As will be shown below, there is a good deal of evidence identifying the risk and protective factors associated with the etiology of child anxiety. We have reliable and valid measurement methods that enable us to identify children at risk, and convincing evidence exists to show that these risk factors are amenable to change through active intervention. Finally, there are many opportunities to apply preventive interventions to children at risk through childcare and education settings, and mental health clinics.

Risk Factors

Our knowledge of factors that place children at risk of developing anxiety problems has increased considerably. Risk factors for the development of anxiety disorders may (a) be nonspecific and applicable to several mental health problems, (b) impact upon anxiety disorders in general, or (c) be specific to one particular anxiety disorder. Much has been written about risk factors in earlier chapters and only a brief summary will be presented here. Taken together the evidence suggests that the development of child anxiety disorders involves a complex interplay between biological, psychological, and environmental factors.

Table 15.1 summarizes some of the many factors which evidence suggests play a role in the development and maintenance of maladaptive fears and

Table 15.1. Risk Factors for the Development of Anxiety Disorders in Childhood

Source of influence	Risk factors	Protective factors
Child characteristics	Genetic constitution	Problem-focused coping skills
	Temperament style (e.g., behavioral inhibition)	Positive self-talk
	Avoidant/emotion-focused coping style	Relaxation skills
	Pessimistic/threat-bias thinking style	
Environmental factors	Sociocultural influences: low SES, poor housing, large family size	Social support
	Family stress and high daily hassles	Modeling of non-fear/ coping skills
	Negative life events, trauma or loss	Latent inhibition: non-traumatic pre-exposure
	Life transitions	
	Parental psychopathology	
	Modeling of fearful responses/observational learning	
	Operant conditioning of fear behaviors	
	Classical conditioning	
	Parental cueing to threat	
	Overprotective, over-controlling, critical parental style	
Child–environment interaction		

anxiety disorders in childhood. It is important to note that, in practice, these influences do not operate in a discrete manner and many of these variables are interrelated, or represent mechanisms through which particular factors exert their influence. For example, it is likely that parental psychopathology exerts an influence upon child anxiety through a combination of genetic and environmental influences. The genetic factors may operate through their effect upon the child's temperament, conditionability, emotional reactivity, and negative affectivity. On the other hand, environmental influences may operate through the impact of parental behavior, such as the modeling and reinforcement of the child's anxious behavior. Thus, the sources of influence outlined in table 15.1 are not proposed to be mutually exclusive nor independent of each other.

Intrinsic Child Characteristics

There is increasing evidence of a genetic influence in the development of anxiety problems in childhood (see Eley, this volume). Anxious children are more likely than their nonanxious peers to have anxious parents (Last, Hersen, Kazdin, Francis, & Grubb, 1987). Similarly, studies show that anxious parents are likely to have anxious children (Turner, Beidel, & Costello, 1987). Familial studies of this type do not, however, indicate the relative contribution of genetic versus environmental influences in the development of childhood anxiety. Recent genetic studies have provided some insights into the extent of genetic influences, with heritability estimates of around 40–50% being found for anxiety symptoms in children (Thapar & McGuffin, 1995). This leaves a great deal of unexplained variance for environmental factors to influence the development of anxiety disorders.

If we accept that genetic factors are important in child anxiety, we still need to consider exactly what is inherited. One likely possibility is that the mechanism of heritability is through temperament characteristics. The work of Kagan and colleagues (e.g., Kagan, Reznick, & Gibbons, 1989; Kagan Snidman, 1991) has been influential in identifying a relatively stable temperament style that they term "behavioral inhibition." The characteristic features of behavioral inhibition include initial timidity, shyness, and emotional restraint when exposed to unfamiliar people, places, or contexts (Asendorpf, 1993). This behavioral pattern is associated with elevated physiological indices of arousal and has been shown to have a strong genetic component (Plomin & Stocker, 1989; DiLalla, Kagan, & Reznick, 1994).

Certain types of childhood temperament have been proposed as risk factors for the development of anxiety. In particular, a temperament style of behavioral inhibition has been shown to increase the probability of the development of anxiety disorders during childhood (Biederman et al., 1993; Kagan, 1997; Rosenbaum et al., 1993). However, early childhood temperament is clearly not a complete explanation for the development of childhood anxiety problems. As Lonigan and Phillips (this volume) point out, child temperament on its own is unlikely to account for more than a small percentage of variance in the prediction of child anxiety. Although behavioral inhibition may be a relatively stable temperament characteristic over time, there are many children who cease to show this pattern and move into uninhibited status. Furthermore, many children who show a temperament style of behavioral inhibition do not proceed to develop anxiety disorders (Biederman et al., 1993; Rosenbaum et al., 1993). One of the challenges for researchers is to identify the moderating variables that influence whether behaviorally inhibited children continue to show this temperament style over time, and whether they proceed to develop an anxiety problem. For example, Fox and Calkins (1993) found that the child's attachment style interacts with child temperament in predicting subsequent levels of behavioral inhibition. Parenting characteristics have also been proposed to play a part in determining the stability of behavioral inhibition and its impact upon psychosocial development. Overprotective and overly critical childrearing styles in particular are proposed to moderate the relationship between a temperament of behavioral inhibition and the development of anxiety. Hirshfeld, Biederman, Brody, Faraone, & Rosenbaum (1997a, 1997b) found that high maternal expressed emotion, in the form of criticism, was associated with child behavioral inhibition, particularly in anxious mothers. Furthermore, maternal criticism was significantly associated with a higher number of child anxiety disorders. In contrast, Kagan (1994) reported that reactive infants whose mothers focused on teaching their childen coping skills, rather than just soothing them, were less likely to show fear and inhibition in subsequent observations. However, if parents were not sensitive enough to their child's distress and attempted to impose excessive socialization demands, then this parenting style was associated with children's increased feelings of guilt and sensitivity to criticism (Kagan, 1994). These findings led Lonigan and Phillips (this volume) to propose that a good balance between comforting and the teaching of coping skills will be most effective in moderating the impact of behavioral inhibition upon the development of child anxiety. Clearly, the relationship between parenting style and child temperament is a complex one, and furthermore it is likely to be reciprocal in nature such that parenting can alter the expression of temperament and temperament can influence the way in which parents respond to their children.

Behavioral inhibition is not the only temperament style that has been proposed to place children at risk for the development of anxiety problems. Lonigan and Phillips (this volume) propose that a combination of high negative affectivity/neuroticism in combination with a pattern of low effortful control predisposes children either directly or indirectly to the development of anxiety.

Extrinsic Influences

It is clear that many psychological problems in childhood are associated with adverse sociocultural factors such as low socioeconomic status, poor housing conditions, large family size, or marital discord. In the case of childhood anxiety disorders, however, the relationship with such variables is unclear and we do not have clear evidence to permit conclusions to be drawn (Gittelman, 1986). Child anxiety disorders are also associated with negative or traumatic life events and stressful life transitions. There is substantial evidence to demonstrate elevated rates of anxiety disorders following major traumatic events such as earthquakes, bush fires, and storms (e.g., Dollinger, O'Donnell, & Staley, 1984; Terr, 1981; Yule & Williams, 1990). Following trauma, children show increased rates of fears relating to stimuli associated with the traumatic event. They may also demonstrate avoidance behaviors, somatic complaints, depression, sleep disturbance and intrusive experiences (Dollinger, 1986; Dollinger et al., 1984). Although such problems ameliorate relative quickly for most children, a significant proportion of children show persistent anxiety symptoms for many months after the trauma (Terr, 1981).

In many instances, a classical conditioning process is likely to explain the development of the phobic response. For example, Dollinger et al. (1984) reported a high level of fear of storms in a group of children who were survivors of a severe lightening strike. A generalization gradient of fears relating to storms, noise, the dark, death, and dying was found, with strongest fear being associated with stimuli most related to storms, and weakest fear being associated with unrelated events such as social or school situations. This effect was not found amongst nontraumatized matched control children.

The occurrence of negative life events, such as parental separations and divorce, death of a family member, family conflict, and repeated moves of school, has also been found to be greater amongst clinically anxious that nonanxious children (Benjamin, Costello, & Warren, 1990; Goodyer & Altham, 1991). However, on their own, negative life events are clearly not a satisfactory explanation for the development of anxiety disorders. Many anxious children do not experience elevated rates of negative life events, and many children survive trauma without clinically significant psychological problems (Goodyer, Wright, & Altham, 1990). This has led to the search for variables that buffer or exacerbate the effects of negative life events upon children's psychosocial development. Factors which appear to reduce the negative impact of aversive life events upon children include availability of social support and problem-focused coping strategies (Compas, 1987). In addition, parental behavior has been implicated as a variable that serves to influence the development of anxiety problems following negative life events. For example, McFarlane (1987) reported that the best predictor of post-traumatic phenomena in children following a bush fire disaster was the mother's response to the events. This effect was even stronger than the degree of exposure to the disaster in determining the child's behavior. The mothers who were most anxious and overprotective following the fire tended to have children who exhibited the most posttraumatic symptoms. Anxious parental behavior has also been shown to have a strong influence upon the degree of anxiety and distress shown by children during painful medical procedures (Jacobsen, Manne, Gorfinkle, & Schorr, 1990; Bush, Melamed, Sheras, & Greenbaum, 1986).

Studies that have examined the relationship between parental behavior and childhood anxiety suggest that, in general, the parents of anxious children behave in ways that increase the chance their child will behave in an anxious manner. From a learning theory perspective, it has been proposed that parents of anxious children tend to model, prompt, and reinforce anxious behavior in their children (Spence, 1996b). Indeed, studies demonstrate that parents of anxious children are particularly likely to communicate the threatening aspects of the world and undermine their child's acquisition of effective coping strategies (Barrett, Rapee, Dadds, & Ryan, 1996; Dadds & Roth, this volume; Krohne & Hock, 1991).

Interactive Risk Factors

Some risk factors reflect an interaction between characteristics of the child and his or her environment. For example, research has recently moved from focusing upon parenting behavior per se as a risk factor for anxiety, towards features of the parent–child relationship. In particular, the role of early attachment style has received attention. For example, Warren, Huston, Egeland, and Srouge (1997) showed that the early attachment relationship is a strong predictor of the development of anxiety disorders in childhood and adolescence. To date, we know very little about the way in which different risk factors interact with each other to influence the development of anxiety disorders. Risk factors may interact in various ways, in some instances having an additive effect, and in others producing a multiplicative effect. Researchers need to examine the interactive effects of multiple risk and protective factors in order to make accurate predictions about who will develop an anxiety disorder (Kazdin & Kagan, 1994).

Protective Factors

It is clear that our knowledge regarding protective factors lags a long way behind the evidence relating to risk factors. A challenge for researchers over the next decade will be to identify further protective factors. This will provide valuable guidelines for the content of preventive interventions. Given that it is unrealistic to eliminate many traumatic and negative life events, and that genetic determinants of anxiety may prove to be extremely difficult to change, the enhancement of protective factors will be important in reducing the development of anxiety disorders. Although the search for protective factors is in its infancy, there is some tentative evidence regarding factors that serve a protective function in buffering the impact of risk factors in the development of anxiety disorders.

In particular, children's coping skills have been suggested to play a role as protective factors. Children differ markedly in their ability to use a range of coping skills that influence the degree of fear, anxiety, and distress experienced in response to unpleasant experiences. Much of this evidence comes from the literature on coping with aversive medical procedures. Methods such as seeking out information, positive self-talk, diversion of attention, relaxation and thought stopping have been demonstrated to be associated with lower levels of anxiety and distress (Brown, O'Keefe, Sanders, & Baker,1986; Peterson, Harbeck, Chaney, Farmer, & Thomas, 1990). The ability to use problem-focused coping strategies rather than avoidant or emotion-focused coping has also been shown to be associate with more positive psychological adjustment in children (Compas, 1987). The availability of social support and children's ability to access this support has also been proposed to play a significant role as a protective factor against the development of a range of child behavioral and emotional problems (Compas, 1987).

Interestingly, there appear to be developmental differences in the way children try to cope with stressful situations. Band and Weisz (1988) proposed a primary–secondary model of coping in children. Primary approaches to coping aim to change the aversive stimulus directly (e.g., attempting to remove the feared event through verbal protest or running away). Secondary coping strategies, on the other hand, accept the occurrence of the aversive situation and focus on methods of producing the least degree of aversiveness and distress. Band and Weisz suggested that children gradually learn that primary coping attempts are generally not successful in preventing the feared situation. Thus, with increasing age, children begin to use secondary coping methods which aim to produce the least degree of distress to the aversive situation. This model fits with evidence that children show increased use of strategies such as positive self-talk or relaxation with increasing age (Brown et al., 1986).

The importance of coping strategies in enabling children to deal with aversive and fearful situations has clear implications for the way in which prevention programs should be designed. The ultimate aim of prevention of childhood anxiety disorders should be to teach children strategies that may facilitate their handling of a wide range of stressful situations. Skills to be taught include relaxation, use of positive self-talk strategies, rational interpretation of events, accurate prediction of outcomes, and problem-solving abilities. In addition to skills that provide a general protective function for a wide range of difficult life events, there are some skills that assist children to cope with specific stressful situations. For example, children transferring from elementary grades to secondary school may find that the transition requires many new skills (e.g., use of public transport, social skills for friendship making, independent study skills).

Our knowledge about risk and protective factors provides a guide to the identification of children at risk and the content of interventions that are likely to be effective in preventing the development of child anxiety disorders. Many of the risk factors in table 15.1 are observable and measurable, thereby allowing us to identify children at risk. Based on the literature reviewed

Table 15.2. Groups at Particular Risk for Development of Anxiety Disorders

1. Children with early symptoms of anxiety who do not yet meet criteria for a disorder
2. Infants and children of anxious parents
3. Infants and children of overprotective/overcritical parents
4. Infants with an anxious/resistant attachment style
5. Infants and children with identified temperament styles of behavioral inhibition or high negative affectivity/neuroticism in combination with low effortful control
6. Children exposed to traumatic events, such as car accidents or environmental disasters
7. Children exposed to stressful life transitions or negative life events, such as parental separations/divorce, hospitalizations, major illnesses, painful procedures, family bereavement

above, it is proposed that the groups listed in table 15.2 are at particular risk for the development of anxiety disorders.

An Integrated Developmental Model for Prevention

It is clear that different risk and protective factors come into play at different developmental stages. This has important implications for preventive programs. Ideally, preventive efforts should provide an ongoing influence across the lifespan in order to tackle those risk factors that are significant at any given age. Nevertheless, there are some risk factors that may occur at any point across the lifespan, such as exposure to traumatic or negative life events, and general sociocultural influences such as poverty, poor housing, and high levels of family stress. Table 15.3 outlines the way in which various risk factors come into play at different developmental stages.

Fortunately a good deal of evidence exists to guide us in ways of modifying these risk factors and enhancing protective factors that may attenuate the risk. Spence (1994) presented theoretical arguments to suggest a range of intervention methods that are likely to be beneficial in preventing childhood anxiety. These methods were selected based upon our knowledge of risk and protective factors for child anxiety, techniques for increasing children's skills to cope with painful and stressful life events, and the treatment of clinically anxious children.

The Child-focused approaches can be summarized as follows:

1. Model coping skills through successful handling of the stressful situation by peers or adults (live or videotaped).
2. Give direct instruction in the use of coping strategies, such as cue-controlled relaxation, positive self-statements, breathing exercises, emotive imagery using hero models, and attention distraction.
3. Employ behavior rehearsal, role-play and practice of coping skills for dealing with the stressful situation.
4. Give positive reinforcement of approach ("brave") behavior and the use of coping skills.

Table 15.3. Risk Factors for Anxiety Disorders and Change Methods Across the Lifespan

Age of influence	Risk factor	Preventive methods
Across the lifespan	Traumatic life events	Coping skills training Trauma counseling
	Negative life events	Preparation for marriage Child coping skills training Divorce counseling
	Genetic predisposition (family history)	
Prenatal period	Genetic history of anxiety disorder	Parenting skills training
	Parental psychopathology	Treatment of parental anxiety and other psychopathology
Infancy	Insecure attachment Temperament of behavioral inhibition	Parenting skills training
	Parental anxiety + anxious parenting	Treatment of parental anxiety
Childhood	Overprotective/ overcritical child-rearing style	Parenting skills training Treatment of parental anxiety
	Temperament of behavioral inhibition	
	Starting school Parental anxiety Early symptoms of anxiety	Child coping skills training
Adolescence	Transition to high school	Adolescent coping skills training
	Parental anxiety	Parenting skills training
	Symptoms of anxiety	Treatment of parental anxiety

5. Provide information (verbally or filmed) about feared situations so that children obtain a sense of control over the stressful event.
6. Allow the child as much control over the situation as possible.
7. Arrange for nontraumatic pre-exposure prior to stressful situations (latent inhibition).
8. Exposure to potentially stressful situations in the absence of feared consequences.

The environmental-change approaches can be summarized as follows:

1. Teach parents to: model appropriate coping behavior; encourage and reinforce their child's use of coping skills; reduce their own anxious behaviors; reduce overprotective and critical child-rearing responses; encourage their child to expose himself or herself to appropriate

situations; ignore and prevent inappropriate avoidance of situations by their child; avoid excessive focus on, and communication of, potential threat.

2. Reorganize the physical structure of environments to facilitate adjustment, such as the school environment (see Felner & Adan, 1988, described below).

3. Reduce the child's exposure to trauma and negative life events (e.g., by programs to prevent parents' marital breakdown, or by preventing motor vehicle and other accidents).

Table 15.3 illustrates how, from a theoretical perspective, some of these techniques might be brought into play at different points in the lifespan as a means of dealing with age-relevant risk and protective factors. However, it is clear from table 15.3 that some preventive interventions appear repeatedly. In particular, the treatment of parental anxiety and parenting skills training appear as important preventive components at many age levels. Both these approaches aim to decrease the tendency of parents to model, prompt, and reinforce anxious behavior, to reduce parental focus upon threat cues in the environment, and to decrease parental use of overprotective and overcritical child-rearing styles.

Research into the Prevention of Anxiety Disorders in Young People

Much has been written about the need to prevent childhood anxiety disorders and some authors have proposed the type of approaches that could be used (e.g., King, Hamilton, & Murphy, 1983; Martinez, 1987; Robinson, Rotter, Fey, & Robinson,1991). However, there has been very little research to evaluate the effectiveness of preventive programs for children's anxiety disorders. Many studies have suffered from a range of methodological limitations that limit the conclusions able to be drawn. Such problems include inadequate sample sizes, absence of appropriate no-intervention control groups, lack of random allocation of participants to prevention and control groups, high attrition rates, poor representativeness of the sample in relation to the population of concern, lack of multiple sources of assessment data, sole reliance on self-report measures, use of measures of questionable reliability and validity, and inadequate long-term follow-ups. Very few studies have succeeded in overcoming these limitations. Nevertheless, the small amount of evidence available provides an optimistic picture regarding the effectiveness of preventive interventions for child anxiety disorders.

Early Intervention and Indicated Prevention with Children Who Show Early Symptoms of Anxiety Disorder

LaFreniere and Capuano (1997) reported a study that sought to prevent the development of childhood anxiety in preschool children who showed anxious–withdrawn behavior. The intervention aimed to increase the mother's understanding of the needs of her child, promote parenting skills in terms of sensitivity to these needs, reduce parental stress, and enhance social support for the family. The rationale was based on evidence that insecure attachment to the primary caregiver is a predictor of later preschool behavior problems, including anxiety, dependency, withdrawal, submissiveness, and internalizing problems in general. The parents of anxious children have also been shown to be low on contingent reinforcement, and high on negativity and intrusive/controlling behavior (LaFreniére & Dumas, 1992). The intervention therefore aimed to increase parental sensitivity to children's needs, to increase the use of positive parenting skills, and to enhance attachment security.

Forty-three children were assigned randomly to either the parental intervention or to a no-intervention control group. The intervention was carried out over a 6-month period and involved 19 home visits. Following the intervention, the mothers in the treatment group showed lower levels of intrusive overcontrolling behavior, and the children showed increased cooperation and enthusiasm in a problem-solving task with their mothers. In addition, teacher ratings showed significant improvements in the children's social competence at preschool. However, on some of the measures the control group also showed significant improvements over time. For example, significant reductions in anxious–withdrawn behavior were found for both the intervention and the control groups. Similarly, maternal stress decreased among mothers in both groups.

The Queensland Early Intervention and Prevention of Anxiety Project (Dadds, Spence, Holland, Barrett, & Laurens, 1997; Dadds et al., 1999) is another example of indicated prevention and early intervention, but in this instance focusing on children who show early symptoms of anxiety. This study evaluated the effectiveness of a cognitive–behavioral, child and parent, group intervention for preventing the onset and development of anxiety disorders in children. Children were identified as being "at risk" for the development of anxiety disorders on the basis of a screening process designed to detect the presence of high levels of anxiety symptoms. Of those children identified by the screening process, 75% met diagnostic criteria for an anxiety disorder, albeit at a relatively mild level of severity, and 25% showed symptoms of anxiety but did not yet meet diagnostic criteria for a clinical anxiety disorder.

A two-stage screening procedure was used. First, a total sample of 1786 children aged 9–14 years completed the Revised Children's Manifest Anxiety Scale (RCMAS; Reynolds & Richmond, 1979). Perrin and Last (1992) have shown that no single self-report measure of anxiety in children can reliably discriminate anxious children from those with other behavior problems. Thus, Screen 1 identified a small number of children with attention deficit and oppositional problems without anxiety problems. In Screen 2, teachers were asked to nominate up to 3 children from each class who displayed the most anxiety (inclusion criterion) and up to 3 who displayed the most disruptive behavior (exclusion criterion). The rate of concordance between teachers' and children's reports was quite low. Of the 361 children found to have anxiety problems using either criteria, only 33 (9.14%) appeared on both teachers' lists and their own self-report. However, structured diagnostic interviews with parents subsequently revealed that each recruitment method resulted in high detection rates of children with anxiety disorders and symptoms, and that each method detected different types of anxiety problems. Teachers were more likely to detect social anxiety, whereas, not surprisingly, parents were more aware of separation anxiety in their children. Thus, both methods may need to be used in parallel in future clinical studies if comprehensive detection of anxiety problems is to be achieved.

The children attended eight schools that were matched in pairs for size and socioeconomic status. Schools within each pair were then assigned randomly to either intervention or monitoring conditions. After recruitment and diagnostic interviews, 61 children were assigned to a 10-week school-based child and parent intervention, and 67 children were assigned to the monitoring group. The intervention was based on an Australian modification of Kendall's (1994) Coping Cat anxiety program. Several controlled trials have demonstrated the effectiveness of this approach with clinically significant anxiety disorders (Barrett, Dadds et al., 1996; Kendall, 1994). For the 10 ten intervention sessions, attendance was high (about 80%). For the three parent sessions, attendance by mothers was moderate (about 58%) but lower for fathers (about 21%).

After the intervention, both intervention and monitoring groups showed improvement, with no significant differences between groups. However, at 6-month follow-up a difference emerged, with only 27% of children in the intervention group showing an anxiety disorder diagnosis compared with 57% in the monitoring condition. At 12-month follow-up, rates of diagnosis for the two groups converged (37% vs. 42%), but by 2-year follow-up a significant difference between groups was again evident: the intervention group showed an anxiety disorder diagnosis rate of 20% compared with 39% for the monitoring group. Interestingly, the 2-year follow-up showed that the likelihood of still having a clinical diagnosis increased as the pre-intervention severity rating of the diagnosis increased (Dadds et al., 1999): approximately 50% of children with a moderate-to-severe clinical diagnosis of an anxiety disorder retained a clinical diagnosis 2 years later if they had not received the intervention. This finding demonstrates the persistence of childhood anxiety disorders if they are left untreated.

The findings were particularly interesting for those children who initially showed symptoms of anxiety but did not actually have a clinically significant anxiety disorder diagnosis. At 6-month follow-up, 54% of these children met criteria for an anxiety disorder if they were left untreated, compared with 16% in the intervention group. However, at 2 year follow-up there was minimal difference between the preventive-intervention and monitoring-only conditions in terms of the percentage of children who showed an anxiety disorder diagnosis (around 11% vs. 16%, respectively). Thus children with anxious symptoms that are of very low severity do not appear to be at high risk of developing a more severe anxiety disorder in the longer term if left untreated. In contrast, those who initially show a clinical diagnosis of mild-to-moderate severity are at risk of maintaining a clinical disorder if they do not receive intervention. Preventive efforts and early intervention may be most valuably targeted towards these children.

Spence and Dadds (1996) discussed several ethical issues emerging in the course of the Queensland Early Intervention and Prevention of Anxiety Project with implications for other preventive interventions. First, children who were allocated to the monitoring group were at risk for, or already had, an anxiety diagnosis. Accordingly, some of these children deteriorated over the monitoring period. Safeguards were built into the design such that any child the clinician rated as having a diagnosis of 6 or greater on the 8-point scale was referred for individual help. If the family accepted assistance, the child was excluded from the evaluation component of the study. Any child whose parents requested help at the follow-up interviews or during the intervening period was also referred for treatment. A second ethical issue concerned the use of teachers to identify and nominate children with psychological problems, as this raised the possibility of adverse labeling effects. However, this sort of identification is common practice for teachers and there is no evidence that it is detrimental to the children. On the contrary, there is evidence that children with anxiety problems are often ignored by teachers, and thus continue to suffer without receiving appropriate services. Third, parents were notified that their child would be interviewed prior to participation in a group educational program (or passive monitoring program). This may inadvertently have conveyed to parents that their child had a problem. However, it is accepted that schools should and do provide feedback to parents on the social development of their child(ren). Parents had previously given permission for their children to be screened and for feedback to be provided. In order to minimize parental concerns, participation in the intervention part of the project was described as a positive skill-building experience rather than a remedial treatment. Participation in the monitoring group was described as an assessment process that would provide feedback to parents in the event that the researchers identified significant problems.

Prevention of Anxiety in the Children of Anxious Parents

One of the risk factors for anxiety includes having a parent with an anxiety disorder (Mattison, 1992). It may be feasible to develop interventions targeted towards parents and children in order to reduce the probability of development of anxiety problems in the child. Such interventions could include training parents to reduce their own anxious behaviors, to model the use of coping skills for dealing with stress situations, and to reinforce their child's use of coping skills and approach rather than avoidance behaviors. Children may also be taught a range of coping skills that could be applied across a wide range of stressful and aversive situations as they arise. These skills could include relaxation, use of positive self-instruction, rational interpretation of events and outcome expectancies, and problem-solving abilities.

There do not appear to have been any controlled evaluations of the effectiveness of parent anxiety-reduction programs in the prevention of childhood anxiety. However, a study by Cobham et al. (1998) suggested that the treatment of parental anxiety might enhance the effectiveness of the cognitive–behavioral treatment of clinically significant child anxiety disorders where the parent manifests high levels of anxiety.

Children with a Temperament Style of Behavioral Inhibition

The temperament style of behavioral inhibition has been implicated as a risk factor for the development of child anxiety disorders, as discussed above. One of the challenges for researchers and practitioners will be the development of effective techniques for the prevention of later anxiety disorders among children who, at an early age, manifest a temperament style of behavioral inhibition. It is clear that not all children with a behaviorally inhibited temperament progress to develop anxiety problems, and many do not remain behaviorally inhibited over extended periods (Reznick et al., Rosenbaum et al., 1993). Given that parenting style is likely to moderate the impact of a behaviorally inhibited temperament style, parent training of the type outlined above is likely to be an important focus in preventive interventions. It may also be possible to intervene with the behaviorally inhibited children themselves, rather than working through the parents. For example, it may be feasible to develop techniques to teach children to modify physiological reactivity to novel and stressful situations through relaxation training and cognitive self-instruction approaches. Training children in coping skills, such as problem-solving, may also provide a protective function with older children.

Helping Children to Cope with Stressful Life Events

Children are required to cope with a wide range of stressful life situations, ranging from events that are common to most children (e.g., starting a new school) to situations that are relatively less frequent (e.g., dealing with the death of a parent).

Facilitating the Transition to a New School. The transition to a new school is one of the most stressful situations with which children are required to cope (Soussignan, Koch, & Montagner, 1988). During such transitions children have to adapt to new buildings, peer groups, teachers, teaching styles, and rules and regulations. Perhaps not surprisingly, school transitions are associated with a range of emotional and behavioral difficulties, including peer relationship problems, school refusal and somatic complaints, academic failure, increased substance abuse, delinquency and school dropout in older children (Hightower & Braden, 1991). In response to this evidence, programs have been devised to prevent or reduce the distress involved. For example, Felner and Adan (1988) ran the School Transition Environment Project (STEP) that aimed to facilitate the development of personal relationships between pupils and staff, and to create subenvironments within the overall large school environment. STEP organizes the physical plan of the school into units with "home rooms," in order to facilitate familiarity with the school environment. Children are taught their core academic subjects in these home rooms. A "home room" staff member has the responsibility for taking the daily attendance list, following up nonattendance and counseling, pupils regarding academic or school adjustment problems. STEP also ensures a coordinated liaison between teaching and school counseling staff. Evaluation of the STEP approach demonstrated that children who participated in the program showed higher levels of academic performance and self-esteem, better school attendance, and lower school dropout rates than control children who did not take part (Felner & Adan, 1988).

Prevention of Anxiety Disorders Following a Traumatic Experience. Given the elevated rate of child psychopathology following exposure to trauma, it is important that communities have in place rapid-response programs to prevent or at least reduce the negative psychological impact on children. Unfortunately, there is very little controlled outcome data relating to the most effective approaches. Owing to the usual unpredictability of these events, it is difficult to plan and implement highly controlled research. Ideally, interventions need to be rapid and should facilitate optimal parental response. Preventive methods also need to take into account the developmental level of the children involved and the nature of the traumatic experience (Sugar, 1989). To date, most reports have involved case reports and descriptive summaries, so it remains to be demonstrated conclusively whether current methods are effective (Bisson, 1997). Others have outlined their recommendations in response to clinical experience. Methods that have been described include encouraging children to describe their reactions, providing reassurance that such reactions are a normal response to an abnormal experience, relaxation training, and exposure to stimuli and memories relating to the trauma event (Yule & Williams, 1990). Yule (1991) emphasized the need for vivid and prolonged exposure to disaster-related cues in order to facilitate emotional processing.

Working with Children Following Parental Divorce. Parental separation is one of the most common and serious negative life events confronting children and adolescents (Hetherington, Bridges, & Insabella, 1998; Hightower & Braden, 1991; Hodges, 1991). Hess and Camara (1979) reported that the emotional and behavioral consequences for some children include depression, anger, conduct disorder, anxiety and withdrawal, particularly in the first two years following the divorce or separation. However, the more recent evidence demonstrates that the majority of children continue to be well adjusted following divorce and the negative consequences are limited to a minority of children (Amata & Keith, 1991; Forehand, 1992). Furthermore, the adverse emotional consequences of parental separation and divorce are influenced by the quality of the relationship between family members before, during, and after the separation. The negative effects are greatly mitigated when positive relationships between the parents are maintained so that the child is able to experience a supportive relationship with the noncustodial parent (Forehand, 1992). It is important, therefore, that legislation and procedures relating to separation and divorce be designed to facilitate positive family dynamics in the face of relationship breakup. Procedures and counseling that enable parents to separate amicably, and to resolve issues relating to custody, access, and property settlement in a harmonious manner, will play an important role in facilitating children's adjustment to divorce.

However, even if amicable relationships between separating parents can be achieved, most children will still experience the family breakup as aversive and distressing. This has led to the development of programs designed to provide children with skills to help them (e.g., Hodges, 1991; Pedro-Carroll & Cowen, 1985; Short, 1998). For example, the Children of Divorce Intervention Project was developed for use on a small group basis within schools. The project aimed to prevent academic, behavioral, and emotional problems using five intervention components. These elements included: (1) development of a supportive group environment; (2) facilitation of the identification and expression of divorce-related feelings; (3) promotion of understanding of divorce-related concepts and rectifying misconceptions; (4) teaching of coping skills, including social problem solving skills; and (5) enhancement of children's positive perceptions of themselves and their families. The program involved 12–16 sessions, involving discussion, role-play, skills training, and home-based tasks. Evaluation of the program demonstrated its effectiveness in producing reductions in anxiety, fewer behavioral problems, greater gains in school competencies, decreased feelings of self-blame, and better ability to solve divorce-related problems, in comparison with children of divorce who did not participate in the project. A 2-year follow-up showed that the benefits were maintained for the majority of children, although only around half the children continued to show the gains they had made over the comparison group at 3-year follow-up (Hightower & Braden, 1991). Programs such as the Children of Divorce Intervention Project offer promise in the prevention of mental health problems in children.

Prevention of Dental and Medical Anxiety. Fear of attending the dentist and subsequent avoidance of dental treatment represents a significant public health problem (Milgrom, Vignehsa, & Weinstein, 1992; Öst, 1987). Research into the development of dental anxiety points to an association with prior aversive experience, suggesting a classical conditioning process. Weinstein (1990) reviewed the literature relating to prevention of dental fears in children. Methods such as providing the child with as much control over the procedure as possible, nontraumatic pre-exposure prior to invasive treatment, and videotaped modeling of another child coping with the same procedure have all been reported to be beneficial in reducing child anxiety about subsequent dental visits (Melamed, Weinstein, Hawes, & Katin-Borland, 1975). Orally administered sedatives and electronic dental anesthesia (EDA) are also found to reduce distress and disruptive behavior during dental procedures. However, these effects are likely to reflect distraction, rather than analgesia per se, as similar results have been found with placebo EDA (Modaresi, Lindsay, Gould, & Smith, 1996).

Many children are required to undergo medical procedures that, in addition to being painful and unpleasant, involve new and novel surroundings and separation from parents (Melamed, 1998; Traughber & Cataldo, 1983). In addition to subjective distress, the behavioral manifestations of anxiety relating to medical procedures may include temper tantrums, running away, and protesting. These behaviors in turn produce considerable distress to parents, nurses, and medical personnel, and may also result in non-compliance with medical regimens. Over the past 20 years, a great deal of research has been conducted into the development of methods to minimize children's anxiety during medical procedures. These techniques are now used widely in hospital settings for helping children to cope with painful and stressful procedures, such as injections, bone marrow aspirations, and changing of burns dressings (Melamed, 1998; Jay, Elliott, Fitzgibbons, Woody, & Siegel, 1995). Such methods include provision of information, modeling demonstrations (usually involving films or puppets), training in coping skills such as cue-controlled relaxation, distracting or coping mental imagery (e.g., use of hero images), and use of comforting self-talk (Melamed & Sieigel, 1975; Melamed, Siegel, & Ridley-Johnson, 1988; Peterson & Shigetomi, 1981). Generally, a combination of these techniques has been found to be most effective in helping children to cope with painful procedures (Jay, Elliott, Katz, & Siegel, 1987; Jay et al., 1995).

As mentioned above, parent behavior influences the level of anxiety experienced by children during medical treatments. Preventive interventions should therefore aim to bring about changes in parent behavior in addition to the enhancement of child coping skills. For example, such programs should include reduction of parent's anxious behaviors, and should increase parental modeling of coping skills and reinforcement of their child's non-anxious/coping behavior.

In addition to the need to assist sick and injured children, studies have also demonstrated the emotional difficulties experienced by the siblings of terminally ill children. This has led to the development of interventions to assist siblings to cope with concerns such as feelings of resentment towards the sick sibling, jealousy about the amount of parental attention directed towards the sick brother or sister, feelings of being neglected by the parents, guilt, anger, loneliness, lack of family recreational activity, and fears of contamination, getting sick, the sibling's death, and their own death (Bendor, 1990; Williams et al., 1997).

Issues for the Future

Although research into the prevention of child anxiety disorders is in its infancy, we have evidence that presents an encouraging picture. Certainly, the evidence suggests that risk factors for child anxiety can be identified and in some instances modified successfully. Preventive efforts can be moderately effective in reducing symptoms of anxiety in response to stressful life events. There is also some encouraging evidence that preventive interventions may be beneficial in preventing the onset of later child anxiety disorders in young children who show early, preclinical symptoms of anxiety. However, we await large-scale replications of these approaches before definitive conclusions can be drawn.

Despite the encouraging picture, there are many unanswered questions that pose a challenge for researchers and practitioners.

1. Will selected and indicated prevention approaches, such as Dadds et al. (1997) or LaFreniere and Capuano (1997), be effective if applied on a universal prevention basis? It is not clear whether such interventions will be either feasible or effective if applied to whole populations of children who have not been selected on the basis of identified risk. Research is needed to demonstrate whether funds for preventive efforts are best directed towards large-scale universal interventions, or towards more intensive programs for a smaller number of children who are identified as being at risk. This raises the issue of a cost–benefit analysis; we need to know whether the benefits of universal interventions, where many of the children are unlikely to develop an anxiety problem, are sufficient to justify the high costs.

2. Can researchers and mental health planners obtain adequate information about cost–benefit ratios for various approaches to the prevention of childhood anxiety? It has been proposed (Spence, 1996a) that one explanation for the lack of government funding is the absence of cost–benefit data from psychologically based prevention studies. In contrast, in the area of physical health, convincing evidence is available regarding the savings involved. For example, Mrazek and Haggerty (1994) cite evidence to suggest that the cost–benefit ratio of the mumps–measles–rubella vaccine program in the US is around 14:1, with the 1983 scheme producing cost savings of $1.4 billion. The benefits of prevention in mental health are much harder to estimate. Although it is relatively easy to determine the cost of interventions, it is more difficult to determine the value of benefits derived from preventing mental disorders. Nevertheless, there are clear indicators that could be used in cost–benefit analyses, such as reductions in mental health consultations, time off work, hospitalizations, and pension payments.

3. To what extent can mental health practitioners be encouraged to transfer their attentions from intervention with established clinical cases towards the prevention of mental health problems? It is proposed here that

this shift in emphasis needs to begin with the training of mental health workers. Currently, most curricula pay little attention to prevention. Thus, many practitioners may not feel they have the skills or confidence to develop and implement preventive programs. Mental health workers also need to have a full understanding of the risk and protective factors involved in various forms of mental illness and to be made aware of programs that have been effective in preventing the onset of such problems.

3. How can research funding bodies be encouraged to provide the level of funding that will permit the use of adequate sample sizes in prevention research? This is a particular issue for studies of universal prevention. In order to evaluate the outcome of a preventive program, studies typically need extremely large sample sizes if the base rate of the disorder in the population is relatively low. Only then is it possible to determine whether the prevalence of the presenting problem is lower in the group receiving the preventive intervention than in the no-intervention control group.

5. Is investment in prevention best geared towards specific clinical disorders or towards mental health problems in general? Munoz et al. (1996) pointed out that there is a high level of comorbidity between most mental disorders. This is particularly true for anxiety disorders, where a high level of comorbidity is found with depression, attention-deficit hyperactivity disorder, and conduct disorders (Mattison, 1992). Furthermore, recent evidence suggests that childhood anxiety may be a precursor for the development of depression in young people, indicating common etiological factors or a causal role for anxiety in the development of depression (Cole et al., 1998). Indeed, many risk factors are common to multiple mental disorders, including parental psychopathology, marital difficulties, family stress and distress, and parental separations and divorce. Similarly, factors such as children's positive thinking style, problem-solving skills, positive parenting skills, high self esteem, social support, and positive peer relationships serve as protective variables against the impact of many risk factors for a range of mental disorders. Thus, it is feasible that preventive efforts would be best focused upon ameliorating generic risk factors and enhancing generic protective factors, with the goal of reducing a range of mental disorders.

6. When is the most appropriate timing for delivery of preventive programs? Given that anxiety disorders have a relatively early age of onset, with a sizeable percentage of the adult population recalling the onset of anxiety disorders during childhood and adolescence, there is a strong case for preventive efforts relatively early in life. There is little point in introducing prevention at age 18 if the majority of cases have already had their onset (Munoz et al., 1996). However, what is not clear is whether prevention is most effective if applied to risk factors that operate in infancy, in early childhood, in the elementary school years, or at adolescence, or whether a lifespan approach is required with multiple intervention points.

7. If preventive interventions are to be applied to children who are deemed to be "at risk" on the basis of some risk factor(s), then we need brief, cheap, reliable, and valid mechanisms to permit identification of these children. Dadds et al. (1997) demonstrated the effectiveness of a relatively brief school-based screening procedure for primary school children. However, if we are to intervene successfully at earlier points, we need to have screening methods that can be used during infancy and pre-school years. Two significant risk factors for this younger age group appear to be a temperament style of behavioral inhibition, and insecure attachment patterns. The identification of both these factors has traditionally involved relatively complex and time-consuming laboratory observations. Such procedures are not realistic as large-scale screening methods, so a further challenge for researchers is the development of reliable, valid, and brief questionnaire methods of screening to identify behaviorally inhibited children and those with insecure attachment style.

References

Albee, G. W. (1996). Revolutions and counterrevolutions in prevention. *American Psychologist, 51*, 1130–1133.

Amata, P. R., & Keith, B. (1991). Parental divorce and the well-being of children: A meta-analysis. *Psychological Bulletin, 110*, 26–46.

Asendorpf, J. B. (1993). Beyond temperament: A two-factor coping model of the development of behavioral inhibition during childhood. In K. H. Rubin & J. B. Asendorpf (Eds.), *Social withdrawal, inhibition and shyness in childhood* (pp. 265–290). Hillsdale, NJ: Lawrence Erlbaum.

Band, E., & Weisz, J. R. (1988). How to feel better when it feels bad: Children's perspectives on coping with everyday stress. *Developmental Psychology, 24*, 247–253.

Barrett, P. M., Dadds, M. R., & Rapee, R. M. (1996). Family treatment of childhood anxiety: A controlled trial. *Journal of Consulting and Clinical Psychology, 64*, 333–342.

Barrett, P. M., Rapee, R. M, Dadds, M. R., & Ryan, S. M. (1996). Family enhancement of cognitive style in anxious and aggressive children. *Journal of Abnormal Child Psychology, 24*, 187–203.

Bendor, S. J. (1990). Anxiety and isolation in siblings of pediatric cancer patients: The need for prevention. *Social Work in Health Care, 14*, 17–35.

Benjamin, R. S., Costello., & Warren, M. (1990). Anxiety disorders in a pediatric sample. *Journal of Anxiety Disorders, 4*, 293–316.

Biederman, J., Rosenbaum, J. F., Bolduc-Murphy, E. A., Faraone, S. V., Chaloff, J., Hirshfeld, D. R., & Kagan, J. (1993). A 3-year follow-up of children with and without behavioral inhibition. *Journal of the American Academy of Child and Adolescent Psychiatry, 32*, 814–821.

Bisson, J. I. (1997). Is post-traumatic stress disorder preventable? *Journal of Mental Health UK, 6*, 109–111.

Brown, J. M., O'Keefe, J., Sanders, S. H., & Baker, B. (1986). Developmental changes in children's cognition to stressful and painful situations. *Journal of Pediatric Psychology, 11*, 343–357.

Bush, J. P., Melamed, B. G., Sheras, P. L., & Greenbaum, P. E. (1986). Mother–child patterns of coping with anticipatory medical stress. *Health Psychology, 5,* 137–157.

Cantwell, D. P., & Baker, L. (1989). Stability and natural history of DSM-III childhood diagnoses. *Journal of the American Academy of Child and Adolescent Psychiatry, 28,* 691–700.

Cobham, V., Dadds, M. R., & Spence, S. H. (1998). The role of parental anxiety in the treatment of childhood anxiety. *Journal of Consulting and Clinical Psychology, 66,* 893–905.

Coie, J. D., Watt, N. F., West, S. G., Hawkins, J. D., Asarnow, J. R., Markman, H. J., Ramey, S. L., Shure, M. B., & Long, B. (1993). The science of prevention: A conceptual framework and some directions for a national research program. *American Psychologist, 48,* 1013–1022.

Cole, D. A., Peeke, L. G., Martin, J. M., Truglio, R., & Seroczynski, A. D. (1998). A longitudinal look at the relation between depression and anxiety in children and adolescents. *Journal of Consulting and Clinical Psychology, 66,* 451–460.

Compas, B. (1987). Coping with stress during childhood and adolescence. *Psychological Bulletin, 101,* 393–403.

Dadds, M. R., Holland, D. E., Laurens, K. P., Mullins, M., Barrett P. M., & Spence, S. H. (1999). Early intervention and prevention of anxiety disorders in children: Results at two-year follow-up. *Journal of Consulting and Clinical Psychology, 67,* 145–150.

Dadds, M. R., Spence, S. H., Holland, D. E., Barrett, P. M., & Laurens, K. R. (1997). Prevention and early intervention for anxiety disorders: A controlled trial. *Journal of Consulting and Clinical Psychology, 65,* 627–635.

DiLalla, L. F., Kagan, J., & Reznick, J. S. (1994). Genetic etiology of behavioral inhibition among 2-year-old children. *Infant Behavior and Development, 17,* 415–412.

Dollinger, S. J. (1986). The measurement of children's sleep disturbances and somatic complaints following a disaster. *Child Psychiatry and Human Development, 16,* 148–153.

Dollinger, S. J., O'Donnell, J. P., & Staley, A. A. (1984). Lightening-strike disaster: Effects on children's fears and worries. *Journal of Consulting and Clinical Psychology, 52,* 1028–1038.

Felner, R. D., & Adan, A. M. (1988). The School Transition Environment Project: An ecological intervention and evaluation. In R. H. Price, E. L. Cowen, R. P. Lorion, & J. Ramos-McKay (Eds.), *Fourteen ounces of prevention: A case book for practitioners* (pp. 111–122). Washington, DC: American Psychological Association.

Forehand, R. (1992). Parental divorce and adolescent maladjustment. *Behaviour Research and Therapy, 30,* 319–327.

Fox, N. A., & Calkins, S. D. (1993). Pathways to aggression and social withdrawal: Interactions among temperament, attachment and regulation. In K. H. Rubin & J. B. Asendorpf (Eds.), *Social withdrawal, inhibition and shyness in childhood* (pp. 81–100). Hillsdale, NJ: Lawrence Erlbaum.

Gittelman, R. (1986) *Anxiety disorders of childhood.* New York: Guildford.

Goodyer, I. M., & Altham, P. M. (1991). Lifetime exit events and recent social and family adversities in anxious and depressed school-aged children. *Journal of Affective Disorders, 21,* 219–228.

Goodyer, I. M., Wright, C., & Altham, P. M. (1990). The friendships and recent life events of anxious and depressed school-aged children. *British Journal of Psychiatry, 156,* 689–698.

Hess, R. D., & Camara, K. A. (1979). Post-divorce family relationships as mediating factors in the consequences of divorce for children. *Journal of Social Issues, 35,* 70–95.

Hetherington, E. M., Bridges, M., & Insabella, G. M. (1998). What matters? What does not? Five perspectives on the association between marital transitions and children's adjustment. *American Psychologist, 53,* 167–184.

Hightower, A. D., & Braden, J. (1991). Prevention. In T. R. Kratochwill & R. J. Morris (Eds.), *The practice of child therapy* (pp. 410–440). New York: Pergamon.

Hirshfeld, D. R., Biederman, J., Brody, L., Faraone, S. V., & Rosenbaum, J. F. (1997a). Associations between expressed emotion and child behavioral inhibition and psychopathology: A pilot study. *Journal of the Academy of Child and Adolescent Psychiatry, 36,* 205–213.

Hirshfeld, D. R., Biederman, J., Brody, L., Faraone, S. V., & Rosenbaum, J. F. (1997b). Expressed emotion towards children with behavioral inhibition: Association with maternal anxiety disorder. *Journal of the Academy of Child and Adolescent Psychiatry, 36,* 910–917.

Hodges, W. F. (1991). Interventions for children of divorce. New York: Wiley.

Jay, S. M., Elliott, C. H., Fitzgibbons, I., Woody, P., & Siegel, S. E. (1995). A comparative study of cognitive behavior therapy versus general anesthesia for painful medical procedures in children. *Pain, 62,* 3–9.

Jay, S. M., Elliott, C. H., Katz, E., & Siegel, S. E. (1987). Cognitive–behavioral and pharmacologic interventions for children's distress during painful medical procedures. *Journal of Consulting and Clinical Psychology, 55,* 860–865.

Jacobsen, P. B., Manne, S. L., Gorfinkle, K, & Schorr, O. (1990). Analysis of child and parent behavior during painful medical procedures. *Health Psychology, 9,* 559–576.

Kagan, J. (1994). *Galen's Prophesy: Temperament and human nature.* New York: Basic Books.

Kagan, J. (1997). Temperament and the reactions to unfamiliarity. *Child Development, 68,* 139–143.

Kagan, J., & Snidman, N. (1991). Infant predictors of inhibited and uninhibited profiles. *Psychological Science, 2,* 40–43.

Kagan, J., Reznick, J. S., & Gibbons, J. (1989). Inhibited and uninhibited types of children. *Child Development, 60,* 838–845.

Kazdin, A. E., & Kagan, J. (1994). Models of dysfunction in developmental psychopathology. *Clinical Psychology: Science and Practice, 1,* 35–52.

Keller, M. B., Lavori, P. W, Wunder, J., Beardslee, W. R., Schwartz, P., & Roth, T. (1992). Chronic course of anxiety disorders in children and adolescents. *Journal of the American Academy of Child and Adolescent Psychiatry, 31,* 595–599.

Kendall, P. C. (1994). Treating anxiety disorders in children: Results of a randomized clinical trial. *Journal of Consulting and Clinical Psychology, 62,* 100–110.

King, N. J., Hamilton, D. I., & Murphy, G. C. (1983). The prevention of children's maladaptive fears. *Child and Family Behavior Therapy, 5,* 43–57.

Krohne, H. W., & Hock, M. (1991). Relationships between restrictive mother–child interactions and anxiety of the child. *Anxiety Research, 4,* 109–124.

LaFreniere, P. J., & Capuano, F. (1997). Preventive intervention as means of clarifying direction of effects in socialization: Anxious–withdrawn preschoolers case. *Development and Psychopathology, 9*, 551–564.

LaFreniére, P. J., & Dumas, A. E. (1992). Behavioral and contextual manifestations of parenting stress in mother–child interaction. *Early Education and Development, 6*, 73–91.

Last, C. G., Hersen, M., Kazdin, A. E., Francis, G., & Grubb, H. J. (1987). Psychiatric illness in the mothers of anxious children. *American Journal of Psychiatry, 144*, 1580–1583.

Last, C. G., Perrin, S., Hersen, M., Kazdin, A. E. (1996). A prospective study of childhood anxiety disorders. *Journal of the American Academy of Child and Adolescent Psychiatry, 35*, 1502–1510.

Martinez, J. G. R. (1987). Preventing math anxiety: A prescription. *Academic Therapy, 23*, 117–125.

Mattison, R. E. (1992). Anxiety disorders. In S. R. Hooper, G. W. Hynd, & R. E. Mattison (Eds.), *Child Psychopathology: Diagnostic criteria and clinical assessment* (pp. 179–202). Hillsdale, NJ.: Lawrence Erlbaum.

McFarlane, A. C. (1987). Posttraumatic phenomena in a longitudinal study of children following a natural disaster. *Journal of the American Academy of Child and Adolescent Psychiatry, 26*, 764–769.

Melamed, B. G. (1998). Preparation for medical procedures. In R. T. Ammerman and J. V. Campos (Eds.), *Handbook of pediatric psychology and psychiatry: Vol. 2. Disease, injury, and illness* (pp. 16–30). Boston: Allyn & Bacon.

Melamed, B. J., & Siegel, L. J. (1975). Reduction of anxiety in children facing hospitalization and surgery by use of filmed modeling. *Journal of Consulting and Clinical Psychology, 43*, 1357–1367.

Melamed, B. J., Siegel, L. J., & Ridley-Johnson, R. (1988). Coping behaviors in children facing medical stress. In T. M. Field, P. M. McCabe, and N. Schneiderman (Eds.), *Stress and coping across development* (pp 109–137). Hillsdale, NJ: Lawrence Erlbaum.

Melamed, B. J., Weinstein, D., Hawes, R. R., & Katin-Borland, M. (1975). Reduction of fear-related dental management problems with use of film modeling. *Journal of the American Dental Association, 90*, 822–826.

Milgrom, P., Vignehsa, H., & Weinstein, P. (1992). Adolescent dental fear and control: Prevalence and theoretical implications. *Behaviour Research and Therapy, 30*, 367–375.

Modaresi, A., Lindsay, S. J., Gould, A., & Smith, P. (1996). A partial double-blind, placebo-controlled study of electronic dental anesthesia in children. *International Journal of Paediatric Dentistry, 6*, 245–51.

Mrazek, P. J., & Haggerty, R. J. (Eds.) (1994). *Reducing the risks for mental disorders: Frontiers for preventive intervention research.* Washington, DC: National Academy Press.

Munoz, R. F., Mrazek, P. J., & Haggerty, R. J. (1996). Institute of Medicine report on prevention of mental disorders: Summary and commentary. *American Psychologist, 51*, 1116–1122.

Murray, C. J. L., & Lopez, A. D. (1996). *The global burden of disease.* Boston: Harvard University Press.

Öst, L.-G. (1987). Age of onset in different phobias. *Journal of Abnormal Psychology, 96*, 223–229.

Pedro-Carroll, J. L., & Cowen, E. L. (1985). The Children of Divorce Intervention Project: An investigation of the efficacy of a school-based prevention program. *Journal of Consulting and Clinical Psychology, 53*, 603–611.

Perrin, S., & Last, C. G., (1992). Do childhood anxiety measures measure anxiety? *Journal of Abnormal Child Psychology, 20*, 567–577.

Pelosi, N. (1996). Reducing risks of mental disorders. *American Psychologist, 51*, 1128–1129.

Peterson, L., & Shigetomi, C. (1981). The use of coping techniques to minimize anxiety in hospitalized children. *Behavior Therapy, 12*, 1–14.

Peterson. L., Hartmann, D. P., Gelfand, D. M. (1980). Prevention of child behavior disorders: A lifestyle change for child psychologists. In P. O. Davidson & S. M. Davidson (Eds.), *Behavioral medicine: Changing health lifestyles* (pp. 195–221). New York: Brunner/Mazel.

Peterson, L., Harbeck, C., Chaney, J., Farmer, J., & Thomas, A. M. (1990). Children's coping with medical procedures: A conceptual overview and integration. *Behavioral Assessment, 12*, 197–212.

Plomin, R., & Stocker, C. (1989). Behavioral genetics of emotionality. In S. Reznick (Ed.), *Perspectives on behavioral inhibition* (pp. 219–240). Chicago: University of Chicago Press.

Poulton, R., Trainor, P., Stanton, W., & McGee, R. (1997). The (in)stability of adolescent fears. *Behaviour Research and Therapy, 35*, 159–163.

Reiss, D., & Price, R. H. (1996). National research agenda for prevention research: The National Institute of Mental Health Report. *American Psychologist, 51*, 1109–1115.

Reynolds, C. R., & Richmond, O. B. (1979). What I think and feel: A revised measure of children's manifest anxiety. *Journal of Personality Assessment, 43*, 281–283.

Reznick, J. S., Kagan, J., Snidman, N., Gersten, M., Baak, K., & Rosenberg, A. (1986). Inhibited and uninhibited behavior: A follow-up study. *Child Development, 57*, 660–680.

Robinson, E. H., Rotter, J. C., Fey. M. A., & Robinson, S. L. (1991). Children's fears: Towards a preventative model. *The School Counselor, 38*, 187–202.

Rosenbaum, J. F., Biederman, J., Bolduc-Murphy, E. A., Faraone, S. V., Chaloff, J., Hirshfeld, D. R., & Kagan, J. (1993). Behavioral inhibition in childhood: A risk factor for anxiety disorders. *Harvard Review of Psychiatry*, May/June, 2–16.

Short, J. L. (1998). Evaluation of a substance abuse prevention and mental health promotion program for children of divorce. *Journal of Divorce and Remarriage, 28*, 139–155.

Soussignan, R., Koch, P., & Montagner, H. (1988). Behavioral and cardiovascular changes in children moving from kindergarten to primary school. *Journal of Child Psychology and Psychiatry, 29*, 321–333.

Spence, S. H. (1994). Prevention. In T. H. Ollendick, N. King, & W. Yule (Eds.), *International handbook of phobic and anxiety disorders in children and adolescents* (pp. 453–474). New York: Plenum.

Spence, S. H. (1996a). A case for prevention. In P. Cotton & H. Jackson (Eds.), *Early Intervention and Preventive Applications of Clinical Psychology* (pp. 1–20). Melbourne: Australian Academic.

Spence, S. H. (1996b). The prevention of anxiety disorders in childhood. In P. Cotton & H. Jackson (Eds.), *Early Intervention and Preventive Applications of Clinical Psychology* (pp. 87–108). Melbourne: Australian Academic.

Spence, S. H., & Dadds, M. R. (1996). Preventing childhood anxiety disorders. *Behaviour Change, 13,* 241–249.

Stemberger, R. T., Turner, S. M., Beidel, D. C., & Calhoun, K. S. (1995). Social phobia: An analysis of possible developmental factors. *Journal of Abnormal Psychology, 104,* 526–531.

Sugar, M. (1989). Children in a disaster: An overview. *Child Psychiatry and Human Development, 19,* 163–179.

Terr, L. C. (1981). Psychic trauma in children: Observations following the Chowchilla school-bus kidnapping. *American Journal of Psychiatry, 138,* 14–19.

Thapar, A., & McGuffin, P. (1995). Are anxiety symptoms in childhood heritable? *Journal of Child Psychology and Psychiatry, 36,* 439–447.

Traughber, B., & Cataldo, M. F. (1983). Biobehavioral effects of pediatric hospitalization. In P. McGrath & P. Firestone (Eds.), *Pediatric and adolescent behavioral medicine: Issues in treatment* (pp. 107–131). New York: Springer.

Turner, S. M., & Beidel, D. C. (1987). Social phobia: Clinical syndrome, diagnosis and comorbidity. *Clinical Psychology Review, 9,* 3–18.

Turner, S. M., Beidel, D. C., Costello, A. (1987). Psychopathology in the offspring of anxiety disorders patients. *Journal of Consulting and Clinical Psychology, 55,* 229–235.

Warren, S. L., Huston, L., Egeland, B., Sroufe, L. A. (1997). Child and adolescent anxiety disorders and early attachment. *Journal of the American Academy of Child and Adolescent Psychiatry, 36,* 637–644.

Weinstein, P. (1990). Breaking the worldwide cycle of pain, fear and avoidance: Uncovering risk factors and promoting prevention for children. *Annals of Behavioral Medicine, 12,* 141–147.

Williams, P. D., Hanson, S., Karlin, R. Ridder, L., Liebergen, A., Olson, J., Barnard, M. U., Tobin-Rommelhart, S. (1997). Outcomes of a nursing intervention for siblings of chronically ill children: A pilot study. *Journal of Social Pediatric Nursing, 2,* 127–137.

Yule, W. (1991). Work with children following disasters. In M. Herbert (Ed.), *Clinical child psychology: A social learning approach to theory and practice* (pp. 349–363). Chichester, England: Wiley.

Yule, W., & Williams, R. (1990). Post-traumatic stress reactions in children. *Journal of Traumatic Stress, 3,* 279–295.

Zubrick, S. R., Silburn, S. R., Teoh, H. J., Carlton, J., Shepherd, C., & Lawrence, D. (1997). *Western Australian Child Health Survey: Education, Health and Competency,* Catalogue 4305.5, Perth, WA: Australian Bureau of Statistics.

III

INTEGRATIVE EXAMPLES

16

The Etiology of Childhood Specific Phobia: A Multifactorial Model

PETER MURIS and HARALD MERCKELBACH

Specific fears of the dark, animals, blood, heights and so on are common in childhood (see, e.g., King, Hamilton, & Ollendick, 1988), yet most of them are short-lived and dissipate within months (Bauer, 1976; Ferrari, 1986). However, in some children, specific fears become severe and invalidating in the sense that they interfere with normal functioning. In these cases, the diagnosis of specific phobia should be considered (see the latest edition of the *Diagnostic and statistical manual of mental disorders* [DSM-IV] published by the American Psychiatric Association in 1994).

The present chapter describes a multifactorial model of the etiology of (childhood) specific phobias. The model that is sketched draws heavily on ideas and concepts proposed by other authors (e.g., Craske, 1997; Taylor, 1998; King, Gullone, & Ollendick, 1998) and attempts to integrate the empirical material that has accumulated over the past years. It rests on the following observations:

1. The majority of children display normal developmental fears that wane with the passage of time.
2. A minority of children have a genetic vulnerability that predisposes them to develop maladaptive fears.
3. This genetic vulnerability manifests itself in certain behavioral patterns.
4. Discrete learning experiences interact with normal developmental fears and genetically linked behavioral patterns to produce extremely persistent fears that culminate in specific phobias.
5. Once a specific phobia exists, it is maintained by cognitive biases.

The sections that follow are organized around these points. The chapter concludes with a critical discussion of the model and its concurrents.

Normal and Abnormal Childhood Fears

Normal Fears

Studies on childhood fears have relied predominantly on surveys that list a broad range of potentially fear-provoking stimuli. A widely used instrument

355

for this purpose is the revised version of the Fear Survey Schedule for Children (FSSC-R; Ollendick, 1983). The FSSC-R asks children to indicate on three-point scales ("none", "some", "a lot") how much they fear specific stimuli or situations. FSSC-R surveys indicate that "normal" children and adolescents report a surprisingly large number of fears. For example, Ollendick, King, and Frary (1989) found an average of 14 fears reported by American and Australian youths aged 7–17 years. There are good reasons to believe that this number is quite similar across different nationalities (e.g., Ollendick, Yang, King, Dong, & Akande, 1996), that girls exhibit significantly more fears than boys (Ollendick et al., 1989), and that younger children endorse more specific fears than older children (Ollendick et al., 1989). A recent study by Gullone and King (1997) showed that, although children's level of fearfulness generally decreased over a 3-year period, initial fear scores were good predictors of follow-up fear scores—suggesting a trait component of fearfulness.

Studies employing the FSSC-R consistently indicate that prevalent fears of children are nearly always related to dangerous situations and physical harm. More specifically, FSSC-R studies revealed the following rank order for common childhood fears: (1) not being able to breathe; (2) being hit by a car or truck; (3) bombing attacks; (4) getting burned by fire; (5) falling from a high place; (6) burglar breaking into the house; (7) earthquake; (8) death; (9) illness; and (10) snakes (e.g., Ollendick et al., 1989; Ollendick, Yule, & Ollier, 1991). It is obvious that this rank order depends critically on the fear items listed by the FSSC-R (see, for a similar argument in the adult literature, Kirkpatrick, 1984). Recently, Muris and colleagues (Muris, Merckelbach, & Collaris, 1997; Muris, Merckelbach, Meesters, & Van Lier, 1997) examined the prevalence of common childhood fears by employing a different approach. In their studies, fear rank orders were obtained by asking children what they feared most without specifying items a priori. Results indicated that the fear rank order based on this "free option" method substantially deviates from that produced by the FSSC-R surveys (see Muris, Merckelbach et al., 1997). For example, whereas the free option method suggests that top intense fears pertain to animals (in particular, fear of spiders), FSSC-R studies indicate that top intense fears have to do with danger and death.

Developmental Patterns

A number of studies have investigated the developmental course of childhood fears (see, for a detailed review, Marks, 1987). In this context, one of the most cited studies is that by Bauer (1976) who asked 4- to 12-year-old children to specify what they feared most. Results showed that 74% of the 4- to 6- year-olds, 53% of the 6- to 8-year-olds, but only 5% of the 10- to 12-year-olds reported fears of ghosts and monsters. In contrast, only 11% of the 4- to 6-year- olds, but 53% of the 6- to 8-year-olds, and 55% of the 10- to 12-year-olds reported fears of bodily injury and physical danger. Similar results were obtained by Muris, Merckelbach, Gadet, and Moulaert (2000) who investigated the content of fear among 4- to 12-year-old children. Their study also illustrates that specific fears are fairly common among 4- to 6-year old children (71.0%), peak between the ages 7 to 9 (87.0%), and then decline in 10- to 12-year-olds (67.8%). Taken together, these results imply that the content of fears changes as children grow older and that fears are most prominent in the 7–9 years age range. In addition, the developmental changes of specific fears follow a highly predictable course, a phenomenon that has been termed "the ontogenetic parade of normal fears (Marks, 1987, p. 109).

Children's cognitive capacities are an important determinant of the onto-genetic parade of fears. This is not surprising given the fact that fear origi-nates from threat and threat has to be conceptualized. Conceptualization, in turn, depends critically on cognitive abilities (e.g., Vasey, 1993). Thus, at very young ages, specific fears are directed at immediate, concrete threats (e.g., loud noises, loss of physical support, separation of mother). As cognitive abilities reach a certain maturational stage, specific fears become more sophisticated. For example, at 9 months, children learn to differentiate between familiar and unfamiliar faces and, consequently, fear of strangers becomes manifest. Following this, fears of imaginary creatures occur and these are thought to be intimately linked to the magical thinking of toddlers (Bauer, 1976). Fear of animals also develops during this phase. These fears are believed to be functionally linked to the increasing mobility of the child. That is, fear of animals would have survival value, as it would protect the mobile child from predators (Öhman, Dimberg, & Öst, 1985). From age 7 onwards, children are increasingly able to infer physical cause effect rela-tionships and to anticipate potential negative outcomes. These cognitive changes probably broaden the range of fear-provoking stimuli and, thus, fear of blood and injury, natural events, and social encounters develop (e.g., Vasey & Daleiden, 1994).

Several recent studies have investigated the prevalence and phenomen-ology of panic attacks in children and adolescents (e.g., Hayward et al., 1992; King, Gullone, Tonge, & Ollendick, 1993). These studies suggest that, whereas only a small minority of young children experience isolated panic attacks, their incidence increases dramatically as children grow older. There is evidence to support the idea that children's interpretation of panic attacks changes as a function of cognitive development. While young children tend to relate panic symptoms to external causes, adolescents attribute panic symptoms to internal sources (Nelles & Barlow, 1988). It is only with such internal, catastrophic interpretations (e.g., "I am losing control", "I am going crazy") that a full-blown panic syndrome may develop. In contrast, external interpretations of panic symptoms may sustain a pathological radi-calization of specific fears, a point to which we will return later.

Severity of Childhood Fears

It is far from clear how serious developmental fears are. In Ollendick and King's (1994) words: "Do children really worry about that many fears on a frequent or regular basis? Do they engage in avoidance behaviors to prevent their occurrence? Do the reported fears interfere with their daily functioning?" (p. 635). Few studies have addressed these questions in a systematic fashion. In a survey by McCathie and Spence (1991), children were asked to complete the FSSC-R and the Fear Frequency and Avoidance Survey Schedule for Children (FFASSC). The FFASSC measures the frequency with which children respond with fearful thoughts and avoidance behavior to fear items listed by the FSSC-R. McCathie and Spence noted that there are robust connections between the most commonly reported fears on the FSSC-R and the frequency of fearful thoughts and avoidance behaviors. Thus, not only did children report having FSSC-R defined fears, they also said that these fears were accompanied by aversive thoughts and avoidance behavior. Likewise, Ollendick and King (1994) found that a large majority of children (more than 60%) reported that their fears interfered substantially with daily activities.

These findings emphasize the point that childhood fears are often seriously distressing. Yet, in order to get a better picture of the clinical significance of these fears, their connection to DSM-defined specific phobias and other anxiety disorders should be considered. A recent study by Muris, Merckelbach, Mayer, and Prins (2000) explored this issue. Fears of 290 children aged 8–13 years were assessed and then their severity was evaluated by means of a structured diagnostic interview measuring anxiety disorders in terms of DSM criteria. Results showed that in a sizeable minority of the children (22.8%), fears reflect significant anxiety disorders, notably specific phobias. There has been a strong tendency in the literature to portray childhood fears as mild and nonpathological phenomena (e.g., Rutter, Tizard, & Whitmore, 1968). While this may be true most of the time, the studies summarized in this section make clear that at least a subgroup of children evidence clinically significant and disabling phobias.

Childhood Specific Phobias

Epidemiological surveys have yielded prevalence rates of childhood specific phobias that vary between 2% and 9% (see, for reviews, Bernstein & Borchardt, 1991; Ollendick, Hagopian, & King, 1997). However, a recent study (Costello et al., 1996) that recruited nonclinical samples from the 9–13 years age range found markedly lower 3-months prevalence rates for specific phobias: 0.42% for girls and 0.13% for boys. Whatever the cause of these discrepancies in prevalence rates, there can be little doubt that specific phobias are one of the most commonly diagnosed anxiety disorders in children.

There is little consensus about the natural course of childhood specific phobias. Whereas there is evidence that a substantial proportion of these phobias remit without treatment (e.g., Agras, Chapin, & Oliveau, 1972), retrospective studies of adult phobic patients clearly demonstrate that specific phobias often have their onset in childhood (e.g., Öst, 1987). As a matter of fact, Thyer, Parrish, Curtis, Nesse, and Cameron (1985) found that almost half of their large sample of patients with specific phobias reported an onset in the preteen years. In agreement with the latter position are the results of Strauss and Last (1993). These authors examined onset ages and other features of specific phobia in children referred for treatment services. The mean age of their sample was 11 years, while the mean onset age reported by this sample was 7.8 years, suggesting that specific childhood phobias have a relatively long history before they enter treatment programs.

Conflicting results about the developmental stability of childhood specific phobias may be more apparent than real. For example, Last, Perrin, Hersen, and Kazdin (1998) reported that 3 years after the initial diagnosis of an anxiety disorder, a large majority of clinically referred children and adolescents no longer met the criteria for their initial diagnosis. However, a substantial percentage of these "recovered children switched to a new anxiety disorder. This is an important finding because it suggests the presence of a general, higher order factor that predisposes to a broad spectrum of anxiety disorders. Last and associates also noted that separation anxiety disorder had the highest recovery rate (96%), whereas specific phobias were characterized by relatively low recovery rates (69%). A survey by Newman et al. (1996) demonstrates that, from childhood to early adulthood, anxiety disorder diagnoses become progressively more stable. Thus it is safe to assume that, while not all childhood specific phobias persist into adulthood, adult specific phobias often have their origins in childhood or early adolescence.

Overall, girls have higher scores on self-report measures of fear than do boys (e.g., Ollendick et al., 1989). Does this mean that they are at a higher risk for developing specific phobias? The answer seems to be affirmative. According to the DSM IV, between 75% and 90% of the adults with animal, situational, or natural environment phobias are female. For blood-injection-injury phobia, the male–female distribution is somewhat more balanced: between 55% and 70% of the individuals with this type of phobia are female (Frederikson, Annas, Fischer, & Wik, 1996). As demonstrated by Muris, Schmidt, & Merckelbach (1999), the skewed sex distribution of specific phobia symptoms is also evident for children and adolescents.

In conclusion, then, specific fears are common in childhood and there are good reasons to believe that cognitive development is linked to the content of these fears. Furthermore, in most children, these fears represent transitory phenomena. Yet, in a subgroup, specific fears become chronic and develop into a phobia. The factors that are involved in this radicalization of childhood fears can be roughly grouped into genetically linked factors and environmental influences.

Genetically Linked Factors

Genetics

Specific fears and phobias run in families. This point is illustrated by the work of Fyer and colleagues (1990) who found that first-degree relatives (i.e., brothers and sisters) of probands with specific phobias more frequently suffered from specific phobias (31%) than relatives of control probands (11%). In addition, 15% of the children of the specific phobia probands were diagnosed with specific phobia, compared with 8% of the children of the control probands. Results also indicated that first-degree relatives of specific phobia probands did not have an increased risk for any psychiatric disorder other than specific phobia. On the basis of these findings, Fyer et al. (1990, p. 255) conclude that "specific phobia is a highly familial disorder that breeds true." This conclusion is further substantiated by recent work of Frederikson, Annas, and Wik (1997) who documented that spider and snake phobic women often report a positive familial history of such phobias.

In general, behavioral–genetic studies have shown clearly that genetic transmission contributes to the familial aggregation of specific fears and phobias. Rose and Ditto (1983) compared the frequency of self-reported fears in monozygotic and dizygotic twin pairs with ages ranging between 10 and 34 years. These authors found that a twin's level of fearfulness could be predicted from the co-twin's score. Also, the frequency of fears was more similar in monozygotic than in dizygotic twin pairs. By and large, these findings were replicated in a twin study of Stevenson, Batten, and Cherner (1992). These authors conducted analyses on FSSC-R scores of monozygotic and dizygotic twins in the 8–16 years age range and this led to two major conclusions. To begin with, whereas heritability (h^2) was significant for the summed FSSC-R scores, the specific FSSC-R components revealed a diverse picture, with some components having a nonsignificant heritability (e.g., medical fears) and others having a highly significant heritability (e.g., fear of injury and small animals: $h^2 = 0.46$). Second, no evidence was found to suggest that heritabilities increase at the extreme end of the fear continuum.

Taylor (1998) reviewed a number of large-scale behavioral–genetic studies concerned with phobias. Although this review was not particularly focused on childhood phobias, his differentiation between general and specific genetic factors is relevant to the present discussion. The general genetic factor acts as a vulnerability factor to a wide range of phobic fears, while specific factors predispose to certain types of fears. Taylor (1998, p. 211) summarized the role of both factors in phobic etiology as follows:

> The general factor tended to make a modest contribution to agoraphobia, situational phobia, and social phobia (7–10% of variance; mean = 9%) and a greater contribution to animal phobia (35%). Conversely, specific genetic factors were more important for agoraphobia, situational phobia, and social phobia (20–29%; mean = 23%) compared to animal phobia (0%).

Taylor points out that the general genetic component may constitute the biological substrate of what is typically referred to as "negative affectivity" or "neuroticism." Evidence for the idea that a general genetic factor contributes to anxiety via temperamental traits comes from a study by Zinbarg and Barlow (1996). That study relied on a large sample of anxiety-disordered adults, including patients with specific phobias. Patients completed a battery of self-report scales selected to provide a broad coverage of the key symptoms of various DSM-defined anxiety disorders. Scores on these scales were subjected to factor analyses and this revealed a general higher order trait common to all anxiety disorder diagnoses. Further evidence for a general higher order trait is provided by Hofmann, Lehman, and Barlow (1997), who noted that having one specific phobia also increases the likelihood of experiencing subclinical fears from other phobia subtypes. An obvious behavioral approximation of this higher order trait is behavioral inhibition.

Behavioral Inhibition

Behavioral inhibition is the tendency of some children to interrupt ongoing behavior and react with vocal restraint and withdrawal when confronted with unfamiliar people or settings. Behavioral inhibition is thought to be a stable and inherited response disposition that characterizes approximately 10–15% of these children (e.g., Kagan, Reznick, Clarke, Snidman, & Garcia-Coll, 1984). Cross-sectional and longitudinal data collected by Biederman and colleagues (1990, 1993) strongly suggest that this response disposition is a risk factor for anxiety disorders. These studies showed that preschool children identified as behaviorally inhibited are more likely to have anxiety disorders (including phobias) than control children. This became even more prominent at a 3-year follow-up: in the cohort of children who were initially identified as behaviorally inhibited, the rates of specific phobias and other anxiety disorders had increased markedly (see, for a review, Biederman, Rosenbaum, Chaloff, & Kagan, 1995). Thus, behavioral inhibition seems to be a vulnerability factor for a broad range of anxiety disorders, among which are specific phobias. It is not surprising, therefore, that it has been linked to higher order constructs such as neuroticism, trait anxiety (Craske, 1997), and negative affectivity (Clark, Watson, & Mineka, 1994).

In line with the results from behavioral inhibition studies, Stevenson-Hinde and Glover (1996) found that extreme shyness in preschool children is accompanied by relatively high levels of negative mood, worry, and fears. Behavioural inhibition, and in its wake shyness, are considered to be enduring temperamental traits that are relatively stable from early to middle and late childhood (Kagan, Reznick, Snidman, 1987, 1988; Scarpa, Raine, Venables, & Mednick, 1995; Gest, 1997). However, few studies have looked directly at the connection between behavioral inhibition/shyness and anxiety symptoms in older children. One exception is a recent study by Muris, Merckelbach, Wessel, and Van de Ven (1999). Children aged 12–14 years were provided with a definition of behavioral inhibition and then asked to classify themselves as low, middle, or high on behavioral inhibition. In addition, children completed questionnaires of worry, depression, and anxiety symptoms. Results showed that children in the high behavioral inhibition category had elevated levels of anxiety, worry, and depression compared with children who endorsed the low or middle behavioral inhibition categories. Moreover, children who rated themselves high on behavioral inhibition more frequently exhibited anxiety disorder symptoms in the subclinical range than did children scoring low or intermediate on behavioral inhibition.

As to the biological underpinnings of behavioral inhibition, relevant parameters have been identified by Schmidt and coworkers (1997). These researchers noted that behaviorally inhibited children exhibit relatively high morning levels of the stress hormone cortisol. They speculated that high levels of cortisol may sensitize subcortical arousal circuits (e.g., amygdala, hypothalamus) and this would make children more prone to develop serious anxiety symptoms. Interestingly, work on psychophysiological parameters that tap subcortical fear responsivity (e.g., the eye blink startle reflex; Vrana, Spence, & Lang, 1988) support such an interpretation. For example, Grillon, Dierker, and Merikangas (1997) measured startle reflexes in children with a parental history of an anxiety disorder (who often meet the criteria for behavioral inhibition; see Rosenbaum et al., 1988) and control children. It was found that startle magnitude was relatively elevated in children of parents with an anxiety disorder. This is in agreement with the notion that anxiety-prone (i.e., behaviorally inhibited) children have hyperexcitable subcortical circuits that may promote fear behavior (see, for an extensive review, Rosen & Schulkin, 1998).

Another promising research area is concerned with the connection between frontal brain asymmetries and behavioral inhibition. A variety of evidence (see, for a review, Tomarken & Keener, 1998) indicates that the left frontal areas sustain approach behavior, while the right frontal areas are involved in avoidance behavior. This raises the possibility that a stable right frontal hyperactivation is a biological substrate of the tendency to react with withdrawal to potentially threatening stimuli. Germane to this issue is a study by Davidson and Fox (1989) who demonstrated that young infants with a strong activated right frontal hemisphere tend to react with crying to subsequent maternal separation. More recent studies suggest that relative right frontal hyperactivation in children is linked to a much broader response style that comes close to behavioral inhibition (e.g., Calkins, Fox, & Marshall, 1996). Perhaps, then, relative right frontal hyperactivation might be a good marker of behavioral inhibition and, possibly, severity of childhood specific phobias. While there have been some studies of EEG asymmetries in adult phobics (e.g., Davidson, 1998; Merckelbach, Muris, Pool, & De Jong, 1998), more research is required to delineate the precise connections between EEG frontal asymmetries, behavioral inhibition, and childhood specific phobias (see, for a critical review, Turner, Beidel, & Wolff, 1996).

Disgust Sensitivity

The studies reviewed above converge on the notion that behavioral inhibition affects a broad spectrum of phobic disorders. Thus, it qualifies as the behavioral expression of what Taylor (1997) termed a higher order genetic factor.

According to this author, lower order (i.e., more specific) genetic factors and their behavioral manifestations seem to play a less prominent role in specific phobias, but one possible exception in this context is disgust. Disgust has been identified as a food-related basic emotion, in part because it has clear biologically prewired antecedents. For example, young babies react with a spitting reflex when they are exposed to bitter substances (Ekman, 1992). Disgust sensitivity can be measured reliably with self-report scales that contain items like "It bothers me to see someone in a restaurant eating messy food with his fingers" (Haidt, McCauley, & Rozin, 1994). Psychometric studies have revealed that scores on such disgust scales are correlated positively with neuroticism and negatively with sensation seeking, although the correlations with these fundamental traits are modest (Haidt et al., 1994; Hennig, Pössel, & Netter, 1996).

Haidt and associates (1994, p. 711) concluded that "Disgust appears to make people cautious not only about what they put into their mouths, but about what they do with their bodies." Yet, recent findings suggest that the contribution of disgust sensitivity to anxiety is much more specific. There is now good evidence that disgust sensitivity is involved in the genesis of certain types of specific phobias, in particular animal phobias and blood-injection-injury phobias. For example, Matchett and Davey (1991; see also Merckelbach, De Jong, Arntz, & Schouten, 1993) found a positive association between measures of disgust sensitivity and scores on the animal phobia scale of the Fear Survey Schedule. A subsequent study (Davey, Forster, & Mayhew, 1993) not only noted a significant correlation between parents' and children's disgust scores, but also indicated that parental disgust sensitivity was the main predictor of offspring animal fear.

Only one study has investigated directly the role of disgust sensitivity in childhood animal phobia. De Jong, Andrea, and Muris (1997) assessed fear of spiders, disgust sensitivity, and spiders' disgust-evoking status in spider phobic girls who applied for treatment, in nonphobic girls, and in the parents of both groups of children. Phobic girls were tested twice, before and after behavioral treatment. The idea that disgust is an important aspect of spider phobia was supported by the following findings. To begin with, compared with control girls, spider phobic girls exhibited higher levels of disgust sensitivity and considered spiders per se as more disgusting. Second, after treatment, the reduction in spider fear was paralleled by a decline in spiders' disgust-evoking status. Third, mothers of spider phobic girls attributed a high disgust-evoking status to spiders. De Jong et al. (1997, p. 559) interpret the latter finding in terms of modeling experiences: "The acquisition of spider fear is facilitated by specific parental disgust reactions when confronted with spiders." Alternatively, it may well be the case that a genetic factor is involved in the familial transmission of disgust sensitivity and, in its wake, animal phobia.

As to the connection between disgust and blood-injection-injury (BII) phobia, Page (1994) has argued that elevated disgust sensitivity is responsible for the fainting component of BII phobia. Consistent with a genetic interpretation are studies that report strong parent–child correspondence for fainting reactions to BII stimuli (e.g., Kleinknecht & Lenz, 1989). Unfortunately, no study has explored the links between disgust sensitivity and BII fear in children. Meanwhile, adult studies suggest that this may be a promising line of rescarch. For example, Tolin, Lohr, Sawchuk, and Lee (1997) demonstrated that both spider phobic and BII phobic undergraduates exhibited elevated disgust sensitivity levels (see, for a similar finding, De Jong & Merckelbach, 1998). Interestingly, Tolin and colleagues found suggestive evidence that spider phobics react with a combination of fear and disgust to spiders, whereas BII phobics react with disgust rather than fear to medical stimuli.

Some authors (e.g., Phillips, Senior, Fahy, & David, 1998) have speculated that the basic emotion of disgust underlies a wide range of psychiatric symptoms. According to these authors, not only certain types of phobias, but also depression, eating disorders, and obsessive–compulsive disorder, would be related to disgust sensitivity. The evidence for such a broad relevance of disgust to psychopathology is, however, meager. In the final analysis, disgust can best be conceptualized as a rather specific factor.

Fear of Suffocation

Panic attacks are discrete episodes of intense fear accompanied by strong bodily sensations (e.g., shortness of breath, dizziness, sweating). Epidemiological surveys indicate that specific phobias are strongly comorbid with panic attacks (e.g., Magee, Eaton, Wittchen, McGonagle, & Kessler, 1996). While DSM-IV descriptions of specific phobias portray panic attacks as secondary consequences of these conditions, evidence from various sources suggests that the role of panic attacks in the etiology of certain specific phobias may be more prominent than previously thought. There is, of course, older work demonstrating that panic attacks may constitute conditioning trials that produce persistent agoraphobic avoidance (e.g., Gorman, Liebowitz, Fyer, & Stein, 1989). Likewise, studies examining key cognitions of claustrophobia show that typical panic thoughts such as fear of suffocation, loosing control, and being trapped dominate this type of phobia and that successful treatment of claustrophobia depends critically on the extent to which these cognitions can be corrected (e.g., Shafran, Booth, & Rachman, 1993).

More recent work indicates an even closer connection between certain specific phobia types and panic. For example, Verburg, Griez, and Meijer (1994; see also Antony, Brown, & Barlow, 1997) exposed patients with animal phobias, patients with situational or natural environment phobias, and control subjects to a 35% carbon dioxide panic provocation challenge. These authors noted that patients with situational or natural environment phobias, but not animal phobics or controls, reacted with an increase in subjective anxiety that was similar to that found in earlier studies with panic patients. According to Verburg et al., situational/natural environment phobias are characterized by excessive fear of suffocation, and panic-like experiences may be responsible for the onset of this category of specific phobias. By this view, isolated panic attacks are attributed by the patient to the context in which it occurred and this could result in a specific phobia. Consistent with such an interpretation are the findings of Himle, Crystal, Curtis, and Fluent (1991), who found that almost half of their sample of situational phobics ascribed the onset of their complaints to a panic-like experience in specific situations that subsequently became phobogenic (see also Merckelbach, De Ruiter, Van den Hout, & Hoekstra, 1989). Further support for the link between certain specific phobia types and panic is provided by the high incidence of natural environment and situational fears among panic disorder patients (De Ruiter, Rijken, Garssen, Van Schaik, & Kraaimaat, 1989; Starcevic & Bogojevic, 1997). In most cases, these specific fears and phobias precede the onset of panic disorder.

Exaggerated fear of suffocation is thought to reflect a biological and possibly heritable trait linked to what Klein (1993) has termed "hypersensitive suffocation detectors." According to Klein, these hypothetical brain detectors trigger panic attacks in response to a broad range of stimuli that may signal a lack of useful air (i.e., suffocation). Support for this conceptualization comes from the finding that respiratory abnormalities in response to challenges occur more often in anxiety disordered children than in controls (Pine et al., 1998), from studies showing that the incidence of anxiety disorders (among which severe specific phobias) is considerably heightened in children with asthma (Bussing, Burket, & Kelleher, 1996), and from a medical condition known as "congenital hypoventilation syndrome" (Ondine's curse) in which children have a deficient suffocation detector and evidence fewer anxiety symptoms (Pine et al., 1994). To the extent that the role of hypersensitive suffocation detectors in situational/environmental phobias is genetically determined, it can be considered as a specific genetic contribution. On the other hand, hypersensitive suffocation detectors trigger isolated panic attacks and it is these panic attacks that are believed to set up conditioning trials leading to phobic avoidance (Forsyth & Eifert, 1996). Thus, panic attacks may also be conceived as learning experiences, an issue to which we turn now.

Environmental Influences

By and large, twin studies have shown that genetic factors play a significant but modest role in the etiology of specific phobias. Most of these studies have come up with heritability estimates for specific phobias that are considerably lower than those for, say, bipolar disorders or schizophrenia. For example, Kendler et al. (1992, p. 279) conclude from their analysis of twin data that "the estimated heritability of liability for phobias (...) indicates that genetic factors play a significant but by no means overwhelming role in the etiology of phobias." A similar conclusion can be drawn from studies concerned with behavioral inhibition in children. About 70% of the children classified as behaviorally inhibited remain free of any anxiety disorder (Biederman et al., 1990). Apparently, then, environmental factors determine whether genetically transmitted vulnerabilities culminate in specific phobias.

Following Taylor (1998), one may differentiate between general environmental factors contributing to all phobias and specific environmental factors unique to each type of phobia. Negative life events and dysfunctional parental rearing behavior constitute such a general factor, while discrete learning experiences correspond to specific environmental factors.

Negative Life Events

Several studies have found an increased incidence of negative life events such as parental divorce or death of significant family members in clinically anxious children (Benjamin, Costello, & Warren, 1990; Goodyer, Wright, & Altham, 1990; Kashani et al. 1990). However, it is unlikely that these life events per se are responsible for the emergence of phobias or other anxiety disorders. Spence and Dadds (1996) argue that the negative impact of aversive life events critically depends on factors that either exacerbate (e.g., behavioral inhibition; cf. *supra*) or buffer (e.g., social support and effective coping strategies) their effects. Interestingly, Hekmat (1987) found some evidence to suggest that environmental stressors produce a larger fear increase in individuals with traits that are related to neuroticism.

A more articulated theory about the contribution of negative life experiences to the etiology of specific phobias was proposed by Jacobs and Nadel (1985). These authors noted that developmental fears may reappear after exposure to stressful events. According to the Jacobs and Nadel model, the slowly maturing hippocampus is responsible for contextual control and inhibition of developmental fears. However, stressful conditions would disrupt hippocampal functioning and this would result in the re-emergence of context-free and stereotyped fear responses that are typical for early maturational stages. While the Jacobs and Nadel theory offers an interesting perspective on the role of negative life events in the radicalization of developmental fears, direct empirical evidence supporting this model is lacking (see, for a critical review, McNally, 1989).

Parental Rearing Behaviors

A number of studies have examined the role of parental rearing behaviors in the development of anxiety disorders (e.g., Rapee, 1997). Basically, these studies have followed one of two research lines. The first line is inspired by attachment theory and focuses on early parent–child interactions. The second line is based on a broader perspective and examines the connection between ongoing parental rearing behaviors (i.e., parental rearing styles) and anxiety.

Attachment theory proposes that children's level of anxiety is affected by the way in which they are attached to their caregivers (Bowlby, 1973). There is, indeed, evidence to suggest that early attachment relationships are connected to fear and anxiety in later childhood. For example, in their prospective study, Warren and colleagues (1997) classified infants as either securely or insecurely attached. When children reached 17.5 years of age, current and past anxiety disorders were assessed by means of an interview schedule. Insecurely attached children more frequently suffered from anxiety disorders than control children. Unfortunately, Warren and associates did not include specific phobias in their analyses. A recent study by Muris, Mayer, and Meesters (2000) further examined the connection between attachment styles and anxiety disorder symptomatology. Children were asked to complete Hazan and Shaver's (1987) single-item measure of attachment style and the Screen for Child Anxiety Related Emotional Disorders (SCARED; Birmaher et al., 1997; Muris, Merckelbach, Schmidt, & Mayer, 1999), an index of DSM-defined anxiety disorder symptoms. In accordance with Bowlby's position, insecurely attached children exhibited elevated levels of anxiety disorder symptomatology compared with securely attached children. However, securely and insecurely attached children did not differ with regard to specific phobia symptoms. Thus, while insecure attachment seems to promote the development of the more complex anxiety disorders (e.g., generalized anxiety disorder), there is no direct evidence that this factor also plays a major role in the etiology of specific phobias.

While attachment researchers emphasize that disturbances in early parent–child interactions promote the development of high anxiety levels in children, others have stressed the importance of particular parental rearing styles. Evidence for this position comes from two classes of studies. The first relies on direct observation of current parent–child interactions. Following such an approach, Dadds and colleagues (Dadds, Barrett, & Rapee, 1996; see, for a review, Dadds & Barrett, 1996) noted that parents of anxious children often encourage their children to rely on avoidant coping strategies. Similarly, a study by Muris, Steerneman, Merckelbach, and Meesters (1996) demonstrated that specific fears reported by the children are a function of the extent to which mothers express their own fears in the presence of their children. A second class of studies makes use of questionnaires that intend to measure children's perceptions of parental rearing behaviors. For example, in a study by Muris and Merckelbach (1998a), normal schoolchildren completed the child version of the EMBU (Egna Minnen Betraffende Uppfostran [My memories of upbringing]; Castro et al. 1993), a questionnaire that taps children's perceptions of four main dimensions of parental rearing behaviors: emotional warmth, rejection, control, and anxious rearing. Additionally, children completed the SCARED (cf. *supra*). Results revealed significant and positive relationships between, on the one hand, anxious rearing behaviors and parental control, and, on the other hand, anxiety disorder symptomatology—in particular, symptoms of generalized anxiety disorder, separation anxiety disorder, and to a lesser degree situational/natural environment phobia.

Specific Learning Experiences

According to Rachman's (1977, 1991) influential three-pathways theory, there are three types of discrete learning experiences that may play a role in the acquisition of phobias: (1) aversive classical conditioning; (2) modeling (vicarious learning); and (3) negative information transmission (exposure to negative information about the phobic object). Rachman (1977) further speculated that severity of fears is a function of acquisition mode. More specifically, fears acquired through vicarious learning or exposure to negative information would be less intense, whereas clinical phobias would be more likely to have a direct conditioning etiology.

Several studies have sought to test Rachman's three-pathways theory (see, for reviews, Menzies & Clarke, 1994; Merckelbach, De Jong, Muris, & Van den Hout, 1996; King et al., 1998; Muris & Merckelbach, 1998b). In most of these studies, adult phobics were asked to what extent the three pathways contributed to the onset of their complaints. Overall, these studies found some (but by no means unequivocal) support for Rachman's hypothesis that direct conditioning is the predominant pathway in clinical phobias, while indirect pathways (modeling and exposure to negative information) more frequently figure in the etiology of mild fears (Öst, 1991). One problematic feature of these findings is that they were based on patients who were asked to assign their pertinent learning experiences to the three pathways 10–20 years after the onset of their specific phobias (e.g., Menzies, Kirkby, & Harris, 1998). While it is true that the unreliability of retrospective reports should not be exaggerated (Brewin, Andrews, & Gotlib, 1993), support for the three-pathway theory would be stronger if it came from children and adolescents who were closer to the onset of their specific fears or phobias.

A number of recent studies have interviewed parents about the etiological pathways of their children's phobias or fears, whereas others have explored etiological routes to childhood specific fears and phobias by asking children directly about their learning experiences. The main findings of both categories of studies are listed in table 16.1.

Graham and Gaffan (1997) compared water-fearful children with nonfearful controls and had mothers of both groups complete a child fear origins questionnaire. Most mothers (78%) of fearful children said that the child's fear had always been present, but they also reported exposure to negative information and, to a lesser extent, aversive modeling and conditioning experiences. Remarkably, such learning experiences were also described by mothers of nonfearful children. Thus, these findings suggest that learning experiences of the sort implicated in Rachman's three-pathway theory are not so much responsible for the origins of fears, but rather play a role in their persistence and radicalization.

Table 16.1. Origins of Childhood Specific Fears and Phobias: Type of Fear, Sample Sizes, and Main Results

Study	Fear/phobia	Sample	Phobic origins	
Parent-based attributions				
Graham & Gaffan (1997)	Fear of water	9	Conditioning	22%
			Modeling	11%
			Negative information	78%
			Don't know	22%
Milgrom et al. (1995)	Dental fear	174	No percentages specified	
Menzies & Clarke (1993)	Water phobia	50	Conditioning	2%
			Modeling	26%
			Negative information	14%
			Always been afraid	56%
King et al. (1997)	Dog phobia	30	Conditioning	27%
			Modeling	53%
			Negative information	7%
			Don't know	13%
Child based attributions				
Ollendick & King (1991)	10 common FSSC-R fears	1092	Conditioning	37%
			Modeling	56%
			Negative information	89%
Muris, Merckelbach, & Collaris (1997)	Top intense fears	192	Conditioning	61%
			Modeling	50%
			Negative information	88%
Doogan & Thomas (1992)	Fear of dogs	11	Conditioning	91%
			Modeling	73%
			Negative information	82%
Merckelbach, Muris, & Schouten (1996)	Spider phobia	22	Conditioning	41%
			Modeling	14%
			Negative information	5%
			Always been afraid	46%
Merckelbach & Muris (1997)	Spider phobia	26	Conditioning	23%
			Modeling	8%
			Negative information	4%
			Always been afraid	62%

Note. In most studies, percentages do not add up to 100% since youths and/or parents could endorse more than one pathway.

In their large-scale study on the origins of childhood dental fear, Milgrom, Mancl, King, and Weinstein (1995) did not specify exact frequencies of conditioning, modeling, and negative information experiences in the subsample of fearful children. However, information about potential learning experiences provided by the mothers was subjected to a regression analysis and this led the authors to conclude that "both direct conditioning and parental modeling factors were significant independent predictors of fear level even when controlling for gender, age, and other sociodemographic and attitudinal factors" (p. 318). At the very least, this suggests that an analysis of childhood fears in terms of Rachman's three-pathways is informative.

Menzies and Clarke (1993) as well as King, Clowes-Hollins, and Ollendick (1997) focused on clinically significant fears. Like Graham and Gaffan (1997), Menzies and Clarke found that the majority of parents (56%) believed that their child's water phobia had always been present. Even so, modeling episodes, exposure to negative information, and to a lesser extent conditioning experiences were reported as either "most influential" (modeling) or "somewhat influential" (negative information) factors in the etiology of their child's phobia. Remarkably similar findings were reported by King et al. In their study, parents endorsed modeling as the most important factor contributing to the development of their child's dog phobia, while very few parents endorsed exposure to negative information as the major pathway.

The studies reviewed so far were based on parental attributions, but as King et al. (1997, p. 77) rightly point out, reliance on parental perceptions of fear acquisition "may be quite invalid in terms of what actually occurred." In what seems to be the largest study on origins of childhood fears, Ollendick and King (1991) evaluated to what extent Rachman's theory of fear acquisition can be applied to the top 10 intensive FSSC-R fears. Children who reported "a lot" of fear to FSSC-R items such as "not being able to breathe", "being hit by a car or truck", and so forth, were given a short questionnaire that asked them whether they had experienced conditioning, modeling, and/ or informational events related to these stimuli or situations. The authors found that a majority of the children (88.8%) attributed their fear to negative information. Modeling and conditioning events were less often mentioned by the children (56.2% and 35.7%, respectively).

In an attempt to replicate these findings, Muris, Merckelbach, and Collaris (1997) had children specify their top intense fear and then asked them whether conditioning, modeling, and negative information played a role in that fear. Like Ollendick and King (1991), these authors found that exposure to negative information was the most prominent pathway to fear mentioned by the children, followed by conditioning and modeling. In the Muris et al. study, children were also explicitly asked to what extent these learning experiences intensified their fears. Thus, whereas Ollendick and King (1991) employed broad definitions of the three types of learning experiences ("Did it play a role?"), children in the Muris et al. study answered the additional question about whether these experiences served as antecedents of a radicalization of their fear. With this more strict definition, 46% of the children endorsed a conditioning pathway, while modeling and negative information were less often mentioned (4% and 35%, respectively).

Consistent with this are the findings of Doogan and Thomas (1992) who found that a large majority of dog-fearful children reported aversive conditioning encounters with dogs. However, the frequencies with which dog-fearful children reported such experiences did not differ from those found in a group of nonfearful children, a finding that parallels the results of Graham and Gaffan (1997). Apparently, then, these learning experiences are not the primary cause of fear.

In a study by Merckelbach, Muris, and Schouten (1996), children with a severe spider phobia were interviewed about conditioning events, modeling experiences, and negative information transmission. To evaluate the reliability of the information provided by the children, parents were interviewed independently about the origins of their child's phobia. Conditioning events were reported by a substantial proportion of spider phobic children and a majority of these events were confirmed by their parents. Interestingly, nearly half of the children (46%) said that they had always been afraid of spiders, but even in this subsample, reports of conditioning and modeling experiences were found. These results were largely replicated by Merckelbach and Muris (1997) who also found a relatively high frequency of conditioning reports that were substantiated by parents.

Three important conclusions can be drawn from the studies reviewed in this section. To begin with, Rachman's three-pathway model is a valuable framework for conceptualizing the role of learning experiences in the development of childhood fears and phobias. Second, the results of clinical studies (e.g., Menzies & Clarke, 1993; King et al., 1997; Merckelbach, Muris et al., 1996) as well as analogous studies (e.g., Ollendick & King, 1991; Doogan & Thomas, 1992; Graham & Gaffan, 1997; Muris, Merckelbach, & Collaris 1997) suggest that conditioning and modeling are more important factors in the etiology of severe fears than negative information transmission. Third, given the high percentage of fearful children who claim to have always been afraid, and the high percentage of nonfearful children who claim to have experienced conditioning and/or modeling events, it is highly unlikely that the learning experiences implicated in Rachman's three-pathways model represent simple etiological antecedents of specific childhood fears and phobias. Rather, research findings are consistent with the idea that in some children such experiences have a stronger impact and thus contribute to a transition of normal, developmental fears into persistent phobias. Note, in passing, that there is a huge literature on personality traits and conditionability, showing that individuals with traits related to neuroticism or behavioral inhibition acquire fear responses with relative ease compared with individuals without such traits (e.g., Eysenck, 1987; see also Gershuny & Sher, 1998).

Maintenance of Fears and Phobias

How are specific fears and phobias maintained, once they have been acquired? The influential two-stage model of Mowrer (1960) suggests that avoidance behavior is responsible for the conservation of phobic fear. More specifically, avoidance would minimize direct and prolonged contact with the fear-provoking stimulus, and, hence, the phobic person would not have the opportunity to learn that it is in fact harmless.

While the role of avoidance behavior in the maintenance of fears and phobias seems self-evident, there are other mechanisms that are highly relevant in this context. Inspired by cognitive psychology, recent studies have sought to elucidate information-processing abnormalities that may play a critical role in the maintenance of anxiety symptoms (see, for reviews, Eysenck, 1992; McNally, 1998). These abnormalities have been termed "cognitive biases" and two of them may be especially relevant for understanding the persistence of specific phobias in children: attentional bias and interpretation bias.

Attentional Bias

A large number of studies have documented that adult phobics display hyperattention toward potentially threatening material. A frequently employed technique for demonstrating this attentional bias is the emotional Stroop task. In that task, subjects are required to name the color in which words are printed while ignoring the meaning of these words. A consistent finding in Stroop studies with, for example, spider phobics is that their color naming of threatening words (e.g., "creepy", "hairy") is slower than that of neutral words (e.g., "shady", "cars"). This is due to the fact that phobics automatically direct their attention to the content of the threatening words and this interferes with their main task of color-naming (e.g., Watts, McKenna, Sharrock, & Trezise, 1986). There are reasons to believe that learning experiences like, for example, aversive conditioning events promote an attentional bias (Merckelbach, Van Hout, De Jong, & Van den Hout, 1990). Also, attentional bias for threat cues disappears in phobics who have been successfully treated (e.g., Watts et al., 1986; Lavy, Van den Hout, & Arntz, 1993). Taken together, these findings indicate that the attentional bias phenomenon is a consequence rather than a cause of anxiety (McNally, 1998). However, this is not to say that attentional bias is an epiphenomenon without clinical ramifications. It is highly plausible that the attentional bias phenomenon leads to an increased encoding of threatening material, thereby elevating fear levels, which in turn intensifies the attentional bias etc. In Mineka and Sutton's (1992), words: "One can easily see how the attentional bias toward threatening information associated with anxiety would tend to perpetuate or even enhance the emotion because of the increased focus on danger and threat cues" (p. 68).

So far, most studies on attentional bias were concerned with adult patients and their symptomatology. Yet, there is evidence that the attentional bias phenomenon also occurs in fearful children. For example, in their Stroop experiment, Martin, Horder, and Jones (1992) found that spider-fearful children exhibited retarded color-naming times when confronted with spider-related words (e.g., "web"), but not when confronted with neutral words (e.g., "fly"). Likewise, using the dot-probe paradigm, Vasey and colleagues (Vasey, Daleiden, Williams, & Brown, 1995; Vasey, El-Hag, & Daleiden, 1996) demonstrated that clinically anxious children and children high in test anxiety were faster to react to a probe if it was preceded by a threatening rather than a neutral word. This differential reaction reflects selective attention to threatening stimuli and was not evident for the control children in the Vasey et al. studies.

Thus, studies on attentional bias in fearful children have produced findings that closely parallel those reported in the adult literature. Yet, there is one exception that is worthy of note. In a series of studies, Kindt and colleagues (Kindt, Bierman, & Brosschot, 1997; Kindt, Van den Hout, De Jong, & Hoekzema, in press) examined response latencies of spider-fearful and control children aged 8–12 years in an emotional Stroop task. These researchers found consistently that attentional bias for spider-related material was not restricted to the highly fearful group, but also emerged in the control group. Furthermore, in the control group, age was found to be negatively correlated with attentional bias, suggesting a decline of attentional bias for spider-related words with age. In contrast, in the phobic group, a positive correlation was found between age and attentional bias, suggesting an increase of bias with age. On the basis of these data, Kindt et al. argue that at early developmental stages, attentional bias for threatening material may be a pervasive and normal phenomenon. As children grow older, they would learn to inhibit selective processing of threat cues. By this view, the development of childhood fears into phobias would be accompanied by a failed inhibition of selective attention. Such an interpretation fits nicely with the well-documented fact that, in most young children, normal developmental fears dissipate.

Interpretation Bias

Attentional bias for threat may be viewed as a fundamental characteristic that operates at the early stages of information processing. Yet, studies on anxious adults have revealed that there are other cognitive biases that operate at the more conceptual stages of information processing. A good example is provided by the interpretation bias. For example, Hadwin, Frost, French, and Richards (1997) confronted children low or high on trait anxiety with ambiguous homophones that had either a neutral or a threatening interpretation (e.g., dye vs. die). High levels of trait anxiety were found to be positively associated with threatening interpretations of homophones. In a study by Barrett, Rapee, Dadds, and Ryan (1996), anxious and nonanxious children received more complex stimulus material, namely ambiguous stories, and were then instructed to interpret them. Results indicated that anxious children were more likely to interpret ambiguous situations in a threatening way compared with nonanxious children. Similar findings were reported by Bell-Dolan (1995) and Chorpita, Albano, and Barlow (1996). The latter study also obtained some preliminary evidence that child–parent interactions might reduce a child's tendency to interpret ambiguous material as threatening.

All in all, it is fair to conclude that the interpretation bias of anxious children is a robust empirical phenomenon. In this respect, the findings are highly similar to those found in the adult literature. Yet, no study has carried out a more thorough analysis of the specificity of this bias. Thus, it remains unclear whether this bias is linked to general characteristics such as trait anxiety or to specific anxiety states.

Conclusion

Our knowledge of factors that are involved in the etiology of childhood specific phobias has increased considerably. The present chapter has made an attempt to structure this knowledge using a tentative model that synthesizes concepts and evidence from various sources. Figure 16.1 presents an outline of the model. It emphasizes a multifaceted etiology of childhood specific phobias and is based on the assumption that there is a continuity between normal developmental fears and childhood specific phobias. However, whereas childhood fears are common, but transitory phenomena in most children, there is a small subgroup of children in whom these fears tend to radicalize owing to a genetic vulnerability. This genetic vulnerability

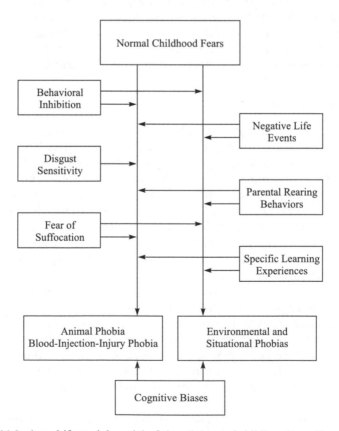

Figure 16.1. A multifactorial model of the etiology of childhood specific phobias.

may manifest itself in certain behavioral patterns (e.g., behavioral inhibition or disgust sensitivity). Stressful life events, parental rearing behaviors, and specific learning experiences (i.e., conditioning, modeling, and negative information) interact with normal developmental fears and genetically based behavioral patterns to produce extremely persistent fears that ultimately take the form of a specific phobia (or another anxiety disorder; see Craske, 1997). Once a specific phobia exists, it is maintained by cognitive mechanisms such as attentional bias.

We do not claim that the present model has the qualities of a scientific model in the strict sense of the word. Clearly, it lacks specificity. Most importantly, the precise dynamics between the various factors that figure in the model are far from clear. For example, do aversive learning experiences like conditioning or modeling contribute to a radicalization of developmental fears only during a critical period (e.g., when a certain developmental fear is at its maximum)? Or is it the case that learning experiences in combination with behavioral inhibition or disgust sensitivity may reinstate developmental fears that disappeared during a previous phase? These issues require longitudinal prospective studies that include various parameters. Of course, such complex prospective studies are not easy to conduct, precisely because they are time-consuming and difficult to get funded. But as Clark et al. (1994, p. 113) point out:

> Until prospective studies have followed individuals—whose premorbid personality and environmental characteristics are known—over sufficiently long periods of time to yield a sufficient base rate of disorder, we will not be able to distinguish causal from concomitant, confounding, or residual factors.

Not only prospective studies, but also comorbidity studies could make a major contribution to our understanding of the etiology of childhood specific phobias. For example, the connection between cognitive maturation and specific phobias can be worked out by examining fear symptoms in samples with clearly defined cognitive dysfunctions. Autistic disorder is a case of point (Muris, Steerneman, Merckelbach, Holdrinet, & Meesters, 1998): children with pervasive developmental disorder not otherwise specified display more frequently specific phobia symptoms than do children with autistic disorder, and this may well have something to do with higher IQ levels in the former group. A closer analysis of such associations would be informative. Much the same is true for the connection between isolated panic attacks and environmental/situational fear symptoms in children with medical conditions like asthma (Bussing et al., 1996).

Our multifaceted model is difficult to reconcile with the so-called nonassociative account of phobic etiology (Menzies & Clarke, 1993, 1995). The basic assumption of this account seems to be that discrete learning experiences play a marginal role in the etiology of specific phobias. According to the nonassociative account, common developmental fears reflect innate and spontaneous reactions to evolutionary prepotent cues. Specific phobias would echo these spontaneous fear reactions. But, if this is the case, one might ask why not all children suffer from specific phobias. Menzies and Clarke (1993, 1995) propose that "poor habituators may remain fearful of innate fear cues. In these individuals, developmental" fears would become chronic and take the form of a specific phobia. Alternatively, nonspecific stressors (e.g., life events) could produce dishabituation and the reinstatement of developmental fears. In either case, specific phobias would originate directly from developmental fears which, in turn, would derive from innate responses to evolutionary dangers. This would also explain why adult patients with specific phobias often report that they have always been afraid of the phobic stimulus.

The nonassociative account is flawed on several counts. To begin with, it assumes that one can relate developmental fears to evolutionary challenges. Admittedly, it is relatively easy to construct an evolutionary scenario for, say, fear of heights or fear of strangers. But consider fear of spiders. In that case, an evolutionary interpretation is more problematic given the fact that only 0.1% of the 35,000 known spider varieties are dangerous. A second point is that the nonassociative account fails to explain *why* some individuals habituate poorly to prepotent fear stimuli. Furthermore, from a scientific point of view, it is not satisfactory to think of phenomena as "spontaneous" or "nonassociative." After all, science is about causal associations, so one would like to know where "spontaneous" phobias originate from (see, for critical reviews of the nonassociative account, Merckelbach & De Jong, 1997; Forsyth & Chorpita, 1997). In other words, etiological models of specific phobias cannot do without the explanatory power of concepts like disgust sensitivity, behavioral inhibition, and aversive conditioning.

The multifactorial model outlined in this chapter draws on extensive empirical work, and in many respects it approaches a consensus among researchers about the complexity of the etiological antecedents involved in phobias. Over the past years, the extensive research in this domain has, indeed, produced a high degree of theoretical sophistication. Paradoxically, theoretical refinements may create a certain risk that researchers or clinicians become attracted to more cavalier-like conceptualizations. This is nicely illustrated by a recent Dutch book on phobias that reintroduces the Freudian idea that specific phobias are symbolic references to internal but unconscious conflicts (Fuldauer, 1998). The author claims, for example, that phobias of spiders would reflect a problematic marriage while phobias of frogs derive from conflict with parents. As another example, recent years have seen the rapid proliferation of power therapies like eye-movement desensitization and reprocessing (EMDR; see, for a critical analysis, Rosen, Lohr, McNally, & Herbert, 1998). These therapies have been promoted as fast cures for all sorts of anxiety disorders, among which are specific phobias. Controlled outcome studies (e.g., Muris, Merckelbach, Sijsenaar, & Holdrinet, 1998) have shown that EMDR adds nothing to the well-established exposure-based therapies. Apparently, theoretical advances may be accompanied by professional ignorance, and this underlines that it is important for professional organizations to encourage consensus development and research-based treatment protocols.

Note

Please address all correspondence to Dr Peter Muris, Department of Medical, Clinical, & Experimental Psychology, Maastricht University, P.O. Box 616, 6200 MD Maastricht, The Netherlands. Fax: +31 43 361 5735; E-mail: p.muris@dep.unimaas.nl.

References

Agras, S., Chapin, H. N., & Oliveau, D. (1972). The natural history of phobia: Course and prognosis. *Archives of General Psychiatry, 26*, 315–317.

American Psychiatric Association (1994). *Diagnostic and statistical manual of mental disorders* (4th ed.). Washington: American Psychiatric Association.

Antony, M. M., Brown, T. A., & Barlow, D. H. (1997). Response to hyperventilation and 5.5% CO_2 inhalation of subjects with types of specific phobia, panic disorder, or no mental disorder. *American Journal of Psychiatry, 154*, 1089–1095.

Barrett, P. M., Rapee, R. M., Dadds, M. R., & Ryan, S. M. (1996). Family enhancement of cognitive style in anxious and aggressive children: Threat bias and the FEAR effect. *Journal of Abnormal Child Psychology, 24*, 187–203.

Bauer, D. H. (1976). An exploratory study of developmental changes in children's fears. *Journal of Child Psychology and Psychiatry, 17*, 69–74.

Bell-Dolan, D. J. (1995). Social cue interpretation of anxious children. *Journal of Clinical Child Psychology, 24*, 1–10.

Benjamin, R. S., Costello, E. J., & Warren, M. (1990). Anxiety disorders in a pediatric sample. *Journal of Anxiety Disorders, 4*, 293–316.

Bernstein, G. A., & Borchardt, C. M. (1991). Anxiety disorders of childhood and adolescence: A critical review. *Journal of the American Academy of Child and Adolescent Psychiatry, 30*, 519–532.

Biederman, J., Rosenbaum, J. F., Bolduc-Murphy, E. A., Faraone, S. V., Chaloff, J., Hirshfeld, D. R., & Kagan, J. (1993). A 3-year follow-up of children with and without behavioral inhibition. *Journal of the American Academy of Child and Adolescent Psychiatry, 32*, 814–821.

Biederman, J., Rosenbaum, J. F., Chaloff, J., & Kagan, J. (1995). Behavioral inhibition as a risk factor for anxiety disorders. In J. S. March (Ed.), *Anxiety disorders in children and adolescents*. New York: Guilford.

Biederman, J., Rosenbaum, J. F., Hirshfeld, D. R., Faraone, S. V., Bolduc, E. A., Gersten, M., Meminger, S. R., Kagan, J., Snidman, N., & Reznick, S. (1990). Psychiatric correlates of behavioral inhibition in young children of parents with and without psychiatric disorders. *Archives of General Psychiatry, 47*, 21–26.

Birmaher, B., Khetarpal, S., Brent, D., Cully, M., Balach, L., Kaufman, J., & McKenzie Neer, S. (1997). The Screen for Child Anxiety Related Emotional Disorders (SCARED): Scale construction and psychometric characteristics. *Journal of the American Academy of Child and Adolescent Psychiatry, 36*, 545–553.

Bowlby, J. (1973). *Attachment and loss: Vol. 2. Separation: Anxiety and anger.* New York: Basic Books.

Brewin, C. R., Andrews, B., & Gotlib, I. H. (1993). Psychopathology and early experience: A reappraisal of retrospective reports. *Psychological Bulletin, 113,* 82–98.

Bussing, R., Burket, R. C., & Kelleher, E. T. (1996). Prevalence of anxiety disorders in a clinic-based sample of pediatric asthma patients. *Psychosomatics, 37,* 108–115.

Calkins, S. D., Fox, N. A., & Marshall, T. R. (1996). Behavioral and physiological antecedents of inhibited and uninhibited behavior. *Child Development, 67,* 523–540.

Castro, J., Toro, J., Van der Ende, J., & Arrindell, W. A. (1993). Exploring the feasibility of assessing perceived parental rearing styles in Spanish children with the EMBU. *International Journal of Social Psychiatry, 39,* 47–57.

Chorpita, B. F., Albano, A. M., & Barlow, D. H. (1996). Cognitive processing in children: Relation to anxiety and family influences. *Journal of Clinical Child Psychology, 25,* 170–176.

Clark, L. A., Watson, D., & Mineka, S. (1994). Temperament, personality, and the mood and anxiety disorders. *Journal of Abnormal Psychology, 103,* 103–116.

Costello, E. J., Angold, A., Burns, B. J., Stangl, D. K., Tweed, D. C., Erkanli, A., & Worthman, C. M. (1996). The great smoky mountains study of youth. *Archives of General Psychiatry, 53,* 1129–1136.

Craske, M. G. (1997). Fear and anxiety in children and adolescents. *Bulletin of the Menninger Clinic, 61,* 4–36.

Dadds, M. R., & Barrett, P. M. (1996). Family processes in child and adolescent anxiety and depression. *Behaviour Change, 13,* 231–239.

Dadds, M. R., Barrett, P. M., & Rapee, R. M. (1996). Family process and child anxiety and aggression: An observational analysis. *Journal of Abnormal Child Psychology, 24,* 715–734.

Davey, G. C. L., Forster, L., & Mayhew, G. (1993). Familial resemblances in disgust sensitivity and animal phobias. *Behaviour Research and Therapy, 31,* 41–50.

Davidson, R. J. (1998). Affective style and affective disorders: Perspectives from affective neuroscience. *Cognition and Emotion, 12,* 307–330.

Davidson, R. J., & Fox, N. A. (1989). Frontal brain asymmetry predicts infants'' response to maternal separation. *Journal of Abnormal Psychology, 98,* 127–131.

De Jong, P. J., & Merckelbach, H. (1998). Blood-injection-injury phobia and fear of spiders: Domain specific individual differences in disgust sensitivity. *Personality and Individual Differences, 24,* 153–158.

De Jong, P. J., Andrea, H., & Muris, P. (1997). Spider phobia in children: Disgust and fear before and after treatment. *Behaviour Research and Therapy, 35,* 559–562.

De Ruiter, C., Rijken, H., Garssen, B., Van Schaik, A., & Kraaimaat, F. (1989). Comorbidity among the anxiety disorders. *Journal of Anxiety Disorders, 3,* 57–68.

Doogan, S., & Thomas, G. V. (1992). Origins of fear of dogs in adults in adults and children: The role of conditioning processes and prior familiarity with dogs. *Behaviour Research and Therapy, 30,* 387–394.

Ekman, P. (1992). An argument for basic emotions. *Cognition and Emotion, 6,* 169–200.

Eysenck, H. J. (1987). The role of heredity, environment, and preparedness in the genesis of neurosis. In H. J. Eysenck & I. Martin (Eds.), *Theoretical foundations of behavior therapy*. New York: Plenum.

Eysenck, M. W. (1992). *Anxiety: The cognitive perspective*. Hillsdale, NJ: Lawrence Erlbaum.

Ferrari, M. (1986). Fears and phobias in childhood phobias: Some clinical and developmental considerations. *Child Psychiatry and Human Development, 17*, 75–87.

Forsyth, J. P., & Chorpita, B. F. (1997). Unearthing the non-associative origins of fears and phobias: A rejoinder. *Journal of Behavior Therapy and Experimental Psychiatry, 28*, 297–305.

Forsyth, J. P., & Eifert, G. H. (1996). Systematic alarms and fear conditioning: I. A reappraisal of what is being conditioned. *Behavior Therapy, 27*, 441–462.

Frederikson, M., Annas, P., Fischer, H., & Wik, G. (1996). Gender and age differences in the prevalence of specific fears and phobias. *Behaviour Research and Therapy, 34*, 33–39.

Frederikson, M., Annas, P., & Wik, G. (1997). Parental history, aversive exposure, and the development of snake and spider phobia in women. *Behaviour Research and Therapy, 35*, 23–28.

Fuldauer, D. (1998). *Dierfobieën en psychosomatische stoornissen (Animal phobias and psychosomatic disorders)*. Leuven, Belgium: Garant.

Fyer, A. J., Mannuzza, S., Gallops, M. S., Martin, L. Y., Aaronson, C., Gorman, J. M., Liebowitz, M. R., & Klein, D. F. (1990). Familial transmission of simple phobias and fears. *Archives of General Psychiatry, 47*, 252–256.

Gershuny, B. S., & Sher, K. J. (1998). The relation between personality and anxiety: Findings from a 3-year prospective study. *Journal of Abnormal Psychology, 107*, 252–262.

Gest, S. D. (1997). Behavioral inhibition: Stability and associations with adaptation from childhood to early adulthood *Journal of Personality and Social Psychology, 72*, 467–475.

Goodyer, I., Wright, C., & Altham, P. (1990). The friendships and recent life events of anxious and depressed school-age children. *British Journal of Psychiatry, 156*, 689–698.

Gorman, J. M., Liebowitz, M. R., Fyer, A. J., & Stein, J. (1989). A neuroanatomical hypothesis for panic disorder. *American Journal of Psychiatry, 146*, 148–161.

Graham, J., & Gaffan, E. A. (1997). Fear of water in children and adults: Etiology and familial effects. *Behaviour Research and Therapy, 35*, 91–108.

Grillon, C., Dierker, L., & Merikangas, K. R. (1997). Startle modulation in children at risk for anxiety disorders and/or alcoholism. *Journal of the American Academy of Child and Adolescent Psychiatry, 36*, 925–932.

Gullone, E., & King, N. J. (1997). Three-year follow-up of normal fear in children and adolescents aged 7 to 18 years. *British Journal of Developmental Psychology, 15*, 97–111.

Hadwin, J., Frost, S., French, C. C., & Richards, A. (1997). Cognitive processing and trait anxiety in typically developing children: Evidence for an interpretation bias. *Journal of Abnormal Psychology, 106*, 486–490.

Haidt, J., McCauley, C., & Rozin, P. (1994). Individual differences in sensitivity to disgust: A scale sampling seven domains of disgust elicitors. *Personality and Individual Differences, 16*, 701–713.

Hayward, C., Killen, J. D., Hammer, L. D., Litt, I. F., Wilson, D. M., Simmonds, B., & Taylor, C. B. (1992). Pubertal stage and panic attack history in sixth- and seventh-grade girls. *American Journal of Psychiatry, 149,* 1239–1243.

Hazan, C., & Shaver, P. (1987). Romantic love conceptualized as an attachment process. *Journal of Personality and Social Psychology, 52,* 511–524.

Hekmat, H. (1987). Origins and development of human fear reactions. *Journal of Anxiety Disorders, 1,* 197–218.

Hennig, J., Pössel, P., & Netter, P. (1996). Sensitivity to disgust as an indicator of neuroticism: A psychobiological approach. *Personality and Individual Differences, 20,* 589–596.

Himle, J. A., Crystal, D., Curtis, G. C., & Fluent, T. E. (1991). Mode of onset of simple phobia subtypes: Further evidence of heterogeneity. *Psychiatric Research, 36,* 37–43.

Hofmann, S. G., Lehman, C. L., & Barlow, D. H. (1997). How specific are specific phobias? *Journal of Behavior Therapy and Experimental Psychiatry, 28,* 233–240.

Jacobs, W. J., & Nadel, L. (1985). Stress-induced recovery of fears and phobias. *Psychological Review, 92,* 512–531.

Kagan, J., Reznick, J. S., Clarke, C., Snidman, N., & Garcia-Coll, C. (1984). Behavioral inhibition to the unfamiliar. *Child Development, 55,* 2212–2225.

Kagan, J., Reznick, J. S., & Snidman, N. (1987). The physiology and psychology of behavioral inhibition in children. *Child Development, 58,* 1459–1473.

Kagan, J., Reznick, J. S., & Snidman, N. (1988). Biological basis of childhood shyness. *Science, 240,* 167–171.

Kashani, J. H., Vaidya, A. F., Soltys, S. M., Dandoy, A. C., Katz, L. M., & Reid, J. C. (1990). Correlates of anxiety in psychiatrically hospitalized children and their parents. *American Journal of Psychiatry, 147,* 319–323.

Kendler, K. S., Neale, M. C., Kessler, R. C., Heath, A. C., & Eaves, L. J. (1992). The genetic epidemiology of phobias in women: The interrelationship of agoraphobia, situational phobia, and simple phobia. *Archives of General Psychiatry, 49,* 273–281.

Kindt, M., Bierman, D., & Brosschot, J. F. (1997). Cognitive bias in spider fear and control children: Assessment of emotional interference by a card format and a single-trial format of the Stroop task. *Journal of Experimental Child Psychology, 66,* 163–179.

Kindt, M., & Van den Hout, M. A., De Jong, P. J., & Hoekzema, B. (in press). Cognitive bias for pictorial and linguistic threat cues in children. *Journal of Psychopathology and Behavioral Assessment.*

King, N. J., Clowes-Hollins, V., & Ollendick, T. H. (1997). The etiology of childhood dog phobia. *Behaviour Research and Therapy, 35,* 77.

King, N. J., Gullone, E., & Ollendick, T. H. (1998). Etiology of childhood phobias: Current status of Rachman's three pathways theory. *Behaviour Research and Therapy, 36,* 297–309.

King, N. J., Gullone, E., Tonge, B., & Ollendick, T. H. (1993). Self-reports of panic attacks and manifest anxiety in adolescents. *Behaviour Research and Therapy, 31,* 111–116.

King, N. J., Hamilton, D. I., & Ollendick, T. H. (1988). *Children's fears and phobias: A behavioral perspective.* Chichester, England: Wiley.

Kirkpatrick, D. R. (1984). Age, gender, and patterns of common intense fears among adults. *Behaviour Research and Therapy, 19,* 109–115.

Klein, D. F. (1993). False suffocation alarms, spontaneous panics, and related conditions. An integrative hypothesis. *Archives of General Psychiatry, 50,* 306–317.

Kleinknecht, R. A., & Lenz, J. (1989). Blood/injury fear, fainting, and avoidance of medically-related situations: A family correspondence study. *Behaviour Research and Therapy, 27,* 537–547.

Last, C. G., Perrin, S., Hersen, M., & Kazdin, A. E. (1998). A prospective study of childhood anxiety disorders. *Journal of the American Academy of Child and Adolescent Psychiatry, 35,* 1502–1510.

Lavy, E., Van den Hout, M. A., & Arntz, A. (1993). Attentional bias and spider phobia: Conceptual and clinical issues. *Behaviour Research and Therapy, 31,* 17–24.

Magee, W. J., Eaton, W. W., Wittchen, H. U., McGonagle, K. A., & Kessler, R. C. (1996). Agoraphobia, simple phobia, and social phobia in the national comorbidity survey. *Archives of General Psychiatry, 53,* 159–168.

Marks, I. M. (1987). *Fears, phobias, and rituals: Panic, anxiety, and their disorders.* New York: Oxford University Press.

Martin, M., Horder, P., & Jones, G. V. (1992). Integral bias in naming of phobia-related words. *Cognition and Emotion, 6,* 479–486.

Matchett, G., & Davey, G. C. L. (1991). A test of a disease-avoidance model of animal phobias. *Behaviour Research and Therapy, 29,* 91–94.

McCathie, H., & Spence, S. H. (1991). What is the revised fear survey schedule for children measuring? *Behaviour Research and Therapy, 29,* 495–502.

McNally, R. J. (1989). On stress-induced recovery of fears and phobias. *Psychological Review, 96,* 180–181.

McNally, R. J. (1998). Information-processing abnormalities in anxiety disorders: Implications for cognitive neuroscience. *Cognition and Emotion, 12,* 479–495.

Menzies, R. G., & Clarke, J. C. (1993). The etiology of childhood water phobia. *Behaviour Research and Therapy, 31,* 499–501.

Menzies, R. G., & Clarke, J. C. (1994). Retrospective studies of the origins of phobias: A review. *Anxiety, Stress, and Coping, 7,* 305–318.

Menzies, R. G., & Clarke, J. C. (1995). The etiology of phobias: A non- associative account. *Clinical Psychology Review, 15,* 23–48.

Menzies, R. G., Kirkby, K., & Harris, L. M. (1998). The convergent validity of the Phobia Origins Questionnaire (POQ): A review of the evidence. *Behaviour Research and Therapy, 36,* 1081–1089.

Merckelbach, H., & De Jong, P. J. (1997). Evolutionary models of phobias. In G. C. L. Davey (Ed.), *Phobias: A handbook of theory, research, and treatment.* Chichester, England: Wiley.

Merckelbach, H., & Muris, P. (1997). The etiology of childhood spider phobia. *Behaviour Research and Therapy, 35,* 1031–1034.

Merckelbach, H., De Jong, P. J., Arntz, A., & Schouten, E. (1993). The role of evaluative learning and disgust sensitivity in the etiology and treatment of spider phobia. *Advances in Behaviour Research and Therapy, 15,* 243–255.

Merckelbach, H., De Jong, P. J., Muris, P., & Van den Hout, M. A. (1996). The etiology of specific phobias: A review. *Clinical Psychology Review, 16,* 337–361.

Merckelbach, H., De Ruiter, C., Van den Hout, M. A., & Hoekstra, R. (1989). Conditioning experiences and phobias. *Behaviour Research and Therapy, 27,* 657–662.

Merckelbach, H., Muris, P., Pool, K., & De Jong, P. J. (1998). Resting EEG asymmetry and spider phobia. *Anxiety Stress and Coping, 11,* 213–223.

Merckelbach, H., Muris, P., & Schouten, E. (1996). Pathways to fear in spider phobic children. *Behaviour Research and Therapy, 34,* 935–938.

Merckelbach, H., Van Hout, W., De Jong, P. J., & Van den Hout, M. A. (1990). Classical conditioning and attentional bias. *Journal of Behavior Therapy and Experimental Psychiatry, 21,* 185–191.

Milgrom, P., Mancl, L., King, B., & Weinstein, P. (1995). Origins of childhood dental fear. *Behaviour Research and Therapy, 33,* 313–319.

Mineka, S., & Sutton, S. K. (1992). Cognitive biases and the emotional disorders. *Psychological Science, 3,* 65–69.

Mowrer, O. (1960). *Learning theory and behavior.* New York: Wiley.

Muris, P., Mayer, B., & Meesters, C. (2000). Self-reported attachment style, anxiety, and depression in children. *Social Behavior & Personality, 28,* 157–162.

Muris, P., & Merckelbach, H. (1998a). Perceived parental rearing behaviour and anxiety disorders symptoms in normal children. *Personality and Individual Differences, 25,* 1199–1206.

Muris, P., & Merckelbach, H. (1998b). Specific phobias. In A. S. Bellack & M. Hersen (Eds.), *Comprehensive clinical psychology: Vol. 6. Adults: Clinical formulation and treatment.* Oxford, England: Pergamon.

Muris, P., Merckelbach, H., & Collaris, R. (1997). Common childhood fears and their origins. *Behaviour Research and Therapy, 35,* 929–937.

Muris, P., Merckelbach, H., Gadet, B., & Moulaert, V. (2000). Fears, worries, and scary dreams in 4- to 12-year-old children: Their content, developmental pattern, and origins. *Journal of Clinical Child Psychology, 29,* 43–52.

Muris, P., Merckelbach, H., Mayer, B., & Prins, E. (2000). How serious are common childhood fears. *Behaviour Research and Therapy, 38,* 217–228.

Muris, P., Merckelbach, H., Meesters, C., & Van Lier, P. (1997). What do children fear most often? *Journal of Behavior Therapy and Experimental Psychiatry, 28,* 263–267.

Muris, P., Merckelbach, H., Schmidt, H., & Mayer, B. (1999). The revised version of the Screen for Child Anxiety Related Emotional Disorders (SCARED-R): Factor structure in normal children. *Personality and Individual Differences, 26,* 99–112.

Muris, P., Merckelbach, H., Sijsenaar, M., & Holdrinet, I. (1998). Treating phobic children: Effects of EMDR versus exposure. *Journal of Consulting and Clinical Psychology, 66,* 193–198.

Muris, P., Merckelbach, H., Wessel, I., & Van de Ven, M. (1999). Psychopathological correlates of self-reported behavioural inhibition in children. *Behaviour Research and Therapy, 37,* 575–584.

Muris, P., Schmidt, H., & Merckelbach, H. (1999). The structure of specific phobia symptoms among children and adolescents. *Behaviour Research and Therapy, 37,* 863–868.

Muris, P., Steerneman , P., Merckelbach, H., Holdrinet, I., & Meesters, C. (1998). Comorbid anxiety symptoms in children with pervasive developmental disorders. *Journal of Anxiety Disorders, 12,* 387–393.

Muris, P., Steerneman, P., Merckelbach, H., & Meesters, C. (1996). The role of parental fearfulness and modeling in children's fear. *Behaviour Research and Therapy, 34,* 265–268.

Nelles, W. B., & Barlow, D. H. (1988). Do children panic? *Clinical Psychology Review, 8,* 359-372.

Newman, D. L., Moffitt, T. E., Caspi, A., Magdol, L., Silva, P. A., & Stanton, W. R. (1996). Psychiatric disorder in a birth cohort of young adults: Prevalence, comorbidity, clinical significance, and new case incidence from ages 11 to 21. *Journal of Consulting and Clinical Psychology, 64,* 552–562.

Öhman, A., Dimberg, U., & Öst, L.-G. (1985). Animal and social phobias: Biological constraints on learned fear responses. In S. Reiss & R. R. Bootzin (Eds.), *Theoretical issues in behavior therapy.* Orlando, FL: Academic Press.

Ollendick, T. H. (1983). Reliability and validity of the revised fear survey schedule for children (FSSC-R). *Behaviour Research and Therapy, 21,* 685–692.

Ollendick, T. H., & King, N. J. (1991). Origins of childhood fears: An evaluation of Rachman's theory of fear acquisition. *Behaviour Research and Therapy, 29,* 117–123.

Ollendick, T. H., & King, N. J. (1994). Fears and their level of interference in adolescents. *Behaviour Research and Therapy, 32,* 635-638.

Ollendick, T. H., Hagopian, L. P., & King, N. J. (1997). Specific phobias in children. In G. C. L. Davey (Ed.), *Phobias. A handbook of theory, research and treatment.* Chichester, England: Wiley.

Ollendick, T. H., King, N. J., & Frary, R. B. (1989). Fears in children and adolescents: Reliability and generalizability across gender, age and nationality. *Behaviour Research and Therapy, 27,* 19–26.

Ollendick, T. H., Yang, B., King, N. J., Dong, Q., & Akande, A. (1996). Fears in American, Australian, Chinese, and Nigerian children and adolescents: A cross-cultural study. *Journal of Child Psychology and Psychiatry, 37,* 213–220.

Ollendick, T. H., Yule, W., & Ollier, K. (1991). Fears in British children and their relationship to manifest anxiety and depression. *Journal of Child Psychology and Psychiatry, 32,* 321–331.

Öst, L.-G. (1987). Age of onset in different phobias. *Journal of Abnormal Psychology, 96,* 223–229.

Öst, L.-G. (1991). Acquisition of blood and injection phobia anxiety response patterns in clinical patients. *Behaviour Research and Therapy, 29,* 323–332.

Page, A. C. (1994). Blood-injury phobia. *Clinical Psychology Review, 14,* 443–461.

Phillips, M. L., Senior, C., Fahy, T., & David, A. S. (1998). Disgust: The forgotten emotion of psychiatry. *British Journal of Psychiatry, 172,* 373–375.

Pine, D. S., Coplan, J. D., Papp, L. A., Klein, R. G., Martinez, J. M., Kovalenko, P., Tancer, N., Moreau, D., Dummitt III, E. S., Shaffer, D., Klein, D. F., & Gorman, J. M. (1998). Ventilatory physiology of children and adolescents with anxiety disorders. *Archives of General Psychiatry, 55,* 123–129.

Pine, D. S., Weese-Mayer, D. E., Silvestri, J. M., Davies, M., Whitaker, A. H., & Klein, D. F. (1994). Anxiety and congenital central hypoventilation syndrome. *American Journal of Psychiatry, 151,* 864–870.

Rachman, S. J. (1977). The conditioning theory of fear acquisition: A critical examination. *Behaviour Research and Therapy, 15,* 375–387.

Rachman, S. J. (1991). Neoconditioning and the classical theory of fear acquisition. *Clinical Psychology Review, 11,* 155–173.

Rapee, R. M. (1997). Potential role of childrearing practices in the development of anxiety and depression. *Clinical Psychology Review, 17,* 47–67.

Rose, R. J., & Ditto, W. B. (1983). A developmental–genetic analysis of common fears from early adolescence to early adulthood. *Child Development, 54,* 361–368.

Rosen, G. M., Lohr, J. M., McNally, R. J., & Herbert, J. D. (1998). Power therapies, miraculous claims, and the cures that fail. *Behavioural and Cognitive Psychotherapy, 26,* 97–99.

Rosen, J. B., & Schulkin, J. (1998). From normal fear to pathological anxiety. *Psychological Review, 105,* 325–350.

Rosenbaum, J. F., Biederman, J., Gersten, M., Hirshfeld, D. R., Meminger, S. R., Herman, J. B., Kagan, J., Reznick, J. S., & Snidman, N. (1988). Behavioral inhibition in children of parents with panic disorder and agoraphobia: A controlled study. *Archives of General Psychiatry, 45,* 463–470.

Rutter, M., Tizard, J., & Whitmore, K. (1968). *Education, health, and behavior.* London: Longman.

Scarpa, A., Raine, A., Venables, P. H., & Mednick, S. A. (1995). The stability of inhibited/uninhibited temperament from ages 3 to 11 years in Mauritian children. *Journal of Abnormal Child Psychology, 23,* 607–618.

Schmidt, L. A., Fox, N. A., Rubin, K. H., Sternberg, E. M., Gold, P. W., Smith, C. C., & Schulkin, J. (1997). Behavioral and neuroendocrine responses in shy children. *Developmental Psychobiology, 30,* 127–140.

Shafran, R., Booth, R., & Rachman, S. J. (1993). The reduction of claustrophobia: II. Cognitive analyses. *Behaviour Research and Therapy, 31,* 75–85.

Spence, S. H., & Dadds, M. R. (1996). Preventing childhood anxiety disorders. *Behaviour Change, 13,* 241–249.

Starcevic, V., & Bogojevic, G. (1997). Comorbidity of panic disorder with agoraphobia and specific phobia: Relationships with the subtypes of specific phobia. *Comprehensive Psychiatry, 38,* 315–320.

Stevenson, J., Batten, N., & Cherner, M. (1992). Fears and fearfulness in children and adolescents: A genetic analysis of twin data. *Journal of Child Psychology and Psychiatry, 33,* 977–985.

Stevenson-Hinde, J., & Glover, A. (1996). Shy girls and boys: A new look. *Journal of Child Psychology and Psychiatry, 37,* 181–187.

Strauss, C. C., & Last, C. G. (1993). Social and simple phobias in children. *Journal of Anxiety Disorders, 7,* 141–152.

Taylor, S. (1998). The hierarchic structure of fears. *Behaviour Research and Therapy, 36,* 205–214.

Thyer, B. A., Parrish, R. T., Curtis, G. C., Nesse, R. M., & Cameron, O. G. (1985). Ages of onset of DSM-III anxiety disorders. *Comprehensive Psychiatry, 26,* 113–122.

Tolin, D. F., Lohr, J. M., Sawchuk, C. N., & Lee, T. C. (1997). Disgust and disgust sensitivity in blood-injection-injury and spider phobia. *Behaviour Research and Therapy, 35,* 949–953.

Tomarken, A. J., & Keener, A. D. (1998). Frontal brain asymmetry and depression: A self-regulatory perspective. *Cognition and Emotion, 12,* 387–420.

Turner, S. M., Beidel, D. C., & Wolff, P. L. (1996). Is behavioral inhibition related to the anxiety disorders? *Clinical Psychology Review, 16,* 157–172.

Vasey, M. W. (1993). Development and cognition in childhood anxiety: The example of worry. *Advances in Clinical Child Psychology, 15,* 1–39.

Vasey, M. W., & Daleiden, E. L. (1994). Worry in children. In G. C. L. Davey & F. Tallis (Eds.), *Worrying: Perspectives on theory, assessment and treatment.* Chichester, England: Wiley.

Vasey, M. W., Daleiden, E. L., Williams, L. L., & Brown, L. M. (1995). Biased attention in childhood anxiety disorders: A preliminary study. *Journal of Abnormal Child Psychology, 23,* 267–277.

Vasey, M. W., El-Hag, N., & Daleiden, E. L. (1996). Anxiety and the processing of emotionally-threatening stimuli: Distinctive patterns of selective attention among high- and low-test-anxious children. *Child Development, 67,* 1173–1185.

Verburg, K., Griez, E., & Meijer, J. (1994). A 35% carbon dioxide challenge in simple phobias. *Acta Psychiatrica Scandinavica, 90,* 420–423.

Vrana, R. J., Spence, E. L., & Lang, P. J. (1988). The startle probe response: A new measure of emotion? *Journal of Abnormal Psychology, 97,* 487–491.

Warren, S. L., Huston, L., Egeland, B., & Sroufe, L. A. (1997). Child and adolescent anxiety disorders and early attachment. *Journal of the American Academy of Child and Adolescent Psychiatry, 36,* 637–644.

Watts, F. N., McKenna, F. P., Sharrock, R., & Trezise, L. (1986). Colour naming of phobia-related words. *British Journal of Psychology, 77,* 97–108.

Zinbarg, R. E., & Barlow, D. H. (1996). Structure of anxiety and the anxiety disorders: A hierarchical model. *Journal of Abnormal Psychology, 105,* 181–193.

17

Posttraumatic Stress Disorder: A Developmental Perspective

ERIC M. VERNBERG and R. ENRIQUE VARELA

Posttraumatic stress disorder, or PTSD, is unique among anxiety disorders in that an identifiable, overwhelming traumatic experience must precede the emergence of core symptoms of the disorder. Core symptoms of PTSD fall into three clusters: re-experiencing phenomena; avoidance of trauma-related stimuli and numbing of general responsiveness; and signs of increased arousal. Related features, not included in the core symptoms but often present, include feelings of shame or guilt, somatic complaints, dissociative symptoms, hopelessness or helplessness, hostility, impaired affect regulation, and impaired relationships with others (American Psychiatric Association, 1994). These symptoms must cause clinically significant distress or impairment in one or more important area of functioning for a diagnosis of PTSD to be given.

Research and clinical work with trauma-exposed children demonstrate that full PTSD occurs in all ages, with the possible exception of infancy, although a case can be made for even this age group (Scheeringa, Zeanah, Drell, & Larrieu, 1995). Symptoms of posttraumatic stress are common in children and adolescents following single-episode stress events such as natural disasters, residential fires, and acts of violence (Vogel & Vernberg, 1993). PTSD can emerge in children and adolescents who were functioning adequately prior to a discrete, identifiable trauma exposure. However, PTSD is also diagnosed often in children who have multiple exposures to trauma over a period of months or years, and whose developmental histories indicate longstanding behavioral or psychological problems. In an all-too-common clinical scenario, children present with histories of chronic exposure to interpersonal trauma such as physical, sexual, or psychological abuse and exhibit numerous symptoms of PTSD (along with symptoms of other disorders). In many instances, the exact nature and extent of traumatic exposure is difficult to determine because the child and/or caretakers are unwilling or unable to describe traumatic events accurately, and because so many traumatic episodes have occurred that it is difficult to know where to start. Comorbid diagnoses are common, appearing to be the rule rather than the exception in studies of the long-term effects of trauma (Hubbard, Realmuto, Northwood, & Masten, 1995).

Differences in developmental repercussions, treatment, and prognosis between single-episode, acute traumatic exposure and multiple exposures to trauma over a lengthy period have led some to propose a formal distinction between an acute or Type I form of PTSD resulting from single-incident traumatic exposure, and a chronic or Type II form associated with multiple exposures to trauma over a lengthy period (Famularo, Kinscherff, & Fenton, 1990; Lipovsky, 1991; Terr, 1991). In Type I PTSD, intrusive thoughts, anxiety, and overt attempts at escape and avoidance of traumatic reminders are proposed to predominate. Type II PTSD is proposed to involve more of the numbing, detachment, and restriction or absence of feeling (Lipovsky, 1991). Such a distinction seems unlikely to be adopted in the DSM nosology, although DSM-IV distinguishes between acute and chronic PTSD based on the duration of symptoms (acute if symptoms persist less than 3 months).

Numerous controversies remain over the cognitive, biological, and social mechanisms which underlie the symptoms defining PTSD (Yehuda & McFarlane, 1995). There is ongoing debate about whether PTSD should remain classified as an anxiety disorder, or instead be considered as dissociative disorder or a component of a new stress response disorder category (Brett, 1997). This debate reflects the fact that there is a great deal of variability in the clinical presentation of individuals who have experienced extreme trauma, and the central symptoms of PTSD are only one aspect of this response.

In our view, a key to continued progress is to propose and evaluate comprehensive conceptual models of the ways exposure to highly traumatic events in childhood and adolescence influences developmental processes. In this effort, the core symptoms of PTSD are important foci, but not the only important outcomes. The larger issue is to understand how traumatic exposure at various points in the developmental period affects developmental trajectories in multiple domains, including biological, cognitive, behavioral, and interpersonal.

Conceptualizing PTSD from a Developmental Perspective

Conceptual models of the impact of traumatic exposure in children and adolescents share a number of features, and empirical evidence supports many aspects of these models. Common structural elements of these models include: nature of traumatic exposure; characteristics of the individual at the time of exposure; qualities of the posttraumatic environment; efforts at processing the traumatic events; and symptomatology (table 17.1). Within these basic elements, a number of factors are proposed to influence the nature and duration of symptoms for individual children. These factors explain in part why children differ markedly in their reactions to traumatic exposure, and how responses other than PTSD may follow in some instances. In the sections to follow, we describe each of these structural elements from a developmental perspective, with an emphasis on the ways traumatic exposure

Table 17.1. Common Elements of Conceptual Models for Understanding the Effects
of Traumatic Exposure on Children and Adolescents

Elements of traumatic exposure
Objective and subjective elements
Duration, frequency, and intensity
Agents and targets of exposure

Characteristics of individual at exposure
Age-related characteristics: biological issues and social–cognitive issues
Gender
Temperament
Prior trauma and psychopathology

Qualities of the posttraumatic environment
Social support
Parental distress and ongoing disruptions
Economic resources

Processing of traumatic events
Social–cognitive issues: emotional, psychodynamic, and cognitive processing
Biobehavioral processing

Outcomes
PTSD
Comorbid conditions
Attitudes, beliefs, and expectations

---

at various ages may exert different effects, and on the mechanisms that may
"carry" these effects forward in time.

Elements of Traumatic Exposure

Several typologies have been offered to allow greater specificity and compre-
hensiveness in describing the nature of exposure to traumatic events (Green,
1990; McFarlane & de Girolamo, 1997; Pynoos, Steinberg, & Goenjian,
1997). These typologies converge in making several important conclusions,
distinctions and qualifications in conceptualizing and assessing exposure.
Traumatic experiences can be categorized on a continuum from low to
high exposure, with the intensity and duration of PTSD and other trauma-
related symptoms in children increasing as exposure increases (Pynoos,
Goenjian et al., 1993; Lonigan, Shannon, Finch, Daugherty, & Taylor,
1991; Vernberg, La Greca, Silverman, & Prinstein, 1996). An accurate understanding of the level of traumatic exposure for an individual child, which is
often crucial for treatment, must take into account both objective and subjective aspects of the experience. In addition to identifying whether specific
forms of exposure occurred, it is important to understand the frequency,
duration, and intensity of exposure. Finally, the agents involved in the traumatic exposure (e.g., natural forces, humans), and the relationship of these
agents to the exposed child, must be taken into account.

Objective Elements of Exposure

Objective aspects of exposure severity include events that can reliably be said to have occurred during traumatization. Specific objective events vary for different types of trauma, yet signal more general categories. Green (1990) identified eight general categories: (1) threat to one's life or bodily integrity; (2) severe physical injury or harm; (3) receipt of intentional injury or harm; (4) exposure to the grotesque; (5) violent, sudden loss of a loved one; (6) witnessing or learning of violence to loved ones; (7) learning of exposure to a noxious agent; and (8) being the cause of death or severe harm to another (see Vernberg, 1999, for a discussion of these in relation to children and families). In work with children, these categories are often represented by event-specific items. A recent measure of children's hurricane-related traumatic exposure, for example, asks about windows or doors breaking, being hit by flying debris, and having to flee in the midst of the storm (life threat), whether the child saw someone hurt badly (witnessing violence) or received a physical injury personally (Vernberg et al., 1996). Many studies with children, covering a range of traumatic events, have found strong relationships between greater numbers of objective elements of exposure and symptom severity and persistence (La Greca, Silverman, Vernberg, & Prinstein, 1996; Pynoos, Goenjian et al., 1993; Pynoos, Sorenson, & Steinberg, 1993; Vernberg et al., 1996; Yule & Udwin, 1991).

Assessment of objective aspects of traumatic exposure with children and adolescents becomes problematic under certain conditions. Younger children may lack the communication skills or cognitive sophistication to give detailed accounts of traumatic experience. Many children, as well as adults, are unwilling to give accurate descriptions when trauma involves threats, intimidation, or legal consequences for family members. Further, repeated questioning, rehearsals, and discussions of trauma may cloud accurate recall (Spaccarelli, 1994).

Subjective Aspects of Exposure

Subjective aspects of exposure focus more on the individual's reactions and interpretation of events. These include perceptions that death or serious harm was likely during the traumatic episode, internally experienced events such as intense fear, panic, or anger, and feelings of unreality or dissociation. Several studies with children have found subjective aspects of exposure to add to the prediction of later adjustment, even once objective measures of exposure are considered (La Greca et al., 1996; Vernberg et al., 1996).

Several developmental features influence subjective aspects of traumatic exposure. The ability to interpret accurately the degree of threat posed by objective events emerges gradually with age. The threshold for arousal, and tolerance for arousal, is related to age (van der Kolk, 1997a). Inhibition of the startle reflex is still developing in middle childhood, and the ability to attend to multiple dimensions of experience (e.g., internal cues, environmental signals) improves with age. Caretakers, especially attachment figures, play important roles in emotion regulation, and perceptions of danger and intense emotional reactions in younger children are believed to depend in part on the availability and reactions of caretakers during exposure (Vogel & Vernberg, 1993). As a consequence of these developmental trends, younger children may be very frightened by events that produce mild fear in adolescents or adults, may attend more selectively or idiosyncratically to signals of threat, and may be more strongly influenced by the reactions of attachment figures during exposure.

Evidence for some of these trends appear in research on trauma. For example, 60% of a sample of 8–11 year old children reported thinking they thought they might die at some point during a hurricane, but only 8% reported being injured, and 18% saw someone else hurt (Vernberg et al., 1996). Presumably, many children feared imminent death when this was not a very realistic concern.

Duration, Frequency, and Intensity of Exposure

Longer, more intense periods of exposure to traumatic events are clearly related to symptom severity in children and adolescents. Prolonged episodes of life-threatening acts of terror, such as the kidnapping of a busload of school children in Chowchilla, California, produced longstanding symptoms in all survivors (Terr, 1983). The duration of sexual abuse or assault episodes, greater violation of body integrity, and the use of force or intimidation are thought to be important influences on the course of post-exposure adjustment (Kendall-Tackett, Williams, & Finkelhor, 1993; Spaccarelli, 1994).

Closer physical proximity to acts of violence (Pynoos & Nader, 1989), transportation accidents (Yule & Udwin, 1991), and lightning strikes (Dollinger, O'Donnell, & Staley, 1984) have all been shown to be related to higher levels of distress in children. These effects are generally explained by the increased personal threat signaled by being physically close when another person is seriously injured, exposure to more dimensions of traumatic exposure (e.g., exposure to grotesque scenes), and more extensive sensory involvement (e.g., sounds, smells, touch, in addition to vision).

Agents and Targets of Exposure

The agents involved in producing trauma, and the characteristics of these agents, are a final important element of exposure. Acts involving human agents, as opposed to natural forces, generally produce more distress and longer-lasting effects (Vogel & Vernberg, 1993). Actions taken with specific intent to harm others (e.g., assaults, sniper shooting, torture) may be more difficult to reconcile than human acts that cause trauma unintentionally (e.g., transportation accidents, structural collapses), because deliberate violence damages basic beliefs about human relationships and society. Shame, embarrassment, and feelings of powerlessness and self-blame may be particularly likely to emerge among victims of intentional violence (McFarlane & van der Kolk, 1997).

Younger children appear more likely than older children to assign human motives and attributes to natural phenomena, and to believe a natural act was intended to hurt them personally (Belter & Shannon, 1993). However, this misunderstanding disappears with age, whereas awareness of the intentional, malevolent nature of some harmful acts haunts trauma survivors for years.

Characteristics of an Individual at Exposure

Although most children with high exposure to traumatic stress show increased symptoms of PTSD, many do not develop sufficient symptoms and impairment of functioning necessary for a diagnosis of acute PTSD, and many of those with acute PTSD do not progress to chronic PTSD (Saigh, Green, & Korol, 1996; Vogel & Vernberg, 1993). Characteristics of children at the time of exposure are associated with variable responses to trauma. Age, and related aspects of developmentally based social-cognitive competencies and biological maturation, deserve prominent attention. Other potentially influential individual characteristics include temperament, pre-existing psychiatric disorders, and prior exposure to trauma. These characteristics also may influence the likelihood of exposure to trauma.

Age-related Characteristics

Biological Issues Immature biological systems are generally more vulnerable than mature systems to environmental hazards, including traumatic exposure, in the sense that the course of maturation may be changed. Direct physical injuries from traumatic events affecting the central nervous system pose threats of learning problems and increased vulnerability to a number of psychiatric disorders (Spreen, Risser, & Edgell, 1995). Brains of younger children appear to have a greater capacity to adapt to structural damage by utilizing intact areas to carry out functions normally performed by other regions; yet this compensation is seldom complete and creates a neurological system that is more vulnerable to future insults. Early damage also causes normal development to slow during physical recovery, and may involve a loss of previously acquired skills. Thus traumatic injury often results in a lost opportunity for acquiring new skills, and in some instances leaves the individual more vulnerable to the effects of future physical insults and normal age-related biological changes.

Aside from direct structural damage, exposure to trauma is thought to influence brain chemistry, which in turn affects neuronal networks and brain architecture (Perry, 1997a, 1997b; Perry, Pollard, Blakely, Baker, & Vigilante, 1995; van der Kolk, 1997b). Neuronal connections and pathways are established and refined throughout childhood, and early neuronal development sets the stage for later patterns. Early, chronic exposure to traumatic events may have especially pernicious effects on network characteristics.

Neurological systems that are actively developing in childhood are thought to be most affected (van der Kolk, 1997b). More primitive, early-maturing regions such as the brain stem and hypothalamus are thought to be less easily modified by traumatic exposure (except when exposure involves physical damage to these systems), whereas the limbic system and neocortex appear more readily shaped by environmental input. Van der Kolk argues that the complexity of brain function makes it unrealistic to expect uniform or discrete structural or neurotransmitter system changes from traumatic exposure in childhood. Recent evidence does suggest, however, that chronically-traumatized children as a group differ from comparison children on multiple indices of limbic and neocortical functions, including cortical synchrony and corticosteroid and thyroid functions (De Bellis, Chrousos et al., 1994; De Bellis, Lefter, Trickett, & Putnam, 1994; De Bellis, Burke, Trickett, & Putnam, 1996).

Social-cognitive Issues. Memory and language change dramatically during childhood and adolescence, leading to tremendous age-related variability in the ability to encode, evaluate, and represent traumatic events. Younger children may derive some protection during traumatic exposure by failing to comprehend the significance of some aspects, such as property loss or events not directly witnessed. Normal "amnesia" for early childhood events exhibited by most children may also offer some advantages. However, limited verbal skills at the time of exposure limits the young child's ability to think about traumatic experience and to explain what has happened.

Limitations in cause and effect reasoning make younger children more likely to think about traumatic events in more egocentric terms, ascribing causality to themselves, temporally related but noncausal aspects of the exposure environment, or unknown, uncontrollable factors. Each of these limitations in reasoning works against the key developmental tasks of gaining a sense of self-efficacy and mastery over the environment.

Traumatic exposure poses specific threats to emerging "knowledge structures." Knowledge structures include a number of concepts derived from diverse lines of inquiry, including working models of relationships, internal representations of self and others, schemas and scripts, and attitudes and beliefs. A key point is the recognition that knowledge structures appear to guide more discrete, reliably measured aspects of social information processing (Dodge, 1993). From this perspective, social information characteristics observed in traumatized children, such as oversensitivity to cues of threat or difficulty assessing one's own emotional and physiological state, are driven by qualities of underlying knowledge structures which are more difficult to measure and modify. Attachment theory provides one example of a knowledge structure possibly influenced by trauma. In this theory, early caregiver–child relationships provide the basis for the development of an internalized, working model for close interpersonal relationships (Bowlby, 1988). This working model is thought to include expectations for protection, emotional responsivity, and nurturance. Traumatic exposure may shape the formation of this working model, especially when such exposure involves a violation of healthy expectations for reliable protection, nurturance, and emotional regulation.

Children with more highly developed, healthy knowledge structures at the time of exposure seem likely to be more resistant to long-term repercussions from traumatic exposure. Again using attachment theory as an example, a child's working model of close interpersonal relationships becomes increasingly internalized and stable with age. An early history of optimal attachment relationships is believed to contribute to resilience in the face of adversity later in life. Conversely, an early history of severely disturbed or disrupted attachment relationships appears to leave children vulnerable to long-term problems in emotional regulation and interpersonal relations. In support of this argument, long-term dysfunction from sexual abuse appears somewhat less global for children who are older at the age of abuse, and less severe when a healthy relationship exists with at least one parent (Cole & Putnam, 1992).

Gender

Many studies report higher PTSD symptomatology in girls than in boys, although gender differences are typically small (Saylor, Belter, & Stokes, 1997; Vogel & Vernberg, 1993). Evidence suggests that gender differences in PTSD increase somewhat with age, as they do for other types of internalizing symptoms (Vogel & Vernberg, 1993). In contrast to the pattern seen for internalizing symptoms, boys appear more prone than girls to exhibit externalizing behavioral problems following traumatic exposure, although once again evidence suggests these gender differences are not extreme (Vogel & Vernberg, 1993).

Temperament

Individual differences in characteristic responses to environmental stimuli are thought to reflect temperament. In young children, dimensions of temperament typically include adaptability, capacity for emotional regulation, reactions to novelty, and sociability. Temperament is thought to be related to biological factors, influenced both by genetics and environmental events. Some evidence exists to suggest that children with a more behaviorally inhibited response pattern are more likely to acquire anxiety-related problems (including PTSD symptoms), possibly because of a biologically based low threshold for arousal in the amygdala and hypothalamic circuits (Biederman, Rosenbaum, Chaloff, & Kagan, 1995). This lower threshold for arousal may allow behaviorally inhibited children to become more easily overwhelmed by traumatic exposure, thus increasing the likelihood of subsequent PTSD symptomatology. In addition, pre-existing difficulties with emotion regulation and social introversion may further complicate recovery from trauma (Strelau, 1995). A difficult temperament appears to be a general risk factor for developing psychiatric problems in response to adversity, yet we know of little research with children and adolescents directly examining the role of temperament in the emergence of PTSD.

Prior Trauma

The effects of trauma exposure are proposed to be cumulative, such that a child with a history of trauma exposure is at greater risk than a formerly unexposed child for responding more severely to a specific traumatic event. Rationale for this position rests on the effects of trauma on the developing brain and knowledge structures, as described above and in later sections. Some of these effects are believed to influence reactions during traumatic exposure, including lower thresholds for initiating fight/flight/freeze responses, lower access to internal cues that might guide behavior, and restricted attention to environmental cues (Perry et al., 1995). Prior trauma exposure is also thought to influence post- exposure adjustment, possibly by strengthening trauma-shaped formulations of knowledge structures and continuing to shape neuronal networks to adapt to a trauma-laden environment. Evidence regarding these propositions is beginning to emerge, yet may best be considered plausible but speculative.

Psychopathology

Children who exhibit greater psychopathology at the time of exposure to trauma are believed to be at greater risk for more prolonged and severe posttraumatic reactions, although research evidence remains limited (Vogel & Vernberg, 1993). Pre-existing anxiety disorders and higher levels of trait anxiety have drawn attention as specific risk factors. Difficulties with anxiety may indicate greater sensitivity to cues of threat, general difficulties with overarousal and worry, or difficulties controlling maladaptive cognitions. These features may contribute to lower thresholds for feeling overwhelmed by traumatic exposure and thus produce higher levels of acute distress during exposure. The tendency of more anxious children to use avoidance as a coping strategy possibly interferes with the healthy processing of traumatic experiences, as described below. Direct evidence for these propositions is scant. However, a recent study with adequate pre-exposure measures of children's adjustment found that pre-exposure anxiety predicted posttraumatic stress symptoms both 3 and 7 months after exposure, even after accounting for level of traumatic exposure (La Greca, Silverman, & Wasserstein, 1998).

Qualities of the Posttraumatic Environment

Social Support

Access to supportive social relationships following traumatic exposure regularly emerges as a significant predictor of recovery (Vernberg et al., 1996; La Greca et al., 1996). Younger children are more dependent on adults for instrumental assistance and protection, but also for emotional regulation. Regaining (or gaining) a sense of security and safety is a basic adaptational task following traumatic exposure, and the ability of caretakers to assist in this task is of paramount importance.

Children with secure attachment relationships and continued access to attachment figures are best situated for limited duration of symptoms after traumatic exposure. Unfortunately, traumatic exposure sometimes includes death or serious injury to attachment figures. In other instances, especially those involving abuse, children are separated from attachment figures during investigative procedures. Spaccarelli (1994) described such separation as an "abuse-related" form of traumatic exposure that adds to the cumulative risk of maladjustment.

Most vulnerable of all are trauma-exposed children with a history of poor attachment relationships, especially when a would-be attachment figure is implicated in the traumatic exposure, either as a perpetrator of trauma or as a nonprotective bystander. Not only are such children less likely to have age-appropriate internal resources related to emotional regulation, support seeking, and positive expectancies; they are also less likely to experience optimal levels of protection, nurturance, and affection following trauma exposure.

Even previously well-functioning families may be affected by social support depletion following traumatic events (Kaniasty & Norris, 1997). For example, following natural disasters in which the entire community is affected, entire families may be temporarily or permanently dislocated from their homes. Shelter and assistance is often provided by relatives or close friends, yet over time the financial burdens, crowded living arrangements, and disruptions of familiar roles and routines tends to produce interpersonal discord.

Parental Distress

In many instances, parents are exposed to the same or similar traumas as their child, and bear continued or increased responsibilities at home and work. Increases in numerous forms of symptomatology, including depression, anxiety, and anger, and suicidality have been documented among adults following traumatic exposure (Green, 1991). Linkages have also been documented between a variety of forms of parental distress and poorer outcomes for children. The mechanisms involved in these linkages vary depending on the form of parental distress and the age of the child. For example, maternal depression is thought to decrease sensitivity and responsiveness to social and emotional needs of children. Irritability and anger in parents provide models for coping with distress with aggression and hostility (Conger, Patterson, & Ge, 1995).

Ongoing Disruptions

Continued disruptions in the form of residential instability, economic strain, and changes in roles and routines appear to contribute to children's adjustment following several forms of traumatic exposure, including natural disasters (La Greca et al., 1996), sexual abuse (Spaccarelli, 1994), and bushfires (McFarlane, 1987). Although these types of disruptions are undoubtedly problematic at all ages, young children typically are quite sensitive to changes in environments (Vernberg & Field, 1990), and a rapid resumption of familiar roles and routines is generally thought to be helpful for more rapid recovery from trauma (Vernberg & Vogel, 1993).

Economic Resources

Economic resources in families of trauma-exposed children may be related to the course of psychological recovery in several important ways. Rebuilding and repairing damage wrought by disasters, for example, typically occurs more rapidly for families with good property insurance coverage and other financial assets. Poorer families are less likely to have adequate personal property insurance, more likely to work in service jobs which are often disrupted following widespread disasters, and have fewer options for housing and childcare. The lack of mental health insurance, or underinsurance, for lower income families, also decreases access to mental health services that potentially help children and families cope with traumatic exposure.

The numerous stresses and daily hassles associated with poverty contribute to parental distress and continued exposure to frightening events, making recovery from acute, severely traumatic events more difficult. Recent research documents extreme variability in exposure to community violence, often related to socioeconomic status (Jenkins & Bell, 1997), and gives testimony to the high level of distress among parents living in impoverished areas with high levels of social toxins. For example, over 50% of mothers in a recent study of residents in an inner-city housing project reported clinically significant levels of depression (Osofsky, Wewers, Hann, & Fick, 1993).

Research on trauma-exposed children living in developing countries provides further evidence that financial resources affect the likelihood of exposure to trauma and the course of recovery. Psychiatric morbidity following disasters in developing countries is much higher than in developed countries, and the level of exposure to trauma much higher for similar types of disasters (Goenjian et al., 1995).

Processing of Traumatic Events

Traumatic exposure presents the serious adaptational task of coming to terms with an overwhelming, horrific experience. The nature of this task, and the various aspects of "coming to terms," is an area of debate, although the issues are defined in increasingly sophisticated terms. Much of the extreme behavior or internal turmoil following trauma exposure is conceptualized as an attempt to cope with this challenge. There is a prevalent belief that some efforts are more likely to produce adequate processing than others, with denial, avoidance, and disengagement leading to poor processing and greater symptomatology (Saylor et al., 1997; Vernberg et al., 1996).

Social–Cognitive Issues

Healthy cognitive processing of traumatic experiences involves a number of tasks. These include coping with frightening thoughts and feelings related to the traumatic exposure, regaining a sense of security and trust, and gaining mastery or making sense of the traumatic experiences. Learning theory conceptualizations of processing emphasize neutralizing emotion-provoking stimuli by repeated exposure to trauma-related stimuli under controlled conditions until exaggerated responses disappear. Foa and Kozak (1986, 1991) conceptualize *emotional processing* as the modification of an emotional memory through the incorporation of corrective information. This perspective postulates the existence of *fear structures* comprised of memory networks which activate escape or avoidance behavior in the presence of perceived threat. Fear structures created or shaped by trauma are a target for intervention, using two basic principles: (1) the fear structure must be accessed in order to be modified; and (2) information incompatible with some elements of the fear structure must be available in order to change the existing fear structure. In treatments based on this model, cognitive strategies (e.g., self-talk and reframing) are used along with behavioral strategies (e.g., relaxation techniques) to help the child tolerate activation of trauma-related fear structures.

Psychodynamic models emphasize the need to re-examine trauma-related experiences, with the goals of placing these experiences in a more understandable, less overwhelming framework. From this perspective, processing involves expression of traumatic experiences in words, images, or behavior, coupled with an exploration of the meaning of these experiences for internal representations of the self and others. Inability to describe or demonstrate what has happened hampers a child's ability to gain mastery over the experience and regain a basic sense of safety and security. This process is sometimes described as integrating a traumatic experience into autobiographical memory, such that the occurrence of the trauma can be acknowledged without being the overwhelming, defining influence of perceptions of the self and others (van der Kolk, McFarlane, & van der Hart, 1997).

Cognitive models of processing traumatic exposure are quite similar to psychodynamic models in focusing on the impact of the trauma on knowledge structures. Again, a desired outcome of processing is to allow the traumatic experience to be viewed as a discrete, time-limited incident, and only one part of life-experience shaping beliefs about the world. Cognitive processing in this context is believed to be facilitated by translating relatively unorganized, iconic memories into language-based thoughts. Language allows the overwhelming trauma to be described more fully, and evaluated in relation to the schema, scripts, and beliefs that guide social information processing and decision-making. This formulation has been used to explain why writing repeatedly about traumatic experiences appears to result in decreases in trauma-related symptomatology, in that writing helps translate images into language and confront, rather than avoid, disturbing material (Pennebaker, 1993).

Developmental features undoubtedly influence social–cognitive aspects of processing traumatic events. Limitations in language make it difficult for younger children to describe traumatic experiences in words. The ability to give accurate descriptions of temporal sequences emerges gradually during childhood, as does the capacity to understand cause-and-effect relationships. Insights about the nature of cognition and emotions develop slowly, along with social perspective taking abilities.

At least three notable complications in social–cognitive aspects of processing trauma follow from these developmental factors. First, detailed verbal, self-report descriptions of traumatic exposures are difficult, if not impossible, for many children to provide. Accurate descriptions from others of what has happened are often difficult to obtain, especially when legal issues coexist, as is typically the case when traumatic exposure involves child abuse. Unfortunately, chronic exposure to child abuse appears to further depress children's ability to describe their thoughts and feelings. Second, limited understanding of cognition and emotions makes it harder for children to understand how effortful processing of traumatic experiences may provide symptom relief. Controlled exposure, either by verbal recounting of experiences or the presentation of trauma-related stimuli, produces discomfort, and it is often difficult to convince children that these activities are in their own self-interest. Third, logical reasoning about features related to traumatic events (e.g., intentionality, causal factors) and the implications of these features for working models of the self and others is much more limited during childhood. Reasoning about traumatic experience must be consistent with the child's cognitive capacity if social–cognitive processing is to be facilitated by adults.

Biobehavioral Issues

Physiological processing of trauma is a multidimensional process. The recurrence of strong, negatively valenced emotions, with accompanying physiological reactions, in response to trauma-related stimuli represents a major struggle for many traumatized children. Control of these reactions is often sought through avoidance by physically staying away from such stimuli, mental disengagement, or both. Younger children tend to respond to overwhelming stimuli with more primitive behaviors, such as overt distress, disorganized physical activity, self-stimulating or self-injurious behavior, or an almost complete cessation of activity and engagement (Perry et al., 1995). With more extreme trauma, older children and adolescents also show these responses.

Some research has assessed trauma-exposed children's physiological responses to trauma-related stimuli (Ornitz & Pynoos, 1989; Perry et al., 1995). Current formulations focus on biological processing relating to arousal and response to threat (e.g., startle responses, sensitized neural response) and emotional regulation. In terms of arousal, acute traumatic exposure is believed to interfere with the development of inhibitory control over the startle reflex by increasing sensitivity to fear-producing stimuli (Ornitz & Pynoos, 1989). From this perspective, traumatic exposure reduces the threshold for producing startle, leading acutely traumatized children to have frequent, environmentally inappropriate episodes of overarousal when confronted with a wide range of trauma-related stimuli. Some have argued that the process of repeated activation of neural systems involved in startle responses leads to a progressively lower activation threshold, working against spontaneous extinction of this response (Perry et al., 1995). From this perspective, specific environmental supports are needed to block or reduce startle activation and avoid chronic oversensitivity. These include clear cues that arousal is inappropriate, which may occur naturally given adequate access to protective adults. Alternatively, intentional behavioral treatments based on classical conditioning (e.g., relaxation, systematic desensitization) may be needed to weaken this conditioned response.

It has also been argued that children show hyperarousal, with concomitant fight or flight behavior, as an initial response to overwhelming trauma, yet progress further into a dissociative continuum marked by freezing, surrender, and, in extreme situations, fainting (Perry et al., 1995). The threshold for activating of this freeze-surrender response is also thought to be lowered by traumatic exposure. From this perspective, children who progress to a freeze–surrender response during traumatization may experience reactivation of this response, rather than hyperarousal, when processing trauma-related stimuli.

Developmental factors are believed relevant to biobehavioral processing of traumatic experiences in several ways. Younger children are less likely to succeed in flight–fight responses, and thus may be more likely to acquire a lower threshold for freeze–surrender (Perry et al., 1995). This response is likely more difficult to observe than a hyperarousal response, but may be equally, or even more, debilitating. Concerns are also raised that trauma-related activation of fight/flight/surrender may have more pervasive, durable effects for younger children because characteristics of neurobiological systems are more easily shaped by the environment during the developmental period (Perry et al., 1995).

Outcomes of Traumatic Exposure

As argued throughout this review, traumatic exposure during childhood is thought to influence development in multiple ways. Although PTSD or sub-clinical manifestations of this disorder are common and important consequences of traumatic exposure, other developmentally relevant outcomes also seem to be influenced by this exposure. At times, these other outcomes are notable and debilitating, with symptoms of PTSD less prominent.

PTSD

There is ample evidence that symptoms of PTSD occur frequently in children exposed to trauma along the lines described in the DSM-IV criteria for this disorder (Vogel & Vernberg, 1993). Early posttrauma levels of the core symptoms of re-experiencing phenomena, psychic numbing, and hyper-arousal following acute, life-threatening, trauma are relatively well explained by the conceptual model described here, although longer-term predictions of persistence of symptoms remain problematic. One set of studies based on this conceptual model (at least one measure from each of the four major factors was taken) explained 62% of the variance in PTSD symptoms reported by elementary-age children 3 months after a natural disaster (Vernberg et al., 1996), 39% at 7 months post-disaster, and 24% at 10 months (La Greca et al., 1996). In these studies, PTSD symptoms declined over time for most children, but remained high at the 10-month point in 43% of those reporting severe or very severe PTSD symptoms at 3 months, giving further evidence of the persistence of these types of symptoms in a subset of exposed children.

Chronic PTSD is thought by many to reflect exposure-induced restructuring of related brain structures and dysfunctional biochemical systems (e.g., Charney, Deutch, Krystal, Southwick, & Davis, 1993; Kolb, 1987; Perry, 1997a; Perry et al., 1995, van der Kolk, 1997b). Although multiple biological effects are postulated, effects on the amygdala, hippocampus, locus coeruleus, and neurochemical systems influencing activity by the hypothalamic–pituitary–adrenal axis have drawn considerable research attention. Much of the research in this area has been conducted with adults who experienced significant traumatic exposure as children, and, in many instances, further exposure as adults. Although still a matter of debate, there appears to be an emerging consensus that trauma-induced alterations in reactivity produce long-term overreactions to trauma-related stimuli in a subset of adults exposed to extreme war-related trauma (Keane et al., 1998). Moreover, this heightened physiological reactivity is linked to a broad range of problems, including PTSD, multiple comorbid conditions, social dysfunction, and occupational and legal difficulties (Keane et al., 1998). Recent research with adult survivors of traumatic sexual abuse during childhood provides similar evidence of long-term differences in physiological reactivity between those who develop chronic PTSD and those who do not (Orr et al., 1998).

Comorbid Conditions

Highly traumatized children and adolescents often meet diagnostic criteria for depressive or anxiety disorders when exposure is high and many of the previously described risk factors influencing symptomatology are present. For example, a study of child survivors $1\frac{1}{2}$ years after the 1988 Armenian earthquake, a disaster in an economically underdeveloped country marked by many deaths, very high exposure to trauma, and massive property destruction, indicated that the majority of children from the most devastated towns met criteria for both PTSD and a depressive disorder, and about 40% also developed separation anxiety disorder (SAD) (Goenjian et al., 1995). In contrast to PTSD and SAD, depression apparently emerged months after the disaster, and was highest among children with chronic PTSD. Here, depression was viewed as a "secondary disorder" arising from bereavement, prolonged social disruptions in the aftermath of the disaster, and as a reaction to chronic PTSD, rather than as a direct consequence of the exposure experience. The authors noted that depression has been suggested to emerge in reaction to the symptoms of chronic PTSD in war veterans, and proposed a similar mechanism in these severely traumatized children. High rates of depression and anxiety disorders are also reported in child survivors of Cambodian refugee camps from the Pol Pot era, years after their relocation to the United States (Kinzie, Sack, Angell, Manson, & Rath, 1986; Hubbard et al., 1995).

Traumatic sexual abuse is believed to be related to the subsequent emergence of several disorders involving interpersonal relations, mood regulation, and impulse control, including borderline personality disorder, dissociative disorders, somatization disorders, eating disorders, and substance abuse disorders (Cole & Putnam, 1992). These disorders are thought to develop as a consequence of repeated violations of physical and social boundaries, especially when perpetrated over an extended period, beginning at an early age, by a primary caretaker who uses physical coercion and threats (Cole & Putnam, 1992; Spaccarelli, 1994).

Attitudes, Beliefs, and Expectations

Aside from psychiatric disorders, traumatic exposure is thought to affect emerging knowledge structures. Garbarino (1995; Garbarino & Kostelny, 1997) outlined probable effects of traumatic exposure in terms of children's "social maps." From this perspective, traumatic exposure, especially chronic exposure, forces children to adjust their understanding of themselves and the world to make sense of an overwhelming experience. Depending on the nature and extent of exposure and other factors presented earlier, these accommodations may include heightened sensitivity to signals of potential danger, diminished expectations for the future, mistrust of others, and readily accessed aggressive or defensive responses to a wide range of cues. Others have outlined specific hypotheses about the effects on knowledge structures of specific forms of traumatic exposure. In the case of sexual abuse, these include negative cognitive appraisals from sexual abuse (e.g., self-blame and loss of self-esteem, negative evaluations of others, bias towards perceived threat of harm) (Spaccarelli, 1994), distorted views of sexual norms and behaviors, and feelings of powerlessness (Finkelhor & Browne, 1985).

Future Directions

The relationship between traumatic exposure in childhood and developmental outcomes is multifaceted and multidetermined. It is heartening that the relationship between overwhelming traumatic experiences and subsequent development is not isomorphic, and we are accumulating increasingly sophisticated models to explain variations in the course of recovery from horrific events. These models allow greater specificity in research designed to refine our understanding of trauma-related phenomena, and offer guidelines for interventions.

At the same time, the toll exacted by highly traumatic experiences is severe, especially when exposure begins early in life, continues for extended periods, and rises to extreme levels for children living in conditions of social and economic adversity. If the effects of traumatic exposure are indeed cumulative, prevention of initial exposure to overwhelming trauma should be a central societal goal. Once traumatic exposure has occurred, conditions known to facilitate recovery ought to be offered as soon as possible. Clinical scenarios such as offered at the outset, coupled with more objective evidence of the frighteningly high levels of traumatic exposure among children and adolescents around the world (Jenkins & Bell, 1997; McFarlane & de Girolamo, 1997; Zeanah & Scheeringa, 1997), shows how far we are from providing developmentally adequate childhoods for many of tomorrow's adults.

References

American Psychiatric Association (1994). *Diagnostic and statistical manual of mental disorders* (4th ed.). Washington, DC: American Psychiatric Association.

Belter, R. W., & Shannon, M. P. (1993). Impact of natural disasters on children and families. In C. Saylor (Ed.), *Children and disasters* (pp. 85–104). New York: Plenum.

Biederman, J., Rosenbaum, J. F., Chaloff, J., & Kagan, J. (1995). Behavioral inhibition as a risk factor. In J. S. March (Ed.), *Anxiety disorders in children and adolescents* (pp. 61–81). New York: Guilford.

Bowlby, J. (1988). *A secure base.* New York: Basic Books.

Brett, E. A. (1997). The classification of posttraumatic stress disorder. In B. A. van der Kolk, A. C. McFarlane, & L. Weisaeth (Eds.), *Traumatic stress. The effects of overwhelming experience on mind, body, and society* (pp. 117–128). New York: Guilford.

Charney, D. S., Deutch, A. Y., Krystal, J. H., Southwick, S. M., & Davis, M. (1993). Psychobiologic mechanisms of posttraumatic stress disorder. *Archives of General Psychiatry, 50,* 294–305.

Cole, P. M., & Putnam, F. W. (1992). Effect of incest on self and social functioning: A developmental psychopathology perspective. *Journal of Consulting and Clinical Psychology, 60,* 174–184.

Conger, R. D., Patterson, G. R., & Ge, X. (1995). It takes two to replicate: A mediational model of the impact of parents' stress on adolescent adjustment. *Child Development, 66,* 80–97.

De Bellis, M. D., & Putnam, F. W. (1994). The psychobiology of childhood maltreatment. *Child and Adolescent Psychiatric Clinics of North America, 3,* 1–16.

De Bellis, M. D., Burke, P., Trickett, P. K., & Putnam, F. W. (1996). Antinuclear antibodies and thyroid function in sexually–abused girls. *Journal of Traumatic Stress, 9,* 369–378.

De Bellis, M. D., Chrousos, G. P., Dorn, L. D., Burke, L., Helmers, K., Kling, M. A., Trickett, P. K., & Putnam, F. W. (1994). Hypothalamic–pituitary–adrenal axis dysregulation in sexually–abused girls. *Journal of Clinical Endocrinology and Metabolism, 78,* 249–255.

De Bellis, M. D., Lefter, L., Trickett, P. K., & Putnam, F. W. (1994). Urinary catecholamine excretion in sexually abused girls. *Journal of the American Academy of Child and Adolescent Psychiatry, 33,* 320–327.

Dodge, K. A. (1993). Social–cognitive mechanisms in the development of conduct disorder and depression. *Annual Review of Psychology, 44,* 559–584.

Dollinger, S. J., O'Donnell, J. P., & Staley, A. A. (1984). Lightning–strike disaster: Effects on children's fears and worries. *Journal of Consulting and Clinical Psychology, 52,* 1028–1038.

Famularo, R., Kinscherff, R., & Fenton, T. (1990). Symptom differences in acute and chronic presentation of childhood posttraumatic stress disorder. *Child Abuse and Neglect, 14,* 439–444.

Finkelhor, D., & Browne, A. (1985). The traumatic impact of child sexual abuse: A conceptualization. *American Journal of Orthopsychiatry, 55,* 530–541.

Foa, E. B., & Kozak, M. J. (1986). Emotional processing of fear: Exposure to corrective information. *Psychological Bulletin, 99,* 20–35.

Foa, E. B., & Kozak, M. J. (1991). Emotional processing: Theory, research, and clinical implications for anxiety disorders. In J. D. Safran & L. S. Greenberg (Eds.), *Emotion, psychotherapy, and change* (pp. 21–49). New York: Guilford.

Garbarino, J (1995). *Raising children in a socially toxic environment.* San Francisco: Jossey–Bass.

Garbarino, J., & Kostelny, K. (1997). What children can tell us about living in a war zone. In J. D. Osofsky (Ed.), *Children in a violent society* (pp. 32–41). New York: Guilford.

Goenjian, A. K., Pynoos, R. S., Steinberg, A. M., Najarian, L. M., Asarnow, J. R., Karayan, I., Ghurabi, M., & Fairbanks, L. A. (1995). Psychiatric comorbidity in children after the 1988 earthquake in Armenia. *Journal of the American Academy of Child and Adolescent Psychiatry, 34,* 1174–1184.

Green, B. L. (1990). Defining trauma: Terminology and generic stressor dimensions. *Journal of Applied Social Psychology, 20,* 1632–1642.

Green, B. L. (1991). *Mental health and disaster: A research review.* Rockville, MD: Emergency Services and Disaster Relief Branch, Center for Mental Health Services.

Hubbard, J., Realmuto, G. M, Northwood, A. K., & Masten, A. S. (1995). Comorbidity of psychiatric diagnoses with posttraumatic stress disorder in survivors of childhood trauma. *Journal of the American Academy of Child and Adolescent Psychiatry, 34,* 1167–1173.

Jenkins, E. S., & Bell, C. C. (1997). Exposure and response to community violence among children and adolescents. In J. D. Osofsky (Ed.), *Children in a violent society* (pp. 9–31). New York: Guilford.

Kaniasty, K., & Norris, F. H. (1997). Social support dynamics in adjustment to disasters. In S. Duck, S. (Ed.), *Handbook of personal relationships* (2nd ed., pp. 595–619). New York: Wiley.

Keane, T. M., Kolb, L. C., Kaloupek, D. G., Orr, S. P., Blanchard, E. B., Thomas, R. G., Hsieh, F. Y., & Lavori, P. W. (1998). Utility of psychophysiological measurement in the diagnosis of posttraumatic stress disorder: Results from a Department of Veteran Affairs cooperative study. *Journal of Consulting and Clinical Psychology, 66,* 914–923.

Kendall–Tackett, K. A., Williams, L. M., & Finkelhor, D. (1993). Impact of sexual abuse on children: A review and synthesis of recent empirical studies. *Psychological Bulletin, 113,* 164–180.

Kinzie, J. D., Sack, W. H., Angell, R. H., Manson, S. & Rath, B. (1986). The psychiatric effects of massive trauma on Cambodian children: 1. The children. *Journal of the American Academy of Child and Adolescent Psychiatry, 25,* 370–376.

Kolb, L. C. (1987). A neuropsychological hypothesis explaining posttraumatic stress disorders. *American Journal of Psychiatry, 144,* 989–995.

La Greca, A. M., Silverman, W. K., Vernberg, E. M., & Prinstein, M. J. (1996). Symptoms of posttraumatic stress in children following Hurricane Andrew: A prospective study. *Journal of Consulting and Clinical Psychology, 64,* 712–723.

La Greca, A. M., Silverman, W. K., & Wasserstein, S. B. (1998). Children's predisaster functioning as a predictor of posttraumatic stress following Hurricane Andrew. *Journal of Consulting and Clinical Psychology, 66,* 883–892.

Lipovsky, J. A. (1991). Posttraumatic stress disorder in children. *Family and Community Health, 14,* 42–51.

Lonigan, C. J., Shannon, M. P., Finch, A. J., Daugherty, T. K., & Taylor, C. M. (1991). Children's reactions to a natural disaster: Symptom severity and degree of exposure. *Advances in Behavioral Research and Therapy, 13,* 135–154.

McFarlane, A. C. (1987). Posttraumatic functioning in a longitudinal study of children following a natural disaster. *Journal of the American Academy of Child and Adolescent Psychiatry, 26,* 764–769.

McFarlane, A. C., & de Girolamo, G. (1997). The nature of traumatic stressors and epidemiology of posttraumatic reactions. In B. A. van der Kolk, A. C. McFarlane, & L. Weisaeth (Eds.), *Traumatic stress: The effects of overwhelming experience on mind, body, and society* (pp. 129–154). New York: Guilford.

McFarlane, A. C., & van der Kolk, B. A. (1997). Trauma and its challenge to society. In B. A. van der Kolk, A. C. McFarlane, & L. Weisaeth (Eds.). *Traumatic stress: The effects of overwhelming experience on mind, body, and society* (pp. 24–46). New York: Guilford.

Ornitz, E. M., & Pynoos, R. S. (1989). Startle modulation in children with posttraumatic stress disorder. *American Journal of Psychiatry, 147,* 866–870.

Orr, S. P., Lasko, N. B., Metzger, L. J., Berry, N. J., Ahern, C. E., & Pitman, R. K. (1998). Physiological assessment of women with posttraumatic stress disorder resulting from childhood sexual abuse. *Journal of Consulting and Clinical Psychology, 66,* 906–913.

Osofsky, J. D., Wewers, S., Hann, D. M., & Fick, A. C. (1993). Chronic community violence: What is happening to our children? *Psychiatry, 56,* 7–21.

Pennebaker, J. W. (1993). Putting stress into words: Health, linguistic, and therapeutic implications. *Behaviour Research and Therapy, 31,* 539–548.

Perry, B. D. (1997a). Memories of fear: How the brain stores and retrieves physiologic states, feelings, behaviors and thoughts from traumatic events. In J. Goodwin & R. Attias (Eds.), *Images of the body in trauma.* New York: Basic Books.

Perry, B. D. (1997b). Incubated in terror: Neurodevelopmental factors in the "cycle of violence." In J. D. Osofsky (Ed.), *Children in a violent society* (pp. 124–149). New York: Guilford.

Perry, B. D., Pollard, R., Blakely, T., Baker, W., & Vigilante, D. (1995). Childhood trauma, the neurobiology of adaptation, and "use dependent" development of the brain: How "states" become "traits." *Infant Mental Health Journal, 16,* 271–291.

Pynoos, R. S., & Nader, K. (1989). Children's memory and proximity to violence. *Journal of the American Academy of Child and Adolescent Psychiatry, 28,* 236–241.

Pynoos, R. S., Goenjian, A., Tashjian, M., Karakashian, M., Manjikian, R., Manoukian, G., Steinberg, A., & Fairbanks, L. A. (1993). Post–traumatic stress reactions in children after the 1988 Armenian earthquake. *British Journal of Psychiatry, 163,* 239–247.

Pynoos, R. S., Sorenson, S. B., & Steinberg, A. M. (1993). Interpersonal violence and traumatic stress reactions. In L. Goldberger & S. Breznitz (Eds.), *Handbook of stress: Theoretical and clinical aspects* (2nd ed., pp. 573–590). New York: Free Press.

Pynoos, R. S., Steinberg, A. M. & Goenjian, A. (1997). Traumatic stress in childhood and adolescence: Recent developments and current controversies In B. A. van der Kolk, A. C. McFarlane, & L. Weisaeth (Eds.), *Traumatic stress: The effects of overwhelming experience on mind, body, and society* (pp. 331–358). New York: Guilford.

Saigh, P. A., Green, B. L., & Korol, M. (1996). The history and prevalence of posttraumatic stress disorder with special reference to children and adolescents. *Journal of School Psychology, 34,* 107–131.

Saylor, C., F., Belter, R., & Stokes, S. J. (1997). Children and families coping with disaster. In S. Wolchik & I. Sandler (Eds.), *Handbook of children's coping: Linking theory and intervention* (pp. 361–383). New York: Plenum.

Scheeringa, M. S., Zeanah, C. H., Drell, M. J., & Larrieu, J. A. (1995). Two approaches to the diagnosis of posttraumatic stress disorder in infancy and early childhood. *Journal of the American Academy of Child and Adolescent Psychiatry, 34,* 191–200.

Spaccarelli, S. (1994). Stress, appraisal, and coping in child sexual abuse: A theoretical and empirical review. *Psychological Bulletin, 116,* 340–362.

Spreen, O., Risser, A. T., & Edgell, D. (1995). *Developmental neuropsychology.* New York: Oxford University Press.

Strelau, J. (1995). Temperament risk factor: The contribution of temperament to the consequences of the state of stress. In S. E. Hobfoll & M. W. de Vries (Eds.),

Extreme stress and communities: Impact and intervention (pp. 63–81). The Netherlands: Kluwer Academic.

Terr, L. C. (1983). Chowchilla revisited: The effects of psychic trauma four years after a school–bus kidnapping. *American Journal of Psychiatry, 140,* 1543–1550.

Terr, L. C. (1991). Childhood traumas: An outline and overview. *American Journal of Psychiatry, 148,* 10–20.

van der Kolk, B. A. (1997a). The complexity of adaptation to trauma: Self–regulation, stimulus, discrimination, and characterological development. In B. A. van der Kolk, A. C. McFarlane, & L. Weisaeth (Eds.), *Traumatic stress: The effects of overwhelming experience on mind, body, and society* (pp. 182–213). New York: Guilford.

van der Kolk, B. A. (1997b). The body keeps the score: Approaches to the psychobiology of posttraumatic stress disorder. In B. A. van der Kolk, A. C. McFarlane, & L. Weisaeth (Eds.), *Traumatic stress: The effects of overwhelming experience on mind, body, and society* (pp. 214–241). New York: Guilford.

van der Kolk, B. A., McFarlane, A. C., & van der Hart, O. (1997). A general approach to treatment of posttraumatic stress disorder. In B. A. van der Kolk, A. C. McFarlane, & L. Weisaeth (Eds.), *Traumatic stress: The effects of overwhelming experience on mind, body, and society* (pp. 417–440). New York: Guilford.

Vernberg, E. M. (1999). Children's responses to disasters: Family and systems approaches. In R. Gist & B. Lubin (Eds.), *Responses to disaster: Psychosocial, community, and ecological approaches.* (pp. 193–209). Phildelphia: Brunner/Mazel.

Vernberg, E. M., & Field, T. (1990). Transitional stress in children and adolescents moving to new environments. In S. Fisher & C. L. Cooper (Eds.), *On the move: The Psychology of change and transition* (pp. 127–151). Chichester, England: Wiley.

Vernberg, E. M., & Vogel, J. (1993). Interventions with children following disasters. *Journal of Clinical Child Psychology, 22,* 485–498.

Vernberg, E. M., La Greca, A. M., Silverman, W. K., & Prinstein, M. J. (1996). Prediction of posttraumatic stress symptoms in children after Hurricane Andrew. *Journal of Abnormal Psychology, 105,* 237–248.

Vogel, J. M., & Vernberg, E. M. (1993). Children's responses to disasters. *Journal of Clinical Child Psychology, 22,* 468–484.

Yehuda, R., & McFarlane, A. C. (1995). Conflict between current knowledge about posttraumatic stress disorder and its original conceptual basis. *American Journal of Psychiatry, 152,* 1705–1713.

Yule, W., & Udwin, O. (1991). Screening child survivors for posttraumatic stress disorders: Experiences from the "Jupiter" sinking. *British Journal of Clinical Psychology, 30,* 131–138.

Zeanah, C. H., & Scheeringa, M. S. (1997). The experience and effects of violence in infancy. In J. D. Osofsky (Ed.), *Children in a violent society* (pp. 97–123). New York: Guilford.

18

Social Withdrawal and Anxiety

KENNETH H. RUBIN and KIM B. BURGESS

During the past two decades, the study of social withdrawal in childhood has taken on a research trajectory that can best be described as voluminous. Yet, the construct itself remains something of a mystery; it appears to carry with it a variety of definitions and a number of very different perspectives concerning its psychological significance. Further, social withdrawal represents a construct that has different psychological meanings as one moves from culture to culture.

From the outset, it is important to note that social withdrawal, in and of itself, is not a clinical disorder. After all, most people would agree that there are some individuals who appear perfectly content to spend most of their time alone. In fact, writing a chapter such as this one requires a good deal of solitary confabulation. Yet, there are those who typically avoid others when in social company; there are those who choose solitude to escape the initiation and maintenance of interpersonal relationships; and there are those who are isolated or rejected in social groups. In these latter cases, social solitude could hardly be construed as normal or as socially or psychologically adaptive. But it is not the display of solitude that is the problem; rather, the central issue is that social withdrawal may reflect underlying difficulties of a social or emotional nature.

To some researchers, a fearful temperament underpins the behavioral expression of social withdrawal (e.g., Kagan, 1989). Yet others believe that children demonstrate solitude not because they are strongly motivated to avoid others, but because they prefer object manipulation and construction (Asendorpf, 1993). Lastly, some researchers believe that socially withdrawn behavior reflects underlying thoughts and feelings of social anxiety, loneliness, insecurity, and depression (e.g., Rubin, Chen, & Hymel, 1993; Rubin, Chen, McDougall, Bowker, & McKinnon, 1995). With such diverse etiological viewpoints, clinical psychologists have been unable to agree about the significance of social withdrawal for the development of psychopathology.

Because there appear to be several different forms of solitary behavior, each of which may not carry the same psychological meaning (Coplan, Rubin, Fox, Calkins, & Stewart, 1994; Rubin, 1982a; Rubin & Mills, 1988), the first goal of this chapter is to define social withdrawal. To understand the psychological implications of not interacting and relating to peers in "normal" ways, the second section addresses the developmental and psychological benefits of children's peer interaction and relationships. The third purpose of this chapter is to reflect on those factors that may undergird the stable, continuous display of social withdrawal during childhood. Fourth, we review the literature on the correlates and predictive consequences of social withdrawal, and make reference to a transactional developmental pathway that has guided our writings on social withdrawal for almost 20 years (e.g., Rubin, 1982b; Rubin, LeMare, & Lollis, 1990). Lastly, we discuss the role of parenting in social withdrawal, as well as epidemiological factors associated with social withdrawal.

Social Withdrawal Defined

It is not uncommon to find psychologists using the following terms interchangeably: "social withdrawal," "social isolation," "inhibition," and "shyness." As a point of departure, we argue that psychological nomenclature is important and that any confusion be quelled. With this in mind, we refer the reader to Rubin and Asendorpf (1993) who have attempted to bring some order into the confusion caused by slippery terms of reference. In their paper, *inhibition* referred to the disposition to be wary and fearful when encountering novel (that is, unfamiliar) nonsocial situations. *Shyness* referred to inhibition in response to novel *social* situations. *Social isolation* had little to do with the behavioral expression of wariness; rather the term reflected the expression of solitary behavior that results from peer rejection. Finally, *social withdrawal* referred to *the consistent (across situations and over time) display of solitary behavior when encountering familiar and/or unfamiliar peers.* Simply put, social withdrawal was construed as isolating oneself *from* the peer group; social isolation indicated isolation *by* the peer group.

According to Rubin and Asendorpf (1993), the underlying motives for withdrawing from the social milieu are multiply determined. Asendorpf (1990; 1993) has reported that some children have a low social approach motive without a high avoidance motive. These children demonstrate more object- than person-oriented activity, and prefer quiescent, exploratory, or constructive solitude to social activity (referred to as "solitary-passive play"; Rubin, 1982b). Other children may be motivated to interact with peers but are compelled to avoid it. When these socially anxious and wary children play alone, they are observed to frequently engage in unoccupied or onlooker behavior (labeled "reticence"; e.g., Coplan et al., 1994). Motivation and terms of reference aside, the following section lays the groundwork for understanding the implications for a lack of social interchange.

The Significance of Peer Interaction for Normal Development

An early source of information pertaining to the significance of peer interaction for normal social, emotional, and cognitive growth came from the writings and research of Jean Piaget. According to Piaget, young children are egocentric and not particularly adept at understanding the perspectives, intentions, and feelings of others (Piaget, 1926). Drawing from this early work, contemporary researchers began to use children's lack of social–cognitive maturity (specifically the immaturity of perspective-taking skills) to explain the behavioral expression of maladaptive social behaviors (e.g., Rubin & Rose-Krasnor, 1992; Selman, 1980). For example, it was proposed that the probability of behaving in an aggressive manner would increase if a person is unable to understand the victim's thoughts and feelings, or realize the consequences of his or her actions.

Given the possibility that social–cognitive immaturity might help explain the expression of incompetent social behavior, the ensuing developmental question becomes: "What accounts for the developmental decline in egocentrism?" From the Piagetian perspective, peer interaction allows children the opportunities to examine conflicting ideas and explanations; to negotiate and discuss multiple perspectives; and to decide to compromise with, or reject, the notions held by peers (Piaget, 1926). In short, social cognitive maturity was largely a function of children's peer interactions; in turn, their ability to think maturely about their social worlds influenced children's social behaviors.

Support for these Piagetian notions derived from research demonstrating that peer exchange, conversations, and interactions produced *intrapersonal* cognitive conflict and a subsequent decline in egocentered thinking (e.g., Damon & Killen, 1982). Evidence was also offered for the associations between the *inability* to perspective-take and the demonstration of *maladaptive* social behavior (e.g., Crick & Dodge, 1994). Finally, researchers found that perspective-taking skills could be improved through peer interactive experiences, particularly those experiences that involved role-play. In turn, such improvement led to increases in prosocial behavior and to decreases in aggressive behavior (e.g., Selman & Schultz, 1990).

The extant literature allows the conclusion that peer interaction influences the development of social cognition and, ultimately, the expression of competent social behavior. Peer interaction also influences children's understanding of the rules and norms of their peer subcultures. It is this understanding of normative performance levels that engenders in the child an ability to evaluate her or his own competency against the perceived standards of the peer group.

According to Mead (1934), the ability to self-reflect, to consider the self in relation to others, and to understand the perspectives of others is largely a function of participation in organized, rule-governed activities with peers. He suggested that peer exchanges, whether in the arenas of cooperation, competition, conflict, or friendly discussion, allow the child to gain an understanding of the self as both a subject and an object. Understanding that the self could be an object of others' perspectives gradually evolves into the conceptualization of a "generalized other" or an organized and coordinated perspective of the "social" group. In turn, recognition of the "generalized other" leads to the emergence of an organized sense of self.

Finally, the personality theorist Sullivan (1953) suggested that the foundations of mutual respect, cooperation, and interpersonal sensitivity derive initially from children's friendship and peer relationships. Sullivan specifically emphasized the importance of chumships, or special relationships, for the emergence of these concepts. Once the concepts of equality, mutuality, and reciprocity were learned via chumships, these concepts then could be applied more generally to other, less special, peer relationships.

From both theoretical and empirical perspectives, therefore, peer interaction is essential for normal social–cognitive development and emotional growth (see Rubin, Bukowski, & Parker, 1998, for an extensive review). Naturally, if peer interaction is important for the development of social competence, peer relationships, and positive self-regard, one wonders about the impact of little social interchange. Refraining from peer interchange may bring with it a number of developmental costs. Therein lies the developmental "place" for the study of social withdrawal. In the next section, we describe the possible developmental "costs" of social withdrawal by reviewing the relevant clinical literature, especially insofar as anxiety is concerned.

Social Withdrawal, Anxiety, and Clinical Diagnosis

In recent years social withdrawal has been viewed as a marker of social and/ or emotional maladjustment (Quay & Werry, 1986). Yet, the phenomenon does not occupy a place of its own in the major diagnostic manuals; instead, in the *Diagnostic and statistical manual of mental disorders* (DSM-IV, American Psychiatric Association, 1994) and the ICD-10 *Classification of mental and behavioral disorders* (ICD-10; World Health Organization, 1993) social withdrawal is subsumed under other categories of disturbance. The current systems, therefore, represent social withdrawal as a symptom rather than as a syndrome with its own etiology and prognoses. Despite the fact that social withdrawal has not been a primary focus of psychiatric inquiry, it has nevertheless been associated with several clinical disorders of childhood and adolescence. These disorders range from autism to anxiety and phobic disorders, major depression, personality disorders, and schizophrenia. In keeping with the focus of this volume, we provide links between social withdrawal and anxiety, depression, and avoidant personality disorder.

Behavioral Inhibition, Anxiety, and Phobic Disorders

Behavioral inhibition, a presumed precursor to the frequent demonstration of social withdrawal, is a temperamental construct reflecting the tendency to be fearful and anxious during the toddler years, and socially wary and withdrawn in unfamiliar situations during the early school-age years (Calkins & Fox, 1992; Calkins, Fox, & Marshall, 1996; Kagan, Reznick, Snidman,

Gibbons, & Johnson, 1988). Several researchers have suggested that behavioral inhibition represents a marker of anxiety and anxiety proneness. For example, a positive relation exists between cortisol production in saliva and the demonstration of extremely inhibited behavior not only in the toddler period (Kagan , Reznick, & Snidman, 1987; Nachmias, Gunnar, Mangelsdorf, Parritz, & Buss, 1996), but also during early and middle childhood (Schmidt et al., 1997). The high cortisol levels of inhibited children may increase corticotrophin-releasing hormones in the central nucleus of the amygdala, exacerbating the social fearfulness response. Further, high cortisol levels may predispose inhibited children to develop a cognitive working model to expect fear and anxiety when facing novelty. It is relevant to note that exaggerated autonomic responses to novelty are associated with internalizing problems such as anxiety (e.g., McBurnett et al., 1991).

Longitudinal data also suggest a link between behavioral inhibition in infancy and early childhood and phobic and anxiety disorders in mid-childhood (Hirshfeld et al., 1992). Behaviorally inhibited children evidence higher rates of phobic disorders (Biederman et al., 1993) and multiple anxiety disorders (avoidant disorder, separation anxiety disorder, and agoraphobia; e.g., Rosenbaum et al., 1988) than uninhibited children. Thus, behavioral inhibition is associated contemporaneously and predictively with indices of anxiety and phobic disorders.

Social Withdrawal and Anxiety Disorders

Anxiety disorders represent one of the most common disorders of childhood (Achenbach, 1982). Whatever it is that causes children's social fears and anxieties, their social interactions and relationships with peers are inevitably impaired. Clearly, the avoidance of social interaction may serve to reduce visceral arousal. If anxiety does decrease following avoidant behavior, then social withdrawal or avoidance will be reinforced, and the probability of recurrence increased (Barrios & O'Dell, 1989). Not surprisingly, therefore, anxiety disordered children often exhibit social withdrawal.

The relation between withdrawal and anxiety may be described as dialectic and cyclical in nature. Anxiety may be "marked" by frequent withdrawal from, and avoidance of, peer interaction. But social withdrawal and avoidance interfere with the normal development of social skills. Deficiencies in social skills will then serve to reinforce social anxiety and to foster negative self-appraisals and negative self-esteem (Boivin, Hymel & Bukowski, 1995; Hymel, Bowker, & Woody, 1993; Messer & Beidel, 1994).

Social Withdrawal and Depression

Similar to anxiety, depression is an internalizing disorder. However, social withdrawal accompanying depression may have different social consequences than does social withdrawal exhibited by anxious individuals. Social withdrawal induced by social anxiety may yield sympathy, interest, and social overtures from others; whereas depressed individuals may elicit support in a way that actually causes others to withdraw from them, even ignore or reject them (e.g., Mullins, Peterson, Wonderlich, & Reaven, 1986).

A partial understanding of why such interpersonal consequences ensue derives from the DSM-IV and ICD-10 descriptions of children who have major depression or dysthymia. These children experience depressed mood, *social withdrawal*, feelings of hopelessness, low self-esteem, and poor concentration, as well as appetite and sleep disturbances; hence, they are not particularly fun to be around. Moreover, others may view depressive behaviors as being within a person's realm of control, in contrast to being a victim of a nervous or anxious disposition.

As well as being a concomitant of childhood depression, social withdrawal appears to be a *predictor* of depression. Rubin and colleagues (1993; Rubin, Chen et al., 1995) found a predictive link between the early display of social withdrawal and later depression in adolescence. Further, Bell-Dolan, Reaven, and Peterson (1993) examined the relation between childhood depression and social functioning in fourth and sixth graders. Results showed that social withdrawal predicted depression as reported by both peers and teachers, and that low social activity predicted self-reported depression.

Social Withdrawal and Avoidant Personality Disorder

Whereas depressive behaviors are viewed as ephemeral and within an individual's control, personality disorders are viewed as longstanding, and temperamentally or dispositionally based. Avoidant personality disorder is marked by excessive preoccupation and fear of criticism, disapproval, or rejection, leading to avoidance of interpersonal contact (e.g., Millan, 1981). Individuals with this diagnosis express a desire for affection, acceptance, and friendship; but they often have few friends and share little intimacy with anyone. Fear of rejection plays a key role in distancing themselves from personal attachments. These avoidant individuals are typically described as timid and withdrawn (Turkal, 1990). They fail to enter into relationships unless the prospective partner provides unusually strong guarantees of uncritical acceptance (Millan & Everly, 1985). In addition, their nervousness often makes companions uncomfortable, and thereby leads to rejection or damages the quality of ongoing relationships (Millan, 1981; Millan & Everly, 1985; Turkal, 1990). Avoidant individuals also cope by hypervigilance and by restricting the range of environmental stimuli; hence, they retreat from novel social experiences. This retreat inhibits the development of social self-efficacy for dealing with interpersonal situations (Costa & McCrae, 1985).

Summary

Social withdrawal surfaces in numerous diagnostic categories of the two major classification systems, DSM-IV and ICD-10. Specifically, social withdrawal is listed as a symptom, or marker, of anxiety and phobic disorders, major depression, and avoidant personality disorder. It may be that the forms of solitude and the motivations underlying these behavioral expressions vary from one disturbance to another. Clearly, the time is ripe for researchers to examine the etiology and developmental course of social withdrawal in childhood. To set the stage for such inquiry, we have described a developmental model (e.g., Rubin, Stewart, & Coplan, 1995), which has been revised in light of recent research findings. Nevertheless, it is the conceptual framework that has provided the basis for our own research on the causes, concomitants, and consequences of childhood social withdrawal.

Developmental Pathways to and from Social Withdrawal in Childhood

Behavioral Inhibition, Physiology, and Affect

Several researchers have argued that the pathway to social withdrawal begins with a dispositional or temperamental trait now widely recognized as *behavioral inhibition*. This phenomenon has been thought to emanate from a physiological "hard wiring" that evokes caution, wariness, and timidity in unfamiliar social and nonsocial situations (e.g., Kagan, 1997; Kagan et al., 1987). Inhibited infants and toddlers differ from their uninhibited counterparts in ways that imply variability in the threshold of excitability of the amygdala and its projections to the cortex, hypothalamus, sympathetic nervous system, corpus striatum, and central gray (Calkins et al., 1996). Two dimensions of infant behavior are particularly predictive of toddlers' fearful and anxious behaviors: (1) frequency of motor activity; and (2) display of negative affect (Calkins et al., 1996; Kagan & Snidman, 1991). The combination of *consistently* expressed motor arousal and negative affect is thought to be a function of elevated excitability in areas of the limbic system involved in fear responses. Infants who are easily and negatively aroused motorically and emotionally have displayed behavioral inhibition as toddlers (Calkins et al., 1996; Kagan & Snidman, 1991).

That there is a physiological basis underpinning social wariness, anxiety, and other problems of an internalizing nature is supported by adult studies. For example, elevated cortisol levels have been linked to fear, distress, and depression in adults (e.g., Bell-Dolan et al., 1993). Abnormalities in ventilatory physiology (e.g., asthma) have been associated with panic and anxiety disorders, not only in adults but also in children (e.g., Pine et al., 1994). Also, adults diagnosed with unipolar depression, even in remission, are more likely to display right frontal EEG asymmetry than are controls (Henriques & Davidson, 1990). Further, adults exhibiting right frontal EEG asymmetries are more likely to express negative affect and to rate emotional stimuli as negative (Jones & Fox, 1992).

This literature has proved evocative for those researchers interested in the origins of social wariness and inhibition. It is now known that infants with right frontal EEG asymmetries are more likely to cry to maternal separation, and display signs of negative affect and fear of novelty (Davidson & Fox, 1989). Further, stable patterns of right frontal EEG asymmetries in infancy predict temperamental fearfulness and behavioral inhibition in early childhood. Fox and Calkins (1993) recorded brain electrical activity of children at ages 9, 14, and 24 months and found that infants who displayed a pattern of stable right frontal EEG asymmetry across this 15-month period were more fearful, anxious, compliant, and behaviorally inhibited as toddlers than other infants. Also, Fox, Calkins and Bell (1994) noted that negative reactivity and right frontal EEG asymmetry in response to mild stress was associated with the display of toddler inhibition.

The findings just described suggest that unique patterns of brain electrical activity may be involved in the expression of fear and anxiety (LeDoux, 1989) and appear to reflect a particular underlying temperamental type. The functional role of hemispheric asymmetries in the regulation of emotion may be understood in terms of an underlying motivational basis for emotional behavior, specifically along the approach–withdrawal continuum. Infants exhibiting greater relative right frontal asymmetry are more likely to withdraw from mild stress, whereas infants exhibiting the opposite pattern of activation are more likely to approach (Calkins et al., 1996).

Another physiological entity that distinguishes wary from nonwary infants/toddlers is vagal tone, an index of the functional status or efficiency of the nervous system (Porges & Byrne, 1992), marking both general reactivity and the ability to regulate one's level of arousal. Reliable associations have been found between vagal tone and inhibition in infants and toddlers (Fox, 1989; Garcia Coll, Kagan, & Reznick, 1984): children with *lower vagal tone* (consistently high heart rate due to less parasympathetic influence) tend to be more behaviorally inhibited.

It is important to note that human physiology is hardly immutable. Thus, we suggest that behavioral inhibition in infancy and toddlerhood, and its physiological markers, may be altered or exacerbated through environmental means. For instance, we have suggested that a temperamentally inhibited infant may prove a challenge or stressor to his or her parents. Thus, an interplay of endogenous, socialization, and early relationship factors might lead to a sense of felt insecurity, and ultimately to the chronic expression of social withdrawal.

Attachment Relationships and Behavioral Inhibition

Attachment theorists have posited that the parent-infant attachment relationship results in the child developing an internal working model of the self in relation to others (Bowlby, 1973). This internal working model allows the child to feel secure, confident, and self-assured when introduced to novel settings. A sense of "felt security" fosters the child's active exploration of the social environment (Sroufe, 1983). In turn, exploration of the social milieu allows the child to address a number of significant "other-directed" questions such as "What are the properties of this other person?"; "What is she/he like?"; "What can and does she/he do?" (Rubin, 1993). Once these exploratory questions are answered, the child can begin to address "self-directed" questions such as "What can *I* do with this person?". Thus, felt security is viewed as a central construct in socioemotional development: it enhances social exploration, which results in interactive peer play. Peer play, in turn, plays a significant role in the development of social competence (Rubin & Rose-Krasnor, 1992).

Children who develop insecure internal working models of social relationships, on the other hand, come to view the world as unpredictable, comfortless, and unresponsive (Sroufe, 1983). This insecure internal representation may lead some children to "shrink from their social worlds" whilst others "do battle" with theirs (Bowlby, 1973, p. 208). That subgroup of insecurely attached young children who refrain from exploring their social environments have typically been classified as "anxious–resistant" or "C" babies. It has been suggested that the "C" baby's lack of exploration eventually impedes social–peer play and, thus, interferes with the development of social competence. In novel settings these infants maintain close proximity to the attachment figure; and when the attachment figure (usually the mother) leaves the paradigmatic "Strange Situation" for a short period of time, "C" babies become disturbingly unsettled. Upon reunion with the attachment figure, these infants show ambivalence—angry, resistant behaviors interspersed with proximity, contact-seeking behaviors (e.g., Greenspan & Lieberman, 1988).

An association between inhibited temperament and attachment relationships has been shown by a number of empirical studies. For example, meta-analyses have indicated that the temperamental characteristic of "proneness to distress" predicts the resistant behavior that partly defines insecure attachment status of the "C" variety (Goldsmith & Alansky, 1987). It is possible that irritability or proneness to distress presents as a significant stressor to parents, and therefore influences the quality of mother–infant interactions and the quality of attachment (Izard, Haynes, Chisholm, & Baak, 1991). The temperament construct of *emotionality*, which comprises irritability and proneness to distress, may lay the basis for the development of insecure attachment relationships. Support for this contention comes from the research of Izard and colleagues who found that infant emotionality, as well as infant resting-state cardiac activity (a physiological index of emotionality and emotion regulation), independently predicted insecure attachment status.

Direct evidence for a predictive relation between infant temperament and insecure "C" attachment status derives from several sources. Thompson, Connell, and Bridges (1988) have reported that infant proneness to fear predicts distress to maternal separation. Such distress is usually allied with a "C" classification in the traditional attachment paradigm (Belsky & Rovine, 1987). Further, infants who are dispositionally reactive to mildly stressful, novel social events are more likely to be classified as insecurely attached "C" (anxious–resistant) babies than their less reactive counterparts (Calkins & Fox, 1992).

Attachment, Inhibition, and Social Withdrawal

The social behaviors of toddlers and preschoolers who have an insecure "C"-type attachment history are thought to be guided largely by fear of rejection. Conceptually, psychologists have predicted that when these insecurely attached children are placed in peer group settings, they should attempt to avoid rejection by demonstrating passive, adult-dependent behavior and withdrawal from social interaction (Renken, Egeland, Marvinney, Mangelsdorf, & Sroufe, 1989). Empirical support for these conjectures derives from data indicating that anxious–resistant ("C') infants are more whiny, easily frustrated, and socially inhibited at age 2 than their secure ("B") counterparts (Fox & Calkins, 1993; Matas, Arend, & Sroufe, 1978). Anxious-resistant "C" babies also tend to be less socially skilled as toddlers and to be rated by their teachers as more dependent, helpless, tense, and fearful than their secure counterparts (Pastor, 1981). Finally, "C" babies lack confidence and assertiveness at age 4 years (Erickson, Sroufe, & Egeland, 1985); then, at age 7 years they are observed to be socially withdrawn (Renken et al., 1989). Booth, Rose-Krasnor, McKinnon, and Rubin (1994) provide additional support for both predictive and contemporaneous connections between insecure attachment and social withdrawal.

Parenting and Behavioral Inhibition

Thus far, we have described factors that may be responsible for the development of behavioral inhibition, and ultimately the demonstration of social withdrawal in childhood—factors such as the child's dispositional characteristics and the quality of the parent–child attachment relationship. But insecure attachment relationships are also predicted by maternal behavior. For example, mothers of insecurely attached "C" babies are more overinvolved and overcontrolling than mothers of securely attached babies (Erickson et al., 1985). Indeed, in our developmental model we have posited that this particular parenting style is especially salient; and the developmental process may be as follows.

Given reticence to explore their environments, socially inhibited children may develop difficulties in solving intra- and interpersonal problems on their own. Parents of socially wary children may sense their child's difficulties and perceived helplessness; and then might try to support their children directly by either manipulating their child's behaviors in a power assertive, highly directive fashion (e.g., telling the child how to act or what to do) or by actually intervening and taking over for the child (e.g., intervening during peer disputes; inviting a potential playmate to the home). For socially fearful children, the experience of parental overcontrol is likely to maintain or exacerbate, rather than ameliorate, their difficulties. Parental overdirectiveness will not allow the child to solve impersonal or interpersonal problems on her or his own. In controlling what their children are exposed to and how such situations are handled, these parents may prevent their children from engaging in necessary, self-initiated coping techniques. Lacking practice in behavioral self-regulation, children who are poor physiological self-regulators may not learn to overcome their dispositional vulnerabilities. Further, such parenting experiences may prevent the development of a belief system of self-efficacy; and likely will perpetuate feelings of insecurity within and outside the family.

Recent research has demonstrated that parental influence and control does appear to maintain and exacerbate children's inhibition and social withdrawal. Rubin, Hastings, Stewart, Henderson, and Chen (1997) found that mothers of inhibited toddlers were "oversolicitous"; that is, they were observed to be highly affectionate and shielding of their toddlers when it was neither appropriate nor sensitive to do so. In a recent examination of reported (rather than observed) parenting styles, Chen and colleagues found that the parents of inhibited toddlers were more likely to endorse statements pertaining to protection, punishment orientation, and a lack of emphasis on independence training (Chen et al., 1998).

From Inhibition to Reticence and Withdrawal

Inhibition during the toddler period has been linked conceptually and empirically to shyness and social reticence in early and mid childhood. For example, investigators have consistently demonstrated that inhibited toddlers are likely to remain inhibited in the early and mid years of childhood (e.g., Broberg, Lamb, & Hwang, 1990; Reznick et al., 1986; Sanson, Pedlow, Cann, Prior, & Oberklaid, 1996). Notably, Kochanska and Radke-Yarrow (1992) reported that *social* (but not nonsocial) inhibition in toddlerhood predicted shy, inhibited behavior at 5 years when children played with an unfamiliar peer. Similarly, when inhibited toddlers were observed again at 7.5 years of age in a group of unfamiliar peers, they were observed to be more distant from their playmates and less likely to converse with them (Kagan & Snidman, 1991). Finally, mothers and fathers who perceive their toddlers to be socially inhibited maintain these perceptions when their children are preschoolers (Rubin, Nelson, Hastings & Asendorpf, 1999).

The Developmental Course of Social Withdrawal

Having described the putative antecedents of social withdrawal in childhood, we now turn to an examination of its correlates and consequences. In our developmental model of pathways leading to and following from social withdrawal, we have argued that reticence to explore novel, out-of-home settings impedes: (a) the possibility of establishing normal social relationships; (b) the experience of normal social interactive play behaviors; and (c) the development of those social and cognitive skills supposedly encouraged by peer relationships and social play (Rubin, Stewart et al., 1995). Further, the developmental process begins with a socially inhibited, fearful, insecure child who withdraws from social interaction and thereby fails to develop those skills derived from peer communication, negotiation, and compromise. This relative lack of peer interaction causes the child to become increasingly uncomfortable and anxious amongst peers, and ultimately leads to isolation from the peer group. We have also posited that the recognition of one's social failure results in thoughts and feelings of negative self-regard. These thoughts and feelings are repeatedly reinforced as the child continues to demonstrate inadequate social skills.

Different Forms of Withdrawal

Support for these conjectures emanates from several sources. First, it is essential to note that, whilst alone, children are not necessarily avoiding their peers. Some children prefer to play alone in the peer group; these children are often observed engaging in exploratory and constructive activity (Asendorpf, 1990, 1993; Coplan et al., 1994; Rubin, 1982a). Other children appear to spend time alone whilst among peers because they are fearful and wary of social interaction. It is this particular group of children who we believe have the biological underpinnings of wariness and anxiety, and who have been socially inhibited as toddlers (Fox & Henderson, 1998).

Reticence and Emotion Dysregulation

Fox and colleagues have demonstrated that reticent, fearful, solitary behavior is associated with greater relative right frontal EEG activation; but constructive solitude is not (Fox et al., 1995). Further, those reticent children who have such EEGs are viewed by their parents as being anxious and as having internalizing difficulties (Fox, Calkins, Schmidt, Rubin, & Coplan, 1996). Interestingly, *sociable* children with demonstrably greater relative right frontal EEG activation are viewed by parents as having externalizing problems (Fox et al., 1996). Fox and colleagues explain these findings by noting that frontal EEG activation may reflect an individual's ability to regulate affective arousal. Many of the cognitive competencies (e.g., analytic abilities, verbal mediation) involved in successful affect regulation may be mediated by left frontal lobe areas. Thus, individuals with greater relative left frontal activation may have the means to successfully regulate affective arousal. On the other hand, individuals with greater relative right frontal EEG activation may not have access to the same language and analytic based strategies, thereby rendering affect regulation more difficult. This would be true whether the affect arousal was extremely negative or positive, although the behavioral consequences would obviously differ. In the case of extreme negative affect arousal, unsuccessful regulation might lead to withdrawal and/or depressive symptoms. In the instance of extreme positive affect arousal, unsuccessful regulation may lead to aggression and oppositional behaviors.

Further evidence for affect dysregulation being associated with social withdrawal is drawn from the research of Eisenberg and colleagues. These researchers found that, among kindergarten to second-grade children, shyness was positively associated with internalized negative emotions such as nervousness, distress, and upset; shyness was negatively related to positive emotions such as enthusiasm and excitement (Eisenberg, Shepard, Fabes, Murphy & Guthrie, 1998). They also reported that the internalization of negative emotions including increased anxiety levels led to children's coping with problematic social situations by avoiding peer interaction.

Social Withdrawal, Social Skills, and Self-regard

If socially withdrawn children are too fearful to engage in peer interaction, it follows that they might not develop those skills that emanate from peer interaction. In this regard, it has been found that socially withdrawn children do lack the social skills that endear themselves to peers or that elicit positive thoughts and feelings about the self. During the preschool and primary-grade school years, these children are less able to comprehend the perspectives of others (LeMare & Rubin, 1987). From mid-to-late childhood withdrawn children are also less competent than are sociable children in using interpersonal negotiation strategies to solve problems and conflicts (Adalbjarnardottir, 1995). Further, withdrawn children are more likely than their more sociable agemates to be adult-dependent and unassertive when faced with interpersonal dilemmas (Rubin, 1982b; Rubin, Daniels & Bream, 1984). When they do attempt to assert themselves or gain compliance from peers, they are more likely than sociable agemates to be rebuffed (Rubin & Krasnor, 1986). Importantly, the social initiations of withdrawn children become decreasingly assertive, and noncompliance to their requests increases from early to middle childhood (Stewart & Rubin, 1995).

This increasing experience of failure following social initiation suggests that a socially withdrawn child may incur peer rejection on a continual basis; such negative experiences may produce unpleasant cognitions and emotions. As a result of frequent interpersonal rejection by peers, withdrawn children may begin to attribute their social failures to internal causes; in other words, they may come to believe that there is something wrong with themselves rather than attributing their social failures to other people or situations. Supporting these notions, Rubin and Krasnor (1986) found that extremely withdrawn children tended to blame social failure on personal, dispositional characteristics rather than on circumstances or external events. The combination of peer rejection and internal (dispositional) attributions for peer noncompliance could be construed as creating a feedback loop whereby an initially fearful, withdrawn child begins to believe that his or her social failures are personality-based, and then these beliefs are reinforced by increasing failure of social initiatives or interactions (Rubin & Stewart, 1996). Ultimately, the consequence of such cognitions may be further withdrawal from the social environment.

As children approach the mid-to-late years of childhood, there is evidence to support an association between social withdrawal or social anxiety and both intrapersonal and interpersonal difficulties. Given that peers often do not comply with, or reciprocate, social initiations beginning in primary school, it makes sense that observational and peer assessments of social withdrawal have been associated with sociometric assessments of peer rejection and unpopularity by middle-to-late childhood (e.g., Harrist, Zaia, Bates, Dodge, & Pettit, 1997; Rubin et al., 1993). Why socially withdrawn children's peers dislike them by mid-to-late childhood despite their not being rejected in early childhood may be explained by the increasing negative salience of playing alone as children get older. With the recognition that social solitude represents a behavior that deviates from the norm, it becomes increasingly viewed as deviant by the peer group (Younger, Gentile, & Burgess, 1993). Moreover, by mid-to-late childhood, children are better able to recognize or perceive peers' "internally driven" problems such as anxiety and hypersensitivity, which often accompany social withdrawal.

Previously, we have argued that the constellation of social withdrawal, social inadequacy, and peer rejection sows the seeds for internalizing problems such as negative self-regard, low self-esteem, anxiety, loneliness, and depression (e.g., Rubin, 1993). In fact, investigators have found that beginning in middle childhood, socially withdrawn children have negative self-perceptions of their social competence and interpersonal relationships (e.g., Hymel et al., 1993; Rubin, Hymel & Mills, 1989). In addition to negative self-perceptions, socially withdrawn children actually do experience feelings of anxiety, loneliness and depressed mood by mid/late childhood (e.g., Boivin et al., 1995; Rubin, Hymel et al., 1989). In pre- to early adolescence they report anxiety, depressive symptoms, and somatic complaints (Burgess & Younger, 1996).

Consequences of Social Withdrawal

Highlighting the potential long-term outcomes of social withdrawal is a recent report which showed that a composite of observed and peer assessed social withdrawal at age 7 years predicted negative self-perceived social competence, low self-worth, loneliness, and felt peer-group insecurity among adolescents aged 14 years (Rubin, Chen et al., 1995). These latter findings are augmented by related research findings. For example, Renshaw and Brown (1993) found that passive withdrawal at ages 9 to 12 years predicted loneliness assessed one year later. Ollendick, Greene, Weist, and Oswald (1990) reported that 10-year-old socially withdrawn children were more likely to be perceived by peers as withdrawn and anxious, more disliked by peers, and more likely to have dropped out of school than their well-adjusted counterparts 5 years later. Finally, Morison and Masten (1991) indicated that children perceived by peers as withdrawn and isolated in middle childhood were more likely to think negatively of their social competencies and relationships in adolescence. In sum, it would appear as if early social withdrawal, or its relation to anxiety, represents a behavioral marker for psychological and interpersonal maladaptation in childhood and adolescence.

Stability of Social Withdrawal

Not only is social withdrawal associated with numerous negative inter- and intra-personal phenomena, it also appears to be an insidiously stable entity. Initial evidence for its stability came from the Waterloo Longitudinal Project (WLP), which followed a normative sample of public-school children from kindergarten to ninth grade. Observed social withdrawal was relatively stable from ages 5 to 9 years (Rubin, 1993); peer assessments using the Revised Class Play yielded significant intercorrelations (all $p < 0.001$) between ages 7 and 10 years. When a categorical approach was used to identify extreme groups of socially withdrawn children in the WLP, approximately two-thirds of the withdrawn children maintained their status across any 2-year period from 5 to 11 years of age (Rubin et al., 1993). Supporting this finding is Kagan and colleagues' (e.g., Kagan, 1989) contention that the developmental continuity of inhibition is strongest when an extreme group (i.e., the top 15%) is selected from the longitudinal sample. It should be noted, however, that different subtypes of withdrawal may be differentially stable depending upon the ages studied and methods of measurement.

In a longitudinal study extending into adulthood, Caspi and Silva (1995) found that individuals identified as shy, fearful, and withdrawn at 3 years of age reported that they preferred to stick with safe activities, be cautious, submissive, and had little desire to influence others at 18 years. A subsequent follow-up at age 21 on interpersonal functioning showed that these same children were normally adjusted in both their work settings and their romantic relationships (Newman, Caspi, Moffitt, & Silva, 1997).

Clinical Status

Most samples described in our review have been nonclinic children. Furthermore, the outcomes of social withdrawal have not typically involved clinical assessments. This leaves open the question of whether clinically assessed psychological disturbance can be predicted from earlier indices of social withdrawal and its concomitants. To address this question, Rubin (1993) administered the Child Depression Inventory (CDI; Kovacs, 1980/81) to the 11-year-olds participating in the WLP. Those whose CDI scores were one standard deviation or more above the mean for their age group were identified; these children constituted the top 8% of children in terms of CDI scores (their scores were above the clinical cutoff for depression). These children were then compared with their nondepressed schoolmates on indices of social and emotional well-being assessed at age 7 years. Follow-back discriminant function analyses indicated that the depressed children could *not* be distinguished from their normal counterparts on the basis of their popularity or aggressive behaviors among peers at age 7 years; however, they could be distinguished on observed and peer-assessed social withdrawal, and self-reported negative self-perceptions of social competence. These results support the model offered above in which social withdrawal is described as a risk factor for the development of internalizing disorders (e.g., Rubin & Stewart, 1996).

Despite this initial support for the model, it is clear that further long-itudinal research is necessary before social withdrawal can be impli-cated causally in the development of maladaptation in adolescence and adulthood.

The Parents of Socially Withdrawn Children

We have noted that when interacting with their *inhibited* young children, parents demonstrate directive and overly solicitous behaviors (e.g., Chen et al., 1998; Rubin et al., 1999). Indeed, we have also found that perceiving one's 2-year-old as socially wary and inhibited actually *predicts* overprotec-tive parenting two years hence (Rubin et al., 1999). These latter findings provide support for our earlier contention that once an *inhibited* behavioral style is established, parents may sense the child's anxieties and insecurities, and seek to help the child's mastery of the environment through authoritar-ian direction, protection, and oversolicitousness (e.g., by solving the child's interpersonal and intrapersonal problems). These links between parenting and both social reticence and withdrawal have been examined in a number of studies.

Parenting Beliefs and Social Withdrawal

Parenting behaviors have been posited to be partly influenced by parents' notions concerning when it is that children come to demonstrate particular behaviors or ways of thinking; why it is that children behave in the ways they do; and how it is that parents can influence growth or inhibit maladaptive behavior (Bugental & Goodnow, 1998). In a series of studies conducted by Rubin and Mills, parenting beliefs about children's socially withdrawn beha-viors were assessed. In one study, Rubin and Mills (1990) presented the mothers of extremely anxious–withdrawn children with stories describing hypothetical incidents in which their own child consistently behaved in a socially withdrawn fashion. Compared with mothers of nonanxious ("nor-mal") children, mothers of anxious–withdrawn children were more likely to suggest the use of high control strategies (e.g., directives) and less likely to prefer low-power strategies (e.g., redirecting the child) and indirect/ no-response strategies (e.g., seeking information from others, arranging opportunities for peer interaction, not responding) in reaction to their chil-dren's demonstration of socially withdrawn behavior. Also, these mothers were more likely to attribute the consistent display of social withdrawal to dispositional sources; and they expressed more anger, disappointment, embarrassment, and guilt about their children's displays of withdrawal.

The finding that these mothers placed greater importance on a directive approach to teaching social skills than did mothers of average children, and that they were more likely to choose controlling strategies for dealing with unskilled social behaviors, suggests that children who are socially anxious and wary tend to have mothers who may be overinvolved. The causal attributions and emotional reactions of these mothers are also indicative of overinvolvement, and provide some tentative insights about why they may be overinvolved. This dynamic is reminiscent of the pattern of anxious, overprotective parenting which has previously been linked to internalizing difficulties in children (Parker, 1983). It may be that mothers of socially withdrawn preschool-age children transmit their own internalizing problems to their children through overinvolved parenting, which creates a sense of felt insecurity. Indeed, preschool-age children of depressed mothers exhibit significantly more inhibited and anxious-withdrawn forms of play with both familiar and unfamiliar playmates than do children of nondepressed mothers (Kochanska, 1991; Rubin, Both, Zahn-Waxler, Cummings, & Wilkinson, 1991). Further, it may be that mothers are highly sensitized to their children's social and emotional characteristics; and such sensitivity may provoke well-meaning overcontrol and overinvolvement. This reaction to their child's social characteristics may produce a mixture of defensive reactions (e.g., downplaying the importance of social skills) and negative emotions. Thus, it would appear as if children's social withdrawal may be a function of the interplay between maternal and child characteristics and the dialectic processes that are produced therein.

Parenting Behaviors and Childhood Social Withdrawal

Given that parental beliefs and cognitions may influence parents' behaviors (Bugental & Goodnow, 1998), it would seem natural to expect that the socialization practices of parents whose children are withdrawn differ from those of parents whose children are "'normal" and socially competent. As noted above, the mothers of anxious–withdrawn children believe strongly in the use of highly controlling behaviors to "deal with" their children's demonstration of social withdrawal in the peer group. That socially anxious and withdrawn children are the recipients of highly directive parenting *behaviors* has been demonstrated by Baumrind (1967). Further, MacDonald and Parke (1984) found that boys perceived by teachers as socially withdrawn, hesitant, and as spectators in the company of peers had fathers who were highly directive and less engaging and physically playful during father–son interactions. The findings were less clear-cut for socially withdrawn daughters. In general, though, the researchers reported that during parent–child play, the parents of socially withdrawn children were less spontaneous, playful, and affectively positive than parents of more sociable children. Further, the mothers of inhibited toddlers have been shown to be "oversolicitous" in their observed behaviors. Maternal overcontrol and oversolicitousness encompass not only restrictions on parenting behavior, but also manifestations of anxiety and concern that convey a lack of confidence in the child (Mills & Rubin, 1998). Such parenting practices may also be accompanied by expressions of criticism and disapproval that attack the child's sense of self-worth.

More recently, Mills and Rubin (1998) found that, relative to mothers of normal children, mothers of extremely anxious–withdrawn children (aged 5–9 years) were observed to direct significantly more *behavior control* statements to their children. Further, mothers of anxious–withdrawn children used more *psychological control* statements (defined by devaluation statements or nonresponsiveness to the child).

Finally, Rubin, Cheah, and Fox (under review) report that the mothers whose preschoolers frequently displayed socially reticent behavior among peers were more likely than mothers whose children rarely displayed social reticence to use control statements during *free play* with the child. Directiveness during goal-oriented tasks may be expected of parents (e.g., Kuczynski & Kochanska, 1995), but there is no compelling reason for parents to control their child's behavior in a pleasant, unstressful play environment. The use of a highly directive parenting style during free-play may suggest that the parent is attempting to protect the child from harm or stress when neither is objectively present. Yet, in the Rubin et al. study, socially fearful behavior among preschoolers was predicted by mothers' displays of highly controlling and oversolicitous behaviors during a free-play session. Thus, these mothers appear to provide guidance and directives when neither is necessary, thereby precluding the child from independent exploration.

Importantly, the findings described above derive from very few databases. Even though the findings support longstanding beliefs about the kinds of parental behaviors that may influence or reinforce socially anxious and withdrawn child behavior, the existing data still do not allow definitive conclusions on the topic of parenting and children's withdrawal. Moreover, a bidirectional relation may operate whereby children's anxiety leads to overprotective parenting (Rubin et al., 1999). Clearly, this is an avenue of research that requires additional attention.

Epidemiological Factors Associated with Social Withdrawal

Gender Differences

During the past decade, a number of longitudinal and correlational studies have suggested a different risk status for boys and girls who may experience social wariness/fearfulness in the company of peers. Morison and Masten (1991) found that the risk of being socially withdrawn (as assessed via peer nominations) may differ depending on the child's sex. For example, withdrawn–isolated boys reported lower self-esteem and less perceived athletic ability in adolescence than did girls. Caspi, Elder, and Bem (1988) reported that men who were shy–withdrawn at age 8–10 years were delayed, relative to the norm, with regard to the timing of marriage, parenthood, and career establishment. These men were also at greater risk for separation and divorce in adulthood. On the other hand, shy–withdrawn females were "on time" and adjusted with respect to adult-role transitions into marriage and home-making; and they did not evidence psychological difficulties. Now that women's roles are changing, however, it remains to be seen how socially wary females fare with regard to nontraditional roles in relationships and in work settings.

A number of recent correlational reports support these longitudinal find-ings with respect to gender differences in social–emotional adjustment. For instance, Rubin, Chen et al. (1993) found that, relative to socially normal children, extremely withdrawn 11-year-old boys, but not girls, described themselves as being more lonely and having poor social skills.

Whether there are parenting differences regarding withdrawn boys and girls has been examined by several investigators. Stevenson-Hinde (1989) and Engfer (1993) reported that the parents of inhibited–withdrawn toddler and preschool-age girls were warm, responsive, and sensitive; although this result was qualified by a subsequent study which also found positive interactions only for *moderately* inhibited girls but less positive interactions for *extremely* inhibited girls (Stevenson-Hinde & Glover, 1996). In contrast, withdrawn boys' parents were cold, less affectionate, and less responsive than were average boys' parents. Stevenson-Hinde and Glover also found that mothers interacted more positively with very shy boys than they did with very shy girls. Whether their measure of warmth could be construed as an index of oversolicitous parenting is a question worth addressing given the Rubin et al. (1997) report that warm, yet intrusive, parenting is associated with socially wary and inhibited behaviors.

Recently, further evidence has been found for sex differences in parenting associated with the demonstration of social reticence (Rubin et al., under review). Preschool-age boys whose mothers perceived them to be unable to regulate their emotions were less socially reticent among peers if their mothers were appropriately controlling in a situation that required parental guidance and support (e.g., a teaching task); whereas for dysregulated boys whose mothers offered little support and guidance, the demonstration of reticent behavior in the peer group appeared to be exacerbated. These rela-tions between maternal guidance and emotion dysregulation were not found for preschool girls. These findings raise the possibility that when mothers provide guidance and support in an appropriate context, they are more likely to have an influence on their sons' anxieties than on their daughters'. Importantly however, these researchers reported that the use of maternal control during situations in which such behavior could be construed as intrusive and inappropriate (e.g., during free-play) was associated with *both* boys' and girls' social reticence in the peer group.

Lastly, the quality of the parent–child attachment relationship has been associated with the display of shyness for boys but not girls. Insecurely attached ("C" status) boys, but not girls, are more likely than their secure counterparts to display passive–withdrawn behaviors in early and mid childhood (Renken et al., 1989).

In summary, the empirical literature suggests that inhibited/withdrawn boys experience different socialization practices/histories and more negative developmental outcomes than do girls. Continuing to study significant adults' and peers' *attitudes* about reticence/withdrawal in boys versus girls, as well as studying parental and peer *behaviors* during interactions with boys versus girls, will undoubtedly prove fruitful if our goal is to understand and alleviate childhood anxiety and withdrawal.

Culture and Social Withdrawal

The research reviewed thus far is derived almost exclusively from samples in the western world—Australia, Canada, United Kingdom, Germany, Norway, Sweden, and the United States. Yet, the evaluation of social behavior is influenced by cultural values and social conventions. Specifically, people view children's behaviors as normal or abnormal from the perspective of cultural norms and ideologies.

Clearly, social attitudes and values help set thresholds for concerns about problematic child behaviors, emotions, and thoughts. This reality has been elegantly demonstrated by Weisz, Suwanlert, Chaiyasit, and Weiss (1988), who compared the judgments of Thai and American parents, teachers, and clinical psychologists about two children, one with overcontrolled problems (e.g., fear, shyness) and one with undercontrolled problems (e.g., disobedience, fighting). Compared with Americans, Thais rated problems of both types as less serious, less worrisome, less likely to reflect personality traits, and more likely to improve with time. Cross-national differences in perceived seriousness were more pronounced for parents and teachers than for psychologists, suggesting that professional backgrounds and higher education may mitigate the effects of national belief systems.

In western cultures, passive, reticent, shy and withdrawn behavior is viewed negatively, not only by parents (Mills & Rubin, 1990) but also by peers (e.g., Harrist et al., 1997). As noted above, children who display such behaviors are considered socially immature, fearful, and dependent (Morison & Masten, 1991). However, children growing up in China are actually encouraged to be dependent, cautious, self-restrained, and behaviorally inhibited (Ho, 1986; Ho & Kang, 1984) because such behaviors are generally considered indices of accomplishment, mastery, and maturity (Feng, 1962; King & Bond, 1985). Similarly, shy, reticent, and quiet children are described as good and well-behaved. Indeed, researchers have consistently revealed that Chinese children, adolescents, and adults are more inhibited, anxious, and sensitive than their North American counterparts (e.g., Chan & Eysenck, 1981; Chen et al., 1998). Unlike North American children, shy–inhibited Chinese children are viewed as socially competent and they are accepted by the peer group (Chen, Rubin, & Li, 1995; Chen, Rubin, & Sun, 1992).

These results suggest that societal values may have a differential effect on the perception and treatment of wary, fearful, and withdrawn behaviors. Given that the majority of the world's inhabitants do not reside in western countries, the studies just described bear careful note. It would appear as if the definitions of normalcy and psychological disorder described in the vast majority of texts may be culture-specific. Assuredly this is an issue that will require further examination, not only for the study of social withdrawal, but also for most other supposed abnormal behaviors in childhood. Relatedly, it would seem in the best interests of the psychological community of scholars not to generalize to other cultures our own culture-specific theories of developmental psychopathology.

Conclusion

The study of social withdrawal has garnered an enormous amount of attention. Most empirical research has focused on the contemporaneous and predictive correlates of social reticence and withdrawal at different points in childhood and adolescence. These correlated variables include those of the biological, intrapersonal, interpersonal, and psychopathology ilk that have been chosen from conceptual frameworks pertaining to the etiology, stability, and outcomes of socially wary and withdrawn behaviors. Thus far, it appears that socially inhibited children have a biological disposition that fosters emotional dysregulation in the company of others. These children, if overly directed and protected by their primary caregiver, become reticent and withdrawn in the peer group. In turn, such behavior precludes the development of social skills and the initiation and maintenance of positive peer relationships. Yet again, this transactional experience seems to lead children to develop anxiety, loneliness, and negative self-perceptions of their relationships and social skills.

Despite these strong conclusions, however, it is important to recognize that the databases upon which these conclusions rest are relatively few. Clearly, replication work is necessary. The extent to which dispositional factors interact with parenting styles and parent–child relationships to predict the consistent display of socially withdrawn behavior in familiar peer contexts still needs to be established. Further, the sex differences discussed in our review require serious additional attention.

Lastly, our knowledge of the developmental course of social withdrawal is constrained by the almost sole reliance on data gathered in western cultures. Little is known about the developmental course of the phenomenon in eastern cultures such as those in China, Japan, or India; and even less is known of social withdrawal in southern cultures such as those found in South America, Africa, and southern Europe. It may well be that depending on the culture within which the phenomenon is studied, the biological, interpersonal, and intrapersonal causes, concomitants, and consequences of social withdrawal may vary. In short, cross-cultural research is necessary, not only for the study of social withdrawal, but also for most behaviors that are viewed as deviant or reflective of intrapsychic abnormalities in the West.

References

Achenbach, T. M. (1982). *Developmental psychopathology*. New York: Plenum.

Adalbjarnardottir, S. (1995). How schoolchildren propose to negotiate: The role of social withdrawal, social anxiety, and locus of control. *Child Development, 66*, 1739–1751.

American Psychiatric Association (1994). *Diagnostic and statistical manual of mental disorders*. (4th ed. revised) Washington, DC: APA.

Asendorpf, J. B. (1990). The development of inhibition during childhood: Evidence for situational specificity and a two–factor model. *Developmental Psychology, 26*, 721–730.

Asendorpf, J. B. (1993). Beyond temperament: A two–factorial coping model of the development of inhibition during childhood. In K. H. Rubin and J. B. Asendorpf (Eds.), *Social withdrawal, inhibition and shyness in childhood* (pp. 265–289) New Jersey: Lawrence Erlbaum.

Barrios, B. A., & O'Dell, S. L. (1989). Fears and anxieties. In E. J. Mash & R. A. Barkley (Eds.), *Treatment of childhood disorders*. New York: Guilford.

Baumrind, D. (1967). Child care practices anteceding three patterns of preschool behavior. *Genetic Psychology Monographs, 76*, 43–88.

Bell–Dolan, D., Reaven, N. M., & Peterson, L. (1993). Depression and social functioning: A multidimensional study of the linkages. *Journal of Clinical Child Psychology, 22*, 306–315.

Belsky, J., & Rovine, M. (1987). Temperament and attachment security in the strange situation: An empirical rapproachment. *Child Development, 58*, 787–795.

Biederman, J., Rosenbaum, J. F., Bolduc–Murphy, E. A., Faraone, S. V., Chaloff, J., Hirshfeld, D. R., & Kagan, J. (1993). A 3-year follow-up of children with and without behavioral inhibition. *Journal of the American Academy of Child and Adolescent Psychiatry, 32*, 814–821.

Boivin, M., Hymel, S., & Bukowski, W. M. (1995). The roles of social withdrawal, peer rejection, and victimization by peers in predicting loneliness and depressed mood in childhood. *Development and Psychopathology, 7*, 765–785.

Booth, C. L., Rose-Krasnor, L., McKinnon, J., & Rubin, K. H. (1994). Predicting social adjustment in middle childhood: The role of preschool attachment security and maternal style. *Social Development, 3*, 189–204.

Bowlby, J. (1973). *Attachment and loss: Vol. 1. Attachment*. New York: Basic Books.

Broberg, A., Lamb, M. E., & Hwang, P. (1990). Inhibition: Its stability and correlates in sixteen-to-forty-month-old children. *Child Development, 61*, 1153–1163.

Bugental, D., & Goodnow, J. (1998). In N. Eisenberg (Ed.), *Handbook of child psychology: Social, emotional, and personality development* (5th ed., pp. 389–462). New York: Wiley.

Burgess, K. B., & Younger, A. J. (1996). Behavioral–emotional functioning of socially withdrawn preadolescents. Poster presented at the XIVth Biennial Meeting of the International Society for the Study of Behavioral Development, Quebec City, Canada.

Calkins, S. D., & Fox, N. A. (1992). The relations among infant temperament, security of attachment and behavioral inhibition at 24 months. *Child Development, 63,* 1456–1472.

Calkins, S. D., Fox, N. A., & Marshall, T. R. (1996). Behavioral and physiological antecedents of inhibited and uninhibited behavior. *Child Development, 67,* 523–540.

Caspi, A., & Silva, P. A. (1995). Temperamental qualities at age three predict personality traits in young adulthood: Longitudinal evidence from a birth cohort. *Child Development, 66,* 486–498.

Caspi, A., Elder, G. H., & Bem, D. J. (1988). Moving away from the world: Life-course patterns of shy children. *Developmental Psychology, 24,* 824–831.

Chan, J., & Eysenck, S. B. G. (1981, August). National differences in personality: Hong Kong and England. Paper presented at the joint IACP-ICP Asian Regional Meeting, National Taiwan University, Taipei, Taiwan.

Chen, X., Hastings, P. D., Rubin, K. H., Chen, H., Cen, G., & Stewart, S. L. (1998). Child-rearing attitudes and behavioral inhibition in Chinese and Canadian toddlers: A cross-cultural study. *Developmental Psychology, 34,* 677–686.

Chen, X., Rubin, K. H., & Li, B. (1995). Social and school adjustment of shy and aggressive children in China. *Development and Psychopathology, 7,* 337–349.

Chen, X., Rubin, K. H., & Sun, Y. (1992). Social reputation and peer relationships in Chinese children: A cross-cultural study. *Child Development, 63,* 1336–1343.

Coplan, R. J., Rubin, K. H., Fox, N. A., Calkins, S. D., & Stewart, S. L. (1994). Being alone, playing alone, and acting alone: Distinguishing among reticence, and passive- and active-solitude in young children. *Child Development, 65,* 129–137.

Costa, P. T., Jr, & McCrae, R. R. (1985). *The NEO personality inventory manual.* Odessa, FL: Psychological Assessment Resources.

Crick, N. R., & Dodge, K. A. (1994). A review and reformulation of social information-processing mechanisms in children's social adjustment. *Psychological Bulletin, 115,* 74–101.

Damon, W., & Killen, M. (1982). Peer interaction and the process of change in children's moral reasoning. *Merrill–Palmer Quarterly, 28,* 347–378.

Davidson, R., & Fox, N. (1989). Frontal brain asymmetry predicts infants' response to maternal separation. *Journal of Abnormal Psychology, 98,* 127–131.

Eisenberg, N., Shepard, S. A., Fabes, R. A., Murphy, B. C., & Guthrie, I. K. (1998). Shyness and children's emotionality, regulation, and coping: Contemporaneous, longitudinal, and across–context relations. *Child Development, 69,* 767–790.

Engfer, A. (1993). Antecedents and consequences of shyness in boys and girls: A 6-year longitudinal study. In K. H. Rubin & J. Asendorpf (Eds.), *Social withdrawal, inhibition, and shyness in childhood* (pp. 49–80). Hillsdale, NJ: Lawrence Erlbaum.

Erickson, M. F., Sroufe, L. A., & Egeland, B. (1985). The relationship between quality of attachment and behavior problems in preschool in a high-risk sample. In I. Bretherton & E. Waters (Eds.), *Growing points of attachment theory and research. Monographs of the Society for Research in Child Development, 50,* (Nos. 1–2, Serial No. 209).

Feng, Y. L. (1962). *The spirit of Chinese philosophy* (E. R. Hughes, Trans.). London: Routledge & Kegan Paul.

Fox, N. (1989). Psychophysiological correlates of emotional reactivity during the first year of life. *Developmental Psychology, 25,* 364–372.

Fox, N., & Calkins, S. (1993). Relations between temperament, attachment, and behavioral inhibition: Two possible pathways to extroversion and social withdrawal. In K. H. Rubin & J. Asendorpf (Eds.), *Social withdrawal, inhibition, and shyness in childhood.* Hillsdale, NJ: Lawrence Erlbaum.

Fox, N. A., & Henderson, H. A. (1998, April). Stability and instability of infant temperament. In N. A. Fox (Chair), *Domains of change or continuity: Why is infancy so important?* Symposium conducted at the 11th Biennial International Conference on Infant Studies, Atlanta, GA.

Fox, N. A., Calkins, S. D., & Bell, M. A. (1994). Neural plasticity and development in the first year of life: Evidence from cognitive and socio-emotional domains of research. *Development and Psychopathology, 6,* 677–698.

Fox, N. A., Calkins, S. D., Schmidt, L., Rubin, K.H., & Coplan, R. J. (1996). The role of frontal activation in the regulation and dysregulation of social behavior during the preschool years. *Development and Psychopathology, 8,* 89–102.

Fox, N. A., Rubin, K. H., Calkins, S. D., Marshall, T. R., Coplan, R. J., Porges, S. W., Long, J. & Stewart, S. L. (1995). Frontal activation asymmetry and social competence at four years of age: Left frontal hyper- and hypo-activation as correlates of social behavior in preschool children. *Child Development, 66,* 1770–1784.

Garcia Coll, C., Kagan, J., & Reznick, J. S. (1984). Behavioral inhibition in young children. *Child Development, 55,* 1005–1019.

Goldsmith, H. H., & Alansky, J. A. (1987). Maternal and infant temperamental predictors of attachment: A meta-analytic review. *Journal of Consulting and Clinical Psychology, 55,* 805–816.

Greenspan, S. I., & Lieberman, A. F. (1988). In J. Belsky & T. Nezworski (Eds.), *Clinical Implications of attachment.* Hillsdale, NJ.: Lawrence Erlbaum.

Harrist, A. W., Zaia, A. F., Bates, J. E., Dodge, K. A., & Pettit, G. S. (1997). Subtypes of social withdrawal in early childhood: Sociometric status and social–cognitive differences across four years. *Child Development, 68,* 278–294.

Henriques, J., & Davidson, R. (1990). Regional brain electrical asymmetries discriminate between previously depressed and healthy control subjects. *Journal of Abnormal Psychology, 99,* 22–31.

Hirshfeld, D. R., Rosenbaum, J. F., Biederman, J., Bolduc, E. A., Faraone, S. V., Snidman, N., Reznick, J. S., & Kagan, J. (1992). Stable behavioral inhibition and its association with anxiety disorder. *Journal of the American Academy of Child and Adolescent Psychiatry, 31,* 103–111.

Ho, D. Y. F. (1986). Chinese pattern of socialization: A critical review. In M. H. Bond (Ed.), *The psychology of Chinese people.* New York: Oxford University Press.

Ho, D. Y. F., & Kang, T. K. (1984). Intergenerational comparisons of child rearing attitudes and practices in Hong Kong. *Developmental Psychology, 20,* 1004–1016.

Hymel, S., Bowker, A., & Woody, E. (1993). Aggressive versus withdrawn unpopular children: Variations in peer and self-perceptions in multiple domains. *Child Development, 64,* 879–896.

Izard, C. E., Haynes, O. M., Chisholm, Y., & Baak, K. (1991). Emotional determinants of infant–mother attachment. *Child Development, 62,* 906–917.

Jones, N., & Fox, N. (1992). Electroencephalogram asymmetry during emotionally evocative films and its relation to positive and negative affectivity. *Brain and Cognition, 20,* 280–299.

Kagan, J. (1989). Temperamental contributions to social behavior. *American Psychologist, 44,* 668–674.

Kagan, J. (1997). Temperament and the reaction to unfamiliarity. *Child Development, 68,* 139–143.

Kagan, J., & Snidman, N. (1991). Infant predictors of inhibited and uninhibited profiles. *Psychological Science, 2,* 40–44.

Kagan, J., Reznick, J. S., & Snidman, N. (1987). The physiology and psychology of behavioral inhibition in children. *Child Development, 58,* 1459–1473.

Kagan, J., Reznick, J. S., Snidman, N., Gibbons, J., & Johnson, M. O. (1988). Childhood derivatives of inhibition and lack of inhibition to the unfamiliar. *Child Development, 59,* 1580–1589.

King, A. Y. C., & Bond, M. H. (1985). The Confucian paradigm of man: A sociological view. In W. S. Tseng and D. Y. H. Wu (Eds.), *Chinese culture and mental health.* New York: Academic Press.

Kochanska, G. (1991). Patterns of inhibition to the unfamiliar in children of normal and affectively ill mothers. *Child Development, 62,* 250–263.

Kochanska, G., & Radke–Yarrow, M. (1992). Inhibition in toddlerhood and the dynamics of the child's interaction with an unfamiliar peer at age five. *Child Development, 63, 325–335*

Kovacs, M. (1980/81). Rating scales to assess depression in school-aged children. *Acta Paedopsychiatria, 46,* 305–315.

Kuczynski, L., & Kochanska, G. (1995). Function and content of maternal demands: Developmental significance of early demands for competent action. *Child Development, 66,* 616–628.

LeDoux, J. (1989). Cognitive–emotional interactions in the brain. *Cognition and Emotion, 4,* 267–274.

LeMare, L., & Rubin, K. H. (1987). Perspective-taking and peer interactions: Structural and developmental analyses. *Child Development, 58,* 306–315.

MacDonald, K., & Parke, R. D. (1984). Bridging the gap: Parent–child play interaction and peer interactive competence. *Child Development, 55,* 1265–1277.

Matas, L., Arend, R. A., & Sroufe, L. A. (1978). The continuity of adaptation in the second year: Relationship between quality of attachment and later competence. *Child Development, 49,* 547–556.

McBurnett, K., Lahey, B. B., Frick, P. J., Risch, C., Loeber, R., Hart, E. L., Christ, M. G., & Hanson, K. S. (1991). Anxiety, inhibition, and conduct disorder in children: II. Relation to salivary cortisol. *Journal of the American Academy of Child and Adolescent Psychiatry, 30,* 192–196.

Mead, G. (1934). *Mind, self and society.* Chicago: University of Chicago Press.

Messer, S. C., & Beidel, D. C. (1994). Psychosocial correlates of childhood anxiety disorders. *Journal of the American Academy of Child and Adolescent Psychiatry, 33,* 975–983.

Millan, T. (1981). *Disorders of personality: DSM-III, Axis II.* New York: Wiley.

Millan, T., & Everly, G. S. (1985). *Personality and its disorders: A biological learning approach.* New York: Wiley.

Mills, R. S. L., & Rubin, K. H. (1990). Parental beliefs about problematic social behaviors in early childhood. *Child Development, 61,* 138–151.

Mills, R. S. L., & Rubin, K. H. (1998). Are behavioral control and psychological control both differentially associated with childhood aggression and social withdrawal? *Canadian Journal of Behavioral Sciences, 30,* 132–136.

Morison, P., & Masten, A. (1991). Peer reputation in middle childhood as a predictor of adaptation in adolescence: A seven-year follow-up. *Child Development, 62,* 991–1007.

Mullins, L. L., Peterson, L., Wonderlich, S. A., & Reaven, N. (1986). The influence of depression in childhood on the social responses and perceptions of adults. *Journal of Clinical Child Psychology, 15,* 233–240.

Nachmias, M., Gunnar, M., Mangelsdorf, S., Parritz, R. H., & Buss, K. (1996). Behavioral inhibition and stress reactivity: the moderating role of attachment security. *Child Development, 67,* 508–522.

Newman, D. L., Caspi, A., Moffitt, T. E., & Silva, P. A. (1997). Antecedents of adult interpersonal functioning: Effects of individual differences in age-3 temperament. *Developmental Psychology, 33,* 206–217.

Ollendick, T. H., Greene, R. W., Weist, M. D., & Oswald, D. P. (1990). The predictive validity of teacher nominations: A five-year follow-up of at-risk youth. *Journal of Abnormal Child Psychology, 18,* 699–713.

Parker, G. (1983). *Parental overprotection: A risk factor in psychosocial development.* New York: Grune & Stratton.

Pastor, D. L. (1981). The quality of mother–infant attachment and its relationship to toddler's initial sociability with peers. *Developmental Psychology, 17,* 323–335.

Piaget, J. (1926). *The language and thought of the child.* London: Routledge & Kegan Paul.

Pine, D. S., Weese–Meyer, D. E., Silvestri, J. M., Davies, M., Whitaker, A., & Klein, D. F. (1994). Anxiety and congenital central hyperventilation syndrome. *American Journal of Psychiatry, 151,* 864–870.

Porges, S. W., & Byrne, E. A. (1992). Research methods for measurement of heart rate and respiration. *Biological Psychology, 34,* 93–130.

Quay, H., & Werry, J. (Eds.) (1986). *Psychopathological disorders of childhood* (2nd ed.). New York: Wiley.

Renken, B., Egeland, B., Marvinney, D., Mangelsdorf, S., & Sroufe, L. (1989). Early childhood antecedents of aggression and passive-withdrawal in early elementary school. *Journal of Personality, 57,* 257–281.

Renshaw, P. D., & Brown, P. J. (1993). Loneliness in middle childhood: Concurrent and longitudinal predictors. *Child Development, 64,* 1271–1284.

Reznick, J. S., Kagan, J., Snidman, N., Gersten, M., Baak, K., & Rosenberg, A. (1986). Inhibited and uninhibited behavior: A follow-up study. *Child Development, 57,* 660–680.

Rosenbaum, J. F., Biederman, J., Gersten, M. et al. (1988). Behavioral inhibition in children of parents with panic disorder and agoraphobia: A controlled study. *Archives of General Psychiatry, 52,* 5–9.

Rubin, K. H. (1982a). Non-social play in preschoolers: Necessary evil? *Child Development, 53,* 651–657.

Rubin, K. H.(1982b). Social and cognitive developmental characteristics of young isolate, normal, and sociable children. In K. H. Rubin & H. S. Ross (Eds.), *Peer relationships and social skills in childhood* (pp. 353–374). New York: Springer-Verlag.

Rubin, K. H. (1993). The Waterloo Longitudinal Project: Correlates and consequences of social withdrawal from childhood to adolescence. In K. H. Rubin and J. Asendorpf (Eds.), *Social withdrawal, inhibition and shyness in childhood.* (pp. 291–314). Hillsdale, NJ: Lawrence Erlbaum.

Rubin, K. H., & Asendorpf, J. (Eds.) (1993). *Social withdrawal inhibition, and shyness in childhood.* Hillsdale, NJ: Lawrence Erlbaum.

Rubin, K. H., & Krasnor, L. R. (1986). Social cognitive and social behavioral perspectives on problem-solving. In M. Perlmutter (Ed.), *Minnesota Symposia on Child Psychology* (Vol. 18, pp. 1–68). Hillsdale, NJ: Lawrence Erlbaum.

Rubin, K. H., & Mills, R. S. L. (1988). The many faces of social isolation in childhood. *Journal of Consulting and Clinical Psychology, 56,* 916–924.

Rubin, K. H., & Mills, R. S. L. (1990). Maternal beliefs about adaptive and maladaptive social behaviors in normal, aggressive, and withdrawn preschoolers. *Journal of Abnormal Child Psychology, 18,* 419–435.

Rubin, K. H., & Rose-Krasnor, L. (1992). Interpersonal problem-solving and social competence in children. In V. B. van Hasselt & M. Hersen (Eds.), *Handbook of social development: A lifespan perspective* (pp. 283–324). New York: Plenum.

Rubin, K. H., & Stewart, S. L. (1996). Social withdrawal. In E. Mash & R. Barkley (Eds.), *Child psychopathology* (pp. 277–307). New York: Guilford.

Rubin, K. H., Both, L., Zahn-Waxler, E. C., Cummings, M., & Wilkinson, M. (1991). Dyadic play behaviors of children of well and depressed mothers. *Development and Psychopathology, 3,* 243–251.

Rubin, K. H., Bukowski, W., & Parker, J. (1998). Peer interactions, relationships, and groups. In N. Eisenberg (Ed), *Handbook of Child Psychology: Social, emotional, and personality development* (5th ed., pp. 619–700). New York: Wiley.

Rubin, K. H., Cheah, C., & Fox, N. A. (under review). Emotion regulation, parenting, and display of social reticence in preschoolers.

Rubin, K. H., Chen, X., & Hymel, S. (1993). The socio-emotional characteristics of extremely aggressive and extremely withdrawn children. *Merrill–Palmer Quarterly, 39,* 518–534.

Rubin, K. H., Chen, X., McDougall, P, Bowker, A., & McKinnon, J. (1995). The Waterloo Longitudinal Project: Predicting adolescent internalizing and externalizing problems from early and mid-childhood. *Development and Psychopathology, 7,* 751–764.

Rubin, K. H., Daniels, T., & Bream (1984). Social isolation and social problem solving: A longitudinal study. *Journal of Consulting and Clinical Psychology, 52,* 17–25.

Rubin, K. H., Hastings, P. D., Stewart, S. L., Henderson, H. A., & Chen, X. (1997). The consistency and concomitants of inhibition: Some of the children, all of the time. *Child Development, 68,* 467–483.

Rubin, K. H., Hymel, S., & Mills, R. S. L. (1989). Sociability and social withdrawal in childhood: Stability and outcomes. *Journal of Personality, 57,* 237–255.

Rubin, K. H., LeMare, L., & Lollis, S. (1990). Social withdrawal in childhood: Developmental pathways to peer rejection. In S. R. Asher & J. D. Coie (Eds.), *Peer rejection in childhood* (pp. 217–249). New York: Cambridge University Press.

Rubin, K. H., Nelson, L. J., Hastings, P. D., & Asendorpf, J. (1999). The transaction between parents' perceptions of their children's shyness and their parenting styles. *International Journal of Behavioral Development, 23,* 937–958.

Rubin, K. H., Stewart, S. L., & Coplan, R. J. (1995). Social withdrawal in childhood: Conceptual and empirical perspectives. In T. H. Ollendick & R. J. Prinz (Eds.), *Advances in clinical child psychology: Vol. 17* (pp. 157–196). New York: Plenum.

Sanson, A., Pedlow, R., Cann, W., Prior, M., & Oberklaid, F. (1996). Shyness ratings: Stability and correlates in early childhood. *International Journal of Behavioral Development, 19,* 705–724.

Schmidt, L. A., Fox, N. A., Rubin, K. H., Sternberg, E. M., Gold, P. W., Smith, C. C., & Schulkin, J. (1997). Behavioral and neuroendocrine responses in shy children. *Developmental Psychobiology, 30,* 127–140.

Selman, R. L. (1980). *The growth of interpersonal understanding.* New York: Cambridge University Press.

Selman, R, L., & Schultz, L. H. (1990). *Making a friend in youth: developmental theory and pair therapy.* Chicago: University of Chicago Press.

Sroufe, L. A. (1983). Infant–caregiver attachment and patterns of adaptation in pre-school: Roots of maladaptation and competence. In M. Perlmutter (Ed.), *Minnesota symposia on child psychology: Vol. 16.* Hillsdale, NJ: Lawrence Erlbaum.

Stevenson-Hinde, J. (1989). Behavioral inhibition: Issues of context. In J. S. Reznick (Ed.), *Perspectives on behavioral inhibition* (pp. 125–138). Chicago: University of Chicago Press.

Stevenson-Hinde, J., & Glover, A. (1996). Shy girls and boys: A new look. *Journal of Child Psychology and Psychiatry, 37,* 181–187.

Stewart, S. L., & Rubin, K. H. (1995). The social problem solving skills of anxious–withdrawn children. *Development and Psychopathology, 7,* 323–336.

Sullivan, H. S. (1953). *The interpersonal theory of psychiatry.* New York: Norton.

Thompson, R. A., Connell, J., & Bridges, L. J. (1988). Temperament, emotional and social interactive behavior in the strange situation: An analysis of attachment functioning. *Child Development, 59,* 1102–1110.

Turkal, I. D. (1990). The personality disorders. *A psychological approach to clinical management.* New York: Pergamon.

Weisz, J. R., Suwanlert, S., Chaiyasit, W., & Weiss, B. (1988). Thai and American perspectives on over- and undercontrolled child behavior problems: Exploring the threshold model among parents, teachers, and psychologists. *Journal of Consulting and Clinical Psychology, 56,* 601–609.

World Health Organization (1993). *The ICD–10 Classification of Mental and Behavioural Disorders.* Geneva: WHO.

Younger, A. J., Gentile, C., & Burgess, K. B. (1993). Children's perceptions of social withdrawal: Changes across age. In K. H. Rubin & J. B. Asendorpf (Eds.), *Social withdrawal, inhibition and shyness in childhood* (pp. 215–235). Hillsdale, NJ: Lawrence Erlbaum.

19

Social Phobia

TRACY L. MORRIS

The experience of social anxiety is an almost universal phenomenon. Most individuals can recall at least one occasion during which they felt uncomfortable in a social situation. The term "social anxiety" refers to a constellation of behaviors that may occur in response to social stimuli (e.g., public performance situations; informal social interactions). Such responses include overt behaviors such as escape and avoidance, cognitions involving a negative evaluatory component, and physiological reactions such as increased heart rate, trembling, and muscle tension (Beidel, Turner, & Dancu, 1985). Fortunately, for the vast majority of the population social discomfort is but a transient experience restricted to isolated contexts. For others, however, social anxiety is ubiquitous, often leading to restricted functioning and concomitant socioemotional difficulties.

Social Phobia: Definition and Clinical Characteristics

Although descriptions of socially fearful individuals have been documented throughout recorded history (Marks, 1985), the term "social phobia" did not enter the diagnostic nomenclature until 1980 with the release of the DSM-III by the American Psychiatric Association. Social phobia currently is defined in the fourth edition of the *Diagnostic and statistical manual of mental disorders* (DSM-IV) as a "marked and persistent fear of one or more social or performance situations in which the person is exposed to unfamiliar people or to possible scrutiny by others" (American Psychiatric Association, 1994, p. 416).

The DSM-IV allows for specification of a "generalized" subtype of social phobia if the individual's fears include most social situations. A "specific" subtype also has been widely discussed in the literature (Heimberg, Hope, Dodge, & Becker, 1990). Specific social phobia involves social fear and avoidance in a particular context such as speaking or performing in public. The generalized subtype has been reported to have an earlier age of onset, more associated clinical symptoms (e.g., depression), and to be of greater severity than the specific subtype (Bruch & Heimberg, 1994; Herbert, Hope, & Bellack, 1992; Turner, Beidel, & Townsley, 1992).

On a final note regarding definition, the term social anxiety disorder was introduced in the DSM-IV as an alternative label for this syndrome, stemming in part from professional disagreement over technical use of the term "phobia." The term social anxiety disorder is rapidly gaining acceptance and is predicted to be the preferred label in any subsequent versions of the DSM. Throughout this chapter, the terms "social phobia" and "social anxiety disorder" may be considered interchangeable.

Epidemiology

Vastly disparate US lifetime prevalence estimates have been presented for social phobia, ranging from 2.4% in the Epidemiological Catchment Area Survey (Schneier, Johnson, Hornig, Liebowitz, & Weissman, 1992) to 13.3% in the National Comorbidity Survey (Kessler et al., 1994). Examination of methodological differences between the studies (e.g., diagnostic criteria, sampling procedures, diagnostic instruments), as well as comparison with international investigations (e.g., Lepine & Lellouch, 1995; Stein, Walker, & Ford, 1994), suggests that the NCS data may be most representative. Furthermore, Kessler et al. (1994) found social phobia to be the third most prevalent psychiatric disorder, falling just behind Major Depressive Episode (17.1%) and Alcohol Dependence (14.1%).

With regard to gender differences, NCS lifetime prevalence estimates were 11.1% for males versus 15.5% for females (Kessler et al., 1994), a male to female ratio that is consistent with that identified through other epidemiological investigations (Mannuzza, Fyer, Liebowitz, & Klein, 1992; Pollard & Henderson, 1988). However, the gender distribution of social phobia among clinical populations has been reported as roughly equal (Last, Perrin, Hersen, & Kazdin, 1992; Turner & Beidel, 1989). Racial and ethnic differences in the prevalence of social phobia typically have not emerged consistently in the literature (Beidel & Turner, 1998), although further investigation is necessary to reach firm conclusions.

The mean age of onset for social phobia has been reported to range from early- to mid-adolescence (Amies, Gelder, & Shaw, 1983; Last et al., 1992; Liebowitz, Gorman, Fyer, & Klein, 1985; Öst, 1987; Turner, Beidel, Dancu, & Keys, 1986). However, it is quite common for adults who meet criteria for social phobia to state that they have been shy and socially anxious throughout their entire life. Increased social demands, coupled with increased metacognitive skills and self-focused attention, likely interact in such a way that many shy children ultimately will breach the clinical threshold for social phobia during adolescence.

Comorbidity

High comorbidity rates have been reported for social phobia. Common comorbid conditions include other anxiety disorders (particularly generalized anxiety disorder) and depression (Schneier et al., 1992; Turner, Beidel,

Borden, Stanley, & Jacob, 1991). Furthermore, the high comorbidity rates (22–89%) between generalized social phobia and avoidant personality disorder (APD) cited in the literature, have prompted many investigators to question the validity of distinctions between the two disorders (Heimberg, Holt, Schneier, Spitzer, & Liebowitz, 1993; Herbert et al., 1992; Holt, Heimberg, & Hope, 1992; Turner et al., 1992). Although comparison studies suggest that APD may be characterized by greater severity of social fear and avoidance, there has been no firm empirical evidence for a *qualitative* distinction between APD and social phobia.

Developmental Progression

As noted earlier, the mean age of onset for social phobia typically has been reported as early- to mid-adolescence (Turner & Beidel, 1989). Although several etiological precursors to the disorder are discussed in this chapter, large-scale longitudinal investigations of the expression and influence of these factors across the lifespan have not been conducted. At present, no long-term prospective data are available to address issues of the developmental progression or stability of the disorder. However, results of retrospective studies (Stemberger et al., 1995) indicate that for many individuals diagnosed with social phobia the developmental pattern reflects an early onset and progressive generalization of social fear. Furthermore, experts working in the field have noted extremely long intervals (e.g., 20 years on average) among their clients between the reported onset of extreme social anxiety and initial attempts to seek treatment—intervals considered to be longer than that for most other psychiatric disorders. These findings suggest a high degree of stability for social phobia in the absence of direct therapeutic intervention or other events (e.g., parental arrangement of socialization experiences leading to sufficient exposure to reduce social fear) that may divert the individual from a maladaptive developmental pathway.

Social Anxiety as a Risk Factor

As noted above, social anxiety has been found to co-occur with a variety of psychological conditions. Although there has been little empirical research on the developmental progression of social anxiety and its temporal relationship with other disorders, there is some evidence to suggest that social anxiety may increase an individual's risk for certain forms of maladjustment. For example, Stein, Tancer, Gelernter, Vittone, and Uhde (1990) found that depression began *after* the onset of Social phobia in the majority of cases. Restriction of social activities in effort to avoid or reduce feelings of social anxiety impedes the development of interpersonal relationships (Schneier et al., 1992) and may adversely impact academic and occupational functioning (Turner et al., 1986). As social withdrawal increases and functioning becomes more impaired, depression is but a likely outcome.

Social anxiety also may increase an individual's risk for substance abuse. Page and Andrews (1996) reported a 27% rate of alcohol problems for adults with social phobia, thus representing risk ratios three (males) to five (females) times that of the ECA population estimates. It has been suggested that individuals who experience high levels of social anxiety may use alcohol in an attempt to lower inhibition and general physiological arousal, and that social phobia precedes alcohol abuse in the majority of cases in which the conditions are comorbid (Kushner, Sher, & Beitman, 1990).

Further research is necessary to elucidate patterns of risk associated with social anxiety. However, at this point it seems clear that high levels of social anxiety do little to promote well-being and may seriously reduce an individual's quality of life. In light of the chronicity of social anxiety and its association with other pathological conditions, the need for early-intervention and prevention programs is underscored. Yet in order to develop effective programs, we must develop a greater understanding of factors related to the development and maintenance of social anxiety.

Factors Related to the Development of Social Anxiety

Figure 19.1 depicts the basics of an exploratory model for the development of social anxiety disorder. The model reflects multiple entry points that may place a child on the path toward social anxiety disorder and, conversely, multiple points at which a child may be diverted from the path. From the outset it must be made clear that all associations are not linear. Furthermore, the possibility of multiple entry points allows for great diversity in individual etiological pathways. The following section of this chapter provides a review of factors recognized to play a role in the development of social anxiety disorder. Consistent with the multicontextual perspective of developmental psychopathology, the review incorporates findings from the psychiatric, clinical, developmental, and social psychology literatures.

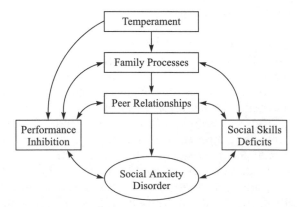

Figure 19.1. Pathways to social anxiety disorder.

Temperament

Very little is known about the possible role of genetic transmission in the development of social anxiety. There are presently no adoption studies available to provide social phobia concordance estimates for biological versus adoptive parents, children, and siblings. However, several twin and family studies have been conducted which shed some light on the issue. Kendler, Neale, Kessler, Heath, and Eaves (1992) conducted a study of 2163 female twin pairs and reported concordance rates of 15.3% for dizygotic pairs and 24.4% for monozygotic pairs, with an overall heritability index of 30%. Family studies have reported increased rates of social phobia among first-degree relatives of persons diagnosed with social phobia (Fyer, Mannuzza, Chapman, Liebowitz, & Klein, 1993; Perugi et al.1990; Reich & Yates, 1988). Furthermore, Mannuzza et al. (1995) reported that relatives of persons with the generalized subtype of social phobia were nearly three times as likely (16% vs. 6%) to meet criteria for social phobia than were relatives of persons with the nongeneralized subtype.

Although the exact mechanism of any biological contribution to the development of social anxiety remains unclear, there is growing evidence to support a connection between temperamental inhibition and social anxiety. Temperament refers to a person's characteristic responses to stimuli based on various behavioral dimensions (e.g., emotionality, activity, sociability) and is considered by many researchers to have a genetic or physiological basis (Buss & Plomin, 1984; Thomas, Chess, & Birch, 1968). Kagan and his colleagues (Garcia-Coll, Kagan, & Reznick, 1984; Kagan, Reznick, & Snidman, 1988) have described a temperamental style termed "behavioral inhibition" which refers to a generally shy demeanor and tendency to approach new situations with restraint, avoidance, and distress. Increased rates of anxiety disorders in general, and social phobia in particular, have been found among behaviorally inhibited children (Biederman et al., 1990; Biederman et al.,1993; Hirshfeld et al., 1992). Approximately one-half of inhibited infants have been found to remain inhibited into their eighth year (Kagan, Snidman, & Arcus, 1993). Research suggests that it is this group of children who express stable inhibition that are at greatest risk for development of an anxiety disorder (Biederman, Rosenbaum, Chaloff, & Kagan, 1995). For a more thorough discussion of temperamental factors the reader is referred to Lonigan and Phillips (this volume).

Family Processes

Attachment. As the relationship among the constructs of attachment and anxiety is discussed in detail by Thompson (this volume), this section serves merely to orient the reader and to provide a general overview of relevant research. The function of attachment behaviors is considered to (a) meet the basic physiological needs of the infant, and (b) provide emotional security to the infant (Bowlby, 1958, 1969). Ainsworth, Blehar, Waters, & Wall (1978) identified three specific patterns of infant–caregiver attachment (secure; inse-cure–ambivalent; insecure–avoidant) based on responses to the classic "strange situation" laboratory task.

A large body of research has indicated that insecure patterns of attach-ment are related to future maladjustment and the development of psycho-logical disorders (e.g., Erickson, Sroufe, & Egeland, 1985; Kobak, Sudler, & Gamble, 1991). Warren, Huston, Egeland, and Sroufe (1997) reported the results of a 16-year prospective study of 172 adolescents who had partici-pated in the strange situation task at 12-months of age. An anxious–resistant attachment style in infancy was associated with an increased risk for anxiety disorders in childhood or adolescence (28% among the anxious–resistant group, compared with 11% of the securely attached group and 16% of the avoidant attachment group). Of the adolescents who had experienced an anxiety disorder, 38% met criteria for social phobia—making it the most commonly occurring anxiety disorder in this sample. Furthermore, attach-ment classification predicted anxiety disorder over and above measures of maternal anxiety and infant temperament.

There is a growing body of literature on parent–adolescent attachment and adult romantic attachment (Armsden & Greenberg, 1987; Berman, Heiss, & Sperling, 1994; Hazan & Shaver, 1987; Van Ijzendoorn & Bakermans-Kranenburg, 1996). Albeit somewhat controversial in terms of reliance on self-report methodology (in contrast to the direct observation methodology utilized in research on infant–caregiver attachment), this research is contributing to our understanding of how family processes may contribute to the development of psychopathology. Although these studies have not specifically assessed social anxiety, associations have been docu-mented between attachment and related variables such as general anxiety, isolation, lack of interpersonal contact, loneliness, and self-esteem.

Parenting Style. Considerable research has been conducted on perceived parenting style and psychopathology (Parker, 1983; Parker et al., 1997). Parenting styles characterized by low levels of care/warmth and high levels of control/overprotection repeatedly have been associated with anxiety and depression (e.g., Duggan, Sham, Minne, Lee, & Murray, 1998; Wiborg & Dahl, 1997). Arrindell and colleagues have reported results of two investiga-tions in which adults with social phobia rated their parents as less warm and caring and more controlling and rejecting than did nonclinical controls (Arrindell, Emmelkamp, Monsma, & Brilman, 1983; Arrindell et al., 1989).

Observational studies of parent–child interaction support results of the retrospective investigations cited above. For example, Krohne and Hock (1991) observed mother–child dyads working together on a puzzle task and found mothers of high-anxious girls to be more controlling than were mothers of low- anxious girls. A more recent observational study (Dumas, LaFreniere, & Serketich, 1995) has suggested bidirectional influences, with mothers of anxious children attempting to control their children by being coercive and unresponsive, and children trying to manage their mothers by being resistant and coercive. Patterns of extreme parental control may serve to communicate an impression that the child is not competent to make decisions without parental input and may foster feelings of helplessness and dependence.

Family Sociability. A sizable literature base has been amassed by developmentalists conducting research in the area of parental influences on children's social behavior (Booth, Rose-Krasnor, McKinnon, & Rubin, 1994; Cohn, Patterson, & Christopoulos, 1991; Darling & Steinberg, 1993; Profilet & Ladd, 1994; Russell & Finnie, 1990). Parents play the central role in providing young children with opportunities for social contacts (Bhavnagri & Parke, 1991; Bryant & DeMorris, 1992; Ladd, Profilet, & Hart, 1992; Putallaz & Hefflin, 1990). Parents who are themselves anxious in social settings may be less likely to facilitate their children's development of social networks and more likely to model strategies of avoidance in an effort to reduce social discomfort (Daniels & Plomin, 1985).

In retrospective investigations, adults with social phobia have described their parents as encouraging family isolation and limiting contacts with neighbors, relatives, and acquaintances (Bruch, Heimberg, Berger, & Collins, 1989; Bruch & Heimberg, 1994). Similarly, Arbel and Stravyinski (1991) found that persons with Avoidant Personality Disorder, in comparison to a nonclinical control group, recalled their parents to have been less sociable, to have experienced more social discomfort, and to have been less encouraging of their children's social activity. A recent study by Rapee and Melville (1997) extends these findings by including reports from individuals diagnosed with social phobia and their mothers. Results, confirmed both by offspring and their mothers, indicated lower family sociability for the social phobia group than for nonclinical controls.

Modeling of Fear. In addition to the direct influence of limiting (or not encouraging) social contacts, parents also may contribute to the development of anxiety in children by providing information that may promote heightened states of arousal and hypervigilance. In a study of the offspring of parents with anxiety disorders, Turner and Beidel (2000) used a "risk room" procedure in which children were given access to a laboratory room furnished with playground equipment. Parents with anxiety disorders were observed to make significantly more comments to their children regarding the potential danger of the situation than did nonclinical control parents (e.g., "be careful"; "don't climb so high").

An innovative series of studies by Barrett, Dadds, and colleagues provides evidence that parents of anxious children are more likely to model threat interpretations to ambiguous cues than are parents of aggressive or nonclinical control children (Barrett, Rapee, Dadds, & Ryan, 1996; Dadds, Barrett, Rapee, & Ryan, 1996). In these investigations, parents of anxious children also were more likely to provide and reinforce avoidant solutions in response to hypothetical social scenarios. Although the studies by Turner and Beidel and by Barrett, Dadds, and colleagues included samples selected for anxiety disorders in general, rather than social phobia in particular, the processes involved are relevant to a thorough understanding of the nature of social anxiety. For a more complete review of parental factors associated with social anxiety, the reader is referred to Masia and Morris (1998) and to Dadds and Roth (this volume).

Peer Relationships

Children's peer relationships are a crucial contributor to social and emotional development (Berndt & Ladd, 1989; Hartup, 1979; Asher & Parker, 1989). Peer interaction not only supplements familial influences, it also contributes uniquely by providing opportunities for learning specific skills that are not attainable through adult–child interaction. Considerable evidence indicates that peer relationship difficulties may be an important risk factor for subsequent psychopathology (Boivin, Poulin, & Vitaro, 1994; Kupersmidt & Patterson, 1991; Ollendick, Weist, Borden, & Greene, 1992; Parker & Asher, 1987). Although much of the literature on the association of peer relationships and psychopathology has focused on externalizing behavior problems (Newcomb, Bukowski, & Pattee, 1993), inclusion of psychometrically sound measures of anxiety and depression has become more common in recent investigations. For example, studies by La Greca and colleagues (La Greca, Dandes, Wick, Shaw, & Stone, 1988; La Greca & Lopez, 1998; La Greca & Stone, 1993) have found peer acceptance to be related inversely to social anxiety in children and adolescents. Similar results were obtained by Inderbitzen, Walters, and Bukowski (1997) who found that peer-neglected and peer-rejected children reported the highest levels of social anxiety among 973 middle-school children. Relatedly, Strauss, Lahey, Frick, Frame, and Hynd (1988) found that children diagnosed with anxiety disorders were more likely to be classified as peer-neglected than were non-clinical control children or children diagnosed with conduct disorders.

The role of social withdrawal in peer contexts is particularly relevant to discussions of developmental factors for anxiety and depression. Social anxiety may lead to social withdrawal, and conversely social withdrawal may interfere with the development of social skills and interpersonal relationships which may in turn lead to increased anxiety in social situations (e.g., Vernberg, Abwender, Ewell, & Beery, 1992). Rubin and his colleagues (Rubin, 1993; Rubin, LeMare, & Lollis, 1990; Rubin & Mills, 1988) have developed an impressive program of research in the area of social with-drawal. The reader is referred to Rubin and Burgess (this volume) for a more thorough discussion of this topic.

Traumatic Conditioning

Apart from the effect of more enduring adverse social experiences such as peer neglect or peer rejection, the possibility that specific traumatic experiences may trigger the development of social anxiety has been explored by several researchers. Retrospective reports of shy adults have implicated unpleasant peer experiences as contributing factors in the development of shyness (Ishiyama, 1984). Öst and Hughdahl (1981) reported that 58.1% of a sample of adults with social phobia recalled direct traumatic conditioning experiences as having been related to the development of their social fears. In a study by Stemberger, Turner, Beidel, & Calhoun (1995), 56% of participants diagnosed with the specific subtype of social phobia recalled traumatic conditioning experiences to be related to the development or exacerbation of their social fears, in comparison with 40% of participants diagnosed with generalized social phobia, and 20% of nonclinical controls. The results from Stemberger et al. suggest that traumatic conditioning may play a more significant role in the development of specific social phobias (e.g., public performance fears) than with the generalized form of the disorder. However, many persons who have had traumatic social experiences do not develop social phobia and a sizeable proportion of those diagnosed with social phobia do not recall any specific traumatic conditioning experiences. It is likely that the long-term effect of such experiences will have differential impact on individuals depending on their prior learning history and temperamental characteristics (for a discussion of conditioning factors, see Mineka & Zinbarg, 1995; Ollendick, Vasey, & King, this volume; and Dadds, Davey, & Field, this volume).

Cognitive Biases

The role of cognitive biases in the development and maintenance of anxiety is receiving increased empirical attention (see Vasey & MacLeod, this volume). Research cited previously on the role of parenting factors clearly suggests selective attention for threat cues among anxious individuals (Barrett et al., 1996). Several studies have suggested that persons with social phobia may underestimate their own degree of social skill, while overly attending to perceived errors in social behavior (Dodge, Heimberg, Nyman, & O'Brien, 1987; Heimberg, Acerra, & Holstein, 1985; Hope, Rapee, Heimberg, & Dombeck, 1990; Maddux, Norton, & Leary, 1988; Rapee & Lim, 1992; Stopa & Clark, 1993). Although few studies have investigated cognitive biases in children with anxiety disorders, initial reports have suggested a similar pattern of findings as that obtained with adults (Chansky & Kendall, 1997; Vasey, Daleiden, Williams, & Brown, 1995; Zatz & Chassin, 1985). The origin of such cognitive biases remains to be explicated through future research; however, early learning experiences such as parental modeling of social fear, and reinforcement of threat interpretations and avoidance strategies likely set the stage for biased perceptions of the social environment.

Social Skills Deficits

While the author was aware of only one study that directly assessed the social skill of children with social phobia (Beidel, Turner, & Morris, 1999), several studies have used behavioral performance tasks to assess whether adults with social phobia exhibit performance deficits in social–evaluative situations (Beidel et al., 1985; Rapee & Lim, 1992; Turner et al., 1986). Although results in the adult literature have been somewhat mixed with respect to the extent of social skills deficits in persons with social phobia, the available evidence suggests that such deficits are more likely to be identified in persons diagnosed with the generalized subtype of the disorder. However, when skill differences are found, it is difficult to ascertain whether lower levels of performance among the social phobia groups reflect genuine skills deficits (i.e., lack of knowledge of, or actual ability to perform, the appropriate behavior) or rather performance inhibition stemming from high anxiety.

Pathways to Social Anxiety

As stated previously, there are multiple pathways to the development of social anxiety. The factors discussed above were presented in isolation, as this is the manner in which they often have been studied. However, each factor may interact with others to ameliorate or exacerbate its effect. For example, research has been conducted linking temperament, attachment, and peer relationships (Asendorpf, 1990; Calkins & Fox, 1992; Fagot, 1997).

When considering pathways to social anxiety disorder, a particularly entrenched path may be developed in the case of a behaviorally inhibited infant who is brought into a family of anxious or unresponsive parents. In this case a poor fit between parent(s) and child may exist, resulting in a poor quality of infant–caregiver attachment (cf. Thomas & Chess, 1977). As the parent–child relationship serves as the model upon which all other social relationships are formed, this inhibited and poorly attached child may have difficulty establishing effective peer relationships. Social isolation restricts the child's opportunities for establishing and practicing effective social skills. All this serves to increase the child's inhibition and discomfort in social settings, thus creating a vicious cycle. Although this may be a prototypical pathway for many individuals diagnosed with the generalized subtype of social phobia, it is by no means the only route. Many individuals who were not particularly inhibited as infants and/or who have fine relationships with their parents may develop problems in peer relationships that place them on a pathway to social anxiety. The possible combinations of risk and protective factors are too numerous to discuss here. However, one would be remiss without noting the multiple opportunities for intervening in such a way to divert an at-risk individual from the path. Virtually at any point in the lifespan some naturally occurring experience or targeted intervention may alter an individual's course. As the effect of risk factors tends to compound as time progresses, making it more difficult to return to a more adaptive path, intervention efforts may have a greater likelihood for success the earlier that they occur.

The Child and Family Social Interaction Project: Investigating Pathways to Social Anxiety Disorder

The remainder of the chapter will be devoted to discussion of research investigations primarily conducted under the auspices of the Child and Family Social Interaction Project at West Virginia University. The preceding portions of this chapter were devoted to the formulation of a heuristic model for the development of social phobia. The focus of the CFSIP is to investigate components of the model in order to further explicate potential pathways to the development of social anxiety. Our work has included various retrospective, prospective, and laboratory analog studies conducted with adults and children drawn from community and clinical settings.

Retrospective Studies of Late Adolescents and Young Adults

Although potential limitations of retrospective designs must be acknowledged, the practical utility of retrospective designs should not be dismissed. Given the vast financial and time commitments involved in longitudinal research, retrospective designs provide an opportunity for investigators to test out possible relationships that may be explored further in laboratory analog and longitudinal investigations.

Over 1200 undergraduate students have participated in various investigations conducted through the CFSIP in an effort to elucidate relationships among parenting style, parent–adolescent attachment, anxiety (general and social), and depression (Morris & Huffman, 1996; Morris & Kuhn, 1994; Spaulding, Morris, & Koudelka, 1995). Results of a recent investigation (Morris & Huffman, 2000) will be presented to illustrate our findings. The sample included 582 undergraduate students (mean age 19 years; 57% female; 89% European American). Participants were administered a protocol including the Social Phobia and Anxiety Inventory (Turner, Beidel, Dancu, & Stanley,1989), the State–Trait Anxiety Inventory (Spielberger, 1983), the Beck Depression Inventory (Beck & Steer, 1987), and the Parental Bonding Instrument (Parker et al., 1979) and two measures of attachment styles (Feeney, Noller, & Hanrahan, 1994; Hazan & Shaver, 1987). Main effects were found for parenting style on all symptom measures. Participants who reported that their mothers engaged in an "optimal" parenting style (high care/warmth, low control/overprotection) reported significantly lower levels of social anxiety, trait anxiety, and depression. The results suggested a pattern of potential differential effects of parenting style whereby general negative affectivity (depression and trait anxiety) was most related to a parenting style of "affectionless control" (low care/warmth, high control/overprotection), while social anxiety was most related to a "neglectful" parenting style (low care/warmth, low control/overprotection). Substantial differences were identified with respect to the proportion of participants exceeding identified cutoff scores on the SPAI by parenting style group. Notably, results reflected a fourfold increase for "probable social phobia" for the neglectful parenting style group (21%), in comparison with the optimal parenting style group (5%). Both the affectionless control and neglectful parenting style groups were characterized by insecure attachment styles (avoidant and anxious). In contrast to affectionless control, little attention has been paid to the effects of exposure to a neglectful parenting style. Our results suggest the need for continued investigation of potential differential effects.

The investigations cited above focused on the parenting style of mothers. We have recently completed a study of over 400 undergraduate students that extends this work by collecting data on the parenting behavior and psychiatric history of both fathers and mothers (Anhalt & Morris, 2000). A study of the impact of sibling relationships and preferential parental treatment on social anxiety currently is in progress. Further research is needed to identify specific processes through which parenting behaviors may maintain and/or exacerbate internalizing problems. From an applied perspective, the association between parenting style and development of psychopathology in offspring suggests the need for early intervention to assist parents in modifying caretaking behaviors.

Assessment of Social Anxiety in Children

Successful investigation of processes related to the development and course of psychopathology often hinges on the availability of sound measures of the phenomenon of interest. Although there are several adequate measures available to assess "general" levels of anxiety in children, until recently there were no specific measures available to assess social anxiety in children. The Social Phobia and Anxiety Inventory for Children (SPAI-C; Beidel, Turner, & Morris, 1995; 1998) was developed to meet this need. The SPAI-C has demonstrated sound psychometric properties (Beidel, Turner, & Fink, 1996; Beidel, Turner, Hamlin, & Morris, 2000; Morris & Masia, 1998) and is being used as a screening and outcome measure in our research with community and clinical samples.

Investigations of Parent–Child Interaction

In contrast to a relatively large literature in the area of disruptive behavior disorders, few studies involving direct observation of parent–child interaction have been conducted in the area of childhood anxiety (notable exceptions include the previously cited research programs of Dadds, Barrett, and Rapee). Moreover, research targeting the family interaction patterns of socially anxious children has been lacking. In a recent investigation (Spaulding & Morris, 1997), approximately 200 children in the fourth to sixth grades were screened for social anxiety using the SPAI-C. Thirty mother–child dyads (15 high social anxiety, SPAI-C >17; 15 low social anxiety, SPAI-C <10) participated in two laboratory tasks. Prior to beginning the tasks, dyads were seated alone in a room and videotaped through an observation window in order to obtain latency to first speech as a measure of behavioral inhibition. Following this observation period, each dyad was presented with two tasks designed to create situations that would provide a context in which mothers may or may not elect to engage in controlling, doubting, or critical behavior. The block task required the mother–child dyads, seated side-by-side, to build a Jenga® block tower in the center of a table. Increasing the height of the tower requires the removal of lower level blocks, thus making the tower increasingly unstable as it becomes taller. Mothers and children were instructed to take turns placing the blocks on the tower for a 5-minute interval. Interactions were videotaped. Following the block-task interaction, dyads were presented with five hypothetical scenarios involving social interaction (e.g., trying out for the school play). Each child and their mother were presented the scenarios in separate rooms and asked for their interpretation of the scenario (or for mothers, their child's interpretation) and what they (or their child) would do in that situation. Then the mother and child were brought into the same room and asked to discuss each scenario. Results indicated that children in the high social anxiety group exhibited longer latency to first speech in the baseline observation period and were more likely to exhibit nondirective and passive behavior (e.g., fewer commands) during the block task. Although merely approaching statistical significance, the data suggested that mothers of children in the high social anxiety group were more likely to exhibit controlling behavior (e.g., more commands, critical statements) during the block task.

With regard to the hypothetical scenarios, mothers of children in the high social anxiety group were more likely to report that their children would perceive the situations as threatening and to propose more avoidant solutions. Of interest, internalizing scores on the Child Behavior Checklist (Achenbach, 1991) correlated significantly with child-proposed negative solutions (avoidant or aggressive) after discussing the scenarios with their mothers, but not before the discussions. Such change suggests that some aspect of the discussion with the mother was influential in modifying the child's response, with feedback from the mother essentially serving to increase the likelihood that children with higher internalizing scores would propose an avoidant strategy. The design of the study limits our ability to draw conclusions about directions of effect. Although the results may merely reflect the accuracy of mothers to predict their children's behavior in social situations, changes in children's responses to the scenarios after discussions with their mothers leaves open the possibility of causal influence.

Following from our retrospective studies and our laboratory investigation with mother–child dyads, we have recently launched a home observation study to identify patterns that may discriminate families of socially anxious and nonanxious children. Continued work in laboratory and natural contexts is needed to expand our knowledge base with respect to potential causal factors in the development of social anxiety as well as to provide information that may assist in the development of intervention programs that incorporate the family (see Barrett, Dadds, & Rapee, 1996, for a discussion of family anxiety management).

Longitudinal Study of Children's Peer Relationships

In 1994, I initiated a longitudinal investigation to examine children's social relationships and the developmental progression of anxiety. At that time, the cohort of children, recruited from a local elementary school, were in the first through third grades. To date, over 500 children have participated in the project. Sociometric nominations (Coie, Dodge, & Coppotelli, 1982) have been collected each fall and spring. Parent- and child-report measures of social anxiety (SPAI-C), anxiety (MASC; March, 1997) depression (CDI; Kovacs, 1992), behavior problems (CBCL; Achenbach, 1991), and diagnostic symptom levels (CSI; Gadow & Sprafkin, 1994) have been collected at periodic intervals for subsets of children (owing to reading limitations, self-report data collection began only when each child reached the 3rd grade). High stability for sociometric classification has been demonstrated across the project period. For example, 84% of the children who were classified as peer-neglected in year 1 were again classified as peer-neglected in year 4 (stability for peer rejection was 70%). Significant correlations have been obtained between sociometric data obtained in year 1 and symptom reports obtained in year 4. To illustrate, like-least sociometric scores were significantly correlated with social anxiety ($r = 0.47$), total anxiety ($r = 0.61$) and depression ($r = 0.55$). With respect to sociometric status, peer-rejected and peer-neglected children have endorsed higher levels of social anxiety, general anxiety, and depression than have popular or average status groups. This cohort of children will be followed into their high-school years to determine (a) normative patterns of change in self-reported social anxiety, and (b) whether sociometric status in the early elementary grades is related to adolescent diagnostic status.

Early Intervention and Treatment

As the available research suggests that socially isolated children are at risk for developing anxiety and/or affective disorders, an important aspect of our research program involves the development of intervention programs to improve children's social status and interaction with peers. In an investigation conducted with colleagues at the University of Mississippi (Morris, Messer, & Gross, 1995), sociometric nominations were obtained for 229 first- and second-grade children. Based on the sociometric data, 24 peer-neglected and 24 popular children were selected for participation in a peer-pairing intervention. Peer-neglected and popular children were assigned randomly to peer-pairing or control conditions. Each peer-neglected child was paired with a popular child from her or his own classroom. Each peer-pair participated in twelve 15-minute play sessions over a 4-week period. Sociometric nominations and behavioral observations were conducted again following intervention and for 1 month after treatment. Results revealed significant improvement on both sociometric status and positive interaction rate. No significant changes were evident for the control group. Results were maintained at follow-up.

Along with colleagues at the Medical University of South Carolina, we have developed a comprehensive treatment package for children with social phobia, called Social Effectiveness Therapy for Children (SET-C; Beidel, Turner, & Morris, 1997; in press). The components of SET-C include education, group social skills training, individual therapist-directed exposure, peer-generalization experiences, and programmed practice. The program includes 28 sessions (16 individual, 12 group) conducted over a 4-month period. An NIMH-funded treatment outcome study of the efficacy of SET-C has been completed, and initial results indicate that the program is effective in reducing social anxiety and increasing social effectiveness (Beidel et al., in press).

Recently, we have initiated a modified version of SET-C to provide access to early intervention for children residing in rural community settings. Unfortunately, the resource-intensive nature of many empirically tested structured treatment programs, such as SET-C, impede their delivery in many community practice settings. Our new school-based version of SET-C (SbSET-C; Morris, 1998) is expected to be a cost-effective, time-efficient, early-intervention program for children experiencing significant social anxiety. The program, which may be administered by community practitioners or school psychologists, includes 12 social skills training and 4 parent training sessions plus weekly phone contacts to monitor programmed practice in the home and community setting. Additionally, a peer-pairing component has been included whereby socially anxious children will be paired with more socially skilled classmates to participate in cooperative activities during recess.

Concluding Comments

Social anxiety is a common experience. However, for those meeting criteria for a diagnosis of social phobia the level of distress experienced in social situations may be incapacitating. In an attempt to manage arousal and distress, individuals with social phobia may increasingly avoid social encounters and activities. Although avoidance may serve to reduce distress in the short term, nonparticipation in social activities may interfere with acquisition of skills necessary for effective social interaction and may have long-term deleterious effects on academic and occupational functioning.

Research on the developmental psychopathology of social phobia is in its infancy. An exploratory model has been presented in this chapter to help integrate existing findings and guide future research. At this stage, the developmental roots of social phobia potentially may be identified through examination of temperamental and family process factors. This presents an exciting challenge, as each advance in our understanding of etiological factors may lead to a new avenue for prevention or early intervention. Explication of developmental pathways will provide an opportunity for targeted intervention across all stages of the lifespan. For example, parents may be trained to modify their interaction styles with inhibited infants; parent–child interaction therapy may be of benefit with insecurely attached toddlers; peer-pairing procedures may be implemented in school settings with socially withdrawn children; and group social skills programs may be provided for socially anxious adolescents.

Clearly much remains to be learned about the developmental psychopathology of social anxiety. However, all indication is that we are on the crest of a wave that promises a flood of new research. Contemporary investigators have incorporated the findings of diverse literatures and are willing to use a variety of methodologies to approach this area of inquiry. Continuing advances in our knowledge base and in our technology undoubtedly will allow us to bridge the gap between theoretical supposition and informed action in our quest to improve the quality of human life.

References

Achenbach, T. M. (1991). *Child Behavior Checklist for Ages 4–18.* Burlington, VT: University of Vermont.

Ainsworth, M. D. S., Blehar, M. C., Waters, E., & Wall, S. (1978). *Patterns of attachment: A psychological study of the strange situation.* Hillsdale, NJ: Lawrence Erlbaum.

American Psychiatric Association (1994). *Diagnostic and statistical manual of mental disorders* (4th ed.), Washington, DC: Author.

Amies, P. L., Gelder, M. G., & Shaw, P. M. (1983). Social phobia: A comparative clinical study. *British Journal of Psychiatry, 142,* 174–179.

Anhalt, K., & Morris, T. L. (2000). The relation between parenting factors and social anxiety: A retrospective study. Manuscript submitted for publication.

Arbel, N., & Stravyinski, A. (1991). A retrospective study of separation in the development of adult avoidant personality disorder. *Acta Psychiatrica Scandinavica, 83,* 174–178.

Armsden, G. C., & Greenberg, M. T. (1987). The inventory of parent and peer attachment: Individual differences and their relationship to well-being. *Journal of Youth and Adolescence, 16,* 427–454.

Arrindell, W. A., Emmelkamp, P. M. G., Monsma, A., & Brilman, E. (1983). The role of perceived parental rearing practices in the etiology of phobic disorders: A controlled study. *British Journal of Psychiatry, 155,* 526–535.

Arrindell, W. A., Kwee, M. G. T., Methorst, G. J., Van der Ende, J., Pol, E., & Moritz, B. J. M. (1989). Perceived parenting styles of agoraphobic and socially phobic in-patients. *British Journal of Psychiatry, 155,* 526–535.

Asendorpf, J. B. (1990). Development of inhibition during childhood: Evidence for situational specificity and a two-factor model. *Developmental Psychology, 26,* 721–730.

Asher, S. R., & Parker, J. G. (1989). Significance of peer relationship problems in childhood. In B. H. Schneider, G. Attili, J. Nadel, & R. P. Weissberg (Eds.),

Social competence in developmental perspective (pp. 5–23). Norwell, MA: Kluwer Academic.

Barrett, P. M., Dadds, M. M., & Rapee, R. M. (1996). Family treatment of childhood anxiety: A controlled trial. *Journal of Consulting and Clinical Psychology, 64,* 333–342.

Barrett, P. M., Rapee, R. M., Dadds, M. M., & Ryan, S. M. (1996). Family enhancement of cognitive style in anxious and aggressive children. *Journal of Abnormal Child Psychology, 24,* 187–203.

Beck, A. T., & Steer, R. A. (1987). *Manual for the Beck Depression Inventory.* San Antonio, TX: Psychological Corp.

Beidel, D. C., & Turner, S. M. (1998). *Shy children, phobic adults: Nature and treatment of social phobia* (1st ed.), Washington, DC: American Psychological Association.

Beidel, D. C., Turner, S. M., & Dancu, C. V. (1985). Physiological, cognitive, and behavioral aspects of social anxiety. *Behaviour Research and Therapy, 23,* 109–117.

Beidel, D. C., Turner, S. M. & Fink, C. M. (1996). The assessment of childhood social phobia: Construct, convergent, and discriminative validity of the Social Phobia and Anxiety Inventory for Children (SPAI-C). *Psychological Assessment, 8,* 235–240.

Beidel, D. C., Turner, S. M., Hamlin, K., & Morris, T. L. (2000). The Social Phobia and Anxiety Inventory for Children (SPAI-C): External and discriminative validity. *Behavior Therapy, 31,* 75–81.

Beidel, D. C., Turner, S. M., & Morris, T. L. (1995). A new inventory to assess child social phobia: The Social Phobia and Anxiety Inventory for Children. *Psychological Assessment, 7,* 73–79.

Beidel, D. C., Turner, S. M., & Morris, T. L. (March, 1997). Social effectiveness therapy for children. In C. L. Masia and T. L. Morris (Chairs), *Treating anxiety disorder in children and adolescents: Cost-effective interventions and clinical considerations.* Symposium presented at the annual meeting of the Anxiety Disorders Association of America, New Orleans.

Beidel, D. C., Turner, S. M., & Morris, T. L. (1998). Social Phobia and Anxiety Inventory for Children. North Tonawanda, NY: Mental Health Systems, Inc.

Beidel, D. C., Turner, S. M., & Morris, T. L. (1999). The psychopathology of childhood social phobia. *Journal of the American Academy of Child and Adolescent Psychiatry, 38,* 643–650.

Beidel, D. C., Turner, S. M., & Morris, T. L. (in press). Behavioral treatment of childhood social phobia. *Journal of Consulting and Clinical Psychology.*

Berman, W. H., Heiss, G. E., & Sperling, M. B. (1994). Measuring continued attachment to parents: The continued attachment scale—parent version. *Psychological Reports, 75,* 171–182.

Berndt, T. J., & Ladd, G. W. (Eds.) (1989). *Peer relationships in children's development.* New York: Wiley.

Bhavnagri, N. P., & Parke, R. D. (1991). Parents as direct facilitators of children's peer relationships: Effects of age of child and sex of parent. *Journal of Social and Personal Relationships, 8,* 423–440.

Biederman, J., Rosenbaum, J. F., Bolduc–Murphy, E. A., Faraone, S. V., Chaloff, J., Hirshfeld, D. R., & Kagan, J. (1993). A 3-year follow-up of children with and without behavioral inhibition. *Journal of the American Academy of Child and Adolescent Psychiatry, 32,* 814–821.

Biederman, J., Rosenbaum, J. F., Chaloff, J., & Kagan, J. (1995). Behavioral inhibition as a risk factor for anxiety disorders. In J. S. March (Ed.), *Anxiety Disorders in Children and Adolescents*. New York: Guilford.

Biederman, J., Rosenbaum, J. F., Hirshfeld, D. R., Faraone, S. V., Bolduc, E. A., Gersten, M., Meminger, S. R., Kagan, J., Snidman, N., & Reznick, J. S. (1990). Psychiatric correlates of behavioral inhibition in young children of parents with and without psychiatric disorders. *Archives of General Psychiatry, 47,* 21–26.

Boivin, M., Poulin, F., & Vitaro, F. (1994). Depressed mood and peer rejection in childhood. *Development and Psychopathology, 6,* 483–498.

Booth, C. L., Rose-Krasnor, L., McKinnon, J., & Rubin, K. H. (1994). Predicting social adjustment in middle childhood: The role of preschool attachment security and maternal style. *Social Development, 3,* 189–204.

Bowlby, J. (1958). The nature of the child's tie to his mother. *International Journal of Psychoanalysis, 39,* 1–23.

Bowlby, J. (1969). *Attachment and loss: Vol. 1.* New York: Basic Books.

Bruch, M. A., & Heimberg, R. G. (1994). Difference in perceptions of parental and personal characteristics between generalized and nongeneralized social phobics. *Journal of Anxiety Disorders, 8,* 155–168.

Bruch, M. A., Heimberg, R. G., Berger, P., & Collins, T. M. (1989). Social phobia and perceptions of early parental and personal characteristics. *Anxiety Research, 2,* 57–65.

Bryant, B. K., & DeMorris, K. A. (1992). Beyond parent–child relationships: Potential links between family environments and peer relations. In R. D. Parke & G. W. Ladd (Eds.), *Family–Peer Relationships* (pp. 159–189). Hillsdale, NJ: Lawrence Erlbaum.

Buss, A. H., & Plomin, R. (1984). *Temperament: Early developing personality traits.* Hillsdale, NJ: Lawrence Erlbaum.

Calkins, S. D., & Fox, N. A. (1992). The relations among infant temperament, security of attachment, and behavioral inhibition at twenty-four months. *Child Development, 63,* 1456–1472.

Chansky, T. E., & Kendall, P. C. (1997). Social expectancies and self-perceptions in anxiety-disordered children. *Journal of Anxiety Disorders, 11,* 347–363.

Cohn, D. A., Patterson, C. J., & Christopoulos, C. (1991). The family and children's peer relations. *Journal of Social and Personal Relationships, 8,* 315–346.

Coie, J. D., Dodge, K. A., & Coppotelli, H. (1982). Dimensions and types of social status: A cross-age perspective. *Developmental Psychology, 18,* 557–570.

Dadds, M. M., Barrett, P. M., & Rapee, R. M. (1996). Family process and child anxiety and aggression: An observational analysis. *Journal of Abnormal Child Psychology, 24,* 715–734.

Daniels, D., & Plomin, R. (1985). Origins of individual differences in infant shyness. *Developmental Psychology, 21,* 118–121.

Darling, N., & Steinberg, L. (1993). Parenting style as context: An integrative model. *Psychological Bulletin, 113,* 487–496.

Dodge, C. S., Heimberg, R. G., Nyman, D., & O'Brien, G. T. (1987). Daily heterosocial interactions of high and low socially anxious college students: A diary study. *Behavior Therapy, 18,* 90–96.

Duggan, C., Sham, P., Minne, C., Lee, A., & Murray, R. (1998). Quality of parenting and vulnerability to depression: Results from a family study. *Psychological Medicine, 28,* 185–191.

Dumas, J. E., LaFreniere, P. J., & Serketich, W. J. (1995). Balance of power: A transactional analysis of control in mother–child dyads involving socially competent, aggressive, and anxious children. *Journal of Abnormal Psychology, 104,* 104–113.

Erickson, M. F., Sroufe, L. A., & Egeland, B. (1985). The relationship between quality of attachment and behavior problems in a high-risk sample. *Monographs of the Society for Research in Child Development, 50 (1–2 Serial No. 209),* 47–166.

Fagot, B. I. (1997). Attachment, parenting, and peer interactions of toddler children. *Developmental Psychology, 33,* 489–499.

Feeney, J. A., Noller, P., & Hanrahan, M. (1994). Assessing adult attachment. In M. B. Sperling & W. H. Beirman (Eds.), *Attachment in adults: Clinical and developmental perspectives.* New York: Guilford.

Fyer, A. J., Mannuzza, S., Chapman, T. F., Liebowitz, M. R., & Klein, D. F. (1993). A direct interview family study of social phobia. *Archives of General Psychiatry, 50,* 286–293.

Gadow, K. D. & Sprafkin, J. (1994). *Child Symptom Inventories Manual.* Los Angeles: Checkmate Plus.

Garcia–Coll, C., Kagan, J., & Reznick, J. S. (1984). Behavioral inhibition in young children. *Child Development, 55,* 1005–1019.

Hartup, W. W. (1979). Peer relations and the growth of social competence. In M. W. Kent & J. E. Rolf (Eds.), *Primary prevention of psychopathology* (pp. 150–170). Hanover, NE: University Press of New England.

Hazan, C., & Shaver, C. (1987). Romantic love conceptualized as an attachment process. *Journal of personality and social psychology, 52,* 511–524.

Heimberg, R. G., Acerra, M. C., & Holstein, A. (1985). Partner similarity mediates interpersonal anxiety. *Cognitive Therapy and Research, 9,* 443–453.

Heimberg, R. G., Holt, C. S., Schneier, F. R., Spitzer, R. L., & Liebowitz, M. R. (1993). The issue of subtypes in the diagnosis of social phobia. *Journal of Anxiety Disorders, 7,* 249–269.

Heimberg, R. G., Hope, D. A., Dodge, C. S., & Becker, R. E. (1990). DSM-III-R subtypes of social phobia: Comparison of generalized social phobics and public speaking phobics. *Journal of Nervous and Mental Disease, 178,* 172–179.

Herbert, J. D., Hope, D. A., & Bellack, A. S. (1992). Validity of the distinction between generalized social phobia and avoidant personality disorder. *Journal of Abnormal Psychology, 101,* 332–339.

Hirshfeld, D. R., Rosenbaum, J. F., Biederman, J., Bolduc, E. A., Faraone, S. V., Snidman, N., Reznick, J. S., & Kagan, J. (1992). Stable inhibition and its association with anxiety disorder. *Journal of the American Academy of Child and Adolescent Psychiatry, 31,* 103–111.

Holt, C. S., Heimberg, R. G., & Hope, D. A. (1992). Avoidant personality disorder and the generalized subtype of social phobia. *Journal of Abnormal Psychology, 101,* 318–325.

Hope, D. A., Rapee, R. M., Heimberg, R. G., & Dombeck, M. J. (1990). Representations of the self in social phobia: Vulnerability to social threat. *Cognitive Therapy and Research, 14,* 177–189.

Inderbitzen, H. M., Walters, K. S., & Bukowski, A. L. (1997). The role of social anxiety in adolescent peer relations: Differences among sociometric status groups and rejected subgroups. *Journal of Clinical Child Psychology, 26,* 338–348.

Ishiyama, F. I. (1984). Shyness: Anxious social sensitivity and self-isolating tendency. *Adolescence, 19,* 902–911.

Kagan, J., Reznick, J. S., & Snidman, N. (1988). The temperamental qualities of inhibition and lack of inhibition. In M. Lewis & S. M. Miller (Eds.), *Handbook of developmental psychopathology* (pp. 219–226). New York: Plenum.

Kagan, J., Snidman, N., & Arcus, D. (1993). On the temperamental categories of inhibited and uninhibited children. In K. H. Rubin & J. B. Asendorpf (Eds.), *Social withdrawal, inhibition, and shyness in childhood* (pp. 19–28). Hillsdale, NJ: Lawrence Erlbaum.

Kendler, K. S., Neale, M. C., Kessler, R. C., Heath, A. C., & Eaves, L. J. (1992). The genetic epidemiology of phobias in women: The interrelationship of agoraphobia, social phobia, situational phobia, and simple phobia. *Archives of General Psychiatry, 49,* 273–281.

Kessler, R. C., McGonagle, K. A., Zhao, S., Nelson, C. B., Hughes, M., Eshelman, S., Wittchen, H., & Kendler, K. S. (1994). Lifetime and 12-month prevalence of DSM-III-R psychiatric disorders in the United States. *Archives of General Psychiatry, 51,* 8–19.

Kobak, R., Sudler, N., & Gamble, W. (1991). Attachment and depressive symptoms in adolescence: A developmental pathways analysis. *Development and Psychopathology, 3,* 461–474.

Kovacs, M. (1992). The Children's Depression Inventory (CDI). New York: Multi-Health Systems.

Krohne, H. W., & Hock, M. (1991). Relationships between restrictive mother–child interactions and anxiety of the child. *Anxiety Research, 4,* 109–124.

Kupersmidt, J. B., & Patterson, C. J. (1991). Childhood peer rejection, aggression, withdrawal, and perceived competence as predictors of self-reported behavior problems in preadolescence. *Journal of Abnormal Child Psychology, 19,* 427–447.

Kushner, M. G., Sher, K. J., & Beitman, B. D. (1990). The relation between alcohol problems and the anxiety disorders. *American Journal of Psychiatry, 147,* 685–695.

Ladd, G. W., Profilet, S. M., & Hart, C. H. (1992). Parent's management of children's peer relations: Facilitating and supervising children's activities in the peer culture. In R. D. Parke & G. W. Ladd (Eds.), *Family-peer relationships* (pp. 215–253). Hillsdale, NJ: Erlbaum.

La Greca, A. M., & Stone, W. L. (1993). Social anxiety scale for children-revised: Factor structure and concurrent validity. *Journal of Clinical Child Psychology, 22,* 17–27.

La Greca, A. M., & Lopez, N. (1998). Social anxiety among adolescents: Linkages with peer relations and friendships. *Journal of Abnormal Child Psychology, 29,* 83–94.

La Greca, A. M., Dandes, S. K., Wick, P., Shaw, K., & Stone, W. L. (1988). Development of the social anxiety scale for children: Reliability and concurrent validity. *Journal of Clinical Child Psychology, 17,* 84–91.

Last, C. G., Perrin, S., Hersen, M., & Kazdin, A. E. (1992). DSM–III–R anxiety disorders in children: Sociodemographic and clinical characteristics. *Journal of the American Academy of Child and Adolescent Psychiatry, 31,* 928–934.

Lepine, J. P., & Lellouch, J. (1995). Classification and epidemiology of social phobia. *European Archives of Psychiatry and Clinical Neuroscience, 244,* 290–296.

Liebowitz, M. R., Gorman, J., Fyer, A. J., & Klein, D. F. (1985). Social phobia: Review of a neglected anxiety disorder. *Archives of General Psychiatry, 42,* 729–736.

Maddux, J. E., Norton, L. W., & Leary, M. R. (1988). Cognitive components of social anxiety: An investigation of the integration of self-presentation and self-efficacy theory. *Journal of Social and Clinical Psychology, 6,* 180–190.

Mannuzza, S., Fyer, A. J., Liebowitz, M. R., & Klein, D. F. (1992). Delineating the boundaries of social phobia: Its relationship to panic disorder and agoraphobia. *Journal of Anxiety Disorders, 4,* 41–59.

Mannuzza, S., Schneier, F. R., Chapman, T. F., Liebowitz, M. R., Klein, D. F., & Fyer, A. J. (1995). Generalized social phobia: Reliability and validity. *Archives of General Psychiatry, 52,* 230–237.

March, J. (1997). *Multidimensional Anxiety Scale for Children.* North Tonawanda, NY: Mental Health Systems.

Marks, I. M. (1985). Behavioral psychotherapy for anxiety disorders. *Psychiatric Clinics of North America, 8,* 25–45.

Masia, C. L., & Morris, T. L. (1998). Parental factors associated with social anxiety: Methodological limitations and suggestions for integrated behavioral research. *Clinical Psychology Science and Practice, 5,* 211–228.

Mineka, S., & Zinbarg, R. (1995). Conditioning and ethological models of social phobia. In R. G. Heimberg, M. R. Liebowitz, D. A. Hope, & F. R. Schneier (Eds.), *Social phobia: Diagnosis, assessment, and treatment.* New York: Guilford.

Morris, T. L. (1998). *School–based social effectiveness therapy for children: Treatment manual.* Unpublished manuscript.

Morris, T. L., & Huffman, D. G. (November, 1996). Influence of parenting style on the development of shyness and social anxiety. Poster presented at the annual meeting of the Association for Advancement of Behavior Therapy, New York.

Morris, T. L., & Huffman, D. G. (2000). Parental influence and social anxiety: An etiological pathway? Manuscript submitted for publication.

Morris, T. L., & Kuhn, B. R. (November, 1994). Association between parenting style and social anxiety: Retrospective report of a college sample. Paper presented at the meeting of the Association for Advancement of Behavior Therapy, San Diego, CA.

Morris, T. L., & Masia, C. L. (1998). Psychometric evaluation of the social phobia and anxiety inventory for children: Concurrent validity and normative data. *Journal of Clinical Child Psychology, 27,* 459–468.

Morris, T. L., Messer, S. C., & Gross, A. M. (1995). Enhancement of the social interaction and status of neglected children: A peer–pairing approach. *Journal of Clinical Child Psychology, 24,* 11–20.

Newcomb, A. F., Bukowski, W. M., & Pattee, L. (1993). Children's peer relations: A meta–analytic review of popular, rejected, neglected, controversial, and average sociometric status. *Psychological Bulletin, 113,* 99–128.

Ollendick, T. H., Weist, M. D., Borden, M. C., & Greene, R. W. (1992). Sociometric status and academic, behavioral, and psychological adjustment: A five-year longitudinal study. *Journal of Consulting and Clinical Psychology, 1,* 80–87.

Öst, L.-G., & Hughdahl, K. (1981). Acquisition of phobias and anxiety response patterns in clinic patients. *Behaviour Research and Therapy, 16,* 439–447.

Öst, L.-G. (1987). Age of onset in different phobias. *Journal of Abnormal Psychology, 96,* 223–229.

Page, A. C., & Andrews, G. (1996). Do specific anxiety disorders show specific drug problems? *Australian and New Zealand Journal of Psychiatry, 30*, 410–414.

Parker, G. (1983). *Parental overprotection: A risk factor in psychosocial development.* New York: Grune & Stratton.

Parker, G., Gladstone, G., Wilhelm, K., Mitchell, P., Hadzi-Pavlovic, D., & Austin, M. P. (1997). Dysfunctional parenting: Over–representation in non-melancholic depression and capacity of such specificity to refine sub-typing depression measures. *Psychiatry Research, 73*, 57–71.

Parker, J. G., & Asher, S. R. (1987). Peer relations and later personal adjustment: Are low-accepted children at risk? *Psychological Bulletin, 102*, 357–389.

Parker, G., Tupling, H., & Brown, L. B. (1979). A parental bonding instrument. *British Journal of Medical Psychology, 52*, 1–10.

Perugi, G., Simonini, E., Savino, M., Mengali, F., Cassano, G. B., & Akiskal, H. S. (1990). Primary and secondary social phobia: Psychopathologic and familial differentiations. *Comprehensive Psychiatry, 31*, 245–252.

Pollard, C. A., & Henderson, J. G. (1988). Four types of social phobia in a community sample. *Journal of Nervous and Mental Disease, 176*, 440–445.

Profilet, S. M., & Ladd, G. W. (1994). Do mothers' perceptions and concerns about preschoolers' peer competence predict their peer-management practices? *Social Development, 3*, 205–221.

Putallaz, M., & Hefflin, A. H. (1990). Parent–child interaction. In S. R. Asher & J. D. Coie (Eds.), *Peer rejection in childhood* (pp. 189–216). New York: Cambridge University Press.

Rapee, R. M., & Lim, L. (1992). Discrepancy between self- and observer ratings of performance in social phobics. *Journal of Abnormal Psychology, 101*, 728–731.

Rapee, R. M., & Melville, L. F. (1997). Recall of family factors in social phobia and panic disorder: Comparison of mother and offspring reports. *Depression and Anxiety, 5*, 7–11.

Reich, J., & Yates, W. (1988). Family history of psychiatric disorders in social phobia. *Comprehensive Psychiatry, 29*, 72–75.

Rubin, K. H. (1993). The Waterloo longitudinal project: Correlates and consequences of social withdrawal from childhood to adolescence. In K. H. Rubin & J. B. Asendorpf (Eds.), *Social Withdrawal, Inhibition, and Shyness in Childhood* (pp. 291–314). Hillsdale, NJ: Lawrence Erlbaum.

Rubin, K. H., & Mills, R. S. L. (1988). The many faces of social isolation in childhood. *Journal of Consulting and Clinical Psychology, 56*, 916–924.

Rubin, K. H., LeMare, L. J., & Lollis, S. (1990). Social withdrawal in childhood: Developmental pathways to peer rejection. In S. R. Asher & J. D. Coie (Eds.), *Peer rejection in childhood* (pp. 217–249). Cambridge, England: Cambridge University Press.

Russell, A., & Finnie, V. (1990). Preschool children's social status and maternal instructions to assist group entry. *Developmental Psychology, 26*, 603– 611.

Schneier, F. R., Johnson, J., Hornig, C. D., Liebowitz, M. R., & Weissman, M. M. (1992). Social phobia: Comorbidity and morbidity in an epidemiologic sample. *Archives of General Psychiatry, 49*, 282–288.

Spaulding, S., & Morris, T. L. (March, 1997). Direct observation of mother–child interaction: An etiological pathway for social anxiety. In C. L. Masia and T. L. Morris (Chairs), *Assessment of anxiety disorders in youth: Innovative techniques for comprehensive assessments of anxiety symptomatology.* Symposium presented at the annual meeting of the Anxiety Disorders Association of America, New Orleans.

Spaulding, S. A., Morris, T. L., & Koudelka, P. A. (April, 1995). Multiple assessment of parenting style and social anxiety: A preliminary study. Poster presented at the meeting of the Anxiety Disorders Association of America, Pittsburgh, PA.

Spielberger, C. D. (1983). *Manual for the State–Trait Anxiety Inventory (Form V)*. Palo alto, CA: Consulting Psychologists Press.

Stein, M. B., Tancer, M. E., Gelernter, C. S., Vittone, B. J., & Uhde, T. W. (1990). Major depression in patients with social phobia. *American Journal of Psychiatry, 147*, 637–639.

Stein, M. B., Walker, J. R., & Ford, D. R. (1994). Setting diagnostic thresholds for social phobia: Considerations from a community survey of social anxiety. *American Journal of Psychiatry, 151*, 408–412.

Stemberger, R. T., Turner, S. M., Beidel, D. C., & Calhoun, K. S. (1995). Social phobia: An analysis of possible developmental factors. *Journal of Abnormal Psychology, 104*, 526–531.

Stopa, L., & Clark, D. M. (1993). Cognitive processes in social phobia. *Behaviour Research and Therapy, 31*, 255–267.

Strauss, C. C., Lahey, B. B., Frick, P., Frame, C. L., & Hynd, G. W. (1988). Peer social status of children with anxiety disorders. *Journal of Consulting and Clinical Psychology, 1*, 137–141.

Thomas, A., & Chess, S. (1977). *Temperament and development*. New York: Bruner/Mazel.

Thomas, A., Chess, S., & Birch, H. G. (1968). *Temperament and behavior disorders in children*. New York: New York University Press.

Turner, S. M., & Beidel, D. C. (1989). Social phobia: Clinical syndrome, diagnosis, and comorbidity. *Clinical Psychology Review, 9*, 3–18.

Turner, S. M., & Beidel, D. C. (2000). Family interaction patterns of anxious children and their parents. Manuscript in preparation.

Turner, S. M., Beidel, D. C., Borden, J. W., Stanley, M. R., & Jacob, R. G. (1991). Social phobia: Axis I and Axis II correlates. *Journal of Abnormal Psychology, 100*, 102–106.

Turner, S. M., Beidel, D. C., Dancu, C. V., & Keys, D. J. (1986). Psychopathology of social phobia and comparison to avoidant personality disorder. *Journal of Abnormal Psychology, 95*, 389–394.

Turner, S. M., Beidel, D. C., Dancu, C. V., & Stanley, M. A. (1989). An empirically derived inventory to measure social fears and anxiety: The Social Phobia and Anxiety Inventory. *Psychological Assessment, 1*, 35–40.

Turner, S. M., Beidel, D. C., & Townsley, R. M. (1992). Social phobia: A comparison of specific and generalized subtypes and avoidant personality disorder. *Journal of Abnormal Psychology, 101*, 326–331.

Van Ijzendoorn, M. H., & Bakermans–Kranenburg, M. J. (1996). Attachment representations in mothers, fathers, adolescents, and clinical groups: A meta–analytic search for normative data. *Journal of Consulting and Clinical Psychology, 64*, 8–21.

Vasey, M. W., Daleiden, E. L., Williams, L. L., & Brown, L. M. (1995). Biased attention in childhood anxiety disorders: A preliminary study. *Journal of Abnormal Child Psychology, 23*, 267–279.

Vernberg, E. M., Abwender, D. A., Ewell, K. K., & Beery, S. H. (1992). Social anxiety and peer relationships in early adolescence: A prospective analysis. *Journal of Clinical Child Psychology, 21,* 189–196.

Warren, S. L., Huston, L., Egeland, B., & Sroufe, L. A. (1997). Child and adolescent anxiety disorders and early attachment. *Journal of the American Academy of Child and Adolescent Psychiatry, 36,* 637–644.

Wiborg, I. M., & Dahl, A. A. (1997). The recollection of parental rearing styles in patients with panic disorder. *Acta Psychiatrica Scandinavica, 96,* 58–63.

Zatz, S., & Chassin, L. (1985). Cognitions of test-anxious children under naturalistic test-taking conditions. *Journal of Consulting and Clinical Psychology, 53,* 393–401.

20

Early Separation Anxiety and Its Relationship to Adult Anxiety Disorders

DERRICK SILOVE and VIJAYA MANICAVASAGAR

Separation anxiety (SA) can be defined according to a combination of behavioral, emotional, and cognitive characteristics that together reflect the core fear of being separated from significant attachment figures or places of safety (Bowlby, 1969, 1973; Gittelman & Klein, 1985). Among the young of many species, including *Homo sapiens*, reliance on primary adult attachments is prolonged, so that vigilance about the proximity of caregivers is important to survival (Bowlby, 1969). Nevertheless, the attachment system can be effective as a survival mechanism only if it is reciprocal; that is, the strength of the caretaker's attachment parallels that of the infant (Bowlby, 1969; Lamb, Thompson, Gardner, Charnov, & Estes, 1984). Thus, it is not surprising that SA can manifest in adulthood, particularly in the form of parental anxieties about the health and safety of their infants (Hock, McBride, & Gnezda, 1989; Deater-Deckhard, Scarr, McCartney, & Eisenberg, 1994).

Although it is recognized that attachment insecurities are prevalent throughout the life course, past research on SA has tended to focus on the early phase of development. One reason may be that separation distress is most evident between the ages of 9 and 13 months, and that infants exhibit their SA openly and unambiguously. It is possible that the manifestations of SA become more covert during later years, thus preventing easy recognition of such anxieties in adults.

Pathological Forms of Separation Anxiety

Anxieties about separation usually are regarded as clinically significant when they are excessive, lead to age-inappropriate behaviors, or interfere markedly with social, family, or role functions (Gittelman-Klein & Klein, 1980). The diagnostic criteria for juvenile separation anxiety disorder (JSAD) specified in DSM-IV (American Psychiatric Association, 1994) and ICD-10 (World Health Organization, 1992), reflect both the observable behaviors associated with severe SA, as well as elements of subjective distress, such as excessive fears of harm befalling close attachment figures, or of being separated from people or places of safety. The phrasing of some criteria (for example, refusal to attend school) support the trend to reserve a diagnosis of separation anxiety disorder to the juvenile years. ICD-10 specifies that JSAD must have its onset in the preschool years and discourages clinicians from assigning the diagnosis beyond adolescence. On the other hand, DSM-IV recognizes the possible progression of separation anxiety disorder into adulthood, but suggests that such an outcome is rare and that the diagnosis should be made only when other possible primary diagnoses such as panic disorder and agoraphobia have been excluded.

A number of key issues relating to the developmental psychopathology of SA will be highlighted in this chapter. Among them is the need to demarcate on the one hand between SA as an adaptive phenomenon that promotes the survival of the species, and on the other hand a subtype of anxiety disorder with a specific pattern of presenting symptoms, longitudinal course, and pattern of family transmission. Developmental models linking early SA to adult anxiety disorders will be considered, with an important issue being the possibility that, in some cases, JSAD may persist into an adult form of the disorder. The chapter is organized according to three major aims: first, to provide an overview of early SA and its possible developmental antecedents; second, to consider adult outcomes of early SA; and finally, to present a recent formulation concerning the developmental roots of a putative form of adult separation anxiety disorder.

Early SA and Its Developmental Antecedents

Prevalence

In the early psychiatric literature, SA and school phobia tended to be regarded as synonymous, since it was assumed that school refusal was motivated primarily by a fear of being separated from attachment figures (Broadwin, 1932; Estes, Haylett, & Johnson, 1956; Coolidge, Hahn, & Peck, 1957). Differences in sampling methods and inclusion criteria have led to variability in the prevalence of school refusal reported in the literature (Chazan, 1962; Kahn & Nursten, 1962; Smith, 1970; Granell de Aldaz, Vivas, Gelfand, & Feldman, 1984). One reason for such variability in rates may be that school refusal is a heterogeneous category that includes several types of emotional disorders. Nevertheless, the overlap of school phobia with SA is substantial, with the former behavior still being included as one of the eight criteria (Criterion A) for JSAD in DSM-IV and ICD-10.

Epidemiological studies using DSM-III and DSM-III-R criteria generally have recorded point prevalence rates of between 2% and 5% for JSAD (Moreau & Weissman, 1993). For example, a study of 1869 families in Canada found a 2.4% prevalence rate for JSAD among 12- to 16-year-olds (Bowen, Offord, & Boyle, 1990). A community study in New Zealand yielded a rate of 3.5% for JSAD among 11-year-olds (Anderson, Williams, McGee, & Silva, 1987), while a study in Puerto Rico estimated the prevalence of that disorder to be 4.7% among 4- to 16-year-olds (Bird et al., 1988).

In outpatient anxiety disorder clinics for children and adolescents, rates of JSAD have been found to be as high as 47%, although substantial levels of comorbidity with other juvenile anxiety disorders are evident (Last, Hersen, Kazdin, Finkelstein, & Strauss, 1987). In particular, comorbidity has been found for JSAD with childhood overanxious disorder (Strauss, Last, Hersen, & Kazdin, 1988; Bowen et al., 1990; Bernstein & Borchardt, 1991), obsessive–compulsive disorder (Valleni-Basile et al., 1994), and depressive disorders (Kovacs, Gatsonis, Paulauskas, & Richards, 1989).

There is virtually no information about the prevalence of SA symptoms in adults. Where SA symptoms have been observed, it has generally been assumed that they form part of, or are secondary to, another diagnosis such as agoraphobia (Hafner, 1981). More recent studies have focused on adult SA as a dimensional form of anxiety, for example, in parents of young children (Hock et al., 1989) and among individuals who fear rejection (Kramer, 1993). Until recently, there have been no studies investigating the possibility that a cluster of SA symptoms may constitute an independent category of anxiety disorder in adulthood.

Etiological Factors

Genetic and Temperamental Factors. Although research data are relatively scant, evidence suggests that juvenile SA selectively aggregates in families and that genetic factors may be relevant (Goldsmith & Gottesman, 1981; Granell de Aldaz, Feldman, Vivas, & Gelfand, 1987). In a recent study by our group (Silove, Manicavasagar, O'Connell, & Morris-Yates, 1995), the Separation Anxiety Symptom Inventory (SASI) (Silove et al., 1993a) (see below) was used to examine the familial aggregation of juvenile SA in 200 twin pairs drawn from a national twin register. Structural equation modeling demonstrated that 39% of the variance in SASI scores was due to genetic effects, with this figure being slightly higher among women (41%).

Indirect evidence for a constitutional factor in SA may be inferred from studies on infant temperament. Although there is still debate concerning the role of temperament in infant development (Chess & Thomas, 1982; Sroufe, 1985), Kagan and his colleagues (Kagan, Reznick, Clarke, Snidman, & Garcia, 1984; Kagan, Reznick, & Snidman, 1987; Rosenbaum, Biederman, Hirshfeld, Bolduc, & Chaloff, 1991) have suggested that the trait of "behavioral inhibition" (defined as a tendency to withdraw from novelty) may be a risk factor for the development of several anxiety disorders in children. Behaviorally inhibited children are described as shy, inhibited and introverted and are reluctant to attend school, characteristics that may overlap with those of SA. As yet, however, little is known about the degree to which the construct of behavioral inhibition relates to that of SA.

Parental Factors. Exposure to aberrant parenting appears to be associated with the development of a range of psychiatric problems in childhood and adulthood (Parker, 1983; Crittenden, 1985; Birtchnell, 1993; Rapee, 1997).

Variations in parental "care" and "protectiveness" have been identified repeatedly as the core characteristics that may lead to psychopathology in offspring (Parker, Tupling, & Brown, 1979). Bowlby (1973, 1977) assigned primacy to early maternal overprotectiveness as the key influence in generating heightened SA in the exposed child. He described several pathogenic variants of overprotective parent–child interactions; in some patterns, the mother's own fears led to overprotective parenting, thereby provoking SA in the child, whereas in others, heightened SA in the child elicited overprotectiveness in the concerned parent.

Bowlby (1973) regarded school phobia in childhood and agoraphobia in adulthood as being the overt clinical manifestations of an underlying SA. Early family descriptions tended to support Bowlby's (1973, 1977) observations of parental overprotectiveness in the families of patients with agoraphobia (Roth, 1959; Solyom, Suberfeld, & Solyom, 1976; Buglass, Clarke, Henderson, Kreitman, & Presley, 1977). Nevertheless, the construct of agoraphobia has evolved over time, with more recent formulations regarding that symptom cluster as being secondary to panic disorder (Sheehan, 1982; Franklin, 1991). It is noteworthy, therefore, that studies using contemporary criteria for diagnosing panic disorder–agoraphobia (PD–Ag) generally have not found that sufferers report past exposure to parental overprotectiveness without associated neglect (de Ruiter & van Ijzendoorn, 1992). In a study comparing 40 agoraphobics with 41 social phobic patients, Parker (1979) found that agoraphobic patients rated their mothers but not their fathers as uncaring, but no differences emerged on the overprotection scale in comparison to control subjects. A study using the Egna Minnen Betraffinde Uppfostran (EMBU) (Perris, Jacobsson, Lindstrom, von Knorring, & Perris, 1980), which measures similar elements of parental style to the PBI, reported that agoraphobic patients characterized their mothers as lacking warmth and having behaved in a rejecting manner (Arrindell, Emmelkamp, Monsma, & Brilman, 1983). Silove (1986) found that agoraphobic patients recorded higher levels of maternal neglect on the PBI than did controls. Overprotection in the presence of adequate parental care ("affectionate constraint") appeared to be of little relevance to risk of agoraphobia, however.

In contrast, two studies have reported high levels of maternal overprotection in patients with panic disorder (Faravelli et al., 1991; Silove, Parker, Hadzi-Pavlovic, Manicavasagar, & Blaszczynski, 1991). Silove et al. (1991) found that patients with panic disorder (PD) reported somewhat higher levels of early maternal overprotection than did those with generalized anxiety disorder (GAD) who, like other anxiety groups, reported excessive exposure to maternal neglect. One possible inference drawn from that study was that there may be a subgroup of PD patients with heightened SA, a form of anxiety that may be specifically linked to earlier exposure to maternal overprotectiveness.

Thus, as a whole, recent empirical research into the parenting received by agoraphobics has failed to provide consistent support for Bowlby's

(1973, 1977) formulation that assigned a primary role to early maternal overprotection as a pathogenetic factor. One of the reasons may be that agoraphobia is no longer defined in a way that equates the disorder with an adult form of SA, an issue that will be pursued below.

Family Factors. Two methods have been used to investigate familial patterns in anxiety, namely, the "top-down" and "bottom-up" approaches (Strober & Carlson, 1982; Puig-Antich, 1984). Top-down studies identify anxious adult probands and then investigate psychopathology in their offspring; whereas bottom-up studies examine for psychiatric morbidity in parents and relatives of an identified proband with the target disorder.

Top-down studies generally have provided tentative, if indirect, support for the familial aggregation of SA (Berg, Marks, McGuire, & Lipsedge, 1974; Berg, 1976; Buglass et al., 1977; Weissman, Leckman, Merikangas, Gammon, & Prusoff, 1984; Silove & Manicavasagar, 1993; Capps, Sigman, Sena, & Henker, 1996). Berg, Marks et al. (1974) found a 7–14% prevalence of school phobia among children of mothers with agoraphobia. Furthermore, the risk of school phobia in a child was increased if the mother herself had suffered from school phobia (Berg, 1976), suggesting, albeit indirectly, the possibility that SA may be the core vulnerability transmitted within families. In a study of 74 adult volunteers with histories of school fears (Silove & Manicavasagar, 1993), those who reported heightened levels of juvenile SA were more likely to have a sibling or child who suffered from similar symptoms.

Bottom-up studies generally have demonstrated increased rates of psychiatric disturbance in the parents of children with school phobia or heightened levels of SA, but parental diagnoses appeared to lack specificity (Berg, Butler, & Pritchard, 1974; Last, Hersen, Kazdin, Francis, & Grubb, 1987; Last, Hersen, Kazdin, Orvaschel, & Perrin, 1991). Berg, Butler et al. (1974) compared school phobic adolescents with those suffering from other psychiatric disorders. One-third of mothers of both groups reported a history of psychiatric illness, more than half of which were affective disorders, but there were no specific associations between type of parental illness and child-hood disorder, respectively. Last and her associates (1987) compared the psychiatric status of mothers of children with JSAD, overanxious disorder, and other psychiatrically disturbed (nonanxious) children. Although the results revealed a strong association between anxiety disorders in mothers and children, no specific transgenerational patterns emerged for subtypes of anxiety. In a later study, first- and second-degree relatives of children with anxiety disorders ($n = 94$) were compared with relatives of children with attention deficit–hyperactivity disorder ($n = 58$) and never-psychiatrically-ill control children ($n = 87$) (Last et al., 1991). Higher rates of anxiety disorders were found in first-degree relatives of children with anxiety disorders, but the predicted association between SA in children and panic disorder in mothers was not demonstrated.

In summary, there is strong evidence that anxiety aggregates in families, but few specific associations have been found linking subtypes of anxiety disorder in parents and their children. There is some evidence to support the hypothesis that SA aggregates in families (Gittelman-Klein, 1975; Berg, 1976; Silove & Manicavasagar, 1993), but such an inference remains tentative given the paucity of available data.

Developmental Outcomes of Juvenile Separation Anxiety

Although there is convincing evidence that early SA may be the harbinger of persisting emotional disorders in adulthood, uncertainty remains about the specific diagnostic outcomes in later years (Silove, Manicavasagar, Curtis, & Blaszczynski, 1996). At least four models of developmental psychopathology may be relevant in considering the possible adult outcomes of early SA. These models are outlined below.

The Continuity Hypothesis

Early-onset anxiety disorders that extend into adulthood, such as social phobia or obsessive–compulsive disorder, conform with a "continuity" model, which suggests that the anxiety subtypes remain relatively consistent in their phenomenology over the course of development. The continuity model of anxiety appears to be in the ascendancy, with DSM-IV heralding a move away from the notion of specific anxiety disorders in childhood and adolescence by omitting previous categories such as overanxious and avoidant disorders. The sole exception is separation anxiety disorder which, although allowable as a diagnosis in adulthood (DSM-IV), appears to be rarely diagnosed in later years (Manicavasagar & Silove, 1997). Evidence will be presented later in the chapter to suggest that greater recognition of continuities between separation anxiety disorder in childhood and adulthood may bring further clarity to the issue of the transgenerational transmission of anxiety subcategories.

Early Separation Anxiety as a Risk Factor for Panic Disorder: The Transformation Hypothesis

Klein (1964, 1980) proposed an important reformulation of anxiety that identified juvenile SA as a specific risk factor to the development of PD in adulthood. It was noted that a distinctive characteristic of adults with PD was the regularity with which they reported a history of early SA, suggesting that the two types of anxiety arose from a common neurophysiological diathesis (the SA–PD hypothesis). That postulated developmental link strengthened the notion that PD and/or agoraphobia represented an unresolved "attachment–autonomy conflict" based on high levels of SA, a model that remains central to prevailing attachment theories of anxiety (de Ruiter & van Ijzendoorn, 1992; Shear, 1996).

Several studies have supported a positive association between early SA and adult PD–Ag. In a series of treatment studies involving phobic patients, 50% of agoraphobics ($n = 58$) reported a history of juvenile SA (Klein, Zitrin, Woerner, & Ross, 1983; Zitrin, Klein, Woerner, & Ross, 1983), while only 17% of patients with simple phobias ($n = 59$) reported such histories. Other studies yielding positive SA–PD associations have, however, reported lower rates of JSAD among PD patients. Breier, Charney, and Heninger (1986) found that 18% of their 60 PD patients reported a history of JSAD, with similar rates of JSAD (20%) being reported by Aronson & Logue (1987) in their group of 64 PD–Ag patients. Taken together these studies indicated that only about one-fifth of PD patients reported histories of JSAD. These observations suggest that the developmental pathways leading to the common final outcome of PD–Ag may be heterogeneous, with early SA being relevant only in a minority of cases.

A smaller number of studies have failed to find an association between early SA and PD–Ag. For example, Thyer, Ness, Cameron, and Curtis (1985) administered a 14-item self-report measure of juvenile SA to 44 agoraphobics and 83 simple phobics. That study failed to find a difference in levels of early SA between the two groups. A further study, utilizing the same questionnaire administered to 23 PDs and 28 small-animal phobics, also failed to find any differences between the two groups in reports of early SA (Thyer, Nesse, Curtis, & Cameron, 1986). A recent study by Lipsitz and colleagues (1994) examined reports of early JSAD in 252 outpatients attending an anxiety clinic. Diagnoses included PD ($n = 156$), social phobia ($n = 107$), obsessive–compulsive disorder ($n = 51$), simple phobia ($n = 57$) and generalized anxiety disorder ($n - 19$). A history of JSAD was found to be greater among patients with two or more lifetime adult anxiety disorders than among those with one anxiety disorder (37% vs. 14%, respectively). There were no differences, however, in rates of JSAD across the PD, social phobia, and obsessive–compulsive disorder patient subgroups, whether or not they had comorbid diagnoses.

As noted above, the changes in the conceptualization of agoraphobia in recent years has led to an increasing tendency to restrict that diagnosis to a constellation of avoidance behaviors that are secondary to PD (Sheehan, 1982; Franklin, 1991). According to DSM-III and DSM-IV, individuals with agoraphobia report fears of suffering from panic symptoms in specific situations such as on public transport, in crowded or enclosed spaces, or while waiting (for example, in a queue). Anticipatory anxiety ("fear of fear") thus centers on the expectation of having further panic attacks in a situation where escape is difficult or where help is unavailable (Chambless & Goldstein, 1981). In contrast, although sufferers of SA may report the occurrence of panic attacks, we postulated (Manicavasagar & Silove, 1997) that these are mainly situation-specific and relate to actual or threatened separations from close attachments, or cognitions that signal such threats. Thus, the apparent avoidance behavior associated with SA arises from an unwillingness to be separated from people or places that represent safety and security. It therefore seems likely that, in comparison with the broader concept of the disorder used by Bowlby (1973), the more restricted definition of agoraphobia characteristic of contemporary usage may not include persons suffering from high levels of SA. Nevertheless, difficulties may be encountered in distinguishing between the two symptom patterns, since SA and agoraphobia both lead to a restriction in independent activities and may be associated with panic attacks.

Inconsistencies in measuring SA symptoms retrospectively have added to the problem of investigating the SA–PD hypothesis, since none of the measures used have been subjected to exhaustive psychometric evaluation. The development of the SASI (Silove et al., 1993a), and the subsequent series of studies conducted using the measure, represented an attempt to address that issue. Because of the potential inaccuracies in making a categorical (present–absent) assignment of SA retrospectively, the 15-item SASI was developed as a dimensional measure. The SASI records adults' memories of SA experiences over the first 18 years of life (Silove et al., 1993a). The measure has a coherent factor structure, satisfactory internal consistency (Cronbach's alpha = 0.86 to 0.88), test–retest reliability (intraclass correlations = 0.86 to 0.98), and generates scores that are not influenced by changes in state anxiety or depression. A square-root transformation is applied to normalize the distribution of scores. In separate studies, concurrent validity was suggested by associations between SASI scores and a history of JSAD in early life (Silove et al., 1993a), and with a history of early school fears (Silove & Manicavasagar, 1993). Furthermore, observer reports within twin pairs have corroborated siblings' SASI scores, providing a crude external validation of the measure (Silove et al., 1993a).

In a preliminary study using the SASI to assess 74 anxiety patients (Silove et al., 1993b), a trend was found for PD patients ($n = 38$) to return higher SA scores than GAD patients ($n = 36$) (3.9 vs. 3.4, respectively) (Silove et al., 1993b). In contrast, a community control group returned a low mean SASI score of 2.7. Differences in SASI scores between the two anxiety subgroups were independent of the severity of general symptoms of anxiety and depression at the time of reporting. We suggested that early SA may exert a graduated risk, with moderate levels predisposing subjects to GAD and higher levels increasing the risk to panic attacks and/or PD.

In a second study (Silove, Harris et al., 1995), 136 economically and socially disadvantaged women living in a government housing estate in Sydney were administered the Diagnostic Interview Schedule (Robins, Helzer, Croughlen, & Ratcliffe, 1981) and the SASI. Subjects with a lifetime history of PD–Ag reported significantly higher levels of SA (3.6) than a composite group with other anxiety disorders without panic (2.9). This distinction was not accounted for by differences in neuroticism or general symptoms of anxiety or depression across the two groups (Silove, Harris et al., 1995). However, there was a high degree of comorbidity in the sample, thus preventing a definitive examination of the association of early SA with "pure" subtypes of adult anxiety disorders.

In a further study, the clustering technique of mixture analysis (Sweeney, 1993) was applied to early SA scores returned by a composite group of adult community and patient samples ($n = 1800$) (Manicavasagar, Silove, & Hadzi-Pavlovic, 1998). Two subpopulations emerged, one with "high" and another with "low" SA scores. Assignment to the "high" early SA subgroup for subtypes of adult anxiety disorder ranged from 37% for simple phobia to 52% for social phobia. Forty-nine percent of PD–Ag subjects were assigned to the high early SA subgroup, and that developmental link was the only association that remained statistically significant in a multiple regression analysis. It is noteworthy, however, that 51% of PD–Ag subjects were not assigned to the high-SA subgroup, suggesting that at least a half of that adult diagnostic grouping do not differ from normals in their levels of early SA.

Uncertainties about the long-term diagnostic outcome of early SA are evident in longitudinal studies. Nevertheless, some studies have suggested, albeit tentatively, that children continue to suffer SA symptoms in adulthood. Adult anxieties include fears of separation from close attachment figures, anxiety about travelling away from home, and an overly constrained approach to life (Coolidge, Brodie, & Feeney, 1964; Weiss & Burke, 1970). The 5- to 10-year follow-up study of school phobic children by Coolidge and colleagues (1964) found that up to 55% were manifesting symptoms related to the original phobia. Weiss & Burke (1970) interviewed 14 hospitalized school phobic children and adolescents between 5 and 10 years after treatment. As adults, 7 of the 14 were judged to be experiencing difficulties in their relationships, and were "constricted" in their affect, in spite of being well-adjusted at work (Weiss & Burke, 1970). Nevertheless, the classification of such adult anxieties has remained unclear, possibly because a diagnosis of adult separation anxiety disorder has not been clearly accepted within prevailing diagnostic traditions.

Separation Anxiety as One Element of General Anxiety or as an Adaptive Response

As discussed earlier, several studies have suggested that heightened levels of early SA may predispose to a variety of anxiety disorders (Tyrer & Tyrer, 1974; Lipsitz et al., 1994) rather than specifically to PD–Ag. Thus, according to a unitary notion of neurosis (Tyrer, 1985), SA might be regarded as only one component of a general neurotic vulnerability. However, genetic data (Silove, Manicavasagar et al., 1995), together with other measures of construct validity (Silove et al., 1993a), have suggested that SA may be distinguishable from the construct of neuroticism, and the diagnosis of JSAD appears to have consolidated its status as a distinctive category in both the DSM and ICD systems.

Nevertheless, it is possible that natural separation fears may be heightened in a nonspecific manner when a person feels threatened or unable to cope for a variety of reasons (Bowlby, 1973, 1977). Such reactions may have an adaptive function in that transiently heightened SA may elicit protection and assistance from attachment figures in times of need. Heightened SA may thus constitute a common reaction pattern to a range of physical and psychological disorders in both childhood and adulthood, and thus may have no specific association with any one type of psychiatric disorder.

Early Separation Anxiety as a Precursor of Personality Disorder in Adulthood

Of the ten major personality disorders listed in DSM-IV and ICD-10, dependent personality is the one with the characteristics that bear the closest similarities to those of separation anxiety disorder. Although persons diagnosed with dependent personality disorder display clinging behaviors and fears of separation, they also exhibit submissive tendencies and experience great difficulty in making everyday decisions or in initiating projects or tasks, characteristics that are assumed to arise from a lack of confidence in being able to function adequately without the help of others (Hirschfeld, Shea, & Weise, 1991). Also, individuals with dependent personality disorder typically are indiscriminate in their dependency behaviors which are directed towards a wide range of others (Livesley, Schroeder, & Jackson,1990; Bornstein, 1992). Thus, if persons with dependent personalities develop anxiety, it is usually related to fears of not being able to cope. Such characteristics, however, are not central to the construct of SA. The anxieties of individuals with heightened levels of SA typically are focused on the safety and whereabouts of a small number of specific attachment figures (Bowlby, 1973), and sufferers are not necessarily inadequate in other aspects of their lives (Manicavasagar & Silove, 1997). Nevertheless, further research is required to examine more fully the relationship between SA symptoms and the development of personality disorders in adulthood.

In summary, several possible developmental pathways may account for the psychosocial impairments suffered by adults who experienced high levels of SA in their early lives. Although there is some empirical support for the hypothesis that SA is linked to risk of later PD, the relationship does not appear to be highly specific or exclusive: early SA may be associated with other anxiety-related outcomes, and a large portion of persons with adult PD do not report heightened levels of early SA.

Recent Formulations Regarding the Adult Outcome of JSAD

Based on clinical observations in treating adult anxiety patients (Manicavasagar & Silove, 1997) and on a study of volunteers recruited through the media (Manicavasagar, Silove, & Curtis, 1997), we have suggested that the most likely pathological outcome of early separation anxiety may be an adult equivalent form of the disorder. In the preliminary clinical study (Manicavasagar & Silove, 1997), three subjects, two recruited from an anxiety clinic and one from a private clinic, were identified on clinical impressions as suffering from an adult form of separation anxiety disorder. The second study (Manicavasagar et al., 1997) explored more systematically the phenomenology, onset, and course of adult SA in a sample of 36 community volunteers. Two provisional measures of adult SA were used: a self-report questionnaire, the Adult Separation Anxiety Checklist (ASA-CL); and the Adult Separation Anxiety Semistructured Interview (ASA-SI).

The two studies indicated that it is possible to identify a primary form of separation anxiety disorder in adulthood and that the core anxieties mirror those observed in childhood, even though some of the features are modified by maturation. The adult volunteers complained of ego-dystonic and unrealistic fears of separation from key attachment figures, as well as extreme anxiety that harm might befall such individuals (Manicavasagar et al., 1997). Sufferers experienced frustrating limitations in their lives imposed by the need to maintain proximity to, or at least telephone contact with, their key attachment figures. Affected adults commonly (but not always) dated SA symptoms to their early years, suggesting that there may be close continuities between the juvenile and adult forms of the disorder.

For many subjects, symptoms were episodic rather than continuous. Detailed assessments suggested that other diagnostic categories, such as agoraphobia, dependent personality disorder, and obsessive–compulsive disorder, were not appropriate as primary diagnoses for these subjects. In the majority of cases of ASAD, time of onset of comorbid disorders and the subjects' own accounts of which symptom clusters were experienced as dominant, supported the conclusion that comorbid symptoms (for example, of panic, depression, or generalized anxiety) were secondary to those of underlying SA. One of the three anxiety patients and about one-third of the volunteer sample reported that their SA symptoms began de novo in adulthood, in all instances, following a major traumatic event or loss (death, divorce).

We have therefore speculated that adults with a putative separation anxiety disorder may be particularly prone to developing severe anxiety symptoms including panic attacks when faced with threats to intimate bonds (Manicavasagar & Silove, 1997). It is also possible that, because of the prevailing tradition of restricting the diagnosis of separation anxiety disorder to childhood, and because affected adults may attempt to conceal their symptoms from others (Manicavasagar & Silove, 1997), older sufferers may present for treatment only when their anxiety becomes extreme, especially when they experience panic. Thus, clinicians may be disposed to making the diagnosis of PD in adults and hence overlook the possibility that persisting separation anxiety disorder underlies the more overt symptoms of panic. Thus, the hypothesis being proposed is that the link between early SA and risk to adult PD, and possibly other anxiety disorders, may be mediated by the persistence of separation anxiety disorder into adulthood.

On the basis of such preliminary findings, a study was undertaken to identify the putative ASAD category amongst adult patients attending an anxiety clinic (Manicavasagar, Silove, Curtis, & Wagner, 2000). Patients assigned to the ASAD category reported higher levels of juvenile SA compared with other anxiety patients. In the absence of ASAD, PD–Ag patients reported levels of early SA that were within the normal range of community samples. There was no specificity in the relation of ASAD with other adult anxiety diagnoses. Where comorbidity existed, symptoms of SA appeared to predate the onset of other anxiety subtypes. This study thus provides further tentative support for the notion that ASAD may be diagnosable in adults and that it may have its origins in heightened levels of juvenile SA.

Two subsequent studies examined familial factors relevant to adult SA. The first involved diagnostic assessments of parents of children attending an anxiety clinic (Manicavasagar, Silove, Rapee, Waters, & Momartin, in press). A high level of concordance was found between a diagnosis of separation anxiety disorder in children and the same putative diagnosis in their parents (63%). No other parental anxiety or depressive disorder was associated with JSAD in children, suggesting a high degree of specificity for the familial clustering of SA symptoms. In a further study, the possibility was investigated that early parenting styles might differentiate between persons assigned to the ASAD category and those with PD–Ag. ASAD subjects reported significantly higher rates of exposure to maternal overprotectiveness than did those with PD–Ag, and the latter category did not differ in their ratings of parental overprotectiveness from general-practice controls. Overlap of diagnostic categories presented a methodological limitation, however, so that a larger sample would be needed to confirm this differential parenting pattern. Also, it remains uncertain whether high levels of maternal overprotectiveness constitutes an etiological factor to SA in offspring, or an understandable parental response to an insecure child.

In summary, our recent empirical work suggests, at least tentatively, that SA symptoms in adulthood may be reliably identified, and in some cases, may coalesce to form a distinct anxiety subcategory; that high levels of juvenile SA are exclusively associated with ASAD rather than with any other adult anxiety or depressive subcategory; and that there may be a high level of familial aggregation of SA, with some specificity in antecedent parental risk factors, especially in relation to maternal overprotectiveness.

A Developmental Model of Separation Anxiety

As indicated earlier, SA has assumed a central place in theories of attachment that are relevant to developmental psychopathology. Nevertheless, although SA has been regarded as an important early risk factor to adult neurotic disorders, the precise nature of the developmental pathways involved has remained somewhat unclear (Silove et al., 1996; Shear, 1996). Interest has tended to focus on the SA–PD hypothesis, with little research attention being given to the possible persistence of SA into adulthood.

The data reported provide the basis for proposing a specific model of SA that is consistent with the broad developmental framework for depressive and anxiety disorders outlined by Brown and his colleagues (Brown & Harris, 1993; Brown, Harris, & Eales, 1993). According to that general model, early family adversity creates vulnerability in the child who is then predisposed to the later development of adult anxiety and depressive disorders under specific conditions of stress. Early vulnerability may be provoked by aberrant styles of parenting, childhood abuse, or frequent changes of caregivers, all of which engender insecurities in the child (Brown & Harris, 1993; Brown et al., 1993). The lasting impact on self-esteem and confidence that such adverse early experiences incur may perpetuate the cycle of vulnerability into adult life (Parker, 1983; Parker, Barrett, & Hickie, 1992).

The model proposed for SA (fig. 20.1) represents a special case of the more general model.

Why some children recover from JSAD while others experience persisting symptoms into adulthood remains to be investigated. Longitudinal studies of school phobic children have suggested that approximately a third (Baker & Wills, 1979) to a half (Weiss & Burke, 1970; Berg & Jackson, 1985) of affected children demonstrate persisting levels of psychosocial dysfunction in later years. Vulnerability to a poor prognosis may be determined by genetic factors, ongoing bonding difficulties, and/or other interpersonal stressors, but the contribution of these factors remains to be investigated further.

In two of the studies reported (Manicavasagar & Silove, 1997; Manicavasagar et al., 1997) we found that SA symptoms appeared to develop de novo in adulthood in a minority of subjects. One possibility is that subjects who reported an adult onset of ASAD had simply forgotten their childhood symptoms of SA. However, it is possible that age of onset of separation anxiety disorder may follow a skewed distribution, with most

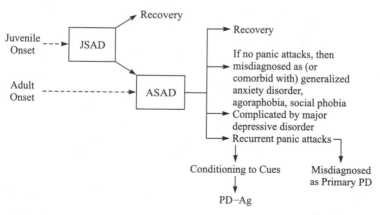

Figure 20.1. A putative developmental pathway leading to adult separation anxiety disorder.

cases commencing in early life, but some being precipitated in early adult-hood. Thus, it is possible that a combination of early protective influences and later provocative factors may delay the onset of separation anxiety dis-order in a minority of cases. For example, highly protective environments in the family of origin may prevent the early expression of SA; but, once the person has left home, precipitating factors such as illness or threats to adult intimate bonds may provoke the underlying diathesis. Thus, the factors that contribute to the adult onset of separation anxiety disorder warrant further investigation.

In all studies reported herein, there was a degree of comorbidity of ASAD with other anxiety and affective disorders, most frequently with major depressive disorder and PD–Ag. It seems likely that agoraphobia in particular could be mistaken for ASAD. Behavioural manifestations of agoraphobia, such as avoiding leaving the home or requiring companionship to do so, are also key features of ASAD. However, the behaviors in agora-phobic subjects arise out of anticipatory fears about being in particular phobic situations that provoke panic or limited symptom attacks. In con-trast, sufferers of ASAD tend to report feeling more secure at home because that location symbolizes security or signifies the proximity of close attach-ment figures. Thus their worries mainly revolve around the whereabouts and safety of their loved ones. Hence, although agoraphobia and SA share some similarities in their behavioral manifestations, they appear to differ funda-mentally in the factors that motivate such behaviors.

Epidemiological studies consistently report that the peak age of onset for PD and agoraphobia is between 20 and 40 years (Robins et al., 1984; Wells, Bushell, Hornblow, Joyce, & Oakley-Brown, 1989; Kessler et al., 1994; Kendler, Davis, & Kessler, 1997). In contrast, separation anxiety disorder generally has its origins in childhood and adolescence (DSM-IV; ICD-10). Thus, epidemiological evidence would support the general contention that where juvenile SA symptoms persist into adulthood and comorbidity with PD–Ag occurs, SA is the pre-existing disorder. Participant reports in our volunteer study (Manicavasagar et al., 1997) supported that sequence in the majority of cases, and subjects identified adult SA as being the direct cause of their disability and distress.

Where ASAD is primary there are several possible links to panic symp-toms (see fig. 20.1). One possibility is that symptoms of panic may be integral to ASAD; that is, where SA fears are sufficiently provoked, symptoms of panic supervene. If persons with ASAD experience repeated panic attacks, however, then panic symptoms may become self-perpetuating (as indicated in fig. 20.1). Thus, although initially triggered by ASAD, panic attacks may become relatively autonomous, with "fear of fear" and other immediate contingencies generating further panic (Clark, 1986). Secondary condition-ing may then lead to the development of agoraphobia, warranting an addi-tional diagnosis of PD–Ag. At that point, the features of PD–Ag may be more obvious than those of SA, thus overshadowing the initial disorder (ASAD).

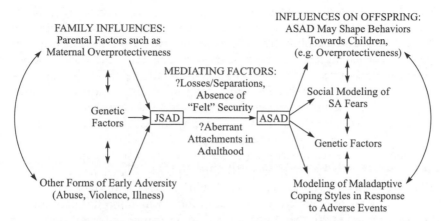

Figure 20.2. A family model for the transmission of separation anxiety disorder.

A Familial Model of Separation Anxiety

The data obtained on adult manifestations of SA allow tentative speculation about the familial transmission of such anxieties (see fig. 20.2).

Genetic factors appear to be influential in the transmission of SA particularly in women (Silove, Harris et al., 1995). Once acquired, SA symptoms in parents may exert direct effects on their relationships with their children (see fig. 20.2). Parents may be a powerful source of social modeling of SA-related fears and behaviors. As indicated by our recent study, a specific type of parenting style, maternal overprotectiveness, may be associated with the development of separation anxiety disorder in adult offspring. Overprotectiveness itself may be a manifestation of heightened SA in parents, thus complicating the etiological relationship between that maternal style and SA in children. Finally, adverse events may act to accentuate SA in both parents and their children. Thus, a complex interplay of genetic, behavioral, and environmental factors may magnify risk of transmission of severe SA within vulnerable families.

Caveats

Other conceptualizations of the data reported herein may have merit. For example, various aspects of anxiety such as panic attacks, avoidance behavior, and SA, amongst others, may represent components of a spectrum concept of panic disorder (Cassano et al., 1997). Alternatively, a focus on temperament (Kagan et al., 1984, 1987; Rosenbaum et al., 1991) may suggest a developmental model that blurs the distinction between personality traits such as dependency, and putative Axis-I symptoms of SA. Further investigations will be needed to test the validity of competing nosological formulations relevant to SA.

The measures used to assess adult SA (the ASA-SI and the ASA-CL) are provisional and the instruments will require rigorous further psychometric evaluation. Such tests should include, inter alia, thorough item analysis, factor analysis using representative samples, and measures of concurrent validity, for example, by using corroborative reports of observed SA behaviors provided by close attachment figures (mothers, spouses, children). Other multivariate statistical procedures, such as cluster analysis or latent class analysis, may be useful in confirming whether SA symptoms form a distinct anxiety subcategory. The identification of biological markers for ASAD may help to delineate the putative disorder further—as yet, neurophysiological evidence relevant to SA is limited to animal studies (e.g., Hofer, 1995; Insel, 1997).

It must also be acknowledged that several of the instruments used in our studies, such as the SASI and the PBI, although psychometrically evaluated (Silove et al., 1993a; Parker et al. 1979; Parker, 1986), are based on retrospective reports and therefore are susceptible to anamnestic inaccuracies. Prospective studies are therefore required to determine more accurately the possible developmental pathways involving SA. Such studies would also allow a closer examination of possible factors, such as early life events, adverse family environments, and history of aberrant parenting, that may contribute to the persistence of SA into adulthood. The relationship between attachment styles and wider social supports to the onset and persistence of SA also remains to be elucidated more fully.

If it is confirmed that ASAD warrants greater recognition as an adult subtype of anxiety, then the inferences drawn from past epidemiological and clinical studies on adults would require revision, since those investigations have failed to include a category of ASAD. It is possible that persons with ASAD have been misdiagnosed (as PD–Ag, GAD, etc.), or omitted altogether from case assignments. Thus, the inclusion of ASAD could alter current notions of the prevalence, patterns of comorbidity, and risk factor profiles for the other adult anxiety subcategories.

If a specific pattern of developmental continuity in SA can be confirmed, it would suggest that the SA–PD hypothesis requires revision. Results of the empirical studies reported herein suggest that the link between juvenile SA and adult PD may be indirect, being mediated by the presence of ASAD. The proposition that a substantial portion of clinical cases presenting with panic may be persons suffering primarily from ASAD thus has potentially important implications for the way in which panic disorder is conceptualized. It suggests that panic disorder may be a heterogeneous category representing a final common pathway for several pathogenic processes, with the persistence of separation anxiety disorder from childhood into adulthood being only one such route.

Conclusions

Attachment behavior and anxieties about the security of interpersonal bonds appear to be fundamental experiences of human existence. The boundary between normal and pathological fears concerning the safety and whereabouts of attachment figures is likely to depend on many influences, including cultural, social, and historical factors. The conceptualization of SA presented herein, and the empirical investigations that were prompted by such notions, invariably were based on a simplification of what is undoubtedly a complex social and psychophysiological phenomenon. Data from multiple sources will be needed, therefore, to delineate in a more comprehensive manner the complex developmental pathways that lead to the persistence of SA symptoms across the life course.

References

American Psychiatric Association (1994). *Diagnostic and statistical manual* (4th ed). Washington, DC: American Psychiatric Press.

Anderson, J., Williams, S., McGee, R., & Silva, P. (1987). DSM-III disorders in preadolescent children: Prevalence in a large sample from the general population. *Archives of General Psychiatry, 44,* 69–76.

Aronson, T., & Logue, C. (1987). On the longitudinal course of panic disorder: Developmental history and predictors of phobic complications. *Comprehensive Psychiatry, 28,* 344–355.

Arrindell, W., Emmelkamp, P., Monsma, A., & Brilman, E. (1983). The role of perceived parental rearing practices in the etiology of phobic disorders: A controlled study. *British Journal of Psychiatry, 43,* 183–187.

Baker, H., & Wills, U., (1979). School phobic children at work. *British Journal of Psychiatry, 135,* 561–564.

Berg, I. (1976). School phobia in the children of agoraphobic women. *British Journal of Psychiatry, 128,* 86–89.

Berg, I., & Jackson, A. (1985). Teenage school refusers grow up: A follow-up study of 168 subjects, ten years on average after in-patient treatment. *British Journal of Psychiatry, 147,* 366–370.

Berg, I., Butler, A., & Pritchard, J. (1974). Psychiatric illness in the mothers of school-phobic adolescents. *British Journal of Psychiatry, 125,* 466–467.

Berg, I., Marks, I., McGuire, R., & Lipsedge, M. (1974). School phobia and agoraphobia. *Psychological Medicine, 4,* 428–434.

Bernstein, G. A., & Borchardt, C. M. (1991). Anxiety disorders of childhood and adolescence: A critical review. *Journal of the American Academy of Child and Adolescent Psychiatry, 30,* 519–532.

Bird, H. R., Canino, G., Rubio-Stipec, M., Gould, M. S., Ribera, J., Sesman, M., Woodburg, M., Heurtas-Goldman, S., Pagan, A., Sanchez-Lacay, R., & Moscoso, M. (1988). Estimates of the prevalence of childhood maladjustment in a community survey in Puerto Rico: The use of comorbid measures. *Archives of General Psychiatry, 45,* 1120-1126.

Birtchnell, J. (1993). Does recollection of exposure to poor maternal care in childhood affect later ability to relate? *British Journal of Psychiatry, 162,* 335–344.

Bornstein, R. E. (1992). The dependent personality: Development, social and clinical perspectives. *Psychological Bulletin, 112,* 3–23.

Bowen, R., Offord, D., & Boyle, M. (1990). The prevalence of overanxious disorder and separation anxiety disorder. *Journal of the American Academy of Child and Adolescent Psychiatry, 29,* 753–758.

Bowlby, J. (1969). *Attachment and loss: Vol. I. Attachment.* London: Penguin Books.

Bowlby, J. (1973). *Attachment and loss: Vol. II. Separation: Anxiety and anger.* New York: Basic Books.

Bowlby, J. (1977). The making and breaking of affectional bonds: I. Etiology and psychopathology in the light of attachment theory. *British Journal of Psychiatry, 130,* 201–210.

Breier, A., Charney, D., & Heninger, G. (1986). Agoraphobia with panic attacks. *Archives of General Psychiatry, 43,* 1029–1036.

Broadwin, I. T. (1932). A contribution to the study of truancy. *American Journal of Orthopsychiatry, 2,* 253–259.

Brown, G., & Harris, T. (1993). Etiology of anxiety and depressive disorders in an inner-city population: 1. Early adversity. *Psychological Medicine, 23,* 143–154.

Brown, G., Harris, T., & Eales, M. (1993). Etiology of anxiety and depressive disorders in an inner-city population: 2. Comorbidity and adversity. *Psychological Medicine, 23,* 155–165.

Buglass, D., Clarke, J., Henderson, A., Kreitman, N., & Presley, A. (1977). A study of agoraphobic housewives. *Psychological Medicine, 7,* 73–86.

Capps, L., Sigman, M., Sena, R., & Henker, B. (1996). Fear, anxiety and perceived control in children of agoraphobic parents. *Journal of Child Psychology and Psychiatry, 37,* 445–452.

Cassano, G. B., Michelini, S., Shear, M. K., Coli, E., Maser, J. D., & Frank, E. (1997). The panic–agoraphobia spectrum: A descriptive approach to the assessment and treatment of subtle symptoms. *American Journal of Psychiatry, 154,* 27–38.

Chambless, D. L., & Goldstein, A. J. (1981). Clinical treatment of agoraphobia. In M. Mavissakalian & D. H. Barlow (Eds.), *Phobia: Psychological and pharmacological treatment* (pp. 103–144). New York: Guilford.

Chazan, M. (1962). School phobia. *British Journal of Educational Psychology, 32,* 201–217.

Chess, S., & Thomas, A. (1982). Infant bonding: mystique and reality. *American Journal of Orthopsychiatry, 52,* 213–222.

Clark, D. M. (1986). A cognitive approach to panic. *Behaviour Research and Therapy, 24,* 461–470.

Coolidge, J., Brodie, R., & Feeney, B. (1964). A ten-year follow-up study of sixty-six school-phobic children. *American Journal of Orthopsychiatry, 34,* 675–684.

Coolidge, J. C., Hahn, P. B., & Peck, A. L. (1957). School phobia: Neurotic crisis or way of life. *American Journal of Orthopsychiatry, 27,* 296–306.

Crittenden, P. (1985). Maltreated infants: vulnerability and resilience. *Journal of Child Psychology and Psychiatry, 26,* 85–106.

de Ruiter, C., & van Ijzendoorn, M. (1992). Agoraphobia and anxious–ambivalent attachment: An integrative review. *Journal of Anxiety Disorders, 6,* 365–381.

Deater-Deckhard, K., Scarr, S., McCartney, K., & Eisenberg, M. (1994). Paternal separation anxiety: Relationship with parenting stress, child-rearing attitudes, and maternal anxieties. *Psychological Science, 5,* 341–346.

Estes, H., Haylett, C., & Johnson, A. (1956). Separation anxiety. *American Journal of Psychotherapy, 10,* 682–695.

Faravelli, C., Panichi, C., Pallanti, S., Paterniti, S., Crecu, L., & Rivelli, S. (1991). Perception of early parenting in panic and agoraphobia. *Acta Psychiatrica Scandinavica, 84,* 6–8.

Franklin J. A. (1991). Agoraphobia. *International Review of Psychiatry, 3,* 151–162.

Gittelman, R., & Klein, D. (1985). Childhood separation anxiety and adult agoraphobia. In A. Tuma & J. Maser (Eds.), *Anxiety and anxiety disorders* (pp. 389–402). Hillsdale, NJ: Lawrence Erlbaum.

Gittelman-Klein, R. (1975). Psychiatric characteristics of the relatives of school phobic children. In D. Siva Sankar (Ed.), *Mental health in children* (pp. 325–334). Westbury, NY: PJD Publications.

Gittelman-Klein, R. & Klein, D. (1980). Separation anxiety in school refusal and its treatment with drugs. In L. Hersov & I. Berg (Eds.), *Out of school* (pp. 321–341). London: Wiley.

Goldsmith, H., & Gottesman, I. (1981). Origins of variation in behavioral style: A longitudinal study of temperament in young twins. *Child Development, 52,* 91–103.

Granell de Aldaz, E., Feldman, L., Vivas, E., & Gelfand, D. (1987). Characteristics of Venezuelan school refusers: Toward the development of a high-risk profile. *Journal of Nervous and Mental Disease, 175,* 402–407.

Granell de Aldaz, E., Vivas, E., Gelfand, D., & Feldman, L. (1984). Estimating the prevalence of school refusal and school-related fears. *Journal of Nervous and Mental Disease, 172,* 722–729.

Hafner, R. J. (1981). Agoraphobia in men. *Australian and New Zealand Journal of Psychiatry, 15,* 243–249.

Hirschfeld, R. M. A., Shea, M. T., & Weise, R. (1991). Dependent personality disorder: Perspectives for DSM-IV. *Journal of Personality Disorders, 5,* 135–149.

Hock, E., McBride, S., & Gnezda, T. (1989). Maternal separation anxiety: Mother–infant separations from the maternal perspective. *Child Development, 60,* 793–802.

Hofer, M. A. (1995). *Hidden regulators: Implications for a new understanding of attachment, separation, and loss.* Reprinted from S. Goldberg, R. Muir, & J. Kerr, (Eds.), *Attachment theory: Social, developmental, and clinical perspectives* (pp. 203–230). Hillsdale, NJ: Analytic Press.

Insel, T. R. (1997). A neurobiological basis of social attachment. *American Journal of Psychiatry, 154,* 726–735.

Kagan, J., Reznick, J. S., Clarke, C., Snidman, N., & Garcia, C. (1984). Behavioral inhibition to the unfamiliar. *Child Development, 55,* 2212–2225.

Kagan, J., Reznick, J. S., & Snidman, N. (1987). The physiology and psychology of behavioral inhibition in children. *Child Development, 58,* 1459–1473.

Kahn, J., & Nursten, J. (1962). School refusal: A comprehensive view of school phobia and other failures of school attendance. *American Journal of Orthopsychiatry, 32,* 707–718.

Kendler, K., Davis, C. G., & Kessler, R. C. (1997). The familial aggregation of common psychiatric and substance use disorders in the National Comorbidity Survey: A family history study. *British Journal of Psychiatry, 170,* 541–548.

Kessler, R. C., McGonagle, K. A., Zhao, S., Nelson, C. V., Hughes, M., Eshleman, S., Wittchen, H. U., & Kendler, K. S. (1994). Lifetime and 12-month prevalence of DSM-III-R psychiatric disorders in the United States: Results from the National Comorbidity Survey. *Archives of General Psychiatry, 51,* 8–19.

Klein, D. (1964). Delineation of two drug-responsive anxiety syndromes. *Psychopharmacologia, 5,* 397–408.

Klein, D. (1980). Anxiety reconceptualized: Early experience with imipramine and anxiety. *Comprehensive Psychiatry, 21,* 411–427.

Klein, D. F., Zitrin, C. M., Woerner, M. G., & Ross, D. C. (1983). Treatment of phobias: II. Behavior therapy and supportive psychotherapy: are there any specific ingredients? *Archives of General Psychiatry, 40,* 139–145.

Kovacs, M., Gatsonis, C., Paulauskas, S. L., & Richards, C. (1989). Depressive disorder in childhood: IV. A longitudinal study of comorbidity with, and risks for, anxiety disorders. *Archives of General Psychiatry, 46,* 776–782.

Kramer, P. D. (1993). *Listening to Prozac.* New York: Viking.

Lamb, M. E., Thompson, R. A., Gardner, W., Charnov, E. L., & Estes, D. (1984). Security of infantile attachment as assessed in the 'strange situation': Its study and biological interpretation. *Behavioural and Brain Sciences, 7,* 127–147.

Last, C., Hersen, M., Kazdin, A., Finkelstein, R., & Strauss, C. (1987). Comparison of DSM-III separation anxiety and overanxious disorders: Demographic characteristics and patterns of comorbidity. *Journal of the American Academy of Child and Adolescent Psychiatry, 26,* 527–531.

Last, C., Hersen, M., Kazdin, A., Francis, G., & Grubb, H. J. (1987). Psychiatric illness in the mothers of anxious children. *American Journal of Psychiatry, 144,* 1580–1583.

Last, C., Hersen, M., Kazdin, A., Orvaschel, H., & Perrin, S. (1991). Anxiety disorders in children and their families. *Archives of General Psychiatry, 48,* 928–534.

Lipsitz, J. D., Martin, L. Y., Mannuzza, S., Chapman, T. F., Liebowitz, M. R., Klein, D. F., & Fyer, A. J. (1994). Childhood separation anxiety disorder in patients with adult anxiety disorders. *American Journal of Psychiatry, 151,* 927–929.

Livesley, W. J., Schroeder, M. L., & Jackson, D. N. (1990). Dependent personality disorder and attachment problems. *Journal of Personality Disorders, 4,* 131–140.

Manicavasagar, V., & Silove, D. (1997). Is there an adult form of separation anxiety disorder? A brief clinical report. *Australian and New Zealand Journal of Psychiatry, 31,* 299–303.

Manicavasagar, V., Silove, D., & Curtis, J. (1997). Separation anxiety in adulthood: A phenomenological investigation. *Comprehensive Psychiatry, 38,* 274–282.

Manicavasagar, V., Silove, D., Curtis, J., & Wagner, R. (2000). Continuities of separation anxiety from early life into adulthood: A clinic study. *Journal of Anxiety Disorders, 14,* 1–18.

Manicavasagar, V., Silove, D., & Hadzi-Pavlovic, D. (1998). Subpopulations of early separation anxiety: Relevance to risk of adult anxiety disorders. *Journal of Affective Disorders, 48,* 181–190.

Manicavasagar, V., Silove, D., Rapee, R., Waters, F., & Momartin, S. (in press). Parent–child concordance for separation anxiety: A clinic study. *Journal of Affective Disorders.*

Moreau, D., & Weissman, M. (1993). Anxiety symptoms in nonpsychiatrically referred children and adolescents. In C. G. Last (Ed.), *Anxiety across the lifespan: A developmental perspective* (pp. 37–62). New York: Springer-Verlag.

Parker, G. (1979). Reported parental characteristics of agoraphobics and social phobics. *British Journal of Psychiatry, 135,* 555–560.

Parker, G. (1983). *Parental overprotection: A risk factor in psychosocial development.* New York: Grune & Stratton.

Parker, G. (1986). Validating an experiential measure of parental style: The use of a twin sample. *Acta Psychiatrica Scandinavica, 73,* 22–27.

Parker, G., Barrett, E., & Hickie, I. (1992). From nurture to network: Examining links between perceptions of parenting received in childhood and social bonds in adulthood. *American Journal of Psychiatry, 149,* 877–885.

Parker, G., Tupling, H., & Brown, L. (1979). A parental bonding instrument. *British Journal of Medical Psychology, 52,* 1–10.

Perris, C., Jacobsson, L., Lindstrom, H., von Knorring, L., & Perris, H. (1980). Development of a new inventory for assessing memories of parental rearing behaviour. *Acta Psychiatrica Scandinavica, 61,* 265–274.

Puig-Antich, J. (1984). Affective disorders. In H. J. Kaplan & B. J. Sadock (Eds.), *Comprehensive textbook of psychiatry* (pp. 1850–1861). Baltimore: Williams & Wilkins.

Rapee, R. M. (1997). Potential role of childrearing practices in the development of anxiety and depression. *Clinical Psychology Review, 17,* 47–67.

Robins, L. N., Helzer, J. E., Croughlen, J., & Ratcliffe, K. S. (1981). National Institute of Mental Health Diagnostic Interview Schedule: Its history, characteristics and validity. *Archives of General Psychiatry, 38,* 381–389.

Robins, L. N., Helzer, J. E., Weissman, M. M., Orvaschel, H., Gruenberg, E., Burke, J. D. Jr, & Regier, D. A. (1984). Lifetime prevalence of specific psychiatric disorders in three sites. *Archives of General Psychiatry, 41,* 949–958.

Rosenbaum, J., Biederman, J., Hirshfeld, D., Bolduc, E., & Chaloff, J. (1991). Behavioural inhibition in children: A possible precursor to panic disorder or social phobia. *Journal of Clinical Psychiatry, 52,* 5–9.

Roth, M. (1959). The phobic anxiety–depersonalization syndrome. *Proceedings of the Royal Society of Medicine, 52,* 587–595.

Shear, M. K. (1996). Factors in the etiology and pathogenesis of panic disorder: Revisiting the attachment–separation paradigm. *American Journal of Psychiatry, 153,* 125–136.

Sheehan, D. (1982). Current concepts in psychiatry: Panic attacks and phobias. *New England Journal of Medicine, 307,* 156–158.

Silove, D. (1986). Perceived parental characteristics and reports of early parental deprivation in agoraphobic patients. *Australian and New Zealand Journal of Psychiatry, 20,* 365–369.

Silove, D., & Manicavasagar, V. (1993). Adults who feared school: Is early separation anxiety specific to the pathogenesis of panic disorder. *Acta Psychiatrica Scandinavica, 88,* 385–390.

Silove, D., Harris, M., Morgan, A., Boyce, P., Manicavasagar, V., Hadzi-Pavlovic, D., & Wilhelm, K. (1995). Is early separation anxiety a specific precursor of panic disorder–agoraphobia? A community study. *Psychological Medicine, 25,* 405–411.

Silove, D., Manicavasagar, V., Curtis, J., & Blaszczynski, A. (1996). Is early separation anxiety a risk factor to adult panic disorder? A critical review. *Comprehensive Psychiatry, 37,* 1–14.

Silove, D., Manicavasagar, V., O'Connell, D., Blaszczynski, A., Wagner, R., & Henry, J. (1993a). The development of the Separation Anxiety Symptom Inventory (SASI). *Australian and New Zealand Journal of Psychiatry, 27,* 477–488.

Silove, D., Manicavasagar, V., O'Connell, D., Blaszczynski, A., Wagner, R., & Henry, J. (1993b). Reported early separation anxiety symptoms in patients with panic and generalized anxiety disorders. *Australian and New Zealand Journal of Psychiatry, 27,* 489–494.

Silove, D., Manicavasagar, V., O'Connell, D., & Morris-Yates, A. (1995). Genetic factors in early separation anxiety: Implications for the genesis of adult anxiety disorders. *Acta Psychiatrica Scandinavica, 92,* 17–24.

Silove, D., Parker, G., Hadzi-Pavlovic, D., Manicavasagar, V., & Blaszczynski, A. (1991). Parental representations of panic disorder and generalized anxiety disorder patients. *British Journal of Psychiatry, 159,* 835–841.

Smith, S. L. (1970). School refusal with anxiety: A review of sixty-three cases. *Canadian Psychiatric Association Journal, 15,* 257–264.

Solyom, L., Silberfeld, M., & Solyom, C. (1976). Maternal overprotection in the etiology of agoraphobia. *Canadian Psychiatric Association Journal, 21,* 109–113.

Sroufe, L. A. (1985). Attachment classification from the perspective of infant–caregiver relationships and infant temperament. *Child Development, 56,* 1–14.

Strauss, C. C., Last, C. G., Hersen, M., & Kazdin, A. E. (1988). Association between anxiety and depression in children and adolescents with anxiety disorders. *Journal of Abnormal Child Psychology, 16,* 57–68.

Strober, M., & Carlson, G. (1982). Bipolar illness in adolescents with major depression: Clinical, genetic, and psychopharmacologic predictors in a three- to four-year prospective follow-up investigation. *Archives of General Psychiatry, 39,* 549–555.

Sweeney, J. A. (1993). Mixture analysis of pursuit eye-tracking dysfunction in schizophrenia. *Biological Psychiatry, 34,* 331–340.

Thyer, B., Nesse, R., Cameron, O., & Curtis, G. (1985). Agoraphobia: A test of the separation anxiety hypothesis. *Behaviour Research and Therapy, 23,* 75–78.

Thyer, B., Nesse, R., Curtis, G., & Cameron, O. (1986). Panic disorder: a test of the separation anxiety hypothesis. *Behaviour Research and Therapy, 24,* 209–211.

Tyrer, P. (1985). Neurosis divisible. *Lancet, i,* 685–688.

Tyrer, P., & Tyrer, S. (1974). School refusal, truancy and adult neurotic illness. *Psychological Medicine, 4,* 416–421.

Valleni-Basile, L. A., Garrison, C. Z., Jackson, K. L., Waller, J. L., McKeown, R. E., Addy, C. L., & Cuffe, S. P. (1994). Frequency of obsessive–compulsive disorder in a community sample of young adolescents. *Journal of the American Academy of Child and Adolescent Psychiatry, 33,* 782–791.

Weiss, M., & Burke, A. (1970). A 5- to 10-year follow-up of hospitalized school phobic children and adolescents. *American Journal of Orthopsychiatry, 40,* 672–676.

Weissman, M., Leckman, J., Merikangas, K., Gammon, G., & Prusoff, B. (1984). Depression and anxiety disorders in parents and children. *Archives of General Psychiatry, 41,* 845–852.

Wells, J. E., Bushell, J. A., Hornblow, A. R., Joyce, P. R., & Oakley-Browne, M. A. (1989). Christchurch Psychiatric Epidemiology Study: 1. Methodology and lifetime prevalence for specific psychiatric disorders. *Australian and New Zealand Journal of Psychiatry, 23,* 315–326.

World Health Organization (1992). *The ICD-10 classification of mental and behavioural disorders.* Geneva: Author.

Zitrin, C., Klein, D. F., Woerner, M., & Ross, D. C. (1983). Treatment of phobias: I. Comparisons of imipramine hydrochloride and placebo. *Archives of General Psychiatry, 40,* 125–138.

21

The Development of Generalized Anxiety

RONALD M. RAPEE

Criteria for generalized anxiety disorder (GAD) are reportedly met by 5% of the population over their lifetime (Kessler et al., 1994). A considerably larger proportion of the population experience high levels of trait anxiety and, despite not having sufficient interference to warrant an official diagnosis, are likely to experience varying degrees of low-level life interference. In fact, Rapee (1991) has argued that GAD can be conceptualized as similar to simply high levels of trait anxiety. Along these lines, GAD has been argued to be the "basic" anxiety disorder, underlying to a greater or lesser degree most of the other anxiety disorders (Barlow, 1988; Brown, Barlow, & Liebowitz, 1994; Rapee, 1991).

For these reasons, improved understanding of the nature and development of GAD is likely to have far-reaching implications. Several studies have indicated the tremendous life interference that can be produced by GAD (Massion, Warshaw, & Keller, 1993; Roy-Byrne & Katon, 1997), and this, coupled with its large prevalence, shows the impact this disorder may have on costs to the community.

This chapter will describe research that bears on the question of the origins and development of GAD. Research in this field is still in its infancy and so, of necessity, many of the conclusions will be limited and speculative. Nevertheless, there is sufficient evidence emerging to begin to elucidate some of the factors that are likely to be involved in the development of GAD. Given the issues raised above, many of these factors will not be specific to GAD, nor will they have been specifically tested in people with GAD. Rather, factors of importance to the development of all of the anxiety disorders and even the mood disorders will have relevance to a model of GAD. By definition, the final model will, in many ways, be a general model of the development of anxiety disorders.

Features of Generalized Anxiety Disorder

GAD can be diagnosed in both adults and children, although most research evidence to date has centered on adults. Females are more likely to meet criteria than males as indicated in both epidemiological and clinical populations (Rapee, 1991). Similarly, measures of trait anxiety are also typically higher in females than in males.

Age of onset has been difficult to assess, largely because many people with GAD report a slow, insidious onset that is hard to pin down (Rapee, 1985). Of importance to developmental models of GAD, the mean and median ages of onset are relatively early (Brown et al., 1994; Rapee, 1991). However, determining a mean age of onset may be largely irrelevant given that a large proportion of sufferers report being anxious for as long as they can recall (Rapee, 1985). This would seem to suggest that GAD, or at least many of its features, are an extension of basic features of the individual's personality. Hence, an explicit age of onset may be difficult (or impossible) to determine and would depend on each individual's definition of "disorder."

The symptoms of GAD are also largely common to all of the anxiety disorders and to high levels of trait anxiety. Symptoms such as poor sleep, irritability, and autonomic arousal are found across anxious individuals, and studies have generally failed to demonstrate distinctions between individuals with GAD and other anxiety disorders based on these physiological symptoms (Barlow, Blanchard, Vermilyea, Vermilyea, & Di Nardo, 1986).

Several authors have argued that the key feature of GAD is worry (Barlow, 1988; Rapee, 1991). The nature and content of worry in GAD is not especially different from that found in nonclinical subjects (Borkovec, Shadick, & Hopkins, 1991; Craske, Rapee, Jackel, & Barlow, 1989; Sanderson & Barlow, 1990). Rather, GAD worry differs from normal in degree and in associated constructs such as the degree of perceived control over worry (Borkovec et al., 1991; Craske et al., 1989). While cognitive activity in the form of worry is common to all of the anxiety disorders, the primary focus of worry may differ somewhat from disorder to disorder. Clearly, in panic disorder the focus is more narrowly on physical catastrophe; and in social phobia the focus is more narrowly on social mishap. In GAD, worry more broadly spans both physical and social dangers.

Reflecting many of the issues described above, studies of the hierarchical structure of the anxiety disorders show that GAD loads largely on the higher-order factor of negative affect (Brown, Chorpita, & Barlow, 1998; Clark, Watson, & Mineka, 1994). In fact, the study by Brown et al., (1998) showed that GAD loaded the most strongly of any of the anxiety disorders on negative affect (neuroticism). In turn, negative affect is common to all of the anxiety and mood disorders. Physiological arousal, believed to be specifically characteristic of anxiety (Clark et al., 1994), was found to relate significantly to GAD as expected, but interestingly, in a negative direction. The authors suggested that this may reflect the hypothesized functional purpose of worry, to reduce emotional processing (Borkovec, Lyonfields, Wiser, & Deihl, 1993; Borkovec et al., 1991). In other words, the high levels of cognitive activity in GAD (worry) may result in lowered physiological arousal as a distinguishing feature, despite the fact that the disorder itself may be characterized by above-average arousal (Brown et al., 1998).

Models of the Maintenance of Generalized Anxiety

Several authors have described factors of importance to the maintenance of GAD once the disorder is established. These models have all been based on data obtained from adults, but presumably very similar factors are likely to be important across the lifespan. Factors important in the maintenance of a disorder need to be established and, as such, similar or even the same factors may also have a role to play in the development of the disorder.

Following the pioneering work of Beck (e.g., Beck, Emery, & Greenberg, 1985), many researchers have emphasized the importance of biased processing of threat in the maintenance of anxiety. Specifically, generally anxious individuals are believed to overestimate both the probability and consequences of danger (Butler & Mathews, 1983). Associated with this bias in interpretation, anxious individuals have also been shown to allocate excessive attentional resources to the detection of threat in situations where resources are divided (Dalgleish & Vasey, 1997; MacLeod & Mathews, 1991; Mogg, Mathews, Eysenck, & May, 1991). In contrast to this emphasis on danger expectations, other authors have argued that anxiety and mood disorders are maintained by low perceptions of control over negatives (Barlow, 1988; Chorpita & Barlow, 1998). According to this perspective, it is not perceptions of danger that lead to anxiety but rather the belief that one has no means to alter or control one's predicament.

Combining these perspectives, Rapee (1991) argued that GAD (as a typical model of any anxiety disorder) involved both a tendency to associate stimuli with threat information (i.e., overestimate danger) and a belief that one's actions are unlikely to lead to alteration of the stimulus (low perception of control). Thus, this model of GAD is very similar to several earlier perspectives on trait anxiety and stress (e.g., Beck et al., 1985; Spielberger, 1975). Empirical evidence has supported the suggestion that perceptions of threat and perceptions of control can be distinguished and that each is independently associated with anxiety (Rapee, 1997a).

In a very similar theory, Woody and Rachman (1994) suggested that the increased threat perceived by people with GAD is, in turn, a lowered perception of signals indicating safety. According to this theory, people with GAD fail to perceive or learn about safety, and they therefore experience prolonged anxiety owing to an inability to determine when or where to expect threat.

Finally, several authors have focused on the concept of worry as a key feature of GAD. It has been suggested that the act of worrying is not only a feature of anxiety, but plays a major role in its maintenance (Borkovec, Shadick, & Hopkins, 1991; Mathews, 1990). According to this perspective, worry, by the fact of its very verbal nature, serves to suppress processing of threat information at an emotional level. This allows preservation of the association between certain stimuli and threat. In this way, worry can be seen as a type of avoidance strategy.

Factors Important to the Development of Generalized Anxiety

Temperament

As described earlier, many people with GAD report a lifetime of anxiety. This fact suggests a potential temperamental or personality style underlying chronic, generalized anxiety. Evidence for the association between temperament and later anxiety has come from both retrospective reports and prospective studies. Few studies, however, have been addressed directly towards GAD, and the research is better conceptualized at this stage as providing evidence pertinent to anxiety as a broader construct.

Several studies have asked adults to report retrospectively on the experience of anxiety disorders or anxious/neurotic characteristics in childhood. These studies have typically shown higher levels of such characteristics among anxious adults than among controls (Lipsitz et al., 1994; Pollack et al., 1996; van der Molen, van den Hout, van Dieren, & Griez, 1989). In our own research, adults with panic disorder or social phobia reported higher levels of introverted behaviors as children than did nonclinical controls, and these reports were supported by the subjects' mothers (Rapee & Melville, 1997).

Few studies have extended this type of research to children. Our own data examined retrospective reports from mothers of clinically anxious and nonclinical children (Rapee & Szollos, 1997). Ninety-four children meeting diagnostic criteria for one of the broad-based anxiety disorders (separation anxiety disorder, social phobia, or generalized anxiety disorder) were compared with 75 nonclinical children. Children were between 7 and 16 years of age and averaged an age of 10.5 years. Mothers of the children were asked to complete a retrospective questionnaire that asked about several features of the child's personality and life experiences in their early years. Of relevance to the current discussion were questions asking about features of the child in their first year of life, specific fears relative to those of other children in their first two years of life, and general difficulties settling after distress. Compared with nonclinical children, mothers of clinical children reported that their children were more difficult in the first year of life. Specifically, this translated to greater reports of crying, difficulties sleeping, and pain and gas. Interestingly, these reports did not differ between disorders; so that all with anxiety disorders, including those with GAD, scored higher on these measures than did nonclinical children. Anxious children were also more fearful in their first two years of life than were nonclinical children. In particular, anxious children scored considerably higher on measures of separation fears, fear of strangers, and fears of the dark. Again, there were no differences between specific disorders. Finally, anxious children showed greater difficulties settling in situations such as daycare, first day of school, and babysitters and, again, there were no differences between disorders.

The data from our laboratory are consistent with findings from several longitudinal studies. In some of the most convincing work, links have been drawn between parents' anxiety, children's anxiety disorders, and behavioral inhibition (Rosenbaum et al., 1993). Behavioral inhibition refers to a temperament category described by Kagan and colleagues that is characterized by proximity to major caregivers, long latency to approach, reduced verbalizations, and apparent distress, especially in the face of novelty and social interaction (Kagan, Snidman, Arcus, & Reznick, 1994). Behaviorally inhibited children are more likely to have a parent with an anxiety disorder (Rosenbaum et al., 1992), and adults with anxiety disorders are more likely to have a behaviorally inhibited child (Rosenbaum et al., 1993). There do not currently seem to be any particular patterns in these data with respect to specific disorders. In addition, children assessed at 21 months as being behaviorally inhibited were more likely than uninhibited children to develop anxiety disorders over the next 5–10 years (Biederman et al., 1993; Hirshfeld et al., 1992). Again, these data do not pertain to any specific anxiety disorder. Parents of behaviorally inhibited children have described their children as having been especially irritable, colicky, and sleepless in the first few months of life (cf. the retrospective reports from mothers of clinically anxious children reported by Rapee & Szollos, 1997). More recently, these retrospective observations have been supported via prospective evaluation. Kagan and Snidman (1991) have shown that children who are identified at 4 months of age as being highly motorically active and crying a great deal are at greater risk for the later development of behavioral inhibition. Similar results have been reported by other researchers (Fox & Calkins, 1993).

Several other longitudinal studies have supported the argument that withdrawn and inhibited temperament at a young age tends to persist and is associated with greater difficulties in adulthood (Caspi, Elder, & Bem, 1988; Caspi, Moffitt, Newman, & Silva, 1996; Oberklaid, Sanson, Pedlow, & Prior, 1993; Rubin, 1993).

The results from both retrospective and longitudinal studies are consistent with an argument that a proportion of clinically anxious individuals develop their disorder following a lifetime of vulnerability. In fact, Roth and Mountjoy (1982) have argued that diagnosing an individual with anxiety in which the disorder appears to have begun suddenly, later in life, may represent a misclassification. Based on the previous results, we might suggest two features of this vulnerability. First, it appears that the vulnerability (or at least those aspects measured here) is likely to be general to anxiety as a broad construct rather than specific to any particular disorder. Second, data from the first year of life suggest that the more early manifestation of this temperament is to be found in high arousal and emotionality. Being so early, it is possible that this represents a large proportion of any genetic vulnerability.

Genetic Factors

It is almost a truism to claim that genes are involved in the manifestation of any mental disorder. Genes are probably involved in basketball ability as well. However, it would be ridiculous to claim that there exists a specific gene locus for the ability to play basketball. Rather, basketball ability is likely mediated by several factors (e.g., height, strength, agility), each of which may be partly genetically determined. Thus, the more interesting question for the psychology of anxiety is not whether there is a genetic component but in what way this component is manifested.

Certainly, several studies have demonstrated a genetic involvement in anxiety disorders in general (Andrews, Stewart, Allen, & Henderson, 1990; Kendler, Heath, Martin, & Eaves, 1987; Torgersen, 1983). Few studies have examined GAD specifically. The often-cited study by Torgersen (1983) failed to indicate a genetic involvement in GAD. In this study, where one twin had GAD the probability of the second twin having any anxiety disorder was 17% in the case of monozygotic twins and 20% in the case of dizygotic twins. However, the number of subjects with GAD was extremely small ($N = 6$) and GAD was diagnosed using DSM-III criteria which placed GAD at the bottom of a hierarchy. More extensive work has been conducted by Kendler and colleagues in a series of studies using large numbers of twin pairs (Kendler, Neale, Kessler, Heath, & Eaves, 1992; Kendler, Neale, Kessler, Heath, & Eaves, 1992; Kendler et al., 1995). These studies have all indicated a moderate genetic involvement to GAD, accounting for around 30% of the variance (Kendler et al., 1992a; Kendler et al., 1995). Again, however, the diagnostic criteria used may limit the results. All three studies reported by Kendler and colleagues relied on a definition of GAD which did not focus clearly on worry as the major feature (cf. Barlow, 1988; Rapee, 1991) and which allowed a brief duration to the problem (1 month). It is very possible, therefore, that the populations included many subjects with transient problems such as adjustment disorders which may underestimate the degree of genetic involvement and may also misrepresent the nature of this involvement.

As mentioned earlier, the extent of genetic involvement in a disorder is probably less interesting than speculation about the nature of that involvement. In other words, what exactly is inherited? To begin to address this question, we might look at the results of several studies that have failed to show a specific pattern of inheritance for any individual anxiety disorder (e.g., Andrews et al., 1990; Torgersen, 1983). Based on the results of these studies, some authors have argued that what is inherited across the anxiety and mood disorders is a general vulnerability or propensity to neurosis (e.g., Andrews, 1996). In support of such arguments are data pointing to the heritability of personality traits such as neuroticism (Eysenck, 1975; Jardine, Martin, & Henderson, 1984). In a similar fashion, some data have supported a genetic involvement in behavioral inhibition (Robinson, Kagan, Reznick, & Corley, 1997). However, it is important to point out that these personality or temperament dimensions cannot constitute the "pure" inherited substrate since the genetic involvement for them is no greater than that involved in anxious symptomatology—around 50% of the variance (Jardine et al., 1984).

To argue more specifically regarding the pure inherited substrate to GAD, and probably all of the anxiety and mood disorders, we must turn more to speculation. Eysenck and Rachman (1965) suggested that two independent mediators of personality, arousal and emotionality, were largely inherited. Arousal is linked to introversion–extraversion while emotionality manifests as neuroticism. This conceptualization is consistent with research relating to higher-order factors underlying the specific anxiety and mood disorders, positive and negative affect (Brown et al., 1998; Clark et al., 1994; King, Ollendick, & Gullone, 1991).

At a neurobiological level, considerable research has related fearfulness to the degree of activity in the limbic system, especially the amygdala (McNally, 1998). Kagan and Snidman (1991) have pointed out that projections from the basal and central areas of the amygdala differ and seem to relate to motor activity and emotional distress, respectively. Interestingly, recent research has shown that the amygdala is not only important in fearfulness but also plays a role in fear-related conditioning (Flint, 1997). Further, specific genetic loci have been identified that influence the degree of fear conditioning shown by mice (Caldarone et al., 1997; Wehner et al., 1997). These recent studies provide an interesting fit with early research on the interaction between aversive conditioning and personality. Several studies have shown that individuals who are higher on trait anxiety learn the relationship between a neutral stimulus and aversive outcome more quickly than do subjects low in trait anxiety (Bitterman & Holtzman, 1952; Spence & Taylor, 1951; Zinbarg & Mohlman, 1998).

The discussion to date ties in well with our earlier discussion of temperament. Both we and, more impressively, Kagan and Snidman (1991) found that infants who are at risk for anxiety show greater levels of both activity (sleeplessness) and distress (crying) The similarity of these features to the constructs of arousal and emotionality are obvious. Interestingly, in a twin study, Kendler and colleagues (1995) indicated two separate genetic factors as involved in several disorders, including GAD, panic disorder, specific phobias, and major depression. Both factors were common to all disorders but each factor showed a slightly different pattern of loading for each disorder. Clearly these findings do not correspond completely and there are still many questions to answer. However, there are sufficient indications coming through to speculate that what is inherited with relevance to the development of GAD (and most likely all the anxiety disorders) relates to an individual's basic level of arousal as well as their tendency toward emotional reactivity. In turn, these factors are likely to strongly influence the rapidity with which an individual is able to draw associations between external stimuli and threat. At present, the data are still too preliminary to determine whether these factors represent two (or more) clearly distinct factors that are mediated by distinct genetic loci, or whether they are inherited through a single set of genes.

Environmental Factors

Twin studies into temperament and personality tell us about the role of genetic mediation in these constructs, but they also tell us a great deal about the environmental input into disorders. For example, studies of genetic involvement in personality and temperament have shown clearly that these constructs are not pure measures of genetic contribution, but likely include an environmental component (Eysenck, 1975; Robinson et al., 1997).

More importantly, these studies have been able to partial the observed variance into that attributable to factors that are shared between twins (shared environment) and factors that are experienced differently by each twin (individual or unshared environment). Studies of the environmental aspects of anxiety have shown an interesting combination of results. In behavior genetic studies of adults with anxiety disorders, most studies have indicated that shared environmental factors account for very little of the variance in anxious symptomatology (Kendler et al., 1995; Jardine et al., 1984; Daniels & Plomin, 1985). Rather, the data indicate that individual environmental factors are more influential. The studies described earlier by Kendler and colleagues (1992a, 1992b, 1995) indicate that a large proportion of the variance in GAD in adults is accounted for by individual environmental factors. Of course, the methodology of behavioral genetics cannot distinguish this component from the effects of measurement error (Kendler et al., 1995; Pike & Plomin, 1996), so it is unclear exactly how much of the variance is due to environmental factors. The study by Kendler et al. (1995) indicated that the nature of this individual environmental influence was largely nonspecific across the anxiety disorders studied, with a somewhat smaller component being specific to each disorder. In other words, a large component in the development of GAD is likely to be due to factors that add to the risk for the development of any anxiety disorder. What these factors might be is still very much open to speculation, but some data are accumulating.

In contrast to studies with adults, behavior genetic studies of anxiety in children provide somewhat less consistent results (e.g., Topolski et al., 1997). However, at least some of these studies have indicated a considerably stronger role for shared environmental factors than have adult studies (Stevenson, Batten, & Cherner, 1992; Thapar & McGuffin, 1995; see also Eley, this volume). One of the major complications in studies with children is the different results that seem to occur depending on the source of reporting, parent or child (Thapar & McGuffin, 1995). It seems likely, then, that both shared and individual environments may be important in the development of anxiety disorders. While children are of the age to live together and remain at home, the influence of shared factors has a better chance of being detected. When individuals move apart and leave the family, the influence of individual environmental factors may become more apparent. It is also important to point out that behavior genetic studies do not generally allow for the possibility of gene–environment interactions which is a central feature of the model presented here. This point will be discussed further later in this chapter.

Transmission of Parental Anxiety

There is a familial basis to anxiety. Several studies have shown consistently that first-degree relatives of people with anxiety disorders are more likely to have an anxiety disorder too (Beidel & Turner, 1997; Fyer, Mannuzza, Chapman, Martin, & Klein, 1995; Noyes, Clarkson, Crowe, Yates, & McChesney, 1987; Stein et al., 1998). In addition, as mentioned earlier, behaviorally inhibited children are more likely to have anxious parents and the children of anxious parents are at higher risk for behavioral inhibition (Rosenbaum et al., 1993). In contrast to twin studies, the transmission in family studies has proven to be relatively disorder-specific (Beidel & Turner, 1997; Fyer, Mannuzza, Chapman, Martin, & Klein, 1995; Stein et al., 1998). For example, Noyes and colleagues (1987) found that the first-degree relatives of people with GAD were more likely to have GAD also than were relatives of control subjects as well as relatives of people with panic disorder, but were no more likely than controls to have panic disorder.

Clearly, part of the familial transmission of anxiety is due to genetic factors. However, as noted above, this cannot account for the entire story and it is likely that transmission of parental anxiety also occurs via environmental processes. Speculatively, two processes that may help to transmit parental anxiety to offspring are verbal instruction and modeling. These processes may involve the effects of either shared environmental influences (i.e., main effects) or gene–environment interactions. In other words, it is possible that verbal instruction, say, has an influence in increasing anxious responding only, given a particular temperament.

In a series of studies, Bruch, Heimberg, and colleagues (Bruch & Heimberg, 1994; Bruch, Heimberg, Berger, & Collins, 1989; Leung, Heimberg, Holt, & Bruch, 1994) found that adults with social phobia retrospectively report that their parents were more likely than the parents of nonclinical subjects to emphasize the importance of other people's opinions and to use shame as a disciplinary tactic. In a similar fashion, some research has found that adults with panic attacks or who are high on fear of physical sensations reported more reinforcement from their parents in response to sick-role behavior than did nonclinical subjects (Ehlers, 1993; Watt, Stewart, & Cox, 1998). These data support a wealth of research showing that a small, but consistent proportion of subjects with specific phobias report verbal transmission of information in the onset of their phobia (Menzies & Clarke, 1995; Ollendick & King, 1991; Öst, 1987; see also Muris & Merckelbach, this volume).

We have recently demonstrated the influence of parent reinforcement of avoidance more directly. In a recent study with anxious children (separation anxiety disorder, social phobia, and GAD), we provided the children with a hypothetical scenario and asked them to indicate their most likely response (Barrett, Rapee, Dadds, & Ryan, 1996). Each child, together with his or her parents, was then asked to discuss briefly the scenario and the most appropriate response for 5 minutes. The child was then again asked to indicate his or her response (either the same or altered). Anxious children showed a dramatic increase in the tendency to report an avoidant response to the scenario from before family discussion to after. In contrast, nonclinical and oppositional children showed a slight decrease. Detailed examination of the interaction indicated that the parents of anxious children were more likely to respond to their child's avoidant responses with indicators of agreement (Dadds, Barrett, Rapee, & Ryan, 1996). Thus it may be that some type of verbal reinforcement and agreement from parents may help to inflate an anxious child's tendency to deal with a situation with avoidance, and hence maintain anxiety.

Several studies have also demonstrated the potential for anxious responses to be acquired via modeling (Bandura & Rosenthal, 1966; Cook & Mineka, 1989). For example, some research has demonstrated that adults with social phobia retrospectively recall their parents as having engaged in less social interaction than do nonclinical subjects (Bruch et al., 1989; Rapee & Melville, 1997). While this difference might well reflect a difference in shared genetics, at least one adoption study has demonstrated a nongenetic aspect. Using a full adoption design, Daniels and Plomin (1985) showed that infant shyness is negatively correlated with the degree of sociability of their adoptive mothers. These data allow for the possibility that modeling of avoidance of social interaction may be involved in the development of social anxiety. Of course, they are also consistent with the possibility that social anxiety is influenced by a lack of experience with, and direct exposure to, social interactions. Which of these mechanisms, if either, is critical awaits further research. In addition, the extent to which these factors are relevant to GAD is still unclear. Nevertheless, similar suggestions from retrospective studies have been reported for subjects with physical fears and specific phobias (Ehlers, 1993; Muris, Steerneman, Merckelbach, & Meesters, 1996; Watt et al., 1998).

If we accept the scant evidence indicating an association between factors such as parents' verbalizations and parents' anxious actions and anxiety in offspring, the question remains as to the nature of such a relationship. The lack of twin or adoption designs applied to the examination of these specific factors allows the possibility that the parental transmission data can be accounted for by shared genetic factors (i.e., parents and offspring share similar genes). The study by Daniels and Plomin (1985) indicates that this may not entirely be the case, since these researchers showed that shyness in offspring was negatively related to sociability in adoptive mothers. Nevertheless, the lack of longitudinal research limits the extent to which causality can be inferred. Further, there are currently no similar studies using subjects with GAD. However, it is at least theoretically possible that parental instruction related to threat and parent modeling of anxious reactions work by increasing an individual's tendency to associate specific stimuli with danger or by inflating the degree of danger expected. In addition, it is very likely that similar messages may be relayed that relate to a perception that one has little control over threat (Chorpita & Barlow, 1998). Should they be demonstrated through later research, such mechanisms would fit nicely with models of the maintenance of GAD (cf. Barlow, 1988; Rapee, 1991).

Parent Reaction

A wealth of research has been conducted over a number of years investigating the relationship between certain parenting styles and anxiety. As reviewed by Rapee (1997b), there are a number of limitations to this research. Most importantly, the vast majority of data are based on retrospective studies using adult anxious subjects and relying on these subjects' perceptions of their parents' behavior. Nevertheless, following a detailed review of the literature, this author concluded that there were some clear consistencies in the literature that allowed some speculation about the relationship between particular parenting styles and anxiety. Specifically, parents of anxious offspring appear to be characterized by both a critical, rejecting style of parenting and a tendency to be overprotective/overcontrolling in their parenting. Of these, the most consistent evidence links an overprotective style with anxiety.

We have recently begun to try and address some of the limitations in the existing literature on parenting and anxiety (Hudson & Rapee, 1998a, 1998b). In our first study, clinically anxious children (including GAD) were asked to complete two complex cognitive tasks while their mothers sat beside them with the solutions to the tasks. Mothers' instructions were to help only if they felt that the child really needed it. Blind raters scored the behavior of the mother and child. Compared with mothers of nonclinical children, the mothers of anxious children were more likely to provide unsolicited help and were more generally intrusive in the task. Similar results have been reported with withdrawn preschool children (LaFreniere & Dumas, 1992).

In the second study, clinically anxious children and a nonclinical sibling were asked separately to complete a similar cognitive task and were compared with nonclinical children and their siblings. In this study, the children were accompanied by either their mother or father in one instance and then by the other parent. Thus, this design allowed examination of mother with clinical child, mother with sibling, father with clinical child, and father with sibling. The previous result, that mothers of anxious children were more intrusive than mothers of nonclinical children, was replicated. However, this effect was not found with the small number of fathers in this study. More interesting were the data comparing clinical children and their siblings. Both mothers and fathers of anxious children were significantly more intrusive and offered more unsolicited help to their clinically anxious child than to his or her sibling. There was a tendency for the mothers of anxious children also to be slightly more intrusive with their nonclinical child than were the mothers of nonclinical children, but this difference did not reach significance.

Naturally, these results do not demonstrate a causal relationship between overprotective parenting and anxiety. However, one study has shown that reducing overinvolvement in mothers of anxious–withdrawn preschoolers did improve social competence and produced a slight reduction in withdrawal (LaFreniere & Capuano, 1997). Future research will need to include the use of twin or adoption designs and longitudinal studies. However, the data do suggest that an overinvolved style of parenting is associated with anxiety. More importantly, our sibling study indicates that this parenting style is not completely the result of factors internal to the parent and would therefore not show up as variance accounted for by shared environmental factors. Rather, this style of parenting is associated primarily with the anxious child, and would therefore contribute to variance seemingly accounted for by genetic factors even though it actually represents a gene by environment interaction. In support of this argument, we have found that parents of anxious children report markedly different interactions with their anxious child compared with other children in the family (Hudson & Rapee, 1998b). Therefore, it is very possible that anxiety will be found to be the result of an interaction between genetic factors (such as greater arousal and emotionality) and overinvolved parenting (see below).

Peer Relationships

There is no published research on the nature of peer group norms and behaviors in anxious children. Yet there is reason to consider that protective and unchallenging peer relationships may help to maintain and possibly fuel anxiety in later childhood and adolescence. Harris (1995) has argued that peer relationships are an especially powerful source of influence on the development of personality. According to Harris, inhibited behavior, especially in boys, may be attenuated by the effects of cultural and peer norms that view anxious behavior in males negatively. In support of this suggestion, a study of Swedish children showed relatively stable levels of inhibition from 18 months to 6 years, but found a decrease in inhibited behavior from 6 to 16 years for males only (Kerr, Lambert, Stattin, & Klackenberg-Larsson, 1994). The authors argued that the reduction in inhibition in males was due to an unacceptability of shy behaviors in boys. On the other hand, like-mindedness within a peer group can help to accentuate certain characteristics (Harris, 1995). Thus, anxious children who socialize with other anxious children may show an increase in anxiety owing to an acceptance of anxious behaviors within that subculture. Other factors such as peer rejection and ostracism may also increase anxiety. Rejection and neglect by peers is not likely to be a random phenomenon but is more likely to be a result of prior temperamental features to which the peers are reacting (Rubin, 1993). In general, anxious children tend not to be rejected, but are more likely to be neglected (Fox & Calkins, 1993; Strauss, 1988). Nevertheless, even peer neglect may reinforce beliefs that one does not have control in the world. Thus, this view sees anxiety as resulting from an interaction with prior temperament and very probably reflects a gene–environment interaction.

Nonspecific Environmental Stressors

In a seminal paper, Finlay-Jones and Brown (1981) reported on the association between the onset of stress and anxiety disorders and further showed that the type of stressful event differed between anxiety and depression. Whereas loss-related events preceded the onset of depression, threatening events were associated with the onset of anxiety. A number of studies have supported this relationship between anxiety and stress across several of the anxiety disorders, especially panic disorder (see Craske, 1999). In the only study examining GAD, a clear association was shown prospectively between life events and development of the disorder. Individuals reporting one or more serious and unexpected life events had three to four times the risk of having GAD than did those with no events. Unfortunately, this study used DSM-III criteria and so it is possible that many of the "new cases" of GAD may be better considered adjustment disorders. In addition, GAD was not assessed at Time 1, so it is not clear how many of the subjects were already anxious before experiencing the stressor. Given our earlier discussion, it is likely that this was the case for the majority.

In our own research with anxious children, we have found that clinically anxious children seem to have had more stressful events in their lives than have nonclinical children (Rapee & Szollos, 1997). However, comparison between the anxiety disorders showed that this effect was primarily a result of the considerably greater number of stressors experienced by children with separation anxiety disorder. Children with GAD did not have significantly more stressors than nonclinical children.

The stress issue in relation to the anxiety disorders is a complex one. How does one reconcile the "truism" that environmental stressors are involved in the development of anxiety with the observation that many anxious individuals report anxiety for as long as they can remember? In a study examining stress at onset in anxiety, we asked subjects with a variety of anxiety disorders to report on events in their lives during the 6 months preceding onset and compared that with the events reported by nonclinical subjects during a retrospective 6-month period (Rapee, Litwin, & Barlow, 1990). No differences were found between groups in the number of stressors or the percentage of the group reporting a stressor. But compared with nonclinical subjects, the anxious subjects reported a significantly greater negative impact of the stressors. This was despite the fact that blind raters did not rate the types of stressors as any more negative in an objective sense. We concluded that, despite the fact that anxious subjects were no more likely to experience a stressor in their lives prior to onset of the disorder than nonclinical subjects, their pre-existing personality or vulnerability made that stressor considerably more distressing when it did occur. In the case of GAD in particular, the long-term features of the disorder make discussion of a specific stressor-related onset somewhat meaningless. But sufferers do often describe an exacerbation of the disorder or onset of a life-interfering quality to the problem following a major life event. Thus it may be better in the majority of cases to consider stressful life events as precipitators of anxiety disorders or exacerbators of anxiety in the context of a vulnerable personality.

What about the possibility that more chronic or early experience with stress might contribute to a vulnerability to anxiety? While this question has not been studied extensively, there are several lines of evidence that provide some support for this conjecture. At least two studies with monkeys have shown that early experience with lack of control over events can increase the degree of fear shown in response to threat, and conversely, that early experience with control can protect against fearful responding (Insel et al., 1986, cited in Barlow, 1988; Mineka, Gunnar, & Champoux, 1986). Several studies have also found that people with anxiety disorders report a greater likelihood of experiencing an adverse environment during childhood (Brown & Harris, 1993; Brown, Harris, & Eales, 1993; Faravelli, Webb, Ambonetti, Fonnescu, & Sessarego, 1985). This includes a greater chance of physical abuse, sexual abuse, and perceived parental indifference.

In contrast to the above, some research has shown that prior experience with stress can reduce the reaction to later stressors. For example, Andrews, Page, & Neilson (1993) showed that students who had been sent abroad to study had a significantly greater decrease on a composite measure of vulnerability (including trait anxiety, locus of control, and defense style) than did students who did not travel during this period. Similar results have been shown in animals (see Barlow, 1988, for a review of "toughening up"). Presumably the effects of early experience with stress will depend on several factors, including existing vulnerability and the nature of the stressors (e.g., controllability, duration, intensity).

A Model of the Development of GAD

Is it possible to pull together the data and speculations described throughout this chapter into a comprehensive model of the development of GAD? First, it must be repeated that such a model will almost certainly be applicable in much the same form to all of the anxiety disorders. Second, we need to remember that, at this stage, many components of the model are necessarily speculative. Finally, it is likely that there are many pathways to anxiety and that a model such as this can summarize the various influential components but does not specify the only possible path. An attempt to summarize the components described in this chapter is shown in fig. 21.1.

According to the model, an anxious parent may produce a child who is born with a vulnerability to anxiety. The specific genetic involvement needs to be delineated with further research, but there is a strong possibility that its main manifestation is via high levels of arousal and emotionality (Kagan & Snidman, 1991). In turn, the anxious parent is more likely to respond to a vulnerable child with excessive control and protection. The suggestion here is that the parent's basic parenting style is not at "fault." Rather, it is more likely that parents of vulnerable children are responding or reacting to apparent distress in the child. Over many years of dealing with a sensitive and highly aroused child, the parent falls into a maladaptive pattern whereby he or she anticipates distress on the part of the child and leaps to the assistance of the child in order to avoid the expected distress. Avoidance of distress

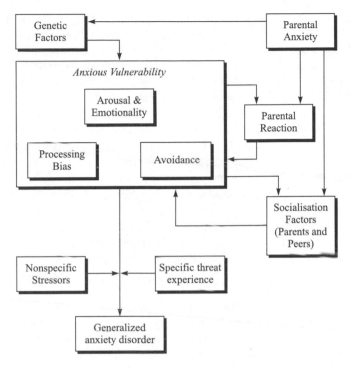

Figure 21.1. A model of the development of generalized anxiety.

would be even more likely if the parent were anxious. Other parental and circumstantial features may also influence the likelihood that a parent will react to an emotional child with overprotection or, conversely, with encouragement to approach. For example, we have found that clinically anxious children are more likely than nonclinical children to have had a birth complication and are slightly more likely to be first-born (Rapee & Szollos, 1997). Either of these factors may influence a parent to be more protective of that child compared with other children in the family. Overprotection provided by the parent is likely to augment the child's vulnerability to anxiety, by strengthening tendencies to avoid threat and by increasing the child's tendency to perceive danger and believe that he or she has no control over danger (Rapee, 1991). On the other hand, parenting that specifically encourages approach and autonomy should reduce anxious vulnerability. Along these lines, some interesting research has shown that temperamentally withdrawn children who attend daycares that encourage social interaction reduce their withdrawn behaviors relative to withdrawn children who attend daycares that ignore them (Volling & Feagans, 1995).

Anxious vulnerability may also be augmented by various social learning experiences. This may occur via interaction with parents in the early years. Specifically, observational learning and provision of specific information from an anxious parent can enhance the child's tendency to avoid and reinforce the message that the world is a dangerous place and the child lacks any ability to control threat. The child's perception that he or she lacks control is consistent with the tendency toward later worry, which seems to involve an attempt to gain control through problem-solving (Borkovec et al., 1991; Vasey & Daleiden, 1994). As with parent reaction, learning from the parent may also interact with an anxious vulnerability. Learning about associations with danger is more rapid in the case of aroused individuals (Spence & Taylor, 1951; Zinbarg & Mohlman, 1998), and processing biases toward threat might also enhance the likelihood of learning about such factors. In later years, anxiety in a child may be maintained and further augmented by acceptance of avoidance behavior and anxious processing through like-minded peers, or through rejection and neglect from the mainstream peer group.

Along the developmental path, the individual will confront both major life events and other stressors as well as specific interactions with threats. While these events can increase anxiety in their own right, they are more likely to have a lasting impact given a background of vulnerability to anxiety (e.g., Rapee et al., 1990).

Finally, the shift from vulnerability to disorder is a vague and fluid one. There is little to discriminate between high levels of so-called "trait anxiety" that are nonetheless "nonclinical," and a clinical diagnosis of anxiety disorder. This point is perhaps best demonstrated in the area of social anxiety, where studies have failed to discriminate clearly nonclinical subjects who score high on measures of shyness from individuals with a clinical diagnosis of social phobia (Turner, Beidel, & Larkin, 1986). Nevertheless, it may be expected that disordered individuals will differ from vulnerable individuals on several parameters, including the degree of anxiety, shifts in anxiety from the individual's usual levels, and life circumstances resulting in interference from anxiety. As an example, a vulnerable individual who is high in trait anxiety may come to be diagnosed with GAD following the loss of a job. At this point, the shift from vulnerability to disorder may be attributable to the increased anxiety experienced as a result of the stressor, the change in anxiety from the person's usual level, and the interference in life caused by the anxiety stopping the person from seeking further jobs.

As mentioned earlier, the model described here does not specify any particular path to anxiety. In fact, it is assumed that none of the factors is necessary and almost any of the factors in the model could be sufficient independent causes of anxiety. Hence GAD could theoretically begin at any age, given sufficient input from a particular factor (e.g., a severe enough life event). However, it is more likely that the interaction between several factors is a much more powerful and common pathway to the development of GAD. In particular, the view taken here is that an early vulnerability to anxiety is the most common factor underlying the later development of GAD. In turn, this vulnerability is influenced by several factors, and itself is central in influencing the effects of these and other factors.

Clearly, while a number of hints and suggestions exist in the literature to support the model presented here, much of the model is highly speculative and considerable research is needed to test its various aspects. There is a clear need for several types of studies, but ultimately the need for well-developed longitudinal studies is apparent. There is no doubt that the model will change many times with empirical testing, but it is hoped that this model can help to formulate questions and channel research efforts.

Note

Please address correspondence to Ron Rapee, School of Behavioural Sciences, Macquarie University, Sydney, NSW 2109, Australia. Email: Ron.Rapee@mq.edu.au

References

Andrews, G. (1996). Comorbidity in neurotic disorders: The similarities are more important than the differences. In R. M. Rapee (Ed.), *Current controversies in the anxiety disorders* (pp. 3–20). New York: Guilford.

Andrews, G., Page, A. C., & Neilson, M. (1993). Sending your teenagers away: Controlled stress decreases neurotic vulnerability. *Archives of General Psychiatry, 50,* 585–589.

Andrews, G., Stewart, G. W., Allen, R., & Henderson, A. S. (1990). The genetics of six neurotic disorders: A twin study. *Journal of Affective Disorders, 19,* 23–29

Bandura, A., & Rosenthal, T. (1966) Vicarious classical conditioning as a function of arousal level. *Journal of Personality and Social Psychology, 3,* 54–62.

Barlow, D. H. (1988). *Anxiety and its disorders: The nature and treatment of anxiety and panic.* New York: Guilford.

Barlow, D. H., Blanchard, E. B., Vermilyea, J. A., Vermilyea, B. B., & Di Nardo, P. A. (1986). Generalized anxiety and generalized anxiety disorder: Description and reconceptualization. *American Journal of Psychiatry, 143,* 40–44.

Barrett, P. M., Rapee, R. M., Dadds, M. R., & Ryan, S. M. (1996). Family enhancement of cognitive style in anxious and aggressive children: Threat bias and the FEAR effect. *Journal of Abnormal Child Psychology, 24,* 187–203.

Beck, A. T., Emery, G., & Greenberg, R. L. (1985). *Anxiety disorders and phobias: A cognitive perspective.* New York: Basic Books.

Beidel, D. C., & Turner, S. M. (1997). At risk for anxiety: I. Psychopathology in the offspring of anxious parents. *Journal of the American Academy of Child and Adolescent Psychiatry, 36,* 918–924.

Biederman, J., Rosenbaum, J. F., Bolduc-Murphy, E. A., Faraone, S. V., Chaloff, J., Hirshfeld, D. R., & Kagan, J. (1993). A 3-year follow-up of children with and without behavioral inhibition. *Journal of the American Academy of Child and Adolescent Psychiatry, 32,* 814–821.

Bitterman, M. E., & Holtzman, W. H. (1952). Conditioning and extinction of the galvanic skin response as a function of anxiety. *Journal of Abnormal Social Psychology, 47,* 615–623.

Borkovec, T. D., Lyonfields, J. D., Wiser, S. L., & Deihl, L. (1993). The role of worrisome thinking in the suppression of cardiovascular response to phobic imagery. *Behaviour Research and Therapy, 31,* 321–324.

Borkovec, T. D., Shadick, R. N., & Hopkins, M. (1991). The nature of normal and pathological worry. In R. M. Rapee & D. H. Barlow (Eds.), *Chronic anxiety: Generalized anxiety disorder and mixed anxiety depression* (pp. 29–51). New York: Guilford.

Brown, G. W., & Harris, T. O. (1993). Etiology of anxiety and depressive disorders in an inner-city population. 1. Early adversity. *Psychological Medicine, 23,* 143–154.

Brown, G. W., Harris, T. O., & Eales, M. J. (1993). Etiology of anxiety and depressive disorder in an inner-city population: 2. Comorbidity and adversity. *Psychological Medicine, 23,* 155–165.

Brown, T. A., Barlow, D. H., & Liebowitz, M. R. (1994). The empirical basis of generalized anxiety disorder. *American Journal of Psychiatry, 151,* 1272–1280.

Brown, T. A., Chorpita, B. F., & Barlow, D. H. (1998). Structural relationships among dimensions of the DSM-IV anxiety and mood disorders and dimensions of negative affect, positive affect, and autonomic arousal. *Journal of Abnormal Psychology, 107,* 179–192.

Bruch, M. A., & Heimberg, R. G. (1994). Differences in perceptions of parental and personal characteristics between generalized and nongeneralized social phobics. *Journal of Anxiety Disorders, 8,* 155–168.

Bruch, M. A., Heimberg, R. G., Berger, P., & Collins, T. M. (1989). Social phobia and perceptions of early parental and personal characteristics. *Anxiety Research, 2,* 57–65.

Butler, G., & Mathews, A. (1983). Cognitive processes in anxiety. *Advances in Behaviour Research and Therapy, 5,* 51–62.

Caldarone, B., Saavedra, C., Tartaglia, K., Wehner, J. M., Dudek, B. C., & Flaherty, L. (1997). Quantitative trait loci analysis affecting contextual conditioning in mice. *Nature Genetics, 17,* 335–337.

Caspi, A., Elder, G. H., Jr, & Bem, D. J. (1988). Moving away from the world: Life-course patterns of shy children. *Developmental psychology, 24,* 824–831.

Caspi, A., Moffitt, T. E., Newman, D. L., & Silva, P. A. (1996). Behavioral observations at age 3 years predict adult psychiatric disorders: Longitudinal evidence from a birth cohort. *Archives of General Psychiatry, 53,* 1033–1039.

Chorpita, B. F., & Barlow, D. H. (1998). The development of anxiety: The role of control in the early environment. *Psychological Bulletin, 124,* 3–21.

Clark, L. A., Watson, D., & Mineka, S. (1994). Temperament, personality, and the mood and anxiety disorders. *Journal of Abnormal Psychology, 103,* 103–116.

Cook, M., & Mineka, S. (1989). Observational conditioning of fear to fear-relevant versus fear-irrelevant stimuli in Rhesus monkeys. *Journal of Abnormal Psychology, 98,* 448–459.

Craske, M. G. (1999). *Anxiety disorders: Psychological approaches to theory and treatment.* Boulder, CO: Westview.

Craske, M. G., Rapee, R. M., Jackel, L., & Barlow, D. H. (1989). Qualitative dimensions of worry in DSM-111-R generalized anxiety disorder subjects and non-anxious controls. *Behaviour Research and Therapy, 27,* 397–402.

Dadds, M. R., Barrett, P. M., Rapee, R. M., & Ryan, S. M. (1996). Family process and child anxiety and aggression: An observational analysis of the FEAR effect. *Journal of Abnormal Child Psychology, 24,* 715–734.

Daleiden, E. L., & Vasey, M. W. (1997). An information-processing perspective on childhood anxiety. *Clinical Psychology Review, 17*, 407–429.

Daniels, D., & Plomin, R. (1985). Origins of individual differences in infant shyness. *Developmental Psychology, 21*, 118–121.

Ehlers, A. (1993). Somatic symptoms and panic attacks: A retrospective study of learning experiences. *Behaviour Research and Therapy, 31*, 269–278.

Eysenck, H. J. (1975). A genetic model of anxiety. In I. G. Sarason & C. D. Spielberger (Eds.), *Stress and anxiety: Vol. 2*. Sydney: Wiley.

Eysenck, H. J., & Rachman, S. (1965). *The causes and cures of neurosis*. London: Routledge & Kegan Paul.

Faravelli, C., Webb, T., Ambonetti, A., Fonnescu, F., & Sessarego, A. (1985). Prevalence of traumatic early life events in 31 agoraphobic patients with panic attacks. *American Journal of Psychiatry, 142*, 1493–1494.

Finlay-Jones, R., & Brown, G. W. (1981). Types of stressful life event and the onset of anxiety and depressive disorders. *Psychological Medicine, 11*, 803–815.

Flint, J. (1997). Freeze! *Nature Genetics, 17*, 250–251.

Fox, N. A., & Calkins, S. D. (1993). Pathways to aggression and social withdrawal: Interactions among temperament, attachment, and regulation. In K. H. Rubin & J. B. Asendorpf (Eds.), *Social withdrawal, inhibition, and shyness in children*. (pp. 81–100). Hillsdale, NJ: Lawrence Erlbaum.

Fyer, A. J., Mannuzza, S., Chapman, T. F., Martin, L. Y., & Klein, D. F. (1995). Specificity in familial aggregation of phobic disorders. *Archives of General Psychiatry, 52*, 564–573.

Harris, J. R. (1995). Where is the child's environment? A group socialization theory of development. *Psychological Review, 102*, 458–489.

Hirshfeld, D. R., Rosenbaum, J. F., Biederman, J., Bolduc, E. A., Faraone, S. V., Snidman, N., Reznick, J. S., & Kagan, J. (1992). Stable behavioral inhibition and its association with anxiety disorder. *Journal of the American Academy of Child and Adolescent Psychiatry, 31*, 103–111.

Hudson, J. L, & Rapee, R. M. (1998a, July). Parent–child interactions and anxiety. Paper presented at the World Congress of Behavioral and Cognitive Therapies, Acapulco, Mexico.

Hudson, J. L, & Rapee, R. M. (1998b, July). Parenting of anxious children and their siblings. Paper presented at the World Congress of Behavioral and Cognitive Therapies, Acapulco, Mexico.

Jardine, R., Martin, N. G., & Henderson, A. S. (1984). Genetic covariation between neuroticism and the symptoms of anxiety and depression. *Genetics Epidemiology, 1*, 89–107.

Kagan, J., & Snidman, N. (1991). Infant predictors of inhibited and uninhibited profiles. *Psychological Science, 2* (1), 40–44.

Kagan, J., Snidman, N., Arcus, D., & Reznick, J. S. (1994). *Galen's prophecy: Temperament in human nature*. New York: Basic Books.

Kendler, K. S., Heath, A., Martin, N. G., & Eaves, L. J. (1987). Symptoms of anxiety and symptoms of depression: Same genes, different environments? *Archives of General Psychiatry, 44*, 451–457.

Kendler, K. S., Neale, M. C., Kessler, R. C., Heath, A. C., & Eaves, L. J. (1992a). Major depression and generalized anxiety disorder: Same genes, (partly) different environments? *Archives of General Psychiatry, 49*, 716–722.

Kendler, K. S., Neale, M. C., Kessler, R. C., Heath, A. C., & Eaves, L. J. (1992b). Generalized anxiety disorder in women. *Archives of General Psychiatry, 49,* 267–272.

Kendler, K. S., Walters, E. E., Neale, M. C., Kessler, R. C., Heath, A. C., & Eaves, L. J. (1995). The structure of the genetic and environmental risk factors for six major psychiatric disorders in women: Phobia, generalized anxiety disorder, panic disorder, bulimia, major depression, and alcoholism. *Archives of General Psychiatry, 52,* 374–383.

Kerr, M., Lambert, W.W., Stattin, H., & Klackenberg-Larsson, I. (1994). Stability of inhibition in a Swedish longitudinal sample. *Child Development, 65,* 138–146.

Kessler, R. C., McGonagle, K. A., Zhao, S., Nelson, C. B., Hughes, M., Eshleman, S., Wittchen, H., & Kendler, K. S. (1994). Lifetime and 12-month prevalence of DSM-III-R psychiatric disorders in the United States: Results from the national comorbidity survey. *Archives of General Psychiatry, 51,* 8–19.

King, N. J., Ollendick, T. H., & Gullone, E. (1991). Negative affectivity in children and adolescents: Relations between anxiety and depression. *Clinical Psychology Review, 11,* 441–459.

LaFreniere, P. J., & Capuano, F. (1997). Preventive intervention as a means of clarifying direction of effects in socialization: Anxious–withdrawn preschoolers case. *Development and Psychopathology, 9,* 551–564.

LaFreniere, P. J., & Dumas, J. E. (1992). A transactional analysis of early childhood anxiety and social withdrawal. *Development and Psychopathology, 4,* 385–402.

Leung, A. W., Heimberg, R. G., Holt, C. S., & Bruch, M. A. (1994). Social anxiety and perception of early parenting among American, Chinese American, and social phobic samples. *Anxiety, 1,* 80–89.

Lipsitz, J. D., Martin, L. Y., Mannuzza, S., Chapman, T. F., Liebowitz, M. R., Klein, D. F., & Fyer, A. J. (1994). Childhood separation anxiety disorder in patients with adult anxiety disorders. *American Journal of Psychiatry, 151,* 927–929.

MacLeod, C., & Mathews, A. (1991). Biased cognitive operations in anxiety: Accessibility of information or assignment of processing priorities? *Behaviour Research and Therapy, 29,* 599–610.

Massion, A. O., Warshaw, M. G., & Keller, M. B. (1993). Quality of life and psychiatric morbidity in panic disorder and generalized anxiety disorder. *American Journal of Psychiatry, 150,* 600–607.

Mathews, A. (1990). Why worry? The cognitive function of anxiety. *Behaviour Research and Therapy, 28,* 455–468.

McNally, R. J. (1998). Information-processing abnormalities in anxiety disorders: Implications for cognitive neuroscience. *Cognition and Emotion, 12,* 479–495.

Menzies, R. G., & Clarke, J. C. (1995). The etiology of acrophobia and its relationship to severity and individual response patterns. *Behaviour Research and Therapy, 33,* 795–803.

Mineka, S., Gunnar, M., & Champoux, M. (1986). Control and early socioemotional development: Infant rhesus monkeys reared in controllable versus uncontrollable environments. *Child Development, 57,* 241–1256.

Mogg, K., Mathews, A., Eysenck, M., & May, J. (1991). Biased cognitive operations in anxiety: Artifact, processing priorities or attentional search? *Behaviour Research and Therapy, 29,* 459–467.

Muris, P., Steerneman, P., Merckelbach, H., & Meesters, C. (1996). The role of parental fearfulness and modeling in children's fear. *Behaviour Research and Therapy, 34,* 265–268.

Noyes, Jr, Clarkson, C., Crowe, R. R., Yates, W. R., & McChesney, C. M. (1987). A family study of generalized anxiety disorder. *American Journal of Psychiatry, 144,* 1019–1024.

Oberklaid, F., Sanson, A., Pedlow, R., & Prior, M. (1993). Predicting preschool behavior problems from temperament and other variables in infancy. *Pediatrics, 91,* 113–120.

Ollendick, T. H., & King, N. J. (1991). Origins of childhood fears: An evaluation of Rachman's theory of fear acquisition. *Behaviour Research and Therapy, 29,* 117–123.

Öst, L.-G. (1987). Age of onset in different phobias. *Journal of Abnormal Psychology, 96,* 223–229.

Pike, A., & Plomin, R. (1996). Importance of nonshared environmental factors for childhood and adolescent psychopathology. *Journal of the American Academy of Child and Adolescent Psychiatry, 35,* 560–570.

Pollock, M. H., Otto, M. W., Sabatino, S., Majcher, D., Worthington, J. J., McArdle, E. T., & Rosenbaum, J. F. (1996). Relationship of childhood anxiety to adult panic disorder: Correlates and influence on course. *American Journal of Psychiatry, 153,* 376–381.

Rapee, R. (1985). Distinctions between panic disorder and generalized anxiety disorder: Clinical presentation. *Australian and New Zealand Journal of Psychiatry, 19,* 227–232.

Rapee, R. M. (1991). Generalized anxiety disorder: A review of clinical features and theoretical concepts. *Clinical Psychology Review, 11,* 419–440.

Rapee, R. M. (1997a). Perceived threat and perceived control as predictors of the degree of fear in physical and social situations. *Journal of Anxiety Disorders, 11,* 455–461.

Rapee, R. M. (1997b). Potential role of childrearing practices in the development of anxiety and depression. *Clinical Psychology Review, 17,* 47–67.

Rapee, R. M., & Melville, L. F. (1997). Retrospective recall of family factors in social phobia and panic disorder. *Depression and Anxiety, 5,* 7–11.

Rapee, R. M., & Szollos, A. (1997, November). Early life events in anxious children. Paper presented at the 31st Annual AABT convention, Miami, FL.

Rapee, R. M., Litwin, E. M., & Barlow, D. H. (1990). Impact of life events on subjects with panic disorder and on comparison subjects. *American Journal of Psychiatry, 147,* 640–644.

Robinson, J. L., Kagan, J., Reznick, J. S., & Corley, R. (1997). The heritability of inhibited and uninhibited behavior: A twin study. *Developmental psychology, 28,* 1030–1037.

Rosenbaum, J. F., Biederman, J., Bolduc, E. A., Hirshfeld, D. R., Faraone, S. V., & Kagan, J. (1992). Comorbidity of parental anxiety disorders as risk for childhood-onset anxiety in inhibited children. *American Journal of Psychiatry, 149,* 475–481.

Rosenbaum, J. F., Biederman, J., Bolduc-Murphy, B. A., Faraone, S. V., Chaloff, J., Hirshfeld, D. R., & Kagan, J. (1993). Behavioral inhibition in childhood: A risk factor for anxiety disorders. *Harvard Review of Psychiatry, 1,* 2–16.

Roth, M., & Mountjoy, C. Q. (1982). The distinction between anxiety states and depressive disorders. In E. S. Paykel (Ed.), *Handbook of affective disorders* (pp. 70–92). New York: Guilford.

Roy-Byrne, P. P., & Katon, W. (1997). Generalized anxiety disorder in primary care: The precursor/modifier pathway to increased health care utilization. *Journal of Clinical Psychiatry, 58 (Suppl. 3)*, 34–38.

Rubin, K. H. (1993). The Waterloo Longitudinal Project: Correlates and consequences of social withdrawal from childhood to adolescence. In K. H. Rubin & J. B. Asendorpf (Eds.), *Social withdrawal, inhibition, and shyness in children* (pp. 291–314). Hillsdale, NJ: Lawrence Erlbaum.

Sanderson, W. C., & Barlow, D. H. (1990). A description of patients diagnosed with DSM-111-R generalized anxiety disorder. *Journal of Nervous and Mental Disease, 178,* 588–591.

Spence, K. W., & Taylor, J. A. (1951). Anxiety and strength of the UCS as determiners of the amount of eyelid conditioning. *Journal of Experimental Psychology, 42,* 183–188.

Spielberger, C. D. (1975). Anxiety: State–trait–process. In C. D. Spielberger & I. G. Sarason (Eds.), *Stress and anxiety: Vol. 1* (pp. 115–143). New York: Wiley.

Stein, M. B., Chartier, M. J., Hazen, A. L., Kozak, M. V., Tancer, M. E., Lander, S., Furer, P., Chubaty, D., & Walker, J. R. (1998). A direct-interview family study of generalized social phobia. *American Journal of Psychiatry, 155,* 90–97.

Stevenson, J., Batten, N., & Cherner, M. (1992). Fears and fearfulness in children and adolescents: A genetic analysis of twin data. *Journal of Child Psychology and Psychiatry, 33,* 977–985.

Strauss, C.C. (1988). Social deficits of children with internalizing disorders. In B. B. Lahey and A. E. Kazdin (Eds.) *Advances in clinical child psychology: Vol. 11* (pp. 159–191). New York: Plenum.

Thapar, A., & McGuffin, P. (1995). Are anxiety symptoms in childhood heritable? *Journal of Child Psychology and Psychiatry, 36,* 439–447.

Topolski, T. D., Hewitt, J. K., Eaves, L. J., Silberg, J. L., Meyer, J. M., Rutter, M., Pickles, A., & Simonoff, E. (1997). Genetic and environmental influences on child reports of manifest anxiety and symptoms of separation anxiety and overanxious disorders: A community-based twin study. *Behavior Genetics, 27,* 15–28.

Torgersen, S. (1983). Genetic factors in anxiety disorders. *Archives of General Psychiatry, 40,* 1085–1089.

Turner, S. M., Beidel, D. C., & Larkin, K. T. (1986). Situational determinants of social anxiety in clinic and nonclinic samples: Physiological and cognitive correlates. *Journal of Consulting and Clinical Psychology, 54,* 523–527.

van der Molen, G. M., van den Hout, M. A., van Dieren, A. C., & Griez, E. (1989). Childhood separation anxiety and adult-onset panic disorders. *Journal of Anxiety Disorders, 3,* 97–106.

Vasey, M. W., & Daleiden, E. L. (1994). Worry in children. In G. Davey & F. Tallis (Eds.), *Worrying: Perspectives on theory, assessment, and treatment* (pp. 185–207). New York: Wiley.

Volling, B. L., & Feagans, L. V. (1995). Infant day care and children's social competence. *Infant Behavior and Development, 18,* 177–188.

Watt, M. C., Stewart, S. H., & Cox, B. J. (1998). A retrospective study of the learning history origins of anxiety sensitivity. *Behaviour Research and Therapy, 36,* 505–525.

Wehner, J. M., Radcliffe, R. A., Rosmann, S. T., Christensen, S. C., Rasmussen, D. L., Fulker, D. W., & Wiles, M. (1997). Quantitative trait loci analysis of contextual fear conditioning in mice. *Nature Genetics, 17,* 331–334.

Woody, S., & Rachman, S. (1994). Generalized anxiety disorder (GAD) as an unsuccessful search for safety. *Clinical Psychology Review, 14,* 743–753.

Zinbarg, R. E., & Mohlman, J. (1998). Individual differences in the acquisition of affectively valenced associations. *Journal of Personality and Social Psychology, 74,* 1024–1040.

INDEX

Affectionless control, 445. *See also*
Parental behavior: criticism and
negativity; overcontrol and
overprotection
Age differences, 27–40
behavioral genetics and, 47, 51–52
in interaction with sex differences, 10
in manifestations of anxiety
disorders, 9–10, 27–40
in prevalence of anxiety disorders, 10,
27–40
in treatment, 307, 311–15
Agoraphobia
anxiety sensitivity and, 168
behavioral inhibition and, 74, 411
genetic influences in, 360
nonassociative factors and, 186–88
risk for anxiety in offspring of parents
with, 46, 74, 287
separation anxiety disorder and,
186–88, 224, 459–75
treatment, 311
Ameliorating influences, 9, 16, 18–22
Anxiety sensitivity, 92–107
attachment and, 106
emotion regulation and, 167–69
parental behavior and, 489
social learning influences and, 235
temperament and, 71
Attachment, 54, 172–76, 293–95
anxiety sensitivity and, 106
attentional bias for threat and, 175
behavioral inhibition and, 79, 176,
414–15, 416
control experiences and, 122–24,
126
emotion regulation and, 122–24,
162–63, 172–76, 222
HPA axis activity and, 285–86
learning influences on, 222
panic disorder and, 464
posttraumatic stress disorder and,
390, 392–93, 395
prevention of anxiety, implications
for, 330, 332, 334, 336–37

protective influence of secure
attachment, 174, 222, 395
quality of, 123–24, 174–75, 284
separation anxiety disorder and, 51,
131, 459
social learning theory and, 295–97,
298
social phobia and, 439–40, 444,
445–46
social withdrawal and, 416, 425–26
specific phobias and, 366–68
temperament and, 16, 79, 176, 284,
285, 286, 414–15
Attentional bias for threat, 116, 253–74,
299
behavioral inhibition and, 113
depression and, 265
developmental perspective on, 269–73
effortful control and, 79–80, 271–73
emotion regulation and, 165, 170–71,
175, 177
general bias toward threat in children,
268–69
generalized anxiety disorder and, 483
parental behavior and, 163
posttraumatic stress disorder and,
392, 394, 399, 401
probe detection studies, 263–66
resolving conflicting findings, 266–68
specific phobias and, 372–73
state anxiety and, 264
Stroop studies, 257–63
temperament and, 70, 79–80
trait anxiety and, 264
Avoidance
competence limiting effects of.
See Limited shopping
excessive reliance on. *See* Coping
behaviors: avoidance, excessive
reliance on
parental. *See* Modeling:
of parental avoidance
temperament and, 78
transactional relations to other risk
factors, 19–22